RATKO
TRAGIC HERO

Ratko Mladić: Tragic Hero

by

Translated, edited and supplemented by

Milo Yelesiyevich

Unwritten History, Inc.
New York, New York

Ratko Mladić: Tragic Hero,
Translated, edited and supplemented by Milo Yelesiyevich
© 2006 by Unwritten History, Inc.

Unwritten History, Inc.
PMB 199, Zeckendorf Towers
111 E. 14th Street
New York, NY 10003

e-mail: unwrittenhistory@hotmail.com
website: www.unwrittenhistory.com

ISBN: 0-9709198-0-8

Library of Congress Control Number: 2005932734

Q: And the rape of Muslim women?
A: It was made-up by the foreign press. Representatives from all [major] international organizations visited our camps and they did not find one single Muslim or Croat woman who had been raped. We are not fighting against the Muslim or the Croat people but against their extremist and fascist leaders. I evacuated 12,000 women and children from Srebrenica. We pulled almost 30,000 [Croatian] civilians [fleeing the Muslims] from Travnik, Vareš and Bugojno. We released soldiers who surrendered their weapons. I allowed the evacuation of wounded soldiers from many villages, about 200 of them from Žepa alone. They were transported by UNPROFOR helicopters. The other side, however, did not allow Serbian civilians to leave Tuzla, Zenica or Sarajevo. We fight on the battlefield. We don't hide behind civilians. They spread monstrous lies through their own propaganda machinery and through the foreign press.
Interview with Ratko Mladić (see p. 434)

"The aide said that guys like me were 'in what we call the reality-based community'.... I nodded and murmured something.... He cut me off.... 'We're an empire now, and when we act, we create our own reality.... and you, all of you, will be left to just study what we do.'"
"Without a Doubt," by Ron Suskind, *The New York Times Magazine*, 10/17/04

CONTENTS

APPENDICES

Abbreviations

ABWEHR	The Nazi secret service
AMBO	The Albania, Macedonian and Bulgarian Oil Company.
ARS	*Armija Republike Srpske*, The Army of the Republika Srpska.
B-H	Bosnia-Herzegovina
BND	*Bundes Nachrichten Dienst*, the name of the German secret service, equivalent to the U.S. CIA
CIA	Central Intelligence Agency
EU	European Union (from 1 November 1993)
FRY	Federal Republic of Yugoslavia
HDZ	*Hrvatska Demokratska Zadruga* or The Croatian Democratic Union (CDU) in English, which is Franjo Tudjman's political party.
HVO	*Hrvatska Vjeće Odbrane* or The Croatian Defense Council
ICC	International Criminal Court
ICRC	International Committee for the Red Cross
ICTY	International Criminal Tribunal for the former Yugoslavia
JNA	*Jugoslovenska Narodna Armija*, the Yugoslav People's Army
KLA	Kosovo Liberation Army
MUP	*Ministarstvo Unutrasnji Posla*,
MPRI	Military Personnel and Resources, Inc.
NATO	North Atlantic Treaty Organization
NDH	Nezavisna Država Hrvatske
NSA	National Security Agency (U.S.)
OSCE	Organization for Security and Cooperation in Europe
PL	the PatriotIc League (Bosnian Muslim)
RS	the Republika Srpska, or the Serbian Republic
RSK	*Republika Srpska Krajina*, the Republic of Serbian Krajina
RTS	*Radio-Televizija Serbije*, Radio-Television Serbia
SDA	*Strana Demokratske Akcije*, Alija Izetbegović's Muslim party.
SDS	*Srpska Demokratska Stranka*, The Serbian Democratic Party, Radovan Karadžic's party.
SFOR	Stabilization Force,
SRNA	Srpska Republika News Agency
SS	*Schutzstaffel*, the Nazi elite guard
UN	United Nations
UNHCR	United Nations High Commissioner for Refugees
UNMIK	UN Mission in Kosovo
UNPROFOR	UN Protection Force

Editor's Note

All translations from Serbian are my own, except as otherwise noted. I have added editorial matter in brackets [ ], and have identified editorial matter that came from other sources.

Even though I tried to impose uniformity in the spelling of Balkan names, they appear in a variety of spellings in sources I have quoted. For example, I settled on Ustashi, which also occurs as Ustasha and Ustashe in English. Proper names are seldom spelled correctly in English. For example, the subject of this book spells his name Mladić, however, his name almost always appears in English as *Mladic*.

Acknowledgements

I want to thank all of those who lent support to this book because "Ratko Mladić: Tragic Hero" could not have been completed without their sustained encouragement. I want to thank former Canadian Ambassador to Yugoslavia James Bissett and David Binder (formerly of *The New York Times*) for reviewing an early manuscript. The resulting book profited enormously from their frank criticism. I want to also thank Prof. Radmila Milentijević, Professor Emeritus, The City College of the City University of New York, for reviewing the manuscript for factual errors and omissions. I want to express my thanks to internet sources that consistently provided reliable information on the former Yugoslavia. These include antiwar.com, serbianna.com, serbianunity.net, srpska-mreza.com, tenc.net, kosovo.com, balkanalysis.com. balkanpeace.org, and apisgroup.org. I owe a debt of gratitude to Carl Savich, whose articles appear on serbianna.com, and to Srdja Trifkovic, whose artricles appear on chronilesmagazine.org, for generously allowing me to use extended quotations from their work. Many thanks and gratitude to Kosa Martjak and Van and Tijana Nikov for the confidence in me and their encouragement. I am enormously grateful to P—— B—— for his unfailing support and for answering my many questions about the fine points of translating Serbian. Many thanks to John Zuccardy for recreating the maps on pages 422 and 423. I owe a debt of gratitude to Cindy Kulongowski and Noah Abrams for proofreading the manuscript at different stages. And I am grateful to Carolina Abrams for translating correspondence into Spanish, and to Yuliya Tsaplina for translating correspondence into Russian. Last but certainly not least, I wish to thank Tim DeBaets and Lisa Digernes of Cowan, DeBaets,

Abrahams and Sheppard LLC for providing their invaluable help in reviewing the manuscript. Their encouragement, support and belief in this book was of inestimable value.

Guide to Pronunciation

Serbian is strictly phonetic. The English-speaking reader will not stray far from the mark if he or she uses broad European vowels and English consonants in pronouncing Serbian, with the following exceptions:

c	is always *ts* as in ha*ts*.
ć and č	are pronounced like *ch* as in *ch*urch. The former is soft, and the latter hard, which is too subtle for the English ear to distinguish.
dž	is pronounced like the hard *j* in *j*udge.
đ	is often written as *Dj* or *dj*, and is pronounced like the soft j in *jay*.
j	is always pronounced like the *y* in *y*ellow.
š	is always *sh* as in *sh*arp.
r	strongly rolled, is sometimes a vowel, e.g. G*r*k, a Greek.
ž	is always pronounced like the *s* in mea*s*ure.

Introduction — Ratko Mladić: Tragic Hero

What is a tragic hero?

A tragic hero is a virtuous individual who is catapulted into a series of intolerable yet unavoidable situations in which he must make difficult moral decisions that ultimately bring misfortune upon himself by means of his own tragic flaw, which is not so much a weakness as an excess of virtue. In the struggle to resolve his dilemma, the tragic hero displays *hubris* while exercising his indomitable will, which is nothing less than a presumption of being godlike and attempting to exceed human limitations in order to find a solution. And misfortune is not brought about by villainy but by an error in judgment. Yet, the hero's suffering and its far-reaching repercussions are much greater than the hero's tragic flaw.

General Mladić is a tragic hero. The following pages will reveal him to be a man not without virtue who made difficult moral decisions throughout his career. When Croat and Muslim soldiers deserted his ranks at the onset of the war, he dropped his adopted "Yugoslav" identity and discovered what made him a "Serb." This was the first step that led him to battle radical Islam and resurgent Fascism in the Balkans, which were being supported by the Western powers. Mladić, however, was inspired by the unshakable belief that his cause was just and that it would eventually prevail. It was the source of his *hubris*, and resulted in his downfall.

Ratko Mladić: Tragic Hero is the first study of the Serbian general to be published in English. It also departs radically from mainstream news coverage because it presumes General Mladić to be innocent of charges of war crimes and genocide until he has been proven guilty. Furthermore, this book presumes that the West is acting against its own best interests by attempting to prosecute General Mladić for alleged crimes for which there is still no proof even after the passage of more than ten years.

Washington is waging a relentless war against al Qaida, yet Mladić was fighting Muslim forces that relied on foreign mujahideen, who were al Qaida's shock troops in Europe. Why is Mladić now a fugitive while others, like Tom Ridge, former Director of Homeland Security, are praised and honored for fighting Islamic fundamentalist terrorism in the U.S.? Mladić fought a resurgent neo-Nazi movement in Croatia, but he was demonized for it, while President Franjo

Tudjman of Croatia, an anti-Semite and Holocaust denier, was invited to the opening ceremonies of the U.S. Holocaust Memorial Museum. Why do Americans who, on the one hand, deplore and oppose globalization, condemn Mladić, who, on the other hand, fought to prevent NATO from taking over his country and divvying it up with U.S. and European multinational corporations? The U.S. "victory" resulted in the creation of a Muslim statelet in Europe that is serving as a launching pad for radical Muslim incursions into the European continent, which has been targeted by them for conquest. General Mladić quite simply thought it was better to fight than to be made a sacrificial pawn of U.S. foreign policy in the Balkans, which sought to appease Saudi Arabia for the support it lent to the U.S. during Gulf War I. Even though Mladić fought bitterly against it, U.S. foreign policy makers did, indeed, make him their sacrificial pawn, and then the U.S. promptly lost its queen a few moves later on September 11, 2001.

Each country has its own characteristics. The U.S. is, or ought to be, defined by The Revolutionary War. France is defined by the Revolution of 1789 just as Germany is by Bismarck's unification. These are unqualified victories. Serbia, however, has been defined by the Battle of Kosovo. Americans are bemused by a peculiar people who apparently celebrate a historic defeat instead of a victory. It is not apparent to Westerners that by fighting against insurmountable odds, the Serbs won by keeping their identity and resisted five hundred years of Turkish occupation that sought to convert them to Islam. How would Americans or Germans or the French hold up against five centuries of genocide, forced conversion to Islam, and cultural extermination? If radical Islam continues making greater inroads in Europe and in America, they may have a chance to test their mettle sooner than they wish.

The Serbs have somehow managed to survive out of sheer determination, spite, and tenacious resistance in the face of overwhelming adversity. An estimated 1.25 million Serbs out of a population just under 4 million, which included 51% of the male population, died in WWI. During the WWII, 750,000 Serbs, 75,000 Jews and 50,000 Roma perished in the Jasenovac concentration camp and others like it in Croatia. An estimated total of 1.5 million people died during WWII, most of them Serbian civilians.

One unpublicized aspect of Jasenovac is the fact that Roman

Catholic priests and Franciscan monks administered it, as they did about half of the other concentration camps in Croatia. The late David Martin, author of *The Web of Disinformation*, wrote that there were:

> numerous reports of entire Serbian communities being locked up in their churches and burned alive. There were reports that the Ustashi were making necklaces of Serbian eyes and adorning themselves with them. So fiendish were the reports that one simply cannot blame the civilized Westerners for initially disbelieving them....[1]

One cannot meet a contemporary Serb who has not lost some family member in at least one of the wars in the twentieth century. One can still meet the survivors of the WWII genocide wherever one goes in Serbia or throughout the U.S. where there are numerous Serbian-American communities.

Tito, however, had Jasenovac bulldozed after WWII. No discussion of war crimes was permitted under his regime. A person could have been imprisoned simply for identifying a war criminal because it was in violation of Tito's official policy of "brotherhood and unity." Few war criminals were, therefore, brought to trial and punished. And Serbs, Jews and Roma received no consolation from the fact that Ustashi war criminals were rebaptized as "anti-Communist guerrillas" and shielded by the Vatican, which obtained passports for almost 40,000 fugitive Nazis and Ustashi.[2] And even greater numbers of Ustasha flocked to Tito's Partisans in 1944 and escaped punishment.

Politics has been rightfully described as the art of confusion. Tito's historical revisionism has given rise to present day media myths. The Communists presented a new version of history that was taught in Yugoslav schools. Some events were given emphasis while others were obscured or hidden in order to present the Communist Partisans as the sole group that liberated the country from the Nazis. The Serbian Homeland Defense Forces of General Draža Mihailovich were grouped with Croat and Muslim Ustashi as "enemies of the people." The genocide conducted against the Serbs was never addressed or acknowledged. The consistent denial of Ustashi WWII crimes prevented Serbs from recovering and making peace with their Croat and Muslim neighbors. The U.S., after all, bombed Serbia for three months in 1944 in order to help Tito invade. Tito had demanded the bombardment, and Washington and London betrayed

General Mihailovich, who represented a constitutional monarchy. What sense was there in bombing Serbia in 1944 in order to impose Communism, and then bombing Serbians again in the 1990s in order to impose "free market democracy"? The senselessness is staggering.

One only has to investigate the lives of American families who lost a family member to murder in order to get a sense of what Serbs have had to face. Lucy L. Friedman, founder of Victim Services Agency in New York City says that:

> the survivors of murder victims are often treated like pariahs, avoided like a source of bad luck. They feel cursed. Even the counselors who work with survivors come to feel stigmatized by their jobs.[3]

As the article notes, as many as nine out of ten criminal cases in the U.S. are settled through plea bargains. Serbian Holocaust survivors were subjected to identical processes with the same results. Prosecutors, defense attorneys and judges cut deals behind closed doors, leaving the victims' families feeling powerless. Such institutional brutality leaves the victims' families trapped in a bereavement process that is much more painful than when a family member dies naturally.

Such was the environment Ratko Mladić was born into. His father, a Partisan, was killed when Mladić was still an infant. His father died fighting Ustashi in Ante Pavelić's native village. When his mother fell sick with typhoid fever and could not breast-feed him, Italian soldiers who were occupying his village saved his life by feeding him soup and milk. And the following pages will reveal how he became a soldier.

General Mladić has no counterpart in the present-day U.S. military. But if one goes back to an earlier generation of military men, Brigadier General Smedley D. Butler comes to mind. General Butler was not, of course, anti-war, as some modern generals pretend to be. He was ready to defend the United States of America at any time, and he, fortunately, never had to face an intolerable and ultimately inescapable situation. He did, however, resent the fact that U.S. corporations were using U.S. soldiers to fight wars abroad where they would kill or be killed in the name of corporate profits.

> "War is a racket," he wrote. "It always has been. It is possibly the oldest, easily the most profitable, surely the most vicious. It is the only one in which profits are reckoned in dollars and losses in lives."[4]

In 1937, Butler asked, "Why don't those damned oil companies fly their own flags on their personal property — maybe a flag with a gas pump on it." In his appreciative article on a new edition of General Butler's book, *War Is a Racket*, Ralph Nader wrote: "Today's reply might say, why should they when they can continue to use the American flag."[5]

Old wine, i.e. imperialism, has been poured into a new bottle called globalization. The economic exploitation and enslavement of peoples still benefits imperial powers that utilize captive markets, monopolies, and transnational corporations to capture and control foreign wealth. Mladić was struggling against the worst aspects of globalization and capitalism gone berserk, all in the service of shoring up a failing U.S. economy.[6]

The Bosnian War was commonly attributed to "Serbian nationalism," and Serbs were handily demonized after they had been falsely likened to Nazis in a PR campaign by Ruder-Finn in 1992 (*see* p. 181). The image stuck. Then U.S. citizens were told that there was a strong "humanitarian aspect" to the intervention in Bosnia, but more than a decade later in 2004, it was revealed that there was oil, after all, in Bosnia (in Tuzla, coincidentally, where U.S. Eagle Base is located).

This is not the impression one gets from reading the mainstream press. Millions of words have been written and published over the last decade about General Ratko Mladić. One would normally expect to find multiple points of view, independent analyses, pros and cons, but in his case, we find merely repetition. The general is a "fugitive from justice"; he is an "indicted war criminal"; he is "responsible for the deaths of "8,000 men and boys" in Srebrenica; and he is wanted for "genocide."

The official story line about what happened in the former Yugoslavia goes something like this:

> The Serbs wanted to create a Greater Serbia from the ashes of the Former Yugoslavia. Slobodan Milošević was the evil genius who advocated this neo-Nazi policy and entrusted its execution to General Ratko Mladić, who used "ethic cleansing," "genocide," and all manner of "war crimes" to achieve this goal, as exemplified by the Srebrenica massacre.

The only problem with this official version is that it is not true. Americans at one time expected a peace dividend after George

Bush proclaimed the *New World Order* in September 1990 after the collapse of the Soviet Union. Instead, there have been more armed conflicts and interventions by the UN since 1989 than during the forty preceding years, and they are destabilizing the entire world. The New World Order is code for U.S. hegemony: control of the world economy by means of GATT, the IMF and the World Bank; control of the UN Security Council in order to meddle in the affairs of sovereign nations and impose embargoes and wars on those who resist; control of Europe's energy corridors through NATO; control of oil reserves in the Gulf; and finally the control of hearts and minds by sustained media disinformation.

The principal cause of the two civil wars in Croatia and Bosnia was the fate allotted to the Serbian minorities. In both cases, the Serbs, who have lived for centuries in these two republics and who were considered "constituent nationalities," refused to become minorities in their own country — Yugoslavia — while being compelled to live under historically hostile regimes.

This was the case in Croatia because of the genocide that had taken place between 1941–1945, and because of the unconcealed anti-Serbian policy of the government led by president Franjo Tudjman; this was also the case in Bosnia-Herzegovina, where President Izetbegović wanted to establish an Islamic fundamentalist state that would relegate Serbs and Croats to an official status of *dhimmis*, officially designated second class citizens, to which they had been subjected under Ottoman rule and against which they had fought for centuries.

In order to forge closer ties with the Bosnian Muslims, Ante Pavelić's[7] Ustashi developed a theory about the Bosnian Muslims, which considered them to be the purest part of the Croatian nation, racially Croatian, and the oldest and the purest part of European nobility. Thus, the Ustashi found their greatest allies in Bosnia among Bosnian Muslims, who formed the regime's shock troops, the infamous SS Division, evocatively named *Handžar*,[8] which distinguished itself with horrible massacres they carried out against the Serbian population of Bosnia-Herzegovina during WWII.

Muslim nationalism in Bosnia began to appear in a separatist form only in 1962 when Tito decided that Muslims could define themselves to be "Muslim" by nationality. It was the first time in history that people professing a religion (Muslims who were in reality Bosnian Serbs or Croats who had converted to Islam) became a nation (Bosnian Muslims).

Europe and the U.S. actually plunged Yugoslavia into a civil war because of the project for European unity. Germany put unbearable pressure on EU members to accelerate the disintegration of Yugoslavia and obtaining recognition for new countries: Croatia and Slovenia. The U.S. pushed for the recognition of Bosnia. Coincidentally, they were all once part of the Austro-Hungarian Empire.

From the beginning, Western policies were marked by a fundamental error: they dismissed any consideration for the strong will of the Serbian people to live in a single country. Any permanent solution for the current conflict must arise from the recognition of Serbian rights in this matter, and the Serbs must be given what others have been generously given: the right to choose.

A U.S. policy based on ultimatums keeps repeating itself, and results in wars. We must stop upholding the fiction that the Serbs alone are responsible for the Yugoslav catastrophe. The Croats and the Muslims share a larger part of the responsibility for the outbreak of war than they care to admit. Then Germany and the U.S. poured gasoline on the flames, as will be amply demonstrated in the following pages.

Before dismissing these accusations as "blame everything on Germany and the U.S.," we ought to take into consideration the plain facts that point to such collusion. Erich Schmidt-Eenboom, a former German BND (secret service) agent, published *Der Schattenkreiger, Klaus Kinkel und der BND* (The Shadow Warrior: Klaus Kinkel and the BND, Econ-Verlag. Dusseldorf, 1995). Mr. Eenboom and Philip Agee, the CIA agent who fled the agency in the 1970s and published the first uncensored expose of CIA operations called *Inside the Company: CIA Diary* (Penguin, 1975), share a great deal in common. Both were patriots who were disgusted by the policies of their respective governments. Mr. Eenboom explains in chapter nine of his book how Germany began planning the dismemberment of Yugoslavia in the early 1960s. Klaus Kinkel, a high-ranking official in the BND, was given the responsibility of plotting and organizing contacts with chauvinist leaders in Communist Croatia. Kohl and Genscher were also involved, and lent wholehearted diplomatic, financial and military support in order to achieve recognition for Croatia, Slovenia and later Bosnia.[9]

The U.S. Congress passed the 1991 Foreign Operations Appropriations Law 101-513 on November 5, 1990, a year before the civil wars in Yugoslavia began. This bill cut all aid, trade credits and loans to Yugoslavia and forced the World Bank and the IMF to follow suit. The bill effectively derecognized Yugoslavia and signaled that the U.S. intended to deal with the constituent republics instead.

The declaration of independence (or secession) by Croatia and Slovenia on June 25, 1991 led to the outbreak of civil war. On June 21, at the end of his visit to Yugoslavia, U.S. Secretary of State James Baker stated that the U.S. supported a democratic and unified Yugoslavia, and that its future should be decided through negotiated agreements. Baker also said that the U.S. would not recognize unilateral secessionist movements. The recognition of Croatia and Slovenia by Germany came on December 25, 1991, followed in mid-January 1992 by the Vatican and the European Union.

In July 1992, although the Administration denied that it was shifting its position toward Yugoslavia, it abandoned its earlier insistence on a single, unified Yugoslav state. It said that it would support independence for secessionist-minded republics if achieved peacefully, while calling for an end to the use of force by the federal [i.e., Yugoslav or Serbian] military.[10]

The U.S. at first withheld recognition, but then it reversed its position on April 17, 1992, and recognized Croatia, Slovenia, as well as Bosnia-Herzegovina. Then came the infamous Bosnian referendum for independence in March 1992, which the Serbs boycotted. The Serbs consistently sued for peace. Under the auspices of the European Community, the leaders of the three groups Alija Izetbegović (Muslim), Radovan Karadžić (Serbian) and Mate Boban (Croatian) signed a peace agreement in Lisbon on February 23, 1992 that would have left Bosnia as a confederation of three different ethnic groups. But U.S. Ambassador to Yugoslavia, Warren Zimmermann, urged Izetbegović to renege.

> Immediately after Mr. Izetbegović returned from Lisbon, Mr. Zimmermann called on him in Sarajevo…. "He said he didn't like it," I told him, if he didn't like it, "why sign it?"[11]

One will find an entirely different Slobodan Milošević depicted in the following pages. Instead of the Butcher of the Balkans, we find

Milošević bending over backward to please President Clinton. Milošević even threatened General Mladić with execution if did not fall into line with Clinton's demands. President Clinton and Secretary of State Madeleine Albright thanked Milošević profusely for his cooperation in Dayton and his "contribution to peace." In retrospect, it is clear that Milošević was being set up to be the fall guy. Since then, President Milošević was kidnapped and illegally remanded to an illegal court in The Hague to face prosecution for genocide. His trial has been conducted in the manner of a malevolent farce. Acquittal was never a possible outcome.

NATO, however, is still looking for Mladić. In March 2004, NATO sent him a birthday card featuring a pair of handcuffs, beneath which was written: "Ratko, we have not forgotten about you … this will be your only present soon,"[12] implying that his arrest was imminent.

NATO forces have routinely broken into Serbian churches in search of suspects and have ambushed and killed other Serbs who simply knew too much. NATO forces, setting a new low for occupation forces, beat a Serbian priest and his son nearly to death in 2004 in their relentless pursuit of alleged war criminals. Paddy Ashdown, the UN High Representative in Bosnia, fires elected officials at will, and seizes Serbian property and assets under the pretext of eliminating support for General Mladić. Ashdown rejected the report prepared on Srebrenica by the Bosnian Serb authorities in 2002 without even having read it, and used extortion to obtain a new Srebrenica Report prepared in 2004 in which the Bosnian Serbs, under duress, accepted culpability for the alleged deaths of 8,000 Muslims in the enclave in 1995.

And what of justice? Madeleine Albright almost single-handedly created the International Criminal Tribunal for the Former Yugoslavia in The Hague, which continues to prove itself to be a kangaroo court where show trials are conducted. The vast majority of those indicted have been Serbs; a token number of Muslims, Croats and Albanians have been indicted for slaughtering each other but almost never for innumerable crimes committed against Serbs.

Ratko Mladić: Tragic Hero attempts to redress the obfuscations, omissions and outright lies the American people have been subjected to. Two of the original media lies circulated and amplified by mainstream news sources, namely, Serbian run death camps and mass rape, have been exposed as lies.[13] Bernard Kouchner admitted in his book, *Les Guerriers de la paix* (Warriors for Peace, Grasset, Paris: 2004, p. 384) that he and Richard Holbrooke visited Alija Izetbegović in Sarajevo on October 2, 2003. *Vesti*, a Serbian-language newspaper in Frankfurt, Germany, published excerpts from Kouchner's book that state Alija Izetbegović, before his death, admitted that there were no Serbian death camps for the systematic extermination of Bosnian Muslims.

Izetbegović was convinced that his claims regarding the existence of Serbian camps would provoke a rapid reaction on the part of the Western forces and NATO operations but, according to his own admission, he was wrong in his estimate according to Kouchner.[14]

Despite this candid admission, Serbs are still being prosecuted and convicted in The Hague for having operated such non-existent "death camps." The Bosnian Muslims, however, operated many genuine death camps for Serbs.[15] Izetbegović was even photographed visiting one of them, and there is evidence given by numerous witnesses that he visited Celibici.[16]

Ratko Mladić: Tragic Hero is divided into three parts. Part I contains an abridged version of Ljubodrag Stojadinović's outstanding study, *Ratko Mladić: Hero or War Criminal* ("Ratko Mladić: Heroj ili zločinac," Evro, Belgrade: 2001). Stojadinović knew Mladić personally, and is able to provide insights that Western journalists have largely been unable to perceive. He presents a straightforward narrative account of Mladić's career as a soldier, and answers questions that have not been asked elsewhere: How good of a general was he? What were his successes? his failures? his shortcomings? his virtues? Is he a hero or a war criminal?

Part II examines Bosnia and Croatia's history in the twentieth century. It begins with Gregory Elich's outstanding essay, *Bringing Democracy to Bosnia*, which explores the undemocratic nature of the "Wild West Democracy" that has been imposed on the region. The following chapters consist of background essays that place the Bosnia war in its historical context. *Bosniaks, Nazi Muslims, Mujahideen and Bin Laden* discusses the role of Islamic fundamentalism in Bosnia as part of a grand scheme by Turkey, Iran and Saudi Arabia to penetrate Europe via Bosnia. It is well known that the Bosnian Muslim government issued Osama bin Laden a passport in

1993. But how many Americans know that one of the 9/11 bombers was a Saudi citizen who entered the U.S. on a Bosnian passport? Or that mujahideen who had fought in the Bosnian civil war had been exported from Zenica to assist in the Madrid attacks? *Ustashi, Murderer Monks, Ante Pavelić and the Modern Croatian State* examines the Ustashi's genocide of Serbs in Croatia during WWII as well as terrorist acts that Croatian Ustashi committed in the U.S., which were a violent preamble to the later war they fought against the Serbs. The resurgence of Croatian fascism in the fall of Yugoslavia is examined, as well as its role in the creation of the modern Croatian state. *Srebrenica, the Phantom Massacre*, is a detailed examination of the alleged "Srebrenica Massacre" that reveals it to be a virulent media lie. It argues persuasively that Muslim casualties in Srebrenica did not exceed 1,800 to 2,000, notwithstanding the forced admission Paddy Ashdown exacted from leaders that he himself appointed of the Republika Srpska.

Ratko Mladić in Close Up presents his speeches and interviews in chronological order. The General speaks for himself, which is something he has not been permitted in the Western press.

Part III consists of Appendices: 1) key articles from the Western press; 2) testimonies of Serbian civilians of Pofalići who faced the first mujahideen assault in Europe; 3) analyses of The Hague Tribunal; and 4) the texts of the indictments issued by The Hague Tribunal against Radovan Karadžić and Ratko Mladić.

Not long ago, the American people were misled by false claims made by President Bush that led us to war with Iraq. The pro-war media campaign availed itself of outright lies (i.e., that Iraq was trying to acquire uranium from Niger), and submitted forged documents as proof. "It begs the question," wrote Jay Bookman of *The Atlanta Journal-Constitution*, "what else are they lying about?"[17] Well, they lied quite a bit about General Mladić and the Serbs, as the following pages will demonstrate.

Daniel Brandt, the author of "Journalism and the CIA: The Mighty Wurlitzer," pointed out that Frank Wisner of the CIA is credited with the development of the first "information superhighway," which he named his "Mighty Wurlitzer" after an organ that was developed especially for film productions. It could generate audio special effects, and mimic the sound of train whistles, rain and thunder, etc.

After WWII, the battle against Fascism became the battle against Communism. The CIA pumped money into Italian elections, Radio Free Europe and Radio Liberty, and embraced the new science of psychological warfare. A new terminology appeared to serve the needs of the government:

> OSS highbrows had already embraced psychological warfare as a new social science: propaganda, for example, was divided into "black" propaganda (stories that are unattributed, or attributed to non-existent sources, or false stories attributed to a real source), "gray" propaganda (stories from the government where the source is attributed to others), and "white" propaganda (stories from the government where the source is acknowledged as such.[18]

The CIA co-opted much of the U.S. media by planting numerous agent-journalists and agent-executives with a variety of media: newspaper, radio and television. Daniel Schorr of CBS leaked a copy of the House investigation of the CIA to the *Village Voice* that mentioned the CIA's "frequent manipulation of Reuters wire service dispatches."[19] Mr. Brandt cites the late economist Sean Gervasi, who extrapolated a figure for the cost of propaganda in 1978 to be around $265 million, which involved 2,000 employees. He concluded that the CIA

> uses far more resources in its propaganda operations than any single news agency.... In fact, the CIA propaganda budget is as large as the combined budgets of Reuters, United Press International and the Associated Press.[20]

The CIA has subsidized news bureaus, radio stations, newspapers, magazines and other media.

At least 22 American news organizations had employed American journalists who were also working for the CIA, and nearly a dozen American publishing houses printed more than 1,000 books that had been produced or subsidized by the CIA. When asked in a 1976 interview whether the CIA had ever told its media agents what to write, William Colby replied, "Oh, sure, all the time."[21]

The 1980s and 1990s brought about mergers in the media that centralized ownership of domestic and international news media. The CIA certainly must have firm hold of the reins now.

It is my earnest hope that this book will contribute to a greater understanding of General Mladić's role in the Bosnian war that will benefit journalists, scholars, historians and students, as well as Americans who are appalled by our military adventures overseas.

Traditional American democracy is based on literacy and public debate. The New Democracy, which made its debut with Ronald Reagan, is founded on image and perception and the mobilizing effects of public relations campaigns. The mode of discourse used for news reporting changed in the 1980s in the U.S. News became entertainment, and entertainment became news. In such a context, Mladić, Milošević, and Karadžić were all cast as prime time villains, and all subsequent news stories took the form of a good-guy-vs.-bad guy melodrama. This book rectifies, to the extent a single book can, the deliberate misrepresentations espoused by the mainstream media. It is a civic duty to perform such a task, because democracy relies on a free press, and a free people must be able to make informed decisions in order to remain free.

> "If a nation, in a state of civilization, expects to be [both] ignorant and free, it expects what never has been and never will be." Folks, we are ignorant, and therefore, not free. We have swallowed lies that rival Goebbels'....[22]

I would like to take this opportunity to identify myself as an unhyphenated American. I was born and raised in the United States. My heritage is, indeed, Serbian. Am I biased? Yes, I am biased in favor of the United States. Am I prejudiced? Yes, I am prejudiced against Nazis and their spawn. And how do I feel about Serbs? I understand their problems and their aspirations, and wish to give them the fair hearing they have never received in the United States. The CIA, on the one hand, has a staff of analysts working on General Mladić and the Serbs as well as the concomitant propaganda campaign; the general reading public, on the other hand, has only this book to inform and enlighten them. Therefore, it is an honor and a privilege to submit this work to the critical eye of the American reading public. Many media lies will be exposed, but it is much easier to reveal lies than it is to correct the damage they have done. It is also easier to see how our "humanitarian interventions" in Bosnia and Croatia hoisted us on our own petard than it is to determine what we must do next as a people and as a nation.

The lesson we in the United States must learn is that we cannot fight Islamic fundamentalist terrorism in the U.S. and in Europe by harboring and supporting Islamic fundamentalist terrorism in Bosnia, in Croatia, in Kosovo, in Macedonia and in Chechnya. The World Trade Center attacks may be viewed as a monument to our corrupt and short-sighted policies that tried to appease radical Islam in exchange for cheap oil and commerce. It is time for us to re-evaluate our role in the Balkans, our relations with the Islamic world, and our own national ideals and aspirations. Truly, we cannot seriously discuss evil unless we acknowledge our own participation in it. And General Mladić, as we shall see, is at the heart of the matter.

Milo Yelesiyevich
New York, New York 2005

ENDNOTES

1 *The Web of Disinformation*, by David Martin, Harcourt Brace Jovanovich, New York, 1990, pgs. 44-46.

2 See *Hitler's Pope*, by John Cornwell (Viking: New York, 1999) and *The Unholy Trinity*, by Mark Aarons and John Loftus (St. Martin's Griffin, New York: 1998).

3 "A Grief Like No Other," by Eric Schlosser, *Atlantic Monthly*, September 1997.

4 "Memoirs of a 'Racketeer for Capitalism'," by Ralph Nader, commondreams.org, 12/30/03.

5 *Ibid.*

6 Michel Collon provides an excellent study of the U.S. and European economic interests in the Bosnian War in *Liar's Poker: The Great Powers, Yugoslavia and the Wars of the Future* (IAC, 2002) (see Bibliography).

7 Ante Pavelić, the *poglavnik* or Führer of the Independent State of Croatia, whose independence he declared on April 10, 1941, the same day Nazi forces entered Zagreb. The Vatican helped Pavelić find refuge in South America after the war. He was never prosecuted for war crimes.

8 *Handžar*, a dagger.

9 *See* srpska-mreza.com.

10 Human Rights Watch, http://www.hrw.org/reports/1992/WR92/HSW-08.htm#P1053_305172.

11 "U.S. Policymakers on Bosnia Admit Errors in Opposing Partition in 1992," by David Binder, *The New York Times*, 8/29/93.

12 "NATO Sends Greetings to a Fugitive," cnn.com, 3/12/04.

13 *Liar's Poker: The Great Powers, Yugoslavia and the Wars of the Future*, pp. 34-40, *op. cit.*

14 "Kouchner: Izetbegović admitted no Serb Death Camps in Bosnia," *SRNA*, 1/17/05.

15 See *Visoko, the Moslem Warprisoners Camp: 1992-1993 (Diaries and Testimonies)*, edited by Dr. Momčilo Mitrović (Vojska: Belgrade 1995).

16 See *Liar's Poker: The Great Powers, Yugoslavia and the Wars of the Future*, by Michel Collon (IAC: New York, 2002), p. 38.

17 "If One War 'Fact' On Iraq is False, What of Others?", by Jay Bookman, *The Atlanta Journal-Constitution*, July 10, 2003.

18 "Journalism and the CIA: The Mighty Wurlitzer," by Daniel Brandt, NameBase NewsLine, No. 17, April-June, 1997. Mr. Brandt's outstanding article should be read in its entirety. It has been widely posted on the internet. Mr. Brandt cites the source for this passage as Philip Agee's *Inside the Company: CIA Diary*, (Penguin Books, 1975), pp. 70-71.

19 "The CIA Report the President Doesn't Want You to Read," *Village Voice*, 2/20/1976, p. 40.

20 "CIA Covert Propaganda Capability," by Sean Gervasi, *Covert Action Information Bulletin*, No. 7, Dec. 1977, pp. 1, 8.

21 "Journalism and the CIA: The Mighty Wurlitzer," by Daniel Brandt, NameBase NewsLine, op. cit.

22 "When Ignorance Kills: The Clinton Administration and Al-Qaeda in the Balkans," W.H. Schindley, serbianunity.net, 11/1/04.

RATKO MLADIĆ:
HERO OR WAR CRIMINAL?
by Ljubodrag Stojadinović*

Ljubodrag Stojadinović is an author and journalist. Besides novels and satiric stories, Stojadinović, has written over one hundred articles and analyses for Politika, NIN, *and* Glas Javnosti, *among others. He served in the JNA and the Army of Yugoslavia for more than twenty-five years until 1995, when he was ousted from the military for the offense of "intellectual non-conformity." He is a recipient of the* Zlatni Jež, *the most presigious award granted in Serbia to distinctive authors of satire. He lives in Belgrade, where he covers military and political developments for* Politika.

Where Is He Hiding?

Is Ratko Mladić hiding anywhere at all? That would be uncharacteristic of him, because it has been reliably shown that he is a man of indescribable courage. Before answering the question of whether or not he is hiding at all, it would perhaps be worthwhile to ask if men of extraordinary courage are capable of being criminals? It's too early to answer, because it could be completely arbitrary and, as such, unreliable.

(...)

The story spread throughout Belgrade that Mladić had left the city for good; that he had lost interest in urban living, and so he settled in a mountainous summer pasture in eastern Serbia with his rams and goats, which had become his chief preoccupation.

(...)

But, there are people who know better, who know exactly where Mladić is and they reject this story as if it were a Serbian legend. The General, they say, left Serbia long ago, and now lives in a friendly country. Look, if you want to know exactly where, they mean Russia. Yeltsin received him and Putin later honored his decision. Ratko is in Siberia. The Russians gave him a great *dacha*, and he stays in shape by clearing tracts of immense forests; then he sits down to compose his memoirs and writes late into the night. No one can find this log cabin in Siberia, and elite KGB units, along with Cossacks, protect him; Mladić neither sees nor hears them because they are not to disturb him.

And this, of course, is not quite true, because Mladić was seen in St. Petersburg with his American biographer, who is financing the whole undertaking; meanwhile, a man who matches the description of Ratko Mladić is freely walking the streets of Moscow. They say he was first sighted leaving Lenin's Mausoleum, and that he then went to light a candle in the church of The Blessed Vasiliye. One man, a sort of Serbian representative in Moscow, photographed him in November 1999 in front of the Tsar's Bells in the Kremlin. That picture made a big hit in Belgrade and is still making the rounds.

Mladić was sighted at the same time in Kiev and Alma Ati, but he was also seen in Belgrade in Terazije where he was buying a newspaper. It is said that he was signing autographs for a crowd of people that had gathered; he was in a good mood and was not hiding from anyone. Why would General Mladić be hiding from anyone at all in Serbia?

(...)

Then there were reports of Mladić being sighted at a wedding in Valjevo. Mladić was said to have been an old friend of the family, so he of course came to their *slava*. He seemed somewhat gloomy; he had put on some weight, but was still as strong as an ox. For the most part, he remained silent, and if he said anything at all, it was about Orthodox Christianity. He partook only a small portion of *slavsko žito* and nothing else. He stayed for a little while, and then left.

Then he was sighted at a soccer game against China, and then on the beach in Ada Ciganlija. He wasn't sunbathing but sitting in the shade reading *Politika*. People were a little agitated: it *is* him, it's *not* him, well, it's *got* to be him. Mladić has no twin. But Mladić paid no attention and just kept reading. Then he got up and got dressed. He had gained a little weight; he was a little rounder, but he was still as strong as a bull. A couple of men awaited him a little farther down the lane, and then they left.

On another occasion, he was seen on a beach in the summer of 2000 near Sveti Stefan. Maybe the place was called Rafaljovići. He was taking it easy, lying under a beach umbrella. He spoke with people in his company whom he obviously knew. Then a Montenegrin policeman showed up and told him that he had orders from the authorities that he had to leave Montenegro immediately. Mladić replied: "Fuck you and the guy who sent you!" So the policeman left for reinforcements, but when they realized that they were dealing with Mladić, they dispersed, and the general continued to relax. He left Montenegro when it suited him.

One late-fall evening in 1999 (October 23), I was sitting in a well-known Belgrade café that is frequented by journalists, and I listened to a few of these stories. Each one of them had a different ending, and the narrator inevitably infused it with some of his own imaginative flourishes.... I didn't get involved, even though I have known Ratko Mladić for twenty-five years, ever since he was a captain in Kumanovo.

Communism and Orthodox Christianity

Mladić was a child of state and army ideology. He was schooled on the firm foundation of worshipping a "congenial personality" [i.e., Tito], but the most dazzling moments of his career occurred when the cult of Communist military leaders had begun to decline, and the cult of a new Serbian military leader, General Mladić, was ascendant. His charisma, even in the early phases of its development, defied logic.

Communism was breathing its last, and the Serbs were finally free to intoxicate themselves with poems and songs about Stevan Sinđelić[1] and Živojin Mišić.[2] Did Mladić understand the objective he was struggling to achieve from the very beginning? Was he fighting against separatists and armed rebels whose goal was to destroy Yugoslavia? That was the only country that the General had loved, the only country to which he had sworn an oath of loyalty and allegiance. In the early days of the war, when the incredible drama over the break up of the country took shape, Mladić believed that the SFRY (the Socialist Federal Republic of Yugoslavia) was indestructible. Many times he had said that "No existing [world] power is capable of destroying Yugoslavia." He was, of course, thinking of Tito's Yugoslavia, and he sincerely maintained this erroneous belief. One might even say that he was a fanatic believer because, right off the bat, he did not want to acknowledge the truth about indomitable Balkan atavisms.

Yugoslavia's former enemies from WWII had risen once again like vampires. It was as if they had arrived on the scene with costuming and art direction in place, and all at once ... appeared Partisans, Chetniks, Ustashi, the Muslim religious police. And in all cases, numerous parodies of military units appeared out of nowhere to tag along behind them, and countless military formations that understood war as an ideal setting for violence and indescribable plunder.

The General did not believe that such a patchwork of motley forces could survive. He was, at first, fighting against distinctions, especially when, almost by force, he took over the responsibilities of the Commander of the Knin Corps from the intelligent but indifferent to a fault General Spiro Novaković. He gathered future fighting men of varying capabilities, backgrounds and levels of commitment "for the Serbian cause" from the remnants of the Corps, which had lost most of its men and technology. Some of them wore cockades,[3] which the General found so intolerable that he took them off soldiers' heads, flung them to the ground, and trampled them beneath his boots.[4]

But, he quickly understood that the Yugoslavia, for whose defense he had been preparing with such love and devotion, was disintegrating, and that all the founders of "brotherhood and unity"[5] were rushing off to create their own states. His political reflex was not to underestimate [his opponents], even though he had declared himself as a Yugoslav in the 1960 census. That was how he had registered himself in the Yugoslav People's Army (or JNA), seeking "from members of other peoples and ethnic groups to do the same".... Yet he would come to sorely regret his belief in Yugoslavia.

Even so, Mladić quickly understood the high stakes at risk for the Serbs in this drama: if everyone set up their own nation state wherever they wanted to, then there would no longer be any place for the Serbs, and they would then be forced to leave in an exodus. His patriotic education then took a dramatic turn. In the new order of things, Tito, in whom he had believed sincerely but not fanatically, had become the architect of this new drama. He no longer believed that the interests of the Serbs could be defended by peaceful means. Today, it is understood that Mladić was not in a position to know that such matters could have been resolved by means other than war. Because, Ratko Mladić was first of all a soldier.

Mladić did not know what his own father looked like. The Ustashi killed him in Sunj (the birthplace of Ante Pavelić[6]) in 1945. "So many Serbs died in various wars that children do not remember their fathers," the General once remarked. But he did not want to be a soldier when he was a child. He had wanted to be a teacher. He changed his mind later because the teacher he had idealized turned out to be rough with his pupils: he slapped them around and insulted them. When he was eleven years old, he decided to be a surgeon. Who knows why he finally settled on soldiering?...

The military academy he attended did not hold the promise of a brilliant career. He was an outstanding student, but he chose a school that was, according to the rules in place at the time, not known as a fast track for advancing a military career. For some reason, he decided on the Military-Industrial school in Zemun, whose graduates almost never entered the ranks of elite soldiers.... Later, Mladić completed his military education with resounding success. He completed Command-General Headquarters Academy with a score of 9.57 out of ten, and graduated first in his class.

(...)

He was a high-ranking captain and battalion commander in Kumanovo in 1978. At that time, teams of officers were constantly coming from headquarters in Skoplje to perform inspections. Their methods did not please Captain Mladić. The young commander treated military training as a top priority. On one spring day that was ideal for exercises, a team of twenty officers, corporals, lieutenants and majors, appeared unexpectedly at his barracks. The leader of this motley group of officers was Corporal Jane Grujevski, who advised Captain Mladić that they had come "for a partial, unannounced inspection."

Captain Mladić responded with unconcealed anger instead. He began inspecting his uninvited guests. That was his state of mind when he said, "Comrade Corporal, I respect military command, which is something sacred for me. Training and maneuvers, as well. Every few days some inspection team shows up to pay me a visit. They go snooping around here, and get in my way the whole livelong day. Understand what I'm talking about; I have nothing against inspections that are beneficial, but you are upsetting my system. On top of that, many of the officers in your team don't know anything about a battalion, and they don't know what to look for during an inspection. So, I decided to first present your team with an examination!"

"What kind of examination, Captain? What kind of nonsense is this?"

"An examination on the problems that you are supposed to be on the look-out for during inspections. I told you, Sir, that people come here who don't have a clue. I know a few fellows on your team. I don't think that they've managed to learn anything since I last saw them!...."

The Corporal interpreted the Captain's actions as a deliberate insult, something bordering on a criminal act "against the people and the state." He replied with a similar remark, said something threatening, and left for Skoplje, where he poured out his grief to the commander of the army, General Lambeta Mihailovski.

The General studied the astonished Corporal, who felt tense and isolated, but he realized, at any rate, that the entire problem did not rest with the Captain's conduct.

"There's something to that. Some officers who go out on inspections don't know what they're doing. Worse, they go to smaller garrisons and the surrounding areas, where they gather paprika, cheese, whatever people give them. You think that the enlisted men don't hear about it? If you start acting this way, officers who are not nearly as crazy as this Captain will give you the boot. What did you say his name was?"

"Ratko Mladić."

"Yeah, him."

Cannons, the King, and Infantrymen

The question is posed today, just as it was five years ago: where, in fact, is Mladić? Is he hiding and who, if he were persistent enough, could find him? And furthermore, it is absolutely necessary to carefully consider the sequence of events. Was the general, therefore, merely a product of an abnormal and unfortunate chapter of Serbian history? Or is the matter completely the reverse: did he have such a forceful personality that he adapted circumstances to suite himself? And is he answerable for the subsequent chain of events, which can never be put right again?

If the second version is more or less true, then why wasn't General Mladić able to resolve two key issues: 1) to achieve his professional objectives; and 2) avoid subjecting himself to a permanent arrest warrant as a war criminal? In fact, the stereotype of the victor in battle unavoidably suits him. If he had, in fact, succeeded in what he had set out to do, he would then indeed have joined the company of history's victors, which would have rendered the charge of "war criminal" null and void. In any case, perhaps the most important question is how General Mladić, a man who possessed indisputably great military qualities, get into a situation where his biography became a symbol of serious, incomprehensible war crimes?

People who know Mladić are ill disposed to link his name to horrible practices that transgress the ethics of warfare. He was a high-ranking commander when the war began, and in his case, he was personally not in an environment that could have produced a syndrome of "murderous passions." Generally speaking, even the greatest opponents of his military concepts could not dispute Mladić's gifts as a commanding officer.

But fame as a commander did not come of its own accord. A shabby officer corps that did not understand what was happening and whose personal disorientation led to catastrophe was the hallmark of the JNA's disintegration. Perhaps even Mladić did not understand what it was all about at first, but he did want to change things. He was a product of the JNA, and the public did not distinguish him from the long series of other officers who were products of the same system. A dramatic transformation took place on August 14, 1991 in Vrlika. Mladić was then a colonel and was leading a column of command corps. Croatian rebels had blocked the road with an empty bus that they had mined. There was a group of journalists on the scene, but Colonel Mladić recruited the noncombatants for an important task. He said, "Comrade journalists, before us is a bus that has been mined. You will take cover over there; I will de-mine the bus."

"This colonel is nuts!" said one of the journalists, loud enough to be heard.

"Your daddy was nuts to bang a moron like you into this life!" replied Mladić without breaking his stride as he entered the bus.

About ten minutes later Mladić emerged from the bus and summoned his entourage as well as "male journalists, who still had some balls left."

"Journalists, fall in!" commanded Mladić, and a group of about ten hack writers who had been conscripted somehow lined up.

"To the bus, double time! Forward!" commanded the Colonel, but the group of journalists was in no hurry to do so. Many of them did not immediately understand what they were going to do inside the bus.

Some of them, after having realized that they had been picked out to witness the removal of explosives, became conspicuously frightened.

"What if it blows up?" someone asked.

"If it blows up — then there won't be any more questions," said the Colonel. "After all, it won't blow up. The explosives are now harmless. You can pick it up like kindling."

"Which wire did you cut," asked a reporter.

"The yellow one!" Mladić calmly replied.

"How did you know?"

"I didn't. I had to chose one."

"I always knew this guy was nuts," mumbled the other journalist so that the Colonel would not hear him. "He wasn't going to slip past me. I can always tell nut job when I see one."

Mladić achieved a number of acknowledged successes with the Ninth (Knin Corps). Much to the surprise of the public and the military, as well as to politicians, he was no longer one of "Tito's officers, of average operational capabilities," as Communist generals were often judged to be. One could already see that the officer possessed trenchant intelligence, great personal courage, and that he left a terrific impression on his men. On the suggestion of Nikola Koljević,[7] Mladić, who was already a general, became the Commander of the ARS. These are well known facts, but most important is his meeting with General Kukanjac[8] at the end of May 1992 in Sarajevo, after repeated tragedies had struck JNA units in Skenderija and on Dobrovoljačka ulica.[9] "Kukanjac was completely heartbroken. It was hard for him," said Mladić. "I understood him as a human being, but not as a commander. The dead bodies of JNA soldiers were lying throughout the city; there was nothing but horror wherever one turned. Then he asked me: 'Brother, can you tell me what to do?' 'Kill yourself, Milutin', I said to him, that's what you should do'."

Kukanjac did not take his advice, even though Mladić says that he seriously considered it. The image of the bodies of JNA soldiers floating in the Miljačka remained lodged in General Mladić's mind, and perhaps it was these very same images that later determined the fate of Sarajevo.

Mladić, as a Serbian commander, met with tragedy in the whole of Bosnia-Herzegovina. Was it at all possible to erect a brutal war crimes machine that was based on the relatively recent concept of a Serbian military renaissance? And, generally speaking, was this a renaissance established on the basis of mutual extermination?

The General had many occasions to announce his position on war crimes. He had a profound faith in Serbian military ethics.

Western generals came to the Balkans to cap off their careers with some "experience" or to take wartime risks. Most of them did not like Mladić, except for perhaps MacKenzie. Michael Rose was convinced of Mladić's charisma, cunning and military capability, but he was troubled by his "strategic dogmatism" (?), his egotism, and even his unkempt appearance....

Philip Morillon, the French general, probably respected Mladić, but he certainly hated him. At a meeting with General Perišić on September 17, 1994, which the author of this book attended, Morillon presented a list of thirty-seven instances of attempts to humiliate him. Morillon (wrongly) believed that Perišić had a great deal of influence on Mladić, and that Perišić would warn him not to attempt further humiliations of the French military. And here is just one example. In June of the same year (1994), Morillon had urgently requested a meeting with General Mladić. There were many topics slated for discussion, and Mladić had agreed to meet him at ARS headquarters on June 11 at noon.

Morillon arrived exactly on time. He waited ten, then twenty minutes. Then a half an hour passed, but Mladić had shown no sign of hospitality. Finally, fifty minutes later, Mladić emerged from his office with a sergeant major, who was carrying a chess set under his arm.

"I emphatically protest, General, Sir!" said Morillon.... "Our meeting was set for twelve hundred hours, and you've kept me on ice for a whole hour!"

"Why such an angry outburst, Commander, Sir?" replied Mladić with astonishment. "You must believe me when I tell you that I have a justifiable reason for this short delay of our meeting, which, in any case, I have been looking forward to with great pleasure."

"I was curious to know whether or not you would say that," said the French general without any visible sign of his fury abating.

"You know," said Mladić, "I'm crazy about chess. I never met a military commander who didn't like the game. Napoleon, if you recall, enjoyed playing simultaneous games against his marshals. My opponents have more modest titles, but they are dangerous fighters, in chess as well as in other matters. Look, that sergeant major that just passed by gave me a really rough time. I was in such a complicated position, and I could not allow a sergeant major to defeat me. As Napoleon with his own marshals."

Morillon related this to Perišić with unconcealed fury. "Do you want another cup of coffee?" asked Perišić.

"If possible, I'd like something stronger, much stronger," replied Morillon.

Fear and Fascination

The world almost became indifferent to war during the 1990s. Great powers provoked wars in order to have opportunities to show off their unequalled military superiority. However, local wars or military actions to bring a "world pariah" to heel became profitable public ventures. The actions of the Coalition forces in Gulf War I began as a serious military-political task but ended as a show-business extravaganza. It was the first televised war in history. One of its results was far more important than mere spectacle: the clear and undeniable evidence of global might.

Things were different, however, in the Balkans. The most powerful media organizations in the world were right on the scene, but the resulting chaos and reigning absurdity were not easily transformed into the news stories the media desired. It was necessary to seek out and find suitable settings for a simple dramatic element in which the distinction between "good guys and bad guys" could function without a hitch. It is perhaps correct to assume that the Serbs were assigned the "bad guy" role by the media as early as April 29, 1992, when the general headquarters of the JNA got the idiotic idea to arrest the legitimate president of Bosnia-Herzegovina, Alija Izetbegović. Afterwards, the massacre on Dobrovoljačka ulica took place, Kukanjac was relieved of duty, and Mladić arrived on the scene.

General Mladić quickly proved to be an irresistible media figure. His dealings with people were characterized by his extreme and contradictory manner: people were afraid of his military rashness as well as of his capabilities as an officer. They had no idea of what he was capable of doing. At the same time, he fascinated them with the sheer force of his self-confidence.

Mladić was no diplomat. In 1993, when NATO threatened to bomb the Republika Srpska, he said this: "If they bomb me, I'll bomb London. Whoever intervenes here will get as much in return, and the first target is going to be Italy if they allow NATO to use their bases to make bombing runs over Bosnia. Foreign soldiers will leave their bones in Bosnia to the extent that they intervene."[10]

The Italians reacted immediately. This meant that they took Mladić seriously, even though it wasn't clear how and by what means Mladić would be able to bomb Italian territory, not to mention London. After all, the Italian defense minister at the time, Fabio Fabri, characterized Mladić's statement as "a sign of weakness, of incomprehensible and indefensible conduct and the fruit of blind and irrational nationalism, which must in no way be taken seriously."

The President of the Republika Srpska, Radovan Karadžić, found Mladić's aggressive outbursts incomprehensible. He was no diplomat, either, but he interpreted the threatening remarks made by his leading general as "sheer idiocy." There are witnesses who confirm that Mladić, in a face-to-face meeting with Karadžić, judged this to be a characteristically "retarded" remark made by his civilian chief, and Mladić advised him of it in a rather indelicate manner.

Robert Block of *The Independent* [U.K.] thought that Mladić
had plenty of reasons to be *Man of the Year*.[11] Laura Silber, a
journalist with the *Financial Times*, is always suspended between
fascination and revulsion when writing about Mladić. "Over the
past 32 months of war, Mladić has gained a reputation for brutal
genius, masterminding the Serb campaign to carve out an ethnically pure state in Bosnia-Herzegovina."[12] Ms. Silber is inclined
to describe Mladić as a man who sat with his soldiers on a moun-
tainside above Sarajevo, firing on the city and conducting long
dinners with plenty of drinks. She claims that UN officers, who
made irascible comments about Sarajevo, could be found with
him. "But," writes Silber, "the cruel soldier occasionally wants to
bestow what he sees as his gift of life on Muslims or Croats.
'When I guarantee something it is the same as the word of the
Almighty', he often says. During the mass exodus of Muslims
from the eastern enclave of Srebrenica, a man of military age was
discovered hiding among hundreds of hysterical Muslims jam-
packed into a lorry. Mladić told the terrified man: 'I will spare
your life, but just remember who did it'."

Not everyone, however, considered Mladić to be merely
"aggressive, thoroughly frustrated, and ruled by nationalism, a
man who is governed by irrational instincts." General Louis
McKenzie considered him to be a tactician and strategist of the
highest order. He was convinced that Mladić was always able to
come up with a solution that, at first glance, no other military
man was able to see....

General Mladić was obviously not able to free himself of
stereotyping in order to draft a laconic military-political analysis
of global dimensions. From his point of view, the world was a
dichotomy or it did not exist at all. World power had to be justly
distributed, otherwise power was excessively concentrated. He
even proposed the defense of Russia as a reason for the strategic
removal of Western military organizations from the region.
Nevertheless, his fatal mistake was underestimating NATO's
resolve. And he overestimated NATO's inertia, and he even neglected the interests of the organization as well as of the West, for
NATO's continued existence no matter what it might entail. He
proceeded to act in accordance with these (erroneous) judgments.
Mladić also miscalculated two other elements: Serbia's total

resources to wage a war, and the collective demonization to which the Serbian people were subjected, which made them a target for collective revenge.

No matter what you might think about it, General Mladić personally facilitated the accumulation of this odium, but as such, it has no bearing on his personal shortcomings, because he did not understand the arrangement, the balance of power. His arrogance, *vis-à-vis* those who were more powerful than he, was not a terrible thing when Mladić was a battalion commander. But when he became a national military symbol, his arrogance became fatal, because it brought forth nothing good — only unproductive, masochistic spitefulness.

Now the conditions were set for the sudden decline and fall of Serbian military and political power, which resulted from a misjudgment of superpower politics. It seems as though Mladić's ability to successfully lead operations along the Posavina Valley, Igman and Bjelašnica — and his ability to wreak vengeance on those who remained in Sarajevo for the slaughter of JNA soldiers on Dobrovoljačka ulica, whose bodies he had seen when he took over General Kukanjac's command — resulted from his personal understanding of the struggle between local and global forces. He did not have to understand the temperament of the great powers, but he had to bear in mind the quickly spent motives for going to war as well as a comprehension of the senselessness of war.

In any case, his visionary tactical and operational achievements were not the lens through which he ought to have seen the world. On this basis, Ratko Mladić stands as a unique symbol of Serbian military depression.

Fascination with General Mladić, as well as with his life story, was treated in a relative manner by those who, at the time, wrote him unmerited odes. But fear remained, fear as a symbol of every war. When war is purged of romanticism, only fear remains.

The Serbian–Srpska Republika Connection

The transfer of Serbs from the JNA to the Western Serbian army progressed slowly and with great difficulty. There were many reasons for this. Yet Serbia and Montenegro created another

Yugoslavia, and even at the beginning it looked like something that had been hastily done. The war in Bosnia-Herzegovina became a brutal and cruel affair, while on May 20, 1992, the Socialist Republic of Yugoslavia promised "to withdraw members of the JNA from Bosnia-Herzegovina who were citizens of Yugoslavia."

That was, of course, difficult to achieve. In Serbia, the massacre on Dobrovoljačka ulica aroused disgust and bitterness as well as fear for the well being of the soldiers who had been put in a military situation full of unknowns. And there was more to fear. The government did indeed promise that the soldiers would return, but the General Staff, with General Blagoje Adžić at its head, did something completely different. They began recruiting soldiers from garrisons in Serbia, regardless of their specializations, and without their commanding officers, to be transferred to Bosnia-Herzegovina.

Families that did not know where their sons had been stationed besieged the building that housed the Federal Ministry of National Defense for days on end. Adžić submitted his resignation; he had been insulted by the removal of Kukanjac and by criticism of the amateurish but peaceful army parade in the middle of Sarajevo, which, after all, was in a state of war. The new head of the General Staff, Života Panić, sent the young General Vuk Obradović to inform the parents, to the extent that he could and was able to, of the fate of the army as well as the people, and to somehow hush up the matter, calm these people down, but not to promise anything he could not deliver.

What promises were impossible to fulfill? At that moment, one could have promised almost nothing. The state and the army were utterly disorganized. The conditions were chaotic; war was threatening to break out on all sides, while young Serbian men had been singled out to be cannon fodder for a chauvinistic settling of scores with oligarchs from the former republics. They desired at all cost to create new states, while the Serbs had the idea that the old state had to be preserved at all cost, even though no one wanted it anymore.

Vuk Obradović appeared before a delegation of some fifty people who had been chosen by the parents of soldiers. They entered the building and gathered in a narrow classroom, number 143 on the fourth floor of Building B of the General Staff.

They were shouting: "Ua, you're a bunch of lying, thieving bums! You can't stay in power by spilling innocent blood! Shame on you!"

Vuk said: "Please, listen to me carefully...."

But hardly anyone paid any attention to him. The uproar was indescribable, and there was an undercurrent of horror.

"You lie as soon as you open your trap!" said a heavyset man of middle height, who was obviously setting the tone. But Vuk added: "No, we're not lying. I'm not going to lie to you!"

"You're a liar, just like all the other officers. You're all incompetent, and you're lying to us and sending our children off to their deaths!"...

"I promise you," replied Vuk, "that if all the soldiers who are citizens of the SRY are not back home by May 20, I will no long serve this army as a general."

"You're lying, General!" shouted the citizens, but they somehow dispersed. They refused snacks, coffee and juice.

Fifteen days later, on the day that General Obradović had promised that the soldiers would be back home, the day on which he had staked his career, one hundred people showed up once again at the Federal Ministry of National Defense building. They were carrying a large poster that read, "Hey, Vuk, keep your word!"

That very day, Vuk Obradović resigned from the Yugoslav army, and took a job in his brother's retail store. Later, he became a building contractor....

Perhaps Vuk Obradović, right at the high point of the drama, was a man who took Serbian national interests into account. After all, Milošević, who was convinced of the definitive productiveness of war, was not in the least bit sorry because Vuk Obradović had resigned from the army.... "At last, we got some good news today," [said Milošević] as he lit up a cigarette.

The war in B-H was characterized by alternating suspicion and enthusiasm, and then by unity and division and struggle until Milošević blockaded the Drina in August 1994.

General Mladić knew better than anyone else that the war could not be won without strategic support from Serbia. The Serbian media created a powerful information lobby that propagated two parallel myths. The first was that the Serbs were unconquerable warriors who could defy one and all because they would surely defeat their enemies if it came down to a decisive battle. A variant of this myth is contained in the conviction that with such a balance of power, no one would dare to attack Serbia. The myth of superiority which, of course, had no real foundation, was built on this new cult. Milošević was pronounced a messiah and Serbian prophet. At last, finally, a man arrived on the scene who would enable the Serbs to win victories in war as well as in peace. This capital error certainly had great effect by encouraging implacability among the Serbs in Bosnia-Herzegovina....

Mladić's entire verbal patriotic opus consisted of calling on Serbia to come to the aid of its brothers across the Drina. In the beginning of July, at a coordination meeting between the General Staff of the federal Army of Yugoslavia and of the army of the Republika Srpska, Mladić said: "My fellow officers, I am ashamed of everything that is going on here. Last night I returned from the battlefield, where our men are dying. We don't have enough soldiers, money, food and ammunition. Especially for artillery pieces. Our tank munitions are at a critical low. But all our soldiers would put up with that, and even hunger and poverty. But today I went past Ada Ciganlija, where 300,000 people were sunbathing and swimming. The war is close by, and an entire brother nation is dying and suffering, but in Belgrade they've gone swimming. Officers, this is a shame, and it's not the way to help your brothers."

Mladić's presentation at that meeting was not characterized by the cold-blooded position of an experienced soldier, but by the pathetic view of a moralist who was not sufficiently bitter to depict his own astonishment....

In October of that year, General Perišić summoned all officers from Belgrade garrisons who were by birth from the Republika Srpska to a meeting in Topčidar. About five hundred of them showed up. Perišić and Mladić addressed them.... At first, Mladić chose his words carefully; then he stopped choosing his words carefully. He told the officers that buses were waiting outside, ready to take the officers to Bosnia. He explained that the Bosnian Serb Army was dying. What had happened — happened. He said that they had not answered the call until now, and that they had good reasons for having done so, but now there were no more good reasons. He said that the Serbs were either going to have a state or the army was going to disgrace itself before the world and before its own people.

But not one officer from that large group volunteered. Mladić had insisted that the officers come to the assembly in order to motivate the others to do so — but that did not happen, either. Then Mladić said: "Over there, in my General Headquarters, I've got a company of female soldiers. They are outstanding fighters, and they can stand shoulder to shoulder with the best fighting men. You don't even stand as high as their skirts. Shame on you! I'm not going to come here any more to call on you, plead with you or try to convince you. The next time, I'm going to send my company of women, an outstanding fighting unit, to hunt you down and catch you in Belgrade and bring you in that disgraceful condition over there [to Bosnia], and then we'll let the people tell you what they think of you. That's what I'll do. I'll send women warriors to arrest you, you cunts!"

Perhaps General Mladić's military talent was needlessly wasted, suspended as it was between an unclear political strategy and a correspondingly shaky foundation for military action. At the moment, official contacts between Serbia and the Republika Srpska were broken, and the ARS had taken the initiative on a front line that was 1,600 kilometers in length. It is amply clear that such a fragmented, inconsistent and volatile front line could not have been defended without the greatest amount of aid possible from the motherland.

Mladić tried to address the problem, but he kept believing in Serbian superiority, even if Serbia had stopped providing even symbolic support....

The Karadžić–Mladić Conflict

There are few politicians who have been able to rise to the top by sheer charisma as Ratko Mladić did. Radovan Karadžić and Slobodan Milošević were, each in his own way, convinced that they deserved credit for "creating" the most popular general in modern Serbian history. They both needed Mladić. In the beginning, they were well pleased with the legendary military leader who won battles easily. But, men whose task it was to hold their people in a state of fascination with their "historic missions" were displeased by competition.... The popularity of General Mladić cast a long shadow over everyone else's actions, and most of all, he overshadowed the two men who had "created" him.

Even at the very beginning, General Mladić and President Karadžić had little sympathy for each other. Mladić doubted that Karadžić, an "inspired" poet, and besides that, a neuropsychiatrist, was capable of leading a state. Karadžić was convinced that this one of Tito's Communist officers was utterly devoid of professionalism and virtue. In fact, Mladić is said to have addressed him as "Mr. President" only when they were first acquainted. Thereafter, he simply called him "Radovan." The general in no way wanted to demean his civilian chief, but only to share responsibility with him equally. How could a president have greater responsibility than a general in a state of war?

Karadžić had a distinct need to purge his official biography of references to Communism. For that reason, he publicly distanced himself from the potential shortcomings of a general from Tito's army. He mentioned it several times in sessions of parliament, especially in Sanski Most, where he asserted that all accounts of failures in military operations occurred because of the "weak level of expertise of officers who still bore Tito's ideological stamp."

General Mladić suffered through this as long as he could, and then, after having heard Karadžić's "expert analysis," he took the podium. He removed a piece of paper from the pocket of his camouflaged jacket and began to read: "Dear Comrade Tito, happy seventy-sixth birthday, with sincerest wishes that you will continue to lead us down the path of glory for a long time to come, and that your visionary qualities remain the bright torch that will illuminate our future. Sarajevo, May 25, 1968."

"So, what is that supposed to mean?" asked Karadžić. "Is that yours, something that you, as a young officer, sent to Tito for his birthday?"

"It's not mine, my dear Radovan. It's yours! I didn't read the signature because I thought you would have recalled what you had written." The parliament broke out in guffaws and uproarious laughter, while Karadžić warned Mladić that this was not the time for frivolities because the destiny of the state was in question.

"It's not only a question of the destiny of the state," replied Mladić, "but also of certain biographical details of one of Tito's officers and one of Tito's poets."

(...)

Mladić was outspoken and he tried to isolate political leaders who had become powerful during the war and who had created their own private armies: "These paramilitary forces were, by and large, hovering around various jewelry shops, banks, well-stocked supermarkets, and there is not a single hill that they either protected or liberated. They merely plundered, and plundered well."

General Mladić did not speak publicly about the heart of his conflict with Karadžić. He thought that such things could be settled behind closed doors so that normal disagreements would not take the form of a strategic defeat. Karadžić discovered his ambition to become commander-in-chief of the armed forces only when Ratko Mladić's operational capabilities were indisputable, and when units of the ARS held an unbelievably long front line....

(...)

In August 1995, Karadžić took that step, which perhaps led to the definitive disintegration of the policies held by both the army and government, which had nation-building ambitions. Karadžić, by means of a presidential decree of dubious legality, made himself the commander-in-chief of the armed forces, and made General Mladić his advisor. He was convinced that he had thus solved two problems that had previously made absolute power unattainable: control over the armed forces, and control over the man who, in that army, was invincible.

The General Staff, however, stood by Mladić, while Karadžić created a position called the Chief of the General Staff, and later filled the post with Pero Ćolić, a relatively undistinguished soldier....

(...)

The General Staff received the sensational move with utter disbelief. A few generals that I spoke with at the time said: "They say that guy [Karadžić] is some kind of neuropsychiatrist, but he's nuts"....

One wonders whether or not Karadžić deliberately chose the day of the fall of the Republika Srpska Krajina to relieve Mladić of duty. The fall of the RSK was, in fact, a strategic model for all subsequent withdrawals in the Republika Srpska, as well as for the fall of individual territories that the army had no real chance of defending.

The same media that had at one time created the undefeated general, and had compared him to the most famous military leaders in Serbian history, now reversed itself and began demonizing the leadership of the entire army in the direst moments of the war when Mladić refused to become Karadžić's advisor. ("I don't have any advice to give him. And normal advice is not what he needs.") As soon as General Gvero made the announcement, the Republika Srpska media reacted, and announced the statements made by the political leadership, along with a withering commentary. Mladić commented: "I listened to the news attack General Gvero while I was driving, and I thought it was coming from a Croatian or Muslim radio station. I noticed, however, that they didn't resort to the usual phrases, like 'war criminal' and 'Chetnik General', which was part and parcel of enemy propaganda. That was how I figured out the news was coming from the Republika Srpska news services."

(...)

But the soldiers ... whose testimonials bordered between warrior-like enthusiasm and pathetic idealism, stood by Mladić. The soldiers and the people admired Ratko Mladić, certainly because of his capabilities, but also because he mythically represented inescapable messianism.

(...)

Nevertheless, how strong was the ARS at that moment? and to what extent had military-political disintegration weakened it? It is, indeed, a difficult question to answer because the facts are insufficient and contradictory, and because of the undeniable fact that the upper limits of its troop numbers had never been completely realized. Different conclusions have been drawn because there was no source of information that could have in any sense been officially verifiable. The propaganda apparatus of the Republika Srpska found itself caught between the twin necessities of demonstrating its own strategic power while concealing aid that was coming from the motherland. Nevertheless ... one can conclude that the ARS, at the beginning of 1994, when the actions it initiated fell short of its goals, had between 80,000 and

100,000 soldiers, 320 tanks, 400 armored vehicles, 796 artillery pieces, 40 airplanes, 22 helicopters, and ten batteries of ground-to-air missiles, with SA-6s, SA-7s and SA-14s that had a range of 30–60 kilometers.

The army held a front line whose length was somewhere between 1,600 to 1,700 kilometers. Foreign analysts did not challenge Mladić's capability but they did have some suggestions. Namely, the ARS was waging a largely positional war against, Muslim and Croat enemy units. In the long run, such a war was regarded as unproductive from all points of view, unless the enemy capitulated quickly. Capitulation, however, was not at all certain. Already by the middle of 1994, the staffs of the enemy armies had obtained instructors, chiefly retired German, Turkish and American officers. They advised them to reply with a guerrilla war that focused on the "weak points in Serbian positions." They reasoned that time was a factor going against the Serbs. Neutral observers, if they existed at all, knew that such a long front could not always be successfully defended for an indefinite period of time. Resources were slowly being used up, motivation was slackening, and Serbia no longer had either the strength or the ability to replenish ARS troops. At the highest political levels, corruption and war profiteering became more important than the war itself, and it soon became clear that the fiercest struggles were being set off by attempts to take advantage of the inexhaustible opportunities war provided for monopolies that arose solely for the accumulation of personal wealth.

General Mladić was never labeled as the kind of officer who took advantage of the war to make himself wealthy. But, his civilian chiefs, if he at all acknowledged them as such, were doing precisely that. Radovan Karadžić, poet and psychiatrist, was inclined to spend large sums of money gambling, which was known before the war, but the large sums of money had to come from somewhere, even during the war.

(...)

Mladić clearly showed how much he thought of Karadžić's presidential authority on February 20, 1994, when NATO issued an ultimatum for the withdrawal of Serbian artillery pieces from the area around Sarajevo. Even though the President of the Republika Srpska had agreed to withdraw heavy artillery, and even though the withdrawal had already begun, Mladić at once announced that the withdrawal had been halted, and that the Army would not withdraw. The February 10, 1994 issue of *Vojska* reported that he said: "And what do I care? For me, the war will be symbolically over when the Muslims hand over their weapons on Dobrovoljačka ulica, the same street where they launched the shameful and criminal attack on a column of troops from the former JNA."

Even Milošević, who had attempted to use his personal authority to profit from resolving "the conflict between authorities," namely, Mladić and Karadžić, thought that things had gone too far because of Mladić's stubbornness and arrogance, so he arranged a meeting with Vitaly Churkin.[13]

Churkin and Mladić held their discussions in the Federal Parliament building. Mladić was rude, even hostile to the Russian representative, but he finally agreed to take some steps.

(...)

Dobrica Ćosić, then president of the Serbian Republic of Yugoslavia, spoke about the conflict between Mladić and Karadžić. When asked what influence Karadžić had on Mladić, he replied: "Modest, insignificant. My many efforts have until now failed. We could have minimized some misfortunes. But not one single war has ever been conducted in a logical manner, and this one isn't any different. Our vital interest is peace. The longer the war, the more dishonorable the compromise."

Labeled a War Criminal

Generally speaking, are there people who are inclined (perhaps genetically) to commit war crimes?... Anyone who is involved in a war must make weighty decisions, many of which bear directly on the life and death of great numbers of people, and such an individual must be conscious of the fact that decisions contain traces of evildoing....

Both criminality and heroism are overvalued in order to take advantage of a military initiative or a post-war milieu. The victors will glorify not only their own heroism, but will also elevate their own humanity.... The defeated are fated to suffer the dictates of the victors, because earlier they had to suffer something much worse: military humiliation....

Wartime at one moment offers a commander limitless power over the lives of the enemy as well as over the lives of his own soldiers. Such undeserved power frequently catapults military leaders into a position where they are soulless masters of people's fate, instead of elevating them to humanists whose mission it is to save the victims of war. What was Ratko Mladić like in such circumstances?

Today, there is no unqualified answer. General Mladić was able to say: "When I promise you something, it's just as if the Almighty himself had said it." There are two possible interpretations of this explicitly egotistical personal principle. Did Mladić at one moment actually begin to believe in his own supernatural qualities?... His successes on the battlefield, no matter how numerous, resulted, at least in the beginning, from relatively low intensity encounters. Mladić was commanding units that had already been trained and organized while his opponents, all the way to the end of 1994, were amateurs, products of neo-nationalistic militarism.

There Mladić was superior, but like a visionary, if he were one, he did not notice two conflicting, but mutually dependent processes. While the operational-tactical potential of the ARS, *vis-à-vis* initiatives and solidly planned operations (Igman, Bjelašnica, Posavska Corridor), was weakening, his opponents had nearly overcome their amateurism with battlefield experience. With the help of the West, their inferiority gradually vanished, while Mladić's military capabilities were unable to neutralize their plan to change the balance of power. It seems as though General Mladić, precisely because of his awareness of his own strength, did not want to or was not able to see the dangers that in the future would turn out to be unavoidable and ruinous.

The second reason he may have had for comparing himself to the "Almighty" could lie in his emphasis on sincerity and honesty. This also clearly indicates a high level of egocentricity, but in any case, it is much less astonishing than the first. He probably wished to leave an impression not only of bravery and reliability, but of a man who was "tough, strict but fair," and accordingly, his public statements and his words could be construed as completely reliable, without regard to whom he may have addressed them.

(...)

Was Mladić himself able to believe this? He was, without a doubt, a man who possessed great military prowess. It is altogether clear that the unanticipated and surprising onslaught of fame put Mladić out of touch with reality. Besides, the entire Serbian military-political elite lived for a few years in a pleasant, blind, and non-existent nationalist glory, in a stratosphere of strategic utopia. Mladić was no genius, and it should come as no surprise that he found himself trapped in a parallel world that he had constructed, which he had attempted to criticize and transform, but whose essence he could not change.

(...)

Generals make irreversible decisions and judgments in wartime. A crime is committed when a judgment is made that oversteps the ethical bounds of military decision-making. General Mladić's obstinacy, which he demonstrated by behaving rudely toward one and all, but especially toward those who wielded the most power, was certainly a prejudice above and beyond any rational decision. A man who wields such power is in no position to control it in wartime, because this power is distributed to lower ranking officers who may have no redeeming qualities. Each one of them dreamed of being General Mladić, and imagined that his own words would be ones that would define life and death.

Consider the testimony of Misha Glenny, a BBC correspondent from Eastern Europe. His book, *The Fall of Yugoslavia**, was published in 1992. General Mladić was at that time still the Commander of the Knin Corps, whose command he had recently assumed from General Špiro Novaković. Here is Glenny's account of the meeting:

> After showing a variety of weapons which he had personally confiscated from defeated Croat and Slovene fighters, General Mladić, who was clearly enjoying his captive audience, chuckled as he prepared us for a tape recording of a recent telephone conversation between himself and the head of the Croat Interior Ministry (MUP) force in the nearby port of Split, one of the most militant homes of the Croatian Democratic Union (HDZ). Although neither was expecting to talk to the other, it emerged almost immediately that the two were acquaintances of old:

"Is that you, Mladić?"

"Yes it is, you old devil, what do you want?"

"Three of my boys went missing near ... and I want to find out what happened to them."

"I think they're all dead."

"I've got one of the parents on to me about it, so I can tell them for certain that they're gone?"

"Yep, certain. You have my word. By the way, how's the family?"

"Oh, not so bad, thanks. How about yours?"

"They're doing just fine, we're managing pretty well."

"Glad to hear it. By the way, now I've got you on the line, we've got about twenty bodies of yours near the front and they've been stripped bare. We slung them into a mass grave and they're now stinking to high heaven. Any chance of you coming to pick them up because they really are becoming unbearable... ?"

This camaraderie between the opposing merchants of slaughter was one of the most horrifying phenomena I observed during the war....

In 1994, critics began to appear in Serbia who openly opposed Mladić's outstanding military skill ... when the war's brutality intensified, most notably during the siege of Sarajevo. The former editor of *Narodna armija* (The People's Army), retired colonel Gaja Petković, wrote an article that appeared in NIN, which went on to say: "[Mladić, *Author's Note*] set up artillery all around Sarajevo in groups of ten large caliber guns, 76mm, 105mm, 122mm, 130mm and 150mm, multiple-barreled 'Plamen' rocket launchers and the 128mm 'Oganj', mortars of 60mm, 81mm, 82mm and 120mm, and it perfectly matched the plans for revenge, whose ideological founders were sitting around in Pale and in Belgrade and who began their long-awaited feast of war."

Colonel Petković claimed that Mladić at that time enjoyed such uncontested military superiority that he was "bombing where he had to as well as where he didn't have to throughout Sarajevo," but chiefly where he didn't have to. Mladić wanted "to knock some sense into Alija," but Muslims, Serbs and Croats were all dying in war-torn Sarajevo.

It is obvious that rational military targeting was not possible from the hills around Sarajevo. From these positions, there was no justification for the heavy bombardment of Sarajevo, and the systematic "murder" of the city.[14] Sarajevo was being murdered from within, and all three sides in the conflict were guilty of inflicting terror, snipering and countless other tragedies. But, such scenes would not have existed, nor would the entire city have been turned into a terrible battlefield of reciprocal ethnic terror if it had not been isolated by a terrifying artillery encirclement. No one was able to get out of Sarajevo without the benefit of connections, a great deal of money or madman's luck.

Why did Mladić single out Sarajevo? Did he have, as one psychologist claimed, "the inferiority complex of a peasant from Božinović near Kalinovik, who must have been underestimated by that city, which did not accept him as one of its own, and deemed him unworthy of it".... Mladić said on many occasions that Sarajevo was a Serbian city, and that the war could end once the city had fallen.

If Sarajevo had, indeed, once been a Serbian city, then why did Mladić destroy it with such zeal? Who was going to benefit if the Serbs helped bring down a Serbian city? The siege of Sarajevo, in the end, was not a noble undertaking for a commander, but a unique sort of military horror, an act of unconcealed sadism.

For some reason, Sarajevo remained a distinctive obsession with Mladić which even today has not been fully explained. After operation "Lukavac 93," he advised the Muslims: "Let them not imagine for a moment that someone is going to come to protect them. They will secure their safety if they lay down their arms. If they drop these [hostile] intentions, they can live in the territories that we leave them. Even that is too much for them. It's up to Alija and those who are advising him to think about what they're going to do. I'm leaving Sarajevo for the end."

Vuk Drašković[15] ... defined the relationship between "the Serbian struggle" and a worldwide conspiracy: "Do we really want such politicians and military leaders as we now have portraying us in this fashion for all the world to see? I will not acknowledge those who put on Vojvoda Mišić's hat and then get the notion that they have Vojvoda Mišić's brains, as Serbs. They go shooting their mouths off on television: 'We take no prisoners, we kill them all'."

(...)

But the label of war criminal, which General Mladić carries, is a serious problem that will be examined for a long time to come.

It is a complicated and contradictory wartime labyrinth, almost a thriller, in fact.... History takes note of only heroes and villains, and ignores ordinary men who have disappeared, through no fault of their own, as the nameless victims of somebody's heroism or villainy. For them, such distinctions are meaningless.

The Markale green market massacre on February 5, 1994.... Nowadays, it is believed to have perhaps been a horrifying Muslim set up designed to provoke the world "to finally begin punishing the Serbs" for their "criminal disobedience." Nevertheless, there is still no convincing evidence for two such extremely contradictory assertions.... The Serbs claim that they are not so crazy that they would do something that was so senseless, because they are neither criminals nor so stupid to hang such an albatross around their neck. The Muslims, on the other hand, claim that their struggle was not founded on fanaticism, so it is madness to accuse them of such a horrifying act of self-mutilation.[16]

Each version of the story has its own good reasons, along with plenty of arguments and denials.

General Michael Rose, a seasoned soldier who achieved fame for his actions to retake the Falkland Islands, as well as for a massacre of Argentinean soldiers, gave perhaps the most detailed reasons for the origin of the charge against the Serbs: "I do not accept Serbian denials, because bombing populated areas is unacceptable."

Sir Michael Rose used a line of logic that threatened the long-established tradition of Serbian military self-respect. At the heart of this premise, those who were bombing populated areas did not care about casualties. It is hard to believe that men who were bombing the city every day chose not to bomb the city on just that particular day when one of the greatest crimes of the war took place. One artilleryman, who was well acquainted with the trajectory of mortar shells, said: "On the technical side, bombing the Markale green market didn't present any kind of a problem. Targeting the mortar is routine, then you fire — and it's all over. It was something easy and possible to do from the mountains outside Sarajevo."

The General Staff in Belgrade thought differently. They organized a news conference, where a technical munitions expert attempted to prove that it was impossible for such a tragedy to arise from a single mortar shell.[17]

But it was difficult to convince the world with evidentiary logic. The story about the Serbs, who were killing a defenseless city, was too strong for anyone to believe this refutation. Such a refutation was incredible, even in the chaos of the war in Bosnia-Herzegovina.

Ratko Mladić was at the center of all these events, regardless of whether battlefield exploits or war crimes were in question.... General Mladić became a symbol of military brutality, regardless of his mission and of the confidence he had in himself and in what he was doing.... The West considered the "war criminal" label to be altogether appropriate and well suited for him. He was proud of it.

Besides, the "Almighty" was not suffering, and he was unrepentant of the destiny he had chosen. He believed that it was merely his assignment, and everyone else's destiny.

Reject the Plan, Win the War

"General Mladić was certain of victory. It was impossible to be with him in the same fighting regiment and not to believe it. No, it was not optimism, nor optimism alone.... It was indomitable energy, which was a common feeling when in the General's company."

These are the thoughts of one a fellow soldier who served under the General during the war. He maintains that Mladić was never given to irrational hopes, and that his military sobriety was never in question, but he was nevertheless convinced that Mladić was something entirely different. "He simply had a contribution to make as a commander. I believed in him then, and I still believe in him today. He is completely different from the notion people have about him as a despotic general. He is an original. It's something like egocentricity, but he is essentially a decent man. He is not corrupt, and he is not a criminal."

(...)

This is what took place at a general meeting between ARS Headquarters and General Perišić when a dispute arose over adopting the Contact Group's Plan (August 12, 1994):

Perišić: "International factors want to reintegrate Yugoslavia in such a manner that it no longer has any winners or large states, and it does not want ethnically pure states. They want to pit us against each other. They want to incite quarrels now with either the prospect of peace or with the continuation of the war. Recommendations: 1) to surpass and excel the cunning of the Muslims and the Croats; 2) to count on that fact that together they will not get more than 49% of the territory; 3) Yeltsin will not honor obligations he had previously signed outside of the framework of the accepted plan. It cannot be certain that they [the Russians] will send their own peacekeeping forces. Maybe they can; maybe they can't. They will because it is necessary for them; they won't because they bombed their own Parliament without even the support of 25% of the Russian electorate.

"Unless it accepts their essential interpretation of the plan, the Federal Republic of Yugoslavia will find itself in a position where: 1) it will be impossible to obtain provisions; 2) it will be impossible to send troops; 3) everything else stops." [This defines of the position of the Federal Republic of Yugoslavia on sending its own soldiers to the Republika Srpska, *Author's Note*.]

Perišić's presentation was fairly confused, or perhaps the stenographer who took down his words was not very precise. But he was Milošević's delegate, and he had to present his mandate.... He said that in the near future the Muslims and the Croats would have the advantage in manpower, and that the relatively small ARS was holding vast territories that it would not be able to "verify." According to Perišić, they would go from total victory to defeat. Furthermore, he said that $3.5 billion was needed for both armies, and of that, only $1.5 billion was earmarked for the Yugoslav Army, while the amount actually budgeted for it was only $750 million. "If we reject the plan, we will not be able to achieve any material results."

Perišić was discussing something that went beyond his mandate; he said that it had come down to an open struggle for power, and that the leadership was making the army take the responsibility. International factors were doing everything they could to pit the Serbs against each other.

Afterwards, Perišić delivered messages from Milošević: 1) that the leadership of the ARS was not to allow itself to be manipulated by the civilian leadership of the Republika Srpska, and that the continuation of the war would be a blow to both the army and to Serbian unity; 2) that the leadership of the ARS reject the authority of its own civilian leadership and pay heed to the leadership of the Federal Republic of Yugoslavia, because the leadership of the Republika Srpska was estranged from the Serbian people and was leading both its army and its people on a path to ruin.

It had not yet happened, but it was coming: the severance of [diplomatic] ties, an end to financial support, as well as an end to all contributions of active military and civilian personnel.

The meeting was dramatic because, without regard to his motives, Perišić was bearing an authentic Stalinist message from his master, who had plunged the Republika Srpska into war, and now sought to disassociate himself from the very men whose intention it was to prosecute the war until there was some kind of victory. Perišić, much like the man who had sent him, felt that the current position of victory was sufficient, and that they ought not turn "Serbian territories into Palestine."

He spoke further about the importance of avoiding in-fighting, while at the same time easing the burdens of each other's tasks. "Your moves determine whether or not my hands are tied. If you tie my hands, they'll replace me; and then someone who won't understand any of this will show up and will blindly go about executing all the orders."

(...)

Mladić remarked: "All I want, it is true, is for us to work on behalf of the people. At least I think so. There is a solution. There has got to be one. All we have to do put our shoulder to the wheel and get through it.

"Many soldiers have died, many were wounded, and a great deal of blood has been shed. We must examine the situation to see what we'll do next. The people can replace us as well as their political leadership. Alija and Tudjman have come together, but we never will."

General Milovanović was candid. He said that there was no tangible guaranty for any plan whatsoever, and that Russia was in no position to act as guarantor. "I'm sorry that the world did not acknowledge the victory of the ARS, and so much the worse for the SFRY. We will never reject the authority of our people's leadership."

General Mladić concluded: "A new meeting is necessary, where we must decide how to prevent a schism among the Serbs, define a clear political, diplomatic and military program, and prevent the army from being used to settle ideological accounts. The army belongs to the people, and everything that has been accomplished results from the people and the army, and everyone else is more or less a bit player. I am forbidden to travel to Belgrade, but Adžić, who withdrew the Army [i.e., the JNA] from B-H and then from the Neretva Valley, and then from the barracks on Dobrovoljačka ulica, is allowed to go Belgrade any old time he wants. An assault was launched against the Republika Srpska Krajina, but the Yugoslav People's Army was asleep.

"The Russians can't guaranty anyone anything. They can't even guaranty anything for themselves, not to mention the Serbs. I suggest that Milošević stop sending us divisive messages, and instead come into the field and help in finding unity. I will offer my own head if it is in the interest of the Serbian people. I will, in any case, keep fighting, and no one has to get behind me. Sever the military payroll immediately [he was addressing Perišić, *Author's Note*], because the pay is next to nothing, anyway. My brother lives without a salary. If Milošević introduces sanctions against us, he will be sawing off the very branch he is sitting on."

The episode with Perišić is extremely interesting. He was trying to do at least three things: to unquestioningly obey Milošević, to avoid criticizing Mladić, and to keep his job. He even went so far as to claim that the entire battle would be meaningless if he were replaced, but, at the same time, he was blackmailing them. If the FRY's ultimatum, i.e., Milošević's, were not accepted, then no more salaries, no more weapons, no more ammunition, and no more manpower.

Mladić's response to Milošević's demand, made by his courier Perišić, that the ARS "reject obedience to the leadership of the RS," and obey the political leadership of the FRY, was interesting. Contrary to his own disposition, Mladić remained silent. Later he spoke of other matters, but General Milovanović, a man who did not get involved in politics and who rarely made his personal positions known outside of tactical military problems, said what Mladić had wanted to say: that Milošević's ultimatum was worse than the West's.

Maps had been hung on the wall during the discussions. According to their depiction of the deployment of forces at that time on the territory, the Muslim-Croat Federation had 37 towns, or 50.68%. The Serbs held 36 towns, or 49.31%. It was almost like Yalta: fifty-fifty.

But, according to the Contact Group maps, the Serbs had to hand over sixteen more towns. The statistical picture looked like this: the Federation would have 53 towns, or 72.6%, the Serbs 20 towns, or 27.3%. However, a precise calculation of the ethnic arrangement of the territory, produced on the basis of real estate registries and a property line computer model called "Spider Web" [Paukova Mreža] showed that the Serbs had 64.8% of the territory, and the Muslim-Croat Federation 35.2%.

These positions and calculations of the loss of territory incurred by not fighting gave rise to disagreements about the Contact Group Plan. The General Staff, with Mladić at its head, thought that handing over conquered towns and disregarding the real estate registries would drastically damage the Republika Srpska, and would nullify the results of these battles. Thus, according to the proposals of the Contact Group, the Muslim-Croat Federation had 56.72% of the total territories, while Serbs had 43.27%, which did not include Sarajevo. At the same time, the principle of dividing the country 51% to 49%, was effectively destroyed, because, allegedly, 21.53% of the territory at that time (in the middle of August 1994) was going to be given to the Muslim-Croat Federation. The Serbs, meanwhile, considered such a qualitative division to be unjust because the Federation had gotten mines, roads and other communications, as well as the ability to strategically control all of Serbian territory.

For that reason, Mladić laconically remarked: "Reject the plan; win the war."

But, could such an idea, given the circumstances, have been realized? The General was constantly trapped between his victor's idealism and its brutal limitations. At a reception for incoming second lieutenants held on August 17, 1994, Mladić gave one of his important wartime speeches.

"You have entered a profession in which one can no longer consider what one may gain from it, but what one must give to it. Experience, life and death — not book learning — have taught me that.

"You are now going to war, and you're going to the front lines, far from the comforts of the military academy right into the battle field to urge men onward. The Serbian people have lost their state with the loss of two Yugoslavias. We Serbs don't have our own state, but it is good that we are stubborn, because the world will then accept us. We still do not have a unified national program. Many Serbs who ought to be in the fighting ranks are not.

"Where are Arkan and Šešelj now? They are gunning people down in Belgrade, and have looted everything there that they could not loot here.

"I'm not going to beg anyone to be in the Army, but I'm not going to force anyone into it either. Listen to ordinary people and do what they want you to do, not for their sake, but for yourselves. Protect the people, and the people will protect you.

"The Army must produce its own food because there are no more stores. Go now and command, that's how you are going to learn your craft and master it."

At a meeting in Han Pijesak on August 25, 1994, General Mladić remarked about the essence of his meeting with Perišić:

"Perhaps Perišić wanted to come here as though he were acting on his own initiative, but he was actually sent. I told him that I wasn't going to bring anyone's head on a platter and give it to a lackey. If they want to help us, that's fine. If they don't, then nothing of it. If I'm forbidden go [to Belgrade, *Author's Note*], I'm not going to beg anyone to let me in. All I care about is avoiding a schism.

"The army doesn't belong to Ratko Mladić or to any other individual or to any political party but to the government."

Mladić didn't say precisely what government he was thinking of. During the meeting, he still emphasized the praise he had received from General Wesley Clark when they met the day before. Clark said that he had not met any contemporary military commander, other than Mladić, who always gave the command, "Follow me!" instead of "Forward!" One typically hears the command, "Forward!" But what about the unified Serbian government, which the generals of the ARS regarded with such long-ing? Looking at it objectively, it was utopian, but subjectively, each one of them, and Mladić most of all, believed in the modern Serbian epic. That was what they told Perišić, right at the moment when he came to bring them the news that Milošević was setting up a blockade along the Drina.

History, at any rate, continues independently of any [imposed] reality. At that moment, no one was in any condition to see it, even though it was apparently clear to all of them. Serbia was divided in half and exhausted by wars, while a group of men who believed in their own permanent historical mission were convinced that the last word rested on military superiority....

On October 3, 1994, Radovan Karadžić, Momčilo Krajišnik, Ratko Mladić, Nikola Koljević, Biljana Plavsić, Manojlo Milovanović, Milan Gvero and Zdravko Tolimir attended the tenth meeting of the headquarters staff of the ARS. Mladić said:

"At this moment, there is no one more answerable than we are for the fate of Serbdom. Our dilemma is whether to accept the plan or defeat our enemy. A political solution is unacceptable for us because it has been designed to be unacceptable."

At that time, the Republika Srpska counted 1,300,000 inhabitants. The haphazard process of arriving at this figure included 160,000 men, along with 180,000 retirees and 200,000 soldiers. Along a broad front line (of about 2,560 km),[18] defined more or less by the following battlefields: Una, Sava, Vlašić, Ozren, Drina, Igman-Bjelasica and Konjic-Neretva.

The problems were enormous. The borders of the projected state were unclear and perhaps even indefinite, and the military effort had not been justly deployed.... There was a great deal of robbery; war profiteering reigned. Mladić proposed to put an end to it, and made an announcement to the attendees that it was necessary to wage a struggle against smuggling....

The largest task facing them after the ominous tidings that Perišić brought was the reorganization of the ARS.

General Tolimir called on the civilian leadership to answer the following question: "The government must advise us of our society's material resources for continuing the war, be it offensive or defensive in nature." Afterwards, a contradictory position was announced: "The international rules of warfare must be respected, but we will not allow them to dictate to us the areas where borders will be drawn. We will not accept it."

Mladić kept a realistic view of things. During such meetings, he did not emphasize idealism and victory at all cost, regardless of the enemy and the balance of power. He did a superb job of justifying the relations on which power was founded: "America will decide when this war will end, and it can end it in three weeks."

Momčilo Krajišnik already had a concept of a defensive war: "We will continue to defend ourselves, and do it successfully. As far as material resources are concerned, we have less and less as time goes on. For that reason, we must put everything we have into the war. If we don't defend our territory, we will lose everything."

Krajišnik found himself in a dilemma worthy of Hamlet. He was torn between a military and political solution, but on his list of priorities, the military variant had, in any case, a slight advantage. He praised the talent of the tacticians who drew up the map, but he was not completely satisfied. "This map, which the army drew up, isn't bad, but we still have this to do: we have to widen the corridor and get through to Una, and drive those Muslims out of there if we can. Then we have to straighten out the situation in Sarajevo, now politically, and later definitively with the army; clean up the Prača River, because of the Sarajevo-Višegrad railway, and we have to make our way at least three kilometers up the Neretva, so that we can create a better situation for discussions with the Croats, and we have to hold on to the areas of Srbobran and Vlašić, which are ours"....

Mladić again tried to say that the people and the state must support the army, and not individual counties that "collect voluntary contributions.... We must guard our dignity and fight for our rights. They [the FRJ, *Author's Note*] don't have the right to shut down all the safety valves."

(...)

In the end, President Karadžić outlined the state's strategic positions, as well as his own, in his summary of the meeting: "America is an unstable ally and an adventurer. The UN sees what it wants to see, and the Muslims are fucking them over and making them look like fools. We must demonstrate flexibility. We must not ballyhoo our successes, because we will appear belligerent. To be gentlemanly but firm in our positions, that must be our guiding principle. Our army must behave in a civilized and honorable fashion at checkpoints."

It is not possible to discern any firm political concepts from Radovan Karadžić's presentation, not to mention military concepts. The headquarters staff was seriously divided between military enthusiasm and ignoring the needs of the ARS.

(...)

In any case, Mladić was sovereignly capable of realistic, tactical thinking at meetings where figures could be quantified, projected on maps or understood in the field. That was his high ground and it played to his advantages, but it was also his shortcoming to happily invoke vague ideological categories (the people, the army), which held meaning only in stimulating conversations.

Karadžić maintained a strikingly low profile while Mladić discussed the advantages as well as the problems the Army was experiencing. The president of the Republika Srpska feared (and justifiably so) that the skillful and loquacious general might make use of the advantages he held. Each and every military victory belonged to him; all of the weaknesses of the government were attributed to Karadžić. Meanwhile, Mladić did not eschew old-fashioned demagoguery, at least where it was not too destructive. He was prepared to criticize himself sharply where it would elevate him ("Here is my head on a platter...."), but he also wanted to call his civilian overseers to the carpet for their involvement in smuggling: "There are people who are sitting right here, and they have every right to have a seat here, because trucks with their cigarettes are crisscrossing the Republika Srpska. I will no longer allow my fighting men to buy smuggled cigarettes at ten times the normal price. Instead, I will confiscate the cigarettes, and I will distribute them to the army. That way, good sirs, there will be enough for us as well as for you. Look, just a few days ago I caught one of these trucks and parceled out the cigarettes."

"Do not speak in generalities, General. Those are gross accusations. Why don't you come out and say whose tow trucks they were?" finally asked Momčilo Krajišnik, the President, during a full session of the Parliamentary of the Republika Srpska.

"I don't want to speak openly about it. Someone's reputation might be ruined. But, if you insist, those tow trucks were yours, Momčilo, yours!"

(...)

Mladić made many important decisions on his own. Either there was no time to convene the headquarters staff or the General thought that such meetings were unnecessary. His decision to blockade an UNPROFOR [UN Protection Force] convoy took place at a meeting of the headquarters staff that was already *post festum* on November 28, 1994. At that time, there was an actual threat of bombardment, while Mladić's ambition was to achieve two effects: 1) to prevent supplies from reaching Atif Dudaković's Muslim 5th Corps; and 2) to blackmail NATO's management of the convoy.

Koljević sought to have the convoy deblockaded, because its effects would then be felt more strongly. Otherwise, it would result in catastrophe. Biljana Plavsić wanted to know what was the point of blockading and deblockading convoys. Mladić explained that the Serbian positions were extremely favorable in this action because of the strong effort put into maintaining the blockade. The Muslims were in a bad position because of Bihać. There, the Muslim 5th Corps had been hunted down, and it was not clear to the Muslims why Mladić wanted to destroy it. According to Mladić, this was not clear to the media.

Mladić proposed a compromise: to deblockade the convoy, but not to allow them to leave; and to introduce rigorous control on gasoline reaching the Muslims around Bihać.

Karadžić said that, on account of the blockade, the Serbs had put British leaders in a bad position. It was impossible to explain why they could not even feed their troops.

Tolimir: "There are at least three levels of cooperation, ways of using UNPROFOR. First of all, they can serve us as a sort of air defense system."

Karadžić: "We'll have to keep to the high moral ground. If we don't let them through, it will be disastrous, simply because they are freezing on the road."

Mladić: "But they've got supplies, and they've got reserves. They're blockading us; we're not blockading them. We're interested in breaking up our enemy's supply lines with this action.

They wanted to bomb us from above and inflict losses, but we turned the tables on them."

Mladić was not even paying attention to the reasons Karadžić and Koljević had for ending the blockade. He arranged to have the convoy held up "until the last minute," at least twenty-four hours, especially the Dutch and the British. "They've been supplying our enemies with war materiel for two years. Without such aid, the enemy could not have launched military actions from Žepa and Srebrenica, towns that Morillon and Andrejev[19] saved."

(...)

A Drama with Pilots

The anti-aircraft defenses of the ARS had at least one important trophy: a French "Mirage" fighter along with the captured pilots.[20]

On December 12, 1995, a delegation from the FRY and the Yugoslavia Army, headed by Zoran Lilić, which also included Momčilo Perišić and Aleksandar Dimitrijević, meet with Mladić.

Mladić said: "Is there such a big problem with the pilots that Milošević had to intervene? What's going on with relations between the FRY and the RS? What's going on with the blockade? I delivered an ultimatum to the French armed forces, and the pilots don't leave until it's resolved."

Perišić was confused. He still didn't know what Mladić thought of him. The head of the General Staff of the Yugoslav Army had not yet heard the judgment Ratko Mladić had pronounced on Perišić: that he was a "flunkey," and that Mladić had no intention of delivering anybody's head on a platter to him. Perišić said (having Milošević in mind because he did not consider Lilić to be any kind of president): "The President has invested all means at his disposal for me to complete this assignment. I have do this because he's waiting for results, and I gave my word that I would do everything I could."

Mladić was angry, and he did not try to conceal it. He raised the tone of his voice a notch; he was red in the face, as Sir Michael Rose confirms, but he acted decisively. His bearing was severe. He reminded Generals Perišić and Lilić that there was no aid coming from the FRY, nevertheless, a few things could be gleaned from old military connections, but that was merely enough to hang on a cat's tail. The motherland allegedly had betrayed its brothers across the Drina in their most difficult hour, and practically put all the territories that the Serbs had conquered on a silver platter for the Ustashi and the "Turks."

"The Dayton Accords are traitorous. Milošević betrayed the entire Serbian nation, especially the Republika Srpska. He gave them what they wanted, and then he gave them what they weren't even asking for. He is a latter day Vuk Branković.[21] But I am not Milošević, and in the interests of the Serbian people, I'm not going to speak about that yet. There's still plenty of time for that."

Then he said he would provide some information about the pilots, but he wasn't going to let them go just like that: "Let the Chief of the French General Staff come here. Let him beg our pardon. We'll go public, he and I, so that I won't have to hide like a prostitute. Everything has to be right out in the open here in the Republika Srpska. There is even a possibility for a political agreement about cooperation with the French armed forces. Along with that, an understanding must be reached about compensation for damages, some sort of financial settlement for children whose parents have been killed in the war. They can make up their minds about the rest, but they've got to be neutral. Their soldiers were killing our kids — but our soldiers weren't killing their kids."

Then he added, just as angrily as he did before, that relations with the other side of the Drina were impossible: "The way things are going, we're not going to put up with the [blockade of the] Drina any more. It'll be shock therapy for us, and it'll be shock therapy for you too. But, my brothers, we're going to have to turn a new leaf."

Perišić: "This is not right. We shouldn't enter such a conflict."

General Krstić: "The Dayton Accords do not provide for relations with the homeland. It is severing those relations. Everything that that we've fought for over the last four-five years is losing its value."

Mladić remarked that people were moving out of Sarajevo because life had become too difficult for them to endure. "We fought for a corridor to Goražde, at least to Ilijaš and Vogošča.

The corridor was wider around Goražde than it was around Brčko. It turns out that we fought for nothing. What are we going to do with all those people from the Serbian territory of Olovo?"

Mladić: "We don't have a secure route leading to Trnovo. You see what's going on over there. People have to flee from their own homes in the Serbian territories that have been handed over! They're all ready to mine their homes and set fire to their property. Some families have given two sons [to the army], and three-four men from the family."

General Manojlo Milovanović remarked that the road leading to the pilots was rather long, and that the General Staff was pointing in that direction. "In due time, the FRY will come out being a bigger loser than we are now. The Dayton Accords are injurious to the Republika Srpska. We lost a corridor as well as our ties with Herzegovina; we lost Sarajevo and we lost access to the sea."

General Milovanović continued on the theme of how only the Serbs made concessions, while the Muslims and the Croats never did. "We don't have anywhere to resettle refugees, and there are going to be more than 150,000 coming from Sarajevo alone. No one is going to help them. Those are merely stories they made up" [i.e., for public consumption, *Translator's Note*].

Milovanović claimed that he did not know a thing about the pilots. He said that discussions with the General Staff were unavoidable regardless of whether they were dead or alive, but only under the condition that there would be compensation for damages, including the annulment of the indictments issued by the Hague Tribunal. "If there are no pilots, then we're obliged, as an army and as a state, to issue a public statement."

General Tolimir spoke more sharply than did anyone else. He maintained that the Dayton Accords were an occupation of the Republika Srpska, pure and simple. "It's worse than 1945, when the Germans were here. At least then we had the right to resist, but not now."

Mladić: "We've got every right in the world to put those pilots on trial if they're alive. They want the pilots back so that we won't be able put them on trial along with NATO and France as war criminals. If we surrender the pilots, then we will no longer hold a trump card in the discussions."

General Aleksandar Dimitrijević: "Right now, these pilots are going for the highest possible price. There is absolutely nothing naïve about this. Tošo [Tolimir, *Author's Note*] examined the situation closely. If the Chief of Staff of the French Army actually does come here, then it will amount to nothing. He will not confront his allies about the pilots. The Serbian side must seize the day and advance its own interests. To insist on holding them captive will have a negative effect on Serbian positions at the upcoming conference in Paris, while all the possible actions we could take to improve the Dayton Accords will drop dead in the water."

Perišić: "We must look at the situation realistically. The New World Order has turned into an East-West axis. We don't have any allies. Bearing all that in mind, we must understand that the Serbian people are not enemies of the New World Order."

Perišić went on further about how the war that the Croats and Muslims intended to wage was being supported by NATO. The question was, thought Perišić, what resources do we have to wage a war? He thought that the Serbs had been satanized, and that not one single advantage existed for them in continuing to wage a war.

"We are all nodding in agreement," said Perišić. "If our politicians had the support that Izetbegović and Tuđman had, we would have had the entire Balkan Peninsula. NATO doesn't want to go to war with us, but they want to establish their interests in the Balkans. Out of these conflicting interests, we have to do the best we can for ourselves...."

"Dead or alive, the pilots are here. If we take advantage of them, we can prevent conflicts from breaking out among the Serbian people (?). An ultimatum is counter-productive."

Mladić: "Tomorrow, Mladić and Perišić will be put in question. We must remove the anathema from the Republika Srpska, so that we can at least have freedom of movement. There are twelve thousand graves in Sarajevo (?), and what's going to happen tomorrow?"

Zoran Lilić: "We see some things better from over there. The Muslims lost the most in Dayton. We're not threatening you, we're not trying to convince you, and we're not begging you. You cannot frighten us with consequences. You neither established a state by yourselves nor did you lose the state by yourselves."

After emphasizing that the Serbs established a state west of the Drina for the first time in history, which was twice as large as Montenegro, Lilić continued: "You will surely get access to the sea. Brčko is a matter for arbitration, but with a mixed commission. Brčko has been decided in favor of the Serbian people. Milošević is guaranteeing you that."[22]

"FR Yugoslavia is guaranteeing the construction of New Sarajevo, which is going to take a year. Accordingly, it's not nice to say that no guarantees exist."

Milošević emphasized that the negotiating positions President Lilić of Serbia, undertaken on behalf of Yugoslavia and the Serbian people, were extremely difficult. And the last four years were the most difficult of all. Particularly difficult had been the position of the RSK, so the FRY decided to help all of them. "I want to help you as people, and I can do that specifically with these pilots. We can sign the Dayton Accords, but they won't be implemented if we don't hand over the pilots, because the French are going to seek a lot of concessions. I see your destiny clearly, but we must not fight a war if we don't have the men or the means to do it. For once, we must be shrewd, and we must win in peace. We simply no longer have the capability to continue waging a war.

"If you've got the pilots, the Chief of the French General Staff is going to come, and then we can discuss it with him. If you don't have them, then we're wasting our time talking about it. I propose a meeting in Belgrade, and let Milošević spell it all out for you."

Mladić: "Am I supposed to go there incognito!?"

Mladić (alone with his aides): "I will do everything I can for the unity of the Serbian people. I am ready to make a sacrifice, but I don't want us to lose face. Nothing can be resolved by avoiding the issue of Serbian graves. The stipulations of the agreement are the removal of the blockade on the Drina; the FRY will not deliver its citizens, except for me, to the Tribunal in The Hague. A just solution for the Serbian people is the favored outcome. We'll resolve the incident with the pilots once these conditions have been met. We don't want to put the FRY in a difficult position."

The French pilots were quickly handed over. General Perišić successfully completed the assignment president Milošević had given him, because he was on hand when a French general took custody of the pilots. There was no compensation; there was no trial; and there was no fund established for Serbian orphans. There were no guarantees to void the indictments issued by The Hague Tribunal for anyone at all.

Did General Mladić know that all this business involved in handing over the pilots would turn out like this? He probably did. It is hard to believe that he was actually expecting such large concessions in exchange for two pilots. It is probably closer to the truth to say that he wanted to confirm the legitimacy of the army that he commanded throughout these negotiations. The isolation in which he found himself was twofold: on the one hand, he was a wanted man; on the other, Milošević had set up a blockade on the Drina. The French pilots were a fundamental means to contact the outside world, which in Pale appeared only as a mirage. They had to get their feet back on the ground.

But, in the end, General Mladić treated the French pilots, who had bombed the Republika Srpska, as gentlemen. They exchanged military salutes and shook hands. "Now go to your own country," said the general. "And you can come back here whenever you like, but only as friends. Tell the French people what the Serbian army and its officers are like."

It is not known what the pilots told the French people upon their return. But days before that, the French, led by their president, prayed for the lives of their pilots, who had, nevertheless, been sent on a mission of aggression. The worst scenarios about what could happen to them were examined in hypotheses presented to the general public.

During that time, however, the pilots had been put up in relatively comfortable surroundings and were being served incomparably better food than that what the officers of the ARS were getting, and they had plenty of interesting company. General Mladić played chess with them whenever he had the time. He would come into the room, set up the pieces, and say: "Come on! Which one of you international grandmasters will go first?"

The pilots quickly got used to his company, but they still couldn't believe that they were playing chess against Mladić. "He's got to be a double!" said one of the pilots through a translator. "Guys like that always have a double."

The Posture of the Mind

Today, so many years after he achieved unparalleled military fame, General Mladić remains a mystery — even as his picture appears on wanted posters....

When Mladić first arrived on the scene, his status as a commanding officer was defined as "a necessary but temporary solution," while he personally was considered to be an officer who possessed "average tactical capabilities."

(...)

Nothing was further from the truth. Ratko Mladić is a man who possesses an unusually keen mind, and is inclined to take notice, from his point of view, of all that is necessary for the task at hand, and he uses all five of his senses as well as his intuition.... He made decisions quickly, which were, for the most part, the right ones to make, yet he did not act impetuously....

But none of this would have been good enough had not the General carefully developed his mind and spiritual life. He read, and perused the memoirs of great military leaders and tacticians, but he did not devote his greatest attention to Zhukov or to Clausewitz,[23] as one might suppose, but to Charles de Gaul and to Dwight Eisenhower. We talked about this many times, even back in the days when we were in Štip and Skoplje....

Mladić respected Zhukov, and he held his "work" on the Eastern Front in high esteem, but for him, Charles de Gaul was the only true measure of creative stubbornness. De Gaul was the general of a great army, but he never wanted his nation — or he himself for that matter — to lose its self-determination and identity.

General Eisenhower organized and executed one of the greatest and most complicated military operations in the history of warfare: the invasion of Normandy. Mladić considered him to have powers of military coordination that went above and beyond all known parameters. Eisenhower had to rabbet together diverse elements so that the ultimate success of his operation would not be jeopardized. But, in any case, General Eisenhower had many ordinary human weaknesses, and the operation had numerous "holes." Such things can be seen only when the everything is over.

He studied the strategy of Vojvoda Mišić,[24] his accomplishments, and the difference between direct creativity in wartime and its representation in literature, especially in the works of Dobrica Ćosić's *A Time for Death*.[25] "Serbian history is full of political miscalculations and bad examples that soldiers had to straighten out."

He read world classics, especially the Russians: Tolstoy, Dostoyevski and Gogol. He enthusiastically commented on the "almost faultless ironic metaphor of the Serbian military being" in Dragoslav Mihailović's[26] novel, *Čizmaši*. One of the officers from government security warned him that Mihailović was a hard core member of the Cominform. Mladić replied: "What does that have to do with anything? I hope that Cominformist Mihailović fucks you along with that Chetnik Draža Mihailović."

The late General Predrag Šulović exerted a great deal of influence on Mladić's military education. He was one of the most talented officers and one of the most original military thinkers Serbia had at the time. When Šulović died of lung cancer in 1988, Mladić remarked: "Only cigarettes were able to kill the finest officer in the Yugoslav army — nothing else."

Mladić would later say that he "learned more from Šulović than from all existing literature." Šulović knew literature, film and theatre better than many accomplished intellectuals. His diction, literacy, gravity and military rhetorical touches were incomparable.

The two of them pioneered the creative tactical work in the JNA, and the military exercises that they created (especially "Jedinstvo 83") on the Krivolak polygon, stood out from the "schemes of the ONO and DSZ" [i.e., Opčenarodna Obrana and Društvena Samozaštita, *Translator's Note*]. With Šulović and Mladić began the practical criticism of "the dilution of military craft," the genesis of the diminution of classical, positional warfare in favor of emphasizing surprise elements in maneuvers, artillery, movement, as well as a factor of operational unpredictability that was planned in their exercises.

It now seems that these were steps in a modern military direction taken from the position of a system that was clinging to its ideological origins.

Even though Mladić was a product of the same system, he tried to oppose it. Despite some impressions which he may have left with certain people, he was not a coarse, irascible officer, whose arrogance set an example at the expense of all others. His struggle with the system had a tactical nature. He wanted to reform it, but he was either unable to do so or he did not dare change it.

(...)

In addition to these characteristics, which are the skeleton of an individual, Ratko Mladić was an extraordinarily brave man. His courage on the battlefield sometimes overstepped the bounds of rational behavior, but the general considered it to be completely normal for the position of a commanding officer. "I'm afraid of death. Who wouldn't be? I'm not insane. But, unless I conquer fear, how will I conquer the Muslims? Here's how to be brave. Start from the premise that there is always someone who is more afraid than you are. And you set an example for him."

Unlikely Decisions

Mladić's colleagues said that he did not go to war to become a hero. He had a profound conviction that he was fighting for the Serbian people. He could not understand why people did not share his convictions, nor could he grasp the reasons they may have had for not taking part in the war. Perhaps he wanted to understand them, but to an impartial observer, it seems that he was unable to do so, and that was his first misunderstanding with reality. No one who actually hadn't been on the scene could have understood this.

(...)

Witnesses say that he was careful about looking after prisoners of war. This may seem incredible, and it may even appear as a baseless defense before a world that, having accused Mladić of being a war criminal, has raised a hue and a cry. General Mladić knew how to tell the difference between a criminal and a soldier. Perhaps today, so many years after the war in Bosnia-Herzegovina, some details will appear to be more important now than they may have appeared at the time. Mladić attempted on many occasions to point out the violent appearance of Islamic fanaticism in Bosnia, which had been penetrated by mujahideens, and their horrifying and bloody reckonings with Serbs. Bosnia became an Islamic state, a literal interpretation of Andrić's famous phrase that described Bosnia as the *tamni vilajet* [i.e., dark province, *Translator's Note*], and the effects of the global jihad in Bosnia are certainly more relevant today ever since the U.S. suffered the terrible suicidal attacks on the World Trade Center.

In July 1995, Mladić did, indeed, meet with prisoners of war in Žepa. On that occasion, he really did separate the men, who had irrefutably been proven to have committed war crimes, from the women, and for this reason, the author of this book spoke with four generals who were members of the general staff at that time in the ARS. Two of them were on the scene, and they stated for the record that Mladić said: "Listen well, all of you who are providing security for this transport. The security of the prisoners of war must be absolute. Those of you who are guarding them have to protect them just as you would one of your own. It's going to be too bad for you if anything happens to any one of them."

Perhaps even then the legend of the "almighty" Mladić was fading, so that Mladić's guarantees did not secure absolute results. Along the way, the transport column carrying the prisoners of war was awaited by the "people," namely, a group of men who wanted to take justice into their own hands. Many of those among the prisoners of war were recognized to be Muslims who had slaughtered innocent "people." Some of them were, indeed, bloodthirsty fanatics who had mercilessly killed women and children. Thus, despite the attempt to create an organized government and to reorganize the army, the people decided to carry out a lynching, which resulted unavoidably in some prisoners of war who had not committed any crimes to be executed. The worst incident was at Konjević Polje, where the residents of Bratunac and Kravice recognized the most notorious Muslim butchers.

These incidents, which could be justified *post festum* as having been committed by the "uncontrollable fury of people," does not absolve General Mladić of command responsibility. The tales about the people, the army, soldier's ethics and honor could not be destroyed by the underlying philosophy of such reprisals.

Despite revanchist elements, not all of the prisoners of war were killed in Žepa. Most of them were taken to Kladanj, Olovo, Sarajevo and Rogatica.

In October 1995, Mladić spoke with prisoners of war in Rogatica. Men from Žepa were imprisoned there. He guaranteed them that the conditions of their imprisonment would be good, and that they would be handed over to "international units." He told them that they were all on the Red Cross list, which was, according to him, a guaranty that they would not be subjected to anything worse than imprisonment.

At any rate, he did not see the orders he had given and the promises he had made subsequently executed, and in this case, his authority fell short of the mark with respect to his own troops as well as with respect to the enemy on the battlefield. The troops were obeying his orders with less and less consistency, because Mladić no longer had a mechanism that would fully execute his orders, while his enemies gave him less and less credence. There were no more guarantees, so promises came instead, which Mladić was unable to control, and which did not absolve him of responsibility. Later, fundamental misunderstandings would arise from these contradictions.

Ratko Mladić was not brutal on the front line. He was uncompromising, and he did not underestimate his enemy. Mladić was able to sneer at his opponents on the battlefield when they acted "amateurishly" or demonstrated obvious tactical immaturity, but he did not do so in such a manner that would lead to underestimating the enemy, but to make a spirited justification of the advantages his own forces enjoyed, along with a reminder to his troops that their opponent's inferiority must not "let them fall asleep at the wheel."

When an opponent with demonstrably overwhelming force appeared (NATO), General Mladić knew that he could not defeat it. He merely wanted to neutralize it. General Wesley Clark had already served as the Supreme Commander, Europe (NATO). This man appeared to be desperate to play war, and bombardments had long been his pathological obsession. Perhaps General Clark is just the perfect example of how diseased ambition and authority, when given a free hand, lead to war crimes. But his ill-temper as a military commander and his "legitimate variety of evil" were absorbed by the power wielded by global institutions. General Ratko Mladić enjoyed no such protection. On the contrary, all the forces that protected Clark had been activated against Mladić. In vain did Mladić explain that he had not attacked anyone and that he had conquered no territory, but had instead only defended his own territory.

Clark, who had up until then waged the war for the Muslims, and, in fact, for "annihilating Serbian tactical advantages," had announced the bombardment of Serbian positions in their name. General Mladić decided to thwart the bombardment by any and all means that were available to him. He told Clark that NATO had no right to bomb Serbian positions, and that the reasons for such action had been fabricated, and that NATO had ignored and tolerated all instances of political and military disinformation that the Muslims and Croats had set into motion.

He advised Clark that he would thwart such actions, and that if he did not succeed, he would continue to struggle against them.

The bombardment began with the pretext that "the Serbs must be punished and they must be forced to accept the authority governing the safe havens." But, Admiral Leighton Smith emphasized the need "to bomb strategic positions held by the ARS in order to achieve a balance of power."

Then Mladić did something that was more spectacular than sensational. He ordered that certain NATO officers be tied to posts on bridges and other sensitive locations that were potential targets of NATO's bombardment.

Generals from his headquarters staff have confirmed that: "He didn't do it to demean the Western officers. Maybe, in the last analysis, it sounds cynical, but he had ordered them to be tied 'with a great deal of respect', so that we do not in any manner destroy their integrity."

That is probably the first time in history of warfare that soldiers were tied to posts [at strategic targets] "with strictly observed respect paid to the individuals." To the astonishment of one and all, the officers of the most powerful countries in the world bore their role as hostages during the bombardment with relative calm, but others were actually amused. Of course, some were concerned, even afraid, but public opinion in Western nations was shocked.

But General Mladić's hostage taking fell short of being a complete anti-aircraft defense system. He took an entire Dutch battalion prisoner, and shut them up in a quarry building just outside of Zvornik. He treated the prisoners with respect, and they treated him with respect as well.

In his contacts [with Western generals] during the course of the bombardment, Mladić threatened them with even more severe measures. Even though Radovan Karadžić had called these threats "idiotic," they did not originate with irrational ambition.... but were instead an effort to erect further obstacles against the decisions of a powerful alliance.

Mladić had told Clark: "You never fought a war in your own country, but you're always fighting wars. I'm fighting a war for the first time, and it's in my country. Which one of us, in that sense, has the right to fight a war?"

Clark and the other generals that Mladić had met (Morillon, Janvier, Smith) did not provide lengthy justifications. They had a different system of values. They were convinced that their patriotism was a global privilege, and that they were serving their country no matter what part of the world they were in. Military service to them was not merely acting as servants of the state — they were professionals who executed orders.

Mladić reminded them of the Nuremberg trials, where Goering, Jodl, Kaltenbruner, Hess and others claimed the same thing: "that they were only following orders." A war crime cannot be justified by an order, no matter where it comes from. Everyone has the right to refuse such an order. It is, in fact, a soldier's duty. That was the substance of what Mladić had to say, having forgotten the principle by which victors determine the fate of their opponents and convict them of the same crimes that they themselves have committed. Even if Mladić had not anticipated such a principle at work, he did not doubt that he would eventually emerge as the victor. At that time, he did not even doubt his own orders.

When the bombardment began, Mladić threatened General Rupert Smith: "If the bombardment does not stop at once, 'tying hostages to posts' is going to be the song that's going to be playing in the background when I take care of you."

Mladić's associates maintain, and the author of this book knows it to be true, that Mladić used diplomatic language with no one. That was not his style. Diplomacy, as a profession, simply did not apply to him. Mladić, having considered diplomacy to be none of their business, spoke with generals in a military fashion. NATO, Karadžić, and Milošević all threatened him and underestimated him both in his official capacity as well as personally.

The president of all Serbs and the master of their destiny threatened him with execution. The General was pleased to hear this in July 1994. There was a whole "crew on duty" from the operations center of the Headquarters of the Army of Yugoslavia. Milošević had at first tried to influence Mladić through General Perišić, but that did not work. Mladić advised him to first talk to "his boss," and told both of them to stay out of his way if they could not be of any help.

Milošević wanted Mladić to get in touch with him as soon as possible, so that he could personally clarify "some illogicalities in connection with previous agreements about certain matters, and Mladić knows what I'm talking about."

When Mladić called, the officers on duty could not resist eavesdropping on the conversation. Milošević raised his voice to an intolerable level. It was a raging falsetto that we do not associate with the charismatic leader of all Serbs. Milošević said, in essence, that he would "relieve him of duty, suspend him from his duties," and there was talk of executing him in cold blood.

Mladić barely managed to listen to the tirade, and freely made a truculent remark: "Listen, you: you don't yell at me. If you've got anything to say, you can come here and say it, but don't you go sermonizing from the pulpit. I've got so many of them here that I can export them!"

Then he slammed the receiver into its cradle. Milošević called headquarters three more times, but Mladić would not answer. Then Milošević tried to get in touch with Perišić, and ordered him to urgently find Mladić and "make him understand." Perišić finally got a hold of him, but Mladić laconically replied: "Come on, let me get some work done!"

Reorganization of the Army

The ARS began and ended the war as a unique military hybrid. It was not a classic army, because it had come into its own in a unique, unclassical fashion. It did not wage positional warfare because the war was, for the most part, unique. The operational and tactical procedures were adjusted to the conditions existing in the territory in a constant attempt to keep the position of the army from being determined by extensive deployment on front line positions.

In any case, at one time, the length of the front lines controlled by the Republika Srpska amounted to 2,000 kilometers. The army did not arise from operational logic, but from political demands, the most basic of which was the necessary control of the territory of the future Serbian state.

Nor was the ARS an *ad hoc* formation created by the dictates of military reality. It consisted, for the most part, of fighting men who were defending their own homes at first. It was a unique throwback to the Partisan-Chetnik tradition from WWII. At the same time, the composition of the corps enabled the successful execution of operations throughout the entire territory.

The commanding officers were recruited from three sources: personnel who came from the JNA, namely the Yugoslav Army; retired reserve officers from the territory of the Republika Srpska, and the training of new officers who were selected on the basis of their abilities as demonstrated on the battlefield.

The officers of the former JNA got labeled as "Commies, and not even General Mladić could shake off the epithet. In the first phase of the war, when the successes of the ARS were uncontested, organizational-formational weaknesses could, to a certain extent, be ignored. But, as the war entered its decisive phase, these weaknesses became increasingly burdensome.

General Mladić had a great, perhaps even a decisive, influence on the formation of this army. He must have been conscious of its unique military dialectic: that the ARS, without reorganization and rigorous military discipline, soon would begin to weaken and lose its initiative. Simultaneously, the enemy army was being hardened by getting its training in battles with the ARS, and since they were receiving aid, they were stimulated by their first great military successes, and eventually became equal opponents on the battle field.

In the ARS, the concept of discipline was some sort of mixture of emphasis placed on military camaraderie and "conscious discipline" inherited from the JNA. General Mladić justifiably doubted that, at the very beginning, "iron-clad military relations" could be instituted. Perhaps, at the beginning, it was not even possible, but a year later it was absolutely necessary. The General believed that all those men who went to war for the most diverse reasons could be reined in by the patriotic idea of a Serbian government and by his reputation as a commander.

Arrogant small-time local commanders, thieves and murderers, who had gained some notoriety, quickly used the war as an alibi to give free reign to their pathological natures. There were numerous incidents where senior officers, even brigade commanders, were murdered. These murders were committed by uncontrollable thugs from the units themselves....

Ideas about regrouping the ARS into divisions within the framework of a corps took precedence over others as a solution to the organizational chaos that reigned in the units. But, no matter how many adherents this idea had, there were many opponents, and obstacles that had been creating organizational confusion in the ARS for so long remained, perhaps, to the very end of the war.

The meeting held in Han Pijesak on October 31, 1995 was largely devoted to the reorganization of the army.

General Mladić spoke of the need for "firmer links" between the ARS and the federal Army of Yugoslavia, and then about the interest Grachov (the Russian Defense Minister at the time) had expressed in the fate of the French pilots. "Look how low Orthodox Christianity has fallen," remarked Mladić.

General Manojlo Milovanović addressed the current organizational structure: The Krajina Corps, the Eastern Bosnian Corps, the Drvar Corps, the Second Corps, and the Herzegovinian Corps along with the Air Force.

All the corps, with the exception of the Air Force, had to be deployed in close coordination within the division structure. That was how the 10th, 11th, 13th, 19th, 21st, 22nd, 24th, 31st, 32nd and 33rd infantry divisions were formed. Each division, depending on its purpose, would be composed of 10,000 to 15,000 soldiers.

The Commander of the First Krajina Corps, General Momir Talić, explained that the brigades within the corps structure would be formed along the principle of territory, and that Prijedor, Kotor Varoš, Banja Luka and Doboj would be divisional centers. In order to achieve flexibility, brigades (whose soldiers would average twenty-five years of age) would be dedicated to maneuvers and operations.

Talić suggested division commanders, along with a reminder that they should chose their own staff.

General Mladić presented the following dilemmas, emphasizing that the reorganization was a difficult and costly undertaking, while "a sheet of paper can take anything you put to it. What can we do about the material aspects of modernization? How much housing do we need? How many new officers? How are we going to build barracks?"

(...)

General Mladić: "The government doesn't care about the army; they want demilitarization, but it's not clear to them what this means. They sent us Arkan, who appraised our handling of the war and our senior officers, but people have no idea what he did while he was here, nor do they [the General was thinking about the SRY, *Author's Note*] exert any control over what he says. We lost thirteen counties, because the state didn't verify them on the international map as a factual condition before their loss. But we're not going to start biting each other's head off, because there is someone waiting for us to do just that."

In conclusion, General Mladić said: "We must form brigades composed exclusively of young soldiers who are not bound to their houses, fields and vineyards. They must be trained and ready for action in diverse places."

"To station such units outside of barracks is to harden them. They are not allowed to have any shortcomings. Training must be rigorous and they must have the discipline of tempered steel. These units must be filled with capable and experienced soldiers."

(...)

Mladić discussed the Contact Group's plan as well as the conduct of those who supported the plan: "They're trying to slip the Republika Srpska on the forty-nine percent like a condom. Power brokers are scattering the army and the General Staff in order to water it down. They are our fourth enemy [the Muslims, Croats and NATO are the first three enemies, *Author's Note*]. They have created a porous fabric and we're going to have a hard time closing the gaps. We can no longer act like dumb cattle that allow anyone to lead them along on a leash. There are far greater rogues still displaying much more authority than we do. We weren't even worth anything to them when we held seventy-four percent of the territory. But now, even our own people, who lost territory, do not hold us in the esteem that they once did."

Mladić was pessimistic about the way the military situation was developing: "NATO isn't going to leave the Balkans. They will go farther by using the Muslims and the Croats. A person has got to be nuts not to believe it. I will not permit defeatism. It is not permitted to speak about the possibility of losing the war in the General Staff."

The story about the reorganization of the army, however, never found its conclusion. It had been left undone even at the end of the war, just as a genuine reorganization was never going to occur in the future. On November 19, 1995, the same things were discussed again. The positions taken were contradictory, a little confused, and the arguments that appeared to be convincing did not bear scrutiny, just as those who were proposing them.

(...)

The Commander of the General Staff then expounded on the guiding principal of the reorganization: "To create an army that will be able to defend the Republika Srpska and its people, whether we have to go it alone or with allies.

"Every change we make must contribute to effective leadership and not diminish it. We must by all means prevent 'outside' influences from effecting the army. I would suggest that the high command undertake this [directive]: go with three corps. The structure must be more tightly bound, stronger and it must start with infantry brigades, artillery, armor and aviation brigades, rocket brigades and artillery regiments, and certain so-called detachments must be eliminated." [Here Mladić was thinking of paramilitary units, groups of criminals, and newly-formed, out-of-control, local county units, *Author's Note.*]

Mladić interceded in favor of functional equality among the formations: "Make corps nearly equal in numerical strength in order to avoid favoritism and privileges."

Mladić certainly knew that units holding down positions couldn't wait for reorganization; they had a difficult job on their hands. In that sense, he was defining the main point of the discussion, which was independent of the difficult process of reform:

"We have to extract a certain amount of manpower and technology in order to guarantee maneuvers on the front lines. But, everything that we extract must be compensated by maneuvers, so that things won't keep going the way they did before: whenever we extracted troops, we created a hole in our defenses: Bijeljina, Banja Luka and Vlasenica were under the direct command of the General Staff.

"For example, we cannot just withdraw the Gardijska Brigade. If we withdraw them, who's going to get Trnovo and Treskavica? We must insure that every brigade is mobile. We must form free-ranging forces that we can use in conjunction with the dictates of the military situation. We have a sufficient number of tanks for three armored brigades."

The discussion about the reorganization of the army continued two days later on November 22. Despite Mladić's opposition to his idea about the division of the army into positional and mobile structures, General Talić came around to agreeing with Mladić: "and along with it, to increase the number of brigades that would have greater maneuverability."

Mladić announced his position in relation to the decision he had made earlier: "We don't have a sufficient number of men to form divisions. Don't you get it?"

Then he spoke about a matter that was more urgent than the reorganization itself: "We must put together a group of corps commanders, and train and discipline the army. We are a state only to the extent that we are capable of defending ourselves. Let's unify our republic with the FR Yugoslavia. Let's not wait for the Eskimos to unite before we do. Our goal is to forge alliances across all four corners of the earth. The West and the Islamic countries will attempt to impose their will on us. We must rely on the FR Yugoslavia for political and military support.

"We must reorganize the army in the most rational possible manner with the manpower and technology we have at our disposal. We can't expect anything from anyone at all." General Mladić had obviously received some important information, because only two days earlier he had said that "the FR Yugoslavia would pay for it."

Mladić pointed out the demographic and territorial problems facing the new Serbian state: "If the Republika Srpska is independent, then its position, without ties to Serbia and Montenegro, will be intolerable. We will have a small number of recruits, and it will be a big problem to call up troops to secure the borders."

(...)

On the last day of November 1995, the General Staff heard a summary report by the delegation of the Republika Srpska that had returned from Dayton.

As it turned out, the delegation did not attend the final plenary meeting.

Fifteen different agreements had been signed. Offensive military action had to cease. The generals asked, "And what type of actions are going to continue?"

Over the course of thirty days, territories had to be abandoned and divided. The division was established with a four kilometer buffer zone. That was a corridor "for amortizing mutual hostilities."

There was going to be a separation of opposing forces in Sarajevo seven days after the signing of the Paris Accords.

No armaments could be brought in over the next ninety days; and over the next one hundred and eighty days, nothing larger than 76 millimeters.

All of the suggestions made by the Republika Srpska had been rejected. That was why official documents regarding military issues had not been initialed.

The Republika Srpska delegation had no influence at all to change any document whatsoever.

Mladić transmitted what Milošević had said about his effective contributions to the Dayton Accords.

Milošević (according to Mladić's reinterpretation) said: "A final solution rests on our intention to radically correct our relations with the United States of America. We must renew our traditional, one-hundred-year-old alliance. In Dayton, the Serbs won a place in America's heart. There is no city on the Sava or the Drina that is not ours. If people are have enough brains to stay in Sarajevo, it will be an international city. Of the US$6.5 billion that has been slated for aid, US$1.5 billion is going to the Republika Srpska. We have a state west of the Drina for the first time in history."

Mladić continued to impersonate Milošević by saying that no one stood behind him, that he was alone, and that he had convinced the Americans of what was best for his people: "I myself squelched Krajišnik's howling about the U.S. being our enemy.

Politically, it's a done deal. The U.S. did not bomb us, but the UN did. The army of the RS lost the war, but Holbrook and I saved what we could. Mladić, of course, made some unjustified suggestions that diplomacy had achieved nothing. If he were thinking of relying on the so-called diplomacy of the Republika Srpska, he was absolutely right. The Parliament of the Republika Srpska is a bunch of dopes."

According to Mladić, Milošević anticipated that Clinton, who was seeking election points, would withdraw his forces before November. He continued: "We are pleased that the army is supporting the peace agreement; the map cannot be changed by force. It is essential that our people see us as friends. We have to get rid of the Russians. They will sell us out for their own interests. They've signed up for the Partnership for Peace. The army has absolutely no need to fire another round. Everyone needs to take a vacation from politics, while the SRY will cede some of its own bases."

Mladić then concluded acidly: the president of Serbia, after having had returned from Dayton, where he defended the interests of all Serbs, further ordered: "We have to stand together with the Americans and to tell them that we will be their friends as we have been for one hundred years. We have to re-establish good relations with all Orthodox countries, and after that with China and Japan."

Momir Bulativić: "The U.S. Congress is using the Muslims as a weapon to destroy Clinton, but we have good relations with the administration."

Before the meeting, Ćosić insisted that Mladić meet alone with Milošević, "even though that guy can't stand him."

Milošević at first insisted that the ARS publicly support the plan, but he relented after Mladić's fierce intervention.

Mladić insisted that no personal questions be raised, and that Karadžić's name not even be mentioned.

Gvero: "What Karadžić? He cannot represent the Serbian people."

Mladić: "At a time like this, we should not be creating problems for ourselves. We must prevent armed conflict. Our goal is not to fight for personal interest and power, but to fight for the interests of the Serbian people."

On February 6, 1996, the reorganization of the Army was slated for discussion by the headquarters staff. Many things had been defined in advance under the dictates of the Dayton Accords. General Mladić submitted the introductory paper, with already familiar themes.

Karadžić said: "The appraisal of the enemy, as well as of our own forces, is exact. The border is long, and we won't be able to defend it without Yugoslavia. It doesn't have to give us formal support, but in essence it would have to.

"We must create an army that will be in a state of readiness to engage the unanticipated strategies of the enemy. Until now, we have not had such an army, and maybe we weren't able to have it because we were defending the territory and its people.

"The army, as a whole, will be in the same condition as our society and state, whatever that may be. The borders are not well sealed, we're stretched too thin, and we've heard about the lack of discipline in the army.

"Until the agreement takes effect, I think that we are still allowed to have 10,000–12,000 soldiers for five more years, as a professional nucleus for combat formations. We still don't know what our perspectives will be or whether or not the war will continue. If it does continue, what will Yugoslavia do? That's the first and foremost question. The people are exhausted, and they have little or no taste for war, but, nevertheless, we were justified in not accepting the plan offered by the Contact Group. I have personally noticed here and there that the army and the police are in a state of chaos."

Then Karadžić discussed the relationship between the standing army and the professional army, which he explained in his own words; and then he anticipated creative political concepts for life in peacetime: "Do everything you can for the life of the republic, so that the people will want to live here and come back. If we had more land, we would not have enough people to settle it. And Serbian propaganda is not going as it should. Every devil in the world, including Radio-Krajina, is ruining Serbdom. We can no longer wage war without each and every Serb standing behind us; we have to act with diplomatic cunning instead, as Dubrovnik does."

General Manojlo Milovanović: "The Serbs aren't going to run away. We have a state. The military course may continue until we establish a stable system. By March 20 [1996, *Author's Note*], we must have a peacetime army. The peace will last a year, and then the Muslims will build up their armaments."

Mladić: "Police forces with short-barreled weapons must be able to enter a two kilometer area, because that's the only thing it [i.e., the Dayton Accords] allows. We have to declare our positions at a distance of ten kilometers. We don't have a single house, not a single bivouac. Are we relying on Serbia or not? After all, it appears as though we have no way out except by relying on ourselves and our strengths. War must not catch us off guard."

General Milovanović: "We need 35,000 soldiers just to maintain combat technology. We must make a decision about the contingent of soldiers required to maintain combat technology."

Karadžić: "There's a lot of unnecessary philosophizing going on here. Can we make a decision about 12,500 professionals? Let's decide if we want three or four corps, and leave the rest for later. Are we going to change anything? And what are the interests of the army and state in doing so?"

Mladić: "We can have a meeting with the FR Yugoslavia. It's possible to have one army from the Federal Army of Yugoslavia to be oriented to our territory as its operational focus. If that is not feasible, then we have to rely on our own concept. We pledge to have three corps that will be organized in such a manner so that it may successfully defend the integrity of the Republika Srpska. We don't want localism in the units. Let them inherit the fighting tradition from their units."

Karadžić: "The concept of three corps is accepted. The rest can be decided later. I believe there will be no more war."

Wartime Diplomacy

The war in Bosnia-Herzegovina ran its course in several parallel currents. Politics and diplomacy, the army and peacekeeping forces, observers and generals, reporters and photo-journalists, terrorists and their understudies, new weapons and ideas about quickly ending the war, all existed simultaneously in a single, chaotic arena.

Even generals participated in diplomatic skirmishes. Not all of them actually headed military units, but even those who did were not denied the opportunity to meet with colleagues from around the world.

General Mladić was not temperamentally disposed to negotiation. He was a man given to quick, explosive decisions, and the dynamics of his personality were not suited to tasks for which patience, infinite tolerance, and Aesopian approaches to problems were required, where language is used delicately, as if it were a formal affair conducted in a tuxedo and white gloves.

Nevertheless, Mladić was not only known for his categorical decisiveness but also for the robust defense of his positions, which might as well have been cast in stone. He is, indeed, a dedicated warrior, but an intelligent conversationalist. And his stubbornness above all results from his own convictions as opposed to adherence to anyone else's dogma.

For those reasons, General Mladić was fully conscious of his limitations in diplomacy. He knew that diplomacy was not his strong suit, so he conducted all of his meetings by speaking the language of a soldier.

It is worthwhile to revisit his 1994 meeting with General Wesley Clark, who was NATO Supreme Allied Commander, Europe (a position he still held when he attacked Yugoslavia on March 24, 1999).

The meeting took place on August 27, 1994 in Banja Luka.

In his opening remarks, General Clark said that he was a division commander in the Gulf War. He had been deployed to Kuwait with orders to prevent an Iraqi counter-attack.

He was a successful commander. "We trained in California for that job," he said.

He spoke of the chances for peace, and inquired whether the [Serbian] people would accept the [proposed] map. He said: "If the

Contact Group's plan is not accepted, UNPROFOR will leave, there will be political pressure to lift the [arms] embargo [on the Bosnian Muslims], and hostilities will break out once again."

Mladić: "I want to welcome you, Sir. I want you to convey my regards to General Shalikashvili [the Commander-in-Chief, United States European Command, *Author's Note*].

"UNPROFOR officers have discharged their orders correctly and responsibly, especially De la Presle and Sir Michael Rose. I am not, however, pleased that UNPROFOR is withdrawing from its neutral status; incidents are taking place from Goražde to Bihać. They are tolerating arms deliveries to the Muslims."

General Mladić greeted General Clark in a grand manner in keeping with the history of [U.S.-Serbian] friendship: "The Serbs have a great understanding of the Americans, the French, the English and the Russians. Our forefathers never fought against you. We saved many [U.S.] pilots during the Second World War."[27]

"Please advise Shalikashvili and Clinton that we are very disappointed about the fact that we were bombarded in Goražde. We protest and we warn you that we're not afraid of you. General Clark, Sir, we are not making any threats, but I'm telling you, it will be hard on those whom powerful nations are now defending.

"We are not leading a war of conquest; we never had soldiers outside of our own territory. We are being forced to wage a war against the very same people with whom we created the first and the second Yugoslavias. Our enemies, unfortunately, have American weapons. Franjo Tudjman has American uniforms, provisions and weapons. So does Alija Izetbegović.

"All we are asking for is a real approach to the problems we're talking about. Serbian mothers feel anxious nowadays whenever they hear the sound of your warplanes; you have given everything to our enemies, but you haven't even thrown an empty carton to the Serbs."

General Clark: "I noticed that the Bosnian Muslims have clothing and weapons that America did not supply; they have Kalashnikovs."

Mladić: "Criminals soaked in Serbian blood are supplying them weapons."

Clark: "Yes, but that's not relevant. The Muslims must defend themselves. Are you going to war?"

Mladić: "You will see my reaction, Sir."

Clark: "I hope that we will not go to war. The possibility for peace exists, otherwise we can lift the embargo. What would your reaction be if the Muslims received additional weapons?"

Mladić: "Advise Shalikashvili that you won't be helping anyone at all if the U.S. starts applying that model. The U.S., as the most powerful nation in the world, is responsible for world peace and must take its finger off the trigger. Why don't you leave us alone? We are neither Nazis nor Fascists. The Serbs do not deserve to be left without a state, and for four years you have seen fanatics killing us off, and you're helping them."

"Banja Luka is our largest city, but it hasn't had electricity for four years. Twelve newborns died because they didn't have oxygen. We don't have any medicine; my people are hungry, but you're bottle-feeding the Muslims.

"We want our own state, otherwise we will become extinct. Why are you trampling on our state, while making it possible for the Muslims to establish an Islamic state right here in the Balkans?"

Clark: "We have carefully analyzed, studied and observed the Serbian soldier and your military tradition. You, General Mladić, Sir, are quite an experienced soldier. I did not come here to threaten you; I admire your courage and patriotism. But we must bear in mind the military and political side of the problem. You and I are not politicians, but it interests us as an unavoidable factor in every war. You have 450 tanks and over 700 heavy artillery fieldpieces. The Muslims have inferior technology and weaponry, but they have more men. What are you going to do when the Muslims finally build up their armaments and level the playing field by making their forces equal to yours?"

Mladić: "Once you start arming the Muslims, all resolutions will cease to be in effect. It would be a big mistake for America. You cannot cut up territories into smaller pieces while ignoring the outcome of battles that determined who gained what territory. But the Serbs have a way out of this situation.

"The way out is by silencing all weapons, and by the commanders sitting down and signing a cease fire. Everyone has to stop where they are. Everything else can be solved through political dialogue.

"We can do all that under the auspices of the United Nations and the great powers (and even Germany, which started this war).

"Forcing each and every one of the commanders to sit down and start talks: Bobetko, Roso, Delić, Petković, Mladić.[28] We do this immediately.

"That is the way to peace; arming the Muslims is the way to war.

"We are willing to hold discussions with everyone just to stop the war."

Clark: "The time is short, in fact, we have very little time left. The next week will be crucial. Shalikashvili hasn't got his finger on the trigger; what you said before is wrong. Bombardment, yes; but now it's in your power to stop it."

Mladić showed the map to General Clark, and pointed out the illogical aspects of the Contact Group's Plan.

Clark: "At the next meeting, let's go over the conditions Karadžić set forth...."

Mladić: "That's an unconditional cease fire; UN forces must guarantee the division of territories and the economy has to start functioning again, and then discussions can begin. The Serbs have already taken the necessary steps."

(...)

Mladić: "What is America's strategic interest in the 51%-49% option?"

Clark: "So that there will be no further war, so that NATO will continue to exist, so that America and Russia will work together to bring everything to a conclusion, and so that the rule of law is established. Without that, there is no peace, and no NATO. The embargo [i.e., the economic embargo against the Republika Srpska and Yugoslavia, *Translator's Note*] is now law; no one can change that. Only you can change that, or after a referendum [he's referring to the referendum in the Republika Srpska to approve the Contact Group Plan, *Author's Note*] you can address the Contact Group."

Mladić: "Will America respect the will of the [Serbian] people?

Clark: "Yes, but if the Serbs say 'no', lay down your arms and try to find a solution. Let the [Serbian] leaders inform the people; use your influence on them."

Mladić: "The will of the people is stronger than the law. The Serbs know what can happen. They don't understand why NATO is forcing democracy on them and imposing their solutions. Many of us don't recall our fathers.[29] Kozara is a monument to the murder of Serbs by Muslims. Jasenovac is the site of the Ustashi concentration camp where nearly 700,000 Serbs were killed [during WWII, *Translator's Note*]. We will not abandon our graveyards as long as we're alive. Our army will defend Serbs, whether they be dead or alive.

"I want the world to accept me; people need to see that I don't have horns. The vilest things are said about me, that I skin people alive. We can't have such an image of ourselves presented. And we know that America is fostering just such an image. Let people hear and see, let them know who we are. In fact, I hope that they will be convinced that we are a peaceful and tolerant people. Let the Muslims live next to us in their own state. But they won't be living with us ever again."

Clark: "No one is presenting you as dangerous and evil."

Mladić, because his intonation, bearing and choice of words, appeared to be "lecturing" General Clark....

General Mladić confidently held his ground in this military-diplomatic duel with General Clark, but he was convinced that he was dealing with a stereotype. He was, therefore, acerbic, especially concerning America's neutrality in the Bosnian conflict, and he sent his own orders to General Shalikashvili through Clark.

His approach may have been more sharply nuanced than his typical approach to such negotiations, but General Mladić stuck to the main point of his argument, which was based on the balance of power at the time. He wanted to have the results of battles honored; he wanted military units to hold their current positions; and he wanted the peace negotiations to be based on these precepts.

General Clark spoke about the need for the warring parties to have a level playing field. To achieve this, the Serbs had to "stop," while the simultaneous "lifting of the embargo" to import arms would give the Muslim side a new stimulus because the Muslims were now being favored, especially as beneficiaries of "Operation Parachute."

General Clark emphasized his respect for General Mladić, denying the charge that Mladić was being presented as "a man who skins people alive" by the U.S. media.

"I'm delighted that you have given me this hat," said Clark to General Mladić at the conclusion of their meeting in Banja Luka.

After the meeting, Clark was photographed wearing the Serbian military cap.

The world saw Clark wearing the cap. Milovan Marić noted that Clark "had to explain his conduct to the State Department the very next day." His friend from Arkansas, President Bill Clinton, allegedly saved his career.

Also attending the meeting, as Marić reported, were General Michael Rose, the Commander of UNPROFOR forces at the time, and one Russian and one French officer. Ratko Mladić was well disposed and in full control of the situation.

Mladić described "good circumstances," and said that they were on the same side, that American, English, French, Serbian and Russian officers were on the side of peace. Meanwhile, he kept tapping General Clark on the shoulder. Clark recoiled but was unable to get out of Mladić's way. He apparently did not realize that the shoulder tapping was Serbian body language that expresses sincerity.

According to General Michael Rose, Mladić treated him as if he were a lower ranking officer: "General Rose, come here and let's get our picture taken!"

Additionally, while the cameras were snapping away, he took General Clark's own cap off his head, asking him if he could keep it.

"Of course. Absolutely, why not?" answered the confused Clark, who then took Mladić's hat. "Can I keep this one?"

"And you keep mine!"

Mladić examined Clark's cap: "It's a little small for me. My size is six and one-fifth."

General Clark now faced the dilemma. He did not know whether to make a statement to reporters or not. He then said he would not.

"Oh, of course he's going to make a statement. Why not? Come on, Wesley, tell the folks what you've got to say. They've got a job to do just like you and me."

Clark, having no choice, gave a statement. It was reluctant and brief: "We, as soldiers, have spoken about the past and the future. And we can always discuss peace with General Mladić."

"I'm delighted that you have given me this cap," said Clark to Mladić in farewell, and he left the meeting with the Serbian military cap in his hand.

What happened later to turn this man into a "pathological anti-Serb"? Was it some psychological complex, which metastasized during his meetings with Mladić and led him to use protracted brutality [in the war against Yugoslavia in 1999, *Translator's Note*]? Or was it a prejudice that had accumulated over the course of his meetings with Milošević?

In his meetings with General Perišić six months before the bombardment [i.e., of Yugoslavia in 1999, *Translator's Note*], General Clark was rude and arrogant in his talks with Serbian military officials; he cut them off, threatened them, and raised his voice. Others who attended these meetings have corroborated this. One of our sources described him as "Holbrooke in uniform." He told Perišić, in a tone of voice that expected the obedient execution of his orders: "General, I am not holding discussions with you; I'm dictating the terms!" Perišić signed a military agreement with Clark, but only on the slender hope that the bombardment [i.e., of Yugoslavia, *Translator's Note*] would not take place.

Mladić met with a military delegation from Russia on September 30, 1995. There Mladić used military diplomacy more vehemently than in his earlier meeting with Clark.

The Russian delegation was led by a deputy from the Ministry of Defense, General Furbenko; with him was Vasilj Burov, head of the Armored-Mechanized Unit. Also in the delegation were Colonel Ivanović (Infantry Commander), Colonel Šarovari (Air Defense Systems) and General Karpov (Communications).

The delegation was serious about its mission. This was obvious from the presence of Colonel Javorski (Commander, Artillery-Missile Division), General Nagulov (Engineering-Communication Division), Colonel Novikov (Airborne-Landing Unit), and Colonel Bobiljev (Information).

At the time, it did appear that the Russians were seriously interested in the events unfolding in Bosnia; perhaps they were swept away by the idyllic and completely unrealistic notion of "the eternal brotherhood of the Russian and Serbian peoples."

Mladić spoke: "We have been left to fend for ourselves while our enemies have kept growing stronger."

He apprised his guests of the damage done by Tomahawk cruise missiles, the actions taken by NATO air forces, and the air-defense system of the Republika Srpska. He warned his guests that the Muslims had ordered MI-17 helicopters. Some Arab and Western [mercenaries] had joined the coalition [against the Serbs], and he compared the enemy then facing the Serbs with Hitler: "Hitler was better."

General Mladić emphasized a geostrategic theme: "the goal of the enemy is to reach Russia. Everyone is helping the enemy, while no one is helping us. The condition of the refugees is humiliating; we have over 200,000 of them. Everybody in the world has allies: Islamic states, the Western world; only the Orthodox peoples have been divided."

General Furbenko: "The events taking place in the Balkans require political and military decisions to be made. The NATO attacks are significant because they are breaking resistance and destroying life. This is the first military delegation to visit the territory of a Serbian state since the war began. It is an important means of keeping ourselves informed of the situation. The English, the French and the Germans are asking us why we came. The goal of our meeting is to sober up NATO. Shalikashvili has been warned of Islamic fundamentalism coming from the south. We told them that if they support the Muslim-Croat federation, we will not abandon our Serbian brothers; this is World War III. We reminded them that previous world wars had started in the Balkans.

"The Serbs are not alone; Russia is with them. We intend to get first-hand knowledge of the situation, evaluate it and determine the possibility of Russia's participation in the continuing development of the situation.

"This is a reason for sending support for organized military action, and it may come to that.

"Our battalion will participate in peace-keeping operations. All of those who are on a mission for peace will act within the framework of the UN, and we must never allow NATO to build military bases here.

(...)

"If we are not allowed to take the path of peace, we will influence the course of events through military action. Russia will not abandon its brothers in times of hardship."

The president of the Republika Srpska, Dr. Radovan Karadžić, commented that "the meeting of Russians and Serbs is a turning point." Maybe he actually believed that.

Mladić said, "The Russian delegation, which is composed of military experts, came of its own accord, and not on behalf of the Bosnian Serbs. They spoke about how much they have lost and how much they will continue to lose, precisely because they did not dare to help the Serbs in spite the opposition of all [i.e., the great powers]. Now, when they see what NATO is doing, how much territory it is taking, and the areas into which it is expanding its strength and influence, maybe they will come to their senses."

During their discussions of the military situation and the balance of power, both the Russian delegation and General Mladić continually found themselves caught between the realities of military expertise and ideology. General Clark said that the Bosnian Serbs would be forced to go it alone, and commanded Perišić to advise his president, Milošević, that the Serbs in Bosnia, cut off from the motherland, could fully expect to be fighting the whole world alone.

Mladić told the Russian delegation that the Serbs in Bosnia could no longer survive on their own, and he insisted on some kind of "Orthodox Christian alliance."

That was a relatively good military-diplomatic ploy, but it was, in the last analysis, unproductive. The Americans (Clark) denied that there was a global campaign to demonize the Serbs, and members of the Russian delegation confirmed that their "Serbian brothers would not be left to fend for themselves."

Each of the two positions was part of a single syndrome, which can be defined as "extreme hypocrisy"; that was why Mladić was right when he doubted both one and the other, but he was wrong when he thought that such a balance of power would result in military victory.

In March 1999, a mutual doctrine of "expansion, stubbornness and epic alliances" emerged. The Americans confirmed that the Serbs were guilty of all of the worst aspects of the war; the Serbian leadership, however, insisted on its uniqueness, victimization and martyrdom, while the Russians always promised aid and support that they never delivered. The American threats were real, but the epic spirit that touted epic alliances was unable to interpret them rationally.

This resulted from unfinished, amateurish military diplomacy, which was unavoidably a part of Milošević's brutally experimental "civilian militarism."

General Mladić, a talented soldier who was an awkward diplomat, left a powerful impression, particularly in the chronicles of Serbian military history. He convincingly demonstrated his unique, and frequently folkloric variant of Serbian *inat* [i.e., incredible tenacity in the face of overwhelming odds, *Translator's Note*], which had its own well-defined connotations in the brutal conditions of warfare.

Military diplomacy is an activity in which politicians reluctantly engage, while military leaders happily play the role. For Mladić, it was a "lively aspect of his personality." Mladić would not have been Mladić without his creative arrogance. If he had behaved as a polished and humble parliamentarian, he would have, if necessary, made new allies, and adapted himself to the situation.

Instead, Ratko Mladić tried to do the opposite, to adapt the situation or at least the presentation of the situation, to himself.

It turns out that such an adaptation was impossible. In the least flattering version of the story, Ratko Mladić is the hero, on the one hand, and the victim, on the other, of his own ideological miscalculations and utopian nationalism. He was a quick-thinking officer who, in any case, made his *salto mortale*. He is going to be a great historical dilemma for the Serbs: how did this man chance into an extraordinarily important leadership position when the Serbs, having been backed into a corner, had to decide whether they wanted to live or to die?

Locked in the Stocks of the Hague Tribunal

At the end of May 1995, Ratko Mladić made an original move to either prevent the bombardment of the RS or to compel the great powers to share the risk of such action. He ordered the ARS to arrest UNPROFOR officers and soldiers, and forced them to be held at sites that were hypothetical targets of the threatened bombardment.

(...)

After these UNPROFOR members had been physically bound to these locations, the soldiers and officers of the ARS would say something like this to them: "Look, now you're here, and we'll let them fly overhead. After all, tell them not to do it, because you're guarding these targets. Tell them that we're working toward a common goal, and it does them no good to interfere..."

That was the informal content of the text they were advised to use. The ARS soldiers added that nobody had anything against them personally, and that the Serbian people respected both their profession and their professionalism, but that their commanding officers had become biased and were helping the Muslims in every possible way, providing them with rations and weapons, and now they were bombing [the Serbs] for the benefit of the Muslims.

After all, even Wesley Clark had acknowledged to Mladić that NATO intended to amputate the military superiority of the ARS in technology and armaments, so that the bombardment had an obvious operational, and perhaps even strategic, goal.

Mladić had warned Clark at the time that he should not do such a thing, "because I'll do something that they would never be able to guess." And that was why hostages had been taken, and it caused a global sensation.

UNPROFOR representatives advised the press in Sarajevo on May 28, 1995 that "Serbian forces in Bosnia are holding at least 288 soldiers and 32 unarmed military observers."

(...)

The U.S. Secretary of State, Warren Christopher was deeply concerned about the "barbarian and uncivilized act of taking UN members hostage and immediately called Milošević, of course, and requested that he exert his influence as quickly as possible.

Milošević remained silent during those critical moments, as far as the public was concerned, but through connections with the General Staff of the Yugoslav Army, he berated Mladić, and swore at him like a trooper. Mladić simply stopped answering his calls.

The American public had an opportunity to get acquainted with a completely new dimension of the global media show. Mladić and Karadžić became mythic anti-heroes in the American media even though their reputations had already been blackened, and they were described in the worst language and referred to as incorrigible criminals.

The media compared Karadžić to Saddam Hussein and Ayatollah Khomeni, while Mladić became "a pitiless executioner" and "a criminal who is free of any fear [of prosecution]." A problem arose: was the spectacular arrest of the UNPROFOR soldiers a terrorist act or a war crime?

(...)

The official announcement made by Miroslav Toholj, the Information Minister of the Republika Srpska, was more detailed: "They cannot be considered prisoners of war in any way, because they are UN soldiers whose movements the Serbs have restricted, and we can call them whatever you want, because there is no problem. This month alone [May-June 1995, *Author's Note*], Serbian civilians from Western Slavonia and Pale were bombed by Croatian, American, Turkish, Spanish, Dutch and French warplanes, as well as by Bosnian Muslim helicopters. Neither the Serbian Army nor the Serbian people of the Republika Srpska nor the Republika Srpska Krajina will tolerate this any longer, and in a battle like this, there is no such thing as fair play."

(...)

After a period of suspense during which he was accused of "sadistic exhibitionism," General Mladić promised that the officers and observers, whom the Serbs were using as "human shields," would no longer be tied to targets that "they were protecting," and that they would instead be assigned each morning to their posts in a humane fashion, and would be asked "to sit down at those sites."

(...)

Each and every attempt to find an analogy in Serbian military history with "Mladić's hostages" is unsuccessful. Such precedents do not exist; it is not a part of the national military tradition. It may be noted that all the European newspapers, during the course of WWI, emphasized the conduct [of Serbs] toward Austrian prisoners of war, who in 1915 built the Paraćin-Zaječar railway. There was not a trace of revanchism that was exhibited against them, even though Austrian soldiers were, at the same time, committing atrocities against the Serbian inhabitants of Mačva and Rapevina.

How had the Serbian officer changed since that time? Did anyone ever consider that, if the time had come for the absence of all ethics in one instance, did it present an ideal justification for the destruction of ethics in general?

What kind and how large of a role did Mladić play in all this? One must immediately add that Mladić had the last word in such matters. Perhaps the idea was not even his, but its execution was. In any case, what were the reasons for these tangled incidents that unavoidably led to military and political defeat?

Before answering this question, it is important to understand the tenor of the Republika Srpska's relationship with the motherland, and the paternalism, which Serbia (namely the Serbian president, its alleged metaphor and symbol) stated as if it were his natural right.

Milošević's relationship to the future Republika Srpska was patriotic in an abstract way, but it was concretely hedonistic with respect to power. Milošević did not realize the depth of the problem; the war, to his pragmatic way of thinking, was merely a mural that contained many scenes, and the more colorful, chaotic and bloody they were, so much the better, because he believed that he held the reigns of power more firmly than ever.

His own role in that complicated story is contradictory. He exerted his influence quickly and efficiently in some cases, while in others he complained that "he had no influence at all on Pale."

Milošević spoke with [French President Jacques] Chiraq on June 2, at the very moment General Perišić was on the way to Pale to do what he could to help free the captured French pilots. Mladić also freed the Russian hostages, and on June 1, he released a much larger group of UN peacekeepers of various nationalities.

The West had judged that "Milošević could do things whenever he wanted to," which acknowledged the Serbian president's power over the Serbs, but it was also a silent prologue to The Hague Tribunal. It was understood that such power, despite the recent blockade of the Drina, was not infallible. At the same time, Milošević presented the Republika Srpska an extraordinary opportunity to drag itself out of the mud, and thereby "find an honorable way out of a dishonorable situation."

That was an ideal opportunity for Milošević "to do a favor for the international community," which strengthened his negotiating position in discussions to end the sanctions [against Yugoslavia].

Milošević eagerly seized the opportunity. At the beginning of June, he sent the chief of DB [*Državna Bezbednosti*, i.e. the Serbian secret service], Jovica Stanišić. There is no doubt that the president of Serbia at the time made the best possible choice, because Stanišić was an intelligent and capable negotiator who had at his fingertips detailed dossiers on all of the major players in the crisis.

Stanišić knew exactly what to say to certain people in order to carry out Milošević's orders. According to eyewitness reports, he came to Pale bearing carrots and sticks. His threats probably had no effect at all on either Mladić or Karadžić. These were men who cared little about what the world thought of them. It is unlikely that Milošević's wrath, which the head of the secret service carried with him in his briefcase, led either of them to believe that their respective positions were in jeopardy.

(...)

The leadership of the Republika Srpska sought its own way out. Now it was no longer simply a question of bombardment, but what to do with the hostages. Mladić no longer had any idea about what to do with them or how to "take advantage of them" because manacling them to targets had provoked worldwide anger and hatred for the Serbs. It was a risky position for anyone who was involved in the chaotic concept of international force, blackmail, debate and absurdity.

(...)

When Stanišić completed his mission, the Muslims realized that they too could cook up a Serbian recipe themselves, so they took a group of UN peacekeepers prisoner in Konjic.

(...)

Stanišić personally brought about the release of UN hostages in Novi Sad. Milošević publicly stated that the effort had been brought to a successful conclusion. Milošević thanked Jovica Stanišić and the members of the state security forces for having discharged their duties in an exemplary fashion.

Stanišić, as befits the head of a secret service agency, made a one sentence announcement at a news conference: "Our mission to mediate the release of the UN peacekeepers has been successfully concluded."

(...)

One of the hostages, Patrick Rechner, a captain from the Canadian army, testified before The Tribunal about the purpose of his being held prisoner, and about the adventure as a whole....

Captain Rechner claimed that the taking hostage and humiliation of UN officers was conducted with the full knowledge and approval of the entire political and military leadership of the Bosnian Serbs. Captain Rechner had either direct or indirect contact, particularly with Karadžić's political advisor, Jovan (John) Zametica, over the course of his twenty-three days of captivity. Allegedly, Koljević twice explained the action as electroshock therapy that "might either kill or cure the patient." Mr. Zametica, according to Captain Rechner's testimony, joked with him, "and he did not even try to conceal his delight over the circumstances in which the UN officers had found themselves, and he asked himself out loud 'what's General Rupert Smith [Commander of UNPROFOR forces in Bosnia] going to do now?'"

(...)

Mladić was waiting for "help" from Serbia, but he had no fixed idea of what Serbia had to do. It was clear to him that every direct intervention made by Serbia led to a full Balkan conflict. Milošević kept repeating that "Serbia is not at war," but people had stopped believing that a long time before. It is possible that Mladić was convinced that he was doing the right thing when the "human shield" operation began. NATO was in the air and on the ground, and the general of the Serbian army doubted the target selection of the threatened precision bombing campaign with each successive public announcement. "They can't bomb us from the air just like that while they've got their people all over the place here at checkpoints, technological centers, and camps. How are they going to distinguish us from the Muslims? Do they see then sticking their ass up in the air when they're bowing to pray? Is that how they're going to spare them?"

No matter how much he doubted the effectiveness of air strikes, Mladić rejected the possibility of intervention by ground forces. He had told Clark: "You need 100,000 soldiers just to take Mt. Igman. And all of Bosnia is like that: it's made up of Mt. Igman. I'm afraid that American public opinion will agree to send boys from Florida into some Bosnian *vukojebina*!"[30]

The interpreter appeared to have a lot of trouble with *vukojebina*, because Clark, thinking that it was about some important strategic objective, demanded a literal, word for word translation. The interpreter was sweating it out, and when he formed a compound word with *wolf* and the corresponding expression, and attempted to turn it into a noun, there was silence, and then an outburst of laughter!

"*Vukojebine* [plural, *Translator's Note*], that's certainly true! *Vukojebine* wherever you go, my dear Wesley!" said Mladić seriously with a note of gloom while the remaining negotiators giggled and leafed through their pocket dictionaries.

Mladić anticipated a number of things in his struggle against the most powerful armies in the world. First of all, he thought that the Americans were bluffing. They had announced bombardments on three-four occasions, only to relent afterwards. Even the first announcements made by Pale were greeted with bon fires. People sang songs in honor of Sinđelić, Mišić[31] and Mladić. *Rakija* was consumed; beer and wine flowed. Oxen and lamb were roasted over coals. Once again, an infernal pagan ambiance was created for a hedonistic Serbian sacrifice. But NATO did not strike on this occasion.

"If they hadn't dared to do it then, then they'll never do it," intoned the Serbs with epic inspiration. "No one dares to raise a hand against the Serbs, and they can't do anything about it."

(...)

Mladić certainly did ignore America's experience in the Gulf War, where U.S. bombers demonstrated near perfect precision with "smart" bombs. He underestimated the vanity of the great powers and their frightful sensitivity; he did not believe that their hypothetical prestige, which was at stake, had to be actualized at any given moment.

(...)

General Mladić interpreted Stanišić's arrival as the mission of a man who could provide help in unpleasant circumstances. He would be the one who would take care of the dirty work. Everyone was confident that they would emerge from all this untainted and ready for new undertakings. Therefore, Mladić did not greet Stanišić as if he were a savior "from a higher nationalistic sphere," nor as a troublemaker from the generally incompetent world of cabinet ministers. Stanišić was showing up on the front lines with his own cowboy laws.

At first, Mladić, refusing to meet any more of "Slobo's couriers," wouldn't even meet with Stanišić. According to eye-witness accounts ... Mladić and Stanišić met "in the field" twice over the course of the security chief's four week stay in Bosnia. Jovica Stanišić "worked" chiefly with General Tolimir and spent long hours in discussions with Karadžić.

He told Mladić: "The chief is really angry!"

"I'm even angrier than he is, but he doesn't care, does he? If he cared as much as he ought to, this wouldn't be happening now," replied Mladić.

"He ordered the hostages to be released; otherwise, the results will be unpredictable."

"They're already unpredictable," answered Mladić. "Maybe they're unpredictable for him, but we know what's in store for us. We have no way out of this except for victory, with you or without you. Maybe he gives you orders, but he doesn't give me orders. If he gave you orders to release them, then go ahead and unshackle them and let them go free."

(...)

General Mladić stated that his army never waged a war in foreign territory. But, without risk of erring very much, binding the hostages to targets to impede or render the bombardment impossible, must be classed as a strategic blunder.

Everything after that led to chaos and disintegration — and Waterloo.

Serbian Boot, Serbian Opanak[32]

Years later, it is indescribably difficult to assign culpability for war crimes that took place during the Bosnian War. There were certainly many of them because conditions had been created to ignore ethics in general. It was a war where hatred and revenge reigned, in which the conditions for an ethnic cataclysm had been created by all available means: a cataclysmic rupture of all interethnic relations, once and for all.

(...)

We already claimed that Mladić, in the opening stages of creating the ARS, had to cope with significant limitations. He was able to carry out his operational planning much more easily than he was able to impose military ethics. Hatred for "Turks and Ustashi" was far more pronounced than a basic respect for the enemy. The brutality of wartime revanchism reared its ugly head, and it produced a destructive spiral into mindless violence.

On the other hand, all Serbs at once became "Serbo-Chetniks," which seemed to justify terrible reprisals exacted by the most primitive and pathological characters who happened to be in uniform, and who committed unthinkable atrocities under the aegis of a national symbol.

The commanders had to know or eventually learn of them, but ... more often than not, such atrocities were allowed to happen, and resulted in "functional blindness" that ignored criminal activity and later led to a tacit agreement with them.

"It's war," people said. "All sorts of things are going on."

Even in 1992, the world was trying to understand what was going on in Bosnia-Herzegovina. It's hardly likely that any of the "expert" commentators on the war ever read Ivo Andrić's *Bosnian Chronicles*, so that they were at least aware of a literary depiction of the dark province[33] and real Balkan chaos.

(...)

However, different notes had been struck. The American President George Bush (Senior) ordered the U.S. secret service to find evidence of the existence of "death camps" for Muslims in the areas of Bosnia-Herzegovina controlled by the Serbs.

President Bush received information that such death camps did not exist. The former American Ambassador in the SFRY, Lawrence Eagleburger, announced that terrible things were happening, but that death camps could not be discussed if one imagined something along the lines of Auschwitz.

But on August 23, while the U.S. secret service was still looking for evidence of death camps, Sarajevo was subjected to heavy bombardment by Serbian artillery.

What was General Mladić doing at the time? The world had already charged the Serbs with committing unheard of atrocities even at the beginning of the war. And the Serbs complained, but, for a variety of reasons, their voice was never heard beyond local broadcasts. In Trnovo County, near Sarajevo, the erstwhile policeman, Edo Godinja massacred, with his "green berets," thirteen Serbs, three entire families named Šehovac, Samardžija and Cvijetić.

Mladić had a completely different point of view on the origin of the war, and he addressed a letter to the UNPROFOR

Commander, the Indian General Satish Nambijar, in which he stated that he had encountered twelve brigades from the Croatian Republic in battles in Bosnia-Herzegovina.

He also informed General Nambijar that Muslim-Croat forces were subjecting Sarajevo to continuous attack, and that the Muslims in the Sarajevo suburb of Alipašino Polje had killed seventeen Serbs who refused to join their units.

(...)

This is what General Mladić had to say about the positions taken by the Muslim political leadership: "It must be made clear to the Bosnian Muslim leadership that they cannot rely on international intervention. Izetbegović has to comprehend that, then I believe he will agree to negotiate with the Serbs of Bosnia-Herzegovina. As things stand now, he won't sit down with us at the negotiating table. Without it [i.e., his cooperation], there will be no negotiations."

Louis MacKenzie denied the hypothesis that the Serbs possessed incomparable technological superiority over the Muslims and said that both sides, unfortunately, were very well armed and that stories about an aggressor who was armed to the teeth and an opposing side, which had to rely on its bare hands to fight, were out of place. There were a considerable number of functioning arms factories under the control of Muslims and Croats and Serbs. United Nations inspections found less heavy artillery [than anticipated], which all sides had. Izetbegović, he continued, wasn't going to like this, but he had to say that according to the information at his disposal, Izetbegović's side had fulfilled less of these obligations than the others.

MacKenzie went on to say that, in any case, he did not have any influence on whether or not Karadžić and Mladić were subject to any control whatsoever from Belgrade. And he thought that they made all the important decisions by themselves.

(...)

The Serbian side, of course, did not succeed in capitalizing on MacKenzie's remark *post festum*, not because it believed some of his erroneous judgments, but because it believed that nothing at all depended on the others. The Serbs held more than seventy percent of the territory in Bosnia-Herzegovina. They were at the height of their expansion. Even irrational satisfaction existed among some officers on the occasion of serious indictments and radical demonization tactics used against the Serbs: "They can say and write whatever they want about us, because they can't do anything to us at all." This was no longer the arrogance of victory, but something much worse, a conviction of invulnerability, an unreal supposition about the destiny of their victorious mission.

It was difficult to control excesses while maintaining such concepts, but it is unlikely that Mladić stimulated them. First of all, it could be said that he ignored them, and believed that incidents in which the basic ethics of warfare had been broken were unavoidable "collateral damage" that would be almost negligible with respect to the final resulting victory.

(...)

Only later, when their resources began to dwindle, did some political leaders understand the second-class position of an exhausted Russia and the unanimous agreement of western governments and the inviolability of American leadership. These parameters, even at the very beginning, had to make them conscious of Serbian inferiority in all of the crucial aspects that determined preparedness for war.

General Ratko Mladić did not have to bear that in mind, but he could have. His initial successes led him too quickly to unexpected intoxication, which later led him to unselectively reject many a rational proposition. The policies that determined the fate of the Serbs as a whole were in the hands of dangerous dilettantes who tried to run a state along the lines of a gasoline refinery or a psychiatric clinic.

In this manner, military leaders were able to feel superior, as if they had reached the summit of an indistinct and abstract glory, meanwhile having surrendered themselves to an epic parody of messianism. Of course, their good intentions are not in question, but this in no way justifies taking the road to defeat. Finally, it became clear that battles had been fought in vain, victories gained transitory, and the accompanying death and catastrophe meaningless.

But Serbian generals were one and all inspired by victories from history that were achieved only after terrific sacrifices. On December 12, 1993, the town of Gornji Milanovac in Serbia hosted the annual celebrations of the victory in the Battle of Kolubara.[34] The glory of history had been impressed into the service of inglorious everyday politics; the war in Bosnia was the central theme; and great words cheaply used inundated the celebration.

The principal guests at the celebration were General Mladić, Momčilo Perišić and Zoran Lilić, the president of the FRY.

"Once more history confirms," said Lilić, "a rule that has been tested many times: aggressors cannot forever enslave a people and a state."

The inspired patriotic speech that Zoran Lilić made culminated with an achievement that concerned "historical analogy." He went on to say: "In this century, only the Serbian people, who, alongside their struggle for liberation in two world wars, have now been imperiled for a third time, and this time by the same people with whom they had lived in a common state."

Mr. Lilić added that the Federal Republic of Yugoslavia "is a genuine state in the context of the former SFRY," and added: "We succeeded in protecting the new generation, but the people are suffering, and the country is suffering from destruction, while at the same time we extended support and material aid to the Serbian people in the Republika Srpska and the Republika Srpska Krajina to aid them in their effort to establish their legitimate national rights."

Lilić concluded his wide-ranging epic speech on a note of certainty: "I am convinced that the Serbian people, even over there where a war is being waged against them, will succeed in defending their freedom, integrity and independence, after all, that has always happened over the course of history. Recalling the meaning of significant dates from the history of our nation convinces us that they will succeed in their efforts."

General Perišić recalled the sacrifices that the Serbs had made in order to achieve great victories: "Serbian soldiers appeared on the Sava and Danube on December 13, 1914. Over the course of the Battle of Kolubara, the Serbs sacrificed around 150,000 lives, while the Austro-Hungarians lost 319,075 soldiers. That was a serious blow to the Habsburg Monarchy and it gave Potiorek[35] a reason to say: 'No one has yet defeated the upturned Serbian *opanak*.'"

General Mladić did not speak, but he was without a doubt the star of the show. He received a great deal of attention wherever he went. People were sincerely enthusiastic about Mladić.

Together with Perišić, Mladić laid wreaths on the monuments erected for the Serbian rebels in Takovo[36] as well as for the soldiers who had given their lives in both world wars.

The generals promenaded through the city. Mladić was alert, cheerful and in good spirits, and he spoke with people.

At that moment, it seemed to one and all that war was perhaps a romantic nationalistic tale, an inescapable destiny that wove its threads throughout history, encompassing today as well as the future. One cannot see a true picture of a war at celebrations, but for the citizens of Gornji Milanovac, there were two generals, contemporary warriors who looked as if they had stepped out of the pages of history; these were men who held a conviction to defend or build a Serbian state, no matter where it was.

The citizens asked Ratko Mladić: "General, have you pacified your enemies?"

"Yes, we've pacified them, but they could be pacified a little more," answered Mladić.

The Hague and Its Gallery of Crimes

How trustworthy are the testimonies given to the Tribunal? Perhaps we can say that they are just as trustworthy as the witnesses who give them. But, war is an environment of extreme chaos; it is difficult to discern any order to things. And ordinary men as well as political leaders and military commanders know that war changes everything in a man: his relationship to his own memory, his ability to feel fear, love, hatred, loneliness and solidarity — civilization is unimaginable without all of these things.

Today, the conviction that the members of the ARS committed serious crimes in Srebrenica holds sway in political and jurisdictional circles. The Tribunal Judge Fuad Riyad (Egypt) said in July 1996: "true scenes from hell were written in Srebrenica on the darkest pages of the human history." Justice Riyad based his judgment on documentation and evidence that had been presented to him. And all of that, he said, "enabled the reconstruction of what took place and confirms the responsibility of those who had ordered it or at least did not prevent it."

The Tribunal's Srebrenica investigation began on July 21, 1995 on territory under the control of government authorities [i.e., the authorities of the Muslim-Croat Federation, *Author's Note*], and on January 21, 1996 on territory controlled by the Republika Srpska, more exactly, the greater Srebrenica region.

Jean Rene Ruez, an agent from the French judicial police, testified before The Hague Tribunal.

He quoted statements made by eye-witnesses and victims, and commented on video documentaries and other materials that were presented to the court.

The attack on the so-called "safe area" began on July 5, 1995. Mladić's forces entered the city on July 11. Mladić arrived himself. A VHS video presented to the court, assumed to be material produced by TV Pale, showed General Ratko Mladić congratulating the soldiers on the completion of military action, and he said: "Finally, after the revolt of the *dahiyas*,[37] the moment has come to take revenge on the Turks in this area."

The translation of this last sentence was read before the Court three times. When the court asked if the General's words were meant to be an invitation to revenge, the witness replied that his words meant just that.

Muslim civilians, said the indictment, sought refuge from Mladić's troops in the Dutch UNPROFOR battalion's base in Potočari, but about 15,000 of them, chiefly men and soldiers, headed through the forests and mountains toward Tuzla. Serbian forces encircled the UN base on July 12, then entered it and began to separate the men from the women and children.

The women and children were then evacuated by bus.

The murders allegedly took place once Mladić left the base at Potočari. According to the findings of the investigation, many other incidents confirmed Mladić's *modus operandi*, with the exception of Karakaj. There, Mladić allegedly attended the executions of a large number of detainees.

In other places — Kravica, Konjević Polje, Nova Kasaba, the executions began, as the prosecution claimed, fifteen minutes after his departure.

The statements of witnesses and surviving victims were important for The Hague investigators. They claimed that they had witnessed mass executions — killings and open slaughter, a true organized massacre of detained civilians or captured soldiers in Potočari, Bratunac, Kravica, Nova Kasaba, Cerska, Konjević Polje, Karakaj, and Pilici or along the roads in which columns of civilians or soldiers tried to get out of the encirclement, but ended up fleeing into ambushes despite their best efforts [to avoid them].

The Hague investigators, as they claimed in their indictments, used satellite imagery as the basis for their investigation and went in search of "suspicious" locations. They allegedly found sufficient evidence in the area near the soccer field in Nova Kasaba, the Tatar area near Bratunac, Sahanići near Zvornik, the agricultural building complex in Pilici to confirm the statements made by witnesses. The investigators claimed that the terrain had been meanwhile "tampered with" in such a fashion that larger mass graves had been dug up and emptied. Some of those actions, they maintained, had even been photographed by satellites and aerial reconnaissance. "Activity" had been spotted in satellite imagery taken of suspicious locations in the area of Bratunac on October 20 and 30, 1995, by large earth moving machines, which transformed the "landscape" of the surroundings, and which did not match earlier imagery of the same terrain.

Tribunal prosecutors reconstructed General Mladić's movements during the fall of Srebrenica: on July 11 he was in Srebrenica; on July 12, he was in Potočari; on July 13 in Kravica, Konjević Polje and Nova Kasaba; on July 14 in Karakaj.... In each of these places, he spoke to those who had been detained and claimed that they would be exchanged, and fifteen minutes after his departure the executions would begin. The one exception was Karakaj.

Judge Riyad, on the basis of sources that he had at his disposal, broadly sketched what the indicted had said about the alleged crimes in Srebrenica. That was how Mladić's explanation that soldiers who had fought and died in battles were buried where they had fallen (which generally accounted for the existence of mass graves) was reduced to "hygienic reasons."

Karadžić, using the same explanation in various interviews and conversations, simply wrote off the claims of massive crimes in Srebrenica as Muslim and other anti-Serbian propaganda. He told *The Times* (London) that no one under his command would have dared to kill soldiers who had surrendered. As far as the Republika Srpska was concerned, it was firmly in his hands.

(...)

Does this story, however, have another side to it? The careful reader will notice that the prosecutor was systematic in enumerating various actions that fall within in the tribunal's purview ... but in its own concluding remarks, it made suppositions that cannot be qualified as evidence, but as personal, political positions, instead.

It is risky to claim that the Tribunal is an exclusively political institution that "brings only one people to trial," but even so, there correspondingly exists no reliable evidence to convince anyone of the principled impartiality of The Hague Tribunal, which is in question here.

For example, Veselin Dimitrov, a Bulgarian national who fought as a volunteer for the ARS, gave an interview to *24 časa* ("24 Hours"), a Sofia newspaper. He talked about the pressure he was put under and the suggestions that had been made to him at The Hague. He was summoned as a witness, but the context of his deposition was the anticipated indictments against General Mladić for his alleged crimes.

"They called me over there, and demanded that I bring charges against General Mladić and other commanders of the ARS," said Dimitrov.

"Not one single general of the ARS," said the volunteer, "was able to order the mass murder of civilians."

He fought with the First Kozaračka Brigade, and, according to his deposition, he frequently saw Generals Mladić and Krstić. From May to June of 1995, he was in the elite corps of soldiers called the "Drina Wolves," who carried out intelligence operations.

Dimitrov was not a mercenary. He received fifty deutschmarks a month like all of his fellow soldiers.

"I was interrogated by prosecutor Alberto Perduta," said Dimitrov. "I was designated the number 'Sst-118', and I had no idea what that meant. The investigators knew that I was a small fry, and they said that they weren't interested in whether or not I had done any shooting or whether I had killed anyone, but only to tell them everything I knew about my unit."

Dimitrov, after having been questioned by the investigators about the orders they received, replied: "We never got orders to commit acts of violence against anyone." He told the investigators that he saw men who had been killed, but that his unit "didn't go into the villages" because their assignments consisted of securing important objectives.

"They interrogated me about Srebrenica," said Dimitrov. "They were particularly forceful. There was terrific psychological pressure. I answered, resolutely and curtly, that I would, if they could provide me with evidence of genocide, accept their version of the story and repeat it before the judge. They didn't have any proof; they just kept showing me pictures of dead soldiers," said Dimitrov.

Is the entire Tribunal indictment against Mladić and Karadžić based merely on the statements of "suitable" witnesses and appropriate materials? And were the witnesses who had a different point of view excluded from the process?

It is, indeed, difficult to answer such a question. But, the hypothesis put forth by two American attorneys, who, over the course of 1996 and 1997, prepared Radovan Karadžić's defense, is interesting. Kosta Čavoški explained the defense strategy: it was a document requesting general amnesty for Radovan Karadžić by attempting to place the ultimate blame on "other Serbian leaders" for the massacres that took place during the Balkan wars. *Le Monde* ... published an article about this on April 17, 1998.

Le Monde quoted an anonymous NATO officer in Sarajevo. The officer said that five months earlier [i.e., on or about December 1997, *Author's Note*], he met with one of Karadžić's two attorneys who submitted to him a defense document that numbered 150 pages, which was written by "an attorney from Serbia, Kosta Čavoški."

"It's a good starting point for a future defense," stated this officer for *Le Monde*, without quite saying why, as a NATO officer, he had undertaken to play such an indirect role.

The document practically refutes the indictment issued by The Hague Tribunal against Radovan Karadžić for his alleged participation in the tens of thousands of deaths over the course of the war in Bosnia (1992–1995), including the [alleged] mass murder of civilians in Srebrenica.

Le Monde published excerpts from Kosta Čavoški's document, which stated that Karadžić lost control of the army in that (critical) phase of the conflict, and that the army had been taken over by his "former" military commander, Ratko Mladić, and more significantly, the Yugoslav President, Slobodan Milošević.

"The individual who led this operations [in Srebrenica, *Author's Note*], could be none other than Slobodan Milošević," stated the defense document. "The Hague Tribunal ordered the arrest of Mladić but not Milošević."

Čavoški's defense document acknowledged that Karadžić "was not unerring," but it claimed that he cannot be held accountable for everything that had taken place in the Bosnian War. "The indicted cannot be held accountable for crimes which each individual Serbian resident committed during the course of the ethnic, civil and religious war that subsumed Bosnia," wrote Čavoški.

Professor Čavoški, who was presented as "a senator of the Republika Srpska," explained his position on the culpability and responsibility for the "incident in Srebrenica" in an interview with the Serbian *Oslobođenje* on May 23, 1998. The questions posed by the unidentified journalist who interviewed the professor about Srebrenica are characteristic, primarily because of their suggestiveness. We will quote it here in full: "There has been a great deal of speculation about who pulled the strings in some spectacular incidents, such as Srebrenica, for example. Do you think that reasons exist to believe that Mr. Karadžić, civilians and the military organs of the Republika Srpska were not those who gave the orders in Srebrenica, and that it was instead, perhaps, someone else from another country?"

Even at the beginning of the interview, Professor Čavoški tried to absolve Dr. Karadžić of any responsibility that related to the chain of military command. He said: "It is an indisputable fact that the alleged command of the army on the part of the civilian chief of state over the course of the war was most often nominal, and that high-ranking officers of the ARS remained loyal to their colleagues in the JNA rather than to Dr. Radovan Karadžić. In the end, this was announced by seventeen generals (all members of the ARS) who rejected the legitimate decree issued by Dr. Radovan Karadžić concerning the removal of General Ratko Mladić from his position."

Senator Čavoški took the position that The Hague Tribunal was biased and illegitimate because it did not respect one essential element of jurisprudence, "which is equality [i.e., before the law].

According to that, either everyone on all sides is responsible or only our enemy is entitled to speak, but not our friends and allies."

Čavoški's understanding of the equality of justice is irrefutable; there cannot be any explicit assignment of guilt solely reserved for General Mladić. In other words, the professor does not recognize the Tribunal, but does not deny that Mladić, Milošević and some members of the JNA could be responsible for committing criminal acts. That practically means that Čavoš, ki attempted to defend Karadžić by acknowledging that Srebrenica was, indeed, a criminal trauma, while maintaining that Dr. Karadžić played no role in it because he was not in command of his state's army.

Did Professor Čavoški, in his defense of Dr. Radovan Karadžić, attempt only to distinguish the general's [alleged] guilt from the president's innocence or something more: to distinguish the rights of "Serbs" from "converts from Communism," and to thus justify Karadžić's innocence in such a prejudicial fashion? Or did it occur to him, as a senator, that the then prevalent dream of a mythical Serbian nation west of the Drina finally became a nightmare, and that perhaps he could "protect" Radovan and thus save him for some more auspicious and glorious time? General Mladić, in this interpretation, does not seem to have done anything significant, although, strictly speaking, Karadžić had much better relations with Milošević than Mladić ever did.

It is perhaps important to introduce the thoughts of Dr. Smilja Avramov,[38] Professor of International Law, in such considerations of innocence and guilt. She was a member of Slobodan Milošević's team of advisors until August 1994, i.e., until the blockade of the Drina. Then she abandoned "Comrade Slobo." In an interview that appeared in *Javnost* on June 29, 1996, Jadranka Pandurević posed this question: "The Tribunal has announced that it will bring criminal charges against Radovan Karadžić and General Mladić. What will happen if such legal procedures are indeed set into motion?"

Dr. Avramov replied: "It will be a historic compromise on their part, and it will remain as material evidence of a motion which is not only void of legal justification, but which will serve as an example of serious missteps made by the international community. It is the initiation of a trial that will not only prosecute Karadžić and Mladić, but the entire Serbian people as well, and we must be conscious of that. They [the international community, *Author's Note*] want to take away our right to exist as well our right to self defense."

Dr. Avramov went on to say that "these two individuals symbolize the Serbian people." She asserted that the people owe them a great deal, and that they will enter history as illustrious figures. "I am deeply convinced that all of the Serbian people stand united in their defense, to the extent that they would do anything for them."

She also said that The Hague Tribunal and its investigators will be compromised as jurists for centuries to come, and that, as such, they will enter the darkest pages of history. "And this is how the Dutch judicial system is compromising itself, because it is tolerating [the existence of] a court that is destroying the entire system of international law on its own territory. We must grant President Karadžić and General Mladić profound recognition for all that they have done and we must stand solidly behind them."

One can note the considerable difference in the positions of the two law professors. While Čavoški does not deny the general's guilt, but only passes judgment on the court, and along with that stipulates that Karadžić must be beyond all suspicion, Dr. Avramov did not mention any possibility at all that Serbs committed any crimes whatsoever. She wholly denies the legitimacy of the Tribunal and her relationship to the "heroes of Serbdom" does not border on pathetic idolatry.

A declaration of the defense of Karadžić and Mladić appeared in Belgrade on October 1997, which was signed by important public figures. It said: "The world powers have begun paralyzing each and every political and social activity of the Serbian people with the attempt to completely isolate Karadžić with their continuing threats of his arrest."

The publicist Slobodan Inić polemicized this position by opposing the significance of any one individual for the Serbian people. He said it was biased. But he was in complete agreement with one of the points announced in the Declaration, which stated: "It is a hypocritical and logically untenable assertion that such allegations of individual guilt will diminish the guilt of the Serbian people as á whole, because Radovan Karadžić and General Ratko Mladić were indicted on the basis of command responsibility, which they, in turn, had received by the consent of the people."

Inić also said that: "It is indeed correct, and it is one of the greatest mistakes made by the international community and The Hague Tribunal. No matter how much this mistake originates with human error, which was meant to give the [Serbian] people a chance to free themselves of total responsibility by claiming Karadžić and Mladić to be guilty, it will not change, as it has not until now, changed the relations of the Serbian people to the two individual leaders who have been indicted for mass murder, even after all that has happened. To this extent, and more, the people will suffer all the consequences."

(...)

In fact, there is a great deal of evidence that the Tribunal, lurching beneath the overwhelming weight of prejudicial political power, behaved one-sidedly in many aspects of its complicated existence and undertakings. In some instances, such one-sidedness was brutally applied, and there is evidence that world public opinion ignored murderous media spectacles [e.g., the Croatian "Operation Storm," which drove a quarter of a million Serbs out of Croatia, *Translator's Note*].

Above all, there are video cassettes that depict crimes committed by mujahideen against Serbs in the Bosnian-Herzegovinian war. These videotapes show the President of the Muslim-Croat federation, Alija Izetbegović, personally giving his blessing to the mujahideen's horrifying mission.

There is not a single shred of evidence indicating that the leaders of the Bosnian Serbs ever committed anything similar to this nor, from a corresponding level, that they ever gave orders to Serbian soldiers to commit crimes. This fact does not in any manner diminish the responsibility of Radovan Karadžić and General Mladić but leads one to suspect the impartiality of the Tribunal.

The video cassettes that show Alija's murderous cries before mujahideen, who were sharpening sabers that they were going to use to lop off the heads of Serbs, would probably have been ignored forever if fanatical Muslims had not attacked the U.S.

The FONET news agency announced on Saturday, September 29, [1997] that a private television station, BN from Bijeljina, had broadcast a portion of the material concerning Mujahideen in B-H, but because of the by-laws of the regulatory agency, it did not broadcast material containing the most horrifying scenes. The broadcast ran almost 90 minutes.

Mirko Šarović, President of the Republika Srpska, brought the video cassette to the television studio. These tapes were broadcast over the course of a televised interview with him. The video tapes had been shot in the spring and summer of 1995, most likely for some Arab television station. Even though the faces of some of the Mujahideen had been concealed, Alija Izetbegović's face could be clearly seen.

(...)

Zvokno Prijović, a reporter from *Glas javnosti*, who saw the uncensored video with all of the horrific scenes committed by the "El Mujahideen" Squad, wrote the following: "In scenes shot in a Mujahideen camp, one first sees captives, who are still alive, lying on the ground. Then, above the bound and gagged Serbian soldiers, one sees a dark-skinned mujahideen with a long beard, who is sharpening a cleaver. The camera moves into a close-up of the detention camp, cries of *Alahu ekbar* are heard and one can see the aforementioned mujahideen swinging the cleaver and decapitating one of the captured soldiers.

"Incoherent chanting followed the brutal execution, which, one may surmise, represented some kind of prayer because of its choral nature.

"Not long afterwards," wrote Prijović, "follows a scene where we see how the mujahideens hand out knives to Serbian soldiers, and trying to incite them to kill one another. 'If you won't kill him, I'll kill you!' they said to the unfortunate men who then began stabbing each other. The Mujahideens then decapitated the wounded men with meat cleavers or chain saws, while those who were left alive had to kiss decapitated heads that had been nailed to trees.

"The captives were either hung by ropes or the mujahideen tied bricks to their sexual organs and threw them into barrels filled with water, where they sank under the weight of the bricks, and eventually drowned."

The videos set new standards for fanaticism ... but the facts set forth here about General Mladić's failings as well as his merits are not sufficient to either make a judgment or to relativize his responsibility.

This is simply the mosaic of war, tesserae, which exist in reality as well as in one's awareness of it in history as well as in the minds of those who make history, who are all too often inclined to start all over from the beginning. To do that, they need to be convinced that important matters of life and death depend solely on them.

General Mladić's story cannot be defined as a wholesale sell-off of brutal crimes committed by the three warring parties; it cannot be defined by the of horror which is stirred up in analyses made long after the war had ended. The Hague Tribunal is an unavoidable reality but Ratko Mladić, who has still not been apprehended, is "a fugitive, a coward, a knight, a bum and a hero," as one fascinated reporter once remarked. "I always have the impression that Ratko Mladić is here somewhere, and that you can imagine him to be anywhere, but you must not expect him. He will never be where most people expect him to be. It is impossible to imagine him sitting before the judges in The Hague. He is too proud let them nail him to a bench."

Capturing Mladić

This is what happened at the conclusion of the Bjelašnica operation, which Mladić commanded and whose operational plan was conceived by Manojlo Milovanović: Mladić, Milovanović (his assistant) and a group of followers reached the top of Mt. Bjelašnica a half hour before ARS units, which were advancing up three sides of the mountain. The operation was led with near perfect command coordination and crushed Muslim units along the way.

Mladić got out of his vehicle, took a pair of binoculars, and studied the slopes of the mountain, watching his units make uninterrupted progress to the mountain top.

But a hundred meters beneath him, the commander of a Muslim company, which was preparing to surrender to the Serbs, saw the smaller group of uniformed Serbs, who looked like easy prey.

"Look, there are Chetniks up there. I'll fuck their mothers!" said the commander. "Let's go, Avdo. Take up firing positions. Those are Serbo-Chetniks...."

"Chief, we got here early. I told you we didn't have to hurry!" said General Milovanović, who was unperturbed. There was a note of disapproval in his voice because the commander had hurried to reach the top of Mt. Bjelašnica, and since there were only seven of them, they realized that they had walked into an ambush. There was no way out.

Mladić kept scoping out the battlefield, and did not even bother to turn to Milovanović, when he said: "Let the Turks go. Deploy the troops, and we'll see what happens."

Manojlo obeyed the orders, but then asked: "There are only a few of us, and our troops are still far away. What are we going to do, chief? These guys are taking up firing positions!"

Ratko Mladić calmly stowed his binoculars in their carrying case, and then headed downward along the slope....

"God help me!" said Milovanović. "This commander of ours is nuts. What is he going to do now?"

Mladić calmly walked toward the Muslims, who were, according to the rules of engagement, scurrying to the top of the mountain.

"Halt!" said the Muslim commander. "Let's see what this Chetnik wants."

Then Mladić stopped, and shouted loudly so that his echo could be heard far and wide along the Bjelašnica Gorge. "Heeey, Tuuuuurks! Come here and catch Mladić!"

"I'll fuck my own mother if that isn't really Mladić," said one of the Muslim soldiers, and he added hastily: "Run! It's Satan himself!"

Nearly all of them threw down their rifles, left their heavy weapons and ran to meet the units that were now arriving.

"That guy is crazy," said Manojlo to himself as Mladić was walking back, chuckling to himself. "Mane [a nickname for Manojlo, *Translator's Note*], take out those maps, and mark the positions our forces are taking. I feel sorry for those Turks I met down there. They would have been better off if they had come up here with us."

"Capturing Mladić" has become an obsession, a complex. There are many people, not to mention international organizations, humbled wartime opponents, and prosecutors from The Hague who would like to see Ratko Mladić deprived of his liberty — i.e., behind bars. Likewise, life on the run is not any sort of ideal freedom, but it stimulates resistance.

Having taken pains to avoid making categorical statements elsewhere, the author of this book has been frequently inclined to claim that Ratko Mladić will never be captured for two reasons: 1) he thinks more quickly than his pursuers; and 2) he makes decisions faster, and he executes them uncompromisingly. Such a categorical statement, of course, may be refuted, but that in no way devalues the stated reasons for making this assertion.

The episode in the Bjelašnica Gorge is an anecdotal war story, but witnesses claim it is true. General Mladić's struggle against the ambitions of his pursuers forms part of his biography from 1991 to this very day.

And there are many true stores about efforts made to capture him, fantastical plans and unsuccessful attempts that have entered legend. They tried to capture Mladić even when he was the commander of the Knin Corps. The attempt made by Major Škaro to capture Mladić is interesting. At one time, he was under Mladić's command as an intelligence officer, but then switched sides and fled to join Croatian rebel units.

While Škaro was serving in the JNA, Mladić did not consider him to be very trustworthy, although he was a solid officer as far as his performance was concerned. But Mladić said at meetings of the corps commanders: "When you, Škaro, make an assessment of a situation, you must be obliged to do the opposite, and then you won't go wrong!"

Major Škaro, who was already nursing the ideal of an independent Croatian state, and who was a passionate chauvinist, hated General Mladić because he was a Serb and because he was a man who treated him high-handedly and laughed in his face because he suspected the truth about him.

When Major Škaro fled and joined the Croatian national defense forces, his *idée fixe* became apprehending and capturing General Mladić. "Just you wait and see. I'm personally going to put the cuffs on him! A dog fuck his mother!" said Škaro, congratulating himself after he became a member of the military branch of the HDZ in Zadar. He wanted to "cleanse" the JNA once and for all from his biography with such battlefield exploits.

Several "moles," Croats, who for practical reasons, had still not yet joined "their own people," remained in the command of the corps. Mladić noticed that "information was being leaked," so he held meetings only for the sake of masking intelligence. Therefore, he spoke only about things that he wanted the HDZ in Zadar to know. Otherwise, he made essential decisions himself, and he communicated them directly before putting them into action.

One evening he held a meeting of "a wide selection of officers," where he put forward "general things" about the tasks facing the command and the entire corps. But at the end, as if in passing, he said: "Tomorrow I'm going to go in the direction of Vrlika. I want a jeep, because I'm going to be setting out early."

At four in the morning, he summoned the commander of a company of military police: "Zdravko, arrange for two officers to sit in my jeep. Let them go first in the direction of Vrliki. One squad of military police must set out immediately, and must set up an ambush at milestone 213. The jeep must pause there for twenty minutes, until the squad is in position. I'm going with the first *Pintzgauer*,[39] and you behind me."

In half an hour, moving through the wooded area, a squad of military policemen set up an ambush by a curve in the road near milestone 213. Mladić and the commander of the company of military policeman waited. The jeep with the JNA emblem appeared, and made its way in a leisurely fashion toward the curve in the road. Škaro was waiting right at the side of the road with a group of ten or so 'Zengi' [Croatian paramilitaries]. They ran out on the road. Škaro held an automatic pistol in his hand and stood on the right side of the vehicle, where the "important prisoner" was supposed to be. "Come on out, Mladić. I fuck your Communist and Chetnik mother. Judgment Day has come for you!"

The military policemen emerged from the vehicle with their hands up. "Well, where's Mladić? I fuck each and every one of your Serbian mothers!" Škaro was screaming now. He could not bear seeing such a spectacle unfold before his eyes.

Then the policemen ambushed Major Škaro and his men. Captain Zdravko ordered them to lay down their arms. "And you, too, Major. Right now. The jig is up!"

General Mladić emerged from his Pintzgauer unarmed, and approached a scene that could be described as "an ambush within an ambush."

"So this is how Škaro sets out to capture General Mladić," said the General. The fugitive Major was quivering with fury. "You don't have enough brains to capture anyone, kid. Simply put, besides being untrustworthy, you're really stupid. You were untrustworthy for us, and now you're untrustworthy for them. What's the name of you're commanding officer? I've got to send him a report on you. You're useless, Major. And you better believe it when Ratko Mladić tells you so."

Major Škaro spent two months in some prison in a garrison in Knin, and an indictment was even prepared against him by a military court. But, he was exchanged in a classic transfer of prisoners. Mladić did not oppose the transfer, but he insisted that he "accompany" Škaro. Mladić told him: "We decided to send you back over there. Why do we need you here taking up space in prison and wasting all that food. You're much more useful to us over there, because you'll be causing them trouble instead of us. But watch out! Don't ever try to capture General Mladić again. If I catch you tailing me one more time, you'll never be seen alive again!"

Witnesses claim that there have been many more dangerous attempts to capture or liquidate General Mladić. Did IFOR [Implementation Force, composed of NATO forces which took military command of Bosnia after the departure of UNPROFOR in order to implemented the Dayton Accord, *Translator's Note*] have the authority to do that? There is no precise information on the subject, because the bits of information that do appear, whether from The Hague or Brussels or from Washington, D.C., are always conflicting.

"IFOR has no mandate to intervene and make criminal arrests, so IFOR won't be arresting anyone," said some IFOR commanders. "If we happen to run into someone, then we have the authority to arrest them," said others. It is nevertheless difficult to accurately reconstruct any of the actions taken to capture General Mladić. The journalist Ljiljana Bulatović claims that Mladić had personally told her that he survived a Muslim terrorist action that targeted him: "A unit of 160 terrorists who had been trained in Iran and Turkey, was assigned to get the General's 'head'. They managed to break through and get close enough to the command center where General Mladić was staying to make a direct attack. The last of the terrorists was killed about twenty meters from his headquarters."

Bulatović did not reveal any other details, certainly because she did not know them. Mladić, apparently, did not want to speak any more about it. But, if there is sufficient depth to this story to permit an instructive re-evaluation of the past, then there is little reason to doubt its veracity: it is a fairytale with Westerners, especially Americans, cast in the leading roles. The moral of the story: America has been in the service of Islamic fundamentalism for too long for it to come out of it in one piece and with its reputation untainted. This is about the desire to get Ratko Mladić, be it war or be it peace.

There is, however, reliable evidence that IFOR did try to capture Mladić on July 6, 1996.

Despite reassurances that it has no mandate to capture fugitives, IFOR set up stake-outs for Mladić over the course of many months from Vlasenica to Pale (*Javnost*, July 13, 1996). The largest number of soldiers, almost certainly special forces, were deployed in the area around Han Pijesak. They did not believe that it was necessary to organize any special action; instead, since Mladić was accustomed to spending time there, they were certain that he would fall into their trap.

But time passed, and no one ever saw Mladić; IFOR commanders then decided to send their units to the Command Center of the ARS.

For this decision to have been made, writes *Javnost*, it would have been necessary to "search the terrain, check the barracks, arms depots, all suspicious sites, question the residents, send observers, and conduct non-stop aerial surveillance by pilotless drones."

But that was not enough. "Quite credible disinformation" was necessary to allege that General Mladić ran into members of an American IFOR contingent, cussed them out, and "sent them packing."

At the same time, it was said — and written — that Mladić was seriously ill, and that he was being treated at the VMA [the military hospital in Belgrade] because he was incapable of fending for himself.

These were indications of a large-scaled action that was going to be undertaken to capture him, which was, according to the sources at our disposal, had to be carried out under the guise of an agreement to remove and destroy heavy weaponry the Serbs possessed.

And the disarmament was carried out in the direct vicinity of the Command Headquarters of the ARS.

The action began on the morning of Friday, July 5, 1996. There were about twenty American planes in the air, and one helicopter unit, and these forces were backed up by armored vehicles and troop transports. Infantry support for IFOR came from the direction of Vlasenica, Sokoca and Podčepla.

The planes kept flying over Han Pijesak and ARS Headquarters all day long.

The residents took notice of the unusually aggressive behavior of the "frustrated Americans and impudent Italians." The residents threatened to give serious resistance, which IFOR forces wanted to avoid, but they still, in any case, wanted to complete their assignment. Before long, IFOR troops realized that it wasn't going to be as easy as they had thought, but they did not let up.

General Vidi, the commander of Rapid Reaction Forces based in Ilidža, arrived at the barracks in Han Pijesak. Meanwhile, a large number of people had gathered around the barracks, and they blocked all the roads. Helicopters hovered above the Command Center.

The people, wherever they had any direct contact with members of IFOR (NATO), expressed unconcealed exasperation and fury, while IFOR troops behaved superciliously but then became visibly nervous. It was easy to detect signs of fear among some of them.

Generals Vidi and Gvero were holding discussions in an office located in the barracks. The discussions became protracted, and the prevailing circumstances produced further anxiety — almost unbearable tension. Gvero claimed that there was no heavy weaponry at the coordinates that had been presented. Vidi was in no mood to show him the images of heavy weapons that the pilotless drones had allegedly taken.

General Vidi tried to enter the suspected area for at least a moment.

More people arrived during the protracted discussions. The press center of the General Headquarters issued no statement. An American colonel named Batista was speaking with Serbian officers. He was domineering and surly. He was already leading IFOR members to a warehouse holding weapons for the Serbian Army. He knew the terrain well. They sent him on tough missions.

Colonel Šarović, a member of the ARS, conveyed a message to Batista from General Milovanović, which said that any attempt to enter the Command Center would be treated as an attack on General Mladić.

Surely Batista must have known what this meant.

Batista had to know.

"We will certainly lose, but we will not allow you access to our commander. All of you will die, but no one will gain admittance," said Šarović.

Colonel Beara[40] suggested to Batista that he seek new permission for aerial surveillance, and that he once again do what had already been done. Namely, he had to present the surveillance imagery that had been taken of the terrain.

"We're not going to get anyone's permission, not for that, and not for anything else we intend to do."

"Good, then we'll see each other in heaven," answered Beara, a little provocatively, but with a note of pathos, as well.

That was the end of the conversation. Batista was furious, and slammed the door behind him when he left. At that moment, he was an uncompromising soldier, a commander who had given an irrevocable order for the unit to move toward the General Headquarters.

But it turned out to be only a bluff.

Still more people arrived, and the angry crowd threatened to lynch members of the American military. Cries were heard: "Occupiers, get lost!", "Get out of our country!", "Get out of here!" Some old men, who were normally as quiet as church mice, began stoning IFOR vehicles.

General Gvero concluded his discussions with Vidi. Then Gvero led him to the "suspicious location," where, allegedly, heavy weapons were to be found. There, however, one could find only tracks. Heavy weaponry had indeed been there at one time, but long ago, at the height of the war. Now grass was growing in the tracks they had left behind.

"You're an honorable man, an honest man," said Vidi to Gvero. "Now our units will withdraw."

General Vidi did not give the Serbian general any additional clarification. He did not say how it happened that the pilotless drones or satellites, as the case may be, had captured images of "heavy weapons" instead of ruts in the ground that were overgrown with weeds.

The goal of the military action was General Mladić.

General Gvero was calming down the people who had gathered. He then asked them to disperse.

One American officer, unhappy about having been outmaneuvered, said to Šarović: "Hats off to you. You pulled this off really well. But we'll be back!"

As IFOR vehicles were vanishing down the road, children wrote graffiti that read: "Tread not on our words!"

When Gvero and Beara were leaving the Command Center, one of the American officers asked them: "Okay, is the chief really here in Han Pijesak?"

"Of course not," answered Gvero.

For now, there is no reliable evidence about how much of the operation was devoted to capturing Ratko Mladić. But, there were certainly more attempts than one can imagine.

It was important to know where, in fact, Mladić could be found before the initiation of any secret operation at all. The MUP [Ministry of Internal Affairs] of Serbia claimed that the general was not in Serbia; the MUP in Montenegro denied that a person fitting that name and description was on its territory.

The same information is coming out of the Republika Srpska: Ratko Mladić is not there.

Is Ratko Mladić, therefore, impossible to catch?

"No one is impossible to catch," said one former officer, a former policeman and bounty hunter. "Except Ratko Mladić!"

But the legend of the impossibility of catching him or, at least lending credence to it, is not universally held. No one can any longer be inclined to believe in myths. Above all, the seriousness and "logical coherence" of the relations between the pursuer and the pursued is in question — of course, on the condition that someone actually succeeds in making General Mladić play the role of the pursued.

Even in February 1996, the chief prosecutor of The Hague Tribunal at the time, Richard Goldstone, said that Karadžić and Mladić were moving ever closer to The Hague: "I don't have a crystal ball in which I can see what the future is going to bring, but the chances today are greater than ever before. We have the strength and the willingness to bring them here very quickly."

Mladić's response was categorical: "They must understand that each and every attempt they make will cost them dearly, and that my people will defend me. It must be clear to them that I am going to defend myself. They ought to bear in mind that it's not easy to capture General Mladić."

Karadžić's reaction to Goldstone's announcement was even more provocative: "NATO forces, now temporarily in Bosnia, are not strong enough to capture me. They will need significantly more men than they have now because they know that I have a dedicated security staff."

Karadžić added that, as far as he was concerned, no one would ever be able to capture him, and that each and every attempt to do so would lead to great losses on both sides: "I think that they know that they have no chance of catching me because they are guests in our houses. This is our house."

Karadžić complained that the photograph of him on the wanted poster was poor: "I could have given them a much better picture. Anyway, they can't catch me. I'll travel whenever I think it's necessary. I meet people all around the country, sometimes publicly, at other times secretly. I don't know how long this farce with The Hague Tribunal is going to last," said Karadžić in an interview he gave to the Greek television channel, *Mega*.

On March 11, 1996, Americans saw some exciting television. They saw General Ratko Mladić skiing on Mt. Jahorina and speaking with reporters from Greek television. He ordered NATO forces to cease and desist from the fool's errand on which they had been sent, because they were never going to catch him, and that they could count on dying by making such abortive attempts.

An American television commentator remarked that "Mladić reminds one more of a carefree tourist who is living it up with winter sports and exclusive company instead of a criminal with a world-wide warrant out for his arrest. This man is not only indescribably arrogant, impudent and cold-blooded, but he is also slapping the face of the strongest country in the world, which was apparently relieved because he didn't punch them in the face."

General Mladić's announcements were judged in Washington to be "irresponsible threats," along with the implied warning that American troops in Bosnia were armed, authorized and ready to answer all provocations without hesitation and with the forces at their disposal while "discharging their regular duties."

The Brussels headquarters of NATO had an answer, too. Karadžić's announcements, but particularly Mladić's, were characterized by them as "irresponsible swaggering." The headquarters of the Western military alliance attempted to rationalize its own impotence with respect to capturing General Mladić. "He [General Mladić, *Author's Note*] knows well that his freedom of movement has been restricted more than he is willing to admit. On the contrary, his movements have been severely restricted, and he must be very careful wherever he goes."

NATO headquarters attempted to explain when it would and when it would not arrest General Mladić. "Of course, we will not arrest him if he shows up at the head of a column of forty tanks at some checkpoint, which is manned by ten lightly armed IFOR members. We'll wait for the balance of power to be, at least by an inverse proportion, in our favor. We're convinced that we will see such a situation materialize sooner or later."

America's failure to capture General Mladić and Dr. Karažić grew into a full-blown complex. In July 1997, the two of them remained, of course, beyond the reach of international forces when the American Defense Secretary, William Perry, made an official visit to Bosnia. A reporter for *The New York Times*, Anthony Lewis, wrote in the July 14, 1997 that the Secretary of Defense, William Perry, was known to be a man who did not lose his temper easily and displayed a great deal of self confidence. But, a few days earlier, while he was making an official visit to Bosnia, he angrily answered a reporter who had asked him why NATO forces had not yet captured Karažić and Mladić.

Lewis confirmed that Perry actually did not have an answer, which was the reason he had gotten angry. Lewis continued by saying that Mr. Perry knew that the United States and its allies were looking like fools before the world because of Mr. Karadžić and his friend, Ratko Mladić, who had been indicted as war criminals, were still at large.

The Americans initiated concrete measures that they had suggested in Brussels (at the beginning of June 1997). A unit of special forces was going to be formed that would go to Bosnia to capture Mladić and Karadžić.

America's allies did not agree to the proposal, but the Americans had already put together "a team to capture Mladić and Karadžić," and those units were ready to go. They had been training in southern Austria, were the soldiers had intensive Serbian language training, and prepared for an attack on Pale and Han Pijesak. The special unit was composed of American and British soldiers, drawn from the Green Berets, Rangers, Delta Forces and the British SAS.

These special forces trained under brutal circumstances. They marched fifteen kilometers a day, and ten kilometers every night; they mastered 130 different ways to liquidate an enemy, torture techniques for interrogation, reconnaissance and laying ambushes. They devoted a lot of attention to parachute jumping and clandestine methods of landing.

The training for this unit was costly: between $25,000 and $40,000 per soldier.

And that was not all. NATO had repeatedly denied that special forces were preparing for action in Bosnia. Yet their mission was no secret: it was the arrest of Mladić and Karadžić. But these special forces never did not set out for Han Pijesak and Pale. President Clinton judged the operation to be too risky, and that there would certainly be many casualties. Moreover, success could not be assured because that is the nature of special forces operations: they are either a complete triumph or a catastrophic fiasco. The Americans at that time were recovering from the Somalia fiasco, where they failed to capture the chief of state at the time, General Aidid. The special forces unit (designated to arrest the general) had quarreled with its advance guard ... and then the whole operation fell apart.

That was why training exercises were organized on the Peloponnesus in October 1997, specifically to train troops to capture Ratko Mladić. Five countries contributed units: the U.S.,

Spain, Italy, Holland and Greece. A reporter from the Greek TV station *Mega* told his audience: "The special operations were not successful, and now NATO is planning a real military invasion. America and its allies have a problem with General Mladić and Dr. Radovan Karadžić. There are 1,500 Marines on the Peloponnesus who are training to capture the two dangerous Serbs in order to send them to The Hague."

The Greek Defense Ministry denied it all, and there was new speculation that Mladić and Karadžić had found sanctuary in Sveta Gora on Mt. Athos. The story about the training exercises and the monastic life of Mladić and Karadžić then quickly fell off the front page with breaking news that NATO headquarters in Brussels once again judged such an invasion to be unproductive, risky, uncertain of success, and run the risk of many casualties.

In any case, witness this bit of writing from *Time* magazine (August 1998) that declared such unsuccessful operations as these to be the "good will" efforts of a "functioning system."

At the beginning of this article, the American and French presidents, Clinton and Chiraq, agreed about "the necessity of capturing these two dangerous Serbs" the same night that the peace treaty for Bosnia had been signed in Paris.

Two secret service agencies allegedly began tracking the movements of Mladić and Karadžić, uncovering hide outs and confirming their habits. The plan to kidnap them suffered a setback when the informers lost track of Mladić, so they concentrated on Karadžić.

The reputed mission plan, detailed with maps, diagrams and operational data, was drafted and printed in April 1997 under the code name "Operation Amber Star." The plan proposed that French troops neutralize the thirty members of Karadžić's personal security forces, while elite American commandos would then spring into action and arrest Karadžić.

One of the higher ranking NATO officers, as quoted by *Time*, stated that French soldiers who were in disguise had Mladić and Karadžić in their gun sights but they were unable to get "the official green light."

How did they have both of them in their sights when they had lost track of Mladić? What kind of action was this supposed to be if the special forces were within reach of their target, but there was no one to tell them what to do? Who had stopped the action if Mladić and Karadžić "were in their sights"? If special forces had undertaken this on their own initiative, they could have made a much more radical move with much less risk.

It appears as though it was a fantastic alibi. The excuse goes something like this: "Well, we could have, but we really didn't want to." But then why did they make any attempt at all? Such levity is utterly unacceptable for nervous and fearful great powers that are unsuccessfully searching for General Mladić. If special forces did, indeed, have him in their sights, it is difficult to believe that they would not have pulled the trigger. They, therefore, must have never had him in their sights.

The French president introduced another problem, which could be interpreted as an explanation of why this "dangerous Serb" has not been caught.

"It was necessary to inform the Russians and Italians, who have soldiers around Pale, about all of this, but if we tell the Russians and Italians, we might as well organize a press conference," said Chiraq.

At the end of August 1998, *The Washington Post* reported that the White House had given up making grand plans to capture Ratko Mladić and Radovan Karadžić. One State Department official said that such an action was not very probable for many reasons, but that "their freedom of movement had been restricted and that sooner or later they will fall from the trees, like ripe fruit."

A little before that, in July of 1998, the Americans announced that they had abandoned their obsession with secret service/special forces operations to arrest Mladić and Karadžić. They acknowledged that they had spent more than one hundred million dollars on "Operation Amber Star." This is interesting, but the Americans suspected the French as much as Chiraq had suspected the Russians and Italians. No one reliably knows with whom the Serbs are working. The "Amber Star" faded from sight. Now they are waiting for General Mladić to simply show up one day or for someone to report his whereabouts or turn him over.

No one in the world is able to do that. Only Serbs can undertake such a mission.

Magic and Oblivion

This book came into being in dramatic times, when the world was re-evaluating the relationship between crime and subsequent reprisals. Perhaps this happened because of a relatively simple reason: an overwhelming and uncontested force distributed its unlimited power to the farthest reaches of the world, and then all that dreadful power blew back to its source in a self-destructive implosion.

This force had obtained a monopoly on all manner of assault. Therefore, it could commit crimes in the name of preserving its "national interests" by taking advantage of every purposeful assault regardless of its origin.

It could punish by force, if it were intent on doing so, even states that were struggling against the use of force. All at once, terrorism, as a model of rule by fear, became a universal trauma, so it is difficult to pinpoint the source of such global panic: is the world afraid of terrorism, its all-encompassing and unselective nature or is it afraid of the violent answer to it?

It doesn't matter what people are afraid of. Fear today rules the world instead of a world power that controls the world with soldierly perfection and brute force; fear rules the world instead of Orwellian regimes that erect a Dzugashvili[41] in the mind of each of us; and fear will rule the world for quite some time to come. It holds sway over the greatest empires in history; this is the overwhelming feeling that unites the planet.

Before such an acknowledgement, the "balance sheet" of the war in the Balkans must be reviewed in order to find the truth about the origins of this great tragedy of the last decade of the twentieth century, and the true reasons behind the reawakening of atavistic hatreds.

In fact, now we must pose this question: is this legendary, authentic, internationally recognized Balkan vehemence really self-destructive provincialism? Or is it tied up with a syndrome that absorbs, then gives blossom to the worst seeds that missionaries of chaos had brought to it?

There is no doubt that the "holy war" on the Balkan Peninsula arrived under the patronage of the great powers, but it will not leave no matter what pressure is applied. The scenes which we witnessed of Alija Izetbegović giving his blessing to mujahideen murderers who were setting out to hunt for Serbian heads is a horrifying document that portrays the transformation of a political leader into a religious fanatic. Thus, each and every general stereotype of Serbs as criminals and Muslims as meek victims vanishes. If any consolation is to be found in the leveling force of the phrase "honor among thieves," each side has its own criminals and its own ideology about them.

The idea of a "Greater Serbia" within a small Yugoslavia was elaborated by domestic amateurs in a planned government, but military leaders attempted to realize it in a narrow sense, and with few exceptions, their achievements were short-term. No one imported that idea to Serbia; it was authentic Serbian alchemy that was cooked up at home.

Crimes that were committed in the name of Serbs and Serbia are not an expression of fanaticism, but the madness of war, material interests, revanchism and revenge. How was it possible to uphold any kind of ethics in warfare when chaos and elation inspired by mythic warriors held sway?

Who is General Ratko Mladić? And what did he have to do with all this?

He unavoidably retained a sufficient amount of JNA ideology. That type of "negative tradition" enabled the apparent officer-like stubbornness of Ratko Mladić to exist, but it also made his objective capabilities a relative matter.

Mladić inescapably retained the recidivism of the past, but he was capable of shaking off his most troublesome burdens. Just as he was once convinced of the future of the "Yugoslav nation" (in the sense of glorifying his own supranationality), he likewise became a Serb after a dramatic "enlightenment," and he became convinced that the destiny of the Serbian people hinged on the way he discharged his duties.

Mladić carried on to excess his "use of the people," just as many other political and military leaders who took "the people" to be an indefinite, abstract category, a value above and beyond all other values, whom they summoned whenever they needed to make sacrifices.

Mladić's appeals to the people were sometimes powerful epic metaphors, but they frequently resembled a pathetic red herring that allowed him to find shelter where it was most certain to be found: in the people. There are two possible reasons for such a symbiosis of authentic and professional patriotism: the first reason could be the need for inspiration; and second, the distribution of personal responsibility for everything that was going to take place, along with the mighty message: "I am not doing this in my own name, but in the name of the people."

Moreover, Ratko Mladić is first and foremost a man who is able to take responsibility, and he stands firmly behind his decisions, but he revises them under the compulstion of emerging events or unassailable arguments.

Numerous variations of General Ratko Mladić's "public image" have circulated in domestic as well as in global media. At first, he was a "commander who had the ability to surprise"; he was the new Serbian military leader who emerged from the JNA, but he was different because of everything that he had seen there; he was a man who, according to all those people who got to know him in wartime, fascinated one and all with his unbelievable courage.

For the Serbian media, he suddenly became a new hero, a magical representation of national, legendary wartime valor; he was a man who could do anything, and other military leaders from past fraternal national associations could not be compared to him.

The European and world media did not accord to him this heroic stereotype, but no one could contest his ability, his self-confidence and his courage. They created their own wartime stereotypes, and quickly turned Mladić into a fascinating, brutal warrior, who cynically played with enemy armies and the lives of their soldiers.

When the war reached its high point, General Mladić had already become a metaphor for an illuminating dichotomy: Mladić was an indisputable hero for Serbs, especially for his enthusiastic supporters, who were inspired by "a foreseeable military victory," and many were already comparing him with *vojvodas* Mišić and Putnik.

Mladić was at the time an "indisputable military victor," but also a man to whom criminal acts had been ascribed; he was a man "who committed them or who did not prevent them."

Finally, General Mladić, gradually departed from the memory of those who admired him after the inescapable Serbian military-political Calvary, while for the rest of the world, he became "a mug shot of a war criminal in the newspapers," who ought to be delivered to The Hague "as quickly as possible."

Objectively, Ratko Mladić is a man who carefully guarded his ethnic status up until the war broke out. He had no shortcomings aside from the customary ideological errors and blindness. He was a talented soldier. It is difficult to extract a criminal from such a combination....

None of this can absolve the General of the events that took place during a war in which he himself participated, and in which his commanding role had a decisive influence. Was it sufficient for him to say, after taking Srebrenica, to the soldiers guarding the captured Muslims: "Be careful. Look after them better than you would look after yourselves!" And afterwards to have *ad hoc* county defense committees and other primitive paramilitaries begin to liquidate the captives at will according to the laws of lynch mob?

Srebrenica will, in any case, remain a mystery. What did Mladić do there? Did he really give his silent approval to mass killings? Is it true that the mass killings began fifteen minutes after his departure? Is it true that he attended the alleged executions in Karakaj?

It is unlikely that Mladić ordered crimes to be committed. He did not, as Alija Izetbegović did, give his blessing to those who were going to go on a killing spree. He gave guarantees that the captured men would be exchanged. Nevertheless, crimes did take place.

Ratko Mladić is not a criminal, but he is responsible for the crimes committed by his army. No matter how great his charisma as a commander may have been, he did not succeed in forging discipline among his troops "with an iron hand." His charismatic influence was greater than his command influence. His mistake was to believe that such circumstances could be a real substitute for an army with rigorous rules and regulations. And he never did succeed in reorganizing the army.

Ratko Mladić is not a hero, either. It is likely that he did not want to be one; he believed in his mission, but with newfound ideological illusions, "like a man who belongs to the people." Universal fame surprised him; personal tragedy caused him serious set-backs, but he was not surprised by how quickly "the people" forgot him, after all.

Ratko Mladić is today certainly ruled by salutary resignation instead of the inexhaustible energy that he once transmitted to all those around him. He is, at last, an "ordinary man" in his own eyes, one who exited the stage of history under an international arrest warrant.

He does not want to avoid being tried if he is guilty nor absolved if he is not, but he will not agree "to be tried by those whom he himself would put on trial."

Ratko Mladić, a man who made decisions about war and peace, arms, plans and lives, his own as well as others, is neither a hero nor a war criminal, and is inaccessible to his persecutors.

"They will never be able to catch me. And when I tell you something, it is as if the Almighty had said it himself."

ENDNOTES

[1] *Stevan Sinđelić*, (?–1809) a hero of the First Serbian Uprising. Turkish troops defeated Serbian formations in Kamenica. The Serbs fled toward Deligrad. The company commanded by Sinđelić, however, offered fierce resistance at Čegar. Seeing that he was outnumbered and could not defend his position, he set fire to his stores of gunpowder, and detonated it, killing himself and his fellow soldiers, along with a great number of the enemy. The Turks erected the Tower of Skulls (Ćele kula) on the site, which incorporated the skulls of fallen Serbian solders into the brickwork.

[2] *Živojin Mišić*, (1855–1921) outstanding Serbian military leader who participated in all the wars fought by the Serbian army between 1876–1918. He was in command of the Serbian I Army when they handed Austro-Hungarian forces a stinging defeat in Kolubara in 1915.

[3] *The Chetniks* wore cockades on their hats during WWII.

[4] The poet Duško Petrović, who was serving in the JNA's Knin Corps at this time, provided the following account of the last days of the JNA. "The first significant mobilization of JNA reserve units in the Knin Corps took place on June 30, 1991. The commander of the Knin Corps at the time was General Trajkovski, a Macedonian, who did not inspire the Serbs with a great deal of confidence. On the same night, my infantry battalion was transferred from the village of Suvopolje, near the Dinara, very close to the Croatian village of Kijevo. About a thousand of us arrived there. Most of us were Serbs even though there was a small number of Croatians. The Croatians had not yet fled from Knin except for individual extremists, but they did not answer the JNA's call for mobilization.

"Ten days later, one soldier hung a Serbian flag in the barracks. A little later the military police arrived and took down the flag without any explanation. The soldier who had put up the flag in the first place got another one, and put it up. When the military police again came to take it down, a group of armed soldiers guarded the flag and would not allow it to be taken down. They told them that we were a Serbian army and that we acknowledged only the Serbian flag.

"Yugoslavia was gone!

"That was a shock for the officers and the next day they summoned the entire battalion to give a talk and resolve the problem. Some colonels came along with Brigade Comander Colonel Djukić. After an inspection and presentations by officers, an unknown colonel was given a chance to speak. His name was Ratko Mladić, and he had just arrived from Priština. He became the chief of staff of the Knin Corps. He immediately began to discuss the problem. He said that Yugoslavia was the only option available to its various peoples. He had already been in the field in Croatian villages and he saw that the Croatians were largely in favor of Yugoslavia. Except there was a small group of extremists against it. The JNA would complete the assignment that had been given to it by the Yugoslav Presidency, and that was to protect the country as well as the brotherhood and unity of our peoples. That was when people started to protest. They did not expect his speech to be filled with such empty phrases. In order to save Mladić from further embarrassment, Colonel Djukić said that his soldiers would "surround, burn and annihilate" anyone who stood in their way, which aroused the soldiers' enthusiasm. Then Colonel Bajić, who was a Croat who allegedly loved Yugoslavia, gave his presentation. Quickly after that, a number of men in the battalion dropped to 600. A large number of Serbian nationalists became disappointed in the JNA officers. Mladić later proved himself to be quite a capable officer. His popularity grew daily. Stories were told about how he defused mines on the front lines, and how he shouted at Croatian officers during negotiations over cease fires or prisoner exchanges. His actual capabilities were fully realized later in the war in Bosnia."

5 *brotherhood and unity*, the Titoist slogan expressing unity among the various nationalities of the former Yugoslavia.

6 *Ante Pavelić*, the leader of the Croatian fascist movement during World War II.

7 *Nikola Koljević*, Shakespearean scholar and Vice President of the Republika Srpska who committed suicide in 1997. According to *Truth in Media*, Koljević received assurances from the British that the Queen of England had no objection to the Bosnian Serbs achieving their objectives on the ground. He realized that Serbian interests had been betrayed in Dayton, where he had been sent as a representative. *See* "Perfidious Ablion Strikes again, Aided by Uncle Sam," by Bob Djordjevich, www.truthinmedia.org.

8 *General Kukanjac*, commander of JNA forces in Sarajevo in 1992.

9 *Dobrovoljačka ulica*, One hundred and twenty-seven JNA soldiers who were traveling in a convoy were killed on Dobrovoljačka ulica by Muslim radicals on May 3, 1992.

[10] May 17, 1993.

[11] *See* Appendix, p. 508.

[12] "On the Front Line: Mladic Almighty War and Peace," by Laura Silber, *Financial Times* (London) 12/31/94. See Appendix, p. 511.

[13] *Vitaly Churkin*, Russian ambassador to the former Yugoslavia.

[14] It should be noted that Muslim forces led by Juka Prazina set up mobile mortar positions in various residential neighborhoods from which they shelled Serbian positions in order to provoke return fire. This was part of the Muslim scheme to generally provoke Serbian artillery fire. The most notorious example of this took place when Muslim forces set up mortar positions on the roof of the Sarajevo Library. The Serbs returned fire, and set the library ablaze. This was a pivotal moment that turned U.S. public opinion against the Serbs as destroyers of culture. Iraqi resistance fighters are using many of the same tactics against American troops stationed there. It should also be noted that the Muslims were bombing Serbian areas around Sarajevo regularly, but no Western reporters ever covered this aspect of the war. When the Serbs were forced to abandon Ilidža after the Dayton Agreement, Western reporters were shocked by the destruction the found there. Mladić always claimed that he was defending the Serbian areas around Sarajevo. Juka Prazina was killed in Belgium in late 1993. His assassin has never been found. [*Translator's Note.*]

[15] Novelist and leading opposition figure at the time; currently Foreign Minister of Serbia-Montenegro.

[16] *Balkan Odyssey*, by David Owen (Harcourt Brace: NY, 1995), p. 260-262. Lord Owen revealed in his memoirs that the Muslims set off the blast in the Markale Green Market. [*Translator's Note.*]

[17] *See* David Binder's article, "Bosnia's Bombers," on p. 513. And *see* Michel Collon's *Liar's Poker*, p. 30-31. He refutes the allegations that the Bosnian Serbs were responsible.

[18] Documents and public announcements by high level government officials in the RS have different figures for the length of the front line.

[19] *Victor Andreyev*, the Russian head of the UN High Commessariat for Displaced and Imprisoned Parties.

[20] The French pilots were shot down on August 30, 1995.

[21] *Vuk Branković* is the infamous traitor who sabotaged Serbian chances for victory in the Battle of Kosovo in 1389.

[22] An arbitration committee removed Brčko from Serbian control and put it under the administration of a commission favorable to the Muslim-Croat Federation. This effectively cut the RS in two.

[23] *Zhukov ... Clausewitz*, Zhukov, Georgy Konstantinovich, a Marshall of the Soviet Union who played a historic role in defeating the Nazis during WWII. In April 1945, he personally commanded the final assault on Berlin. Carl

Phillip Gottfried von Clausewitz (1780-1831), Prussian soldier and intellectual, author of *On War*, perhaps the most important theory of warfare and strategy every written.

[24] *Vojvoda Mišić,* Živojin Mišić (1855-1921), one of the most outstanding Serbian military leaders. He served in all the wars Serbia fought between 1876-1918. He commanded the First Army during the Battle of Kolubara, when the Serbian Army, against all odds, handed a stinging defeat to the Austro-Hungarians.

[25] *A Time of Death,* by Dobrica Ćosić, translated by Muriel Heppel (Harcourt, Brace & Jovanovich: New York 1978).

[26] *Dragoslav Mihajlović* (b. 1930), a noted Serbian novelist who is best known for his novel, *Kad su cvetale tikve* (1968), which was translated into English as *When Pumpkins Blossomed* (Harcourt Brace Jovanovich: New York, 1971).

[27] General Mladić is referring to *Operation Halyard,* successfully conducted in December 1944. The operation involved the rescue of more than 500 U.S. airmen who had been shot down over Yugoslavia by Nazi anti-aircraft fire. General Draža Mihailović, the leader of the Chetnik resistance movement, sheltered the airmen and initiated and organized the Serbian side of the rescue mission. A New Yorker, U.S. Major Richard Felman (1921–1999), one of the rescued airmen, campaigned tirelessly on behalf of Mihailović, who was executed after having been convicted in a show trial by Tito on false charges of collaboration with the Nazis. With the help of Congressman Edward J. Derwinski (IL), Felman was able to reveal that President Truman had posthumously awarded Mihailović the Legion of Merit, the highest honor that the U.S. can bestow on a foreign national. The State Department kept this secret until 1974. [*Translator's Note.*]

[28] *Bobetko, Roso, Delić, Petković,* are, respectively Croatian General Janko Bobetko (died 2003), who was accused by the ICTY of war crimes against Serbian civilians in the Medak Pocket near Gospić; Bosnian-Croatian General Ante Roso, who served in the French Foreign Legion; General Rasim Delić, Chief of Staff of the Bosnian Muslim Army; Milivoj Petković, former Chief of Staff of the HVO (*Hrvatsko Vijće Odbrane,* or Croatian Defense Council, i.e., the Bosnian Croat's armed forces), who was accused of the systematic mistreatment of Muslim civilians living in his area of control.

[29] General Mladić was an infant when his own father was killed fighting the Ustashi.

[30] *vukojebina,* a wilderness so desolate that only wolves would go there to fuck.

[31] *Sinđelić, Mišić* ... see footnotes 1 and 2.

[32] *Opanak,* a moccasin with an upwardly curved, pointed toe, worn as part of the Serbian national folk costume.

[33] Bosnia is known in Serbian as the *tamni vilajet,* the "dark province."

[34] *The Battle of Kolubara*, (1914) is the greatest military victory of the Serbian Army in WWI, where, against all odds, it inflicted a devastating attack on Austro-Hungarian forces.

[35] *Potiorek*, Oskar (1853-1934) Austro-Hungarian general who commanded forces in the Battle of Kolubara. Potiorek, after having lost the battle, was relieved of his duties by Kaiser Wilhelm.

[36] *Takovo*, a small town of some eight hundred inhabitants, northwest of Gornji Milanovac, where, on April 11, 1815, a decision was made to begin the Second Serbian Uprising.

[37] *revolt of the dahiyas*, The *dahiya*s (Turk.) were unruly and indomitable senior janissaries; they became powerful in the second half of the eighteenth century, and instituted a reign of terror among the Serbs in order to exact exorbitant taxes from them and thereby enrich themselves at the expense of the *spahis*, the former administrators of the pashalik of Belgrade. The *dahiya*s murdered Serbian leaders in 1784. The Serbian people petitioned the Sultan to put down the rebellion, thus laying the groundwork for the First Serbian Rebellion. The *dahiyas* were defeated in June 1804.

[38] Dr. Smilja Avramov, distinguished Serbian academic and jurist whose testimony opened the defense phase of the Milošević trial in The Hague.

[39] *Pintzgauer*, an Austrian-designed all terrain vehicle that is now exclusively manufactured in the U.K.

[40] *Colonel Beara*, Ljubiša, a colonel and the chief of security for the Bosnian Serb Army, surrendered to The Hague Tribunal in early October 2004. He was accused of genocide in the alleged massacre of 8,000 Muslim men and boys, and of being part of a joint criminal enterprise headed by Gen. Mladić. The Western media reported that he had surrendered voluntarily, yet in his statement to the press, Beara implied that his family had been threatened.

[41] *Dzugashvili*, Joseph Stalin's family name.

BOSNIA AND CROATIA IN DEPTH
Bringing Democracy to Bosnia-Herzegovina
by Gregory Elich[*]

Gregory Elich is an independent journalist and researcher who has published articles on the Balkans and Southeast Asia.

In the popular imagination, the Western presence in post-war Bosnia-Herzegovina is seen as a selfless humanitarian effort. NATO's mission, it is believed, is to inculcate democratic values in an uncivilized and irrational people. Behind the façade of Western peacekeeping in the Balkans, though, lies a darker reality. The benevolence of a Western civilizing mission in post-war Bosnia-Herzegovina is never questioned. Yet an examination of NATO's peacekeeping operation reveals a process of colonization as deep and thoroughgoing as any seen in the 19th century.

Establishing Western Values
Few question the assertion that Western intervention is bringing democracy to the people of Bosnia-Herzegovina, but what is the real nature of this intervention, which has assumed many forms, both direct and indirect? Under terms of the Dayton peace agreement, Bosnia-Herzegovina consists of two entities, the (Bosnian Serb) Republika Srpska and the Muslim-Croatian Federation. Throughout the civil war, the Muslim-Croatian Federation was seen as a client state, and indeed, the Federation itself was a result of an agreement forged under Western pressure. More direct intervention, though, was necessary to place the Republika Srpska under Western control

The first task the West faced following the war was the dismantling of the existing governing structure in the Republika Srpska, and in this task the West found a pliant partner in that entity's President, Biljana Plavsić, a right-wing monarchist. In November 1996, Plavsić, who had frequently complained that the Republika Srpska Army was riddled with "reds," issued a decree dismissing General Ratko Mladić and over 100 leftist officers. Western officials were heavily involved in selecting the officers who would be dismissed and those who would be promoted in their place. Prior

---

to the decree, Colonel Milovan Milutinović warned that "some of our generals are being visited by foreign representatives, at the request of our state organs, and offered leading positions in the army..."[1] When the dismissed officers balked at their removal, Interior Ministry special police units blockaded army barracks, some army buildings had their water and electricity turned off, and the progressive army-run Radio Krajina was closed down. Army Headquarters responded with a statement denouncing these moves, saying they were "carried out by the Interior Ministry against the army on orders from foreign mentors," and pointing out that "a NATO spokesman publicly said that anything that weakens the unity of the Republika Srpska Army's Main Headquarters and the army itself is in NATO's interest."[2] Combined pressure from the Interior Ministry and NATO eventually forced the resignation of these officers on November 28.

Plavsić next turned on the civilian governing structure. In January 1997, after weeks of failed efforts to obtain approval from the People's Assembly for her choice of prime minister, Plavsić waited until opposition deputies walked out of an Assembly session to push through her surprise nomination of another man, Milorad Dodik, for the post. Carlos Westendorp, chief of Western civilian operations in Bosnia, immediately hailed Dodik's appointment, and NATO troops were dispatched to surround the Interior Ministry in a belligerent show of support. The selection of Dodik was an interesting one, as his party held only two seats in the Assembly. How did a man whose party was barely represented in the Assembly gain the nomination? The instantaneous Western show of support for the last-minute appointment hints that the selection may not have been entirely Plavsić's. Several months beforehand, a report in the Bosnian Serb press alleged that Dodik "is under the direct control of the U.S. intelligence service, the CIA," and that some deputies "say that he has already traveled abroad several times for consultations and direct instructions."[3] The effusive praise Western leaders since lavished on Dodik lends support to that accusation.

On June 28, 1997, Plavsić dismissed Interior Minister Dragan Kijac. Five days later, in violation of the constitution, she dissolved the People's Assembly. Western officials were quick to back Plavsić, and David Foley, a spokesman for the Organization for Security and Cooperation in Europe (OSCE) announced that the Assembly "no longer exists." A diplomatic source in Sarajevo admitted, "The Americans have probably pushed Plavsić to act in such a way."[4] The matter was referred to the Constitutional Court, which ruled against Plavsić. The court's ruling was simply brushed aside, as U.S. State Department spokesman James Rubin asserted that "challenges to [Plavsić's] actions are not legally valid," and that Serbs who fail to comply with Western demands are "stupid."[5] A report in the Yugoslav press alleged that three weeks prior to the crisis, "$5 million of the promised $30 million" were deposited into a Swiss bank account in Plavsić's name. "The funds were transferred from the United States," according to "top-level civilian and military security sources" in the Republika Srpska. The report claimed that "the transaction is directly linked to Biljana Plavsić's recent political activities..." Many of the people Plavsić appointed to work in her office came from abroad, "most of whom are supporters of the royalist movement" the report added.[6] The Ministry of Internal Affairs revealed that it had "announced our plan to take legal measures" against one of these men "on the well-founded grounds that he was working for a foreign intelligence service," and that the Ministry had warned Plavsić on "several occasions" of "intelligence activities" by members of her staff.[7]

In the first of many such actions, on August 20, 1997, NATO troops, supported by U.S. Apache helicopter gunships, seized police stations in Banja Luka, ejecting police officers.[8] NATO directly hired new policemen, who then attended training courses run by Western police instructors.[9] UN police spokesman Liam McDowall said of the training classes, "We basically let them know what is expected of a normal police force; not a socialist police force, not a wartime police force, but a police force of a normal democratic society."[10] Evidently, police forces in "normal democratic societies" are dismissed, recruited, and trained by foreign powers.

Four days later, NATO began its campaign to impose censorship on media in the Republika Srpska. A transmitter near Banja Luka was reprogrammed to turn the signal over to Plavsić's control, and two days later NATO troops seized a Serb Radio-TV transmitter near Bijeljina. As NATO forces surrounded Bijeljina and blocked all access roads to the city, thousands of citizens turned out in a mass demonstration. Low-flying NATO helicopters harassed the demonstrators. The next day, NATO forces took another transmitter near Doboj and arrested its staff. Each of the seized transmitters was turned over to Plavsić's control. At 4:00 AM on August 28, NATO troops moved into the town of Brčko. Air raid sirens sounded an alert, and thousands turned out in a mass demonstration. Demonstrators fought NATO troops with sticks and rocks, while NATO troops fired tear-gas canisters and warning shots. Tanks and armored vehicles were sent into the town, but were eventually forced to withdraw after seventy of them were damaged.[11] Infuriated, NATO Secretary-General Javier Solana warned that NATO "will not hesitate to take the necessary measures, including the use of force, against media networks or programs" that denounced Western occupation.[12] Further threats and pressure constrained opposition, and by the end of November, NATO had completed its systematic seizure of Serb radio and television transmitters and police stations.

In April 1998, Western officials announced the creation of a tribunal to monitor and govern media in Bosnia-Herzegovina. The tribunal not only arrogated to itself the power to shut down radio, television and newspapers that voice criticism of NATO's occupation of Bosnia-Herzegovina, but also the authority to write laws regulating broadcasting. Simon Haselock, spokesman for Western civilian operations in Bosnia claimed, "It's not about censorship," but what else is it when foreign powers dictate what media can and cannot say, and revoke the licenses of media which present alternative viewpoints? What else is it when elected representatives are not permitted to write laws regulating broadcasting in their own nation, but must have these laws written and submitted by foreign powers? Was it not censorship when the tribunal ordered Television Kanal S in the Republika Srpska to "immediately cease broadcasting" on April 14, 1999? According to the tribunal, Television Kanal S did not carry Western news programs, and committed "a serious violation" when it broadcast a message from Sarajevo University students in which citizens of the Republika Srpska "were invited to join the students in a peaceful protest" against NATO's bombing of Yugoslavia.[13]

Western policy in ruling Bosnia-Herzegovina is direct and heavy-handed. On December 17, 1997, Westendorp simply imposed a new citizenship law after the Bosnia-Herzegovina parliament failed to meet his arbitrary 48-hour deadline for passage of the law.[14] Similarly, he unilaterally imposed a new Western-designed flag and Western-designed and produced currency, the "convertible mark." Political candidates have been stricken from election lists, based on the flimsiest excuses. In the November 1997 election, the OSCE election commission eliminated three candidates of the Serbian Democratic Party (SDS) because posters of former Republika Srpska president Radovan Karadžić had appeared. The SDS was not permitted to replace these candidates. The following year, nine candidates of the Serbian Radical Party were deleted from election lists because a television station in neighboring Yugoslavia broadcast an interview with the party's presidential candidate, Nikola Poplašen. During the same election, two SDS assembly candidates were disqualified because, as a spokeswoman for the OSCE said, "twice at [an election rally] an SDS supporter held up a portrait of Karadžić." The OSCE also eliminated four assembly candidates of the Croatian Democratic Union and the mayor of Orasje because of "biased" television reports in neighboring Croatia. It is curious logic to assert that television reports in an adjacent nation result in a biased election, and that the solution is for foreign powers to dictate whom voters may or may not vote for.[15]

Western officials reacted angrily when Nikola Poplašen unseated Plavsić in the September 1998 presidential election in Republika Srpska, and immediately began to pressure him to appoint Dodik as his Prime Minister. According to Poplašen, Western officials "demanded" the appointment of Dodik "unconditionally." They also pressured Poplašen to "break off relations" with Yugoslavia and in effect treat it as an "enemy nation", and his refusal to bow to either demand triggered tremendous Western hostility.[16] Such disobedience brought a swift response, and on March 5, 1999, Westendorp issued a statement declaring the removal of Poplašen from office "with immediate effect."[17] The primary justification given was Poplašen's insistence that he had a constitutional right to choose who he would nominate for the post of Prime Minister. This *coup d'etat* by decree deposed the legally elected president of the Republika Srpska.

Immediately after Poplašen's removal, the Republika Srpska government operated under the sole leadership of Dodik, backed by

NATO troops. However, Dodik's term ended with the electoral defeat of Plavsić, and there was no legal basis for his continuing to hold office. The removal of the legally elected government in the Republika Srpska was not sufficient, though. There was still the risk that Republika Srpska citizens might freely exercise their right to vote in upcoming elections, so Western officials began to dismantle Poplašen's party, the Serbian Radical Party (SRS). On October 5, 1999, the Office of the High Representative and the OSCE jointly sent a letter to the Serbian Radical Party, demanding the removal of Poplašen and two other officials from leadership positions in the party because they had criticized NATO. "Failure to remove these persons from leadership positions in the SRS," the letter said, "will result in ... not allowing the SRS to participate in the municipal elections in April 2000."[18] They were as good as their word. Twenty days later, the OSCE's Provisional Election Commission ruled that neither the Serbian Radical Party, nor a smaller party, "will be registered for the municipal elections in 2000 and will not have candidates competing for local offices."[19] The outright banning of a major political party passed without comment in the Western press. No pretense of democracy is made. Western dictate is "democratic," simply by virtue of being Western.

On the same day that saw Poplašen's removal as president, Robert Owen, Western arbitrator for the status of the town of Brčko, announced a decision that effectively split asunder the Republika Srpska. The two halves of the Republika Srpska were held together by a narrow three-mile wide strip, in which lies Brčko. The decree removed Brčko from the Republika Srpska and created a special district to be held jointly by the Republika Srpska and the Muslim-Croatian Federation. Under terms of the decree, Bosnian Serb armed forces could not move from one half of their territory to the other without permission of NATO. The decree also specified that Brčko may at any time be transferred from a "non-complying entity" and placed "within the exclusive control of the other."[20] The decision was met by universal Bosnian Serb rejection and U.S. envoy Robert Gelbard threatened that "the territory of Brčko could still revert to the entity which is in compliance."[21] Following Dodik's resignation over the Brčko decision, Western officials scrambled to talk him out of it. As Gelbard explained it, progress on plans to privatize state assets "is really due to Dodik's leadership."[22] It was not long before Dodik withdrew his resignation and announced his acceptance of the Brčko decision. Dodik's resignation was merely playacting, a bow to local public opinion. He subsequently demonstrated that he would carry out every order, and on October 2, 1999, following his return from meeting with American officials in the United States, he dutifully called for the overthrow of the Milošević government in Yugoslavia.[23]

Wild West Justice

The International War Crimes Tribunal proved to be a useful political tool for NATO, enabling it to seize, or even murder political enemies. On January 30, 1996, two leading Bosnian Serb generals, Djordje Djukić and Aleksa Krsmanović, were invited to meet with Western civilian and NATO officials in Ilidza, at that time, a Serbian suburb of Sarajevo. The meeting was a ruse. A trap had been set, and both men were seized and imprisoned by Bosnian Muslim soldiers. According to a British officer, the kidnapping was a result of NATO passing information to Bosnian Muslim forces. A high-ranking Western European intelligence source revealed that the U.S. Defense Intelligence Agency (DIA) was behind the seizure. "The DIA took a fantastic quantity of bugging and surveillance equipment there," he said. "The vehicle in which the Serb officers were traveling was followed from the air." The DIA, he added, expected the generals to be "the most valuable sources of information. Also do not forget that a not at all negligible number of The Hague investigators are CIA and DIA members."[24]

Two weeks later, the men were transferred to The Hague, where they were subjected to repeated interrogations and pressured to accuse other Bosnian Serb officials and officers of crimes. Djukić's lawyer said, "It was suggested to Djukić that the court would have a better understanding for him in the future if he testified," and tribunal spokesman Christian Chartier said that the fate of the men "very much depends ... on what they might tell us."[25]

Both men refused to talk, however, and punishment was swift in coming. On March 1, Djukić was charged with the "crime against humanity" of being "assistant commander for logistics," including such heinous acts as "proposing appointments of personnel" and "issuing orders relating to the supply of materiel for units of the Bosnian Serb Army." In a pique, chief prosecutor Richard Goldstone said he indicted Djukić because of his refusal to talk.[26] Not even as flimsy a charge as this could be concocted against Krsmanović, who was held without charge for several more weeks of interrogations. At the time, Djukić was suffering from an advanced case of pancreatic cancer. Despite his pain, interrogation sessions continued unabated, but he refused to talk to the end. In late April he was released to return to his family, where he died on May 19.

On July 10, 1997, a joint American-British operation swooped down on two Bosnian Serbs, despite the lack of a public indictment against either man. Four NATO members gained entrance to the Prijedor Medical Center by claiming to deliver a Red Cross package, and arrested the hospital's director, Milan Kovačević. The arrest provoked an angry demonstration by 400 of the hospital's medical staff and several hundred citizens. Former Prijedor security chief Simo Drljaca was less fortunate. Shortly after he returned from fishing, still dressed in a bathing suit, to enjoy breakfast with family and friends, NATO troops burst into his yard. A witness recounts, "Music was playing. I was sitting. Then suddenly I heard screams: 'Simo, Simo!' I turned around. Soldiers were armed ... I saw Simo getting up. At that moment, I heard bullets being fired and they fired at him. Then I saw Simo laying down on sand near a beach. He was laying on his side and shaking. Then a soldier came close to him and fired another bullet at him and finished him off."[27]

Another NATO ambush took place on January 10, 1999, targeting a car occupied by Dragan Gagović and five children from his karate class. One of the children, Sonja Bjelović, described the ambush: "We ran across iron bars on the road. Dragan braked to stop the vehicle, because we could not pass ... then we heard shots. Our coach said, 'down, you can be hit.' He tried to protect us and pass around the iron bars. However the car was hit, tires went flat and it overturned. I saw our coach covered with blood." Another child, Milica Džoković, reported, "When the coach told us to go down I hid under the seat and closed my eyes. When I opened my eyes I saw the coach covered with blood and [NATO soldiers'] gun-barrels pointed at us."[28]

On July 6, 1999, Radislav Brdjanin, leader of the People's Party, was kidnapped from his home in Banja Luka and flown to The Hague, where he was imprisoned. A month and a half later, on August 25, Republika Srpska Chief of Staff General Momir Talić, who had been invited to a conference in Austria, was arrested there and flown to The Hague. Neither man had been publicly indicted. The arrest of these men under "secret indictments" is an effective recipe for silencing free speech. Inevitably, people will feel a reluctance to speak out against NATO occupation, lest they make a target of themselves.

Stanislav Galić's mistake was in accepting an appointment as military advisor to Nikola Poplašen. While Galić was driving his car on December 20, 1999, several vehicles suddenly blocked his path. NATO soldiers sprang out and smashed Galić's car window, roughly dragged him out and placed a hood over his head. Galić was flown to The Hague, where he was imprisoned.

High Commissioner Carlos Westendorp revealed much about the imperial attitude as he delivered his last speech before turning over the reins to his successor, Wolfgang Petritsch. Westendorp expressed his "wish to quote from another famous historical figure, who said not that much could be achieved with a kind word, but a kind word and a gun. This figure was Al Capone. Joke! I've been here too long… I actually prefer Teddy Roosevelt's 'Walk softly and carry a big stick'. The gun or stick in this context is the continuing presence of SFOR [NATO Stabilization Force] and the International Community."[29]

Covert Involvement and Military Aid.

According to a report in the *Los Angeles Times*, "The CIA station in Bosnia is now reputed to be one of the largest in the region."[30] By early 1996, the total number of CIA operatives active in the region had risen to 2,500, almost half of whom were stationed at the agency's regional headquarters in Tuzla.[31] The DIA was also very active in the region, working in close cooperation with the CIA. These agencies not only engage in intelligence gathering, but also shape events, both directly and indirectly. Most of the international organizations present in Bosnia are dominated and run by American officials. Local news reports are "reshaped", that is, censored, by American officials, and compliant media receive Western financing, largely through the U.S. Agency for International Development (USAID). A report in the Yugoslav press claims that in 1996, approximately half a million dollars were funneled to media in both of Bosnia's entities.[32]

The implementation of the U.S. Train and Equip plan pumped more arms into the region. Under the plan, the U.S. initially supplied Federation forces with tens of thousands of M-16 assault rifles, over 100 armored personnel carriers, several dozen tanks, over 100 155-mm howitzers, communications equipment, helicopters, and myriad other weapons. Arms supplies from other nations were arranged by U.S. officials, and one shipment alone, from the United Arab Emirates, consisted of 50 French AMX-30 tanks and 41 armored vehicles.[33]

The plan also provided for American and Turkish training of Federation forces. The Pentagon contracted with Military Professional Resources Incorporated (MPRI) to conduct training. MPRI had earlier successfully trained the Croatian Army in preparation for its brutal invasion of Krajina, in which over 200,000 Serbs were driven from their homes in a matter of days. Training sessions included the use of advanced battle simulation computer software, as was used in preparation for Desert Storm. Funding was also provided to open arms factories in the Federation. In all, eight Federation arms factories operated under NATO supervision, and a Federation defense ministry spokesman announced that half of these factories produce 122mm howitzers for its army.[34]

Officially, American officials asserted that Train and Equip was necessary to ensure peace. Quietly, they had another purpose. Alarmed at the extent of the Federation military buildup, Russian commanders passed NATO satellite photos of Muslim training camps to Bosnian Serb generals. According to information received by a Western diplomat, "The Bosnian Serb generals were stunned. The mood in the room was very black." In the event of an attack, a high-ranking NATO commander said, "We also expect most all of the Serbs [in the Republika Srpska] to be driven into Serbia..."[35] The Train and Equip plan was a useful means of dictating policy to the Republika Srpska, which effectively limited how independently Republika Srpska could act. Western officials regularly threatened that if their demands were not met, then the Muslim-Croatian Federation could receive a go-ahead for an invasion. The Train and Equip plan can be a two-edged sword, though, and in April 1999, U.S. envoy Robert Gelbard temporarily suspended the program for four months in order to force a reorganization of the Federation Army along lines demanded by Western officials.

Reshaping the Economy

The heart of Western policy in the region is the promotion of Western corporate interests. In late 1996, a "peace implementation conference" was held in London, during which much of Bosnia-Herzegovina's future was forged. According to a report by the Press Association, the conference "won a commitment from the Bosnian leaders to reconstruct the shattered economy along free market economy lines, including significant privatization and close cooperation with the World Bank."[36] Laws are penned and imposed by Western officials. Less than one year after the conference, Haris Silajdžić, co-chair of the Bosnia-Herzegovina Council of Ministers, announced that "U.S. Finance Secretary David Lipton will come here bringing draft laws on privatization at the state level" to be submitted to the Assembly for vote. Existing draft laws on property relations and privatization, he said, "will be modified according to regulations the U.S. finance secretary will bring."[37] On July 2, 1998, Westendorp founded a commission to manage the privatization process in Bosnia-Herzegovina. Each privatization, including prior actions, would be subject to review and approval by Western commission officials.[38]

An earlier law on privatization in the Republika Srpska was previously in place. On December 4, 1997, Robert Farrand, of the Office of the High Representative, issued an "Order on Privatization," in which he mandated a "delay" of the Republika Srpska privatization process, "so that international assistance could be provided to make it a credible process leading to successful transition to a free market economy," adding that "current RS [Republika Srpska] legislation on privatization lacks a sound technical framework and in its current form can lead only to large scale fraud."[39] Looking beyond the vague nature of the complaint, and ostensible concern about "fraud," what actually motivated the order suspending the law? Documents from the American Embassy in Sarajevo paint a more honest picture: "The privatization framework is being overhauled and will create more opportunities for involvement of potential foreign investors," adding that a "fundamental flaw" of the previous process "was the allocation of 47 percent of companies' shares to seven government-managed funds." Clearly, the "fraud" that concerned Western officials was that Western corporations could not dominate the process and seize the best assets. The embassy's documents reassured investors that "The new RS government has pledged to overhaul the privatization framework and annulled all previous privatization laws. Assistance is now being provided by the World Bank and USAID to develop new laws similar to those adopted by the Federation." Western officials reshaped privatization in the Republika Srpska, as they did in the Muslim-Croatian Federation, to favor the interests of Western investors.

The Foreign Investment Law, effective on March 1998, and applicable to both entities, "establishes the policy standards of promoting foreign investment and protecting foreign investor's rights," an embassy document declared. "The Entities will amend existing foreign investment laws to conform to the state-level legislation." Western officials were thorough in ensuring their interests. The law "is progressive in terms of its final aim which is to promote foreign direct investment." An important feature was a provision that "protects the rights of foreign investors....there are no restrictions on foreign investment" except armaments and media. "The entities are directed to establish progressive and favorable tax conditions that encourage foreign investment." Furthermore, the law "expressly forbids expropriation or nationalization actions against foreign investments."[40]

And what role is envisioned for the people of Bosnia? The American embassy had an answer for that, too. "Foreign investors can utilize low-cost labor (the lowest in the CEE [Central and Eastern Europe]) while gaining proximity and access to important markets in the EU [European Union] and the CEE." Bosnian people have the privilege of joining the Third World. Because Bosnia-Herzegovina is essentially land-locked, access to the Adriatic Sea was an important prerequisite for exploiting this "low-cost labor." Despite strong Bosnian Muslim reservations concerning certain provisions, an agreement on special relations was signed with neighboring Croatia, in which the Federation was given free transit to and use of the Croatian port of Ploče. According to a report in the Croatian press, agreement from the Bosnian Muslim delegation came "as a result of pressure from the United States."[41] In preparation for the expansion of trade through Ploče, the World Bank financed a $22 million project for the reconstruction of the main pier, and Sealand won a grant from the U.S. Trade and Development Agency to perform "a feasibility study on the development of container terminal facilities and the corridor from Ploce to Sarajevo (and eventually the Sava River)."[42] Following the removal of Brčko from the Republika Srpska, Brčko Supervisor Robert Farrand signed an agreement for the U.S. Trade and Development Agency to solicit bids from American firms to conduct a six-month feasibility study of the Brčko port on the Sava River.[43]

When deemed necessary, Western officials were quick to use threats in order to achieve their goals. A Western diplomatic source revealed that "in diplomatic talks behind closed doors, we are, sort of, intimidating [Republika Srpska] politicians" with the possibility of invasion by Federation troops. "The tendency is to stimulate and open up economically" the Republika Srpska, he added. "When, in some diplomatic efforts, we try to 'soften' their stances, we always hint at their possible war defeat. We always use the illustration of Krajina."[44] Threats against the Federation were less aggressive, if no less effective. On November 10, 1998, the Contact Group, which oversees policy in Bosnia, and is chaired by the U.S., issued a statement threatening a cutoff of millions of dollars in aid to the Federation. An American spokesman bluntly stated that "the time has come and, in fact, is overdue for the governments of Bosnia to be making the transition - and [they] should be making it rapidly - to a sustainable market economy. We are prepared to cut off projects, programs, anything to get their attention..." The spokesman demanded "much more progress on privatization" and foreign investment.[45]

NATO has established a permanent presence in the Balkans. NATO's savage bombing of Yugoslavia was motivated solely by the desire to establish a NATO-run colony in Kosovo and to weaken the nation. The Yugoslav government consistently called for the return of all refugees, greater autonomy in Kosovo, and an international presence in Kosovo. The only divisive issue was the nature of that presence, with NATO insisting on its control of the province. NATO bases have been established throughout the Balkans. A poor Bosnian Serb, Radoslav Skrba, wondered, "How is it that all these Western armies now have bases here? Could it be that it was their strategy all along? During the Communist time we were warned that the West wanted to come here and now here they are."[46]

ENDNOTES

1 Colonel Milovan Milutinović, "Loss of Supreme Command," *Nin* (Belgrade), November 1, 1996.

2 "Don't Push Us Into a Fratricidal War!", *Blic* (Belgrade), November 13, 1996.

3 Nikola Zeklić, "Dancing to the CIA's Rhythm," *Oslobodjenje* (Sarajevo - Bosnian Serb), April 4, 1996.

4 "OSCE Says Pale Assembly 'No Longer Exists," *Agence France-Presse* (Paris), July 4, 1997.

5 "U.S. Supports Bosnian Serb President in Court Case," *Reuters*, August 15, 1997.

6 "U.S. Allegedly to Deposit $30 Million in Plavsić Account," *Beta* (Belgrade), July 1, 1997.

7 "Plavsić Aides Accused as Spies," *SRNA* (Pale), August 24, 1997.

8 Colin Soloway, "NATO Forces Seize Police Stations in Bosnian City," *Washington Post,* August 21, 1997.

9 Chris Stephen, "IPTF Screens, Retrains Police in RS," *Agence France-Presse* (Paris), August 22, 1997. "IPTF Trains Republika Srpska Police Officers," *Tanjug* (Belgrade), August 26, 1997.

10 Srečko Latal, "Bosnian Serb Military Warns President Against Dividing Bosnian Serb Territory," *Associated Press*, August 22, 1997.

11 Edward Cody, "Bosnian Serb's Backers Stone American Troops," *Washington Post*, August 29, 1997. Misha Savić, "Serbs Force U.N. Team to Withdraw," *Associated Press*, August 29, 1997.

12 Misha Savić, "NATO Commander Warns Bosnia Media," *Associated Press*, August 30, 1997.

13 "Media Monitoring Commission Shuts Down Kanal S TV," *BETA* (Belgrade), April 14, 1999

14 "Westendorp Proclaims Citizenship Law," *B92 Open Serbia* (Belgrade), December 17, 1997.

[15] "OSCE Strikes 3 Serb Candidates Off SDS Election List," *SRNA* (Pale), November 21, 1997. "Bosnia Serb Party Sanctioned for Karadžić Picture," *Agence France-Presse*, September 1, 1998. "Nine Delisted for Bosnian Serb's TV Interview," *Agence France-Presse*, September 21, 1998. "Bosnian Croat Candidates Disqualified by TV Bias," *Reuters*, September 4, 1998.

[16] "Poplašen Defends Actions While in Office," *SRNA* (Pale), March 7, 1999. Interview with Nikola Poplašen, by Branislav Radivojsa, "Poplašen: Assembly Must Oppose Unconstitutional Behavior of Dodik's Government," *Politika* (Belgrade), September 3, 1999.

[17] Office of the High Representative, "Removal From Office of Nikola Poplašen," *OHR Press Release* (Sarajevo), March 5, 1999.

[18] *Joint OHR/OSCE Press Release*, "SRS Must Refile Application for Party Registration," October 5, 1999.

[19] *OSCE Mission to Bosnia and Herzegovina Press Release*, "PEC Denies Certification for Serb Radical and SRSS Parties for Municipal Elections 2000," Sarajevo, October 25, 1999.

[20] "Final Award, Arbitral Tribunal for Dispute Over Inter-Entity Boundary in Brčko Area." March 5, 1999.

[19] "Mediators Warn Bosnia Serbs to Comply with Brčko Ruling." *Agence France-Presse* (Paris), March 19, 1999.

[20] "US Envoy Hopes Moderate Bosnia Serb PM Will Stay," *Reuters* (London), March 10, 1999.

[21] "Dodik Returns from US, Backs Anti-Milošević Rallies," *BETA* (Belgrade), October 2, 1999.

[22] Vesna Hadživuković, "Americans Preparing New Kidnappings," *Telegraf* (Belgrade), February 14, 1996.

[23] "Serb Officers Might be Witnesses in The Hague," *Associated Press*, February 23, 1996.

[24] The Prosecutor of the Tribunal, CASE No IT-96-20-I, "Against Dorde Dukic (sic) Indictment."

[25] Broadcast, *Srpksa Televizija* (Pale), July 10, 1997.

[26] "Children Describe Gagović's 'Brutal Murder'," *Tanjug* (Belgrade), January 10, 1999.

[27] *Office of the High Representative*, "Speech of the High Representative Carlos Westendorp at the Stability Pact Dinner," Sarajevo, July 29, 1999.

[28] Tracy Wilkinson, "In Bosnia, U.S. Creeps Deeper, *Los Angeles Times*, November 11, 1997.

[29] "From the Jungle to the Balkans," *Politika Ekspres* (Belgrade), January 22, 1996.

[30] "Daily Criticizes USAID Funding of B-H Independent Media," *Beta* (Belgrade), April 29, 1997.

[31] "New Weapons Shipments for Bosnia's US-Led Rearmament Programme," *Agence France-Presse* (Paris), October 13, 1997. A Prlenda, "Weapons for

Peace and Stabilization," *Oslobodjenje* (Bosnian Muslim), November 22, 1996. Nick Gowing, "Return to War," *The Sunday Telegraph* (London), December 1, 1996. "Arms Shipment from Turkey Arrives in Ploce Port," *HINA* (Zagreb), July 26, 1997. Srečko Latal, "United States Helping Rearm Muslim-Croat Army: Allies Object," *Associated Press*, May 23, 1996.

32 James Drake, "Old GIs Fade Away – to Bosnia," *Baltimore Sun*, November 12, 1997. Nedim Dervišbegović, "Bosnian Firms Produce Artillery with U.S. Aid," *Reuters*, October 17, 1997. "U.S. Envoy Visits U.S-Aided Bosnian Army Factory," *Agence France-Presse* (Paris), September 5, 1997.

33 Chris Hedges, "Bosnian Muslims Said to Intensify Efforts to Rearm in Secret," *The New York Times*, October 3, 1997.

34 Charles Miller, "Tough Action Agreed to in Hunt for Bosnia's War Criminals," *Press Association* (London), December 5, 1996.

35 A Pilav, "Draft Laws Arriving from the US!", *Dnevi Avaz* (Sarajevo), October 7, 1997.

36 Sead Numanović, "Westendorp Forms a Commission," *Dnevi Avaz* (Sarajevo), July 2, 1998.

37 Office of the High Representative, "Order on Privatization," December 4, 1997.

38 *American Embassy, Sarajevo*, "The Commercial Guide to Bosnia and Herzegovina," June, 1998.

39 "Croatia, Federation Sign Special Relations Agreement," *HINA* (Zagreb), November 22, 1998. "Bosnia, Croatia Form Special Relations," *UPI*, November 22, 1998. "Croatia Opens Up Key Port to Bosnia in Thawing of Relations," *Agence France-Presse*, November 22, 1998.

40 *American Embassy, Sarajevo*, "The Commercial Guide to Bosnia and Herzegovina," June, 1998.

41 *OHR Press Release*, "Brčko Port Feasibility Study Agreement Signed," June 4, 1999.

42 Edina Bečirević, "If the Refugees Do Not Return Next Year, the World Will Tolerate That as Well!", *Slobodna Bosna* (Sarajevo), September 21, 1997.

43 Carol Giacomo, "U.S. and Allies May Turn Off Aid Tap," *Reuters*, November 9, 1998. "U.S. Threatens Aid Cut," *UPI*, November 9, 1998. "Contact Group Signals It Wants to Cut Bosnian Aid," *Reuters*, November 10, 1998.

44 Mike O'Connor, "Bosnian Serbs, Unhappy in Serb Republic, Fear Return to Bosnia," *The New York Times*, September 18, 1998.

Bosniaks, Nazi Muslims, Mujahideen and bin Laden

by Milo Yelesiyevich

On September 20, 2001, President Kostunica gave an interview to the Belgrade daily *Politika* in which he discussed the 9/11 bombings of the Pentagon and the World Trade Center. Since Yugoslavia had been bombed by the U.S. in 1999 for fighting Islamic terrorism in Kosovo, it was pungently ironic to find that the tables had now turned. Kostunica made incisive comments. He claimed that the Clinton administration had exacerbated the conflict between co-existing civilizations by a foreign policy of "playing the role of world policeman and by wanting to dominate almost all spheres of life. These are the true deep roots and the true reasons that triggered the birth of terrorism and its development."

President Kostunica then launched a blistering attack on the NATO bombing of his country, and he did not spare the U.S. in his criticism. He stated that the U.S. needed to rethink its role in the world if it wanted to avoid such attacks in the future. He remarked that the U.S. was "a world policeman who can function quite easily when he needs to bomb a country, such as Yugoslavia, for 78 days. When this country is also faced with terrorism in its most fanatical form, as happened on September 11, then things look rather different." He further stated that until a country experiences such an attack, it is impossible for the people to know how it feels.[*]

Yugoslavia was fighting the Kosovo Liberation Army (KLA), which was replete with Islamic terrorists. The KLA had furthermore been sponsored by the U.S., and Yugoslavia became a "rogue state" tarred with accusations of "ethnic cleansing" when it tried to defend itself. This was, in fact, a reprise of the accusations Yugoslavia had suffered when it tried to contain Islamic fundamentalism in Bosnia during the 1992-1995 war.

During that war, the U.S. backed Alija Izetbegović's radicalized Bosnian Muslims at the expense of the majority of moderate Muslims represented by Fikret Abdić. Bosnia became both a haven for mujahideen and a forward base for Islamic fundamentalism in Europe. Thousands, not hundreds, of mujahideen from throughout the Muslim world joined the Bosnian Muslim-KLA

---

[*] *See* "Osama in the Balkans," by Justin Raimondo, 10/29/01, antiwar.com. These two paragraphs paraphrase the opening of Mr. Raimondo's essay.

insurgency. Many were granted citizenship and refuge after the war was over. It is certain that two 9/11 hijackers from San Diego had fought in Bosnia and belonged to al Qaeda for six years. Another Bosnian war veteran recruited the Hamburg al Qaeda cell, which included Mohammed Atta, who played a pivotal role in 9/11.[1]

> Bosnia became the safe haven for bin Laden's al Qaeda terrorists. The U.S was finally persuaded to oppose the presence of mujahideen as a part of the Dayton Accords. The concern was the future threat to the U.S. peacekeepers. After the war, Izetbegović alienated his Western backers for allowing mujahideen to remain in the country and serve as a springboard for the European and even the U.S. jihad. Izetbegović argued that they came to Bosnia when nobody else would. He allowed them to marry Bosnian Muslim women and obtain Bosnian citizenship. However, 99% of the reporters and politicians fail to make the point that Izetbegović was directly responsible for bringing thousands of mujahideen and military equipment from Central Asia and the Middle East to the heart of Europe, to Bosnia, to launch jihad alongside the Bosnian Muslims against the Christian Serbs and Croats. *De facto*, the Bosnian war taught mujahideen how to operate abroad.[2]

The West has a wide array of high-tech weaponry; but the Muslims have a demographic bomb that they keep resorting to. The Muslim population of Great Britain exploded from less than 100,000 in the early 1970s to more than two million today. Germany hosts four million Turks; France is home to five million largely North African Muslims. Italy and the Netherlands each have a million Muslims, and Spain half a million. Entire unassimilable Muslim quarters have taken root in major European cities like Berlin, Paris and Amsterdam.[3]

Politically correct Western intellectuals carefully examine these realities and promptly deny them. Political correctness has declared Christianity to be an "enemy of freedom and modernity," and thus allows Muslims to live in a state of uneasy truce in the West and conceal the true nature of their religion. Let us ask ourselves whether or not such corresponding religious freedom is permitted to Christians in Muslim countries. Regrettably, it is not so. The practice of Christianity is forbidden in Saudi Arabia. One can be imprisoned for merely possessing a Bible, not to mention conducting the Divine Liturgy in one's own home. Greek

Orthodox churches in Istanbul are regularly subject to attack by extremists in Turkey. Chaldeans and other Christians are under siege in Iraq. Albanians waged a pogrom (underreported in the West) against Serbs in Kosovo, killing scores of people and destroying some 35 churches over the course of two days of rioting in March 2004. One can enumerate further examples, but to what end as long as there is such a deep current of denial and deliberate not-knowing among politically correct pundits, academicians, and spin masters. Now we are told that we ought celebrate our "multi-cultural society" because we are so free that we even have Muslim comics to disarm us. "One of the unexpected consequences of the 9/11 attacks in the United States is an upsurge in humour by and about Muslims, which has begun to be enjoyed by a wider American audience."[4]

Perhaps the fundamental error in judgment is that a value-free democracy driven by a market economy is the highest development mankind can reach. Western society is rooted in: 1) Greek philosophy and mythology; 2) Christianity, which absorbed and retransmitted classical philosophy and mythology; 3) the Renaissance, the rediscovery of Greek and Roman literature and philosophy; and 4) the Enlightenment, which gave rise to our secular culture. An informed Westerner has experienced these four stages of development because they never vanished in the first place. These elements uphold American democracy, as conceived by the Founding Fathers, just as a mountain gives rise to a tree at its crest.

On the one hand, any New Yorker or Parisian or Londoner or Belgrader can tell you what living in a "multicultural" society means; on the other hand, any Muslim will view "multiculturalism" in a completely different fashion. More often than not, a Muslim will contend that Islam is "multicultural" because there are European Muslims, Arab Muslims, African Muslims, Asian Muslims — non-Muslims, unfortunately, cannot be counted as part of their experience or world view.

The Serbs have been the most notable victims of such Muslim antipathy. Ever since the Great Schism, the West has been inclined to place Orthodox Christians on the same footing as Muslims. This is the same thinking that was going on in the 14th Century when the Serbs, the Greeks and the Bulgarians faced Ottoman conquest. Slobodan Radulj, advisor to the Serbian

member of the Bosnia-Herzegovina presidency, revealed an offer
mujahideens made to the Serbs in Bocinj, near Maglaj.

> The mujahideen told their Serbian neighbors that they should convert
> to Islam if they wanted to live in peace and safety. He [Radulj] went
> on to state that this was proof that the village of Ozren had been
> turned into a camp to train Islamic terrorists.[5]

Mr. Radulj went on to say that ideological training was aimed at
those who were preparing to give their lives for Islam. He added
that the so-called humanitarian organizations that came to Bosnia
are providing training, which is for the most part conducted in
religious centers, such as schools and mosques.

Al-Qaeda's firm presence in Bosnia remains an unspoken
taboo among journalists, and denials have sadly become routine.
Meanwhile, the U.S. keeps offering the Serbs the same deal: submit to Western economic and strategic demands or you will be
thrown to the dogs.

Islamic Fundamentalism's Historic Nazi Ties

The Grand Mufti of Jerusalem, Amin al-Husseini (or Husayni)
(1895-1974), is a pivotal figure in the introduction of Nazi
thought and practice to the Arab world, because they shared similar goals. The Nazis wanted to exterminate the Jews of Europe;
al-Husseini wanted to exterminate the Jews of Palestine. Al-
Husseini met with Hitler on November 25, 1941 in Berlin. Hitler
spoke highly of al-Husseini, and promised that he would send the
Wehrmacht to the free the Muslim world from British occupation.

> Nazi Germany established for *der Grossmufti von Jerusalem* a Bureau
> from which he organized the following: 1) radio propaganda on
> behalf of Nazi Germany; 2) espionage and fifth column activities in
> Muslim regions of Europe and the Middle East; 3) the formation of
> Muslim Waffen SS and *Wehrmacht* units in Bosnia-Herzegovina,
> Kosovo-Metohija, Western Macedonia, North Africa, and Nazi-occu-
> pied areas of the Soviet Union; and, 4) the formation of schools and
> training centers for Muslim imams and mullahs who would accompa-
> ny the Muslim SS and *Wehrmacht* units. As soon as he arrived in
> Europe, the Mufti established close contacts with Bosnian Muslim
> and Albanian Muslim leaders. He would spend the remainder of the
> war organizing and rallying Muslims in support of Nazi Germany.[6]

Al-Husseini came to Nazi Germany with solid credentials. His grandfather and his half brother had been Muftis in Jerusalem in the 1890s. Al-Husseini studied Islamic philosophy in Cairo briefly before he went to serve in the Ottoman Turkish Army as an artillery officer. When he returned to Palestine, he was appalled by the Jewish immigrants who were arriving there. He feared they would jeopardize Muslim predominance. He subsequently organized riots in 1929 and in 1936 against Jews as well as moderate Muslims. He had an early grasp of official disinformation, which he demonstrated by publishing photographs of murdered Jews and identifying them in the press as murdered Muslims. This was a technique that was used many times during the Bosnian War by both the television and print media. There were many cases of Orthodox Serbs who were photographed (sometimes in cemeteries that prominently displayed crosses) but who were identified in news broadcasts as being Bosnian Muslims.

In 1917, the British government issued the Balfour Declaration, which made a formal commitment to the establishment of a Jewish homeland in Palestine. Al-Husseini rejected the British policy of settling European Jews in Palestine. After inciting riots against Jews in 1920, al-Husseini was tried and sentenced *in absencia* to a ten years prison term.

> On July 1,1920, Sir Herbert Samuel, himself a British Jew, appointed the first British High Commissioner for Palestine, assumed control. Samuel sought to reconcile with the Palestinian population by pardoning Husseini. Sir Robert Storrs, the then governor of the city, appointed him Mufti of Jerusalem. He was also the president of the Supreme Muslim Council, and, later, the Arab Higher Committee. He was thus the religious and political leader of the Palestinian Muslims.[7]

Husseini became one of the most influential and powerful leaders in the Islamic world after he restored the Dome of the Rock Mosque in Jerusalem, which he plated in gold. The impressive Dome, the third most sacred Islamic site after Mecca and Medina, enhanced the status of Jerusalem in the eyes of Muslims throughout the world.

> Husseini was at the forefront of Islamic militancy and 'terrorism' directed against the British/French/US occupation. Hassan el Banna formed the Muslim Brotherhood in Egypt in 1928. The Muslim

Brotherhood had links to the Grand Mufti and worked with him in Palestine, sending volunteers in support of the Palestinian uprisings in 1936, 1939, and during the 1948 war. The Muslim Brotherhood sought to establish Muslim states based on the Sharia, Islamic law, and the Caliphate system of political rule, wherein each Islamic state would be ruled by a Caliph. Islam is 'creed and state, book and sword, and a way of life.' In Pakistan, Syed Abdul Ala Maududi founded the Jamaat Islami movement with the goal of establishing Muslim theocratic states based on Koranic law. Egyptian Sayed Qutb of the Muslim Brotherhood continued the movement after World War II. The Muslim Brotherhood had offshoots: the Egyptian Islamic Jihad and Hamas. Haj Amin el Husseini, the Muslim Brotherhood, Jamaat Islami, Islamic Jihad, all form the roots and historical background for the emergence of the Al-Qaeda network, the mujahideen of Afghanistan, and Osama Bin Laden. Ayatollah Khomeini and Bosnian Muslim leader Alija Izetbegovic would be influenced by the anti-secular, anti-Western, radical Muslim nationalist movements. In his book *The Islamic Declaration*, ("Islamska Deklaracija," 1970; republished, 1990), Izetbegovic rejected the secular conception of an Islamic state espoused by Kemal Ataturk. Izetbegovic sought to create an Islamic state based in the Sharia, a state where religion would not be separate from the state, i.e., an Islamic theocratic state. Izetbegovic established close links to Osama Bin Laden and al-Qaeda and invited mujahideen forces to join the Bosnian Muslim Army. Izetbegovic later would give Osama Bin Laden a special Bosnian passport and the mujahideen 'freedom fighters' would receive Bosnian citizenship and passports. One of the hijackers of the second attack on the World Trade Center on September 11, 2001, possessed a Bosnian passport.

During WWII, al-Husseini traveled to Bosnia many times to recruit Bosnian Muslims and Albanians to serve in the Nazi Handžar Division, which engaged in the outright slaughter of Jews and Serbs in Nazi-occupied Yugoslavia. These Muslim troops were directly under the command of the Nazi *Wehrmacht*, which forged a direct link between the ambitions of the Nazi Party and Islamic fundamentalism. The Serbs retained vivid memories of the WWII slaughter, which is the reason they so adamantly refused to be part of a Muslim dominated statelet fifty years later.

The Nazis, as well as their Croatian puppet state, saw the value in forging an alliance with the Bosnian Muslims. On July 6, 1941, Mile Budak, Ustasha Education Minister, defined the Bosnian Muslim role in Croatia: "The Croatian state is Christian.

It is also a Moslem state where our people are of the Mohammadan religion." Ante Pavelić referred to the Bosnian Muslims as "the flower of Croatia," the oldest and most noble descendants of Croats who had converted to Islam.

Al-Husseini had already publicly announced his intention to establish an "Arab Brigade" to answer the creation of the "Jewish Brigade" by the British in Palestine. The Handžars took their name from a dagger that was traditionally worn by Ottoman Turkish officers. Their numbers eventually grew to about twenty-two thousand men, and they enjoyed the distinction of being the third largest unit of the Waffen SS.

One of the first military actions conducted by the Handžar Division was to send a four man death squad to murder Serbian monks in a monastery in the village of Fojnica. Brother Nikola Miličević, thirty-nine, was shot dead on the spot when he argued with the death squad. Brother Mato Migić, fifty-six, was wounded, and then given a *coup de grace* with a bullet in the neck. Alija Izetbegovic, who was a young Handžar recruiter at the time, sent his condolences.

The Mufti instigated and organized Muslim riots against Palestinian Jews in 1920, 1921, 1929, and 1936. In 1921, the Mufti organized the *fedayeen*, Muslim suicide squads. Following the 1936 riots, fearing imprisonment, he fled to Lebanon. In 1939, the Mufti established his headquarters in Baghdad, Iraq, where he set up a 'political departments' that maintained ties to Germany and Italy. Germany sought to create a Berlin-Baghdad Axis and instigated a pro-Nazi coup. Iraqi General Rashid Ali el Gailani, a militant Muslim nationalist, and the Golden Square, a group of pro-Nazi Iraqi officers, took over the Iraqi government. The Mufti sent representatives to Berlin and a letter to Adolf Hitler. In a reply by German State Secretary Freiherr von Weizsaecker, the Mufti was told that 'the Fuhrer received your letter dated January 20th. He took great interest in what you wrote him about the national struggle of the Arabs. Germany is ready to cooperate with you and to give you all possible military and financial help. Germany is prepared to deliver to you immediately military material.' *Abwehr*, German intelligence, established contacts with the Mufti at this time.

After meeting Hitler and Ribbentrop in Berlin in 1941, the Mufti was approached by Gottlob Berger, head of the SS Main Office in control of recruiting, and by Reichsfuehrer-SS Heinrich Himmler, who made him a part of the SS apparatus. In May, 1943, the Mufti was moved to the SS main office where he participated in the recruiting of Muslims in the Balkans, the USSR, the Middle East, and North Africa. The Grand Mufti was instrumental in the organization and formation of many Muslim units and formations in the Waffen SS and Wehrmacht. Hundreds of thousands of Muslims fought for Nazi Germany in the following formations and units

Al-Husseini, after the failure of a pro-Nazi coup in Iraq, for which, incidentally, he held the indigenous Jewish community culpable, sought refuge in Germany during WWII. After Germany's defeat, al-Husseini was tipped off that Yugoslavia and Hungary were preparing a case against him at the Nuremberg Tribunal and that he was about to be charged with crimes against humanity. He succeeded in escaping from Europe and found refuge in Cairo.

At the Nuremberg Trials, Adolf Eichmann's deputy Dieter Wisliceny (subsequently executed as a war criminal), testified that: "The Mufti was one of the initiators of the systematic extermination of European Jewry and had been a collaborator and adviser of Eichmann and Himmler in the execution of this plan... He was one of Eichmann's best friends and had constantly incited him to accelerate the extermination measures. I heard him say, accompanied by Eichmann, he had visited incognito the gas chamber of Auschwitz." In fact, Husseini had plans of his own to build a death camp, modeled after Auschwitz, near Nablus.[8]

In 1944 al-Husseini launched a chemical warfare assault on the Jewish community in Palestine. Five parachutists were sent with a toxin to dump into the water system of Tel Aviv, a predominantly Jewish city. The police caught the infiltrators in a cave near Jericho, and according to Jericho district police commander Fayiz Bey Idrissi, "The laboratory report stated that each container held enough poison to kill 25,000 people, and there were at least ten containers."[9]

It is not farfetched to suppose that Alija Izetbegović had met al-Husseini during his numerous trips to Bosnia, and that he admired him. Izetbegović deployed many of the same tactics against the Bosnian Serbs that al-Husseini had used against the Jews and moderate Muslims of Palestine during the 1920s and 1930s.

Alija Izetbegović

Alija Izetbegović, who became president of B-H, is chiefly responsible for introducing Islamic fundamentalism in the former Yugoslavia. It required a massive PR campaign and the assistance of numerous U.S. State Department press releases and Pentagon involvement to conceal Izetbegović's past and sell him to the American public. This is how he was depicted in the U.S. press:[10]

> According to *Newsweek* magazine: "The government of Bosnian President Alija Izetbegović ... has always been committed to a multi-ethnic society."[11]

> *Knight-Ridder News Service* reported that: "The Bosnian [Muslims] are struggling for democracy, human rights, and a multiethnic country."[12]

> And Warren Zimmermann, former US Ambassador to Yugoslavia, wrote in *Foreign Affairs*: "Izetbegović was ... a devout Muslim but no extremist, he consistently advocated the preservation of a multinational Bosnia."[13]

The U.S. routinely uses dual track strategies. Izetbegović was praised in order to show the world Muslim community that the U.S. was doing something for Muslims in Europe in Bosnia and Kosovo, which demonstrated its even-handedness, and mollified the fierce criticism the U.S. received from Muslim countries for its close relationship with Israel, as well as its hostility to Iraq. The U.S. also invokes the threat of fundamentalist terror in order to justify military adventures abroad, but it covertly sponsors Muslim terrorism around the world, as it did in Bosnia, Kosovo, Chechnya and Afghanistan.

Mr. Izetbegović was a stubborn man and it was not at all easy to get him to pose in front of the Eiffel Tower in 1995 with a beret on his head for the benefit of the Dayton negotiations. He did not want to do it, but reluctantly agreed in order to cast himself in the role of a latter day French Resistance fighter during WWII. Izetbegović was, in fact, quite the opposite during WWII. Besides being one of the principal recruiters for the Bosnian Muslim Nazi SS Handžar Division, he was an Abwehr agent, and he worked closely with the Gestapo. He was convicted of Islamist crimes after WWII and served a two-year sentence (1946-1948). In 1983, he was again convicted of "hostile and counterrevolutionary acts derived from Muslim nationalism" in Sarajevo. He was sentenced to fourteen years in prison, but ended up serving six years (1983-1988). The Yugoslav prosecutor had charged Izetbegović with conspiracy to make B-H an "ethnically pure Islamic republic."[14]

The question may be reasonably posed: why does the U.S. support Islamic fundamentalism in the former Yugoslavia, while fighting Islamic fundamentalism in Afghanistan and in the Middle East? James Baker put it succinctly: "We only need to oppose Islamic fundamentalism to the extent that it is in our interest to do so."[15] It is regrettable that the U.S. did not oppose the creation of a Muslim fundamentalist state in Bosnia; it created one, instead.

The Islamic Declaration and The Political Program of Izetbegović's Party, the SDA

This section draws on Prof. Miroljub Jevtić's From the Islamic Declaration to Religious War in Bosnia-Herzegovina *(Od Islamske Deklaracije do Verskog Rata u BiH: Filip Visnjic, 1993), which gives an excellent account of the origins of the war in Bosnia.*

After his release from prison in 1988, Alija Izetbegović founded the SDA (*Strana Demokratske Akcije*) as the Yugoslav Muslim Party in March 1990. The name was changed to suit the then-current law that banned the formation of parties along national or religious lines. During the party's inaugural congress, which took place on May 26, 1990 in Sarajevo's Holiday Inn, Izetbegović first prayed in Arabic. The program notes emphasized that the SDA was a religious organization, i.e., "a Muslim Party," and that Bosnia's Muslims were "a native Bosnian nation ... with its own historical name, its own soil under the feet ... and its own religion."

Prof. Jevtić commented on Izetbegović's statement:

> Let us disregard the false claim that Bosnia existed for a thousand years as a separate entity, because from 1463 onward it was part of the Ottoman Empire. Let us also disregard the false claim that a huge part of the present Bosnia was not part of the Ottoman Empire. Much more important is the fact that Izetbegović wanted to claim with this statement that Muslims now living in Bosnia have been there for all

of the thousand years that Bosnia has allegedly existed — as 'a separate political entity' — which is of course not true.

In other words, Bosnia was never a country; it was a region.
The Bosnian war broke out because the SDA could not achieve
its objective peacefully. The war became part of the process of
carving out an Islamic fundamentalist state on the territory of
Bosnia-Herzegovina.

Preporod, the official newspaper of the *mešihat*, the executive
political body of the senior members of Bosnia's Islamic
Community, published a text that had the weight of a *fatwa*, a
judicial opinion about the religious character of the armed conflict. Among other things, it stated:

> Enter the battle … with full confidence in Allah — if you survive, you
> will be *gazija*;[16] if you die, *šehit*.[17] Otherwise, you will lose both.
>
> If possible, enter the battle after taking *abdest*[18] with God's name in
> your heart.…
>
> During an attack on the enemy or during clashes with them, shout:
> *Alahu-ekber!*[19]
>
> If possible, carry a copy of the Koran with you. After all, a Muslim
> must know that he is fighting on the side of justice and on the path of
> God. God's help is guaranteed to such people. No one can defeat a
> Muslim who has Allah on his side. This world as well as the next
> belongs to him.

This was a genuine threat of war, a *jihad*. In addition to this call
to believers, Islamic organizations took many other steps to present the armed conflict as a holy war.

Volunteers needed to be recruited to fight the *jihad*, and
weapons needed to be delivered to Bosnia. Sefko Omerbašić, the
president of the *mešihat* for Croatia and Slovenia, played a significant role in delivering these arms. Policeman from the
Republika Srpska seized huge quantities of weapons that
Omerbašić had sent to fighters in Bosnia-Herzegovina.

Alija Izetbegović published his tract, *The Islamic Declaration: A
Program of Islamization of Muslims and Muslim Nations*, in 1970.
He stated his intentions clearly: "Our goal is the Islamization of
Muslims! Our slogan is: Believe and fight." Izetbegović addressed
the declaration to: "Muslims who know where they belong and
who clearly feel in their hearts what side they are on." This declaration represented a call to action to those people to prepare for the

necessary consequences. Izetbegović warned that the Muslim world was erupting with change, and as these changes spiraled out of control, whatever their outcome, he was certain of one thing: "It will no longer be the world of the first half of the twentieth century. The passive and docile era has ended forever."

Izetbegović estimated that there were 700 million Muslims in the world who were living in servitude. "There is no force capable of stopping a new Muslim generation from putting an end to that abnormal condition," and furthermore, the declaration required that Muslims "move from ideas to organized action to realize these goals."

Set forth below are some representative quotations from *The Islamic Declaration* in which Izetbegović describes the Muslim theocracy he envisioned for Bosnia, which was a step toward the creation of a unified world-wide Muslim caliphate.

> The short definition of the Islamic Order is the unity of religion and law, education and forces, ideals and interests, spiritual community and state, and of voluntarism and coercion.

Izetbegović is describing a theocratic Muslim state that controls all aspects of society and excludes all secular principles. There is no room for secularism in his vision of Bosnia: no public school system, no non-Islamic trade unions, no non-Islamic political organizations, and no non-Islamic mass media.[20]

> As a synthesis of these components, the Islamic Order has two fundamental presumptions: Islamic society and Islamic authority. Islamic society without Islamic authority is imperfect and weak; Islamic authority without Islamic society is either utopia or violence.

This was a veiled threat against the secular order existing in Bosnia-Herzegovina at that time. As we will see from his involvement with the Patriotic League, Izetbegović was prepared for violence long before the Serbs even had a glimmer of an idea that there would be an outbreak of war.

> It is not in fact possible for there to be any peace or coexistence between 'the Islamic religion' and non-Islamic social and political institutions.

Since Izetbegović rules out peaceful coexistence, then Islam is at war with all non-Islamic cultural and political institutions. In other words, it's a permanent war or *jihad* against "infidels."

> Recognition of Allah's absolute ruling power means the absolute non-recognition of any other authority of power.

In other words, secular institutions, the Serbian Orthodox Church, the Roman Catholic Church, Jews and others would be entitled to no recognition beyond their status as *dhimmis*, or officially designated second class citizens.

> The education of the people and in particular, the mass media — the press, radio, television and films — must be in the hands of people who possess impeccable Islamic moral and intellectual authority.

Education and mass media will be under the supervision of and controlled by Islamic councils, in other words, Muslim fundamentalists.

> By announcing this renaissance, we are not announcing a period of security and calm, but a period of unrest and trials. There are too many things that are praying for their destroyers to come. That is why these will be days not of prosperity but days of dignity. Only blows can awaken people who are asleep. Those who wish our community well do not have to spare it from tension, danger, and misfortune. On the contrary, he must do everything in his power so that the community will use all of its forces to test its abilities, to take risks — in a word, not to sleep, but to live. Our community can find itself and its own path only if it awakens and takes action.

This passage stands as an outright call for revolution.

> An Islamic Order can only be established in the countries where Muslims form a majority of the population. Without this majority, Islamic rule is reduced to authority (because the other element, an Islamic society, is missing) and the situation can become violent.

This explains the strategy that Izetbegović had about the use of "ethnic cleansing." On the one hand, Serbs, Croats and Jews had to be driven from territories held by Muslims; on the other hand, Muslims living in Serbian and Croatian areas had to be driven from their homes in order to bolster the population of the Muslim territories and to prove that any communal life with non-Muslims was impossible. Later, when the war broke out, Muslim extremists would disguise themselves as Serbian paramilitaries and threaten Muslim citizens in order to instill antagonism and fear of Serbs.[21]   It was a technique that al-Husseini would have approved of.

> Non-Muslim minorities who form part of the Islamic state enjoy religious freedom and protection, provided, however, on the condition that they are loyal citizens.

Loyal citizens, in this case, is code for submitting to Islamization. Serbian and Croatian troops, who initially fought with the Bosnian Muslims for what they thought was going to be a multi-ethnic Bosnia, found out to their dismay that pressure was put on them to convert to Islam.

> Muslim minority communities who form a part of non-Islamic communities, who enjoy guarantees of all religious freedoms and normal life and development, are loyal and are obliged to perform all their duties toward that community, except for ones harmful to Islam and Muslims.

Many residents of the Sandzak came to Bosnia to fight for the Bosnian Muslims. In fact, they initiated many of the initial attacks against Serbs in Sarajevo. Today, Serbs are being driven from the Sandzak, where mufti Muamer Zurorlić extended holiday greetings to believers last year along with wishes for a pleasant holiday; however, he also drew attention to "certain manifestations" which, in his opinion, represent a threat to Islam in Sandzak. He especially emphasized the point that he sees the events accompanying St. Sava's Day and other similar programs as an attempt to "assimilate" his people. He emphasized that was why he does not accept the invitations of the Serbian Orthodox Church and the Government of Serbia to be a guest at these and similar celebrations.[22] Therefore, Serbs living in the Muslim part of Bosnia would be performing duties that were harmful to Islam and Muslims by observing religious holidays like the feast of St. Sava or Christmas. We have seen such attitudes displayed already in Kosovo, where KFOR has banned the ringing of church bells in the Serbian Orthodox Church of St. Sava in Southern Mitrovica. Tanjug reported this story on May 27, 2001: "Representatives of KFOR introduced this ban with the explanation that Orthodox church bells irritate the Albanians," says Father Velimir. But one can year the call of the muezzins every day, five times a day, from the minarets in the southern part of Kosovska Mitrovica. (*See* "KFOR Forbids the Use of Church Bells," www.pravoslavlje.ru.)

Macedonian and Serbian security forces are increasingly paying attention to the partially Muslim-inhabited Sandzak region, a small, rugged territory straddling the Montenegro-Serbian borders and suspected of supporting foreign and Bosniak mujahideen, as well as Albanian militants from Kosovo.[23]

In January 2005, the Serbian Orthodox Church reported that a group of Muslim youths ambushed and beat up an Orthodox priest, Jovo Andan. Eyewitnesses recognized the son of one of the richest men in Prijepolje among the attackers. This was only the latest in a series of increasingly frequent attacks on Serbs and Serbian Orthodox churches in Raska.[24]

The idea of an Islamic state in this area dates from the time when Muslims arrived as conquerors in Bosnia-Herzegovina, and it was only the military defeat and the retreat of the Ottoman Empire that caused the Islamic state to disappear. The SDA regards the Ottoman Empire and its governing institutions as an inspiration to create a Muslim fundamentalist state in Bosnia. According to Izetbegović:

> The Islamic Order results from the union of religious and socio-political systems. Does the path to the Islamic Order lead to religious renaissance or political revolution? The answer to this question is this: the Islamic revival cannot begin without a religious revolution, but it cannot be successfully realized without a political revolution.

It should come as no surprise that Izetbegović was sentenced to a prison term in 1982 for inciting religious hatred and intolerance. And upon his release, he was the perfect proxy-revolutionary to turn Bosnia into a cauldron of religious hatred and open warfare.

The SDA Organizes War in Bosnia-Herzegovina[25]

The *Patriotic League* paved the way for war in Bosnia. Munib Bisić, then Assistant Secretary of Defense in the Bosnian Muslim government, described the genesis of the Patriotic League.

> Sometime in April 1991, I spoke with a number of people who understood that war in Bosnia-Herzegovina was inevitable. We shared the opinion that it was necessary to organize the defense of the Republic. When I contacted Sule [Sulejman Vranja], we drew up a manual that covered organization and field maneuvers. For the most part, we

> depended upon people from the SDA to seek out sympathizers. Sule
> and his Sarajevan associates named the organization the "Patriotic
> League" in May 1991.
>
> Beginning in September 1991, we noted that former JNA officers
> were enlisting *en masse*. The recruitment was carried out in conspir-
> atorial secrecy through recommendations made by trustworthy indi-
> viduals. The headquarters of the Patriotic League was greatly
> enlarged by the addition of these JNA officers. Almost every county
> in Bosnia-Herzegovina had a local chapter....
>
> The Patriotic League proposed to start the war at the very moment
> when fighting broke out in Croatia. We proposed destroying the
> bridges on the Drina when reservists entered Herzegovina. The polit-
> ical mood would not allow it, however, because Bosnia was not ready
> militarily, politically or psychologically for war. At the beginning of
> this year [1992] the Patriotic League came up with the plan of
> blockading communications and military bases to halt the strategic
> withdrawal of the JNA from its combat positions. Did the Patriotic
> League make a mistake? I think that Izetbegović's variant was
> wiser.[26]

Assistant Secretary of Defense Bisić further stated that two
other similar autonomous organizations existed in Sarajevo at the
time the Patriotic League was founded. These were the "Green
Berets," led by Emin Svrakić, and "Bosna," led by Kerim
Lončarević. Both groups joined the Patriotic League in February
1992.

Sefer Halilović, Chief of Staff of the Bosnian Muslim Army,
also participated in the formation of the Patriotic League.

> In spite of the danger of simply vanishing mysteriously, Sefer
> Halilović painstakingly widened his circle of collaborators through-
> out the entire Republic. [Halilović had been a high-ranking JNA offi-
> cer until then.] Meetings were held on streets, in forests and in
> mosques. At the beginning of the war, the Patriotic League had 9
> regional headquarters, 103 county chapters, and an estimated 98,000
> fighters....
>
> On the eve of war, the Patriotic League held a conference in Travnik
> where it made a proposal to the political leadership of the Republic to
> provoke armed resistance throughout the Republic as soon as the first
> inch of territory was attacked. But the political leadership had anoth-
> er idea and Bosanski Brod and Bijeljina[27] happened....[28]

Members of the Patriotic League had sent *jihad* fighters to
Bosanski Brod and Bijeljina.

Lieutenant Mustafa Mlinarić also served in the Patriotic League, and described how he and his fellow jihadists learned the secrets of guerrilla warfare:

> There were a lot of rumors about the Patriotic League, and about how we had to defend ourselves. So I made up my mind in January 1992. A couple of us left for military training, which was facilitated by Emin Svrakić. The training lasted for twenty days in an inconspicuous town in Croatia.[29]

Mevludin Smajić was a member of the Department of Security in the headquarters of the Bosnian Muslim Army. Smajić described his involvement in the purchase and delivery of weapons and explosives in the summer of 1991:

> You can imagine how dangerous it was to travel through Croatia, which was at war last summer. I procured weapons on the orders of the Patriotic League. Every other day I drove explosives from Vitez![30]

Smajić further described the intensity of Muslim military preparations. He brought 120 kilograms (263 lbs.) of explosives to Sokolac and distributed it to his fellow "patriots," and showed them how to make bombs. In December 1991, he worked on forming units, enlisting fighters, distributing weapons, sending people out in the field, reconnoitering the area around Romanija.[31] In January 1992, a Patriotic League unit was formed in Sokolac that numbered 866 members, 40% of them armed.

Osman Brka was a founding member of the Board of Directors of the SDA. He had intimate knowledge of the SDA's military actions. As early as 1993, he felt comfortable saying that:

> Everything that was done in the defense of Bosnia was the work of the SDA. The formation of the Patriotic League as well as the first armed resistance were led by people from SDA.[32]

Faruk Jazić was the president of Crisis Headquarters in Vratnik, the old part of Sarajevo. The Crisis Headquarters was among the first to be organized, and that as early as March 23, 1992 an order was issued forbidding the movement of JNA military vehicles; when the military base in Zmajevac was evacuated, the residents of Vratnik sent a whole column to Kovaci, where a large *dženaza*[33] was held. A JNA military convoy carrying weapons was stopped, and as Jazić says, "We lifted the weapons." Jazić added:

> When it started, we were the only ones who were organized because we had been preparing for it for months. We had organized a medical corps, amateur radio operators and soup kitchens…. 1,250 of us were armed in Vratnik.[34]

Sefer Halilović summed up Alija Izetbegović's role in the SDA preparations for war this way:

> The SDA established the Patriotic League and other formations that not only served as the core of the politically unaffiliated, non-SDA army, but as the state army, the Bosnian Muslim Army of Bosnia-Herzegovina. The role of President Izetbegovic and his closest aides was decisive in all phases: organization, armament, international support and assistance, among other things.[35]

Alija Izetbegović, as president of the Republic of Bosnia-Herzegovina, summed up his preparations for the war in this fashion:

> On June 10, 1991, right before the war in Slovenia and Croatia began, and ten months before the outbreak of war in Bosnia, the SDA held a conference of leaders from all parts of Bosnia, where it formed a National Defense Council. That was the famous conference in the Militia Building in Sarajevo. The newly formed council was put in charge of the Patriotic League as well as preparing people for defense and providing them with arms. If it weren't for that, Bosnia would have quietly failed; in this manner, the thunder of our resistance could be heard to high heaven.[36]

The Clinton Administration Creates a New Muslim State in Europe

Michael Moore, in his film *Fahrenheit 9/11*, made much of the Bush family's business connections to the Saudis, and made it seem as though a Democratic victory in the 2000 presidential race might have saved us from 9/11. Nothing could have been further from the truth. The Clinton administration had just as many unsavory connections to Islamic fundamentalism, and fostered its growth in Bosnia, Kosovo and Macedonia[37] after the Reagan administration had created the global *jihad* in order to use them as proxy forces in a war against the Russians in Afghanistan. Zbigniew Brzezinski, the architect of the policy, has yet to recant it or recognize the terrible repercussions the West has suffered and will continue to suffer. Srdja Trifkovic quoted Mr. Brzezinski on the subject:

> A year earlier, in his now famous interview with *Le Nouvel Observateur*, Dr. Brzezinski described how the Carter Administration had instigated Islamic resistance to the pro-Soviet government in Afghanistan and thus maneuvered Moscow into military intervention. Asked if he had any regrets about the consequences of that operation, Brzezinski was indignant:
>
> B: Regret what? That secret operation was an excellent idea. It had the effect of drawing the Russians into the Afghan trap and you want me to regret it?
>
> Q: And neither do you regret having supported the Islamic fundamentalism, giving arms and advice to future terrorists?
>
> B: What matters more to world history, the Taliban or the collapse of the Soviet empire? Some stirred-up Moslems or the liberation of Central Europe and the end of the cold war?
>
> Q: Some stirred-up Moslems? But isn't Islamic fundamentalism a world menace today?
>
> B: Nonsense! There is no global Islam.[38]

The Official Dutch inquiry into the alleged Srebrenica massacre contained some of the most shocking revelations ever made public about western intelligence operations. Professor Cees Wiebes of Amsterdam University was granted the freedom to explore the archives of the Dutch intelligence services. He published his findings in *Intelligence and the War in Bosnia, 1992-1995*,[39] an exhaustive study that includes confidential interviews with high-level diplomats and military personnel who questioned the prevailing views of the Bosnian War. Prof. Wiebes gives a clear account of the clandestine alliance the Pentagon forged with Islamic fundamentalist groups in order to assure the Bosnian Muslims of an artificial victory. These Islamist groups are, indeed, the very same ones the U.S. is supposed to be fighting in the "war against Terrorism."

"I found there was much sympathy for the Bosnian Muslims, especially among journalists; and sometimes I think there is an inclination to silence things that do not fit with their view of the war." concluded Prof. Wiebes. "Some people seem pissed off that I did not take sides over the war in Bosnia. I suppose I was more interested in reporting all of the facts,"[40] Prof. Wiebes frankly confessed.

Richard J. Aldrich, a Professor of Politics at the University of Nottingham, revealed Prof. Wiebes most sensational findings in an article for *The Guardian* (UK):[41]

1) The U.S. was providing the Bosnian Muslims with militarily support because the Pentagon owed Islamists groups for their help in both Afghanistan and the Gulf. By 1993, these groups, supported by Iran and Saudi Arabia, were calling in their debts with the Americans. Bill Clinton and the Pentagon wanted to prove their creditworthiness and paid them back with an operation modeled on Iran-Contra, which was in complete violation of the UN Security Council arms embargo against all the combatants in the former Yugoslavia.

2) The resulting secret arms pipeline was arranged by the secret services of the U.S., Turkey and Iran along with a variety of radical Islamist groups that smuggled weapons through Croatia.

3) The U.S. was "very closely involved" in transporting not only weapons but mujahideen fighters who were used as shock troops for especially hazardous operations.

4) The volume of weapons clandestinely flown into Croatia was enormous because the Croatian government imposed a stiff "transit tax," and took 20% to 50% of the weapons right off the top as payment. This was easy to do because the clandestine flights flew from Teheran to Zagreb. The Croats also illegally obtained arms from Germany, Belgium and Argentina.

5) The German secret services were fully cognizant of the illegal trade in weapons.

6) The Pentagon was behind these operations. UNPROFOR relied on the U.S. and other nations that contributed troops for intelligence. This allowed the Pentagon to manipulate the embargo by having American AWACS turn a blind eye to the frequent nightime flights. When Norwegian officials noticed these shipments, the Americans pressured UNPROFOR to rewrite the reports, and "when Norwegian officials protested about the flights, they were reportedly threatened into silence."

7) Iranian and Afghan veterans had established training camps in Bosnia. The Dayton Accords, which were signed in November 1995, stipulated that these foreign forces be withdrawn. The CIA's principal opponents in Bosnia were now the mujahideen fighters whom the Pentagon was supporting and supplying with arms only a few months earlier.

8) Meanwhile, the secret services of the Ukraine, Greece and Israel had been arming the Bosnian Serbs. Mossad was particularly active, and provided substantial supplies of artillery shells and mortars in exchange for securing the safe passage for the Jewish population out of Sarajevo.

The Dutch government resigned because of the report, however, it soon became apparent that the purpose of the report was not to document an alleged massacre in Srebrenica but to reveal U.S. intrigues with Islamic fundamentalists in order to circumvent the embargo on weapons shipments to the Bosnian Muslims. The corporate media tried to put us at ease by claiming that Prof. Weibes' revelations "did not alter the known facts," however, it is self-evident that these revelations do alter the known facts. Mossad knew what was going on, and they were aware of the Serbs' long standing friendship and identification with Jews, and, of course, could count on the Serbs' help to get Sarajevo's Jews out safely because Sarajevo was becoming increasingly hostile to them. The mainstream media, however, rewarded the Serbs by persuading American Jews to side with the Bosnian Muslims, by using the outrageous proposition that the Bosnian Muslims were "victims of genocide" just as Jews had been during WWII. James Harff, director of the Ruder-Finn public relations agency which handled the Bosnian Muslim account, explained how it was done.

> We outwitted three large Jewish organizations: the B'Nai Brith Anti-Defamation League, the American Jewish Committee, and the American Jewish Congress. We suggested that they publish an advertisement in *The New York Times* and organize a protest at the United Nations. It worked out wonderfully well; Jewish organizations joining the fray on the side of the Bosnian Muslims was an extraordinary winning bluff. We were immediately able to identify the Serbs with the Nazis in public opinion.[42]

The Serbs never wanted to be pawns sacrificed for better positioning on the grand chessboard, and they fought to desperately prevent such a sacrifice from taking place. In the meanwhile, radical Islamists consolidated their power base. "Russian and Yugoslav intelligence sources claim that more than 150 Islamist radicals from more than 50 countries held a secret congress in Travnik, Bosnia and Herzegovina."[43]

The Stratfor article revealed that Islamic fundamentalists were settling their internal quarrels in order to conduct a focused *jihad* against the "European race," namely, Americans and Europeans because they have become "voluntary slaves to Israeli Jews." They were planning a "powerful strike" against the EU. Bosnia has become a global Islamist forward base because the U.S. is still officially siding with the Bosnian Muslims against the Serbs, despite the fact that the Serbs were the first to fight al-Qaeda's incursions into Europe. Bin Laden viewed the former Yugoslavia as a key element in al-Qaeda's global strategy. The "powerful strike" against the EU materialized in March 2004, about a year and a half after this Stratfor report was written: it was the brutal Madrid attack.

Yet official media reports kept denying that Bosnia was fertile soil for Islamic fundamentalism. In Bosnia, NATO troops nabbed a fellow named Sabahudin Fijuljanin, a thirty-two-year-old Muslim. Authorities found a rocket propelled grenade launcher in his apartment and a variety of passports in his own name.[44] The article padded the story with the mantra that it was important not to confuse Bosnian Muslims, who were the victims of "genocide in Srebrenica," with Muslim fanatics from Saudi Arabia and terrorists from other Muslim countries. This is rather disingenuous because Sabahudin Fijuljanin is a Bosnian Muslim name. Denials such as these preponderate in western media coverage.

In another instance, the U.S. and Saudi Arabian governments did agree on something besides a petroleum deal. In December 2002, they together requested that the UN designate Vazir, an NGO which was a branch of a Saudi charity, as a terrorist entity, and to add its representatives to the list of individuals linked to al-Qaeda.[45] U.S. authorities recovered a list of 20 financiers suspected of funneling money to Osama bin Laden and other extremist Muslim causes. The cache of documents provided insight into the financing of terrorism.[46]

More documents were seized in March 2002 from the Bosnian offices of the Benevolence International Foundation, an Islamic charity based in Illinois. Authorities found a list of donors and the money transfer structure. Even though the head of the suburban Chicago office, Enaam Arnaout (who is a Jordanian national, however, his name is Albanian) had proven al-Qaeda contacts, he was allowed to plead guilty to lesser charges of illegally buying boots and uniforms for mujahideens in Bosnia and Chechnya. In exchange for his cooperation, charges that he aided bin Laden were dropped.

Washington, however, has paid little or no attention to the Balkans since the 9/11 attacks, and it has been hedging its bets. Clinton administration appointees are still running Bosnia, even though they risk allegations that they aided and abetted al-Qaeda, which may soil the current image of the Bosnian Muslims as innocent victims of Serbian aggression. The Bosnian Serbs have long argued in vain that the reappearance of Islamic fundamentalism in Bosnia means the extermination or forced conversion of all Christians to Islam, and that Islamic fundamentalism in the Balkans can blow up in Washington's face at any time. Even so, Bosnia's International High Representative, Paddy Ashdown, has dismissed such allegations as "insulting and inaccurate prejudices from afar" and reiterated his belief that Bosnia "is not a terrorist base nor will it become one…. Those of us who live in the Balkans have yet to see any evidence of Islamic terrorism."[47]

"Tolerant" Islam

Articles in the mainstream media routinely characterize the Ottoman occupation of the Balkans as an example of "tolerant Islam." The phrase conjures images in the Western mind of liberal Protestants, Reform Jews, Freethinkers. What, may one venture to ask, did such "tolerant Islam" actually tolerate? It tolerated the eating of pork and the drinking of *rakija* (brandy) among its Serbian, and to a lesser extent, Croatian converts. It certainly did not tolerate Jews and Christians (either Orthodox or Roman Catholic).

The Serbs have traditionally viewed themselves as "the bulwark of Christianity." A brief sketch of Islam, its history, its beliefs, and its growth at the expense of non-Muslim neighbors over the centuries will explain why the Serbs have regarded themselves as defenders of Christian Europe.[48]

Islam is not merely a "religion." It is an all-encompassing way of life that pervades all aspects of society and its political and legal affairs. The principal tenet of the faith is: "There is no God but Allah, and Mohammed is His Prophet."

The Koran's principal theological belief is Allah's absolute omnipotence. The free will of human beings, central to Western thinking, is denied. Any idea of freedom apart from total submission to Allah is impossible. Freedom, as we Americans understand it, is a sin.

Mohammed established the "five pillars" of Islam that form the basis of its practice. Srdja Trifkovic pointed out that "all but one — *jihad*, are rooted in pre-Islamic, pagan beliefs and practices. Jihad is Mohammed's one fully original contribution to humanity."

The Koran incites the believers against infidels. And Mohammed applied such unified theory and practice to the three Jewish tribes of Medina, whom he destroyed, and thus established a model for all future relations between Muslim conquerors and non-Muslim subjects. Even modern Muslim scholars believe that Islam must one day rule the world, and that Muslims will continue to sacrifice their lives until it does.

The victims of the casual cruelty of the Ottoman occupiers were *dhimmis*, officially designated second class citizens who were not allowed to own property or bring lawsuits against Muslims, among other things. A Muslim who killed a *dhimmi* was not subject to severe punishment, if any at all. This was how Christian communities in the Mediterranean and Southern Europe were beaten down and eradicated. Some, like the Serbs, endured centuries of agony resisting Islamization. In each case, the Islamic goal was to subjugate Christian majorities by turning them into religious minorities. Taking the case of India, Pakistan, before Partition, had a twenty-five percent Hindu minority in 1941. By 1991, the Hindu minority had dwindled to 1.5%.

The Western mainstream media has been reluctant to characterize the Bosnian Muslim's war against the Serbs as a *jihad*. But the Muslim media had no such compunctions. Pakistani Parliamentary leader Qazi Hussain Ahmed demanded that President Musharaf enact within Pakistan his call to the Organization of Islamic countries for Muslim unity. He cited Alija Izetbegović as a Muslim who devoted himself entirely to the liberation of his "country."

> He revealed that Pakistan had given its unqualified support for the Bosnia 'war of independence'. "He [Izetbegović] visited Pakistan and the government gave him everything he demanded for *jihad*."[49] [Emphasis added.]

Former Information Minister Syed Mushahid Hussain had revealed earlier that the Pakistani government had provided arms to Bosnian insurgents.

> "We went to Bosnia with our Prime Minister Nawaz Sharif and supported their cause. Later we gave them arms for their *jihad*," he said. Former Foreign Minister Sartaj Aziz said that the Bosnian *jihad* was the greatest fight in European history and Muslim leaders should follow the life of Ali Izat Begovich.[50] [Emphasis added.]

And how does the mainstream media address this point? Witness this rebuttal to charges that al-Qaeda was recruiting "white" mujahideen from the Balkans to carry out attacks in Europe and the United States:

> Balkans Islamic scholars told Reuters the "white al Qaeda" scare relies on ignorance of the faith and of Muslim gratitude for America's role in stopping Serb aggression.[51]

If statements like these were not enough, here is the conclusion of the Reuters article:

> The soil for extremism, as Ashdown said, is no more fertile here than in U.S. or Western European cities where the September 11 hijackers planted their cells. Even if it were, tolerating extremism would be the fastest way to kill U.S. support for united Bosnia and Kosovo's hopes of independence from Serbia.[52]

Paddy Ashdown, in addition to being a despotic ruler, is a clever politician: he knows how to pitch a tough sell to the skeptical Western public. It's a great deal easier to do than to admit that the entire occupation of Bosnia was misconceived, born of imperial hubris and folly, and that it is equally deadly to both Serbia and the United States in the long term. It is easier to lie outrageously than to admit that Western civilization, if such a thing exists any longer, has taken a viper to its breast.

The United States tacitly approved of the arrival of thousands of Arab-born mujahideen to the former Yugoslavia in the early 1990s to serve as shock troops in the opening assaults against the Orthodox Serbs in Bosnia. Many of these mujahideen were inspired to go to Bosnia by Osama bin-Laden, who portrayed their role as defenders of the Muslim population in their *jihad* against Orthodox Serbs and Roman Catholic Croats. (*See* "Pofalići" in the Appendices on p. 519 for three eyewitness accounts of the first mujahideen attack in Europe.)

Osama bin-Laden provided direct financial support to the Bosnian Muslims at first, and later to Kosovo Albanians. It is, to say the least, paradoxical that the U.S. entered a marriage of convenience with bin Laden and his supporters in these instances. We may legitimately ask, what is the principle of American foreign policy? Upon closer inspection, we will see that there is none. There are only U.S. interests that must be protected, and the business of protecting such interests. Therefore, U.S. public officials are free to say anything to anyone to sustain the American Empire.

Set forth below is a summary of al-Qaeda involvement in terrorism that connects Bosnia to global terrorism.[53]

Links to Osama bin Laden

1. French authorities arrested Christian Ganczarski, a German-born convert to Islam, on June 6, 2003. French intelligence services determined that Ganczarski was in personal contact with bin-Laden himself. Ganczarski was phoned by an al-Qaeda suicide bomber minutes before the suspect blew himself up at a Tunisian synagogue in April 2002. Ganczarski made several visits to Afghanistan and Bosnia.

2. Karmim Medhi (34) is a Moroccan national who was arrested by French authorities at Charles de Gaul Airport. He was reported to have links to the Hamburg cell that had ties to the September 11 attacks in New York. Medhi was planning to attack tourist centers in Reunion, a French territory in the Indian Ocean. Sources reported that Medhi had received mujahideen training in Afghanistan and in Bosnia. He is also reported to have been an associate of Ziad Jarrah, a member of the Hamburg cell who died during the 9/11 attacks aboard Flight 93 that crashed in a Pennsylvania field.

3. The Bosnian Embassy in Vienna issued Osama bin Laden a Bosnian passport in 1993.[54]

4. Osama bin Laden was connected to an arms smuggling fiasco that took place in the Maribor (Slovenia) airport in 1992. Four cargo planes from the Sudan carrying humanitarian supplies were subjected to security checks. More than 100 tons of weapons destined for Bosnia (still under an arms embargo at the time) were discovered.

5. The arms confiscated in Slovenia at the Maribor airport had been ordered by Elfatih Hassanein, a Sudanese citizen and head of Third World Relief Agency (TWRA), a humanitarian organization based in Vienna. Alija Izetbegović (a personal friend of Hassanein) provided guarantees for TWRA to open a bank account in Vienna in 1993.

6. Enaam M. Arnaout, (see page 182), who became an American citizen in the early 1990s, received Bosnian citizenship just a few years later. Arnaout was indicted for leading a criminal enterprise

that took charitable contributions from unsuspecting American Muslims and funneled them to bin Laden's al-Qaeda network. In his offices, the FBI found military manuals for small arms and explosives, photographs of bin Laden and Arnaout together, as well as photographs of Arnaout holding a shoulder-fired rocket launcher.

7. On December 14, 1999, Ahmet Ressemi, an Algerian national, was arrested at the U.S.-Canada border crossing in British Columbia with a van full of nitroglycerin and bomb-making materials. Apparently, he intended to blow up a major building in the U.S. to kick off the new Millennium. Ressemi had ties with former members of the "El Mujahadeen" unit that served in Bosnia.

Links to September 11

8. Abu Zabair al-Haili (a.k.a. Mohamed Haydar Zammar, "the Bear"), a German citizen of Syrian descent, was the chief organizer of the Hamburg al-Qaeda cell that aided and abetted the 9/11 hijackers. He honed his craft as a senior commander of a Mujahideen battalion that served in Bosnia. Incidentally, his a.k.a., "Mohammed Haydar," is the way Adolf Hitler's name has been translated into Egyptian Arabic.

9. German investigators discovered that Abu Zabair al-Haili or "Mohamed Haydar Zammar," as the case may be, brought Mohammed Atta, the pilot of one of the planes that crashed into the World Trade Center, into the al-Qaeda network.

10. Nawaf Alhazmi and Khalid al-Mihdhar were aboard the American Airlines Flight 77 that crashed into the Pentagon. They were Saudi militants who had served as mujahideen in Bosnia.

11. "'Thirteen of nineteen hijackers who destroyed the World Trade Center buildings in New York and attacked the Pentagon were in Kosovo-Metohija and Bosnia. For a while, they were in the house of an American citizen of Bosnian origin', said Dr. Miroljub Jevtić, a Political Science Faculty Professor and expert for Islam."[55]

12. French military doctor Patrick Barriot, defense witness at the trial of former president of Serbia and Yugoslavia Slobodan Milošević before the Hague Tribunal, presented a French intelligence document which stated that Muhammad Atta, pilot of a plane that hit the World Trade Center in New York on September 11, 2001, was in Bosnia-Herzegovina on three occasions between 1994 and 1999. Both Milošević and Col. Barriot, who serves on the anti-terrorism task force of the French government, said that this document offered proof of "deep-rooted Islamic terrorism in Bosnia."[56]

Other Mujahideen Alumni from Bosnia

13. Bosnian police arrested an Egyptian national who was suspected of belonging to Jamaa Islamiya, a banned Islamic extremist group. The suspect was traveling with his wife and three children. The suspect, identified by his initials, J.A., had held Bosnian citizenship which had been revoked during the crackdown in 2001. Jamaa Islamiya took responsibility for the attack in Luxor, Egypt, which killed 58 German tourists.[57]

14. Ahmad Omar Saeed Sheikh, 28, a UK-raised and educated Muslim of Pakistani origin, received the death sentence for his role in luring *Wall Street Journal* reporter Daniel Pearl to his death in Pakistan. Omar visited Bosnia, where he was radicalized. *Time* magazine[58] reported that the man who actually beheaded Daniel Pearl was Khalid Shaikh Mohammed, a Kuwaiti of Pakistani origin. U.S officials believe that Mohammed was a key organizer of the 9/11 hijackings. Mohammed served as a mujahideen fighter in Bosnia in 1992.

15. "Abdulaziz Issa Abdul-Moshin al-Muqrin is a well-known Saudi al-Qaeda leader who is the most wanted man in Saudi Arabia. He is a veteran of the war in Bosnia and one of a hit squad that tried to kill Egyptian President Hosni Mubarak in Ethiopia in 1995. After two years in prison, he was extradited to Saudi Arabia."[59] He orchestrated a shooting spree in Khobar, Saudi Arabia on June 6, 2004, that killed twenty two people. He was killed on June 18, 2004 after his group claimed responsibility for beheading American Paul M. Johnson, Jr.

16. The director of the the the Republika Srpska Police, Dragomir Andan stated that 11 of the individuals responsible for the terrorist attacks on Madrid on March 11, 2004 "were trained in Bosnia-Herzegovina." He went on to say that "the detonators used in the attacks were produced in BiH."[60]

Al Qaeda is also staging a general mobilization to combat U.S. forces in Iraq. The Syrian route draws al Qaeda operatives from Central Asia, Chechnya, the Balkans — mainly Kosovo and Bosnia — Saudi Arabia, the Gulf states and even Iran.[61]

The Bosnian Serbs

The origin of al-Qaeda has often been traced to the Afghan war of 1979-1992, but few writers and journalists care to mention that these leftover fighters migrated to Bosnia to fight against the Serbs. Their invasion of Bosnia gave them valuable cross-border experience. Thus, Western intervention in Bosnia globalized the mujahideen.

> The Bosnian war taught Islamic terrorists to operate abroad. For all the millions of words written about al-Qa'eda since the 9/11 attacks two years ago, one phenomenon is consistently overlooked — the role of the Bosnian war in transforming the mujahideen of the 1990s into the roving Islamic terrorists today.[62]

Serbia is the focal point for increasing Islamist-controlled territory in Europe. The caliph's design is to create a fundamentalist Muslim region consisting of Bosnia, Kosovo, Macedonia and adjacent areas that will re-integrate the Green Highway leading into Europe. This is the greatest opportunity Islamists have had since the siege of Vienna in 1683, and they are fully aware of it.

> Numerous Islamist sources have indicated that they believe that this "return to Europe" is now within their grasp, offering enormous political symbolism of the success and power of the radical Islamists to the Muslim world, particularly if such an achievement is made as a result of great loss by the West.[63]

The Bosnian Islamist Senad Memić admitted to Yugoslav state security officials in 1991 that Sarajevo Muslims made deliveries of arms and ammunition to Raška (the Sandžak region) with the consent and support of Alija Izetbegović's party, the SDA. Hasan Čengić, another SDA official who had served with the 13th Waffen SS division of the German Army during WWII, had direct ties with Iranian terrorists. He is an Islamic theologian, who was later a general in the Bosnian Muslim Army. He arranged for the influx of foreign mujahideen fighters into Bosnia during the 1990s and was a member of the management committee of TWRA (Third World Relief Agency). He has been implicated in a variety of al-Qaeda sponsored terrorist groups. Western interventionists focused on the task at hand, but not on the long-term consequences, insuring that their moral blind spot with respect to Bosnia would remain.

> [F]rom their enthusiasm with using imported Islamic fighters in not only Bosnia but Kosovo, one would suspect that the policy makers had forgotten about the Afghan experience of the 1980s; lamentably, they would only remember it after September 11th, 2001. Hopefully they won't suffer more persistent and vivid reminders than that of this bad decision in the years to come.[64]

Novi Pazar (in the Raška region of Serbia) is the center of the Muslim fundamentalist effort to construct a land bridge from Albania and Kosovo to Bosnia. If the Serbian government, however, were forced to suppress an uprising in the Sandžak, it would once again be blamed for a "genocide against Muslims" there.

Richard Holbrooke, who once held the position of America's chief Balkans peace negotiator, a title which can now be regarded humorously in retrospect, remarked that the arrival of the mujahideen was a "pact with the devil." Is Holbrooke just reaching for a convenient metaphor or is he at all aware of the consequences Faust suffered when he signed such a pact?

The Clinton administration soon discovered that it was much easier to sponsor the growth of mujahideen than to curb their newly discovered power. Despite the obvious new vulnerabilities to which he was exposing the West, Clinton again sided with Islamic fundamentalists during the Kosovo War against Christian Serbia. "It seems that, for all its hand wringing, the USA just couldn't break the pact with the devil."[65]

Zenica was and still remains a key base for al-Qaeda. Mujahideen fighters were reorganized as a special, foreign legion unit within the Bosnian Muslim Army. Al-Qaeda was supported by the Bosnian government, which provided Zenica's large Vatrostalna Factory building for its headquarters. The "Clinton administration was presented with a classified ... report on the Bosniak issue; it warned of a problem of such size and scope that it 'shocked everyone'."[66] Secretary of State Albright was then brought in to lay down the law to Izetbegović, who was told that "the entire U.S.-Bosnia relationship will change from friends to adversaries" if foreign mujahideen were not expelled from Bosnia."[67]

> Izetbegović later turned up in Zenica to preside over a Bosnian army military parade where "10,000 Bosnian troops and several allied 'elite units' (including foreign mujahadeen) marched in front of Izetbegović and his commanders shouting *Alahu Akhbar!* and 'American tanks will not scare us!'" Later, Izetbegović wrote an angry letter to his senatorial friends, Bob Dole and Joseph Lieberman, that it is "incompatible with the moral principles of our people to expel the people [al-Qaeda] who fought on our side."[68]

So much for Clinton's attempts to remove al-Qaeda from Bosnia.

"Ultimately," concluded Mr. Kohlmann, the author of this article, "American and European demands for the Bosnians to cast out their former Arab-Afghan allies went substantially unfulfilled until even after 11 September 2001. By then it was already too late — generations of new foreign mujahideen were given safe haven, training, financing and ideological inspiration by supposedly demobilized al-Qaeda fighters hiding in Bosnia."

Yossef Bodansky[69] noted that Al-Muhajiroun, a London-based Islamist organization that acts as one of bin Laden's principal European media outlets, issued a statement that explained why the UN building in Baghdad was attacked:

> Verily it was the UN soldiers in Bosnia who were recorded to have stood by when the barbaric Serbs massacred Muslims. The UN first decided to take away the weapons of the Muslims (fearing that they might actually defend themselves and establish Islamic rule) and thereby facilitated their massacre, and were then even photographed helping in the mass murder and gang rape of Muslim women and children. The wounds are still fresh.[70]

Bodansky remarked that this statement was meant to bolster the media lie that 7,000 Muslims had been killed in Srebrenica, even though hard forensic evidence points to Muslim casualties that are far lower. By repeatedly asserting such an inflated numbers of Muslim casualties in Srebrenica, Islamists divert attention from the Muslim massacres of Serb civilians in Srebrenica.

Bodansky also emphasizes that such statements, along with the opening of the Potočari Memorial, which he refers to as "an Islamist shrine" for the alleged victims in September 2003, "all support analysis that a significant new wave of terrorism, this time by many European Islamists, is to begin soon."[71]

Why is Bosnia conspicuously absent from accounts of the rise of the mujahideen? First of all, it is embarrassing. Secondly, its denial. Many commentators, especially liberals, built their reputation on selling Western intervention in Bosnia as "the right thing to do." To this day, questioning the unimpeachable integrity of Western intervention in Bosnia remains taboo.

Stratfor.com analyzed the U.S. situation in the Balkans in the following fashion.[72] The U.S. war against the Islamic world is three-dimensional in nature. It is being waged domestically in the U.S. against foreign terrorists; it is being waged in Islamic countries where fundamentalists struggle against their own governments; and it is being waged along the frontiers of the Muslim countries where non-Muslims are engaged in battle. This means Palestine, Chechnya, the Philippines and the Balkans.

Washington viewed the Milošević regime as the problem, and treated the matter as a police action in order to contain a nation that was not adhering to international norms of behavior. Washington sold the Balkan Wars of Succession, especially the Kosovo War, as "humanitarian efforts" that ultimately benefited trade and stability. Washington portrayed itself as not taking sides. Despite its neutrality, it was siding with underdogs against a "rogue state," Serbia.

Intervention was, nevertheless, seen as taking the side of the Muslims. No one in the Balkans could understand Washington's reasoning. Various reasons were given: the Saudis had promised to cut the price of oil; the Israeli's needed negotiating room with the Palestinians; it was a message to Russia that the U.S. was backing the Chechens.

Stratfor, however, believes that President Clinton, Secretary of State Albright and National Security Advisor Sandy Berger simply blundered. They assumed that the U.S. was facing no major threats. They did not foresee 9/11 or the imminent confrontation with the Muslim world. In short, they designed the Bosnian and Kosovo interventions without reference to the three-dimensional nature of the conflict.

But the U.S. intervention on behalf of Islamists in Bosnia and Kosovo has not even given Washington any credibility with Islamists because it did not address al-Qaeda's interests. Clinton never could link the intervention to a war in favor of the Muslim world. The U.S. believed that it was intervening on behalf of stability instead of Islamic forces, and the Clinton administration could not admit to the obvious.

> Clinton sided with the KLA in order to protect a \$40 billion investment by an international oil consortium in Azerbaijan. He behaved the same as he did in Bosnia and sided with Muslim fundamentalists. And Clinton walked away from the war with a smile on his face, because he was able to negotiate the construction of a trans-Balkan pipeline from Burgos in Bulgaria to the port city of Durres in Albania. Camp Bondsteel in Kosovo is meant to provide security for this pipeline.[73]

Now the problem has grown ten-fold. Mujahideen have established themselves in Albania and Bosnia. Peacekeeping forces stationed there are insufficient in numbers to be effective in defending themselves against attacks. "The region could explode in Washington's face at any time."[74]

The paradoxical conclusion Stratfor reached is this: If Islamic fundamentalists strike in Bosnia or Kosovo or elsewhere in the region, the U.S. and the EU must take action. And the only regional power that has an interest in controlling Islamic expansion is Serbia. "Different time, different regime, but same national interests. What could happen is that, in the end, the United States must rely on the Serbs to deal with the current war."[75]

> The sands have now shifted. The Serbs are being asked to fight Muslim terrorists once again. This time they would be in a different league as minor players on a different team. The Serbian government should not be surprised if there is not a rush of Serbs to offer help to the U.S.A. which had attacked them almost five years earlier in their fight against Albanian terrorists in Kosovo.[76]

ENDNOTES

[1] "Alija Izetbegovic," by Vojin Joksimovich, srpska-mreza.com.

[2] *Ibid.*

[3] "Jihad, Then and Now, Parts I & II," by Srdja Trifkovic, Islam, the West, and the Serbs: Matica Srpska, September 11, 2003, chroniclesmagazine.org. This paragraph and the next one draw from Mr. Trifkovic's article, which is well worth reading in its entirety.

[4] "Dark Humour for Dark Times," by Stephen Evans, *BBC News*, 10/16/04.

[5] "Bosnia and Herzegovina: Bocinja — Camp for Training Islamic Terrorists," seeurope.net, 09/25/03.

[6] Quotations for this section have all been drawn from "Islam under the Swastika," by Carl Savich, serbianna.com.

[7] *Ibid.*

[8] www.answers.com/topic/amin-al-husayni.

[9] *Ibid.*, which cites "The Quest for the Red Prince" by Michael Bar-Zohar and Eitan Haber, 1983, as its source.

[10] The following three quotations are drawn from "Who was Izetbegovic? Moderate Democrat or Radical Islamist?" by Francisco Gil-White, *Emperor's Clothes*, tenc.net, 3/10/03.

[11] *Newsweek*, December 18, 1994, U.S. Edition, National Affairs, p. 32, "Sarajevo on the Spot," by Russell Watson and Rod Nordland.

12 "Bosnia Suffers Genocide as the World — And America — Remains Silent," by Jennifer Scarlott, Knight Ridder/Tribune News Service, Dec. 21, 1993.

13 "The Last Ambassador: A Memoir of the Collapse of Yugoslavia," by Warren Zimmermann; *Foreign Affairs*, March-April 1995, v.74 n.2, p. 2.

14 "Islam, Catholicism, and Orthodoxy: The Civil War in Bosnia-Herzegovina, 1992-1995," by Carl Savich, 2002, serbianna.com

15 *Le Soleil d'Allah aveugle l'occident*, by P-M Gallois, 1995; also quoted in *Liar's Poker: The Great Powers, Yugoslavia and the Wars of the Future*, by Michel Collon: *op. cit.*, p. 181.

16 *gazija* (Ar.), a hero in war; a conqueror.

17 *šehit* (Ar.), a Muslim who dies a heroic death while fighting for his faith; a martyr.

18 *abdest* (Persian), ritual washing performed by Muslims before prayer.

19 *Alahu-ekber* (Ar.), "God is great!"

20 "Who Was Izetbegović? Moderate Democrat or Radical Islamist?" by Francisco Gil-Whitel, *Emperor's Clothes*, tenc.net, 3/10/03.

21 See *Report about Case Srebrenica* (the 2002 Srebrenica Report issued by the Republika Srpska), p. 102.

22 "Growing Islamic Fundamentalism in Raska district (Sandzak)," *Apis Group*, Belgrade 2/1/04.

23 "Terrorism in the Balkans — Enter Sandzak?", by Christopher Deliso, balkanalysis.com, 10/24/04.

24 "Muslim Youths Attack Orthodox Priest in Serbia's Sandzak," *BBC Monitoring* (source: SRNA), 1/31/05.

25 This section is also drawn from Prof. Miroljub Jevtić's book, From *The Islamic Declaration to Religious War in Bosnia-Herzegovina* ("Od Islamske Deklaracije do Verskog Rata u BiH," Filip Visnjic, 1993).

26 Oslobođenje (9/13/92)

27 *Bosanski Brod and Bijelina*, two Bosnian towns that fell to the JNA.

28 "Walter Again Defends Sarajevo," *Naši Dani* 9/25/92. Walter was one of Tito's code names during WWII.

29 *Večernje Novine*, 7/23/92.

30 "The Story of a Patriot," *Oslobođenje*, 9/24/92.

31 *Romanija*, a mountain in Bosnia, east of Sarajevo, covered with forests and pasturelands, and traditionally inhabited by Serbs.

32 *Naš Svijet*, September 1993.

33 *dženaza* (Ar.), a Muslim funeral procession.

34 *Oslobođenje (Muslimansko)*, 8/4/93.

35 "The SDA — The Pillar of the State-Building Conscience of the Bosnian Muslims," an interview with Sefer Halilović, *Ljiljan*, 6/15/94.

36 "Thousands of People Carry Our Flag and Will Continue to Carry It," *Ljiljan*, 2/14/94.

37 *See* "Clinton-Approved Iranian Arms Transfers Help Turn Bosnia into Militant Islamic Base," Congressional Press Release, U.S. Congress, 1/16/97.

38 "1204 and All That: Turning Allies Into Foes," by Srdja Trifkovic, chroniclesmagazine.org, 12/14/04

39 *Intelligence and the War in Bosnia, 1992-1995*, by Cees Wiebes, LitVerlag, Munster, Hamburg, London, 2003.

40 *See* "The Battle al-Qaeda Hasn't Lost Yet," by M. Bozinovich, serbianna.com.

41 *See* "Americans Used Islamists to Arm the Bosnian Muslims," by Richard J. Aldrich, *The Guardian* (UK), 04/22/02.

42 See *Liar's Poker*, by Michel Collon, *op. cit.*, p. 36, which cites *Toutes les verités yugoslaves ne sont pas bonnes à dire*, by Jacques Merlino (Albin Michel: Paris, 1993), pp. 128-129.

43 "Islamist Militants May Seek to Unite, Strike in Europe," 10/16/02, stratfor.com.

44 "Bosnia Peace Force on Alert for al Qaeda," by Guy Taylor, *The Washington Times*, 12/15/02.

45 "U.S. and Saudi Arabia Request UN Designation of Bosnian 'Terrorist' Group," 12/24/02, menareport.com.

46 "Bosnia Raid Yields al-Qaeda Donor List," by John Simon, *AP*, 02/19/03.

47 "Al Qaeda Bogeyman at Work as US Rethinks Balkans," by Douglas Hamilton, *Reuters*, 06/10/03.

48 *See* "Jihad, Then and Now, Parts I & II," by Srdja Trifkovic, Islam, the West, and the Serbs: Matica Srpska, September 11, 2003. The next six paragraphs summarize key points from Mr. Trifkovic's article.

49 "Pakistan Provided Bosnians with Arms," by Khurram Shahzad, 10/16/03, dailytimes.com.pk.

50 *Ibid.*

51 "Al Qaeda Bogeyman at Work as US Rethinks Balkans," by Douglas Hamilton, *Reuters*, 06/10/03.

52 *Ibid.*

53 This list of points is drawn from "Bosnia, 1 degree of Separation from Al-Qaeda," Analysis, July 2003, balkanpeace.org.

54 *Dani* (Bosnia), 09/24/99.

55 "Al Qaeda Roams in Serbia," *Nacional* (Croatia), 05/12/04.

56 "Patrick Barriot testified in the Hague Tribunal: Terrorist from New York Was in Bosnia," *Blic*, (S-M), 1/13/05.

57 "Suspected Egyptian Islamic Extremist Arrested in Bosnia," 08/01/03, *Agence France-Presse*.

58 "Who Killed Daniel Pearl?", *Time Magazine*, 2/3/03.

59 "Militants Give Blow-by-Blow Account of Saudi Massacre," Jason Burke, *The Observer* (UK), 6/6/04.

[60] "Bosnian Serb Police Chief Says Madrid Terrorists Trained in Bosnia," *BBC Monitoring*, 5/10/05.

[61] "Al Qaeda Mobilizes All Its Forces for Iraq," 8/26/03, *DEBKA-Net-Weekly*, debka.com.

[62] "How We Trained Al-Qa'eda," by Brendan O'Neill, *The Spectator* (UK), 09/12/03.

[63] "The Coming New Surge in European Islamist Terrorism: The Momentum Has Begun," *Defense & Foreign Affairs Strategic Policy*, September 2003, pp. 9, 12-13 , by Gregory R. Copley, Editor.

[64] "Al Qaeda's European Attack Route Is the Balkans, New Report Claims," by Christoper Deliso, 10/30/03, balkanalysis.com.

[65] "How We Trained al-Qa'eda," by Brendan O'Neil, *The Spectator* (UK), 9/12/03.

[66] *Al-Qaeda's Jihad in Europe*, by Evan F. Kohlmann, Berg Publishers, 2004, quoted in "The Battle al-Qaeda Hasn't Lost Yet," by M. Bozinovich, serbianna.com.

[67] *Ibid.*

[68] *Ibid.*

[69] "Osama bin Laden Focuses on the Balkans," by Yossef Bodansky, *Defense & Foreign Affairs Strategic Policy*, 09/19/03.

[70] Al-Muhajiroun Press Release, 8/24/03, almuhajiroun.com.

[71] "Osama bin Laden Focuses on the Balkans," by Yossef Bodansky, *Defense & Foreign Affairs Strategic Policy, op. cit.*

[72] "The Balkan Theater of Operations," stratfor.com, 09/22/03.

[73] "Which Shoe? Which Foot?" by William J. Hutton.

[74] "The Balkan Theater of Operations," stratfor.com, op. cit.

[75] *Ibid.*

[76] "Which Shoe? Which Foot?" by William J. Hutton.

Ustashi, Murderer Monks, Ante Pavelić and the Modern Croatian State

by Milo Yelesiyevich

Roman Catholicism is one of the world's great religions. It has served as a beacon for faith for millions of believers throughout the world. The following discussion of the WWII Croatian Ustashi puppet state of necessity must take into consideration the conduct of the Roman Catholic clergy as well as that of the Franciscan Order. It is not this present writer's intention to open wounds, insult believers or bash Roman Catholics. Nevertheless, vital historical facts have been suppressed, and even though their discussion may at first be painful, it is unconscionable to remain silent. Hubert Butler called the clero-fascist campaign to murder, expel and convert Orthodox Serbs, Jews, and Roma from Croatia "the most bloodthirsty religio-racial crusade in history, far surpassing anything achieved by Cromwell or the Spanish Inquisitors."[1]

In 2004, the Vatican issued a formal apology for the sacking of Constantinople during the Fourth Crusade. One earnestly hopes that less than eight hundred years will pass before the Vatican issues an apology and seeks forgiveness for the crimes committed in its name during the Ustashi regime in Croatia, however, the following pages suggest that such an apology is not forthcoming. If this is the case, then Christians of all denominations must ask themselves if the faith is all but dead, because secularists will never pose the question in the first place. It is worth recalling the words of the late Byzantine historian, Steven Runciman, who remarked that Roman Catholicism and Protestantism have reformed themselves to such an extent that if such "reform" continues unimpeded, the Orthodox will then be the only remaining Christians a hundred years from now.

The Ustashi[2] and Croatian Serbophobia

The Serbs never had a history of racism or anti-Semitism. The Serbian idea of national identity rests fundamentally on the concept of a people instead of a race precisely because history compelled the Serbs to migrate so often.

Nevertheless, a growing Croatian nationalist movement began to cultivate Serbophobia as one of the essential planks of its political platform. Such hatred, which had earlier been espoused chiefly by the Croatian clergy, Austrian Jesuits and the Austro-Hungarian government, took broad, popular dimensions with Ante Starčević

Ante Starčević (1823-1896), a Croatian historian, is considered the father of the Croatian nation. He was the founder of the Croatian national doctrine and dreamed of establishing Croatia as the most powerful country in the Balkans. This Croatian state would be founded on two main principles: an alliance with Austro-Hungary and anti-Serbian racism.

> To Starčević we owe the thesis, albeit a fantastic one, that Croats are of Iranian decent, therefore "Aryans." He was the first to write that the only remedy for Serbs was "an ax in the neck," and that for "this foul race, everyone is at once a judge and executor, as for a rabid dog."[3]

During WWI, the Austrians made it a policy to breed and sustain animosity between the Croats and Serbs who were living within their dominions because Austria was fighting a war with Serbia and Montenegro. Austria's goal was to block the creation of a unified Serbian state that would, of course, have included the Serbian areas of Bosnia-Herzegovina. Austria also formed an alliance with Bulgaria, which, despite being an Orthodox country, was Serbia's traditional enemy because it did not want a large unified Serbian state on its borders. Austrian foreign policy traditionally sought to pit Serbia and Bulgaria against each other in order to poison their relations.

Austria, in order to advance this policy, supported a new Serbophobic movement that took root in Croatia in 1884. Josip Frank, a Jewish convert to Roman Catholicism, established an organization called the *Pravaši* or the *Frankovci*. This was an extremist Croatian nationalist movement established to sow hatred between Serbs and Croatians. Its members included the Zagreb elite, Roman Catholic priests, provincial petit bourgeoisie, and criminal elements from Croatian society who organized local terror gangs.

> One of its members in the early 20th century was Ante Pavelić, later to become the head of the so-called "Independent State of Croatia." These Frankovci were used by the Austrians for terrorizing the Serbian inhabitants of Bosnia, where they succeeded in murdering quite a few Serbian clergy.[4]

The Serbs lost one-third of their population in WWI. Despite the massive destruction, Serbs shared their war reparations with the Croats and the Slovenes, both of whom were former Austro-Hungarian territories and had fought against Serbia but whose territories had not been ravaged by warfare.

After WWI, many Croatian intellectuals, inspired by pan-Slavism, actively sought to create a common state with the Serbs. This resulted in the creation of the state of Yugoslavia in 1919. However, Ante Pavelić redefined and regrouped the Frankovci as a terrorist organization that would be known as the Ustashi. Pavelić was preoccupied with training recruits in Italy and Hungary. Anti-Serbian and anti-monarchist terrorist groups were established in Bulgaria, just outside the border with Macedonia, and some of them forged alliances with the Ustashi. In 1934, Pavelić helped establish a terrorist training camp in Janka Puszta in Hungary, where assassins trained to kill King Alexander of Yugoslavia. These terrorists enjoyed the protection of the Horthy government in Budapest.

King Alexander of Yugoslavia was assassinated in Marseilles on October 9, 1934, along with French Foreign Minister Louis Barthou. At the time, the assassins were described as Bulgarians but they were later revealed to actually be Croatian Ustashi. One of the organizers was Ante Pavelić, who ten years later became *poglavnik* (Führer) of the Independent State of Croatia, Hitler's puppet state during WWII.

> Pavelić was sentenced to death by the French court *in absentia* because he was being held in an Italian prison in Turin. During his eighteen months of imprisonment, Pavelić wrote a novel called *The Lovely Blonde*, which gives many details of how the assassination was prepared and carried out.[5]

The death of King Alexander threw the country into turmoil. His son, Peter, was in his teens, so a regency was established, which was headed by Prince Paul, who was not well liked. He favored Western European culture and felt out of place in Yugoslavia. The Regency signed two unpopular agreements: 1) the Concordat with the Vatican, which granted the Roman Catholic Church privileges that were denied to the Orthodox Church; and 2) the Sporazum, which created the autonomous *banovina* of Croatia, which included territories where there was a majority Serbian population. And even this legislation did not appease the Croats. Not a week passed after the Sporazum was signed before WWII broke out.

On March 25, 1941, the Regency succumbed to German pressure and signed the Tripartate Pact with Germany and Italy (i.e., Hitler and Mussolini). Spontaneous demonstrations broke out all over Serbia. The demonstrators chanted, *Bolje rat nego pakt* ("War is better than the pact"), and *Bolje grob nego rob* ("The grave is better than slavery"). On March 27, 1941, a group of officers carried out a *coup d'etat*. Prince Paul fled the country, and one week later Serbia was at war with Nazi Germany. The Serbs were aware that they would lose, but they preferred destruction to treachery and dishonor. The eminent military historian John Keegan described the Serbian revolt as "one of the most heroic acts of defiance to tyranny in European history."

Hitler was enraged, and ordered the bombardment and invasion of Yugoslavia.

On Easter Sunday, April 6, 1941, Belgrade was attacked by 450 German bombers, and fell to Nazi troops on April 17. 20,000 people died during that one day of bombardment, which is more than the entire number of people killed during the London Blitz. Serbs fought the invading Nazi armies but were defeated by overwhelming force and Croatian sabotage. The National Library was bombed, and thousands of mediaeval manuscripts vanished. By standing at the top of the fortress in Kalemegdan Park, one can see precisely where the Luftwaffe bombed by the new buildings that cover the devastation.

On April 14, the Yugoslav command surrendered, but the Yugoslav government declared on May 4 that it would continue its struggle against the occupiers. The resistance was led by Draza Mihailovich, which was the first organized resistance movement to fight the Nazis.

German troops entered Zagreb on April 10, where they were greeted with wild enthusiasm. On that day, Ante Pavelić proclaimed the Independent State of Croatia (*Nezavisna Drzava Hrvatske* ("NDH")). Many Croats were blinded by chauvinism, and enlisted in the invader's armies. Ustashi took public oaths in Roman Catholic churches, and swore to exterminate the Serbs and eradicate Orthodoxy. Archbishop Alojzije Stepinac of Zagreb gave his blessing to the new Croatian state and promised to collaborate closely with it. In this fashion, Archbishop Stepinac reigned over a strange unification of fascist and Roman Catholic ideologies. The horror of the Nazi genocide lay in its emotionless undertaking of the mass extermination of Jews, however, the Ustashi genocide was primitive and sadistic, and it was characterized by the pleasure taken by Ustashi in torturing and murdering their victims.

The Ustashi stood out in sinister prominence during the Nazi invasion. They directed military attacks on the rear guard of Yugoslav units, and carried out fifth-column activities that disrupted the Yugoslav army. The chaos created by Roman Catholic extremists was so effective that it resulted in being one of the principle factors in allowing the swift Nazi conquest of Yugoslavia.

Hitler rewarded the Croats for their loyalty, and they quickly became the Nazi's staunchest ideological and military allies. Proof of this was the fact that Croatia raised the largest army in proportion to its population of any Nazi ally. Hitler drew boundaries for Croatia that included Serbian lands with a population of 2.5 million, thus fulfilling the Vatican's goal of "liberating" Roman Catholic Croatia. The Nazi puppet state occupied the territory that is today comprised of Croatia and Bosnia-Herzegovina, as well as the Srem region going all the way to Belgrade.

The Genocide

Ante Pavelić passed a decree on April 30, 1941 that took the Nuremberg laws as a model. It declared Croats to be Aryans. The first massacres of Serbs began at the same time.

Mile Budak, Minister of Education and Religion, stated in an address delivered in Gospić on July 22, 1941: "We shall kill some of the Serbs, we shall expel others, and the remainder will be forced to embrace the Roman Catholic religion. This last part will in due course be absorbed by the Croatian population." These edicts were inspired by the legal decree Ante Pavelić passed on April 30, 1941. Andrija Artuković,[6] the Minister of Internal Affairs, issued an order banning "Serbs, Jews, Gypsies, and dogs" from entering parks and restaurants, and from using public transportation in Zagreb. Soon the private as well as public use of the Cyrillic alphabet was banned, and Serbs were ordered to wear an armband with the letter "P" (for *Pravoslavac,* i.e., Orthodox). One Roman Catholic periodical praised Pavelić as an Ustashi *Krizar* or "Crusader":

> Raised in the spirit of radical Catholicism, which knows no compromises as far as principles are concerned, that never knew what it meant to give in or abandon any part of the program of Croatian nationalism.[7]

Thus, the master plan for the conversion and/or extermination of the Serbs was launched. The Roman Catholic clergy placed this program in the tradition of the mediaeval crusades that were undertaken to destroy the enemies of the Roman Catholic Church. Archbishop Stepinac regarded the Serbs as schismatics, an evil "almost greater than Protestantism." In 1944, a Berlin newspaper wrote:

> An extraordinary ecclesiastical struggle is going on in Croatia. The Ustashi government is persecuting the Orthodox Church and is trying to convert as many Orthodox people as possible to Catholicism by means of intimidation and all kinds of devices. At the opening of the so-called Croat Assembly, Pavelić said that religious freedom did exist in principle, but it did not include the Orthodox Church. Apart from nationalistic reasons, Pavelić endeavored to represent himself as a missionary by virtue of his work on behalf of the church, thus desiring to acquire greater prestige. We still recall his visit to the Pope at the time when he was just organizing his 'State'.[8]

A diary entry outlines the first meeting Stepinac had with the *poglavnik*, and points out his agreement to the elimination of rival faiths:

> The Archbishop gave his blessing for his work.... When the Archbishop had finished, the *poglavnik* answered that he wanted to give all his help to the Catholic Church.... He went on to say that he would not show tolerance toward the Orthodox Serbian Church because, as he saw things, it was not a church but a political organization. All this left the Archbishop with the impression that the *poglavnik* was a sincere Catholic....[9]

The persecution of Serbs began immediately following the Ustashi seizure of power on April 25. The Ustashi massacred 184

Serbian peasants at Gudovac near Bjelovar on April 27-28 and 250 at Blagaj in Kordun. On May 11-12, the Ustashi massacred 300 Serbs in Glina; in early June, 140 Serbs were massacred in Ljubinje in Herzegovina; and 180 were killed in Korita near Gacko. The Ustashi repeated this massacre pattern throughout the NDH, which was especially pronounced in Serbian-inhabited areas of Croatia and Herzegovina. The Ustashi drew their strongest support from these regions.

The Ustashi would come to a town and summon the Serbs to assemble. They would then order them to convert to Roman Catholicism. Those who declined to convert, as most did, were ordered to assemble at the local Orthodox church. The Ustashi would arrive, lock the parishioners in the church, and set it on fire.

The Ustashi killed their victims in a bestial manner. They rounded up 173 Serbs in the Herzegovinian town of Nevesinje in May-June 1941. These people were tortured before being killed:

> they were set upon with hammers, picks, rifle butts and knives; the
> had their ears, noses, sexual organs and fingers cut off; their eyes
> gouged out; their hair, beards and eyebrows ripped out and stuffed in
> their mouths.[10]

"Anyone who cannot rip a baby out of its mother's womb with a knife is not capable of being a good Ustashi," said Ante Pavelić to his troops.[11]

> In the town of Orocar, the Ustashi officer Ivan Sajfer arrested the
> Orthodox priest, Branko Dobrosavljevic, who was a Serbian repre-
> sentative, along with his son and 331 other Serbs. The criminal had
> them executed by hatchets. The priest and his son were tortured last:
> the child was hacked to pieces before his father's eyes, who was then
> obliged to recite a prayer for the dying.[12]

More than 100,000 people were killed in June 1941.

> Mass executions were common where the victims had their throats
> slit, were sometimes quartered, and also now and then hung in butch-
> er shops with the sign: "human flesh." Cruelties occurred along side
> of which the deeds of the German thugs of the KZ paled by compar-
> ison. The Ustashe loved games of torture with nightly orgies; they
> stuck burning nails under fingernails, poured salt into open wounds,
> cut off all possible body parts and determined by noble competition
> who was best at cutting throats. They burned churches full of people,

impaled children in Vlasenika and Kladany, preferred to cut off noses and ears and poked out eyes. The Italians photographed one Ustashe around whose neck hung two chains of human tongues and eyes.[13]

When Ustashi started losing control of the highland mountain regions, it became increasing more difficult to carry out village massacres. Therefore, the Ustashi regime focused its efforts on concentration camps to eradicate the non-Roman Catholic population. Twenty-two camps were established on the territory of the NDH. The largest camp was Jasenovac, and it was second only in size to Auschwitz. According to the Simon Wiesenthal Center, approximately 600,000 prisoners, predominantly Serbs, were killed there.[14] The Nuremberg Tribunals used the figure of 750,000 Serbs, 75,000 Jews and 50,000 Roma killed in Jasenovac. Historians call this camp the "Auschwitz of the Balkans." It was conveniently located on the Belgrade-Zagreb train line which facilitated bringing victims to the site, which was just north of the juncture of the Una and Sava rivers. Here, the Croatian government conducted the mass torture and extermination of hundreds of thousands of men, women and children. Jasenovac also had the only known concentration camp exclusively devoted to children. This children's camp was operated by Roman Catholic nuns who would "rescue" a small number of children marked for death in order for them to be raised as Roman Catholics. The Nuns organized a "Benevolent Society" by the name of "Caritas" (whose continuing existence is itself shocking) to conduct these activities.[15] It was without a doubt the most barbaric and inhumane episode of WWII. Even Nazi SS troops were appalled by the savagery.

A prisoner at the women's camp in Stara Gradiska, Marijana Amulić, offered the following eyewitness testimony of the murder of Serbian children:

> The children were lying there helpless, even too weak to cry. They were dying slowly and quietly. About 20 female prisoners, themselves as helpless as the children, were taking care of them. Once we were ordered to fetch all the sick children and to house them in the attic rooms of the infamous tower. Then Ante Vrban, the commandant of the camp, had poison gas injected into the rooms. Then there was an eerie silence in the camp, as if life itself had been extinguished.[16]

Jasenovac, as well as half the other twenty two camps, were administered by Roman Catholic priests. The Croatian government had established a committee to collaborate with Pope Pius XII's personal representative, Mgr. Marcone, to conduct the two-pronged policy of forced conversions and extermination of the Serbian Orthodox population. Archbishop of Croatia, Alois Stepinac, served as Supreme Military Apostolic Vicar of the Ustashi Armies and was a member of the Croatian government throughout the war. Ante Pavelić met several times with Pope Pius XII in 1941 and 1943 at the height of the genocide. Stepinac was pleased with the new regime, and praised its new laws that handed out the death penalty for abortion and thirty days in jail for swearing.[17]

Croatian society cannot be held solely responsible for the genocide. Evidence suggests that they would not have pursued a policy of genocide if it had not been for the constant urgings and calls for blood made by Roman Catholic priests and other religious leaders. The slaughter of the Serbs was bitterly ironic because they were the only ethnic group in Europe recognized as having no anti-Semitic history. Furthermore, the Orthodox faith does not engage in missionary work or seek converts.

The Croatian government next forged an alliance with Bosnian Muslims in the NDH. The Vice-President of the NDH was a Bosnian Muslim, Osman Kulenović from Bihać. He was succeeded by his brother, Džafer Kulenović, who held the post from November 1941 to April 1945. "Džafer Kulenović ordered that the Serbian Orthodox Church at Brčko be destroyed, the cemetery dug up, and the bones of the Orthodox Serbs be dispersed. In the Croat-Muslim NDH, not even the dead were spared."[18]

Kurt Waldheim, two-term United Nations Secretary-General, was elected president of Austria in 1986. He had concealed his wartime activities in Yugoslavia. In 1942, *oberleutnant* Kurt Waldheim was an ordnance officer serving in the 714th Infantry Division of the German Army (*Wehrmacht*) at the time of the Kozara action, one of the most brutal acts of genocide and ethnic cleansing committed during World War II in western Bosnia against the Orthodox Serbian population. Approximately 68,600 Serbian Orthodox civilians, including 23,800 children from the Kozara region were driven from their homes and resettled in concentration camps. About 140 Serbian villages were depopulated and leveled to the ground.[19] Waldheim was never tried for the war crimes he committed against the Bosnian Serb population.

In January 1942, the engineer Hinko Picili converted the tile oven in a factory into a crematorium that incinerated the dead as well as the living. Sado Cohen-Davko explained that first the inmates were shut in a building beside the crematorium:

> Here the prisoners were ordered to strip, in order to bathe and be disinfected. The poor women and children had no idea where they were going. At the exit, behind the door, there stood two executioners with mallets. As each passed through for "disinfection," he was hit by one with a mallet and another immediately threw him half-dead into the oven. This oven swallowed up a good thousand victims, especially women and children.[20]

The Jasenovac concentration camp had a number of commanders between 1941 and 1945, but Frater Miroslav Filipović-Majstorović, a former Roman Catholic friar, known as "Brother Satan" (*Fra Sotona*), who was in charge of Jasenovac from June to October 1942, was most often noted for his cruelty and savagery. He was ordained a Roman Catholic priest in 1939, and served as a chaplain in an Ustashi brigade which massacred over 2,200 Serbian civilians near Banja Luka. He was accused of inciting this mass murder of Bosnian Serbs, and was brought before a German military court. But Vjekoslav Luburić, another Jasenovac commander, brought him to Jasenovac on June 10, 1942. Filipović-Majstorović, who was tried as a war criminal after the war, admitted that he oversaw the extermination of at least 30,000 inmates. Ivica Brkljačić, another former priest, replaced Filipović-Majstorović as commandant of Jasenovac in 1943.

Jasenovac survivor Egon Berger recalled an incident where Filipović-Majstorović seized children from three women, who begged for mercy and offered themselves in place of their children. According to Berger:

> They threw two children to the ground, and the third into the air like a ball. Fra Majstorović, holding a spike pointing upwards, pierced it three times, while the fourth time, to the accompaniment of both lamentation and laughter, the child remained impaled on the spike. The mothers were thrown to the ground, tearing their hair, and when

they began a terrible screaming, Ustashi of the 14th Osijek Company
took them off and liquidated them.[21]

Another Jasenovac commandant, Ljubo Miloš, was also known
for his sadism. Miloš, according to survivor Jakov Atijas,
"stabbed a Serb in the chest with his dagger and saying that
'Serbian blood is sweet' drank it from his palm." Egon Berger
observed how fourteen-year-old Croat children were brought to
the camp "with the aim of training them to be murderers." Berger
described the murder of five Serbian Orthodox priests at
Jasenovac:

> Five Orthodox priests were led out.... They were ordered to sing
> hymns.... One of them, a man of over eighty, ... was immediately beat-
> en with rifle butts... One of the Ustashi — a child of twelve years old
> — bent over the old man, and took out his dagger. In a moment, he
> had cut off both the priest's ears. He turned grinning to his compan-
> ions, saying: "I'll show them at home tomorrow what sort of ears a
> Vlach priest has!" The Ustashi seized the other four.... Miloš set their
> beards on fire. Then, after such terrible tortures, they killed them.[22]

As the war drew to a close, the Ustashi blew up the camp and
killed most of the remaining inmates in order to destroy evidence
of their crimes. Tito demolished the crematorium and remaining
buildings in 1948, which left virtually no trace of the death camp.

What was the total number of the victims of Jasenovac? In
1952, the Union of Jewish Councils of Yugoslavia, relying on the
reports of Jewish survivors, concluded that, in the Jasenovac
camp alone, "500,000-600,000 people were slaughtered, among
whom were about 20,000 Jews." Menachem Shelah in *The
Encyclopedia of the Holocaust* (1990) gives the following figure:
"Some six hundred thousand people were murdered at Jasenovac,
mostly Serbs, Jews, Gypsies, and opponents of the Ustashi
regime. The number of Jewish victims was between twenty thousand and twenty-five thousand." The Ustashi commander at
Jasenovac, Frater Miroslav Filipović-Majstorović, during questioning after the war, stated that "according to reports of Maks
Luburić ... about a half million Serbs were killed in the NDH during these four years."

Archbishop Stepinac did, however, personally intervene to
save a small number of Jews and Serbs from the Ustashi. This led
Pavelić to secretly appeal to the Vatican for Stepinac' removal.

Since then, Croatian nationalists have appealed to the Israeli Yad Veshem to add Stepinac name to the role of the Righteous because of such intermittant acts of humanitarianism, but their petition has been refused not once, but twice.[23]

In the later years of the war, when the tide had turned against Germany, Stepinac' hatred of Communism became his *idée fixe*. His notion of Catholic Croatia as a bulwark against Orthodoxy was replaced by the idea that Croatian independence had to be upheld at all cost as a bastion against godless Communism. When defeat was looming for the Ustashi, he took control of the archives and a portion of the gold that the Ustashi had looted.[24]

Franjo Tudjman, however, claimed in his book, *The Wasteland of History*, that "about 60,000 perished in all the camps and prisons." According to Tudjman, only 30,000 victims died at the Jasenovac camp.

Franjo Tudjman and Resurgent Croatian Fascism

Franjo Tudjman was Tito's youngest general during WWII. During his service for the Partisans, thousands upon thousands of Ustashi switched sides and joined the Partisans in 1944 when the tide of the war had turned against them.

Tudjman, much like his Bosnian counterpart, Alija Izetbegović, acted as a historical bridge between the Nazis and his modern state. His book, *The Wasteland of History*, effectively denies the Jewish Holocaust ever took place, and claims that only 900,000 Jews died at the hands of the Nazis.

The Simon Wiesenthal Center remarked on the dangerous political signals President Tudjman began sending after and his nationalist party won a majority in the Croatian Parliament in 1990. A Wiesenthal Center press release noted that Tudjman had reduced the number of Jewish victims of the Holocaust from six million to one million in *The Wasteland of History*, and Tudjman stated that historical data about Jasenovac is "inflated." He further alleged that Jews participated "in the liquidation of gypsies in Jasenovac," and accused Jews of having taken "the initiative in preparing and provoking not only individual atrocities but also a 'mass slaughter' of non-Jews, Communists, Partisans and Serbs...." The press release also noted that: "Meanwhile, the new Croatian Democratic Union (CDU) [Croatian abbrev. "HDZ"] government has taken steps to form a special police force made up of ethnically 'pure Croats without mixture of other blood'."[25]

It was a long road for Franjo Tudjman. He had served two prison sentences on charges of nationalism after his falling out with Tito. Professor Nora Beloff, who covered the Balkans for many decades for the British press, had this to say about him:

> By the time I first met him in 1980, he was already *pathologically anti-Serb*. He has allowed himself to be *surrounded by ustasha sympathisers*, many of them returning from Canada and Australia.[26] [Emphasis added.]

President Tudjman began arming his supporters as soon as he took office. Even though they were unable to attack majority Serbian areas in Croatia, which were well defended, they made life for Serbs all but impossible in areas where Croats were the majority. At first, Serbs had to take loyalty oaths to Croatia or lose their jobs. Then they were fired anyway. Serbian homes were burned down. Professor Beloff noted:

> Tens of thousands fled long before the federal army and the international community intervened.... Zagreb simply turned its back on the past. *Today again, the Ustasha flag has been raised....*[27] [Emphasis added.]

By 1991, Croatian Jewish leaders were unanimous in reporting that they found disturbing parallels between the Nazi and Ustashi massacres that took place during WWII and the current nationalist regime that was seeking to break away from Yugoslavia. This provoked anxiety among Croatian Jews. In August 1991, bombs were set off in a Jewish community center, and bombs damaged a Jewish cemetery in Zagreb, where Jews began receiving death threats and were subjected to other forms of intimidation.

> "What worries us is that those in power in Croatia NOW are largely *the same as during the Nazi era*," said Dr. Klara Mandic, a senior Jewish community leader.... "In some cases they are *exactly the same people*, now in their seventies and *back from exile* under the Communists. *In other cases, they are the children of the ustasha.*"[28] [Emphasis added.]

One of the Jews interviewed said that the Croatians were wearing "the same black shirts, the same black trousers," and that many carried knives they called by the old Ustashi expression

"Serbo-seks" (Serb cutters). "Tudjman ... has prepared an atmosphere similar to that at the start of the Second World War."[29]

Many found this reunion of former WWII allies, Germany and Croatia, repulsive. By 1994, the Croatian government had fully resurrected the accouterments of the Nazi puppet regime of the early 1940s. Streets and squares were renamed after Ustashi heroes. The *kuna*, the currency in use during the fascist era, came into use again; the Croatian flag was once again adorned with the *šahovnica*, the red and white checkerboard heraldic shield that symbolized the Nazi puppet state, a symbol which would have been equivalent to the recently reunited German state adopting the swastika as its national symbol. The Croatian government then made the first of many proposals to rebury the Ustashi dead alongside the Serbian and Jewish victims of Jasenovac and the other twenty-two Croatian concentration camps. Croatian citizens found themselves to be a living in a police state. Independently-minded newspaper and magazine editors received invitations to visit the police offices who could offer them "guidance." Mr. Kenneth Roberts, author of the *Spectator* article quoted below, was at a loss to explain the "lack of international reaction to the *resurgent fascism so evident* in the building of the new nation." [Emphasis added.] He continued his dismal appraisal of the new Croatian state.

> British suggestions of economic sanctions on account of Croatia's military involvement in Bosnia have been repeatedly blocked by Germany.... Germany is siding with Croatia ... former partners in tourism and *genocide*. On the American side, *there are none so blind as those who will not see. Swastikas, black uniforms, rape and pillage* fade into insignificance beside the demonic image the State Department has built for the Serbs.[30] [Emphasis added.]

After the current Independent State of Croatia revived all the Ustashi paraphernalia, it then revived its other hallmark: state sponsored atrocities toward Serbian civilians. Simultaneously, Franjo Tudjman pursued an official policy of falsifying Croatia's participation in the Holocaust during WWII. A historian writes histories with original documents and research assistants; Franjo Tudjman rewrites history with a spade and a team of gravediggers.

Tudjman persisted in his efforts to rebury Ushashi murderers along with their victims. For Tudjman, the Ustashi extermination of Serbs, Jews and Roma was a burdensome and inconvenient relic of ancient history, which was the reason Tudjman sought to minimize the number of victims. Tudjman was quoted as saying that the generally accepted figure of six million Jews dying in the European Holocaust was based on "emotionally biased testimonials and exaggerated data." Tudjman also claimed that typical Jewish traits included "selfishness, craftiness, unreliability, miserliness, underhandedness and secrecy." Tudjman was criticized severely for these remarks, and later apologized for them, but these were empty words without any accompanying deeds, and he kept trying to realize his plans for Jasenovac anyway. The memorial, he said, would be "a tribute to all the victims" on Croatia's "way to independence and sovereignty" and that it would reconcile "the dead as well as the living, their children and grandchildren." (*See* "Impending Extradition Forces Croatia to Tackle Its Past," by Judith Gruber, 5/15/98, *Jewish Telegraph Agency*.) And he offered a straightforward justification: "Because of historical and also current political reasons, the Jasenovac memorial should be altered so as to become a memorial of all Croatian war victims." Tudjman wanted to persuade a new generation of Croatians, as well as the rest of the world, that the remains of all the victims of WWII in Croatia were morally equal. He wanted to bestow the innocence of the victims on those who had murdered them. Thus, the Ustashi regime could be rehabilitated. Meanwhile, he rehabilitated the reputation of the Ustashi regime's murderous leader, Ante Pavelić.

Such actions by Tudjman would profane sacred ground. Worse, it would obfuscate what actually happened there for future generations of Croatians, who might simply assume that there were no mass killings, no Holocaust, and that there were never any Serbs in Croatia. Such a forgery would inspire other European countries to revise their own Holocaust histories. The Croatians were risking all on this gambit. Their country was polluted by the blood of Serbs, Jews and Roma from WWII, to which the most recent carnage in the 1990s has been added.

Despite vigorous protests, Mr. Tudjman was invited to the opening of the Holocaust Memorial Museum in Washington, D.C. as an honorary guest. Not one Serb was invited. Not one![31]

In 1991, two Serbs prepared English and French translations of Tudjman's book, which was later published in English as *The*

Horrors of War: Historical Reality and Philosophy (*Bespuća povjesne zbilje*) (M. Evans and Company, revised edition, 1997) after it was heavily revised to remove objectionable anti-Semitic passages and his denial of the Jewish Holocaust. The book was practically an apologia of Germany's as well as Croatia's policies toward Jews during WWII. *Publishers Weekly* reviewed the book, and had this to say: "Morally and intellectually, this book ranks somewhere between O.J. Simpson's *I Want to Tell You* and Sammy Gravano's *Underboss*, and seems to draw inspiration from Lewis Carroll's Wonderland queen, who asserted that when she used a fact it meant only what she wanted it to mean."

When the book first appeared in 1989, the Jews of Europe and the U.S. took note of its anti-Semitism. Tudjman's fellow Croatians were long familiar with his public pronouncements on these matters, as when he remarked before his election in 1990 that he was happy that his wife had no Serbian or Jewish blood.

In his book, President Tudjman said that the "final solution" for the Jews had to be viewed in terms of Germany's ambition to rule Europe: "For this reason the establishment of Hitler's new European order could be justified by the need both to remove the Jews (undesirable more or less in all European countries) and to correct the French-British wrongs of the Versailles system."

President Tudjman came up with some gems that did not survive in the American edition of his book. He sought confirmation in the Old Testament that, for the Jews, "genocidal violence is a natural phenomenon, in keeping with the human-social and mythological-divine nature. It is not only allowed, but even recommended." And Tudjman was generous with his praise for the Austrian government, which became his principal supporter and arms supplier in his quest to create a 'nation': "In the mid-80s, world Jewry still has the need to recall its 'holocaust', even by trying to prevent the election of the former UN Secretary General, Kurt Waldheim, as president of Austria." Yet he tastefully omitted the fact that Waldheim served in occupied Yugoslavia, and aided the Croatian Nazi puppet state.

> It is here that Tudjman's book becomes really repulsive…. the communist government after the war did not allow a proper investigation of the Ustasha atrocities. The communists did not want to acknowl-

> edge that what they called an "anti-fascist" struggle was really a religious massacre on a scale unparalleled in history.[32]

Tudjman made an important point when he claimed that we do not know the full truth about Jasenovac. But Father Filipović-Majstorović, a.k.a. "Brother Satan," knew a thing or two about it. Tudjman dismissed the evidence that was presented in Brother Satan's trial (*see* p. 206), and offered his new theory of how the camp operated. Jasenovac was in fact run by a small group of Jewish inmates who used their positions to rob and murder their Serb and Gypsy fellow prisoners. Such allegations

> should make the rest of us wary of recognising his new independent state of Croatia.[33]

After Tudjman died, a BBC correspondent in Zagreb reported that many heads of state declined to attend Mr. Tudjman's funeral, which reflected the relative isolation in which Croatia had found itself. "His funeral was attended by President Demirel of Turkey and by the prime ministers of Slovenia, Bosnia, Macedonia and Hungary."[34] But that did not stop Javier Solana from paying tribute to the late President Tudjman for being a major figure of the Balkans. At the same time, Mr. Solana saw opportunities for the European Union with new leadership in Zagreb.

> The importance of Croatia in the region, in the Balkans, you know it very well, is very great, very important and we would like to see Croatia play a positive role in the future.[35]

Croatian Ustashi
Acts of Terrorism in the United States[36]

After the fall of their Nazi puppet state, many Ustashi fled the country and took up residence in the West. The escaped with the help of the Vatican's Ratlines. Many went so far as to gain entry to U.S. intelligence services as "freedom fighters" who lent their knowledge and expertise on Yugoslavia to U.S. policymakers.

Petar Radielovic was one such shadowy figure. He was the director of the "Croatian Information Service," based in Arcadia, California, and is the author of a book intriguingly titled *Croatia — Myths and Reality*. Here is what Petar Radielovic had to say about the miscarriage of justice that occurred when the Yugoslav government tried to extradite Andrija Artuković (*see* p. 657, fn 27) in the mid-1980s, which was due to the efforts of Jewish — not Serbian — groups.

> Petar Radielovic, president of the Croatian Information Service in Arcadia, Calif., dismissed the charges as Communist propaganda. "In our eyes they are lies," he said. Whatever killings occurred, he said, were attributable to civil war and were "not under his jurisdiction."[37]

The Los Angeles Times described the tight security in the small magistrate's court and the tensions among those who had come to witness the proceedings.

> Outside the courthouse, Irv Rubin, head of the Jewish Defense League, *engaged in a shoving and shouting match with Petar Radielovic*, president of the Croatian Information Service. Rubin denounced Artukovic's supporters as "nazi pigs" and hailed Brown's ruling as appropriate justice for Jewish victims of the Holocaust.[38] [Emphasis added.]

Petar Radielovic's father "was a Nazi officer in Mostar, and a supporter of Pavelic."[39] His daughter, Mira Radielovic Baratta, was the Croat-American foreign policy adviser to Senator Bob Dole. Balkan-archive.org says the following about her job:

> He [Dole] got the money to pay her [at least in 1994] from some sort of Observer Group which was initially set up to oversee Soviet and American adherence to Nuclear arms control treaties. The article which mentioned this info was in 'Roll Call,' June 5. Apparently, there have been numerous attempts to shut down this organization but $580,000 from it has been 'padding' Senate staff positions each year.[40]

Naturally, Mr. Dole advocated Croatian independence. "Ms. Baratta, whom at least one Hill staffer refers to as 'the Croatian Mata Hari', was singled out by Senator John Warner for praise in framing and helping in the passage of Senate bill S-21, of July 26, 1995, which sought to lift the arms embargo on Bosnia's Izetbegovic regime."[41] Ms. Baratta, as late as 2001, was serving as Deputy Assistant Secretary of Defense for Eurasia in the U.S. Department of Defense.

In Ms. Baratta's case, one might argue that her presence on Dole's staff and later in the Department of Defense is a concrete example of how the Ustashi transferred state terrorism from Zagreb to Washington, D.C. This is, indeed, interesting, because

Croatian Ustashi extremists began honing their terror skills in the U.S. long before al-Qaeda did.

Croatian Ustashi terrorists were inventive and resourceful. They were the first terrorist group that threatened to plant bombs on aircraft. JAT, the Yugoslav national airline, was the first air carrier to institute baggage and body searches. Ustashi agents managed to circumvent these security measures and succeeded in planting a bomb on a JAT DC9 that blew up over Czechoslovakia in 1972.[42]

Years later, the mujahideens who invaded Bosnia entered through Croatia and the Croatian intelligence agencies were fully apprised of their organization, habits, connections and sponsors. Tudjman's regime welcomed terrorists from all over the world as long as they believed in the "Croatian cause." It included not only mujahideens but also extremists from the Croatian diaspora who had organized attacks on Yugoslav diplomatic offices.

> The authorities which came to power last year have not managed to solve one single case of planted explosives, such as the one at Zagreb Mirogoj and in front of the Assembly of Zagreb, or the murder of the Hague witness Milan Levar.[43]

Federal authorities reported that Croatian "nationalists" (or Ustashi) had been responsible for at least twenty-one acts of terror in the U.S. between 1976 and 1980. Eight of these attacks occurred in the New York area, and they included the death of a New York City bomb squad officer who died when he tried to defuse a bomb; the hijacking of a TWA jetliner; the mailing of a book bomb to a New York City publishing company; the bombing of a travel agency in Astoria that arranged trips to Yugoslavia; and in 1980, these Croatian "freedom fighters" set off a bomb in the museum section of the Statue of Liberty, where, coincidentally, there was an oversized portrait of Nikola Tesla, a Serb who was born in what is present day Croatia.

> The wave of attacks began in May 1975 when a Yugoslav diplomat and his wife were assaulted in New York City. The following month, the Yugoslav Mission to the United Nations was bombed. Later, there were bombings and assassination attempts in Chicago, Milwaukee, Cleveland, Pittsburgh, Los Angeles and San Francisco.[44]

In June 1977, three Croatian terrorists shot their way into the Yugoslav mission of the United Nations, wounding a guard in the process. They tricked police officers for a few hours into believing that they had a female hostage who was barricaded behind doors. The terrorists barricaded themselves in an office of the mission, and began throwing leaflets, which called for Croatian independence, into the street below.

> The incident was the second time in a year that Croatian nationalists have carried out a terrorist act in New York City. Last September a TWA jetliner with 86 passengers was hijacked at Kennedy Airport and taken to Paris by five Croats.[45]

The federal charge alleged that the three men planned to seize the Yugoslav ambassador, Jaška Petrić, and hold him in order to publicize their political cause.

> The raid on the mission was one of a series of worldwide terrorist acts by Croatians determined to win independence for their Balkan state from Yugoslavia.[46]

One journalist described the Croatians "freedom fighters" as one of the three most visible terrorist groups operating in the country, and quoted the words of an FBI terrorism expert who remarked that they were "fighting their war on U.S. soil."[47]

The Croatian freedom fighters' boldest move was the hijacking of a NY-Chicago bound TWA 727 on September 10, 1976. The hijacking was the first major incident of domestic air piracy to take place since extensive airport security measures were instituted in 1972, after the JAT airliner was blown up over Czechoslovakia, and it caused officials to rethink how they were going to deal with terrorists who put the lives of hostages in jeopardy.

> They apparently are seeking to publicize [their] campaign for Croatian separation from [the] Yugoslav federation, and they chose [a] method of planting [a] bomb with [a] communiqué on their position in a locker at Grand Central Terminal, NYC.[48]

In June 1981, nine Croatian nationalists were arrested by Federal agents who said that they had scotched "the most violent terrorist group in the United States."[49]

Another Croat, Mr. Deglin, was accused in 1985 of smuggling bombs, weapons, and ammunition from Germany to Yugoslavia, and he was also accused of planting bombs in public buildings. "He was also charged with forming enemy groups and endangering the territorial integrity of Yugoslavia by advocating the establishment of a separate Croatian state."[50]

The Croatian terrorist attacks abated after 1981, certainly because word must have reached the Ustashi diaspora that Germany was committed to Croatian independence, and that the U.S. would eventually take their side. So, the Ustashi diaspora began returning to Yugoslavia to wreak havoc there.

Twenty years after the last Croatian terrorist attack on U.S. soil, we got a taste of Ustashi blowback. In October 2001, a deranged man wielding a box cutter slashed the throat of a Greyhound bus driver and crashed the bus off a Tennessee highway, killing five passengers. This occurred in the wake of the 9/11 attacks after airport security measures had become much more stringent. This incident put beleaguered travelers on notice that not even taking the bus was safe any more. The FBI identified the twenty-nine-year-old attacker as Damir Igrić, a Croat who entered the U.S. in March 1999 on a one-month visa. He also died in the early morning crash.[51]

Many of the stories covering this savage and pointless attack emphasized Mr. Igrić's derangement, and investigations stopped there. Stella Jatras, a brilliant and indefatigable researcher who has earned a reputation for reliability and consistency over the years, remarked:

> What might very well explain this young man's bizarre behavior? According to a Sept. 5, 1995 "Regional Briefing" report in *The Washington Times*, Croatian soldiers at the central Italian drug rehabilitation center said Croatian army infirmaries gave them twice-daily doses of heroin to help them face up to the horrors of war. "To attack [Serb] villages, to cut throats and to kill [Serbs] in cold blood you need a strong anesthetic," said a Croatian soldier identified only as Davor. "A shot of heroin or cocaine was ideal," he said. The account of soldiers being given hard drugs by the government was confirmed in an Aug. 31, 1995 report, "Croat troops 'given drugs'" in London's *Guardian*.[52]

Imagine Ante Pavelić's disappointment. Now a good Ustashi needed heroin to be able to rip a child from its mother's womb with a knife. Another news report carried a story about

> [Toni, aged 23, a member of the Croat irregular forces] said drug-taking was accepted and tolerated by the military hierarchy and was widespread at the front. He claimed that soldiers looted captured villages and dead bodies to raise cash to buy heroin.[53]

All of these Ustasha acts of terrorism in the U.S. and elsewhere were merely a rehearsal for the war they intended to fight against the Serbs, the war that Dagmir Igrić fought in, and the war he brought back to a Greyhound bus in Tennessee.

The War in Croatia

Tudjman's far-right wing government declared its independence on June 25, 1991, along with Slovenia. *The New York Times* reported at the time that Tudjman's HDZ party was financed by members of the Croatian diaspora, in particular the survivors of the Ustashi movement in the U.S., Canada and Australia.[54] War broke out shortly afterwards in Serbian majority areas of Croatia, as in Vukovar and in the Krajina.

The Fourteenth Conference of the European Democratic Union, which assembled the leaders of Christian democratic parties, liberal and conservative European parties, as well as the prime ministers, ministers and representatives of Croatia, Slovenia and Bosnia-Herzegovina in Paris in August 1991, did not hesitate to declare themselves in favor of independence for these three Yugoslav republics. Bosnian independence would follow in April 1992.

The Habsburg's conflict with the Ottomans devastated and depopulated the Serbian borderlands in Bosnia and Croatia, which later came to be known as the *Krajina* (the "Military Frontier"). It separated Ottoman controlled areas from those controlled by Austria. Ottoman Turkish oppression drove the Serbs out of these Muslim-controlled areas, and they fled into these depopulated districts. In 1527, Ferdinand I took steps to make the Serbian settlers migrating to Habsburg regions permanent residents, *graničari* or border guards, who were granted privileges in exchange for military service. The Serbs were given homesteads. Croat and Hungarian nobles were against it because these privileges accorded to the Serbs undermined the feudal system they governed. The Roman Catholic clergy was against it, as well. But the Habsburg policy encouraged Serbian immigration in order to protect the empire's southern borders. In 1630, Ferdinand II demanded that the *graničari* serve in all battles fought by the Habsburg Empire.

Despite having been granted privileges, chiefly religious freedom, the Serbs were nevertheless pressured to accept the Uniate church or to convert completely to Roman Catholicism.

The Habsburg Empire encouraged the Serbs to rebel against the Ottomans in Kosovo in 1690 with the aid of Austrian troops. The rebellion failed. The Serbs retreated with the Austrians to Vojvodina and Eastern Slavonia, where they became a majority. The Croat and Hungarian nobility clamored to regain control of the Serbs as serfs by persecuting them. Maria Teresa reasserted the Serbs' privileges, which the Serbs enjoyed until the end of the nineteenth century. Sremski Karlovci experienced a Serbian revival. Free peasants did well, in fact many made fortunes in Vojvodina and Srem. Many later moved to Serbia when it gained independence, and laid the foundations for Serbian government, education and health care. Thus, the Krajina Serbs had a martial tradition, and did not shrink from defending themselves. They saw that Tudjman's Croatian regime was clearly fascist, and the war broke out because they refused to be dictated to by such a regime.

> On September 28 [1991], Croatian paramilitary forces demolished the Baroque complex of the Pakrac Bishops built in 1732. They set fire to the seminary, and in the cathedral they burnt icons and the bishops' library containing almost 6,000 books, many of historical importance. Fifty of the books dated back to the 18th Century and included a unique copy of a Sabornik, printed in Venice circa 1536.[55]

The Bishop of Slavonia remarked that "They burned our church, offices, hall, museum and library because they want to destroy all proof that the Serbs have been here at least as long as the Croats." Twenty-five thousand Serbs were driven from Western Slavonia in November 1991.

The UN entered the area in 1992, and created "pink zones" that were supposed to be protected Serbian areas. But Serbs had been leaving Croatia ever since the end of the WWII genocide. No amount of "brotherhood and unity" could wipe out the memory of genocide. The pre-WWII Serbian population of Croatia was between 2.5 and 3 million. By 1990, Croatia's Serbian population had fallen to roughly 750,000. The Serbs, contrary to having been depicted as anti-Muslim, took in 40,000 Muslim refugees when Fikret Abdić's enclave around Bihać was taken by Croatian armed forces in 1994. The UN withdrew from the "pink zones" in 1995, and left them vulnerable to attack. The same thing happened to Croatian refugees from central Bosnia and Travnik in 1993.

The Serbs were the most numerous people living the former Yugoslavia. Their problem was that about a quarter of the population resided outside Serbia. Croatia coordinated its drive to create an independent Croatia within the borders of the former Yugoslav with the international community, which had lost its patience with Serbian insistence, and rejected their repeated requests for autonomy or some kind of protected status.

The Badinter Committee emphasized that the minority rights of the Serbs in Croatia, as well in Bosnia and Herzegovina, had to be guaranteed by international law. So the international community pressured Croatia to enact a Constitutional Law on Human Rights to protect ethnic minorities. The Serbs responded in April 1991 by establishing three autonomous areas in Croatia: Krajina, Western Slavonia, and another in Slavonia, Baranja and Western Srem. The declaration of independence by these autonomous regions left the international community's plans in shambles, even though others had contributed to sabotaging them. So the Serbs were blamed. The ICTY went on to indict Milan Babić and Milan Martić, both leaders of the Republika Srpska Krajina (i.e., the Serbian Republic of Krajina).

When Croatia balked on enacting a Constitutional Law on Human Rights to protect ethnic minorities, the UN sent UNPROFOR to protect the Serbs in Croatia, but Croatian forces ended up attacking UNPROFOR, which had been stationed in areas in which Serbs constituted the majority or a substantial minority of the population and where incidents of armed conflict had already occurred, namely, Eastern Slavonia, Western Slavonia and Krajina. After the Republika Srpska Krajina declared its independence, UNPROFOR's mandate was broadened to include support for the Yugoslav National Army (JNA) in the "pink zones." Croatian forces, however, immediately began harassing the UN mission. On January 22, 1993, the Croatian Army attacked "pink zones" in the southern part of UNPROFOR's command. The Croatian government claimed that it launched the attack because it had lost patience with the negotiations over the ownership of various economic enterprises located in these "pink zones."

The U.S. planned, coordinated, and supervised the Croatian Army attack, Operation Lightning in spring 1995, which took the UN Protected Area of Western Slavonija. Milan Martić, the President of the Republika Srpska Krajina, fired a handful of missiles at Zagreb, which resulted in few casualties. The ICTY charged Martić with war crimes. In contrast, Tudjman fired over 2,000 missiles at Knin, but was not charged with war crimes. Obviously, a double standard was at play. The U.S. government and the mainstream media stood behind the genocide and ethnic cleansing. That is the reason why Serbian attempts to survive in Croatia were met with negative publicity if not outright scorn.

Throughout 1995, the Contact Group was mediating peace negotiations in Geneva between the government of the Republika Srpska Krajina (RSK) and the Croatian government. On August 3, 1995, Milan Babić, the Prime Minister of the RSK, announced that he had agreed to the "Z-4 Plan," which planned for the re-integration of the RSK into the Croatian state while preserving autonomy for the Serbs living there. Babić had reached a breakthrough in the negotiations with Peter Galbraith, U.S. Ambassador to Croatia the day before. Babić said in a press conference that Galbraith had promised him that the U.S. would protect the Krajina Serbs from Croatian military actions. Despite the goodwill on the Serbian side, the Croatians were apparently negotiating in bad faith. Croatia rejected the Z-4 Plan and launched Operation Storm the next day (August 4, 1995).[56]

Babić's statements were confirmed by the *The Herald* (Glasgow), which reported:

> Last night [August 3, 1995], an American negotiator said a leader of the rebel Krajina Serbs had offered significant concessions so that there was now no reason for Croatia to go to war.[57]

Earlier, Ret. U.S. General John Galvin had arrived in Croatia as a mercenary through Military Personnel and Resources, Inc. ["MPRI"] along with a number of other retired U.S. Army officers, and spent seven months training the Croatian army for Operation Storm. The U.S., sometimes openly and other times clandestinely, armed, trained, and supplied, and planned military operations for the Muslims and Croats. The CIA established air bases, and centers were created to link up with U.S. spy satellites and download information that was given to the Muslims and Croats. The Croatian government next acted with impudent disregard for its international obligations by launching Operation Storm on August 4-7, 1995, which destroyed the Republika Srpska Krajina. Two hundred thousand and fifty thousand Serbs were driven out of Croatia over the course of a single weekend. Between 4,000 and 7,500 civilians were killed. Many of the elderly or infirm who refused to leave their homes were killed on the spot. What had been begun by the Ustashi troops in conjunction with Nazi troops (Lieutenant Kurt Waldheim among them) in the Kozara action in 1942, where 68,600 Serbs were ethnically cleansed from the region, was now completed with Operation Storm by the descendent of the Ustashi and U.S. military advisors with the support of the Clinton administration. Patrick Barriot, in his testimony at the Milošević trial in The Hague Tribunal, remarked that even U.S. armed forces had participated in Operation Storm.[58]

> On August 25 ... Croatian troops entered Grubori and killed everyone they found. These included: Marija Grubor, 90, whose charred remains were found in her burned house ... Milos Grubor, 80, an invalid ... shot once in the head ... Jovo Grubor, 65, whose throat was slit and who had been stabbed repeatedly.[59]

Lest there be any doubt, a transcript of talks was discovered that the late President Tudjman conducted with the political and military leadership of Croatia on July 31, 1995 in Brioni, which insisted that the Serbs must vanish from Croatia. It was reported in Croatia that Tudjman ordered the military leaders to "strike in a way to make sure that the Serbs will practically disappear from Croatia."[60]

The Plight of Croatia's Remaining Serbs

The Croatian Helsinki Council for human rights reported that Serbs remain the most threatened minority in Croatia.[61] The Council's 2003 Report stated that Croatia continued to ignore crimes against Serbs. There were 384 reported violations of human rights against Serbs, compared to one for Bosnians and 22 for Croats. Large numbers of Serbs have also filed suits against their employers for having been illegally dismissed from their jobs. The report also finds that even though the number of physical attacks on Serbs has decreased, the threat is ever present. The Croatian government has also postponed for the third time returning property to Serbs who fled during the war. The report also called attention to the continued slandering of Serbs in the Croatian media.

> The chairman of the Serb National Council, Milorad Pupovac, stated that a significant number of Serbs in Croatia have changed their first and last names, national and religious identity in the last 14 years, but that he did not have [an] exact figure about this despite the fact that he asked the relevant bodies to provide him with this information six years ago.[62]

Pupovac remarked that he was certain that Serbs had resorted to disguising their identity for fear of reprisals. He said that the largest number of Serbs changed their identities in the early 1990s.

The case of Ivanka Savić provides an example of the form reprisals take. She is a seventy-eight-year-old Serbian woman from Vukovar who was convicted of war crimes and was sentenced to four and one half years of imprisonment without any evidence of wrongdoing having been presented. Her case also illustrates the lack of professionalism at the heart of war crimes prosecutions in Croatia. Her crimes were allegedly committed in Vukovar after it fell to the Yugoslav army in 1991. Savić had been tried *in absencia* in 1993-1994, and was granted a retrial in Vukovar in 2001, for which she was present. The Vukovar court ruled that she had "denounced" (identified at the request of Serbian forces) three men who were taken to Serbia where they were subjected to mistreatment. Human Rights Watch stated that there was no evidence presented at the trial that supported the conviction. The Vukovar court also found that Savić had intimidated and mistreated an ethnic Croat woman from Vukovar by forcing the woman to serve and cook for her, and that Ms. Savić had stolen valuables from the aforesaid woman's house. Human Rights Watch reported that these findings were based on blatant distortions of key witness testimony. Ms. Savić is appealing her conviction, and is not obliged to begin serving her sentence until her appeal has been heard.[63]

Another vast criminal enterprise has been undertaken in real estate. Representatives of the Independent Democratic Serb Party asked the Croatian government to prevent the government real estate agency from purchasing and selling any further real estate until its records department had verified the purchases of almost 10,000 homes that were once owned by Serbs. One of the representatives, Milorad Pupovac, said that the government real estate agency was buying the houses of returnees without their knowledge or assent. "This is daylight robbery under the protection of the state in cooperation with organized crime," remarked Pupovac. A representative from the government real estate agency's managing board denied the charges.[64]

The Simon Wiesenthal Center has not fared any better in its own efforts. In July 2004, the Wiesenthal Center reported that their associates in Croatia, who were assisting in the task of tracking down WWII war crime suspects, had received death threats. The Center stated that "Operation Last Chance," an effort to bring remaining WWII war crimes suspects to trial, would continue despite these threats.

> A Croatian organization called the Anti-Jewish Movement warned that if any Croat was arrested, jailed, or harmed as a result of the Operation, the group would "begin murdering Croatian Jews."[65]

The Wiesenthal Center must be congratulated for its persistence in such adversity. In November 2004, the Center sought the extradition of Milivoj Aschner, a ninety-one-year-old Nazi-era war crimes suspect who had recently fled to Austria. The suspect had lived in Croatia for years before he was identified by Alen Budaj, a twenty-seven-year-old amateur researcher who was studying his family history when he came upon Aschner's nefarious wartime role. Budaj received an award of $5,000 from the Wiesenthal Center as part of "Operation Last Chance." Austria, however, has an uneven record in prosecuting WWII war criminals, and may reject a request for Aschner's extradition. Efraim Zuroff, the chief Nazi hunter for the Wiesenthal Center, remarked, "If he is healthy enough to run away from justice, then he is healthy enough to stand trial."[66]

The Wiesenthal Center has not been alone in receiving death threats. In May 2003, Cali Ruchala, the founder and editor of a Holocaust education and research project called The Pavelic Papers (*see* www.pavelicpapers.com) reported receiving death threats because of his investigations. Mr. Ruchala's fault was to have published a paper on six members of an Ustashe successor organization named, strangely enough, "Otpor," which was founded by Max Luburić, one of the commanders of the Jasenovac Concentration Camp. These six members were convicted in the 1980s in New York State under the RICO act for a variety of crimes, included the attempted assassination of prominent Croatian-American leaders who disagreed with the Ushashi neo-Nazi *weltanschauung*. The intended victims included a journalist and a Roman Catholic priest. The relevant court papers associated with the trial were published in The Pavelic Papers website.

> "I never understood why it was so difficult to find information in English about Pavelic and the Ustase," Ruchala says. "That was one of the reasons I began this project. Now, I understand why that could be." The death threat originated in Croatia, he says, which leaves some doubt as to what United States law enforcement could do.[67]

In Croatia, however, Ustashi thugs can act with impunity. In August 2004, two men wrecked a store and café belonging to Serbian owners, and assaulted the Serbian owner in Karin Donji, Croatia. Even though Croatian police arrested the attackers, the Serbs in the town kept receiving threats. The sister of the owner, Anka Ubrica, told B92 that the two assailants destroyed everything they could get their hands on in the café and in the store. They smashed windows and destroyed inventory. The men pointed a knife at the owner, and told him that Serb returnees were unwelcome in Croatia. Police arrived after about ten minutes, and arrested the two vandals, but others who participated in the attack kept on trashing the café for another ten minutes despite the presence of the police officers. After the police left, passers-by threatened to kill the Serbs if they stayed in Croatia. After one man threatened them with a gun, the police came and made out a report, but took no action against the man who had wielded the gun. A Zadar police official, who was asked to comment on whether or not the assault was a hate crime, replied:

> I cannot comment on that. We do not know what motivated the attack, regardless of the fact that the victims of the crime were of Serbian nationality.[68]

Only 17% of the pre-war Serbian population has returned to Karin Donji. A recent survey showed that about 85% of the Serbs who fled their homes in Croatia during the 1991-1995 war are not prepared to return because they feared discrimination and mistreatment. Croats were polled as well by the same agency (Puls), and almost two-thirds said that they did not want to see the Serbs come back.[69] Only 13% of the Serbs were willing to come back, but only if their basic human rights were to be guaranteed.

The case of Petar Kunić is worth examining in detail. Mr. Kunić fled Croatia in 1995 when the Croatian army reclaimed the area around Zagorje, which is about an hour's drive from Zagreb. He left behind a four-star family run restaurant called "K Svajceru." He sought refuge in Bosnia; meanwhile, a Croatian family took over his restaurant. He ended up having to file a lawsuit with the European Court of Human Rights in Strasbourg in order to get the Croatian government to evict the squatters, which they finally did do. Now, however, Mr. Kunić is a pariah. He is described as "the guy who evicted a Croat." He has even been refused loans by all the local banks even though Croatians obtain loans without difficulty. He has been refused medical treatment by Croatian doctors. "I fear for my life because of anti-Serb discrimination," he said.[70] Mr. Kunić has a lot of courage. Despite the animosity, he hopes to complete the renovation of his restaurant, and once again serve the finest food in the region. He thought things would change when the center-right government came into power, but he remains disappointed. "Everything is still the same, Serbs face huge problems."[71]

Contrast the problems faced by big-time Croatian drug dealers with those of Mr. Kunić. In August 2004, the Croatian weekly *Globus* reported fugitive Croatian general Ante Gotovina, who has been indicted for war crimes against Serbs during the 1991-1995 war, had been implicated in arms and drug smuggling. He was linked to an attempt to smuggle 600 kilos of cocaine, which was uncovered by authorities in the coastal town of Rijeka in 1999. Was Gotovina also involved in supplying the Croatian Army with cocaine and heroin during the 1991-1995 war? Bosnian Croat General Ivan Andabak was also charged with drug trafficking, but was later released.[72]

Also in August 2004, there was a brouhaha over a memorial plaque. Croatian President Stipe Mesić lashed out at a proposal by a group of Croats from the Canadian and Australian diaspora to erect a monument to Mile Budak, who was the Ustashi Minister of Education and Religion for the Croatian Nazi puppet state during WWII (*see* p. 201). Trained as a lawyer, he authored the Croatian racial laws that deprived Serbs, Jews and Roma of their civil rights, and forced them to wear armbands to identify themselves. He happily followed the German models, the Nuremberg Laws. Budak was later executed as a war criminal on July 7, 1945.[73]

The monument was to be erected in the town of Gospić, where some of the fist massacres against Serbs took place during WWII. The diaspora group contended that the monument was meant to memorialize his novels and poems and not his political deeds. Mesić remarked that: "Monuments should not be erected for fascist leaders or their deputies."[74]

It is illuminating to briefly examine Mr. Budak's literary career. He is actually listed in the *Jugoslovenski književni leksikon* (Matica Srpska, 1984), and it tells us a few things about him. He fought with the Serbs during WWI against Austro-Hungary, and participated in the bitter retreat through Albania. He published several novels: *Doktor Križanić* (Dr. Križanić), *Rascvjetana trešnja* (The Cherry Tree in Blossom), and *San o sreći* (A Dream of Happiness). He published poems, stories and articles. His most mature work is considered to be his four-volume novel, *Ognjište* (The Family Hearth, 1938). Ante Pavelić also wrote a novel, called *The Lovely Blonde*, which reportedly casts some insight into the machinations behind the assassination of King Alexander and French Prime Minister Barthou in Marseille in 1934. But Pavelić is not mentioned in the *Jugoslovenski književni leksikon* at all. I have not read either of these works, so I am not competent to render an opinion on their literary quality, however, one may conclude that Budak's work had, at least, some lowest common denominator of literary merit to be worthy of inclusion in a standard reference work. The titles of his early works suggest formulaic romantic themes, while his "mature work" rings of a family saga. All these novels sound rather kitsch, but they must have represented his vision of life, which ultimately evolved into a vision of genocide. It may very well be that Mile Budak's works can be for Holocaust scholars what the works of Henry Darger (who may or may not have murdered a young girl in his youth) have become for post-modernists: the mechanism of a deranged, compulsive imagination laid bare.

Is Mr. Budak entitled to a commemorative plaque or not? Here in the United States, we have the case of Ezra Pound, a brilliant poet, who, after long residence abroad, lost touch with America and was seduced by Italian Fascism. He was spared execution after his trial for treason (he had made radio broadcasts to the U.S. from Fascist Italy) because he was judged to be insane. He was, however, honored with a commemorative plaque at his former residence in London on Kensington Church Walk, where he lived from 1909 to 1914. It was in this apartment that he promoted James Joyce and T.S. Eliot, who were unknown at the time.

> The plaque, from English Heritage, is a first chink of light in the cloud of infamy and disgrace which hangs over Pound's memory, although he was the godfather of literary modernism and midwife to some of the 20th century's greatest works — notably TS Eliot's poem *The Waste Land*.[75]

In New York, however, Pound was denied a plaque in The Poets Corner at St. John the Divine Cathedral in 2002 because some parishioners objected to his anti-Semitism. The little plaque was to read: "Ezra Pound, 1885-1972/What thou lovest well remains/the rest is dross" (from Canto LXXXI).

So how can we come to a decision? Mile Budak is certainly no Ezra Pound, and Ezra Pound is certainly no Mile Budak. We need to probe just a little further in order to draw a conclusion about whether we should be for or against such a plaque.

A little research reveals that Stipe Mesić wrote a book, too! It was published in English as *The Demise of Yugoslavia* (CEU Press, 2003). Its title also underwent some heavy revision by the U.S. publishers. It was originally published as *Kako sam srušio Jugoslaviju* (How I Destroyed Yugoslavia), and then it was retitled with the verb cast in the passive voice, *Kako je srušena Jugoslavia* (How Yugoslavia Was Destroyed). Here are some of Mr. Mesić's key statements.

> It is our sacred duty, in the course of 24 months to cleanse Croatia so that not a single "opanak" [Serb peasant shoe] treads the sacred soil of Croatia any more. (Stipe Mešić, 1989)

> I will be the last president of Yugoslavia. (Stipe Mešić, 1991)[76]

And President Mesić's family is noteworthy enough to appear in books like *Croatian Domobranhood in World War II*, by Ivan Kosutić (Školska knjiga,1992). Page 229 features a photograph of Mr. Mesić's uncle, Marko Mesić, a commander of an artillery unit in WWII, wearing an Ustashi SS volunteer uniform. The caption beneath the photo says: "Commander of artillery unit, officer Mesić gives orders at battlefield before an attack."[77]

Perhaps we have enough to go on now. Let us recall Mr. Mesić earlier remark that: "Monuments should not be erected for fascist leaders or their deputies." This sounds a little like one rule for Mr. Mesić and another for Mr. Budak. If Mr. Mesić is not embarrassed at all about his family's Ustashi past, then he really ought not to be ashamed of Mr. Budak's Ustashi past either, and allow a commemorative plaque to be erected in his native village. Mr. Mesić, in the end, did not allow the plaque to be put up. But the matter did not end there.

Villagers in Lovinac who were on their way to church for Sunday Mass saw that the monument had anyway been erected near the church. The press disingenuously reported that no one knew who had put it up, but it was in all likelihood members of the Canadian and Australian Croatian diaspora. Even Prime Minister Ivo Sanader jumped into the fray, and urged local officials to remove the plaque, saying "it damages the region, Croatia and its national interests."[78]

Soon afterwards, 120 Croatian intellectuals issued a public appeal to the government for a retrial for Mr. Budak. Right-wing academics, writers and artists claimed that his trial, which ended in Mr. Budak's execution by hanging, was a farce. His trial, they contended,

> was conducted in one afternoon ... without defence or the hearing of defence witnesses, even without the right to appeal.[79]

Then the Simon Wiesenthal Center issued an official protest over the erection of the plaque.

> I am certain that you fully realize the implication of such a step which seeks to glorify a person who was an active member of the Ustasha government which carried out a policy of genocide against Serbs, Jews, and Gypsies during WWII.[80]

The Center urged Croatian authorities to take whatever steps were necessary to remove the monument as quickly as possible. Just two days later, armed security forces arrived in the village and removed the plaque amid heavy security on the orders from Zagreb.

> It was the first such "de-Nazification" action since the country became independent in 1991.... The Ustasha era is seen elsewhere as a black mark on Croatia's history. But few Croatians show shame about the country's support for Hitler.[81]

Villagers in Lovinac were reported to have wept as workers, who were guarded by special service policemen, took the plaque away. Another plaque dedicated to another Ustashi, Jure Frančetić, that was erected in a nearly village was also removed. Frančetić was the leader of the infamous Black Legion that fought in Bosnia.

The *Telegraph* article gave a clue to understanding this perplexing little drama in the last paragraph. Croatia is preparing for talks in 2005 to enter the European Union, and Croatia must demonstrate that its track record on human rights and democracy meet the criteria set by Brussels. Croatia wants to be a thoroughly modern European country.

Croatia Today

Since the writings of Croatian leaders were discussed earlier, it is instructive to examine the reading habits of contemporary Croatians. Diana Johnstone remarked that when she visited Croatia in 1996, the book that received the biggest window displays in leading bookstores in Zagreb was the infamous anti-Semitic classic, *The Protocols of the Elders of Zion*. The memoirs of Ante Pavelić came next. Ms. Johnstone went on to note that 1999's best seller was Adolf Hitler's *Mein Kampf*. New publications in 1999 that held promise were *The Protocols of Zion, the Jews and Adolf Hitler*, by Mladen Schwartz, the head of the Croatian neo-Nazi Party (the New Right), and *Talks with Hitler*, by his aide, Herman Rauschning. And there were plenty of WWII Ustashi memoirs.[82]

Stevan Vranešević and Mirijana Djerković, two Serbian students, decided to tweak the Croatians' nose. They went to Zagreb and photographed each other in Bane Jelačić Square in downtown Zagreb while holding a picture of Draza Mihailovich, the legendary WWII Serbian resistance leader. Passers-by were angered by the photo session, and the police had to intervene in order to save the students from being mobbed and beaten. The students were next found guilty on counts of disturbing the peace and, curiously enough, "insulting the moral feelings" (!) of Zagreb's citizens. All of this makes much more sense when it is recalled that Draza Mihailovich led the first organized resistance to Hitler, the patron saint of both the WWII Nazi puppet state and the contemporary Republic of Croatia. Vranešević claimed that the photographs were taken for artistic reasons and denied that there was any political statement at all.

The Croatians have simply been swept away by a tide of anti-Serbian and anti-Semitic racism that has inundated all aspects of public life, and when no Serbs or Jews are in striking distance, anyone else will do. UEFA, the United European Football Association, insisted that it would punish Croatia after fans chanted racist abuse and brandished white supremacist banners during a match between France and Croatia. The French striker, Sylvain Wiltord, who is black, suffered a barrage of racist abuse during the match which ended in a 2-2 draw. UEFA spokesman William Gaillard was quoted as saying: "You can rest assured we'll take measures.... We are gathering all the evidence we have on their behaviour."[83]

Croatian schoolbooks have come under scrutiny too. Natasha Jovicich, the new director of the Holocaust Museum in Jasenovac, initiated a study to call attention to the values being taught to Croatian schoolchildren. The results of her study indicated that: "Croatian textbooks are teaching violence and intolerance."[84] The results were published in *Globus*, a Croatian weekly newsmagazine. The following examples were highlighted from a textbook used by eighth graders:

- British Prime Minister Winston Churchill was portrayed as a bulldog squatting on a British flag.

- A picture of the star of David was depicted on the same page, with a caption reading: "The Jews had to wear a special mark." The discrimination against Jews and their extermination in Croatia was not mentioned.
- The same history book featured a photograph of Ante Pavelić with a caption that reads, "jurist, politician, and founder of the Ustashe movement."

The study concluded that: "This textbook is a dangerous manipulation of history"[85] and that the textbook was responsible for marginalizing fascism and the struggle waged against it to such an extent that the two appeared morally indistinguishable.

In February 2003, Croatian Prime Minister Ivan Račan once again had to condemn the use of Nazi slogans and salutes at a reception in Zagreb for the Croatian national handball team. He warned that such conduct "could not be tolerated in Croatia … fascist salutes are unacceptable … and shame us in the eyes of Europe."[86]

This was not the first time, of course, that Croatian politicians had to reprimand the citizenry for enthusiastically resorting to fascist salutes and Nazi slogans. Next, the handball team asked Marko Perković-Thompson, who is described as a folk singer, to perform at the reception. He incited the crowd by shouting a fascist slogan that was used by the Ustashi: "Za dom!" he shouted, and the crowd responded with "Spremni." It is the Ustashi equivalent of "Sieg, heil!" Despite the criticism, a veterans association defended Perković-Thompson by saying that it was a "traditional Croatian salute."

Mr. Perković-Thompson, though, slings his guitar on his back and goes from one sell-out concert to another, impervious to the criticism leveled against him. His recordings are available everywhere, and he has a devoted following. He embarrassed Croatian authorities yet again in January 2004 with a new song, which goes, in part, like this:

Jasenovac and Gradiska Stara, the home of Maks's butchers
Lorries are speeding through Imotski, carrying [WWII commander]
Jure Francetic's Blackshirts
Many Serbs were slaughtered in Capljina and carried by the [River]
Neretva
The Neretva flows on and takes the Serbs to the blue Adriatic.[87]

"Gradiska Stara" was one of the camps located within Jasenovac that was devoted to the extermination of Serbian and Jewish women and children. The Ustashi disposed of the bodies by throwing them into the river. Maks, of course, is Maks Luburić, one of Jasenovac' commanders. Mr. Perković-Thompson also had a few choice words for Ivan Račan, who had criticized him earlier for his conduct during the reception of the Croatian national handball team in Zagreb. He showed none of the restraint, for exagmple, that Dragan Kalinić demonstrated when Paddy Ashdown dismissed him from the Republika Srpska parliament. (*See* p. 308)

> Our Lady of Sinj, if you can, take Stipe [Mesić] and give us back
> Franjo [Tudjman]
> Hey [Ivica] Racan, may dogs fuck your mother and the mothers of
> your voters
> Shiny star above Metkovic send our greetings to Ante Pavelić

Stipe Mesić actually appeared on a television program to condemn the song. And Slavko Goldstein, who is routinely described as a Croatian Jewish intellectual, appeared, as well, to mumble something about Perković-Thompson being a "horrific paradox." Mr. Goldstein is so often asked to comment on Ustashi embarrassments in contemporary Croatian society that one receives the unfortunate impression that he is the only Jew in Croatia.

Naturally, there were repercussions. The Croatian Parliament had voted, after all, to ban the glorification of Nazism, fascism and all totalitarian regimes, which was "a significant move for a country where many have yet to come to terms with its Nazi past."[88] One has to admire the understatement of the AP report. It should be noted, however, that this ban was instituted six months before Mr. Perković-Thompson's above-referenced song was released. The ban, evidently, has no teeth.

In November 2004, a Serbian basketball player was denied entry to Croatia because of a "controversial tattoo" on his arm. It was a tattoo of General Draza Mihailovich, whom "Croats perceive … as a villain whose fighters killed Croatian soldiers." Croatian authorities claimed that the tattoo of General Mihailovich amounted to displaying "fascist symbols" and represented "an incitement … of racial, national or religious hatred," which is banned by Croatian laws.[89] Obviously, a tattoo of General Mihailovich is treated as a far more dangerous matter than any one of Mr. Perković-Thompson's songs.

One Croatian writer described the new nation-state as being seriously ill, and that it had started making some strange, hitherto unknown signs on its death bed. He cited the results of an opinion poll published recently in *Večernji List* reveal that barely more than half of Croatia's citizens were convinced that it was worth fighting for Croatia, while as many as 25 percent were convinced that Croatian independence was definitely not worth a war.

The poll also indicated that as many as 51 percent of those polled believed that they live worse today than they did ten years ago. This mass of disappointed people were described as

> sobered up supporters of independence who realized that their own nation-state can oppress and steal as well as or even better than somebody else's state.... International recognition ... was supposed to solve the Croatian national problem. Instead it fanned the flames of Croat nationalism and deified the nation, so that only recently we've seen first signs of the realization that the nation is supposed to serve citizens, not the other way round. [90]

To conclude this chapter, I defer to an anonymous internet author who wrote eloquently about the plight of the Croats.

> Are the Croats evil? Not at all, they just had the bad luck of having a new government in Belgrade in 1941, which offended Hitler. They had the misfortune of having madmen imposed upon them as rulers. They had the misfortune of having an odd archbishop, later Cardinal Stepinac, who suffered from a pathological fear of his Serb neighbors and felt that the Nazis were decent although overly eager allies in a good cause. The Croats had the misfortune of having a pope in Rome who did not see it appropriate to order his priests and bishops to stop organizing the genocide of Serbs. Once again, in 1990, the Croats had the misfortune of having a pope in Rome who did not know that Catholic priests and monks had physically participated in the genocide against the Serbs. Since he did not know, he did not see fit to apologize for it or work against the revival of hatred. On the contrary, he saw fit to kneel at the tomb of the strange Cardinal Stepinac. He had him beatified, thus creating the cult of a man who had not been neutral in World War II. Stepinac had been very strongly and openly pro-Axis. Thus Pope Wojtyla legitimized the WWII Croat Nazis as well-meaning nationalists and legitimized their hatred against the Serbs. Such

hatred had never been a mainstream feeling in Croatia; the parties that espoused such hatred had never obtained more than a tiny percentage of votes and achieved power only through German arms and money. The moral legitimization of such hatred allowed it to become acceptable. In some countries similar hatred permeates the whole of society. Poland, the country of birth of Pope Wojtyla, is a good example. There the hatred of the Jews achieved such a pathological level that during WWII a major activity of non-communist Polish guerrillas was the hunting down of escaped Jews. When the survivors of Auschwitz returned to their homes they found themselves targets of attack and mass murder at the hands of Polish Catholics. Poland gave us the wonder of the practice of "anti-Semitism without Jews." The last surviving Jews have all fled, but the "Jewish Problem" is still part of the political discourse in Poland into the present day. No wonder that a person who was inured to such political pathology would not notice that he was legitimizing murderous anti-Serb hatred in Croatia.[91]

ENDNOTES

[1] *Escape from the Anthill*, by Hubert Butler, p. 284. Quoted from "The Stepinac File," by Chris Agee (2000), archipelago.org.

[2] *Ustashi* is used here as an indeclinable adjective which is also used as a noun. It also appears in English as Ustasha (singular), and as Ustashe (the plural).

[3] This quotation, as well as the three preceding paragraphs, were drawn from *Le nouvel ordre mondial et la Yougoslavie*, by Gerard Baudson, Gil Wern, Paris: 1996, p. 120.

[4] "On the Serbian Orthodox New Martyrs of the Second World War, A Brief Historical Background," by Joachim Wertz, orthodoxinfo.com, which is the principal source for this section.

[5] See *A History of Yugoslavia*, by V. Dedijer, I. Božić, S. Ćirković, and M. Ekmečić, McGraw-Hill, 1974, p. 545-546.

[6] *See* "The Artukovitch File," by Hubert Butler, which can be found in his book of essays, *Independent Spirit*, (Farrar, Straus & Giroux: NY. 1996). This essay is also posted on archipelago.org. Artuković found refuge in the United States after World War II and lived unmolested in Los Angeles until the 1980s, when, as a senile old man, he was returned to the former Yugoslavia to be tried for war crimes. He died in custody in Zagreb.

[7] "On the Serbian Orthodox New Martyrs of the Second World War, A Brief Historical Background," by Joachim Wertz, orthodoxinfo.com, *op. cit.*

[8] *Ibid.*

[9] *The Silence of Pius XII*, by Carlo Falconi (Little, Brown: 1965), p. 273, quoted in "The Patron Saint of Genocide: Archbishop Stepinac and the Independent State of Croatia," by Bill Stouffer, www.pavelicpapers.com.

[10] "The Ustasha Genocide," by M. A. Hoare, *The South Slav Journal*, 8/11/04.

[11] *Assassins au nom de Dieu*, by H. Laurière, Paris: L'Age d'Homme, 1993.

[12] *Liar's Poker: The Great Powers, Yugoslavia and the Wars of the Future*, by Michel Collon, op. cit., p. 78.

[13] *With God and Fuhrer*, by Karlheinz Deschner, p.280-281, quoted in "The Patron Saint of Genocide: Archbishop Stepinac and the Independent State of Croatia," by Bill Stouffer, posted on pavelicpapers.com.

[14] The Simon Wiesenthal Center, Museum of Tolerance website, http://motlc.wiesenthal.com/gallery/pg46/pg9/pg46999.html.

[15] The Vatican ran a similar operation in France with Jewish children. It secretly issued instructions to the Catholic church in France not to return Jewish children to their families after WWII. The children had been entrusted to the church's care to save them from death camps, however, if the parents survived the war and came forward to reclaim these children, the Vatican ordered the children were only to be returned "provided [they] have not received baptism." See "Saving Jewish Children, but at What Cost?", *The New York Times*, 1/9/05. Caritas appeared once again in the former Yugoslavia in the 1990s as a "humanitarian" organization. One of its humanitarian tasks was to clandestinely ship weapons to the Croats during the collapse of Yugoslavia. See *Liar's Poker*, by Michel Collon, *op. cit.*

[16] "Jasenovac," by Carl Savage, serbianna.com.

[17] "The Patron Saint of Genocide," by Bill Stouffer, www.pavelicpapers.com, *op. cit.*

[18] "Jasenovac," by Carl Savich, www.serbianna.com.

[19] *Ibid.*

[20] *Ibid.*

[21] *Ibid.*

[22] *Ibid.*

[23] "The Patron Saint of Genocide: Archbishop Stepinac and the Independent State of Croatia," by Bill Stouffer, www.pavelicpapers.com, , *op. cit.*

[24] See *Unholy Trinity*, by Mark Aarons and John Loftus (New York, St. Martin's, 1991/1998), Chapter 6.

[25] The Wiesenthal Center's World Report Aug. 1990, Vol 11 No 3 Circ. 376,280, Page 9.

[26] "Hope and History in Yugoslavia," by Nora Beloff, *Guardian Weekly* (UK), 12/1/91.

[27] *Ibid.*

[28] "War Raises Old Anxieties for Croatian Jews," *The Independent*, October 21, 1991, page 10.

[29] *Ibid.*

[30] "Unreconstructed Nazism On Display," by Kenneth Roberts, *The Spectator* (UK), 3/19/94, pages 16, 17, 18.

[31] *See* srpska-mreza.com.

[32] "An Apologist For Hitler," by Richard West, *The Guardian*, 10/21/91, p. 23.

[32] Ibid.

[34] "Croatia Mourns as Tudjman is Buried," *BBC News*, 12/13/99.

[35] "Tudjman," by Ron Pemstein, *VOA News*, 12/12/99.

[36] This section draws from the SANE (Serbian American Alliance of New England) digest of article abstracts that focuses on extremist Muslim terrorism in the Balkans and Croatian Ustashi terrorism worldwide. *See* sane-boston.org.

[37] *The New York Times*, 11/15/84, pg. 15.

[38] *The Los Angeles Times*, 1/31/85, pg.1.

[39] "The Croat in Dole's Office," *Counterpunch.org*, 10/1/95.

[40] Balkan-archive.org.yu.

[41] "Bob Dole and Yugoslavia; Concurrent Resolution 150 and Other Puzzle Pieces," by Benjamin C. Works, *SIRIUS*, siri-us.com, 5/6/99.

[42] See *Tito and the Rise and Fall of Yugoslavia*, by Richard West (Sinclair-Stevenson: 1994), p. 302-303.

[43] "Croatia after Terrorist Attacks against the USA," by Jelena Lovric, *AIM*, (Zagreb), 9/20/01.

[44] *The New York Times*, 7/23/81.

[45] "Croat Terrorists Held in N.Y. Shooting," by William Claiborne, *The Washington Post*, 6/15/77.

[46] *The Washington Post*, 6/17/77.

[47] "Ethnic Nationalists Fight their Wars on American Soil," by Charles R. Babcock, *The Washington Post*, 4/20/80.

[48] *The New York Times:* Information Abstracts, 9/14/76.

[49] "Arrest of 9 in Terrorist Group Brings Uneasy Calm to Croatian Americans," *The New York Times*, 7/23/81.

[50] "Croat Gets 20 Years for Bombs," by B. Petrovic, *The Guardian* (UK) 4/27/85.

[51] "Greyhound Driver Knifed, 5 Die in Crash," *New York Daily News*, 10/4/01.

[52] *The Washington Times*, 10/9/02.

[53] "Croat Troops 'Given Drugs'," *The Guardian* (UK), 8/31/95.

[54] "Franjo Tudjman, Ex-Communist General Who Led Croatia's Succession, Is Dead at 77," *The New York Times*, 12/11/99.

[55] "For Serbians, Fears of a German Axis Rise For The Third Time This Century," by T. W. Carr, *ISSA Special Reports*, Balkan Strategic Studies, 12/31/1992, http://128.121.186.47/ISSA/reports/Balkan/Dec3192-2.htm.

[56] "The Z-4 Plan and the Run-up to Operation Storm," by Andy Wilcoxson, slo-bodan-milosevic.org, 8/28/04.

[57] *The Herald*, Glasgow (UK), 8/4/95.

[58] "Patrick Barriot testified in the Hague Tribunal: Terrorist from New York was in Bosnia," *Blic* (Serbia-Mont), 1/13/05.

[59] "Elderly massacred in Krajina attack," by T. Hundley, *Chicago Tribune*, 9/11/95.

[60] "Tudjman's Orders to Expel the Croatian Serbs Found?", oneworld.net, 10/10/04.

[61] *SRNA*, 7/16/04.

[62] "Significant" Number of Serbs Changing their Nationality in Croatia — Official," *SRNA*, 7/20/04.

[63] "Croatia: Conviction Spotlights Justice Failings," *Human Rights Watch*, 7/19/04.

[64] "Croatian Serbs Say Refugee Homes Sold without Owners' Consent," *BBC Monitoring*, 12/13/04.

[65] "Wiesenthal: Croatian Associates Get Death Threats," *DPA* (Deutsche Presse Agentur), 7/23/04.

[66] "Wiesenthal Center Seeks Croatian Nazi-Era Suspect," haaretz.com, 11/18/04.

[67] *See* pavelicpapers.com/documents/ljubas/al0001.html.

[68] "Serbian Businessman Attacked in Croatia," *B92*, 8/4/04.

[69] "Most Serb Refugees Unwilling to Return to Croatia — Poll," *AP*, 9/16/04.

[70] "Serb Struggles for Croatian Home, by Marko Kovac, *BBC News*, 9/23/04.

[71] *Ibid.*

[72] "Fugitive Croat General Involved in Smuggling," jang.com, 8/11/04.

[73] "Croat President Blasts Plans for Monument to Member of Nazi Quisling Regime," *AP*, 8/12/04.

[74] *Ibid.*

[75] "Blue Plaque Ends 60 Years in the Cold for Ezra Pound," by John Ezard, *The Guardian* (UK) 8/12/04.

[76] I am grateful to Prof. J.P. Maher for posting these quotations on stopnato.uk.org.

[77] *See* srpska-mreza.com.

[78] "Croatia Fumes over Nazi Plaque," cnn.com, 8/24/04.

[79] "Croatians Demand Retrial of Country's 'Goebbels'," *AFP*, 8/25/04.

[80] "Wiesenthal Center Protests Erection of Monument Honoring World War II Croatian Minister Mile Budak," *The Simon Wiesenthal Center*, 8/26/04.

[81] "Croatians Weep as Nazi Pride Is Erased," *Telegraph* (UK), 8/28/04.

[82] "Nazi Nostalgia in Croatia," Diana Johnstone, 9/6/99, tenc.net.

[83] "Croatia Face UEFA Rap for Racist Fans," by Ian Orr, *Daily Record* (UK), 6/25/04.

[84] "Croatia's Textbooks: 'The Jews had to wear a special mark'," *JTA*, 12/19/02.

[85] *Ibid.*

[86] "Croatian PM Condemns Nazi Salutes," *BBC News*, 2/6/03.

[87] "Croatian Fascist Song Discussion on TV Zagreb," *BBC Monitoring*, 1/23/04.

[88] "Croatian Parliament Bans Glorification of Nazism and Totalitarianism, *AP*, 7/10/03.

[89] "Serbian Basketball Player Rejects Criticism over Controversial Tattoo," by Misha Savic, *Canadian Press*, 11/18/04.

[90] "Balance Sheet of Independence," by Marinko Culic, *Feral Tribune* (Croatia), 1/18/02.

[91] "Bringing Peace to Croatia, Bad Luck and Nazis," http://www.kosovoforum.net/croatiacleanse.htm.

Srebrenica: The Phantom Massacre
by Milo Yelesiyevich

Overview

Srebrenica has been regularly described as "the worst massacre since WWII." This statement merits further examination. The 7,000 alleged deaths are far fewer than the massacres that took place in Rwanda (500,000 to 1,000,000 dead in 1994) or, for example, in Cambodia under Pol Pot (2,000,000 dead between 1975-1979). Srebrenica, however, is further described as the "worst case of genocide since WWII." Comparing the extermination of 6,000,000 European Jews to the alleged deaths of 7,000 Bosnian Muslim soldiers is merely reducing the word "genocide" to a figure of speech. For those who are statistically minded, the alleged number of Bosnian Muslim deaths in Srebrenica equals .0012% of the number of Jews exterminated during WWII. And the following pages will demonstrate that far fewer than the alleged 7,000 deaths occurred. In fact, the correct figure is 1,500 to 1,800 deaths of primarily Muslim soldiers in battle.

Why were Naser Orić's Bosnian Muslim death squads attacking Serbian farming villages? Not one of them could have been considered a strategic target. The Muslims of Bosnia chiefly resided in cities, whereas the Serbs lived in the rural areas and, therefore, occupied about 70% of the land in Bosnia. The key lies in the name Zetra, which was given to the Olympic stadium in Sarajevo. Zetra is an abbreviation for *Zelena Transversala*, the "Green Transversal" or the "Green Highway," which is the Muslim name for the continuous land bridge leading from Istanbul to Europe through the former Yugoslavia. It is the goal of Bosnian Muslim fundamentalists to re-establish this land bridge by depopulating the rural regions of Serbs, gaining Muslim control and domination over these regions, and connecting them. In 1683, when the Green Highway was at its height, Sultan Suleiman II led the Ottomans to attack and lay siege to Vienna for two months.

Western thinking, however, has not been unified by such single-mindedness.

Step 1: What the West Is Planing[1]

NATO was struggling to redefine itself after the collapse of the Soviet Union; namely, it was looking for a new enemy. Meanwhile, Germany had been actively planning a war to break up Yugoslavia since the 1960s. It began making clandestine arms shipments to the Croats and Slovenians immediately after Tito's death. The subsequent war in the former Yugoslavia temporarily rescued NATO from obsolescence. The U.S. was not unprepared. It had also laid plans long ago to gain control of the former Yugoslavia, where it spearheaded the use of "military humanitarianism." Yet there is absolutely nothing humanitarian about Western intervention in the former Yugoslavia.

Short Term Goals: 6 months–1 Year

The Bosnian Muslims led a failed counter-offensive against the Serbs in 1995. The West needed to find some way to reverse Bosnian Muslim losses and regain the initiative. The Muslims were holding on to Srebrenica as a bargaining chip to exchange for Serbian areas around Sarajevo. There were negotiations between Alija Izetbegović and Radovan Karadžić about a peaceful exchange of territory, but they failed. Even though the Bosnian Serb Army was stretched thin and under-supplied, General Mladić defied the West, and took Srebrenica with four hundred troops, one hundred of whom were alleged to have been Greek volunteers.[2] There were another 1,000 to 1,500 rear guard Serbian troops who had encircled the city.

Meanwhile, fifteen senior U.S. military advisers headed by retired two star General Richard Griffiths had been dispatched to Croatia barely seven months before Operation Storm.[3] Among them was a retired U.S. general, John Galvin, who, like the others, went to work for the Croatian Army through MPRI. He planned a military operation to drive the remaining Serbs out of Croatia. Spectacular accusations of an alleged "massacre" at Srebrenica would act as a diversionary tactic that would draw attention away from Operation Storm, which drove 250,000 Serbs from Croatia. At least 4,000 civilians were killed over the course of a single weekend. Allegations of a massacre in Srebrenica were going to insure that no one was going to hear about Operation Storm.

Mid-Term Goals: 5–10 Years

The Albanian port of Durres was going to be transit point for the oil pipeline, which was foreseen to traverse Bulgaria and Macedonia. Oil was also discovered in Tuzla in the early 1990s on the eve of the war, but was kept secret until 2004.[4] The oil pipeline would not succeed unless the Serbian people had been conquered, divided, and subjugated and key U.S. military bases installed in the country. An important part of this strategy was to keep Bosnia unstable. To that end, the U.S. had needlessly prolonged the Bosnian war for years. The U.S. also devised a permanent means of criminalizing the Serbian people by establishing The International Criminal Court for the Former Yugoslavia in The Hague. High on the agenda were the penetration of western capital, the repayment of debts to Saudi Arabia, and the promotion of Turkey's entry into the European Union.

Long Term Goals: 30+ Years

Zbigniew Brzezinski outlined the long-term goals for the region in his book, *The Grand Chessboard*. The U.S. is financing alternative oil pipelines in order to cut Russia out of the oil and gas business. Meanwhile, the U.S. has begun construction of another military base in Burgas, Bulgaria. Coincidentally, the aforementioned pipeline will run from Burgas to the Albanian port city of Durres. The U.S. built camp Bondsteel in Kosovo, the largest U.S. base on foreign soil since the Vietnam war, to protect this pipeline. AMBO (the "Albanian, Macedonia and Bulgarian Oil Company"), a private company which was formed in 1996 in Pound Ridge, New York, will operate the pipeline. By running the pipeline through puppet states that it has created, the U.S. hopes to weaken Russia by cutting into its oil revenues, and ultimately break Russia up into three smaller countries. The U.S. also wants to control Europe by gaining control of the oil and gas routes that it relies upon, hence, the rivalry between Europe and the U.S. in the region.

> In reality, creating inextricable situations is not a mistake but a tactic. The U.S. created an unworkable, unviable state in Bosnia, which is the perfect excuse for a durable protectorate.[5]

Step 2: Images that Shock Public Opinion

Darko Bandic/AP Wide World.
Used with permission.

The Image Stayed With Them
The West had to reverse the Serbian victory in Srebrenica.

A lot of people in Britain remember the death of Ferida Osmanović, a Bosnian woman who hanged herself after the fall of Srebrenica in July 1995. Not so many recall how many boys and men ... were murdered by Bosnian Serb[s] ... but the image stayed with them.[6]

Version 1 — Husband Killed in Srebrenica
Selman [her husband], a locksmith, had refused to leave them and flee to the hills from the Serb forces as they entered Srebrenica. He was pulled away from his hysterical wife by Serb soldiers, and his family never saw him again.[7]

Version 2 — Raped in Srebrenica
David Rohde gave this account of Vice President Gore speaking about Ferida Osmanović's suicide after he read a front page story in the *Washington Post* that described her as a rape victim.

"The worst solution would be to acquiesce to genocide and allow the rape of another city and more refugees," he said. "At the same time, we can't be driven by images, because there's plenty of other places that aren't being photographed where terrible things are going on, but we can't ignore the images either."[8]

ANALYSIS
The Muslims of Srebrenica were eager to leave the town where they had been exploited and mistreated by Naser Orić's troops. Col. Karremans, Gen. Janvier and others attest to this. It is regrettable that Ferida Osmanović chose to take her own life, however,

it ought to be noted that she committed suicide at the UN Base in Tuzla, and not in Srebrenica. One story alleges that her husband was taken away by Serbs and summarily executed. Is it possible that he was a soldier in the Bosnian Muslim Army? If he were a soldier, why didn't he surrender? Could it have been because he was guilty of war crimes himself? Let us now consider the second alternative. If Ms. Osmanović were raped in Srebrenica, who could have been the perpetrator? In this case, it is unlikely that it was a Bosnian Serb soldier. There were many documented rapes of Muslim refugee women in Srebrenica that were committed by Bosnian Muslim soldiers under the command of Naser Orić. The Serbs took in many of them who managed to escape. Vahida Delić and Serifa Selimović, for example, managed to flee Bratunac in April 1994. Here follows an excerpt from Vahida's testimony:

> Five months ago I had to get married, as the other girls had to, and give birth to children on Naser's orders. I married Ševal Huremović. I had to run away from Ševal a month ago, because of constant beatings and his drunkenness. My parents did not take me back, so they placed me with someone named Muša. Then it became a real hell. The next evening Naser Orić came with some woman and a couple of men. He stayed in Muša's room but Sead and Ibro from Glogova and another guy whose name I don't know burst into my room. Sead asked me to take off my clothes. I didn't want to, so he started to slap me around, and then they ripped off my clothes and all three of them took turns with me. I lost consciousness when the third one assaulted me. That was the first time. Then they started coming at any time of day or night, and raped me, and if I resisted, they would beat me....[9]

As far as the media was concerned, the true version was the one that motivated public support to the bombardment. In either case, the Serbs were successfully demonized and the public supported military action.

Tellingly, the discussion centered around the decontextualized *image*, in this case, a photograph, and not the event. For Julian Borger, *it is an image that may change history.* For Vice President Gore, the image is essential, too: *we can't be driven by images ... but we can't ignore the images either.* The tone is one of advocacy journalism, and of responsibility to perceptions created by *images*, and not to events themselves or sober and dispassionate accounts of them in prose. The late Ms. Osmanović was successfully reduced to a propaganda *image* that mobilized public opinion to prepare for an attack against the Serbs, regardless of the tragic and inscrutable reasons she had for taking her own life. After the bombardment, the same image was used to justify attacks on the Serbs.

Step 3: The Media Makes Accusations without Investigation

The International Committee for the Red Cross (ICRC) released the names of 10,000 people who were listed as missing in Srebrenica. The figure of 10,000 was arrived at in this fashion. The ICRC received 10,000 inquiries about civilians who had been transported from Srebrenica to Tuzla. About 2,000 inquires came from family members.

Overnight, "the missing" were redefined as "the dead" by a *New York Times* article, "8,000 Muslims Missing" (Sept. 15, 1995).

> About 8,000 Muslims are missing from Srebrenica ... the Red Cross said today. (...) Among the missing were 3,000, mostly men.... After the collapse of Srebrenica, the Red Cross collected 10,000 names of missing people, said Jessica Barry, a spokeswoman. In addition to those arrested, about 5,000 "have simply disappeared," she said.

Srebrenica also got its own tag line: "the worst genocide since WWII."

This ICRC list served to launch the indictment against Radovan Karadžić and Ratko Mladić on charges of genocide, which provided the "legal" basis for punitive action (military, economic, and political in nature) against the Bosnian Serbs.

Svetlana Radovanović, a university professor and demographer, gave testimony on behalf of the defense at the ICTY on June 21 and 22, 2004. She rendered an opinion on a study performed by Helge Brunborg, in which Brunborg reasoned that 7,475 Muslim men and boys had been killed. Radovanović said candidly, "It is unacceptable as a piece of scholarly research."[10] She objected to the methodology used in the study, and pointed out the existence of duplicate names. "This is not demography," Radovanović testified. "This is statistical exhibitionism."[11] Yet the 8,000 figure still stands, unsupported by any evidence at all.

Step 4: The Western Objective Is Realized
Short Term Goals

The U.S. and NATO used the pretext of the Markale Market place bombing in Sarajevo (where 67 people were killed), as well as the alleged Srebrenica "massacre," to trigger the bombardment of the Bosnian Serbs into submission in August 1995.[12] Schools, hospitals, power plants, bridges, roads, television and radio transmitters were bombed in the Republika Srpska. During the negotiations at Dayton, the Bosnian Serbs were not allowed to represent themselves after having been stigmatized by the massacre allegations. Instead, President Milošević negotiated on their behalf. They later accused him of having given the U.S. and the Muslims everything that they had asked for as well as everything they had not asked for. President Clinton and Secretary of State Madeleine Albright hailed President Milošević as indispensable to the negotiations. The Croats successfully executed Operation Storm and drove 250,000 Serbs out of Krajina.

Mid-Term Goals

Bosnia was successfully reduced to a puppet state, and the first High Representative of the UN, Carlos Westendorp was installed. The High Representative was granted the power to override all decisions made by the Bosnian legislature. The High Representative controls aid, and can dismiss elected officials at will. Bosnia was successfully separated from Yugoslavia, and the Serbs in Bosnia were divided from Serbia by U.S. military force. The U.S. built the Eagle military base in Tuzla, which will be used as "a 'lilly pad' facility from which the military could launch forces for world-wide contingencies."[13]

Long Term Goals

The Hague Tribunal received a new list of high profile indictments that appear to justify a U.S./NATO presence in the former Yugoslavia. After the Dayton Agreement, prospects for the oil pipeline looked favorable. It was one of the reasons for America's pro-Croatian strategy. Michel Chussodovsky wrote that "Chicago-based Amoco was among several foreign firms that subsequently initiated exploratory surveys in Bosnia. The west is anxious to develop these regions." He added that there were "substantial petroleum fields" in the then-Serb held territories "just across the Sava River from the Tuzla Region."[14] The area would be later incorporated into Croatia. Brzezinski's vision, as expressed in his book, *The Grand Chessboard*, was coming together piece by piece.

In January 2005, the Prime Ministers of Bulgaria, Macedonia and Albania signed a political declaration giving their approval for a 900 km oil pipeline to connect the Bulgarian Black Sea port of Burgas with the Albanian Adriatic port of Vlore.

Step 5: The Correction of Erroneous News Reports: Too Late and No Impact

An examination of the Red Cross list of the missing showed numerous names appeared in duplicate and triplicate. A third of the names, strangely enough, have no birth date. An analysis of the remaining names yields two categories: 5,000 inquires about people who left Srebrenica before it fell; the other 3,000 inquiries concern people who were legally arrested by Bosnian Serb Forces.[15]

A local election was held in Srebrenica in 1997 under the supervision of the OSCE; the Muslim faction won the election, however, some 3,000 people from the list of the missing voted in this election. Although the local Serbs filed a complaint, the OSCE ignored it. As a result, the Serbs decided not to recognize the legitimacy of the Assembly.[16]

Various news reports from both Western and Bosnian Muslim news sources indicated that at least 3,000 to 4,000 troops from Srebrenica arrived safely in Tuzla.[17]

> "They had made their way from Srebrenica 'without their families being informed,' a spokesman [i.e., for the ICRC] said, adding that it had not been possible to verify the report because the Bosnian Muslim government refused to allow the Red Cross into the area."[18]

The Bosnian Serbs issued a report in 2002 (the "2002 Srebrenica Report") that indicated that 1,500 to 1,800 Bosnian Muslim soldiers had been killed in battle, and that perhaps 100 or so had been summarily executed. The Bosnian Serb army sustained casualties of 500 deaths during these battles. Paddy Ashdown, the UN High Representative, rejected the report and ordered the Bosnian Serb government to produce a new one consistent with Western claims.

Al-Qaeda links to Srebrenica's Muslim defenders were uncovered by the Dutch government's lengthy report on Srebrenica, and by a U.S Republican Party Press Release.[19] The Dutch

Report also revealed that President Clinton had supported the Bosnian Muslims to pay back Muslim fundamentalists for staying out of Gulf War I.

These candid revelations of Bosnian Muslim casualties in Srebrenica and other reports of Islamic fundamentalist activity in Bosnia had no impact and remain underreported.

The Srebrenica 'Massacre': The Making of a Myth

David Rohde, at the time a cub reporter for the Christian Science Monitor, *won a Pulitzer prize in 1996 for his stories about Srebrenica. In 1997, he published his book-length study of the alleged Srebrenica massacre,* Endgame: The Betrayal and the Fall of Srebrenica, Europe's Worst Massacre since World War II. *His book supposes that a "massacre of 7,000 Muslim men and boys" did take place. He based his case on nothing more than "a pair of eyeglasses, a walking stick and a putrefying leg sticking out of the ground" near Srebrenica, where fighting had been raging for three years. Taking into consideration his proven track record, if either* The New York Times *or the* Christian Science Monitor *deigned to send Mr. Rohde to the North Pole to write a global warming story, we can rest assured that Mr. Rohde will find snow there.*

Rohde's principal witness to the alleged massacre was Melvudin Orić, who later went on to deliver crucial testimony to The Hague Tribunal that would convict Bosnian Serb General Krstić of genocide charges. Not long afterward, a Croatian weekly news magazine revealed that Melvudin Orić was a cousin of Naser Orić. Mr. Rohde quoted him extensively in Endgame. *In his footnotes, Mr. Rohde often cites sources, and just as often omits the names of his "sources," who asked not to be named in order to "protect them from retaliation." Mr. Rhode is more likely than not concealing U.S. intelligence sources.*

Even though his chief witness has been discredited, and his sources unverifiable, Rohde wrote an article called "The Warehouse of Death" that set the tone for thousands of other Srebrenica articles. The collapse of the allegations that a genocide against Albanians had taken place in Kosovo in 1999 was answered with renewed allegations that a genocide had indeed taken place in Srebrenica.

The Warehouse of Death

In Bosnia, Massacre Victims Lie While the Living Bicker,
by David Rohde, *The New York Times*, 03/11/01
Copyright © 2001 by The New York Times. Reprinted with permission.

During the summer of 1995, Serb soldiers carried out the single worst massacre of the war in Bosnia. Thousands of Bosnian Muslim men — who had given up their arms after the United Nations pledged to protect them — were killed in a series of ambushes and mass executions in and around Srebrenica. According to the International Committee of the Red Cross, more than 7,000 disappeared and are presumed dead.

The 4,420 body bags being held in a Tuzla warehouse for burial are the product of five years of exhumations by war-crimes investigators. Because of procedural delays and money shortages, the search is expected to drag on for another two years. Many bodies may never be found, thanks to the passage of time and a Serb campaign to hide the evidence by digging up the corpses and reburying them in remote locations.

There are 1,895 full bodies in the bags. Beyond that, the exact number of victims is unknown: 1,799 bags hold the body parts of a single person; 694 hold the body parts of two or more people. Thirty-two bags have not been autopsied. Only 81 of the victims have been identified. Most of the corpses are so badly decomposed or maimed as to be unrecognizable.

Disputes over the number of victims, and where and how to bury them, are keeping the bodies in limbo. Serb nationalists insist that the number of victims has been wildly exaggerated. In fact, despite the overwhelming evidence to the contrary, some deny any massacre took place at all. Srebrenica's widows say that the total number of victims is closer to 10,000.

Just how many there are is a pivotal issue. The power of the bodies is that they control how history will be told. And all sides realize that controlling history in the Balkans, a region where the past sometimes seems to define the present, is a key to controlling power.

DNA samples have been taken from 1,500 bodies in the warehouse, and those men are ready for burial. (The remains will be identified later through matches with relatives.) But then there is the battle over where they should be buried. The widows want them interred along the main road into Srebrenica. Forcing the Serbs to view thousands of graves every day, the widows say, is the only way to make them face the blood on their soldiers' hands. Serb nationalists, who still control the area, oppose the idea.

The Serb leaders indicted as war criminals for overseeing the executions remain free. Despite numerous opportunities, NATO soldiers in Bosnia have failed to arrest Radovan Karadzic, the former Bosnian Serb president, who is now thought to be hiding in the mountains of eastern Bosnia. And the new Yugoslav government has so far allowed Gen. Ratko Mladic, the former Bosnian Serb Army commander, to live comfortably in a villa in Belgrade, 100 miles from the warehouse of death.

The "massacre" is presumed to be factual.

This is an outright lie. The Bosnian Muslim "men" were actually soldiers who *never* gave up their arms.

The ICRC list of 10,000 names has, after the removal of duplicate and triplicate entries, only 2,000 names of missing men.

Rohde is hedging his bets. The Serbs did not have the manpower, the equipment or the interest to perform such reburials. The 31 new mass graves revealed in June 2004 turned out to be, in fact, only 4 new mass graves. Since these bodies have not been identified, one cannot presume they are Bosnian Muslims. How many of the unidentified are Serbs who were killed by Muslims? As long as the bodies remain unidentified, we will never know. The fact that the Hague Tribunal does not allow the exhumation of Serbian mass graves in Bosnia only gives further cause for suspicion.

Why have only 81 bodies been identified six years after the alleged massacre?

Rohde dismisses the Serbian response to the allegations (by mere rhetorical acknowledgement) without even examining their substance.

The Association of the Widows and Mothers of Srebrenica has less than 100 members. Where are the remaining widows and mothers of the remaining 6,900 men?

Islamists, who frequently invoke Srebrenica in their recruitment videos for mujahideen, cite the death toll as 15,000.

So this is not about establishing a sober and dispassionate account about what took place in Srebrenica, but about "how history will be told." The Srebrenica "massacre" finds its origin in a list of the missing, who were then transformed into the "dead" and were finally mythologized as "victims."

The question of the burial place was resolved when Paddy Ashdown, UN High Representative to Bosnia, ordered the Bosnian Serbs to pay for the Potočari Memorial Monument. When President Clinton made the opening address at the unveiling of the cemetery, there were only 882 bodies buried there,[20] and another 107 were buried there the day Clinton gave his speech, bringing the total to 989.[21]

The closing paragraph is meant to stir up indignation and outrage, which is meant to prevent any objective and rational discussion of what took place in Srebrenica.

250 ♦ *Ratko Mladić*

Srebrenica — The Backstory

"Before WWI, Serbs accounted for 75% of the population of the municipality of Srebrenica. Before WWII, they accounted for 50% of the population. Before the outbreak of the Bosnian War, they accounted for only 30% of the population. This tremendous population decline was not caused by a drop in birth rate or migration. It was a direct result of genocide carried out by Muslim and Croat neighbors."[22]

More than 3,000 Serbian civilians were killed in Srebrenica and its surroundings since the start of the Bosnian civil war. Some 150 Serbian villages were attacked and razed. The most horrible attack came on Orthodox Christmas Day (January 7, 1993) in the village of Kravice where dozens of Serbian civilians were killed. Naser Orić, a former special operations officer with the SUP (Interior Ministry) in Belgrade and bodyguard for President Milošević who had been fired for theft, resurfaced in Srebrenica as a Muslim commander. He led well-armed Muslim forces in surprise attacks against the unprotected Serbian civilian population. These Muslim forces were composed of thugs who had been trained professionally during the war in Croatia the year before, where they had committed war crimes against Serbian civilians. They plundered Serbian villages, burned Serbian homes, and killed and tortured Serbian civilians.

ICTY Prosecutor Dermot Groome asked Morillon a question about the Kravica attack on Orthodox Christmas: "General, your statement details attacks by Naser Orić, particularly the Orthodox Christmas Eve attack." Morillon replied: "The actions that you are referring to were one of the reasons for the deterioration of the situation in the area, especially in the month of January. Naser Orić engaged in attacks during Orthodox holidays and destroyed villages, massacring all the inhabitants. This created a degree of hatred that was quite extraordinary in the region, and this prompted the region of Bratunac in particular — that is the entire Serb population — to rebel against the very idea that through humanitarian aid one might help the population that was present there."[23]

The only Serbs who survived were those who fled. The mainstream media in the West did not mention that "ethnic cleansing" or "genocide" was taking place. But in April 1993, when General Mladić was on the verge of taking Srebrenica, the conscience of the Western media was awakened and it sprang into action. The civilians in Srebrenica had to be saved (along with 10,000 Muslim soldiers) from "unprovoked Serbian aggression." On March 12, 1993, French General Morillon talked his way through the Serbian front lines and entered the town. He declared, without any authorization from his superiors at the UN, Srebrenica to be a "safe haven," and put the town under "the protection of the UN." General Mladić proposed either the demilitarization of Srebrenica or the evacuation of civilians. His demands were rejected.

Humanitarian Aid to Srebrenica

General Morillon's *beau geste* won world-wide sympathy for the Muslims. Appeals were made for humanitarian aid deliveries. However:

- Despite the call for aid deliveries, not one single case of death from starvation was registered on the Bosnian Muslim side in Bosnia during the war, as reported by the Bosnian Muslims;

- The Bosnian Muslims in Srebrenica launched larger offensive operations during winter of 1992 and spring of 1993 after each such delivery of "humanitarian aid";

- There are many indications that the entire campaign to deliver "humanitarian" aid and open up corridors through Serbian territory began in order to supply the Muslims with weapons, logistics, and military equipment. The delivery of weapons was done by air, while food and medicine were mostly delivered by road.[24]

The Srebrenica "safe area" was supposed to be demilitarized, but this did not stop Naser Orić's soldiers from raiding nearby Serb villages. The "safe area" survived for two years. Then a Bosnian Muslim raid, occurring soon after the collapse of the heavy-weapons exclusion zone around Sarajevo, plus the slow formation of the West's Reaction Force, gave General Ratko Mladić the reasons he needed for extracting the thorn of Srebrenica from the Bosnian Serbs' eastern side. But Mr. Orić escaped.[25]

Set forth below is an eyewitness testimony[26] concerning only one of Naser Orić's attacks:

STATEMENT

"The Village of Zalazje," by Velisav Vasić, known as Veljko, the son of Sreten, born 1962 in Radosevići-Srebrenica. Occupation: Laborer, Serbian.

After the fall of Srebrenica and the capture and destruction of many Serbian villages by the Muslims, I found myself in the village of Zalazje as a refugee. Like the other villagers, I joined the defense of the last Serbian village in the region of Srebrenica.

At about 5:15 a.m. on May 8, 1992, the Muslims attacked us from the surrounding Muslim strongholds on all sides. The defense of the village lasted until 3:00 p.m. We defended it and repulsed the attack, but there were 6 dead and 12 wounded peasants who had taken part in defending the village. That day the Muslims had managed to capture a part of the village and put it to the torch, but we succeeded afterwards in driving them out of the village. The next day after the fighting, we collected 5 dead Muslims and exchanged them for the peasants in the burned village of Čumavići.

Following this attack on the village, and advance party of the Muslim army from the surrounding villages, consisting of 5 armed Muslims and two women, attacked our watch in Zalazje and I was wounded on that occasion.

After recovering from the wound I returned to the village of Zalazje to help defend the village.

On July 12, 1992, on the Serbian Orthodox feast of St. Peter, at about 9:00 a.m., the Muslim fundamentalists attacked us on all sides. The village was defended by 47 villagers and the cook Radinka Cvjetinović. Željko Giljević from Srebrenica, a Croat who joined in with his family in the defense of the village of Zalazje and Momčilo Rakić from Zalazje, were killed immediately when the attack began.

The fighting lasted all day. At about 7:00 p.m., we were short of ammunition and more and more people started getting killed. Five people managed to get to a vehicle and escape, but two were unable to get into the car and were killed. The vehicle was full of bullet holes. The following people managed to get away under the fire: Nenad Grujičić, Gavro Pajić, Slavko Pajić, Tomo Jeremić and Branislav Stanojević. I watched as six of our men were captured: Miodrag Rakić, the brothers Branko and Pero Simić, Milisav Ilić, Slobodan Ilić, a judge from Srebrenica, and Miladin Tubić. We were on the other side of our car and were unable to withdraw. Since six of us were left, we climbed to the attic of a new house.

The Muslims had already entered the village and began to set fire to the rest of the houses and kill the village defenders who were wounded, while only one was unhurt, a child who I think was called Milan Jeremić. That day his brother and two cousins and a considerable number of his family were killed. The house, where we had hidden in the attic, was first plundered by the Muslims and then set on fire. We lowered ourselves out of the burning house on which the roof was already blazing, by means of a piece of cable we found, at about 10:00 p.m. and then made our way to Sase. It took us nine hours to travel the three kilometers from the burning house.

While we were inside the burning house, we watched our men being taken prisoner, the houses being pillaged, we heard the Serbs being cursed and saw the houses being set on fire and then they ran wild through the village. The enemy force lined up in front of the house where we were. With me in the attic were: Milomir Lazarević, Gojko Jevtić, Milan Jeremić and another two villagers whose names I cannot remember now.

The enemy force lined up in front of Naser Orić, a policeman from Srebrenica I know well. During the fighting and after the enemy force had lined up I was able to see clearly who were the leaders in slaughtering the Serbian population:

1. Zulfo Turšunović
2. Hakija Meholjić, a policeman from Srebrenica
3. Amir Mehmedović, known as "Geza"
4. Senahid, a policeman from Bratunac and I heard one of the policemen call him Nurija. He was think and dark.

   Each of them lined up their units and with them was a unit of Gypsies headed by a Gypsy from Kazan, whom I knew by his nickname "Hake."

   Of the fighters in the Muslim units who attacked Zalazje and committed the aforesaid massacre, I also recognized:

5. A person by the nickname "Beno," a worker in the "Sase" zinc and lead mine, born in Srebrenica.
6. A person by the nickname of "Mijač" from Srebrenica
7. A person by the nickname of "Kreja," also from Srebrenica.
8. A person called "Đuli" from Srebrenica
9. Velid Delić from Srebrenica
10. Sarija Mulalić from Bajramovići, municipality of Srebrenica
11. Šukrija Ćelo from Potočari, who worked in the battery plant
12. A person who played football and is also called "Ćelo" from Srebrenica
13. Husić, I don't know his surname, known as "Hake," from Srebrenica, otherwise a teacher from Potočari.

After being treated in the hospital, of the five of us who were wounded, two suffered serious nervous breakdowns and are completely disabled.

Here's how Naser Orić described one of his other attacks against a Serbian village, which he had videotaped. The reporter referred to the video tape as Nasir Orić's Greatest Hits, which featured houses set on fire, corpses, decapitated heads, and fleeing refugees:

> Orić grinned throughout, admiring his handiwork.
>
> "We ambushed them," he said when a number of dead Serbs appeared on the screen.
>
> The next sequence of dead bodies had been done in by explosives: "We launched those guys to the moon," he boasted.
>
> When footage of a bullet-marked ghost town appeared without any visible bodies, Orić hastened to announce: "We killed 114 Serbs there."
>
> Later there were celebrations, with singers with wobbly voices chanting his praises.[27]

From the onset of the Srebrenica crisis, Bosnian Muslim propaganda claimed that there were 120,000 civilians in the area. But when Srebrenica did fall, there were only 40,000, including 10,000 solders among the civilians, who were found there. They played the same numbers game around Žepa, Goražde, and Bihać.

Dubious "ham radio operators" created fabricated news reports during a number of battles (*viz*, Srebrenica, Goražde, and Bihać). The mainstream media picked up the desperate pleas and warnings of impending doom from these unidentified ham radio operators and broadcast them unchallenged. The medium of live broadcast radio itself added a note of urgency. In reality, these reports were often entirely fabricated accounts that were produced by the Bosnian Muslim government in Sarajevo.

The Bosnian Muslims were adept at controlling the info war. They had successfully bombed their own people in Sarajevo on two occasions: the Markale Market Place Massacre and the Breadline Massacre on Vasa Miskin Street.[28] And the Bosnian Muslims, with generous western media support, managed to convince world public opinion that these massacres were attributable to the Serbs.[29]

The alleged massacre at Srebrenica has been described as "the worst massacre since WWII, where 7,000 Muslim men and boys were slaughtered." This mantra has been repeated billions of times. It is a pity that none of it is true.

Srebrenica — Exploitation of Muslim Refugees

Naser Orić demonstrated little concern for the Muslim refugees who had sought refuge there. They had already fled fighting in Eastern Bosnia in the spring 1993, and were desperate to leave Srebrenica ever since they arrived. "Instead, they have been forced to remain by the local Muslim warlord, Naser Orić, who drove around town in a Mercedes while the refugees sustained on meager UN handouts and were, occasionally, sold water by Srebrenica residents during the brutally-hot summers."[30]

Orić and the Bosnian Muslim government understood that if the refugees were transferred to safety in Tuzla, they would lose UN protection, and would not be able to hold the enclave, which was surrounded by Serbian forces.

The refugees in Srebrenica were subjected to horrible treatment. The Dutch peacekeepers suffered at the hands of the Bosnian Muslim Army, as well, and they made no effort to disarm Bosnian Muslim soldiers in Srebrenica. In fact, one wonders how they could have agreed to undertake such disarmament. There were 200 Dutch peacekeepers "protecting" between 10,000 and 15,000 Bosnian Muslim solders. On the one hand, Orić's elite death squads continued attacking Serbian villages, while, on the other hand, they freely terrorized Muslim refugees (rape, extortion, price gouging). When the refugees elected a representative to seek better treatment form Orić, the representative was murdered within hours of his election. The Bosnian Muslim Army even fired on Dutch UN peacekeeping personnel carriers that had formed a line of defense against the advancing Bosnian Serb Army, but the anti-tank rocket missed.[31] "The captured observation posts came under tank fire, and a peacekeeper was shot dead, the 67th to be killed in the conflict by Bosnian government forces, as the Dutch troops retreated from the advancing Bosnian Serb forces."[32] The wording of the articles conceals the fact that the only UN peacekeeper to be killed in Srebrenica had been killed by the Bosnian Muslims.

The Dutch soldiers unanimously asserted that "the Bosnian Muslim soldiers who had been under siege in Srebrenica for three years abandoned the town two days before it fell," and that Dutch soldiers saw that "in two locations there was fighting between those who wanted to stay and those who wanted to go."[33] The number of Bosnian Muslims who died fighting one another will remain a mystery, but the Bosnian Muslim government will never acknowledge this.

The Bosnian Muslims, in fact, put up only token resistance.[34] This is strange because the Bosnian Muslim Army had shown that it had improved considerably as a fighting force as was demonstrated in its most recent attacks on Serbian villages. As mentioned earlier, there were 10,000 to 15,000 Bosnian Muslim Army troops in the town. Meanwhile, the Serbian force that actually entered the town consisted of 400 men and five tanks. This was, by any measure, a low-level operation. There were another 1,200 to 1,500 rear guard Serbian troops that took part in the operation. The main Serbian force merely bypassed the Dutch base by taking a road about a mile south of the town.

Even though the Muslims, who were adequately armed for street fighting and outnumbered the Serbs by perhaps five-to-seven to one, fled. This suggests that the Muslims deliberately "lost" the town. "The Bosnian government deliberately increased the suffering of the Muslim refugees fleeing Srebrenica to put pressure on the international community, according to the documents made available to the *Daily Telegraph*."[35]

Among the aforementioned documents were instructions to the UN from the Izetbegović government that the refugees had to be transferred to a single location rather than be distributed to numerous other available refugee centers. The subsequent news footage and print stories highlighted stressed-out and short-handed aid workers in Tuzla coping with the flood of refugees, which created a mediagenic environment for provoking an international response on behalf of the refugees. This was where Ferida Osmanović had hanged herself.

These tactics are redolent of those used during the Markale Green Market Massacre and the Vasa Miskin Bread Line Massacre. Attack one's own people, then blame it on the official enemy. The Bosnian Muslim government in Sarajevo stepped up the pressure on the UN by claiming that up to 15,000 people had been massacred.

Investigators for the ICTY arrived a year later to search for evidence. They found the proof they were looking for, which consisted of four corpses.[36] Yet, as early as August 1995, the "missing enclave troops" were reported to have arrived safely in Tuzla.[37]

The Bosnian Muslim Army had, in fact, been ordered by the Savajevo government not to surrender to the enemy, and to attack the northern flanks of the Bosnian Serb Army positions. Serbian troops, who were outnumbered, were in no position to "massacre" the Bosnian Muslim Army troops — they were instead fighting off a Bosnian Muslim fighting retreat. Three to five hundred elite Serbian troops were killed in these encounters.

UN Secretary General Boutros Boutros-Gali attempted to counter the deliberate false impressions of Srebrenica that had been presented by the Bosnian Muslims to the Security Council. On May 30, 1995, the Secretary General argued in an official document that no enforcement mechanism had ever been established for the "safe area" concept with respect to the six Muslim towns that had been "surrounded" by the Serbs. The Security Council did not demand that the Bosnian Muslim government withdraw its forces and winked at their continued attacks against Serbs.

In response to reports of the alleged Srebrenica massacre, the Secretary general stated publicly that:

> "The international press ... made the battle for Srebrenica sound like Stalingrad.... There is a kind of dialectical relation between the attention of a great power and the power of the media," he said. "It creates a distortion in our work. What I am trying to do, without great success, is to correct this distortion."[38]

Finally, the Dutch troops themselves, who are by any account unbiased witnesses, had this to say: "Dutch Commander Lt.-Col. Ton Karremans said he and his men had seen no evidence to corroborate reports from fleeing refugees of mass killings by Bosnian Serb Troops."[39]

A representative of the UN High Commissioner for Human Rights, Hubert Weiland, was appointed to investigate. He spent five days interviewing refugees from Srebrenica during his investigation into alleged human rights abuses during the fall of Srebrenica. "But we have not found anyone who saw with their own eyes an atrocity taking place."[40]

The only thing that is certain about the official claims of a "massacre" having taken place in Srebrenica is that it completes the hat trick begun with the Markale Market Place "Massacre" and the Vasa Miskin Breadline "Massacre." It was merely a public relations confection created by the Bosnian Muslim government. Alija Izetbegović consistently chose to victimize Bosnian Muslims as well as Serbs and Croats in order to create a Muslim state in Europe, regardless of the cost in human life.

The Hague Tribunal then issued indictments against Radovan Karadžić and Ratko Mladić, accusing them of the massacre of 7,000 "men and boys" who were allegedly separated from the women and children, and then bused to Kladanj, Bratunac and other locations where they were machine-gunned *en masse*.

The Bosnian Serbs Reply

The Bosnian Serbs replied to these allegations with a report on Srebrenica prepared by the Republika Srpska Office of Relations with the International Criminal Tribunal for the Former Yugoslavia. This report, authored by Darko Trifunović, was published in September 2002.[41]

Seldom has an official government report provoked such unanimous censure, condemnation and ridicule as when the Bosnian Serbs issued the "Report about Case Srebrenica" in 2002 (hereinafter referred to as the "2002 Srebrenica Report"). International diplomatic circles made it clear to the Bosnian Serbs that the facts presented in the report were unacceptable, and that if they hoped to get any support from the "international community," they would have to change their tune. The outright rejection of the 2002 Srebrenica Report zeroed in on one single aspect: the Report's statement that a total of roughly 1,500-1,800 Bosnian Muslim soldiers had been killed when the Bosnian Serb Army, commanded by General Ratko Mladić, took the town in July 1995.

Set forth below is a summary of the Report's key findings.

The 2002 Srebrenica Report

The 2002 Srebrenica Report is what NPR would call a "deeply contextual analysis." Chapter one describes the current despair of the Serbs in Srebrenica, most of them IDPs (Internally Displaced People) who have no means of support and eke out a living on the lowest possible subsistence. The miniscule amount of Western aid that does reach the Bosnian Serbs avoids making Srebrenica a beneficiary of it.

The 2002 Report then describes how the Serbs went from being a majority in Srebrenica to a minority. During WWII, the Serbs of Srebrenica were repeatedly attacked by the Handžar Division, which numbered around 20,000 troops. The Handžar Division was organized under the auspices of the Nazi SS, and was composed exclusively of Bosnian Muslims. They attempted to exterminate the Serbs once and for all. The appalling cruelty they used was inherited from the Ottoman Turks, and they used rape, the gouging of eyes and castration against civilians. Alija Izetbegović was revealed to have enthusiastically collaborated with the Nazi ABWEHR and Gestapo, and worked as a recruiter for the "Young Muslims" (*Mladi Muslimani*), who went on to serve in the Handžar Division. The 2002 Srebrenica Report highlights Izetbegović's political agitation, whose goals he outlined in his book, *The Islamic Declaration* (1970), which advocated intolerance of other religions and proposed the introduction of Sharia law in Bosnia. The Muslim National Council, whose goal was the formation of an Islamic state in Bosnia, summoned Muslims from throughout Bosnia-Herzegovina to gather in Bratunac, "the geographical center of all Muslims in Yugoslavia" on the first day of Bajram in 1992. There, Muslims were called upon to take up arms against the Christian Serbs. It was at this time that Naser Orić became a key figure in the development of militant Islam, and later became the commander of the Territorial Defense Forces of Srebrenica.

The Muslim citizens of Srebrenica were just as afraid of what was happening as the Orthodox Christians were. Besim Ibišević (Muslim), who was the former President of the Srebrenica Township Assembly, recounted to a Sarajevo magazine that average Muslim citizens had gathered in large numbers in the Srebrenica Culture Club in April 1992, and chanted the slogan, "Peace at any price!" The Muslims of Srebrenica did not allow extremists like Naser Orić and Zulfo Turšunović (a criminal who was sentenced to 15 years imprisonment in 1986 for the murder of three Muslims, but who was pardoned by Izetbegović in 1991 and appointed Orić's deputy commander) to enter the town at first. Mr. Orić himself described how he had to hide in the forest with his companions in the beginning, and even had to obtain food clandestinely. Meanwhile, *Vox*, a radical Muslim Magazine in

Sarajevo, published the names of Serbs from Srebrenica who were to be killed because they had fought as Partisans against the Handžar Division. Only a feather touch was needed to incite a conflict between Christians and Muslims.

Ethnic Cleansing of Serbs

According to Sefer Halilović, former Chief of Staff of the B-H Army, the Muslim military strategy for Srebrenica was the total dependence on the food supplies and properties belonging to the Serbs. "The only source of our supplies was Chetnik (i.e., Serbian) stores and their production."[42]

Serbs were fired from jobs in government, education, the police force and other public institutions in Srebrenica. Then, after Orić and Turšunović infiltrated the town, and they began organizing attacks on and murders of Serbs in the region. The Serbian exodus from Srebrenica began on May 8, 1992, with the murder of Judge Goran Žekić, who was the leader of the Serbian Democratic Party (the *Srpska Demokratska Stranka* or SDS). Mr. Žekić was an elected representative in the B-H Parliament. On May 6, the Serbian hamlets of Blječeva and Gniona were torched and looted. On May 7, seven Serbs who were attempting to leave Srebrenica were killed in their automobiles. On May 15, the villages of Viogar, Orahovica, Rano, Civeci and Radoševi were attacked. The 2002 Srebrenica Report goes on to state that 192 Serbian villages were destroyed and put to the torch between May 1992 and January 1994. During the same period, 8,000 Serbian houses were attacked, and 5,400 were completely destroyed. More than a thousand people were killed, including men, women and children. The 2002 Srebrenica Report emphasized that 90% of them were killed during the six months following May 1992, despite the fact that the vast majority of them were civilians. Naser Orić also video-taped murders of Serbian civilians as war trophies. (*See* p. 254.)

> Nasir Oric's war trophies don't line the wall of his comfortable apartment — one of the few with electricity in this besieged Muslim enclave stuck in the forbidding mountains of eastern Bosnia. They're on a videocassette tape: burned Serb houses and headless Serb men, their bodies crumpled in a pathetic heap.
>
> "We had to use cold weapons that night," Oric explains as scenes of dead men sliced by knives roll over his 21-inch Sony. "This is the house of a Serb named Ratso," he offers as the camera cuts to a burned-out ruin.[43]

When Orić and his troops abandoned Srebrenica, they left behind these videotapes and a great many documents detailing the torture of civilians. This material was kept by the RS Commission of Legal Experts as evidence of crimes against Serbs. The 2002 Srebrenica Report provides this edifying example:

> One of the reports by the Muslim forces, number 06-08/95, details the death of a Serb man, Milko Marković, who remained in Srebrenica after the death of Judge Zekić. The report says: Milko Marković was arrested and taken to see Mish ["Mouse," a nickname, trans. note]. Mish tortured him, stabbed him with a knife and then slit his throat. However, as Milko was still alive, Mish took him to the small river in the center of Srebrenica and resumed torturing him. When Milko lost consciousness, Mish revived him by pouring water on him. Mish then set him on fire while he was still alive.

Mish is said to be "currently living in Tuzla without any problems." In June 1993, Dragomir Djokić, the *chargé d'affairs* of the Yugoslav Embassy in the United Nations, submitted a report and evidence of crimes by Muslims against Serbs in the region of Srebrenica to the General Assembly and the Security Council of the United Nations; however, no one ever condemned the crimes. Naser Orić was only charged ten years later with war crimes by The Hague Tribunal, and quite pointedly not for genocide. He was indicted only after the tragic events of 9/11, when his ties to mujahideen and al-Qaida could no longer be ignored.

The Future Muslim State and Its Corridors

The Muslim leaders intended to unite the territories of Srebrenica, Žepa and Goražde into a larger territory representing a corridor between a future Muslim state and Serbia. In the spring of 1993, Muslim forces began to run out of food and made the decision "to make use of their own civilians and the UN to further their cause." The Muslim leaders tried to prevent the fall of Srebrenica at all cost, even going as far as using the town as a human shield and refusing to evacuate civilians to other territories. "When the UN decided to evacuate 15,000 people at the end of March and beginning of April 1993, the Muslim leaders were furious, claiming that the UN operation was equivalent to ethnic cleansing and they decided that the convoy must not enter Tuzla, a Muslim-held territory." The same Muslim leaders later told a reporter working for *The Independent* the real reason for their decision: as long as civilians and refugees were present, the Serbs could not carry out a comprehensive attack. The UN Security Council declared Srebrenica a "demilitarized zone" under UN protection even though Muslim soldiers were allowed to keep their weapons and continued to launch attacks on the Serbs from the enclave. The 2002 Srebrenica Report states that:

> Under the command of a unit of the Eighth Operational Group, the 28th Division [of the BH Army] attacked the same Serb villages which had already been attacked in 1992 and 1993. Most of the attacks were terrorist acts committed by small groups of soldiers. More than 500 Serbs were murdered in attacks carried out from the 'safe haven' and the brutality of the attacks remained unchanged.

Furthermore, up to about a month before the fall of Srebrenica, Muslim forces from Srebrenica worked together with units of the Second Corps from Sarajevo to cut off road connections for Serb forces in the Vlasenica region. The author of the study also claims that the political and military leadership of Republika Srpska did not plan to conquer Srebrenica and quotes the former commander of Serb forces, Ratko Mladić, as having said that he "would not have to attack enclaves if the Muslim soldiers in them had been disarmed."

Estimates of Bosniak Casualties

The author, describing the situation after Srebrenica fell into the hands of Serb forces, states that General Mladić organized the evacuation of the residents of Srebrenica after negotiations with the Dutch representative of UNPROFOR and representatives of the Muslim civilians. The 2002 Srebrenica Report states that:

> Mladić kept telling them to tell their soldiers to turn in their weapons within 24 hours. He told them that if they turned in their weapons, the Muslim soldiers, even those not in uniform and those who were war criminals, would be treated according to the Geneva Convention. This did not occur due to the fact that many of the Muslim soldiers had Serb blood on their hands from the period from 1992 to 1995. Fearing Serb revenge and hoping to remain unpunished, they decided to conduct a military breakthrough toward Tuzla to the territory under the control of the so-called B-H Army.
>
> (…)
>
> Mladić told General Smith on July 19 that he had opened the corridor toward Tuzla for Muslim soldiers who had left the enclave around July 10 and 11.

According to estimates cited in the 2002 Srebrenica Report, Muslim forces sustained casualties of approximately 2,000 soldiers, who were killed in a fighting retreat when Serb forces conquered the former safe haven July 1995. Approximately 1,800 Muslim soldiers were killed fighting Serb forces during their retreat and about 100 more died as a result of exhaustion.

> The number of Muslim soldiers killed by Bosnian Serbs out of personal revenge or lack of knowledge of international law is probably about 100.... It is important to uncover the names of the perpetrators in order to accurately and unequivocally establish whether or not these were isolated incidents.

This part of the 2002 Srebrenica Report met with the fiercest criticism.

Fleeing through the Forest

The 2002 Srebrenica Report, citing numerous sources, states that between 10,000 and 15,000 Muslim soldiers

> fled Srebrenica through the forest.... Fierce battles were waged between these Muslim soldiers and the Bosnian Serb soldiers. The battles were intense because the Muslim soldiers had to pass through Buljim, Kravica, Pobudje, Bajkovica and Crni Vrh after coming out of the forest. Since the Bosnian Serb forces had anti-aircraft artillery, they had only to wait and open fire on masses of Muslim soldiers coming out of the forest; nevertheless, the Bosnian Serb forces lost in several locations, such as Bajkovica and Krizevac, and sustained losses of between 300 to 500 soldiers.
>
> (...)
>
> Dr. Ilijas Pilav, who succeeded [making] this journey, said that he noticed many drowned men when he crossed the Jadar River.[44]

The 2002 Srebrenica Report, taking into consideration the considerable losses incurred y Serb forces, estimated that the Muslim forces sustained losses of approximately 2,000 soldiers. These clashes did not occur on the major thoroughfares used by automobile and bus traffic but on rural roads. UNHCR sources stated that approximately 6,000 Muslim soldiers arrived in Zenica through the forest.

> In his book *Lukava Strategija* ("A Cunning Strategy"), [former BH Army commander] Sefer Halilović also confirms that the 28th Division of the Muslim Army was reorganized after its withdrawal

from Srebrenica, and that it was comprised of 6,000 soldiers who broke through the lines of the Bosnian Serbs.

According to the Republika Srpska Office for Relations with the ICTY, approximately 25,000 to 40,000 Muslims, primarily women, children and old people, decided to surrender and gathered in Potočari. Men of fighting age "comprised two to three percent of the total number." The women, children and old people were transferred to Kladanj in Muslim-held territory while the men who turned themselves in,

a total of some 500 to 750 of them were transferred to Bratunac where they were checked for war crimes and divided into three groups: those who had no criminal record, those who required additional checks and those who were known to be war criminals.

The first group of about 500 men was taken to Kladanj in Muslim-held territory immediately after the check. On July 14 the second group was transferred to the collection center Batkovce in Bratunac. The third group was sent from Bratunac to the prison in Zvornik.

The 2002 Srebrenica Report denies the allegation that thousands of Muslims from Srebrenica were murdered in a school in Karakaj near Zvornik. School was in session on July 13 (with class attendance records as proof) and quotes testimony by two Muslim women from Mali Zvornik who said that they heard no gunshots from the other side of the river on that day. The 2002 Srebrenica Report goes on to add that it is highly likely that some Muslim soldiers were

summarily shot out of personal revenge, taking into account that some Serbs were killed during 1992 and 1993 by their Muslim neighbors in extremely brutal fashion.

For example, according to one Dutch soldier, a Muslim in Potočari on July 13 was pulled out of a group and shot. Another Dutch soldier saw Bosnian Serbs "leading a group of ten Muslim soldiers on July 12; nine bodies were later found in the location where they were last seen," says the study, adding that some of the older Serbs indicated that General Mladić personally opposed "every form of illegal behavior and conduct on the part of his soldiers."

List of Missing Persons

The 2002 Srebrenica Report, in further support of its claim that the figure of 6,000 to 8,000 Bosniak casualties is inflated, states that no date of birth was given for 3,381 of the 6,610 persons listed as missing in Srebrenica in the "Book of the Missing," which was compiled by the International Committee of the Red Cross.

> Of the first ten thousand requests filed by families of missing persons, two thousand were duplicates and five thousand named people who had already left Srebrenica before it fell to the Serbs.

The author of the 2002 Srebrenica Report personally visited Srebrenica and discovered that some of the names on the list of missing persons are actually names from the gravestones of people who had long been deceased. He determined that 180 of the inquiries of missing persons on the list left the enclave prior to its fall and, based on documentation left by the Muslim forces in Srebrenica, that 190 out of 3,110 inquiries for people whose names appeared on the list of the missing were deceased prior to the fall of Srebrenica.

"The most recent investigation located 700 additional people from the ICRC list of missing persons," emphasized the 2002 Srebrenica Report. It anticipates that the number of valid inquiries will ultimately drop to between 2,000 and 2,500.

> Another factor is efforts of Muslim soldiers to conceal their identity in order to avoid the war criminal charge from Bosnian Serb forces. They gave false identities to international organizations when they wanted to get out of Srebrenica, and they gave their real name when they arrived at a Muslim territory. Thus, false names remained in the missing list. In Srebrenica, the author noticed that some of the names on the grave stones were identical with the names in the missing list. Probably, they used the names of their dead friends or relatives.

On the other hand, associations of families of missing persons from Srebrenica claim that in July 1995 ten thousand Bosniak civilians were killed in Srebrenica. No mention is made of armed Muslim soldiers under the command of Naser Orić. It is also surprising that official international institutions (the United Nations, The Hague tribunal) do not have reasonably accurate numbers for Srebrenica casualties. These international organizations not only insult the victims of Srebrenica but also demonstrate their lack of readiness to establish the full truth of the Srebrenica tragedy.

Otherwise, The Hague Tribunal would have allowed the exhumation of Serb victims in this region and would have reacted in a more timely fashion to the indictment against Naser Orić forwarded by the Republika Srpska Government in 1993.

One thing is certain: until it is publicly acknowledged that approximately 3,200 Serbian civilians, if not more, were killed during the last war in the Srebrenica and Bratunac region and until those responsible for these crimes are indicted by the Hague Tribunal, the Serbs will not be ready to face what in fact happened in Srebrenica in July 1995.

Lord Ashdown's Handling of Srebrenica

Exacting a False Confession under Duress

Lord Paddy Ashdown, UN High Representative in Bosnia, dismissed the 2002 Srebrenica Report filed by the Bosnian Serb government as an "interim report," and other international officials branded it as a disgrace that attempted to minimize the number of victims in Srebrenica. The aforementioned report highlighted established facts (to which Dutch officers had testified) that the Bosnian Muslims had killed one another in disputes over whether or not to abandon Srebrenica. Ashdown would have none of it, and described the report as a "disgraceful whitewash."

Ashdown, as the top UN official in Bosnia, had the power to impose laws and remove officials if they did not comply with his interpretation of the Dayton Accords.

Then Ashdown worked in concert with U.S. Ambassador David Hays to pressure the Bosnian Serbs to issue a new falsified Srebrenica report in which the Republika Srpska would admit that it was responsible for murdering the requisite number of 8,000 Muslims in Srebrenica.[45]

The timing of the demands coincided with the unveiling of a memorial monument and cemetery that is dedicated solely to the alleged Muslim victims of Srebrenica. The unveiling was slated for September 19, 2003. Former U.S. President Bill Clinton was scheduled to attend the ceremonies in order to counter a growing body of documents and disclosures that portrayed his administration as a prime sponsor of radical Islamic fundamentalism in the Balkans. These underreported revelations are now crucial to re-evaluating the Clinton presidency. Many Islamic terrorist organizations had important ties with Bosnian Muslims, to whom Clinton had given limitless and uncritical support.

The U.S. Embassy contributed one million dollars to the construction of the Srebrenica Memorial, despite the fact that impartial investigations have demonstrated that the allegations of a "massacre" in Srebrenica are baseless and without merit.

It is worth noting that New York City Mayor Michael Bloomberg, a man who is reluctant to forgo any venture that yields a profit, rebuffed offers to establish a sister-city relationship with Srebrenica after the 9/11 attacks because the U.S. secret services presented a direct connection to Bosnian Islamic fundamentalists and the terrorist attack on the World Trade Center in New York City and the Pentagon in Washington. As mentioned earlier, "Thirteen of nineteen hijackers who destroyed the World Trade Center buildings in New York and attacked the Pentagon were in Kosovo-Metohija and Bosnia. They were for a while in the house of an American citizen of the Bosnian origin," said Dr. Miroljub Jevtić, a Professor of Political Science and expert on Islam at the University of Belgrade.[46]

We must bear these points in mind: 1) the only dispute about Srebrenica is the number of victims; 2) Ashdown demanded that the Bosnian Serbs issue an apology to the Bosnian Muslims because their official documents contradicted the claims of Bosnian Muslim propaganda; 3) Ashdown demanded that the Bosnian Serbs establish a new commission of inquiry that would "conduct more research" into the events that took place in Srebrenica. Furthermore, Ashdown stipulated that the Republika Srpksa would be responsible for financing the new commission.

Defense and Foreign Affairs Daily also reported that the Bush Administration turned a blind eye to Islamist entrenchment in the ex-Yugoslavia because of its obsession with Iraq and the "war against terror." Clinton Administration appointees, who are working closely with the Soros Foundation (which is openly anti-Serbian), have consolidated their hold on the former Yugoslavia. One moderate Muslim source in Sarajevo felt that the Bush administration had to act quickly because terrorism would soon spread from the Balkans to the rest of the world. The source thought that Bush was letting Clinton "cover his tracks."

> The radicals not only destroyed the Serbs, they also destroyed the
> lives of moderate Muslims. Now they will start another war. Why is
> the Bush Administration following the policies of the Clinton
> Administration? Why are Clinton people still running all the key posts
> in American embassies in the region?"[47]

Then in October 2003, Paddy Ashdown imposed a six-month
deadline on the Bosnian Serb government to disclose the fate of
the thousands of alleged Bosnian Muslim soldiers who remained
missing after the events that took place in Srebrenica in July
1995. Ashdown was quoted as saying that ascertaining the facts
of the missing Muslims was "taking far too long."

> "It is simply unacceptable that getting the truth from the (Bosnian
> Serb) government is like extracting rotten teeth," he said.[48]

The long-sought forced admission arrived not a month later in
November 2003, *The Independent* (UK) reported that the
Bosnian Serbs admitted for the first time that their forces were
responsible for the "mass slaughter" of Muslims in Srebrenica.
The article went on to say that a new report on Srebrenica had
been "compiled under pressure from Paddy Ashdown."[49] This
admission was based on testimony given at the Hague Tribunal
by Momir Nikolić, who was allegedly key to the cover up operation. Nikolić, pleaded guilty as charged. Dragan Obrenović, a
deputy commander who participated in the operation, said that he
was sorry for the crimes he had committed and offered an apology to the families of the victims.

The Republika Srpska, as it was ordered to do, established a
special commission to investigate the alleged deaths in
Srebrenica. Ashdown, who had issued his diktat in October 2003,
set a deadline of March 2004 for the new report.[50]

In April 2004, the Republika Srpska authorities revealed the
locations of six mass graves in the Srebrenica area. "The disclosure came after Paddy Ashdown … ordered Bosnian Serb authorities to cooperate — or lose their jobs."[51]

When the Republika Srpska authorities "failed to act," Ashdown
used his dictatorial powers to fire Gen. Cvjetko Savić, the Chief of
Staff of the Republika Srpska Army, and Dejan Miletić, the RS
official in charge of cooperation with the U.N. War Crimes
Tribunal in The Hague. Ashdown threatened the president and the
prime minister of the RS if the commission did not complete its

work by June 2004, the new extended deadline. "The Bosnian Serbs have been under great pressure to acknowledge that their forces committed atrocities in Srebrenica."[52]

Then more mass graves were found in the Srebrenica area in mid-May 2004. One of them was exhumed in Zalkopac in May 2004. The supposed victims, Bosnian Muslims, were alleged to have been killed at the outbreak of the Bosnia War by Bosnian Serb forces. "Experts were certain that the remains belonged to 72 Muslim civilians, including 16 children and 10 women."[53] The article went on to say that scattered human bones had also been found in the nearby town of Vlasenica. Only time will tell if they are victims of Bosnian Serb forces. Vlasenica was a Serbian town, and twelve Serbian civilians were murdered there in December 1993. This begs the question: Are the unidentified remains of Serbian civilians being counted as "Muslim victims"? And are victims brought from elsewhere being passed off as victims of the Srebrenica massacre? As long as the bodies remain unidentified, the question will remain unanswered. And the fact that the Hague Tribunal has forbidden the exhumation of Serbian mass graves only gives further cause for suspicion.

Then in early June 2004, the Republika Srpska government, under great international pressure, announced that it had found 31 new mass graves containing remains of alleged victims of "the Srebrenica massacre." The Republika Srpska government did not indicate how many victims were expected to be found in these gravesites. Amor Masović, a representative of the Bosnian Muslim-Croat Federation Commission for Missing Persons, indicated that "the graves *could* hold up to 2,500 bodies."[54] [Emphasis added.] Even so, it is doubtful whether these 31 new "mass graves," of which only four are actually new, will yield more than a hundred or two hundred bodies. At the very end, the article revealed that these were "secondary graves," allegedly reburied to hide traces of the massacre.

Finally, in early June 2004, Ashdown got what he had wanted all along: a Bosnian Serb admission that a "massacre of Muslims took place in Srebrenica."[55] The UN and Muslim authorities claimed to have found the remains of 5,000 victims in eastern Bosnia, and they find new remains every month. Quite pointedly, the article states that "nearly 1,200 Srebrenica victims have been identified through DNA analysis." The new report, so satisfactory to Lord Ashdown, reveals that the perpetrators "undertook measures to cover up the crime by moving the bodies" to other burial sites. This tactic allows people who were not even killed in Srebrenica to be counted as Srebrenica victims. Once again, Dražen Erdemović's false testimony[56] was resurrected. He claimed that his battalion alone had killed up to 1,200 people. Then Ashdown fired several Bosnian Serb officials who refused to provide the right kind of information, and he threatened others as well. Dejan Miletić, Head of the RS Secretariat for Cooperation with the ICTY, was among those dismissed. Ashdown stated that "a dynamic of obstructionism on war crimes issues is being replaced by a dynamic of greater cooperation." It just goes to show that the UN High Representative uses extortion and blackmail as normal management techniques.

The new 2004 Srebrenica Report issued by the Bosnian Serbs followed Ashdown's requirements to the letter, just as if it were a homework assignment. It repeated key elements the instructor wanted included, otherwise, the student would have been flunked. The 2004 Srebrenica Report now stated that Bosnian Serb forces had decided on a three-stage operation: first the town would be attacked; then the men would be separated from women and children; and lastly the execution of the men. The report affirmed that military and police units, along with units from the interior ministry, participated in the murders. Yet, the earlier 2002 Srebrenica Report discussed this and did not deny it. Buried at the end of the BBC article cited below, it states that only 4 of the new grave sites are original sites, while the other 28 were "secondary sites." And lastly, the article informs us that only 1,332 of the alleged victims have been identified, which falls right in line with the original estimates made by the 2002 Srebrenica Report. Beneath the high-decibel headline, there was nothing new at all.

Milan Bogdanić, the Bosnian Serb official who was in charge of the 2004 Srebrenica Report, said "This report will have a historic character." It is instead anti-historical — a fairy tale told by the emperor to his subjects as a bed time story. In a futile effort to prostrate himself before Lord Ashdown, Mr. Bogdanić remarked: "We have reached historic perceptions and we will have to face ourselves."

Then the next day the BBC carried the dramatic admission made by Dragan Ćavić, the Bosnian Serb President, who called the Srebrenica "massacre" a "black page in the history of the Serb people." Using George Bush I verbiage, he said in a special televised broadcast that he "understood the pain of the families who died in Srebrenica."

> Mr Ćavić's statement is also significant because he comes from the same political party as the former Bosnian Serb wartime leader Radovan Karadzic, who is wanted by the war crimes tribunal in The Hague to face genocide charges over what happened at Srebrenica.[57]

The article concluded, naturally, that nothing short of a full apology for Srebrenica would be accepted by Bosnia's Muslim community.

However, nothing is so instructive as having such success blow up in your face. After SFOR intelligence and counter-terrorism agents halted deliveries of weapons that were destined for mujahideen in Iraq, Paddy Ashdown himself was forced in June 2004, by SFOR leaders, to reinstate Dejan Miletić. Miletić had refused to accept responsibility for the "Srebrenica massacre" and his Commission delivered substantial evidence that refuted Ashdown's allegations.[58] Miletić's reinstatement was a sharp rebuke to Ashdown because he had obstructed western intelligence efforts in the Balkans. This was the only instance of an official in Bosnia being restored to his post after having been dismissed.

Ashdown has continued to turn a blind eye to Islamic terrorist links in Bosnia to the 9/11 and Madrid attacks and has continued to obstruct counter-terrorism efforts. He is obsessed with safeguarding his reputation as well as that of his Bosnian Muslim cronies, who have since revealed themselves to be Muslim fundamentalists instead of liberal democrats. One SFOR source remarked, "Ashdown is a big part of the problem."[59]

Dragan Ćavić, the Bosnian Serb President, expressed his regrets to Bosnian Muslims for the alleged massacre at Srebrenica and fulfilled Ashdown's request. He called it a black page in the history of the Serbian people.

Paddy Ashdown then rewarded the subservience of the Bosnian Serbs only two weeks later. He summarily dismissed 60 Bosnian Serb elected officials after having accused them of failing to help apprehend Radovan Karadžić.

"The Serb Republic has been in the grip of a small band of corrupt politicians and criminals for far too long," administrator Paddy Ashdown told reporters, referring to the zone of Bosnia that is controlled by the country's ethnic Serbs."[60]

The dismissals reflected mounting pressure on the Bosnian Serbs by foreign powers. NATO leaders in Istanbul had days earlier rejected Bosnia's petition to join NATO's Partnership for Peace program. The reason given was that the Bosnian Serbs had not apprehended either Radovan Karadžić or General Ratko Mladić. Ashdown expressed his frustration with the Bosnian Serb police forces: "What's not missing is information. It's the political will."[61] He spun the story well and made himself look good. In fact, it was the infiltration of Bosnia by Islamic fundamentalists that nixed NATO membership.

Ashdown also seized the bank account of the SDS as well as that of several major Bosnian Serb companies for allegedly shielding Karadžić and Mladić from arrest. Needless to say, the effect was to paralyze the largest Bosnian Serb political party as well as the Bosnian Serb economy.

"We hope that they will conclude that it is no longer worth it,"[62] said Ashdown's spokesman, Julian Braithwaite, of the dismissals and the seizure of the bank accounts.

The SDS's party coffers contained only 500,000 euros. The reason given for freezing the party's assets was that it had failed to ensure that SDS money did not go to support Karadžić from evading justice. Never mind that Ashdown could not prove that SDS funds had gone to support Karadžić. To add insult to injury, Ashdown used his far-reaching powers to donate the confiscated assets to the three Bosnian state institutions charged with tracking down war criminals.

Dragan Kalinić, MP Republika Srpska, who was also dismissed by Ashdown, said in his farewell address on July 2, 2004, that he planned to take his case to the European Court of Human Rights in Strasbourg because he had exhausted all of his legal options in Bosnia. "Such options exist, naturally, because of the semi-colonial system of government in this country, extremely limited and dictated to fail in advance."[63] He went on to say that:

I have been banned from all political and public work; entry into my office, my pay has been revoked, as well as my pension and social insurance. It is a paradox, but no one will any longer be able to hold me politically accountable for everything that will happen in the party and in the Republika Srpska.... Everything is open to criticism and so is my work and my behavior.

I have also been removed because the SDS did not make possible the arrest of Radovan Karadžić. This type of responsibility, which is being asked of one party (and the SDS is only one part of the current government) is without precedent in political or legal practice....

To those who have used my sentence without a trial and there, the most prominent places were held by Messrs. Bond, Ashdown and a few others, I would like to say the following: "The manners [sic] in which I was raised prevents me from sending you to the place where I believe my dearest, whom I had sacrificed for the Republika Srpska, would send you. I forgive you, even though you did this in a cowboy and colonial manner, in violation of the Constitution, the law and the elementary respect for the democratic will of the voters."[64]

Ashdown's Obsession

Ashdown, after having rejected the 2002 Srebrenica Report, compelled the Republika Srpska to pay for the Srebrenica Monument. In October 2003, Ashdown delivered a eulogy at the funeral of Alija Izetbegović that openly displayed his bias in favor of the Bosnian Muslims. "[H]e spent years in prison for the sake of a political vision that was often caricatured — and just as often misunderstood,"[65] said Ashdown, perhaps referring to Izetbegović's convictions for Nazi collaboration during WWII and the inciting religious hatred in 1982.

Thus, Ashdown's firings of elected officials created untold obstacles to counter-terrorism efforts in Bosnia-Herzegovina.[66] The Defense and Foreign Affairs article went on to quote an SFOR official:

[Ashdown's] only concern is to protect his own reputation and his old Muslim friends who have turned out to be radical Islamists and not the democratic moderates he thought them to be.[67]

As Nebojša Malić wisely pointed out in his thoughtful article, "Srebrenica Revisited," even though Ashdown succeeded in coercing a "confession" for Srebrenica, he was going to raise the bar even higher. Next, he demanded the arrest of Karadžić and Mladić. Whether the unlikely possibility of arrests would take place or not, Ashdown intended to use the new demand to leverage Bosnian Serb integration into Muslim government structures.

Recall Prof. Paunović's statement that a legal foundation was being established in order to declare the Republika Srpska a product of genocide.

Mr. Malić makes the shocking revelation that the new Commission Ashdown had instituted, which of course could not produce an impartial report under such circumstances, simply *copied* significant passages concerning the history and context of the alleged massacre from the recitation of facts contained in The Hague's verdict in *Prosecution* v. *Radislav Krstić*.[68] It is also noteworthy to recall that Melvudin Orić, Naser's cousin and David Rohde's source in *Endgame*, provided "key" testimony that resulted in General Krstić's conviction.

This case bears further scrutiny. Gen. Krstić was convicted of "genocide" on the basis of 46 deaths in what was a military action. The Hague Tribunal later actually "redefined" the term "genocide" in order to win Gen. Krstić's conviction. This is a lie, of course, but it is more devious than simply being a lie, which, once uncovered, is dispelled and never again considered except with contempt and amusement. Instead, this is the corruption of language, a perversion of words, which has lasting, deleterious consequences. The word "genocide" was coined to define the extermination of European Jews during WWII at the hands of the Nazis as well as the deaths of millions of Armenians at the hands of the Turks, which, incidentally, the U.S. government still does not officially recognize. Further, my Polish friends called to my attention that six million Poles also died during WWII at the hands of the Nazis. And, in addition to the Holocaust, let us take into consideration the fact that an estimated 30 million Slavs (Russians, Serbs, Bulgarians, Poles, Czechs, Slovaks, Ukrainians, etc.) perished during WWII. I rue the fact that the word "slavicide" had not been coined. It would have been apposite for the twentieth century. Now, with its new meaning, the word "genocide" has application in the case of a mere 46 deaths in a military action, but retains the primary connotation of the Jewish and Armenian exterminations. It is an insult to the genuine victims of genocide and their survivors, among whom we may honestly count staggering numbers of Serbian civilians who died during both WWI and WWII.

The prosecution in the Krstić case presented no evidence that 7,000-8,000 Muslims were "massacred." The burden of proof, according to The Hague, shifted to the defendant, Gen. Krstić, whose defense was unable to contest the charge. Of course, this does not prove that the charge is true.

Ashdown got his way finally. The publication of the 42-page 2004 Srebrenica Report by the Bosnian Serb government yielded global headlines along the lines of "Bosnian Serbs Own Up to Srebrenica Massacre." Unquestioning public opinion accepted this as definite proof that the alleged massacre of 8,000 "men and boys" was premeditated genocide, just as Alija Izetbegović, the Western news media, and the paralegal Hague Tribunal have maintained all along.

The 2004 Srebrenica Report is a document produced under duress, and, as such, is inadmissible in any court of law. This report is a product of Ashdown's threats, blackmail, extortion and summary dismissals of Bosnian Serb elected officials. Ashdown was obsessed with doing as much damage to the Bosnian Serbs as possible to please his own paymasters. The 2004 Report sheds new light on the events that took place in July 1995 only for "those today who continue to waive them [i.e., the distorted facts] about like a bloody shirt."[69]

The Bosnian Serbs never denied that Muslim POWs had been executed in the 2002 Srebrenica Report. This is not a confession to charges of genocide nor is it acknowledgment that "8,000 Muslim men and boys" had been "massacred."

The Hague Tribunal

The Hague Tribunal is a false institution, a kangaroo court whose role, on the one hand, was to launch and sustain a propaganda campaign to collectively demonize the Serbian people and, on the other, to advance U.S. interests, namely, those of multinational corporations, in the Balkans.

The court was established through the efforts of U.S. Secretary of State Madeleine Albright in 1993. It was set up by the UN Security council which took advantage of a loophole in its Charter. Even though the ICTY is in The Hague, it is not a legitimate international institution like the World Court, which is also located in The Hague.

The ICTY is financed and controlled by the U.S. and a disproportionate number of Muslim countries. It changes its rules of procedure at will, issues secret indictments, trumps up evidence, kidnaps suspects and tortures detainees. Let us recall that one of the great advances in American jurisprudence was trial by a jury of one's peers, along with the presumption of innocence. Let us not forget that the Scheveningen Prison, where The Hague holds its prisoners, was used by the Nazis during WWII to incarcerate, interrogate and execute Dutch anti-fascists. American law is not being practiced in The Hague — it is rather American jurisprudence going native while on a prolonged sojourn abroad — guilty until proven innocent.

The indictments that have been issued follow a predictable pattern: Serbs are indicted for genocide committed against the Bosnian Muslims and Croats; Muslims are charged with simple war crimes against Serbs or Croats; Croats are indicted for war crimes against Muslims; and no one is prosecuted for either genocide or war crimes committed against Serbs. The one exception is the Croatian General Ante Gotovina, who was accused of war crimes against the Serbs during Operation Storm in 1995. Even so, he is held accountable for only 150 deaths of Serbian civilians. At least 4,000 Serbian civilians were killed during Operation Storm.

The ICTY has played the leading role in establishing the alleged Srebrenica massacre as a legal factoid. It is essential to summarize the key cases and the witnesses who were called to testify in order to create and sustain the illusion that a "massacre" had actually occurred in Srebrenica. It is also worth recalling that in these proceedings The Hague Tribunal has not allowed the exhumation of Serbian victims from the Srebrenica area, and has made no effort to identify them.

The Hague Tribunal has stooped to kidnapping and abduction. Dragan Nikolić, a Bosnian Serb information officer who had served under Mladić in Srebrenica, settled in Smederevo in Serbia. He was kidnapped there, and spirited across the border to Bosnia where was then sold to SFOR for cold cash. But there have been other kidnappings. Slavko Domanović, who was the mayor of Vukovar before the outbreak of the war, was duped by American General Jacques Paul Klein into attending a meeting in a protected zone in Croatia under the pretext of giving Domanović a photograph from a recent friendship visit that featured the two men. Domanović later hanged himself in his prison cell in The Hague.

The ICTY is relying on the testimony of very few witnesses to issue indictments against Bosnian Serb political and military leaders. One alleged survivor, Hakija Husejnović, testified that on July 13, 1995, Bosnian Serb forces crammed 2,000 Muslim men into a warehouse in Kravica, where the Bosnian Serbs allegedly used hand grenades and machine gun fire to kill the men. Husejnović claimed that he survived by pretending he was dead. His testimony contradicts the testimony given by another witness, who claimed that 2,000 Bosnian Muslims who had surrendered were transported to Zvornik, where they were lined up and shot. This witness also claimed to have played dead in order to escape. "It is impossible for both of these stories to be true."[70]

Madeleine Albright claimed in August 1995 that the U.S. government had evidence that 8,000 to 12,000 Bosnian men from Srebrenica had been executed by the Bosnian Serbs. For those who weren't sure what this meant, Ms. Albright dramatically waved some satellite photos she was clutching in her hand, and added that they could "locate bodies decomposing under ground." She then urged the War Crimes Tribunal in The Hague, which she had established, to indict Radovan Karadžić and General Ratko Mladić.

The ICTY complied with its founder's urging and presented the aforesaid satellite photographs (provided by U.S. intelligence services) that claimed to reveal a mass grave in a football field in Nova Kasaba. The satellite surveillance presented not one jot of hard evidence that a massacre had occurred. U.S. intelligence services also claimed to have recorded incriminating audio tapes made from intercepted phone calls between Serbian officials who were discussing Srebrenica, but these turned out to be groundless, much like the ham radio stories cited earlier. "John Shattuck admitted in an interview in the German magazine *Der Spiegel* that there was no evidence the tapes exist."[71]

Few journalists besides Linda Ryan bothered to question the timing of the release of the satellite photos, one full month after Srebrenica fell, but mere days before the Croatian *Operation Storm* was set in motion, which drove 250,000 Serbs from their homes in Krajina. The U.S., which had given full backing to the mass "ethnic cleansing" operation by the Croats, was deploying a classic diversionary tactic. The Croats slaughtered 4,000 fleeing Serbian civilians over the course of a single weekend. Needless to say, those who were too old or inform to flee were slain on their doorstep. A phantom massacre thus concealed a real massacre. Thanks to the release of the "Srebrenica satellite photos," most Westerners, if they had even heard about Operation Storm at all, thought, "well, the Serbs are getting their just deserts." In fact, it was a real massacre of the civilian population by armed soldiers. Croatian jets even strafed refugee columns. The U.S. Airforce also lent a helping hand by bombing the few radar installations the Krajina Serbs had. There was no outrage at all. It was treated as the march of progress.

The Srebrenica indictment, issued by The Hague on November 14, 1995, dealt with the command and control responsibility over the Army of the Republika Srpska by Radovan Karadžić and Ratko Mladić. The indictment against Radislav Krstić, issued on October 30, 1995, claimed that Republika Srpska armed forces were under the command and control of Ratko Mladić and Radislav Krstić.

> The indictment against Krstić claims that on July 12 Ratko Mladić in hotel "Fontana" in Bratunac "explained that he would oversee 'the evacuation' of the refugees from Potočari and that he would like to see all Bosniak-Muslim men aged between 16 and 60 in order to make sure that there are no war criminals among them".
>
> Therefore, the responsibility for the selection of men has been for the first time pinned on Mladic, but still there is no explanation of who ordered the evacuation of the inhabitants of Srebrenica and with what motivation.[72]

It is important to note that The Hague Tribunal first indicted Karadžić and Mladić, and only then sought evidence to convict them.

The Hague Tribunal finally revealed its hand during the Milošević trial, when it tried to link Milošević to Srebrenica through the chain of command responsibility (Milošević-Perisić-Mladić-Krstić).

The first significant witness The Hague presented with regard to Srebrenica was Dražen Erdemović. He was rewarded for his cooperation by receiving a five year prison sentence in 1996. He was freed in 2001. Mr. Erdemović is a Bosnian Croat who came from a mixed Croat-Muslim family. He was sent to The Hague at his own request. He confessed to the murder of nearly 100 Muslims from Srebrenica, and confessed to have witnessed the murder of about 1,200 others. He also promised to give testimony against higher-ranking officers that would aid the ICTY in "building its case." Extenuating circumstances in his case were given weighty consideration: Mr. Erdemović was a mere lad (only twenty-six years old); he was the issue of a mixed marriage, held a low rank, and fought for all three warring parties (Muslim, Croat, and Serb). The ICTY judged these facts to be proof of his lack of "commitment" to any ethnic group in Bosnia, and to testify to his "honest disposition."

> Although Dražen Erdemović (a Croat) appeared to be the only [witness who gave] substantial evidence for the alleged systematic ethnic cleansing of Bosnian Serb forces, it has not been [sic] well-known that [the] Yugoslav government submitted him to [the] ICTY after it had diagnosed him as being mentally sick [sic]. When he confessed in Yugoslavia that he [had] executed more than 70 Muslims by [sic] ABC [News] broadcast in May 1996, [the] Yugoslav police immediately arrested him in order to investigate. However, as his statement and behavior had many contradictions, the doctors diagnosed him as mental disease [sic].[73]

Unfortunately, no one really investigated who, in fact, Mr. Erdemović really was, and what connections he had with intelligence services, particularly those of the Croats and the French.

When General Radislav Krstić was convicted by the ICTY, the "massacre" was sublimated to "genocide," at least on paper, on the basis of 46 deaths.

The verdict in General Krstić's trial admits that "it is impossible to precisely determine the number of men" executed by Bosnian Serb forces after the taking of Srebrenica, and quotes as 2,028 "the minimum found in mass graves so far."[74]

Before discussing the manner in which The Hague Tribunal treated testimony regarding the alleged Srebrenica massacre, it is illuminating to quote the great Serbian playwright Branislav Nušić on the subject of testimony:

> SPASOJE: ... You have to be ready to testify against him if it comes to that.
>
> NOVAKOVIĆ: What do we have to testify to?
>
> SPASOJE: Anything that will smear his reputation, anything that can establish him as a subversive, as a foreign agent, an anarchist, anything that can destroy him. Get it?

ANTA: Even about things we haven't seen and heard?

SPASOJE: No, not about *things we haven't seen and heard* but just about *nothing that we have seen or heard*. That's what you have to testify about.[75]

In January 2003, Dragan Nikolić, the Bosnian Serb intelligence officer who was being held by the ICTY (*see* p. 276), agreed to a plea bargain whereby he would "testify," giving evidence:

against Vidoje Blagojevic and Dragan Jokic, Bosnian Serb officers indicted for war crimes alongside him. In May, prosecutors agreed to drop a genocide charge against him and seek a lesser sentence of 15 to 20 years, and in return he changed his not guilty plea to an admission that he committed crimes against humanity. [76]

Nikolić's testimony was supposed to connect Ratko Mladić directly to the alleged massacre.

Nikolić testified that he had ordered the summary execution of 1,000 unarmed Muslims in a warehouse in Kravica,[77] and that he had ordered other mass killings in Sandići. Nikolić then made the implausible claim that General Mladić had actually met with Naser Orić on July 11, 1995 in order to obtain the right to screen Bosnian Muslim men leaving Srebrenica to detain suspected war criminals. Nikolić went on to outline the structure, the chain of command, and logistics of the Bosnian Serb Army. He claimed in his testimony that he himself had suggested several sites that were used as killing fields:

we discussed two locations which were outside Bratunac town. These were: State company "Ciglane" [the Brick Works] and a mine called "Sase" in Sase.[78]

Nikolić went on to claim that Mladić had given him the task of:

"supervising the 'evacuation' of refugees from Potočari" because Mladic "wanted to see all military-aged Bosnian Muslim men so they could be screened as possible war criminals."[79]

Nikolić then named locations where the alleged "massacres" had taken place.

Even though Nikolić had not personally witnessed the killings, he heard hearsay reports of prisoners being executed outside of Potočari. He testified that he thought his commanding officer, Vidoje Blagojević, knew that prisoners were going to be executed.

"General, what will happen to these men?" Nikolić asked. Mladić made a swift move with his hand — "as if cutting grass," said the witness. The prosecutor asked Nikolić what he understood by this gesture. After a moment's silence, he replied, "I knew what would happen to them. *I knew that these men would be captured and killed.* I knew it.[80] [Emphasis added.]

The ICTY took Nikolić's account of Mladić's "swift move with his hand," a mere gesture, to be satisfactory legal evidence that proved Mladić had ordered the alleged executions.

Mr. Nikolić gave some of the most dramatic testimony about Srebrenica on record at the ICTY. When asked by the defense attorney why he did not follow regulations and protect prisoners of war as required by the Geneva Conventions,

> Mr. Nikolic responded sharply: "Do you really think that in an operation where 7,000 people were killed that somebody was adhering to the Geneva Conventions? First of all, they were captured, then killed and then buried, exhumed once again, and buried again. Nobody, Mr. Karnavas, adhered to Geneva Conventions."[81]

One court official opined, "They've practically written the judgment."[82]

This was a hot story. It not only appeared to confirm that the massacre took place, but linked the alleged Srebrenica massacre to General Mladić. The Hague Tribunal congratulated itself for its hard work, and all the supporters of the "humanitarian intervention" held their heads high. Then Nikolić dropped the bombshell.

> "I did not tell the truth when I said that," he stated under oath on September 29, 2003. "I apologize."[83]

Mr. Nikolić's American attorney, Michael Kavarnas, wanted to know if the defendant had to provide the prosecutor with "something he didn't have." He proceeded to question the defendant.

> "You wanted to limit your time of imprisonment to twenty years, that was a part of the arrangement, yes? Quid pro quo?"

> "I wanted the [plea bargaining] agreement to succeed," replied Nikolić."[84]

Naser Orić, who, by some accounts, defended Srebrenica, but by other accounts, abandoned it days before the Serbs attacked, had his day in court too. He appeared before The Hague Tribunal almost ten years after Serbs began to call for his arrest. In April 2003, Mr. Orić was charged by the ICTY—not with genocide—but with a mere six counts of violations of law and the customs of war, including murder, cruel treatment, wanton destruction and plunder. It follows the ICTY indictment scheme outlined earlier, where Muslims and Croats are never accused of genocide against Serbs.

The Bosniaks were furious when Orić was arrested. Passions ran high following his arrest and Muslims referred to him as a national hero.

> One of the wartime army commanders in Srebrenica, Zulfo Turšunović said, "Nasser's army did not kill women and children, which is why he is not a war criminal but a national hero."[85]

This is much like having Al Capone as a character witness. Recall that Mr. Turšunović was a convicted murderer who was released by Izetbegović from prison in 1991, and assigned to work with Orić (*see* p. 259). Furthermore, Turšunović himself was named as one of the Bosnian Muslims responsible for slaughtering Serbian civilians in an eyewitness account of the attack on the village of Zalažje (*see* p. 253), in which Mr. Turšunović himself was responsible for the deaths of a few women and children.

Western news articles cast Orić in the role of a hero and defender of Srebrenica, when nothing could have been further from the truth. He specialized in attacking civilians, farmers and peasants. He was helicoptered out of Srebrenica by the UN three days before the city's fall. Then he was awarded the "Golden Lily," the Bosnian Muslim Army's highest military honor, which was not awarded for the defense of Srebrenica, but for turning a long expected military defeat into a stunning PR coup. He was indicted for pillaging a mere 15 Serbian villages.

When Momir Nikolić and Dragan Obrenović pleaded guilty to helping plan the Srebrenica "massacre," *The New York Times* published an op-ed piece:

> ….Mr Nikolic's confession — in which he described in chilling detail how he helped organize the mass execution and burial and an extensive cover-up, all of which he says army superiors ordered him to carry out — punches a big hole in the Bosnian Serb wall of denial. Serbs should have no reason to doubt his admission. Mr Nikolic has nothing to gain by exaggerating.[86]

It is a pity the Mr. Suljagić, the Bosnian Muslim author of this piece, did not follow up with a second article after Nikolić had admitted to lying under oath in order to get his plea bargain to work. It is also a shame that *The New York Times* did not reveal Mr. Suljagić's identity. He was a major source for David Rohde's book about what he thought had happened in Srebrenica, *Endgame*. Both Mr. Rohde, who won a Pulitzer Prize for his book, and Mr. Suljagić, have a vested interested in promoting the phantom massacre as a real event.

It was also a tough act for Marlise Simons of *The New York Times* to follow. When Nikolić had first "confessed," Ms. Simons related how he "described with cool precision the steps he took in coordinating the logistics, moving between army and police units, avoiding phones and radios, as preparations for the mass executions were under way."[87] She also chose to remain silent when Mr. Nikolić recanted his testimony, as did the rest of the mainstream media. Not one single news source issued a retraction. Nebojša Malić quoted Chris Stephen of the IWPR, who wrote critically of the ICTY for the first time, saying that

> Nikolic "was so desperate to get a deal with prosecutors that he was willing to lie to them." This revelation "will undermine confidence in other details he has supplied about the Srebrenica killings in July 1995, and raises questions about how plea-bargain agreements are negotiated with those accused of war crimes."[88]

The article also revealed that Mr. Nikolić "was not even present" when the alleged executions took place. Mr. Malić went on to note that the IWPR replaced its original article, which was entitled "Key Srebrenica Admits Lying" with another called "Key Srebrenica Witness Apologizes for Lies." Mr. Malić goes on to say that "[t]he above-cited passages are gone, replaced by editorial guidance and spin."[89]

Later, Mr. Malic reported that Chris Stephen, the author of "Key Srebrenica Witness Admits Lying," had been forced to resign from IWPR.[90]

Further proof came of Nikolic's bogus testimony from the ICTY itself, but it made no impact at all on the media. Borivoje Jakovljević was a military policeman who had served with the Bratunac Brigade. He appeared as a prosecution witness at the trial of Vidoje Blagojević. Jakovljević also revealed that Nikolić had lied under oath when he claimed to have been present at the time Mladić allegedly made the hand gesture because Jakovljević himself was accompanying General Mladić at the time, and Nikolić' as it turned out, "was not even present" on that occasion, too.

> Kavarnas: Okay. Well, that's what my question is. Because we've heard testimony from Momir Nikolić, no less under oath, where he stated — and this can be found on the record, for those who may wish to know, on page 1718, that is 1.718 here when his testimony was taken on Monday, 22nd September 2003 — but he stated at that point in time, General Mladić was out of the vehicle, he approached General Mladić to give some sort of a report, that he was able to notice some prisoners, and that upon asking General Mladić what the fate of the prisoners would be, General Mladić made the hand gesture like this. And in fact, we can see that on the video, on the video transcript of his testimony. Sir, did you see Momir Nikolić approach General Mladić for a — what we could call a *téte-a-téte* for Momir Nikolić to give a report to General Mladić at Konjević Polje on 13 July 1995, as he would have us believe?
>
> Jakovljević: I don't recall seeing Momir Nikolić there at that time.
>
> * * *
>
> Kavarnas: Sir, are you — was Momir Nikolić there? Did you see him?
>
> Jakovljević: I did not see him.[91]

Nikolić, the "star witness," was nothing but an ordinary perjurer. This comes as no surprise to anyone who has been following the show trial of President Milošević in The Hague. And this story was hastily consigned to oblivion. A mere ten days after Mr. Malić's article, AFP published a story that emphasized the twenty-year sentence prosecutors were seeking against Nikolić for the "key role he played in the massacre of thousands of Muslims in Srebrenica."[92] And the IWPR fought back, revisiting the Nikolić trial on 10/30/03[93] when it reported that Momir Deronjić, who testified on October 28 against Nikolić, alleged that Radovan Karadžić had ordered the Bosnian Serb Army to kill all the men from Srebrenica. Nikolić was described in the article as "the first Bosnian Serb officer to plead guilty for the Srebrenica massacre." The article made no mention of perjury, either. And who authored the article? Our old friend Emir Suljagić, David Rohde's source for *Endgame*, and author of the weighty *New York Times* op-ed piece, "The Truth at The Hague," which was quoted above.

Nikolić was trotted into court once more to issue a tearful apology.

> I want to express my sincere regret and repentance, I want to apologise to victims, their families and Bosniaks (Bosnian Muslims) for my participation in Srebrenica.[94]

And who is the author of this IWPR article? Once again, it is Emir Suljagić.

The next significant headline in this dismal procession is "Karadžić Wanted Srebrenica Muslims Killed — Witness" (Reuters, 11/21/03). Miroslav Deronjić testified that he met with Radovan Karadžić in early July 1995, shortly before the Serbs attacked Srebrenica. He told the court that Karadžić had said to him that "all the Muslims need to be killed." He also testified that Ljubiša Beara, who reported directly to Mladić, had told him that he had "orders from the highest places, from the top, that all prisoners should be executed." The article, of course, went on to state that the evidence Deronjić gave "matched that of the former Bosnian Army commander, Momir Nikolić"!

The farce, having been prolonged for months on the basis of Nilolić's discredited testimony, needed another dramatic turn. Miroslav Deronjić once again took the stand in the ICTY, this time to testify against Vidoje Blagojević (a colonel in charge of the Bratunac Brigade) and Dragan Jokić (a major, chief of engineering in the 1st Zvornik Infantry Brigade), two Bosnian Serb officers who were on trial for their alleged roles in the alleged Srebrenica massacre. The prosecution had touted Deronjić as another "star witness" who would produce damning evidence. But Deronjić's testimony fell apart when Blagojević's defense attorney poked his testimony full of holes and forced Deronjić to admit that he had gleaned evidence from other prisoners that he provided to the prosecuting attorney. They had another perjurer on their hands!

> As part of his obligation under the terms of his plea agreement, Deronjić provided a written statement to the prosecution detailing what he knew about the Srebrenica massacre.
>
> Exactly what his statement said is unclear, because although the statement was not confidential, the tribunal did not make it available for the public to see.[95]

The upshot of it all was that Blagojević and Jokić were acquitted of half the charges relating to the alleged Srebrenica massacre. The judges determined on April 7, 2004 that the prosecution had failed to provide evidence to prove the officers personal involvement.

> This is the first time in the history of the tribunal that defendants implicated in the Srebrenica massacre have been acquitted of charges relating to personal involvement.[96]

Milan Paunović, Professor of International Law at the Faculty of Law in Belgrade, thought that the conviction of Gen. Radislav Krstić for genocide was laying the groundwork for judging the Republika Srpska to be "a product of genocide," and by extension, Serbia-Montenegro guilty of genocide in order to make them liable for war reparations.

> "Based on the Krstić sentence, Radovan Karadžić and Ratko Mladić have been sentenced before even appearing in court. Consequently, difficult days may be ahead for Republika Srpska and its survival as an entity within Bosnia-Herzegovina," Paunović said in an interview for the Belgrade daily *Blic*.

> "After the Krstić decision, the International Court is missing but a single link to proclaim our country (Serbia) responsible for genocide and charged with payment of compensation," added Paunović.[97]

French General Phillipe Morillon testified against Slobodan Milošević at the ICTY on February 12, 2004. Morillon was presented as the last major prosecution witness. His testimony was supposed to link the genocide charges against Milošević to the fall of Srebrenica.

In 1993, Gen. Morillon prevented the fall of Srebrenica to Bosnian Serb forces by designating the town as a "safe haven" (a theretofore unheard of concept), but he admittedly never demilitarized the area, which was one of the key conditions set forth by Gen. Mladić. Morillon did not live up to his word. He did not stab Mladić in the back, but stabbed him Hollywood style — in the face. "Naser Orić was able to deploy the Bosnian Muslim 28th Division in Srebrenica after it became a safe area or haven."[98] But Gen. Morillon must have had second thoughts about his actions in Srebrenica.

According to Carl Savich, Gen. Morillon's testimony drew the following conclusions:

> The fall of Srebrenica in 1995 was the "direct reaction" to the massacres of Bosnian Serbs by Naser Orić's forces in 1992-1993.

> Morillon acknowledged that Orić's troops had committed war crimes in eastern Bosnia. Morillon personally witnessed the exhumation of the bodies of Bosnian Serb civilians and soldiers who had been tortured, mutilated, and executed. He saw with his own eyes the Serbian villages that had been burned to the ground in the Srebrenica pocket. More than anyone else, Morillon understood the level of devastation in eastern Bosnia and the extent and nature of the massacres of Bosnian Serbs.[99]

Morillon also testified that Milošević was going to be "satanized" if Srebrenica were to fall to Serb forces. His testimony once again clearly demonstrated that Naser Orić openly used Srebrenica as a military base. Orić exacerbated the crisis in many ways. Not only did he personally lead attacks against Serbian villages and their civilian population, but his constant hit and run attacks and the Bosnian Serb Army's counter-attacks made the delivery of humanitarian aid to the area impossible.

Orić systematically executed Serbian prisoners of war, but he has not been charged with genocide, a charge that has been reserved, as we have seen, exclusively for Serbs, which adequately reveals the bias and psywar aspect of the ICTY. It is intended to sustain the impression that Bosnian Muslims were the sole victims.

Here is what Morillon had to say during his testimony about the treatment of Bosnian Serb POWs:

> Naser Orić was a warlord who reigned by terror in his area and over the population itself. I think that he realized that these were the rules of this horrific war, that he could not allow himself to take prisoners. According to my recollection, he didn't even look for an excuse. It was simply a statement: One can't be bothered with prisoners.[100]

Morillon also testified that he expected Serbian retaliation:

> I feared that the Serbs, the local Serbs, the Serbs of Bratunac, these militiamen, they wanted to take their revenge for everything that they attributed to Naser Orić. It wasn't just Naser Orić that they wanted to revenge, take their revenge on, they wanted to revenge their dead on Orthodox Christmas.[101]

One of the new terms introduced by the media during the Balkan Wars of Succession (e.g., in addition to "collateral damage" and "ethnic cleansing") is "revenge killing." Killing another human being is commonly understood as murder. There are few mitigating circumstances: self defense comes to mind, as well as the killing of invaders or enemy soldiers. Murder is ranked in three degrees, and is distinguished from manslaughter by malice and forethought. "Revenge killing" is a manufactured term to excuse certain legally certifiable murders in the press in order to stymie investigation or serious consideration. The term also nefariously imputes collective guilt to the victims. Whatever extrajudicial executions may have taken place during the fall of Srebrenica, they are never described as excusable "revenge killings." However, when Serbs are killed in Bosnia, Croatia or Kosovo, their murders are routinely characterized as "revenge killings."

> Morillon concluded that the fall of Srebrenica in 1995 was due to the massacres committed by Naser Orić's forces in 1992 and 1993. Judge Patrick Robinson asked Morillon: "Are you saying, then, General, that what happened in 1995 was a direct reaction to what Naser Orić did to the Serbs two years before?"

Morillon replied: "Yes. Yes your Honour. I am convinced of that."[102]

Morillon was convinced that certain powerful interests in Sarajevo and New York were manipulating the evolution of the Srebrenica crisis for their own purposes.

> "I was convinced that the population of Srebrenica was the victim of a higher interest ... this higher interest which was located in Sarajevo and New York." Morillon talked about how Mladić had been tricked into attacking Srebrenica. Orić had been evacuated by helicopter to Tuzla. The Bosnian Muslim political and military leadership had abandoned Srebrenica after provoking a Bosnian Serb attack.[103]

Branislav Tapušković, the Amicus Curae, questioned Morillon about this meetings with Naser Orić. Morillon replied:

> "Naser Orić, every night, raided Bosnian Serbs outside town." When General Morillon opposed him on this score, he said that this was the only way he had to get hold of weapons and ammunition. "He admitted killing Bosnian Serbs every night."

> Morillon repeated the admission to him by Orić that he never took any Bosnian Serb POWs: "Orić said that those were the rules of the game, and that in this type of partisan warfare, he cannot take prisoners." Morillon confirmed that Naser Orić was getting his directives and instructions from Alija Izetbegović in Sarajevo: "Naser Orić's reign implied a thorough knowledge of the area held by his forces. It appeared to me that he was respecting political instructions coming from the Presidency" in Sarajevo.[104]

Naser Orić's forces committed serious violations of the Geneva Conventions, among other international laws, on the territory of the former Yugoslavia. Article 3 of the Geneva Conventions pertains to civil wars, and stipulates that POWs must be treated humanely. Murder, mutilation, torture, and cruel treatment are strictly forbidden. POWs may not be executed unless they are publicly tried, given due process, and the right to appeal.

Morillon's testimony plainly demonstrated that Bosnian Muslims and Croats were busy "mass murdering" Serbian civilians even before the onset of war. Furthermore, Morillon disclosed that Izetbegović openly used Muslim civilians as shields in Sarajevo and Srebrenica to win sympathy from the West and establish propaganda themes that are still in effect today. Morillon also testified that the siege of Sarajevo began when the Muslims surrounded and attacked the JNA as they were withdrawing, killing 172 soldiers on Dobrovoljačka Street. Their bodies were burned and mutilated, and their charred corpses lined the streets. They were killed only because they were Serbs. General Mladić was haunted by these murders, and responded in a corresponding fashion. Yet, it must be clear to one and all that the Bosnian Muslim faction provoked the violence.

Another witness at The Hague Tribunal delivered some compelling testimony during the aforementioned Blagojević trial. Unlike Gen. Morillon, this was a "protected witness," meaning that the witness's identity had been concealed. The defense had absolutely no opportunity to corroborate or contest the testimony. The protected witness in question had occupied a command post only a few kilometers away from the alleged mass graves that were alleged to have been dug on July 13 and 14. The witness denied any knowledge of mass murders or mass graves. "It's like a scenario from a film," he said. "I have the impression it is somebody's screenplay."[105]

The Milošević trial in The Hague provided some outrageous revelations that were devoted zero news coverage. Defense witness, French Col. Patrick Barriot testified that Mohammet Atta was present in central Bosnia-Herzegovina in 1994, 1995 and 1999. (See p. 187) Col. Barriot, a medical doctor who served as a humanitarian aid worker in Krajina, refuted claims that the Serbs were ethnically cleansing Bosnia. He pointed out that

scores of Muslim refugees, followers of Fikret Abdic, who fled
the 5th Corps of the Bosnian Muslim Army, sought refuge with
the Serbs, who gave safe haven to over 40,000 such Muslim
refugees, who were attacked by Izetbegović's fundamentalists
because they were on good terms with the Serbs.

Col. Barriot testified that he had the opportunity to speak with
Gen. Mladić in August 1995, a month after the fall of Srebrenica.
Milošević asked Col. Barriot what Mladić had told him about
Srebrenica.

> Mladić told Barriot that there were a handful of summary executions
> (less than 100) carried out by local Serbs who recognized certain
> Muslims who had perpetrated attacks on the surrounding Serbian vil-
> lages. Mladić emphasized that he did not order any executions, and
> this his objective in Srebrenica was to neutralize the 28th Infantry
> Division of the B-H army — not to harm the civilian population, or
> alter the ethnic make-up of the enclave.[106]

Mladić also told Barriot that the Army of the Republika Srpska
took 750 prisoners during the Srebrenica operation, and then
released 500 of them. Only 250 were held. Mladić also related to
Col. Barriot that there were 15,000 armed Muslims in the woods
around Srebrenica who were fighting their way out in order to
reach Tuzla. The Serbs took approximately 500 casualties in
these running battles, while Mladić estimated Muslim losses to
be between 1,500 and 1,800. The Tribunal judges, however, did
not allow Col. Barriot to relate all of what Mladić had told him.
Judge Robinson suggested that Milošević should call Gen.
Mladić as a witness. "After a short silence, Milošević replied:
'Well, if you plan to arrest him, I will certainly not do so'."[107]

Children Must Be Taught to Hate

Don't the victims of the Srebrenica "massacre" deserve a proper burial? Of course, just as the victims of Naser Orić's death
squads do. So what objection can be raised over the Potočari
monument to the Srebrenica victims?

> [T]he radical Islamists have created a new "Trojan Horse" to ensure
> that their actions in the Balkans remain free from scrutiny ... it [is]
> the monument built in Srebrenica to ostensibly commemorate the
> Muslim victims of Serb "genocide" in 1995 ... creating the first
> Muslim "holy place" in Europe.[108]

Bill Clinton, a great supporter of Alija Izetbegović, reportedly received his standard $250,000 speaking fee to attend the dedication of the Potočari monument. This "Trojan horse" for Islamic fundamentalism was built with one million dollars that were provided by the U.S. Embassy in Bosnia. Another four million Bosnian marks (equal to $1,000,000) was extorted from the Republika Srpska by Paddy Ashdown to complete the financing. This decision "settled a lawsuit filed by 49 families who lost relatives" in Srebrenica.[109] No one investigated why the families of the remaining 7,000 Muslims allegedly massacred in Srebrenica did not also bring charges.

Phillip Corwin, the author of *Dubious Mandate*, a memoir of his service as the UN Civilian Affairs Coordinator at the time Srebrenica fell, wrote:

> What happened in Srebrenica was not a single large massacre of Muslims by Serbs, but rather a series of very bloody attacks and counterattacks over a three-year period which reached a crescendo in July of 1995.[110]

And he went on to add:

> I was the United Nations' chief political officer in Bosnia the day that Srebrenica fell. Coincidentally, it was the same day that the Bosnian Government tried to assassinate me as I drove over Mount Igman on the way to Sarajevo.

Regardless of such comments made by dispassionate observers, the U.S. has accepted, lock, stock and barrel the Islamic fundamentalist interpretation of the events that took place in Srebrenica in July 1995. In fact, the timing of Clinton's visit was meant to coincide, as closely as possible, to the commemoration of the 9/11 attacks. "Mr. Ashdown promoted a schedule based on the availability of Mr. Clinton,"[111] just as one would book a washed-up movie star for a cameo appearance in a big budget picture that needed a little commercial boost from old fans.

Ashdown was trying to provide "closure" for the Srebrenica "massacre" in precisely the same manner that Tito provided "closure" for the death of 750,000 people who were murdered in the Jasenovac Concentration Camp. Tito bulldozed Jasenovac after the war and effectively prevented any accounting of the dead from ever taking place. Clinton bulldozed the dead of Srebrenica with a media spectacle. Tito did not resolve the truth by illuminating it with a hard Sophoclean light, but questioned its authenticity so that future generations would doubt whether or not it was a genocide that merited the memorialization accorded to the Jewish or Armenian Holocausts. And Clinton followed Tito's footsteps more closely than those of his American predecessors in the Oval Office.

Before we examine Bill Clinton's ten-minute $250,000 speech at the Potočari Monument, let us examine another instance of an American president giving a heartfelt speech at the graves of Nazis, SS Troopers no less. That was the Gipper, Ronald Reagan, who in 1982 laid wreaths on the graves of SS soldiers who had been killed in WWII. This took place in Bittberg, Germany. Reagan, notwithstanding his lifelong superficiality (a quality that made him an ideal pitch man), was ostensibly senile by that time, so he may be forgiven for such a startling lapse. The real power resided, of course, with Vice President George Bush, former CIA Director, who certainly must have arranged the affair with German Chancellor Kohl. Let us not forget that President George Bush Senior's father, Prescott Bush, was banker to the Nazis in the U.S. at the firm Brown Brothers Harriman until the Federal government seized the bank's assets under the Trading with the Enemy Act in 1943

"Dutch" Reagan later claimed that he did not know that the graves in Bittberg belonged to fallen SS soldiers. And he probably didn't know. But Kohl knew. And so did Bush. So, when Bush Senior became president in 1988, he visited Kohl in Germany once again, this time to declare Germany a "special partner" in the New World Order. No one in the mainstream media bothered to comment on the origin of this expression. It came straight out of Hitler's mouth: "Neue Weltordnung," which is how Hitler described the world vision of the Third Reich. It is not farfetched to conclude that George Bush Senior introduced a Fourth Reich in 1988, whose capital was not Berlin, but Washington, D.C.

Now Bill Clinton knew all of this, too. But he had a public role to play. He knew only one foreign language — and he was fluent in it: German. When Clinton paid his own visits to Kohl, they spoke German together instead of English. The U.S. media never questioned the rich subtext of a scene where an American president speaks German with his German counterpart. It stands in vivid contrast with John Kerry's case in 2004 during his failed bid for the

U.S. presidency: he was reviled because he spoke good French, and he shied away from speaking the language within earshot of American reporters. This in itself made him unworthy of the office that Thomas Jefferson once held.

Clinton was a great supporter of the Bosnian Muslim cause. He must have had secret service reports that Alija Izetbegović, was a recruiter for the Muslim Handžar Division, which was organized under the Nazi SS. But Clinton must have intuitively felt that Izetbegović was a man he could trust, a leader he could do business with because perhaps they had something in common beyond their mutual admiration for WWII Germany.

If any doubt remains of ex-President Clinton's veracity and trustworthiness, let us recall the depths to which Clinton happily stooped during his impeachment proceedings. He had the bold faced audacity to challenge the meaning of "is," which is also the title of an illuminating book about the ex-president. Bob Barr, the author, represented the 7th District of Georgia in the U.S. House of Representatives from 1995 to 2003, serving as a senior member of the Judiciary Committee. Mr. Barr was surprised that it was the Monica Lewinsky case that led to Clinton's impeachment. Here is a succinct judgment of the ex-President.

> This is not to say that lying under oath and obstructing justice are not impeachable charges or that the remedy we chose was inappropriate. However, these charges pale in comparison to the systematic damage Bill Clinton did to American national security, the office of the presidency, and the civil liberties of individual American citizens....
>
> Bill Clinton will go down in history as a failed president, because he had the intelligence and opportunity required for greatness, but suffered from fundamental character flaws.... There is no core to Bill Clinton, no principle he will not sell out, no lie he will not tell, no rule he will not break, if he believes doing so will best serve his immediate interests.[112]

Bearing this judgment in mind, let us now examine ex-President Clinton's speech in Potočari, which is a manual of rhetorical debasement. The first paragraph contains rhetorical devices common to any memorial of the dead, with key words like "mother," "father," "family," "victims," "remembrance," "crime," and, of course, "genocide."[113] He did not, of course, admit to the possibility that he was honoring fallen al-Qaeda fighters who were buried there.

The second paragraph broadens his theme politically to the end of the Cold War, and its disappointments, among which are "dark claims of religious and ethnic superiority." In a sentence bound to be recalled by future generations, Clinton sermonized the Srebrenica "massacre" as follows: "Bad people who *lusted* for power killed these good people simply because of who they were." [Emphasis added.] One cannot help but regard his choice of verbs, "lusted," as being purely Clintonian and evoking merriment and contempt. But Clinton paid off in the last sentence: "It enabled me to secure NATO support for the bombing that led to the peace that put Bosnia and Herzegovina back on the long road to a normal life."

Paragraph 3 admits a "debt of gratitude" to the 60,000 occupation troops.

Paragraph 4 extols The Hague Tribunal as an instrument of exacting justice, and is peppered with key words such as "punishment," "atrocities," and "leaders, [who] have not been apprehended," a thinly veiled reference to Karadžić and Mladić. He ends this paragraph with a perfunctory appeal to execute these arrests because it is owed to "Bosnian children yet unborn to see that justice is done."

Paragraph 5 celebrates the U.S. military actions "to stop aggression and genocide in Bosnia." He gently berates Bosnians, Croats and Serbs (yes, he actually mentions Serbs, albeit last) for their "inability to get along with one another," implying a lengthy military occupation.

Paragraph 6 invokes the living to mourn the dead and "overcome fear and mistrust," which CIA and BND agents had planted in the first place by supplying the Muslims with clandestine arms shipments, then cultivated fear and mistrust with rebellion in order to finally harvest the bloody fruits of war.

Paragraph 7 calls for refugee (i.e. Muslim) returns to Srebrenica. Of course, Clinton made no call for the return of Serbian refugees anywhere. Rhetorical contrasts are made between one ethnic group's "dignity" at the expense of another group's "humiliation." The knowledgeable reader has to admire Clinton for being able to deliver such a speech with a straight face. Clinton himself armed the Bosnian Muslims by contravening the UN arms embargo. And his partners in crime were Iran and Turkey.

Paragraph 8 speaks of "progress" and eventual integration in "Europe and the global community." Evidently, Clinton believes 40% unemployment, massive infiltration by al-Qaeda operatives and military occupation are emblematic and noteworthy examples of such "progress." He promises that American peacekeepers will stay on and on and on. He omitted mentioning the oil fields around Tuzla, where U.S. Eagle Base is located.

Paragraph 9 is merely a segue leading to the stunning conclusion in paragraph 10, which begins: *"Children must be taught to hate*; I hope that you will teach them instead to trust, to chose the open hand over the clenched fist," etc., etc. [Emphasis added.] The speechwriters surely wrote: "Children must *not* be taught to hate; I hope that you will teach them instead..." This used to be called a Freudian slip, a misstatement that is motivated by and reveals a repressed aspect of the subconscious mind. Behavior modification and its twelve step descendants have knocked Freud out of the picture. Just as science has replaced religion, behavior mod has replaced any notion of soul or personal mythology with a personal behavior mechanism. Thus, Clinton's PR people could explain away this Freudian slip away as a simple misstatement. In other words, there was no revelation of a secret wish or a hidden agenda because the speech had no content to begin with. It was merely the omission of a one syllable word, a harmless glitch, a flub. Clinton didn't even bother to comment on it. The BBC report was actually fastidious enough to take his words out of quotation marks, and revise the lines he had blown. The BBC account reads: *Children should be taught to trust, not to hate, he added — "to choose the open hand over the clenched fist."*[114]

But "teaching children to hate" is what the Potočari Monument is all about. Despite the Ottoman invasion and occupation, "ethnic hatred" did not begin then; systematic genocide began during WWII with the Nazi puppet state of Croatia and its Ustasha regime, and the Nazi trained Bosnian Muslim Handžar Division. And this is the legacy that Clinton wished to transmit to future generations. Clinton probably had no idea that in 1463 in the town of Jajce, which is only about one hundred miles west of Potočari, 10,000 Serbian landowners and people of good stock converted to Islam in a single day before Sultan Mehmed II. The Bosnian Muslims and the Serbs have much more in common than they do dividing them. Clinton was, in fact, preaching words of healing to those whom he had himself gashed, and he was pouring salt on still open wounds.

The opening of the Memorial was professionally managed and there were video cameras, make-up artists, production managers and gofers, and a phantom massacre, too. And there were a few graves! The BBC article cited above noted that 882 people were buried there, and another 107 were buried there on the day Clinton delivered his speech. 882+107=989, a far cry from the alleged 8,000 victims.

This is how dancing girls costumed in white flowing robes, a washed-up U.S. president, words corrupted into senselessness, and 989 graves arranged in the shape of flower petals erase the memory of the Jasenovac Concentration Camp where 750,000 died; it erases the memory of the forced conversion of as many as 500,000 Serbs to Roman Catholicism in Croatia; it erases the memory of the expulsion of 250,000 Serbs from Krajina in Croatia during Operation Storm in 1995, weeks after the fall of Srebrenica; it erases the 3,200 Serbian civilians who were killed in the area surrounding Srebrenica. This is how history is rewritten.

A group of people described as "Srebrenica survivors" filed suit against the Dutch government in order to gain compensation because the Dutch Battalion in Srebrenica had failed to protect them during the fall of Srebrenica. The widows, *forty* in number, were joined in the suit by ten orphans. It has been reported that the membership of the Association of Srebrenica Widows runs as high as 86. It is a pity that the number of orphans and widows is not higher to lend some credibility to the claim that "8,000 men and boys" had been killed.

On July 12, 2003, 20,000 Muslims from all over the world converged on Srebrenica. They mourned the "victims." Mustafa Ćerić, the head of Bosnia's Muslim community, said "There cannot be revenge, because revenge is not in our faith...." Another pro forma and contentless statement. And there were renewed calls for the arrest of Karadžić and Mladić.

Clinton's closing paragraph in his address urged the audience to recall Allah's behest to get to know one another, and invoked God's blessing on the "men and boys of Srebrenica and this sacred land that remains their grace." One cannot imagine more venomous words, spoken in bad faith, that will have long lasting, deleterious effects, much like the depleted uranium weaponry that Clinton ordered to be used against the Serbs, but which kills Muslims and Croats, as well. The next chapter will examine Clinton's deadly legacy for all the people of the former Yugoslavia, as well as for future generations of Americans.

ENDNOTES

1   The form of the following analysis of the events that took place in Srebrenica is based on Michel Collon's examination of the Markale and Vasa Miskin Massacres in *Liar's Poker, op. cit.*

2   "Greece Faces Shame of Role in Serb Massacre," by Helena Smith, *The Observer* (UK) 1/5/03

3   "Generals for Hire," by Mark Thompson et al, *Time Magazine*, 15 January 1996, p. 34.

4   "Oil Discovered in Bosnia: Find Hushed Up for Years, Official Says," by Christopher Deliso, balkanalysis.com, 6/1/04.

5   *The Rape of Kosovo (Monopoly*, EPO: Bruxelles, 2001) by Michel Collon, p. 208.

6   "The Image that May Change History," by Julian Borger, *The Guardian* (U.K.) 10/05/00.

7   "The Single Tragedy that Symbolised Srebrenica," by Anthony Loyd, domovina.net.

8   *Endgame: The Betrayal and the Fall of Srebrenica*, by David Rohde, Farrar, Strauss and Giroux, New York, 1997. pp. 320-321.

9   *General Mladić*, by Ljiljana Bulatović, Evro, Belgrade: 2002, p. __, quoting Miroslav Toholj's *Crna Knjiga: patnje Srba u Bosni-Hercegovini od 1991-1995* (Sveta Gora, Cetinje, 2000) ("The Black Book: the Suffering of the Serbs in Bosnia-Herzegovina from 1991-1995").

10 "Karremans Recalls Srebrenica Fall," by Rachel S. Taylor, *IWPR* (06/25/04).

11 *Ibid.*

12 *Liar's Poker: The Great Powers, Yugoslavia and the Wars of the Future,* by Michel Collon, *op. cit.*, presents a fuller treatment of the Markale bombing, as well as David Binder's article, "Bosnia's Bombers," which is included in the Appendices.

13 "Fate of Eagle Base Debated as Bosnia-Herzegovina Handover Nears," by Sandra Jontz, *Stars and Stripes*, July 14, 2004

14 "Oil Discovered in Bosnia: Find Hushed Up for Years, Official Says," by Christopher Deliso, balkanalysis.com, *op. cit.*

[15] ICRC News No. 37, as quoted in "What's in a Mass Grave?", by Linda Ryan, *Living Marxism*, March 1996.

[16] "Ethnic Conflicts during the Civil War in Bosnia," by Takako Sakamoto and Darko Trifunović.

[17] *The New York Times*, by Chris Hedges, July 17, 1995.

[18] "Missing Enclave Troops Found," by Michael Evans and Michael Kallenbach, *The Times*, August 8, 1995.

[19] "Clinton-Approved Iranian Arms Transfers Help Turn Bosnia into Militant Islamic Base," *Congressional Press Release*, U.S. Congress, 1/16/97.

[20] "Srebrenica Victims Reburied at Massacre Site," *AFP*, 3/31/03.

[21] "Clinton Urges Reconciliation in Bosnia, Arrest of War Criminals," *AFP*, 9/20/03.

[22] "Srebrenica Before It Happened," www.balkan-archive.org

[23] "Srebrenica and Naser Oric: An Analysis of General Philippe Morillon's Testimony at the ICTY," by Carl Savich, serbianna.com, 04/27/04

[24] These points were drawn from "Srebrenica Before It Happened," www.balkan-archive.org, *op. cit.*

[25] *The Economist*, 15-21 July 1995

[26] *The Eradication of the Serbs in Bosnia-Herzegovina*, 1992-1993, edited by Drago Jovanović, Gordana Bundalo, Miloš Govedarica: Montreal, 1995, pp. 107-110.

[27] "Fearsome Muslim Warlord Eludes Bosnian Serb Forces," by Bill Schiller, *Toronto Star*, 7/16/95.

[28] *See* Appendix: "Bosnia's Bombers," by David Binder.

[29] See *Liar's Poker: The Great Powers, Yugoslavia and the Wars of the Future*, by Michel Collon (IAC, NY: 2001), pages 28-33.

[30] *Globe and Mail*, (UK) July 12, 1995.

[31] *The Electronic Telegraph*, July 11, 1995.

[32] *The New York Times*, Chris Hedges, 1995.

[33] *The New York Times*, July 23, 1995.

[34] *The Times* (UK), July 14, 1995

[35] "Muslims Manipulate Refugees' Agony," *The Daily Telegraph*, July 15, 1995,

[36] *Reuters*, May 29, 1996.

[37] *The Times* (UK), August 2, 1995.

[38] "Calling Bosnia Crisis Overrated, UN Chief Focuses on Africa," by Barbara Crossette.

[39] *BBC Ceefax*, 23 July 1995.

[40] "Serb Atrocities in Srebrenica Unrpoved," *The Electronic Telegraph*, July 24, 1995.

[41] "Report about Case Srebrenica (The First Part)," www.slobodan-milosevic.org.

[42] *Lukava strategia*, by Halilović, Sefer. 1997, Sarajevo.

[43] "Weapons, Cash and Chaos Lend Clout to Srebrenica's Tough Guy," by John Pomfret, *The Washington Post*, 2/16/94. Note that "cold weapons" is a literal translation of the expression "hladno oružje," which actually means "edged weapons."

[44] The 2002 Srebrenica Report quoted this passage from *Srebrenica: Record of a War Crime*, by Jan (Willem) Honig, Penguin, 1996, p. 58.

[45] "US Official Implicated with Bosnian High Representative Ashdown in Attempting to Force Fabricated Report on Srebrenica," *Defense & Foreign Affairs Daily*, September 11, 2003

[46] "Al Qaeda Roams in Serbia," *Nacional* (Croatia) *op. cit.*, posted on the Serbian Unity Congress' website: http://news.suc.org/bydate/2004/May_12/2.html?w=p.

[47] "US Official Implicated with Bosnian High Representative Ashdown in Attempting to Force Fabricated Report on Srebrenica," *Defense & Foreign Affairs Daily, op. cit.*

[48] "Bosnian Serbs get Six Months to Reveal Truth," *Irish Examiner*, 10/15/03

[49] "Bosnia Serbs Finally Admit Truth of Srebrenica Deaths," by Vesna Peric Zimonjić, *The Independent* (UK), 11/05/03).

[50] "Bosnian Serbs Name Srebrenica Probe Panel," *VOA News*, 12/26/03.

[51] "Bosnian Serbs Say Six Mass Graves Found," *AP*, 04/30/04.

[52] *Ibid.*

[53] "Bosnian Muslim Grave Exhumed," aljazreera.net, 5/22/04.

[54] "Bosnian Serbs Reveal 31 New Srebrenica Mass Graves," by Maja Zuvela, *Reuters*, 06/04/04.

[55] "Bosnian Serbs Admit Massacre of Muslims," by Samir Krilić, *AP* (06/12/04).

[56] *See* pp. 278-279.

[57] "Serb Leader's Srebrenica Regret," *BBC NEWS* (06/23/04).

[58] "Balkan Islamists Note Continued Push for Olympics-Related Action Despite Support for Iraq Exclusive," *Defense & Foreign Affairs Daily*, Monday, June 21, 2004, Strategic Studies Association - June 21, 2004.

[59] *Ibid.*

[60] "60 Bosnian Serb Officials Fired Over War Suspect," by Daniel Williams, *Washington Post Foreign Service*, 07/01/04.

[61] *Ibid.*

[62] "60 Bosnian Serbs Dismissed for Aid to War Crimes Figure," Nicholas Wood, *The New York Times*, 07/01/04.

63 "Dragan Kalinić, Republika Srpska MP, Farewell Address after Having Been Removed by Paddy Ashdown and US Ambassador Bond," July 2, 2004, serbianunity.net.

64 *Ibid.*

65 "Speech by the High Representative Paddy Ashdown at the Funeral of Alija Izetbegović," 10/22/03.

66 "Balkan Islamists Note Continued Push for Olympics-Related Action Despite Support for Iraq," *Defense & Foreign Affairs Daily*, Monday, June 21, 2004.

67 *Ibid.*

68 "Srebrenica Revisited: Reports, Confessions and the Elusive Truth," by Nebojša Malić, antiwar.com, 06/24/04.

69 *Ibid.*

70 *See* "What's in a 'Mass Grave'?", by Linda Ryan, Living Marxism, March 1996. This paragraph and the next three summarize Ms. Ryan's key findings.

71 *Ibid.*

72 "Dangerous Investigation," by Esad Hecimović, *Dani* (Sarajevo, B-H) 07/09/99.

73 "Only the Monster Can Save SFOR," *NIN* (Belgrade, Yugoslavia) (08/02/01).

74 "Knife, Wire Srebrenica: What Would be Left of Ratko Mladic's Heroic Image after His Court Appearance?" by Lj. Smajlović, *NIN* (Serbia) 01/30/03). Even though I have quoted this article in defense of Gen. Mladić, the article actually presupposes his guilt.

75 *The Deceased: A Comedy with a Prelude and Three Acts*, by Branislav Nusić. The Serbian Classics Press: New York, 2004, p. 133.

76 "Key Srebrenica Witness Admits Lying," by Chris Stephen, IWPR (10/4/03).

77 *Nota bene*: this figure conflicts with the one given by Hakija Hasejnović, who, in his dubious account, alleged that 2,000 had been crammed into the Kravica warehouse and killed. See p. 277.

78 *Prosecutor* v. *Momir Nikolić* [2003] ICTY 10 (3 Dec 2003), Case No. IT-02-60/1-S, paragraph 33. *See* http://www.worldlii.org/int/cases/ICTY/2003/10.html#B65 for full text of the Sentencing Judgment.

79 *Ibid.*, paragraph 40.

80 "Two Days in Srebrenica," by Emir Suljagic, IWPR, 9/26/03.

81 "Officers Say Bosnian Massacre Was Deliberate," by Marlise Simons, *The New York Times*, October 12, 2003.

82 *Ibid.*

83 "Key Srebrenica Witness Apologises for Lies," by Chris Stephen, *IWPR* (10/04/03).

84 *Ibid.*

85 "Bosnian Fury at Oric Arrest," by Amra Kebo, *IWPR*, (4/18/03).

[86] "Truth at the Hague," by Emir Suljagić, *The New York Times*, 06/01/03.

[87] "Officers Say Bosnian Massacre Was Deliberate," by Marlise Simons, *The New York Times*, 10/12/03.

[88] "Agents of Empire: The Infrastructure of Intervention," by Nebojša Malić, www.antiwar.com (10/16/03), quoting from "Key Srebrenica Witness Admits Lying," *op. cit.*

[89] *Ibid.*

[90] "Twisted Words, False Justice: Prosecuting War Crimes Imperial Style," by Nebojsa Malic, 12/11/03, antiwar.com.

[91] The Testimony of Borivoje Jakovljevic, International Criminal Tribunal for the Former Yugoslavia, May 26, 2004, pp. 9946-9948.

[92] "Prosecution Seeks 20 Year Sentence over Srebrenica Atrocities, *AFP* (10/27/03).

[93] "Karadzic 'Ordered' Atrocity," by Emir Suljagić, *IWPR* (10/30/03).

[94] "Srebrenica Apology," by Emir Suljagić, *IWPR*, (10/30/03).

[95] "Srebrenica Prosecution Blow," by Karen Meirik, *IWPR* (01/23/04).

[96] "Key Srebrenica Charges Dropped," by Ana Uzelac in The Hague, *IWPR*, 04/08/04.

[97] "Setting the Stage to Proclaim Republika Srpska a Product of Genocide," *SRNA* (Republika Srpska News Agency), 04/25/04.

[98] "Srebrenica and Naser Orić: An Analysis of General Philippe Morillon's Testimony at the ICTY," by Carl Savich, serbianna.com, 04/27/04.

[99] *Ibid.*

[100] *Ibid.*

[101] *Ibid.*

[102] *Ibid.*

[103] *Ibid.*

[104] *Ibid.*

[105] "Bosnian Serb Forces in Chaos at Srebrenica," by Rachel S. Taylor, *IWPR* (06/04/04).

[106] "Tribunal Blocks Evidence Regarding Srebrenica and Islamic Terrorism in the Balkans," by Andy Wilcoxson, www.slobodan-milosevic.org, 1/12/ 05.

[107] *Ibid.*

[108] "The Srebrenica Icon: How a Trojan Horse for Islamist Terrorism Was Built With Western Help in the Heart of Europe," *Defense & Foreign Affairs Strategic Policy*, September 2003, pp. 4-8.

[109] "Serbs Ordered to Pay Compensation," by Daniel Simpson, International Herald Tribune, 3/8/03.

[110] *Dubious Mandate: A Memoir of the UN in Bosnia, Summer 1995*, by Phillip Corwin, Duke University Press, Durham and London, 1999. I am grateful to

Gregory Copley for pointing out these two quotations in his article, "Exaggerated, One-Sided Victim Numbers Fuel Hatred."

[111] "The Srebrenica Icon: How a Trojan Horse for Islamist Terrorism Was Built With Western Help in the Heart of Europe," *Defense & Foreign Affairs Strategic Policy*, September 2003, *op. cit.*

[112] *The Meaning of Is: The Squandered Impeachment and Wasted Legacy of William Jefferson Clinton*, by Bob Barr, Stroud & Hall Publishing: 2004; the quotation is drawn from the forward by R. Emmett Tyrrell, Jr. Editor in Chief, *The American Spectator*.

[113] Address by Former US President Bill W.J. Clinton at the Opening of the Srebrenica Genocide Memorial Sept. 20, 2003.

[114] "Clinton Unveils Bosnia Memorial," *BBC News*, 9/20/03.

FORESHADOWING
INSTEAD OF A CONCLUSION
by Milo Yelesiyevich

Absurdity was an attempt made by writers, who thought of themselves as individuals, to deal with horror in the post-WWII era; generally speaking, the post-modern sensibility denies the existence of the individual, and treats the self as a locus where various systems of signification intersect. Such thinking easily accommodates what the previous generation called mind control, and it has the added dimension of appreciation of the techniques of such control. In contrast, I put forth the premise is that only tragedy and comedy can restore a human shape to life. General Mladić's tragedy, as we have seen, has far-reaching consequences that have touched us intimately and directly. And our own looming tragedy will, if it has not already, engulf his. Perhaps only now can we see him as a human being instead of a cartoon villain or a revenant from Grand Guignol.

One would think that the unimaginable horrors of the wars in Bosnia and Croatia would have inspired tragic drama. But tragedy was pronounced extinct as a literary form even after WWII, when the human mind was first rendered insensible by an inconceivably titanic scale of atrocities. Instead, the modern mind shifted to absurdity to explore loneliness, desolation, purposelessness and futility. When news became narrative entertainment, another transformation occurred. American novelists have still not fully responded to the fact that sensational news stories, no matter how superficially told, appear far more powerful, absurd and real than the stories novelists themselves conceive. Post-modern society is besieged by one media epic after another that sustains the required level of media intoxication. Post-modernist society favors a suspension of the suspension of disbelief in favor of a virtual audio-tactile media environment that is accepted as "true." No one believes movies are real anymore, but everyone believes in going with the media-engineered flow of sound bytes and images that evolve around us like a grave sitcom, blending farce and gravitas, like the 9/11 Hearings.

The Congressional 9/11 Hearings

The 9/11 Panel has inspired some peculiar behavior on the part of witnesses who were scheduled to testify. The case of Sandy Berger, who served as President Clinton's national security advisor, is noteworthy. He was implicated in secret and illegal arms shipments from Iran to the Croats and Bosnian Muslims that violated the arms embargo during the war,[1] and was instrumental in launching attacks against the Bosnian Serbs and the bombing of Belgrade. In other words, he was helping al-Qaeda gain a foothold in Bosnia, and then later in Kosovo and Macedonia.

Now Mr. Berger stands accused of having stolen and destroyed classified documents relating to terrorism.

> In 2003, when Berger was preparing to testify before the national commission investigating the Sept. 11 terrorist attacks ... he spent roughly 30 hours reviewing classified materials in a secure reading room. Berger was seen placing documents in a leather portfolio and stuffing papers in his jacket and his pants.[2]

It is always amusing to see a practiced liar like Sandy Berger in action after having been caught red-handed. These documents in all likelihood contained material damaging to his own reputation, but he said it was "an honest mistake." And when the National Archives demanded that Berger return the documents, he produced only a few and then claimed that he had "inadvertently" destroyed the rest. His shocking conduct, repugnant to all Americans who yearn for responsibility and straightforwardness from public officials, overshadowed the actual content of the documents he had stolen and destroyed. It is open to speculation whether or not these classified materials contained damaging material about the Clinton administration's relationship to al-Qaeda in Bosnia and Kosovo, but the uproar over the missing documents suggests they contain far more damaging material than has already been presented here. In light of the 9/11 hearings, what else could the classified material have been about? House Speaker Dennis Hastert, R-Ill., asked a series of pointed questions.

> What information could be so embarrassing...? ... Did these documents detail simple negligence or did they contain something more sinister? Was this a bungled attempt to rewrite history and keep critical information from the 9/11 commission...?[3]

Then it was the Republicans' turn to block thousands of pages of classified documents that the Commission demanded to see, thus showing themselves to be no better than Mr. Berger.

> The commission investigating the Sept. 11 attacks said on Thursday that it was pressing the White House to explain why the Bush admin-

istration had blocked thousands of pages of classified foreign policy and counterterrorism documents from former President Bill Clinton's White House files from being turned over to the panel's investigators.[4]

It is not the first time Democrats and Republicans have covered each other's tracks.

Mr. Walter Cronkite discussed the initial refusal of President Bush to let his national security advisor appear under oath before the 9/11 Commission and other incidents of secrecy and dishonesty among public officials.

> But this is a dangerous condition for any representative democracy to find itself in. The tight control of information, as well as the dissemination of misleading information and outright falsehoods, conjures up a disturbing image of a very different kind of society.
>
> Democracies are not well-run nor long-preserved with secrecy and lies.[5]

Is anything else needed to prove Gore Vidal's argument that the Democratic and Republicans parties are merely subchapters of the "war party"?

Richard A. Clarke, former White house anti-terrorism official who served under both presidents Clinton and Bush, turned out to be no hero, either. He caused a fifteen-minute sensation on March 22, 2004 with the publication of his book *Against All Enemies: Inside America's War on Terror*. In it, he took Bush to task for his failure to treat the terrorist threat seriously in the months before 9/11 and for misdirecting American resources by waging a war against Iraq. Clarke also tried to absolve Bill Clinton and his national security team (including Sandy Berger) of charges that he was to blame for the United States' failure to understand and take action against the looming terrorist menace. And what did Mr. Clarke have to say about Bosnia? He defended Clinton's destructive policies, and he did his best to place Alija Izetbegović in a favorable light. He described the Bosnians as being "hard-pressed," and speaking of Izetbegović's recruitment of foreign mujahideen, Clarke said that the "Bosnian president Alija Izetbegović decided to take aid where he could."[6]

Meanwhile, Michael Scheuer, a senior CIA counter-terrorism official, defied orders to stop publicly criticizing the U.S. government's response to al Qaeda. He charged that no one has been held responsible for the failures that helped lead to the 9/11 attacks and warned that continuing management problems would keep exposing Americans to risk.

> One whistle-blower expert said that Scheuer's decision to publicly defy the CIA was unprecedented. "I've never seen someone at that level come forward in the way that he has. It just doesn't happen," said Kris Kolesnik, executive director of the National Whistleblower Center.[7]

Scheuer criticized the 9/11 commission for "not naming names" when it issued its 567 page report. He states that pre-9/11 intelligence failings were caused, instead, by bad decisions and other mistakes by identifiable individuals, who in some cases, are "unelected, unaccountable officials who made an art of outlasting their elected superiors."[8]

Here are three questions that ought to be posed at the 9/11 hearings.[9]

> Q: Mr. Clinton, isn't it true that you declined an offer to have bin Laden extradited to U.S. custody?

> Q: Isn't it true that by delivering arms illegally to Bosnia you allowed Iranians, Saudis and other radical Islamists to infiltrate the Bosnian government?

> Q: Isn't it true that Mohammed Atta visited Bosnia three times during the 1990s? What do you think he was doing there?

Western "humanitarian intervention" on behalf of the Bosnian Muslims, who are still viewed as the injured party, has been and still is regarded as indisputably correct. Such uncritical support

> appears to have given rise to a Bosnian state that is far from liberal ... and that it allowed the Mujahideen a mission and a focus during the 1990s remains underreported. The Bosnian war, it seems, has been looked at in black and white for too long.[10]

Mustafa Ćerić's "Tolerant" Islam

Stories about Bosnia's wonderfully tolerant "European" version of Islam still predominate in the media, along with continued denials of any terrorist activity taking place there. For example:

> "If I were a terrorist group member I would think twice about coming to this country," says Senad Slatina, an analyst for the International Crisis Group.... "On top of that, Bosnian Muslims are so European that the radical form of Islam has absolutely no chance of spreading here."[11]

The article downplays the number of mujahideen who came to Yugoslavia, and admits to a total number of 200. Even though U.S. concerns over these groups increased after Sept. 11, 2001, the article went on to quote the Grand Mufti of Bosnia, Mustafa Ćerić, who assured Americans that they have nothing to fear.

> "I want to assure each and every American that as far as Bosnia is concerned, they can sleep safely," says Dr. Ćerić.[12]

Mustafa Ćerić has portrayed Bosnian Islam as a tolerant, European Islam, open to both East and West, yet holding steadfastly to its beliefs. He rejects the idea of the "clash of civilizations," and believes that the world is moving toward freedom and democratic states based on the rule of law. "The world can thank Western civilization and especially Europe for this trend," he said.[13] Islam in Bosnia "threatens nobody and is directed neither against other peoples nor against its own society."

This ought to be welcomed as good news, indeed, however, Dr. Ćerić has shown from past public statements that he is not trustworthy. Christians in Bosnia, both Serbs and Croats, are deeply suspicious of him and think that he is quietly working to establish an Islamic state. Dr. Ćerić studied in Cairo, and took a degree in the United States, so he knows how to speak to an American audience, but he doesn't speak the same way at home. Here are some of his frank remarks about Serbs:

> "The problem isn't in politicization but in the internal sickness which the Serbian Orthodox people currently has." And then once again he gave his diagnosis: "This is the best of advice and the best thing that they can be told. Because drug addicts, too, who are under the influence of drugs will never admit they are under the influence of drugs."[14]

Dr. Ćerić was not very interested whether or not "there are any good Serbs," but held forth about the bad ones:

> "Someone raised these people, someone taught them to hate, someone taught them to be aggressive. It wasn't me; they don't go to my mosque, *they go to some church*, they attend some school."[15] [Emphasis added.]

Dr. Ćerić then revealed his soul, and did not spare the dead in his remarks, either, especially if they were Orthodox. He declared that Serbs had their own *Mein Kampf.*

> "They are reading some kind of books, probably Njegos' *The Mountain Wreath*,[16] a book which has more hate in it than any other book in the world," he fumed.[17]

Preporod, the radical Muslim publication that did so much to incite war in Bosnia, published an article entitled "American Friends," which quotes Dr. Ćerić as saying that Americans are indeed friends of the Bosnian Muslims, even though he wished that the U.S. had a different policy in the Middle East. In an eye-opening inversion, the article also quoted Richard Holbrooke, who happily referred to General Ratko Mladić and Radovan Karadžić "the Osama bin Laden and Saddam Hussein of Europe."[18]

No one is paying attention to the people who pay attention to Dr. Ćerić. In August 2004, the Association of Former Camp Inmates of the Bosnian Serb Republic (Republika Srpska) issued a strongly worded condemnation of the statements Dr. Ćerić made during the opening ceremony of a mosque in Janja. Dr. Ćerić had said that there were no concentration camps or mass graves where there were mosques. The Association called to Dr. Ćerić's attention that there were 124 concentration camps that held mainly Serbian civilians in Sarajevo, a city that has 78 mosques.

> "[T]he entire public should know that between 8-10,000 Serb civilians were killed in the so-called multiethnic Sarajevo and that there were 536 concentration camps on the Bosniak side during the war, exactly on the same spot where the mosques are now," the deputy chairman of the Association of Former Camp Inmates, Slavko Jovičić, has told SRNA.[19]

Dr. Ćerić knows that between the Land of Peace (*Dar al-Islam*) and the Land of War (*Dar al-Harb*) there is a middle ground called *Dar al Sulh*, which is applied when Muslim expansion temporarily pauses. Muslims put it to use when they find it necessary to provisionally adopt a conciliatory attitude in order to conceal their true intentions against their neighbors. This is Mr. Ćerić's strategy.

Consider how Dr. Ćerić supports Sulejman Tihić, the Bosniak member of the Bosnia-Herzegovinian presidency and SDA leader, who called for the discontinuation of the Republika Srpska. Dragan Kalinić, the speaker of the Republika Srpska parliament and president of the SDS, warned that such a policy of pressure, blackmail and calls for the liquidation of Republika Srpska were an attempt to reignite the flames that the Dayton Peace Accord had already extinguished.[20] In other words, the Bosnian Muslims want to destroy all remnants of both secular and Christian society in Bosnia.

If any doubt still remains, consider the inflammatory remarks made by Džemaludin Latić, a poet who had been sentenced together with Alija Izetbegović in the 1983 trial of Muslim radicals for inciting religious hatred. The 468th anniversary of the Gazi Husrev-Begova Madrasa (a school) in Sarajevo provided Mr. Latić with an occasion to call for a "Bosniak cultural revolution and the revitalization of Islamic-Ottoman civilization."[21] And he also called for the creation of a "strong and orderly state, of a Muslim media system, and of a Bosniak cultural identity."

In other words, Mr. Latić was calling for the creation of a Muslim fundamentalist state which needed an Islamic university to establish Sarajevo as the pan-Islamist center in Europe. The subtext was: "let the Christians be damned!" And the article went on to note that Izetbegović's party, the SDA, in conjunction with the Islamic community in Bosnia-Herzegovina, created the preconditions for the resurrection of "Islamic-Ottoman civilization" in the Balkans, which is what the Serbs have claimed all along, and which was denied by Washington, which consistently claimed that Izetbegović wanted to create a "multiethnic Bosnia." This is not a credibility gap but a credibility chasm.

Dr. Ćerić used this occasion to call for "the establishment of Bosniak political domination in B-H since the Bosniak Muslims are the most numerous nation in the state."[22] The key words are "most numerous nation in the state," which indicates that Dr. Ćerić feels strong enough to move against the Christian areas of Bosnia-Herzegovina, and impose Shari'a law on them. And he had the cunning and guile to advise Americans that "they can sleep safely," but Serbs and other Christians aren't going to sleep safely.

Such conduct has not prevented Dr. Ćerić from receiving the UNESCO Peace Prize for Promoting Interfaith Dialogue in September 2004.[23]

Meanwhile, a senior European intelligence operative said the international undercover effort in Bosnia was part of an "invisible but real struggle with the bad guys" that he says could start bomb attacks in Europe — or in the U.S.[24]

> In mosques and storefront Muslim charities, U.S. and European intelligence agencies are engaged in a covert conflict in postwar Bosnia, tracking up to 300 suspected Islamic militants and shutting down those funding them.[25]

As the number of Muslims in Europe keeps growing, it is inevitable that they will insist on "more rights," just as they did in Bosnia. In the West, Bosnia was sold to the public as a model for a "humanitarian intervention." But in the Muslim world, Bosnia is sold to the public as a model of territorial expansion through jihad. Thus, Europe is within reach:

> The ratio of Muslims to the total population of the EU countries ranges between 3.5 and 5.5%. However, the ratio of Muslim youth (between 45 and 50% of the Muslims) to EU youth is between 16 and 20%. In other words, in a few years Muslims will constitute 16 to 20% of the European workforce, and could therefore influence policies and decision-making.[26]

Islam is also making inroads in the U.S., where it is the third-largest and fastest growing religion. Michael Wolfe, apparently an American convert to Islam, wrote a lengthy article that tried to make a favorable presentation of Islam to Americans. "The U.S. began as a haven for Christian outcasts. But what religion fits our current zeitgeist? The answer may be Islam."[27]

What follows is a 1,500-word tract that tries to place Islam as a faith that fits squarely into the American way of life. It reads like a promotional brochure. Mr. Wolfe argues that if the Pilgrims came to seek religious freedom, why can't Muslims? He calls to our attention to the fact that more than 50% of America's six million Muslims were born here. Then comes the chilling question: "Is America a Muslim nation?" He provides seven reasons why the answer may be yes: 1) Islam is monotheistic; 2) Islam is "democratic" in spirit; 3) Islam has an attractive mystical tradition; 4) Islam is egalitarian; 5) Islam shares America's new interest in food purity and diet; 6) Islam is tolerant of other faiths; and 7) Islam encourages the pursuit of religious freedom. Of course, points 1 and 5 may be true, but all the others are false. Nevertheless, these reasons will be trotted out again and again by Muslims in their ceaseless campaign to find converts in the U.S.

As the U.S. spreads "democracy" and "market capitalism" throughout the world, the Muslims are spreading Islam throughout the world. Islam is coming to America and it is getting acquainted with value-free market capitalism. And Islam is finding fertile fields for growth in America's spiritual void. And as their numbers grow, there will be an America Mufti one day, who, like Dr. Ćerić, will call for the imposition of Shari'a law, and dream of turning the Washington Monument into a minaret. This is not an exaggeration for rhetorical effect. The Ottomans turned the Parthenon into a mosque with the addition of a minaret, which was only dismantled after the Greek War of Liberation.

The consequences of Muslim immigration to Europe will be examined later in this chapter. Radical Islam experienced a parallel development with the Nazi movement. It is worthwhile examining the influence of Nazi thinking and practice in U.S. public life and discourse.

Nazi Thinking and Practice Penetrates the U.S.

The U.S. has drifted so far to the right over the past twenty-five years that we have become insensible to the Nazi programs, policies and legislation that have penetrated our society. It began with enthusiasts like Henry Ford and Charles Lindbergh, whose beliefs were judged aberrant or kooky in light of their other redeeming features, but later Nazification took much more ominous turns.

> The Central Intelligence Agency has for the first time confirmed that a high-ranking Nazi general placed his anti-Soviet spy ring at the disposal of the United States during the early days of the Cold War.[28]

The National Archives issued a press release that stated the CIA had filed an affidavit in U.S. District court "acknowledging an intelligence relationship with German General Reinhard Gehlen that it has kept secret for 50 years."[29] This meant that the newly formed CIA had absorbed a network of thousands of former Nazi spies who were rebaptized as anti-Communist freedom fighters. The same men and women who had been plotting to conquer the world with Hitler were now providing raw data for the composition of country reports, analyses of political leaders, and strategy papers that State Department officials, congressmen, senators and presidents read. Eventually, some of these former Nazi spies saw their children rise in the ranks of U.S. intelligence and defense, as in the case of Mira Baratta, which was discussed earlier.

Others in American public life were revealed to have Nazi connections.

> George W. Bush's grandfather helped finance the Nazi Party. Karl Rove's grandfather allegedly helped run the Nazi Party, and helped build the Birkenau Death Camp. Arnold Schwarzenegger's Austrian father volunteered for the infamous Nazi SA and became a ranking officer.[30]

The article goes on to discuss Arnold Schwarzenegger's personal friendship with Kurt Waldheim, whom he had invited to his wedding to Maria Shriver. The authors of the article quoted a illustrative passage from *Arnold: An Unauthorized Biography*, by Wendy Leigh (Congdon & Weed: 1990).

> "My friends don't want me to mention Kurt's name, because of all the recent Nazi stuff and the U.N. controversy," Arnold said. "But I love him and Maria does to, and so thank you, Kurt."

"Kurt," as we may recall, was an intelligence officer in Germany's Army Group E when it committed mass murder against the Serbs in the Kozara region of western Bosnia in 1942. Genocide has been reduced to "Nazi stuff." Waldheim and Schwarzenegger had been seen together as recently as 1998.

Senator Orin Hatch (Utah) is a great supporter of Mr. Schwarzenegger, and is the point man for an effort to amend the Constitution so that a naturalized citizen like Mr. Schwarzenegger can become president. Rove, who is sometimes referred to as "Bush's Brain," and who is also based in Utah, lent considerable behind-the-scenes support to Schwarzenneger's gubernatorial campaign. Mr. Schwarzenegger remarked in a 1977 interview:

> I admire Hitler, for instance, because he came from being a little man with almost no formal education, up to power. I admire him for being such a good public speaker and for what he did with it.[31]

Mr. Schwarzenegger later apologized for the remark, denounced Hitler, and lavished contributions on the Simon Wiesenthal Center to make amends. The sincerity of his actions, however, remains open to question. Franjo Tudjman later went through the same routine, and look what happened.

According to Bob Woodward's *Bush at War*, the President attended a Yankees game not long after the 9/11 attacks. He threw out the first pitch, and the fans roared. Thousands in the crowd raised their arms with thumbs up. Karl Rove, who was sitting in box seats, compared the roaring crowd to "a Nazi rally." The man knows what he's talking about.[32]

But comparisons to Nazis have become commonplace. Saddam Hussein was compared to Hitler, as was Slobodan Milošević, and numerous other perceived enemies. During the bombardment of Serbia in 1999, Radio Television Serbia (RTS) aired pictures of Clinton and Blair with Hitler mustaches, and was bombed shortly thereafter. The attack killed sixteen technicians, including a makeup girl.

It was, of course, only a matter of time before Bush II was likened to Hitler here in the U.S., but the consequences were not as drastic as those for RTS.

> The controversy over comparisons between George W. Bush and Adolf Hitler in two ads submitted to the anti-Bush ad contest run by the online activist group MoveOn.org says less about the state of left discourse than it does about the double standards at Rupert Murdoch's News Corporation.[33]

MoveOn.org removed the ads when complaints were made. The next day the Fox News Channel dwelled on the comparison. Sean Hannity, who hosts a show on Fox, remarked: "You guys on the left are going so far over the cliff. You're making comparisons to the president and Adolf Hitler."[34] *The New York Post*, however, also owned by Rupert Murdoch, retaliated with a column that portrayed Democratic presidential candidate Howard Dean as a follower of Josef Goebbels, and referred to him as "Herr Howie," labeled his supporters "the Internet Gestapo," and compared them to "Hitler's brownshirts." So, as far as Murdoch's News Corp. is concerned, Nazi comparisons are deplorable only when Republicans are the target. In the end, it was a mere squabble in the permanent casting call for new Hitlers.

But when enemy troops are concerned, Nazi paraphernalia is requisite art direction.

> During the 1989 invasion of Panama, American soldiers showed reporters Hitler's portrait hanging in Manuel Noriega's home — a U.S.

> Army colonel later admitted psychological warfare experts had planted
> the Fuhrer's portrait and a voodoo altar shown to TV cameras.[35]

It begs the question: are the psywar experts twelve years old?
and what about the viewers who believed it?

Bruce Ramsey of the *Seattle Times* wrote succinctly about such
comparisons of foreign and domestic public figures to Hitler.

> In today's America, whenever certain topics arise — and war is at the
> top of that list — somebody plays the Hitler card. A comparison is
> made to der Fuhrer. It is the signal for George Orwell's Two Minutes
> of Hate…. It shuts down discussion. It's a sledgehammer.[36]

He rightly considered comparisons to Hitler a signal to shut down
all thought processes and become belligerent. He took Slobodan
Milošević's case into consideration. No one had heard of him in the
U.S., but once he was likened to Hitler, everyone knew what to do.

Not only is Hitler's name frequently invoked, but Nazi terminology has invaded the American language. There have been
many incidents of Nazi nomenclature that have been absorbed in
the U.S., most notably, the New World Order (*Neue
Weltordnung*). They range from the workplace, where we have a
"team leader" (*ubergangfuhrer*), to military operations such as
the 1999 bombing of the Serbs, called "Operation Punishment,"
which was exactly what Hitler had called his illegal aggression
against Serbia in 1941.

The Nazis had a gift for naming their military operations with
alluring, seductive names. The U.S. "Operation Iron Hammer"
(*Eisenhammer*) was launched to ferret out the Iraqi insurgents in
Baghdad who killed scores of U.S. troops. "The U.S. military's
code name for a crackdown on resistance in Iraq was also used by
the Nazis for an aborted operation to damage the Soviet power grid
during World War II."[37] A Pentagon spokesperson, of course,
denied any knowledge of a connection to the Nazi operation.

Adolf Hitler returned like a revenant to haunt the Yugoslav crisis, too. The scandal caused by Hitler's reappearance is attributable to those who have denounced Milošević as a latter day
"Hitler," because they were actually using propaganda techniques that were developed and effectively deployed by Hitler
himself during WWII.

It is fitting to examine some of Hitler's own remarks on the subject of propaganda culled from *Mein Kampf*,[38] for they will shed

some light on today's situation. Hitler, for example, maintained that the repetition of "very few points" and slogans would focus attention on certain key factoids, processes and necessities. "The greater the mass that propaganda is intended to reach, the lower the purely intellectual level of the propaganda will be."[*] The repetition of Srebrenica as "the worst massacre since WWII" thus provides The Hague with "suspects" to prosecute, a process that implicitly casts the U.S. in the role of "good guys" and cements the growth of the American Empire. A factoid becomes a process that is a necessity. We saw the method applied in Iraq.

Hitler also believed that "propaganda is a weapon, and a frightful one in the right hands." He discussed the use of this new "weapon," which could sway the hearts and minds of the population and persuade them to believe the most outrageous things. And he insisted that propaganda had to be drilled into the public until everyone fell into line.

The Bosnian war, as well as the wars in Croatia and Kosovo, were shaped by two slogans: "ethnic cleansing" and "humanitarian crisis." The Clinton administration repeated the phrase "ethnic cleansing" *ad nauseam* in order to win public backing for the bombardment of the Serbs, the allegedly guilty party, who were likened to Nazi Germany. Then NATO went on to claim that the Serbs were committing a contemporary holocaust to drive the point home.

> "Humanitarian crisis," on the other hand, is something that the US, the UK and NATO helped to create by escalating a serious situation to catastrophic proportions.[39]

Hitler also contended that the "power to forget is enormous." Such "power to forget" is aided and abetted by critical omissions in reportage, which also serve as a propaganda tool. Serbia used to be a "friend" of the United States. President Wilson proclaimed June 28 to be Serbia Day after WWI. The Serbs were the first to stand up to Hitler in WWII, and initiated the first guerrilla resistance movement against the Third Reich. Yet, these his-

---

[*] © 1999 by New Dawn Magazine, www.newdawnmagazine.com. "The Public Relations of Modern Warfare: Will the Real Nazis Please Stand Up!" by Susan Bryce. Summarized with permission of the publisher.

toric ties to the U.S. did not shield them from subsequent demonization. In the 1980s, Slobodan Milošević got along very well with Washington, and he even began to reform market policies and began to dismantle state-owned industries. But the rules of the game had changed by the 1990s, and President Milošević became the "butcher of the Balkans." And while attention was isolated to a few key points in the Bosnian War, no one seemed to notice that there were one million refugees in Serbia.

Many commentators have echoed Henry Kissinger's remark that the U.S. has neither permanent friends nor permanent enemies, only permanent interests. But no one has asked if this lack of character is our character.

Propaganda succeeds to the extent that the press has been put under government control. Thus, the media mergers of the 1980s and 1990s paved the way for boldfaced and blatant censorship of news coverage in the former Yugoslavia, and elsewhere, as it focuses on "very few points." The Nazis shut down domestic newspapers and magazines that did not toe the party line; NATO shut down the press in Serbia by bombing television stations and the power grid; here in the States, media giants gain control of the competition by simply buying them out.

All levels of the information gathering and broadcasting process during Balkan Wars were censored. It began with restricting the ability of journalists to report "in the field" and went all the way to Pentagon briefings and diplomatic meetings. It was common knowledge that Western reporters holed themselves up in luxury hotels in Sarajevo during the Bosnian War and relied on NATO briefings. Roy Gutman was reported to have written his Pulitzer Prize winning story, "Serbs Organizing Death Camps in Bosnia," from a Zagreb luxury hotel room. It was a great story. Too bad it wasn't true.[40]

No Western reporters ever went to Ilidža (a Serbian-held suburb of Sarajevo) until after 100,000 Serbs abandoned the area after the Dayton Peace Accords were instituted. Reporters were shocked at the damage caused by Muslim bombardment there, which was far more extensive than the damage caused in Sarajevo.

In the end, the IMF and the World Bank are supposed to help rebuild Serbia, which will repay such loans with its abundant store of natural resources. These include rich "deposits of lead, zinc, cadmium, silver and gold and an estimated 17 billion tons of coal reserves."[41]

> The UK government and U.S. administration, along with NATO, used lies and untruths in order to win support for a bloody war in Yugoslavia. Such untruths are the same as propaganda used by Hitler during World War Two. Representing key corporate and institutional interests, NATO waged a war of aggression, without UN sanction, against an independent and autonomous state.[42]

Adolf Hitler predicted that fascism would rise again eighty years after his death, but it has not taken that long. What is fascism? To paraphrase Mussolini, it is running a state like a business, or the state merging its interests with those of its commercial enterprises. The Nazification of U.S. thinking unofficially began with the absorption of Nazi intelligence officers into the CIA. It began officially with Ronald Reagan laying flowers on the graves of fallen SS soldiers at the Bittberg cemetery in Germany in 1982. Later, George Bush, Sr. announced a special relationship with Germany after the Berlin Wall fell. Then the came the tragic U.S. and German support lavished on Franjo Tudjman of Croatia, Alija Izetbegović of Bosnia, and the KLA in Kosovo, each of whom reawakened political parties and terrorist groups that had historic Nazi ties: the Ustashi in Croatia, the Handžar Division in Bosnia, and the Bali Kombitar in Kosovo.

And there was a ready-made anti-Serbian campaign. Much like a creatively bankrupt Hollywood producer, the U.S. State Department began rummaging through old screenplays and story lines. It unearthed old Austro-Hungarian anti-Serbian propaganda from WWI that denied Serbia's right to exist and used as its slogan "The Serbs must die" (*Strieben muss Serbien*). Then there was a treasure trove of anti-Serbian propaganda generated by Nazi Germany during WWII, because the Serbs, being Slavs, had been categorized as a "subhuman race" along with Jews. There were legions of professional writers, pundits, journalists, speech writers and PR men and women who were willing to do the rewrite of history and put the right spin on it in order to create a "marketable story." And who would catch on to the ruse, after all?

Today, the world fears America the way an earlier generation feared Hitler. According to a recent BBC poll, 52% of its international respondents replied that globalization and the U.S. pose a greater threat to world peace than the war on terrorism.[43]

And Americans regarded themselves differently after 9/11. It was no longer ridiculous to speak of an "American Empire" or to use the expression "the world's only superpower," phrases that became lounge furniture for the mind. But don't "superpower democracy" and "imperial democracy" still sound ridiculous?

> [T]hey seem not only contradictory but opposed to basic assumptions that Americans hold about their political system and their place within it. Americans are now facing a grim situation with no easy solution. Perhaps the ... Declaration of Independence might remind us that "whenever any form of Government becomes destructive ... it must be challenged.[44]

It is important to note the work of John Loftus, former U.S. Deputy Attorney General, because he has not only written on the subjects discussed here, but has taken legal action as well.[45] Mr. Loftus is a perhaps best known for his book, *Unholy Trinity*, which exposed the role of the Vatican, the Nazis and Swiss banks in looting gold from Jewish and Serbian Holocaust victims. Twenty-five years ago, Mr. Loftus, who was working for the U.S. Attorney General, came across twenty vaults of files on the Muslim Brotherhood, and read them. He appeared on "60 Minutes" in 1982, when he revealed that the CIA had put Nazis, whom Mr. Loftus had been assigned to prosecute, on the U.S. payroll. He dedicated himself to educating a new generation of CIA agents about the Muslim Brotherhood, a fascist organization that was retained by Western intelligence, and that over time evolved into what is today called al-Qaeda. The Muslim Brotherhood was established in the 1920s by an Egyptian named Al Bana, who was a great admirer of Adolf Hitler. By the 1930s, the Muslim Brotherhood had become a division of Nazi intelligence. The Palestinian section was headed by the Grand Mufti of Jerusalem, al-Husseini (*see* pp. 164-169). After the end of WWII, the British were going to use the Muslim Brotherhood to crush the infant Israeli state, but they failed. Afterwards, the British sold the Arab Nazis to the OSS, a predecessor of the CIA, and the U.S. put the Muslim Brotherhood on its payroll. Nasser ordered the Muslim Brotherhood out of Egypt in the 1950s, so they moved to Saudi Arabia, where Osama bin Ladin became a student at one of the Muslim Brotherhood's schools. In 1979, the CIA decided to deploy the Arab Nazis in Afghanistan against the Russians.

> And the CIA lied to Congress and said they didn't know who was on the payroll in Afghanistan, except the Saudi's. But it was not true. A small section of the CIA knew perfectly well that we had once again hired the Arab Nazis and that we were using them to fight our secret wars.[46]

Thus, the Muslim Brotherhood envenomed and infected the entire Middle East, and after 9/11, it spread from one end of the world to the other. And a whole generation of CIA employees was ignorant of this.

Mr. Loftus began to question the extent of radical Muslim fundraising through charities in the United States. He began to wonder why radicals like Dr. Sami al-Arian, who was employed at the University of Southern Florida, were raising money for the express purpose of killing Jews in Israel. When Mr. Loftus asked why al-Arian had not been prosecuted, the reply he got from his friends at the FBI and the CIA was that they would have loved to prosecute him, but that they had been told by superiors that they could not touch him because al-Arian was receiving money from the Saudis, and that the FBI and CIA were under strict orders not to do anything to embarrass the Saudis. Mr. Loftus took the initiative. He made a contribution to the charity that served as a terrorist fund, and then he sued to find out where the money was going because he had a right to do so under Florida law. In March 2002, he drafted a lawsuit exposing Professor Sami al-Arian and named the crimes he had committed. He also mentioned in the suit that the Saudis were convinced that the U.S. government would not prosecute them for political reasons. The day before he filed his lawsuit, he got a frantic phone call from the U.S. Department of Justice, which begged him not to file the lawsuit. The Dept. of Justice was going to raid the Islamic charities in question. Mr. Loftus told them that he was filing his complaint at 10:00 a.m. And sure enough, at 10:15 a.m. of the same day, the U.S. government launched Operation Greenquest, which shut down Saudi money-laundering and charities in America in one hour. Mr. al-Arian is now in federal prison, and 32 other people were indicted in the U.S. as a direct result of these efforts.

> Al Qaeda simply didn't spring up on its own. The evil route was
> Nazism. The al Qaeda Doctrine is the same as the Arab Nazis held.
> They hated Jews, they hate democracy, and they hate ... Western
> Culture. Al Qaeda is nothing more than the religious expression of
> Arab Fascism.... and it has come back to haunt us.[47]

And the trail of Nazi gold, or more precisely, Ustashi gold, is
still being traced in America. U.S. courts are going to reconsider
a dismissed lawsuit that alleged that the Vatican Bank laundered
assets stolen from Serbian and Jewish victims of Croatia's Nazi
puppet regime during WWII.[48] This includes the gold that
Archbishop Stepinac took custody of near the end of WWII. The
survivors alleged in a lawsuit filed in U.S. federal court in 1999
against the Vatican Bank and the Franciscan Order, which
charged them with laundering stolen gold and other assets during
WWII. The case was dismissed in 2003. The attorney for the
plaintiffs argued that the lower court ignored precedents of courts
settling political claims, and cited class-action suits that motivated settlements related to German slave labor and Swiss banks.
The Vatican bank attorney did not dispute that such murders,
theft, and money laundering had occurred, and argued instead
that foreign policy, not lawsuits, should address such historical
claims. "Losses that occur in the chaos of war need to be handled
by the state which suffers the loss," he said. "It is well beyond the
provenance of the district court to manage."[49]

This discussion of the Nazification of America cannot be concluded without examining Richard Holbrooke, the architect of
the Dayton Accord. He branded members of the leading Serbian
party in Bosnia "Nazis."[50] Holbrooke made these remarks in
Sarajevo during his visit with Bernard Kouchner to the ailing
Izetbegović. What Holbrooke, in fact, said was: "They are Nazis
who should disappear." Holbrooke then praised Alija
Izetbegović, and claimed that the country could not have existed
without him. This was the occasion that Kouchner wrote about
later in his whimsically titled memoirs, *Les Guerriers de la paix*,
in which Izetbegović made the astonishing revelation that *the
Serbs had no death camps* for the systematic destruction of
Bosnia-Herzegovina. According to Kouchner's book, Izetbegović
was convinced that claims regarding the existence of Serbian-run
death camps would have provoked rapid Western military inter-

vention, but he admitted he was wrong to suppose that.[51] This did not prevent Kouchner from launching a massive ad campaign that claimed just that.[52] Holbrooke also frequently resorted to such false allegations against the Serbs during the Bosnian War.

Holbrooke made these accusations against the Bosnian Serbs knowing full well that the true heirs to Nazi dogma and praxis were Izetbegović and Tudjman, his allies of choice during the Bosnian War, so he conveniently transferred their guilt to the Bosnian Serbs. He was working in concert with President Clinton, Secretary of State Madeleine Albright and others to deliberately implement Hitler's WWII vision and division of Yugoslavia. Does such implementation of Hitler's foreign policy make Holbrooke a Nazi? or a pragmatist? The question itself is irrelevant when the ends justify the means, when America has no permanent friends — only permanent interests.

The War on "Terror"

Michael Scheuer, the author of *Imperial Hubris*, hit the nail on the head. On the one hand, Americans are being advised that they are winning the war on terror against al Qaeda that began on 9/11; on the other hand, if Americans probe these news stories more deeply, they learn that al-Qaeda is more powerful than ever before.

> I believe the answer lies in the way we see and interpret people and events outside North America, which is heavily clouded by arrogance and self-centeredness amounting to what I called "imperial hubris."[53]

It results, says the author, from Americanizing the world as we interpret it. One of the ways we Americanize the outside world is by creating vast PR campaigns that sell war criminals like Alija Izetbegović to Americans as a "democrat," and "tolerant Islamic leader." We Americanize Franjo Tudjman by calling him "Croatia's democratically elected president," and by inviting him to the opening of the Holocaust Memorial Museum in Washington, D.C. But lying is a double-edged sword: if we deceive others about one thing, then we necessarily deceive ourselves about another. Mr. Scheuer is targeting the "no permanent friends but permanent interests" theme that has dominated American foreign policy.

President Bush, after having won his second term in office, promised in his victory speech to "fight this war on terror with every resource of our national power." It is still open to debate whether he is protecting us from "terrorism" or whether he has militarized the nation's energy policy in the Balkans, Afghanistan, and Iraq. Next, the Bush administration began selling the American public on asymmetrical or "fourth-generation" warfare, which pits a nation-state against a "non state actor." Such a war is fought covertly, and even its successes remain secret.

> In broad terms, fourth generation warfare seems likely to be widely dispersed and largely undefined; the distinction between war and peace will be blurred to the vanishing point. It will be nonlinear, possibly to the point of having no definable battlefields or fronts. The distinction between "civilian" and "military" may disappear.[54]

If you live in New York, a city which was and remains a terrorist target, there are many visible signs that a war is going on. Rockefeller Center was swarming with anti-terrorist units armed with automatic weapons when the Christmas tree was on display. No one could miss the National Guardsmen patrolling the subways during the Republican National Convention, or the closing of the Statue of Liberty to visitors, or NYC police officers swarming through Wall Street.

Different pundits have taken equally different points of view on the "war on terror." Richard Pipes was able to reanimate his cold-war stance *vis-à-vis* Russia when the Beslan tragedy struck. He argued that the attacks in New York and the Pentagon were unprovoked attacks on non-Islamic civilization, whereas the attack on Beslan, where 300 school children were killed, was not an attack that sought to destroy Russia — therefore, the Russians could seek to compromise with the Chechens, however, the U.S. could never negotiate with al-Qaeda.[55] Taking leave of such fatuous sophistry, we find Norman Podhoretz making the sensible argument that even if Israel had never existed, the United States would still remain as a symbol of everything that the Muslims consider to be evil.

> His objective is not merely to murder as many of us as possible and to conquer our land. Like the Nazis and the Communists before him, he is dedicated to the destruction of everything good for which America stands.[56]

We cannot fight terrorism at home by supporting terrorism abroad in Bosnia, Croatia, Kosovo, Macedonia and Chechnya. Yet, the task has become more difficult because the language of public discourse has been polluted. When politicians and pundits use the word "stability," they mean that investment banks and multinational corporations will get their money and their markets. When politicians use the word "democracy," they mean television-driven elections in which the candidate with the most money wins simply because he or she can buy more air time for political advertising. And when politicians use the word "terrorism" (or the "war on terrorism" — history's first war against an abstract noun), it means depriving U.S. citizens of their rights, whether it be the right to organize a labor union or the right to smoke a cigarette in a bar or a restaurant. (Hitler, incidentally, banned smoking in Germany when he assumed power.)

Stella Jatras provided a striking example of such U.S. two-fold support for terrorism. Presidential candidate John Kerry invited Hashim Thaci, the Albanian KLA terrorist leader, whose *nom de guerre* was "the Snake," to the Democratic National Convention![57] The KLA financed its terror campaign against the Serbs in Kosovo with its lucrative heroin and white slave trade. Thaci actually went to Boston, where he was promised "that the Democratic authorities would recognize and respect the will of the people of Kosova[58] for self-determination." In other words, the Democrats promised him Kosovo's independence. What on earth were the Democrats thinking? William J. Hutton's article about Serbia's decision to send 1,000 troops to Afghanistan ought to have knocked some sense into people. "The Serbians could make a special contribution (i.e., in Afghanistan) because of their experience in fighting the KLA terrorists."[59] The ironic tragedy the Serbs have been dealt is that they are not allowed to fight Islamic fundamentalist terrorism in Bosnia and Kosovo, but have been subcontracted to fight Uncle Sam's war in Afghanistan. Finally, the media had recognized that the Serbs had been fighting al-Qaeda terrorists in their own country, but no one linked this to Mr. Thaci's visit to the DNC except for Ms. Jatras.

A recent Dutch documentary, *De Brooklyn connectie* (The Brooklyn Connection) shows Florin Krasniqi, a KLA member from Brooklyn, attending a John Kerry fund raiser with several other KLA members, where he writes a check, and then makes it clear that he expects a *quid pro quo*.

> "With money you can do amazing things in this country. Senators and congressmen are looking for donations. If you fund them and raise the money they need for their campaign they pay you back," Krasniqi says in the documentary.[60]

The documentary later shows Krasniqi shopping for weapons in an American gun store. He discusses the fact that in the past, weapons, disguised as humanitarian aid, were smuggled into Kosovo. Krasniqi is also shown in the documentary introducing himself to Gen. Wesley Clark.

> Krasniqi says, "Mr. Clark. This is your group, your KLA." Clark then praises the group saying, "They fought against tremendous odds."

If that were not enough, Kerry's senior foreign policy advisor and former Assistant Secretary of State for European Affairs under Clinton, Richard Holbrooke, who apparently knew one of the KLA members, joined the group and jokingly remarked, "He almost got me killed!"

In another sequence, Krasniqi and a mule driver set off from Albania for Kosovo with the words "Now let's go kill some Serbs."[61]

Examples such as these are not superfluous. They demonstrate why we cannot have a serious discussion about evil unless we discuss our own participation in it.

If one looks at the problems the former Yugoslavia had with Islam, we will clearly see our own. On the two-year anniversary of the trial of Slobodan Milošević, Julia Gorin, writing for *The Nation*, drew a skillful and frightening comparison between the war on terror and the fate of multi-ethnic Yugoslavia. She discussed the case of a U.S. Army sergeant, a convert to Islam, who fragged his fellow soldiers during the invasion of Iraq, and then shot those who tried to flee, killing two and wounding fourteen. She compared the Muslim sergeant's actions to a 1987 incident in which an Albanian conscript in the Yugoslav Army killed four of his fellow Slavic soldiers and wounded six as they slept. She concluded,

> As we feel justified in going halfway around the globe to fight terrorism, to do essentially what Belgrade was trying to do in its own back-

yard before we bombed it and killed 2,000 Serb civilians, perhaps we can finally start to appreciate what the country was up against.[62]

It is a foregone conclusion in the post-9/11 period that we can expect such seditious acts by Muslim conscripts in the U.S. armed forces. And now, we can enjoy the spine-tingling pleasure of Islamic fundamentalism nesting in the U.S. Horror, of course, is beholding terrible things happening to others; terror is experiencing terrible things one's self.

One such horror was the beheading of *Wall Street Journal* reporter Daniel Pearl in Pakistan in 2002. It shocked Americans, but did not bring them to their senses. Then, in 2004, Americans saw another snuff video. Five men wearing headscarves and black ski masks entered the frame and took positions over a bound man in an orange jump suit, who faced the camera and said:

"My name is Nick Berg, my father's name is Michael, my mother's name is Suzanne," the man said on the video....[63]

His last words eerily echoed those of Daniel Pearl. Then, one of the masked men put a knife to Mr. Berg's neck. A scream was heard, accompanied by cries of "Allahu Akbar!" Then the executioner held Mr. Berg's head before the camera for all the world to see.

Yet, the Serbs were the first Western victims of Islamist beheadings. (*See* p. 493). The British government, in fact, banned an exhibition of photographs showing atrocities committed against Serbs in the Yugoslav civil war. The exhibition, which was put together in Belgrade, was banned by the British Department of Trade and Industry on January 13, 1993, even though Croatian and Muslim groups had been permitted to stage their own exhibitions of atrocity photographs in Britain.[64] Bojana Isaković, the curator of the exhibition, remarked:

It is understandable that the Americans and Europeans don't want to show our pictures to their people — because they are the authors of these pictures.[65]

Other massacres also got a face lift in the media. The Markale market massacre was the subject of a recent BBC news report.[66] The article resurrected the charges against the Serbs after an apparent presentation of the two conflicting accounts of the bombing, even though Lord Owen admitted in his memoirs that the Muslims had set off the blast.[67] This is the conclusion the BBC article instead reaches.

> Perhaps the final verdict on the Markale incident lies with the War Crimes Tribunal in The Hague. Last month the court sentenced Bosnian Serb General Stanislav Galic to 20 years in prison for his part in the attack on civilians, including the Markale massacre.[68]

The BBC journalist goes on to defer to the ICTY, which is following a policy of inventing a crime and then finding a suitable person to indict, for a "final verdict." And the serial kidnapping of suspects who have been remanded to the ICTY and their subsequent convictions (no one has been found innocent yet) continue like a parade of prisoners of war led into the Coliseum to be cast to the lions before the roaring approval of the plebes. (For a more detailed examination of The Hague Tribunal, *see* the Appendices .)

The U.S. set a groundbreaking precedent for intrigue, secrecy, and outright manipulation during the Milošević trial after the it demanded and received the right to censor the testimony given by Gen. Wesley Clark at the International Criminal Tribunal for the former Yugoslavia (ICTY). The retired General had at the time, after hesitating in his choice between the two major parties, declared himself to be a Democratic presidential candidate. And he won Michael Moore's support! Much more significant than his choice of parties was the strange views he held on fighting terrorism.

> The media refer to Clark's impressive military credentials but they fail to note that his main accomplishment under President Clinton was presiding over the establishment of a base for radical Islamic terrorism, including bin Laden, in Kosovo.[69]

Clark was widely quoted in the media when he asserted that the U.S. war against Iraq was based on little or no direct evidence. And he ought to know. He waged the Kosovo war on behalf of Clinton on false claims of "genocide." The U.S. and NATO military intervention in Kosovo broke all the rules of international law, a far bolder move than engineering a regime change in Iraq.

Then Clark had the shameless audacity to write a column for *Time* magazine called "How to Fight the New War,"[70] in which he said, "We need face-to-face information collection: Who are these people, what are their intentions, and what can be done to disrupt their plans and arrest them?"

> For the answer, Clark should ask his old friend, Hashim Thaci, the commander of the KLA.... The KLA's ties to Osama bin Laden also well known and reported.[71]

Intelligence reports regularly describe Bosnia, Kosovo and Albania as hotbeds of Islamic fundamentalism. Clark is responsible for this, but he could rest assured that no big name newscaster would ever ask him these tough questions, even when he was running for president. And they didn't, even though they were happily attacking Bush for going to war with Iraq on the flimsiest of evidence, which turned out to be fabricated, after all.

Michael Sheuer believes that the United States will eventually lose the war on terror.

> When asked if the United States could win the "war on terror," which was undertaken following the Sept. 11 attacks, Sheuer said: "No. It can't be won. We're going to eventually lose it."[72]

Did Mr. Sheuer have Mr. Thaci in mind, among others? He went on to discuss the bureaucratic obstacles involved in transferring terrorist suspects to countries that have the death penalty, like the U.S. European law prohibits such transfers. Arab countries are prevented from acting because of bin Laden's popularity. Mr. Scheuer added that al-Qaeda was winning the propaganda war on the internet because it was defining political, military and religious discourse. He believes that the heart of the movement is made up of true believers, and they are suspected of having success in infiltrating the U.S., Saudi and Jordanian military and security services. "They've beaten our pants off," said Mr. Scheuer.

The "war on terror" at home and across the world is so expensive that it will bankrupt us. Its successes have been meager, and three years after 9/11, we have spent billions and are not one jot safer. "Our greatest and most alarming vulnerability is not to terrorist bombs but to 'self-inflicted harm to our liberties and way of life'."[73]

It is regrettable that the course the U.S. and Europe have taken in Bosnia is not going to change anytime soon, despite overwhelming evidence that it should.

Recent Developments — The Bosnian Muslims

Bosnia has, indeed, developed into an Islamic fundamentalist forward base.

Croatia's *Slobodna Dalmacija* newspaper reported that Italian authorities were exploring a possible link between Bosnian Muslim fundamentalists and the Madrid bombings. Their investigation revealed that mujahideen who fought in the Bosnian civil wars had been recruited from an al Qaeda training camp near Zenica to execute the Madrid bombings. The Italian authorities fear other attacks being planned.

> The specter of Bosnia-trained Islamic terrorists attacking Western Europe while their well-concealed Arab organizers conduct "business" with equally well-ensconced Albanian Mafiosi is not only alarming — it's also an expression of everything that has gone wrong for Europe because of Western intervention in the Balkans.[74]

And how did Paddy Ashdown's respond? He invited tourists to come to Bosnia-Herzegovina for a holiday because it was safe! He launched a campaign in London to win over British tourists. "The country's move to peace has been in my view miraculous."[75]

Not a month later, the BBC dutifully followed up with a story about Zijad Jusufović, a tour guide who takes tourists to internationally known locations in Sarajevo. "And this is the market place where the infamous mortar attack took place in February, 1994," he tells the tour group. "Sixty-eight were killed, 200 wounded." Ten years after the Markale green market mortar attack took place, a tour guide now disseminates the media lie that Serbs bombed the market, which, in fact, was bombed by the Muslims in order to provoke Western intervention! And Mr. Jusufović takes the tourists to Srebrenica and to Pale to visit Radovan Karadžić's house. We can only imagine what he has to say at these locations. "Visitors want to know what happened, why it happened and how Bosnia is today. In the end, my message is always the same. War is stupid. Everybody loses," he said.[76] This must have a powerful and sobering effect on tourists. And if any of those tourists would like to take home some souvenir snuff videos, Mr. Jusufović can take them to the Begova *džamija* (mosque) where videos featuring the beheading of Christians (Russians, Serbs and Americans) are for sale at a little makeshift stand that offers digital copies of the Koran and multimedia CDs of Izetbegović's funeral, among other things.[77]

The peculiar aspect of these two stories is that they share a common source: the BBC. The story about Mr. Jusufović appeared in the BBC World Service, while the story about the Begova Džamija was reported by BBC Monitoring, which is much less widely read. It makes one wonder whether or not the BBC reads its own reports.

Meanwhile, the Bosnian media carried extensive reports about young Bosniaks who were recruited to go to Arab countries, purportedly for education and jobs, after undergoing "theoretical preparations by religious instructors in that country."[78] After they receive training in terrorist camps, they are sent on missions to other countries or simply return to Bosnia as "sleepers," ready to act when they are summoned. Reliable sources have indicated that these "sleepers" typically get jobs with international organizations and even SFOR. *Nezavisne novine* carried a story in January 2004 about young Muslim men from Bosnia-Herzegovina who have been sent to Iraq, Afghanistan and Chechnya to fight for Islamic groups, and who have been aided by former mujahideen and organizations that are suspected of having al-Qaeda links. An article in the Banja Luka-based *Reporter*, which quotes a German analysis published in December 2003, provides a detailed description of the "green highway" that goes from Turkey through Albania, Kosovo and Sandzak to Bosnia-Herzegovina. The green highway affords Islamist terrorists two-way traffic that permits them travel under the guise of "Islamic humanitarian organizations." For these people, the road to Western Europe leads through the former Yugoslavia. The German intelligence analysis describes religious and military training camps in the areas of Bosnia-Herzegovina under the control of Bosnian Muslims. Despite the fact these articles appeared in the Republika Srpska, which is traditionally antipathetic to Bosniaks, the number of similar reports from foreign sources is on the rise.[79]

And Paddy Ashdown, a former non-entity for the insignificant Liberal Democratic Party in England, has come into his own as an imperialist pasha in Bosnia.

> Paddy Ashdown's multiculturalism is decidedly lop-sided.... At the
> recent reopening of the old Turkish bridge at Mostar, he sanctioned a
> parade dressed as Turkish Janissaries. To the Christian Serbs and
> Croats alike (who together outnumber the Muslim Bosniaks), this was
> about as culturally sensitive as an SS parade in Tel Aviv.[80]

To make matters worse, "Chronicles Intelligence Assessment"
estimated that 6,000 members of al-Qaeda are operating on the
territory of Macedonia, Albania, Bulgaria, Kosovo and Bosnia-
Herzegovina. Shahid Emir Musa Aizi, an Afghan veteran, is
recruiting Muslim of Slavic origin, "white al-Qaeda," to infiltrate
Europe.[81] This is a far cry from the 200 alleged mujahideen
attested to by the IWPR earlier.

Next come reports of prosecutors in Bosnia being threatened
for trying to fight organized crime and corruption. Ahmed
Ishtikar, a Pakistani by birth who lives in Zenica, is suspected of
being involved in threats targeting prosecutors. Istikhar is
"allegedly involved in human trafficking and contraband
trade."[82] The U.S. prosecutor, Jonathan Schmidt was advised by
the U.S. government not to return to Bosnia from a private trip to
the U.S.[83]

If all this were not bad enough, both Serbians and Muslims in
Bosnia are dying from high cancer rates caused by NATO's use
of depleted uranium (DU) munitions against the Serbs in 1995.
Consider the Serbian village of [Japaga] [the spelling of the name
of this village appears to have been corrupted, *Editor's Note*]:

> Around 100 people live here but in 1996 many people died from can-
> cer. The first was the army base cook, Mrs Ljeposava, who died aged
> 45, as did Mrs Todic. Then it was Budimir Bojat, who died aged 60,
> and Goran Basteh who died at 45, all from cancer.[84]

Muslims are dying from cancer in equally great numbers in the
Sarajevo suburb of Hadzici. Both the U.S. and NATO used DU in
armor-piercing shells for tanks as well as planes. "The aim was
to disrupt the Bosnian Serb forces' command and control structure and degrade their fighting capabilities."[85] This is disingenuous, because DU has a half life of 4.5 billion years. It will eventually kill everyone in the region unless the DU waste is cleaned
up and areas decontaminated, but neither the U.S. government
nor NATO intend to clean up the radioactive poison factory they
have created.

Bosnia is hemorrhaging money. "As much as a billion dollars has disappeared from public funds or been stolen from international aid projects through fraud."[86] The antifraud unit of the Office of the High Representative issued a 4,000 page report whose contents were made available to *The New York Times*. The missing funds were intended to rebuild Bosnia's infrastructure as well as to restore municipal services to towns. "Ten foreign embassies and international aid agencies lost over $20 million deposited in a Bosnian bank."[87] Alija Izetbegović routinely denied these charges, even though his son, Bakir, is one of the most powerful men in Bosnia. He controls The City Development Institute, which is authorized to determine occupancy rights of 80,000 publicly owned apartments in Sarajevo. Needless to say, many apartments owned by Serbian and Croatian residents were handed over to members of Izetbegović's party. Anyone else who wants their occupancy rights restored must pay Izetbegović $2,000. Diplomats who wished to remain anonymous said that Bakir Izetbegović owns 15% of Bosnia Air, and gets a percentage of extortion money collected by Sarajevo gangsters.

The Bosnian Muslims, in addition to their numerous other afflictions, suffered another setback when their former Ambassador to the United Nations, Muhamed Sacirbey, was charged with embezzlement in 2003 in New York City. He was released after posting $6 million bail. In 2000, he used checks and bank orders to withdraw more than $610,000 from his mission's bank account, and deposited the funds into his own personal bank account. He is also charged with siphoning off $1.8 million from an account controlled by his government's investment fund ministry. He was arrested in March 2003, and was released on bail in July 2004. Sacirbey denied misconduct and suggested that the allegations were trumped up by political enemies who wanted to destroy his credibility. "Clearly, it was part of a smear campaign to discredit me," he said.[88] In January 2005, a New York judge ordered Sacirbey's extradition under a 1902 treaty between the U.S. and The Kingdom of Serbia. Cherif Bassiouni, Sacirbey's attorney, said he would fight the extradition.

And there is a new Bosnian scandal brewing. Ali Ahmad Ali Hamad is serving a twelve-year prison sentence in Zenica for a car bomb explosion in Mostar and aggravated assaults on a Croat married couple near Travnik, as well as for an assault on a U.S. military instructor in Zenica. He served in Afghanistan, then in 1992 he was sent to Bosnia-Herzegovina by plane to Zagreb, and then by bus to Split and Travnik. He helped establish a mujahideen training camp in Mehurici, outside of Travnik. These mujahideen were linked to the Bosnia-Herzegovinian Army through the Muslim Seventh Corps. Ali Hamad is now writing a book on international terrorism and al-Qaeda in Bosnia-Herzegovina. He claims that al-Qaeda sent mujahideen to Bosnia not to help their Muslim brothers but to expand their network across Europe. Ali Hamad now feels unsafe in prison because his former fellow mujahideen are threatening to kill him. He alleges that many international and local political and military officials are afraid of the content of his book, which is slated for publication in 2005.[89]

Hamad is prepared to testify against a Rasim Delić, the Muslim commander charged by the ICTY with crimes against Serbian and Croatian civilians between 1993 and 1995, even though an attempt was made on Mr. Ali Hamad's life in prison. It's not just the SDA that wants him dead.

> [I]t's clear that Ashdown is becoming embarrassed by the constant revelations that the al-Qaida terrorists in Bosnia have been working all along with the Bosnian Islamist leaders. If anything happens to Ali Hamad, it will be because Ashdown has deliberately ignored the warnings and left Ali Hamad to his fate."[90]

Bosnian's prime minister, Adnan Terzić, planned to submit a formal request for the release of six Bosnian citizens being held in the U.S. military detention center in Guantanamo Bay, Cuba.[91] "Bosnian citizens," in this case, means that these six men were Algerian mujahideens who married local Bosnian women in order to gain citizenship and remain in the country. They were arrested in October 2001 after U.S. intelligence learned that they were planning attacks on the U.S. and British embassies in Sarajevo, as well as on U.S. Eagle Base in Tuzla. This may seem like a bad time to ask for the release of mujahideens, but Mr. Terzić doesn't have to worry about being insensitive. He knows the Bosnian Muslims can do no wrong in Washington.

Dragomir Adnan, the Bosnian Serb police chief who was quoted earlier, broke the news that all eleven of the terrorists responsible for the Madrid Bombing had passed through Sarajevo before arriving in Spain. It was also reported that the explosives used in the terror attack were produced in Bosnia. Furthermore, Chief Adnan claimed that the Madrid terrorists received training at al Qaeda training camps in Bosnia-Herzegovina.[92]

Chief Adnan added that the Republika Srpska "is first dam to Europe, and we expect full support from the international community." He also noted that RS Ministry of Interior has a "list of 200 Bosniaks [Bosnian Muslims] who were members of the mujahideen units, trained by the Al-Qa'idah in BiH."[93]

Former Gendarmerie commander Goran Radosavljevic-Guri, now an analyst for the Center for the Fight against Terrorism, warned at an international conference called "The Terrorist Threat to Southeastern Europe" that the "Balkans have become a springboard for Islamic terrorists."[94] Zenica was of course the most important training center, but those training camps have disappeared, and appear to have been removed to more remote and isolated mountainous regions.

And how did High Representative Paddy Ashdown react to all of this? He demanded that Chief Adnan retract his remarks concerning the Islamic terrorists responsible for the Madrid bombing that had prepared themselves for the attack in Bosnia-Herzegovina.

> A report Ashdown received from EUPM Commissioner Kevin Carty found that Andan's allegations were unfounded. "It is clear from his report that Mr Andan made these claims without having any firm evidence," the Office of the High Representative said.[95]

Here in the United States, the State Department accepted the credentials of Ms. Bisera Turkovic as the new Bosnian Ambassador to the United States. She comes from a long line of Muslim fundamentalists. Congressman Trent Franks (AZ) expressed his concerns over her designation.

> Bisera Turkovic is one of the founders of the radical Islamist Muslim SDA Party in Bosnia, a party that has had, since its foundation, strong links with al Qaeda, numerous other terrorist organizations, and even the intelligence mechanisms of Iran.
>
> In 1939, Bisera Turkovic's father, Alija Izetbegovic, started a group called the Young Muslims. After World War II, they were prosecuted as Nazi war criminals and spent time in prison together. Over the

years, Dr. Turkovic was promoted by Izetbegovic and then founded the SDA Party in 1990.

(…)

Mr. Speaker, soon after the beginning of the Bosnian civil war in 1992, Dr. Turkovic was accredited as Bosnian ambassador to Zagreb. It was this post, coordinating with others, that was constantly used by the SDA and their leadership to provide Bosnian passports, visas, humanitarian worker status, and logistical support to radical Islamist mujahideen coming into Bosnia to fight their own jihad there….

In violation of the U.S. embargo, the SDA also organized a massive flow of weapons from Iran through Croatia during Bisera Turkovic's time as ambassador.

(…)

The people of this Nation deserve better than to be served by a State Department that aids our enemies and then lies to cover its actions.[96]

The very next day, President Bush, who ignored Congressman Trent's remarks, defended the war in Iraq by telling the American people that the United States was "forced into the war because of the September 11 terror strikes."[97] He was using "the excluded middle" technique discussed earlier.

Karl Rove came to Manhattan to expatiate on the twilight of liberalism in politics, and blamed it on the Democrats for responding weakly to 9/11. He tried to disarm further criticism by claiming that criticism of Republican policies "placed American troops in great danger." Then he delivered his payoff line:

Conservatives saw the savagery of 9/11 in the attacks and prepared for war; liberals saw the savagery of the 9/11 attacks and wanted to prepare indictments and offer therapy and understanding for our attackers.[98]

Would it then be too much to ask Mr. Rove to explain why Nicholas Burns of the State Department was linking the fall of Srebrenica to an independent Kosovo? Or why Mr. Burns headed the U.S. delegation to the Srebrenica commemoration? The Bush administration is offering therapy and understanding for those who used Bosnia and Kosovo as a launching pad to attacked us. Messrs. Bush and Rove are politicians; Peter Goss, CIA Director, is not. He made a personal visit to Sarajevo in late June 2005 with a list of 900 al Qaeda members in connection with an Islamic fundamentalist network. Darko Trifunovic (author of the 2002 Srebrenica Report, *see* p. 258-266) remarked that:

certain congressmen are asking for a change in US policy towards the Balkans, as it can clearly be seen that US policies do not correspond with information on the ground.[99]

Recent Developments — Croatia

In what was described as a "significant gesture," the Croatian Prime Minister, Ivo Sanader, condemned Croatia's WWII atrocities and paid tribute to the victims of the Jasenovac concentration camp. His chose to express himself in elevated rhetoric, and magnanimously condemned all forms of extremism, racial, ethnic and religious hatred.

> "No goal, political or any other, could justify crimes. That is a principle defended in modern Europe, and Croatia, on the path of integration, is also part of that," Sanader told state television.
>
> "I condemn all forms of extremism and racial, ethnic or religious hatred as well as intolerance."[100]

But he omitted to mention the Serbs who had been driven from Croatia in 1995 during Operation Storm. Then, Sanader began plea bargaining.

> Lies of 700,000 Jasenovac victims and the thesis of the genocidal nature of Croatians served as the basis for aggressive [*sic*] policy of carving up [sic] Greater Serbia.[101]

The article went on to note that some historians claim only 50,000 people were killed there, while the U.S. Holocaust Memorial Museum in Washington, D.C. generously "puts the figure at up to 100,000." This is how seven hundred and fifty thousand victims become 100,000 victims, and then finally half that amount, who have been characterized by the Croatians as "Croatian anti-Fascists." If this interpretation is accepted, then the myriad Serbian victims who's bones cry out for justice will be erased from the memory of mankind, and Croatia may then commence its newfound statehood with a clean slate instead of being treated as the product of genocide, which it most certainly is.

The Simon Wiesenthal Center estimates the number of dead in Jasenovac at 600,000. Testimonies given by Nazis on trial in Nuremberg place the figure at 750,000. Fr. Filipović-Majstorović himself admitted to at least 500,000 deaths in Jasenovac during his trial.

Slavko Goldstein, Croatia's best known token Jew, who was named as the head of the Jasenovac Memorial Council, backed up Sanader's statements. He claimed that the tragedy of Jasenovac was two-pronged. On the one hand, it concerned the suffering of the death camp's victims; on the other, it concerned "manipulations with their numbers." He went on to claim that the number of victims had been inflated, and that Slobodan Milošević had seized this inflated number to "infect" Serbs with political propaganda in order to achieve a "Greater Serbia." Why would Mr. Goldstein doubt the estimates made by the Simon Wiesenthal Center and the prosecutors of the Nuremberg War Crimes Tribunal? One earnestly hopes that he might answer this question one day to the satisfaction of the Wiesenthal Center.

In December 2002, the Croatian government sought to arrange the transfer of five Croatian nationalists who had hijacked a Chicago-bound airliner after it left La Guardia Airport in September 1976. One NYC police officer was killed trying to defuse a bomb the terrorists left in a public locker in Grand Central Station, another was partially blinded, and two more were injured. Zvonko Busic and his American-born wife, Julienne, were sentenced to life in prison for air piracy resulting in death. But one can't underestimate Croatian obstreperousness. The Croatian government presented this insensitive request to transfer the prisoners as a "humanitarian issue" only one year after the 9/11 attacks. Terence McTigue, the officer who was blinded in one eye by the bomb that was planted in Grand Central, remarked that if Mr. Busic had been sent to Croatia, "he would be put in a country club" there.[102]

And tourists are returning once again to the bogus Medjugorje shrine in Croatia, where six children claimed they saw a vision of the Virgin Mary on June 25, 1981. The Vatican, which had no qualms about beatifying Archbishop Stepinac, has never recognized this alleged visitation of the Virgin Mary. Steve Shawl, who books tours for Medjugorje, remarked that the "shrine" still attracts tourists but "all around is not good [sic]. The war has left the people free from Communism but also with an ineffective government. Many families have less than when it was Communist. It is sad."[103] There was no mention of the six hundred Serbian civilians who were slaughtered by Ustashi during WWII and thrown into a gorge near the "shrine."

Brother Satan, Cardinal Stepinac and Pope Wojtila

On October 4, 1998, Pope John Paul II went to Croatia to beat-ify the remains of Croatia's patron saint of genocide, Archbishop Alojzije Stepinac, who is considered to be a martyr and national hero. The official Vatican position is that Stepinac was a martyr who fought against Communism. But by making this extremist a saint, the Pope underhandedly absolved Stepinac of his involve-ment in the genocide against Serbs, Jews and Roma. This act of beatification contradicts the Roman Catholic Church's recent public relations campaign about facing its past. The beatification of Stepinac places the Pope squarely with holocaust deniers, and stands out as an attempt to bury one of the darkest chapters in the Roman Catholic Church's twentieth century history. Saint Stepinac now blocks the path of memory, absolves responsibility and poisons reconciliation for future generations.[104]

Thousands of police were deployed during the Pontiff's visit. Police marksmen surveyed the crowd, and NATO helicopters hovered overhead.

The Simon Wiesenthal Center appealed to the Pope to post-pone the beatification "until after the completion of an exhaustive study of Stepinac's wartime record." The Vatican did not reply publicly to the request. Instead, Pope John Paul II beatified Cardinal Alojzije Stepinac at a huge open-air service at the shrine of Marija Bistrica, the most important place of pilgrimage for Catholics in Croatia. The 78-year-old Pope was welcomed in per-son by President Tudjman.

The Pope, acting with full conviction in the "infallibility" con-ferred upon him, addressed a large crowd in front of Zagreb Cathedral. He expressed the hope that the conflict-torn Balkan region would find "a true and lasting peace, which is always built upon justice, respect for others, and the co-existence of different peoples and cultures."

His speech also seemed to contain mild criticism for his hosts, when the Pontiff remarked that "the degree of a nation's civilisa-tion is measured by the compassion it shows for its weakest and most needy members,"[104] which appeared to refer to Croatia's Serb minority. He, of course, offered no apology for Operation Storm, and he did not call for the return of Serbs who had been expelled. Rather than a mission of reconciliation, the pontiff's visit only deepened the schism between the Roman Catholic and Orthodox Churches.

Then Pope John Paul II visited Banja Luka on June 22, 2003. His trip was billed as a mission of reconciliation to urge forgiveness for the crimes committed in the past by Roman Catholics. "I ask Almighty God to have mercy on the sins committed against humanity, human dignity and freedom, also by children of the Catholic Church, and to foster in all the desire for mutual forgiveness," he was quoted as saying.[105] This article, representative of mainstream press coverage, incidentally mentions that:

> during his mass at the ruins of the monastery flattened by Serbs during the war, the pope ... also beatified Catholic theologian Ivan Merz, who brought about a religious revival in Croatia in the beginning of the 20th century.[106]

Quite pointedly, Serbian Orthodox Patriarch Pavle did not come to Banja Luka despite the Pope's calls to meet with him. Why? One has to read Ana Dacic and Peter Makara's article[107] to decode the mainstream press coverage. Ivan Merz was the founder of an organization called the "Croatian Eagles," a Croatian version of *Hitler Youth*. The unnamed monastery that the Serbs had flatted is Petričevac, a Franciscan Monastery. On February 7, 1942, Fr. Tomislav Filipović-Majstorović (*see* p. 206-207), who was a member of the Croatian Eagles during his youth, led Ustashi forces from this monastery to massacre 2,730 Serbs, including 500 children. The horror reached its climax when sixty children were slaughtered in school. The authors quote from Prof. Marko Ruchnov's book, *Zašto Jasenovac*? ("Why Jasenovac?" Nikola Pašić, Belgrade: 2004):

> The following is the transcript of a Croatian witness' account, given at the sentencing of Fr. Filipovich who was tried for his crimes after World War II:
>
> "The slaughter began in this way. Before slaughtering the child of one Djura Glamochanin, namely his little daughter Vasilia, Father Animal [Fr. Filipovic] said these words, which are fitting only for Satan himself: 'Ustashas! I am doing this in the name of God! I am Christening these scum. And you are to follow my lead. I will accept this entire sin on my soul. And when we are done I will absolve you and relieve you of all guilt'...

> "Then, he took out a knife and uttered the following words: 'Look, children!' And with those words he started to slaughter the children. Some he only cut but did not finish completely. So these half-slaughtered children, covered in blood, ran in circles screaming horribly. These children were hunted by the other Ustashas who would finish the children [off] with the butts of their pistols."[108]

This is the same Fr. Filipović who later became a Commander at the Jasenovac concentration Camp. The nickname "Fr. Satan" stuck.

> "It is a creepy fact that the Pope holds a Mass at Petricevac," said Jovan Babic, who has investigated the massacre. Other Bosnian Serbs whose forebearers were murdered by Ustashe forces said that the Pope was not welcome in Banja Luka.[109]

Julia Pascal visited Sibenik in Croatia in the summer of 2003 to participate in the Sibenik International Children's Theatre Festival. She found the "U" symbol (for Ustashi) ubiquitous. One of the directors of the festival remarked that her troupe was

> "not English, they're Jews." ... The few remaining Serbs and Bosnians here are fast changing their names and converting to Catholicism.[110]

She met Serbs who fought with the Croatian army but who had, nonetheless, been ostracized by Croatian society. She met a seventy-six-year-old woman who fought with the Partisans and still had shrapnel fragments in her body, whose pension had been revoked by Franjo Tudjman's government.

> "I am a Yugoslav," she insists. "I spent my whole life fighting nationalism. And it was all for nothing."[111]

Ms. Pascal learned that other elderly citizens who had fought against Croatian fascism committed suicide rather than face indignity and humiliation.

The hotel where she was staying featured a Caribbean evening. The musicians wore rasta wigs and appeared in blackface to serenade the hotel guests. When Ms. Pascale mentioned to them that such a get-up would have been considered offensive in the UK, one of the musicians replied, "Look, we are not racist. We don't even dislike black people. We just hate Serbs."[112]

Recent Developments — The Bosnian Serbs

A recent poll revealed that one third of all Bosnians were prepared to leave the country once and for all, while almost half would leave the country temporarily. "One of the most burning issues in Bosnia, whose economy was hard-hit by the 1992-1995 war, is a high unemployment of more than 40 percent."[113]

Those who stayed in Bosnia witness first-hand how history is being rewritten by means of censorship. Now the European Union is censoring the textbooks of school children in the Republika Srpska by banning the works of Ivo Andrić, the Nobel Laureate who is best known in the West as the author of *The Bridge on the Drina* (*Na Drini Ćuprija*). The content was judged to be "offensive."[114] Not only that, the old WWI song, *Tamo Daleko*, which could be heard at any Serbian-American wedding from San Francisco to Brooklyn, was banned. Musical instruments have not escaped this fate. The *gusle*, a single-stringed instrument played with a bow, used to accompany oral folk epics that celebrated Serbian resistance to the Ottomans, has been banned lest it reawaken national feeling among them. The EU representative warned the Serbs "that unless we accept the renovation of the symbols of [Turkish] occupation, unless we accede *in toto* to the demands of the EU, we will not be accepted."[115]

In the meantime, the Bosnian Serb army has been decimated to 4,000 active troops. Furthermore, Ashdown plans to abolish the defense ministries of the two states comprising Bosnia-Herzegovina, replacing them with the Federal Ministry of Defense, which is dominated by the Bosnian Muslims. His actions are in complete violation of the Dayton Accords, "which allowed the two constituent states to retain their armed forces and their ministries of defense."[116] NATO officials have time and again confirmed that the Republika Srpska police were indispensable in monitoring terrorist training and planning operations in Bosnia and kept them in check. One NATO source said that only Islamic radicals and drug dealers will benefit from this move. "They've paid off so many people, and now they're seeing the reward for their payoffs."[117] The Serbs have thus been deprived of the right of self defense. And Paddy Ashdown keeps dismissing selected Serbian elected officials, ensuring that the Bosnian Serb government's functions are constantly disrupted.

When police in Montenegro arrested Luka Karadžić, brother of Radovan Karadžić, he had some interesting things to say about Paddy Ashdown, which help explain his irrational, anti-Serb bigotry.

> Luka Karadžić ... accused the high representative [Paddy Ashdown] of accepting a bribe from the Bosnian Serb wartime leadership in 1992 to lobby on their behalf in Western Europe. "Mr Ashdown, Radovan still possesses bills and documents that are going to prove how much we paid you for advice and lobbying," wrote Luka Karadžić.[118]

In April 2004, a brutal raid was conducted in Pale. Jeremija Starovlah, a Serbian Orthodox priest and his son were seriously injured when they were nearly beaten to death by IFOR commandos (who were later alleged to have been identified as Croats and Slovenes working in conjunction with British SAS forces). It was another failed attempt to arrest Radovan Karadžić.

> "What do they want from us?" the daily [Avnaz] quotes a "distressed" local woman protester as saying.

> "Why haven't they indicted war criminals Tudjman and Alija Izetbegović instead of searching for our own Mladić and Karadžić? I am Karadžić and Mladić," she says.[119]

At the same time, the NATO-led force in Bosnia was running ads on Bosnian Serb TV that appealed for information about war crimes suspects. The ads featured a house of cards collapsing and encouraged viewers to call a hotline to volunteer information anonymously. "It's just a matter of time until we get you — soon," the voice-over said.[120] Despite the $5 million reward for information leading to the arrest of Messrs. Karadžić and Mladić, there were no takers for the offer.

Then, in November 2004, a remarkable story emerged. A German woman who was living under a witness protection program wrote a book called *I Was Married to a Holy Warrior*, which she published under the assumed name of Doris Glück. It was a memoir of her love affair with an Egyptian man who became gradually more militant until he finally devoted himself to the global jihad. Ms. Glück converted to Islam and traveled to Bosnia-Herzegovina with him in the mid-1990s, where her ex-husband had gone to lend his support to the Bosnian Muslims. His role was to make videotapes of anti-Muslim atrocities and anti-Serb resistance. One day, she was taken to the foot of a mountain where she witnessed the execution of three Serbian men. The first victim was shot to death by a group of women who had lost husbands and sons.

> "Then there was a second man, a Serb, on his knees," Ms. Glück said. "I saw a big knife and then I saw his head cut off. I sleep with this memory every night. Afterwards, the mujahideen played football with the head. Then a third Serb was shot by the men.[121]

She fears that she herself would be tortured or beheaded if her ex-husband's friends learned of her whereabouts.

The 90th anniversary of the assassination of Archduke Ferdinand was observed on June 28, 2004. It comes as no surprise that most western coverage focused on whether or not Gavrilo Princip, the teen-aged assassin, was a hero or a terrorist. Muslims and Croats tend to regard Princip as a Serbian assassin and terrorist, while Serbs unwaveringly regard him as a national hero. One silly article described Princip as a student who "became involved in underground Serbian nationalist movements which wanted to snatch parts of Bosnian territory from the Austro-Hungarian empire."[122] Neither this article, nor the many others like it, bothered to mention that Serbs were actually serfs under Austro-Hungarian rule. Princip was born into an impoverished family, whose members were not allowed to leave the land on which they were born. Furthermore, his family had to turn over nearly half of the produce of their farm to their Muslim overseers. Slavery had been abolished in the United States in 1865, but in 1914, a Serb in Bosnia was still a serf. Few contemporary accounts of the Balkans ever mention that Austro-Hungary gained control of Bosnia-Herzegovina in 1878 after having assumed the administration of Bosnia from Turkey, then the "sick man of Europe," and perpetuated Ottoman injustices against the Christian population. The Nevesinje Rebellion, a genuine Serbian liberation movement, was the first serious challenge to Austro-Hungarian rule. Austro-Hungary then used black mail, pressure, lies and lame excuses to violate international law to annex Bosnia-Herzegovina in 1908. It is no wonder that Princip and his colleagues assassinated Archduke Ferdinand. The unfortunate act triggered WWI, but what were the Serbs to do? Wait for centuries for the Austro-Hungarian occupation to collapse under its own weight? Notwithstanding the aforementioned, the Bosnian authorities would like to re-erect the original memorial for Archduke Ferdinand on the site of the assassination, beside a plaque marking the spot where Princip stood when he fired the fatal shots. The Association of Sarajevo Serbs publicly announced that a memorial to Ferdinand would celebrate "the occupiers," and went on to remark that erecting such a statue next to Princip's plaque would be "provocative." Some Muslims agreed. "There will be people who would lay flowers on one monument and spit on the other," said Amna, a salesclerk.[123]

An anonymous internet posting, a parody of a tourist guide book, expresses the despair of the Bosnian Serbs as no Westerner is able to.[124]

Welcome.

Welcome to the land of economic and power-hungry holocaust.

Welcome to the land of unemployment. Poverty. To the land which still boasts the existence of miners [by that, please understand that the author means the kind of miners who crawl into the mines as little boys and crawl back out again aged forty or so and looking 103, to die shortly afterwards of lung diseases and heart diseases and of simply wearing out their mortal bodies well before their time...]

Welcome to the land of religious and ethnic hatred, to the land of gender, race, religious, ethnic, and a slew of other discriminations — to the land of pain and suffering, to the land of medical discards and the legacy of depleted uranium.

Welcome to the land of envy, assassinations, bombs; the land of chauvinism and protectionism.

Be very welcome in the land of drugs and prostitution, in the land where people can still be literally bought and sold on the market.

Welcome to the land of full bars and nightclubs, where alcohol is both cause and solution of all life's problems.

Welcome to the land of war profiteers, of ex-"soldiers" who wander the country without jobs or futures.

Welcome to the land of shattered families, razed homes, communities, cities ... to the land of destroyed lives ... of unmarked mine fields... the land which once held the Olympic Games where sport is now dead ... where intellectualism is dead ... where conscience is dying.

Welcome, above all, to the land of politics, thievery, bribery and corruption. To the land of crime and the local version of the Mafia. To the land where police are powerless and the administration is bloated.

Welcome to the land of the Dayton Accord. To the land of the poor and the poorer.

Welcome to the land of mountains. We are particularly proud of the beauty of our mountains. It's a shame they're sown with landmines.

Welcome to the land of Balias, Ustashe, Chetniks. The land which is one country, but is really two, and in practical terms three.

Welcome to the land in which being a pensioner means living on the very edge of bare human existence.

Welcome to the land where your purchasing power depends on whether you can pay in Deutschmarks. To the land of the thoroughly modern feudal monarchy. The land of serfs and vassals. And lords and masters, naturally.

Welcome to the land of bought and paid for diplomas. The land without a dream, without a vision; the land of bricked-up horizons.

In this day and age, welcome to the land where only 27% of people even know what the Internet is, and only 6% actually knows how to use it.

Welcome to the land of lawlessness, of anything-goes. The land of pirated software, pirated music, pirated videos, pirated digital TV. Quite simply, to the land of pirates. Privateers. To the land of black market and smuggling. Of violence against women. Festering distrust and hatred.

Welcome to the land where an extra cup of coffee is no longer set aside, in case some other friend should happen by.

Do come in. Welcome. There is no reason why you too should not experience life in our 3-D horror movie...

Welcome to Alija Izetbegović's legacy.

The Global Freedom and Democracy Revolution

Observers of the Ukrainian elections in 2004 could not help but notice their resemblance to the Serbian elections in 2000, where the media presented a fairy tale of young demonstrators who ousted an authoritarian regime with rock concerts, plasma screens and laser shows in a downtown plaza. Washington, of course, welcomed "the people versus the power" in the Ukraine.

No one seemed to notice that the "pro-democracy group," Pora, had postered the Ukraine with images of a jackboot crushing a cockroach, implying that was what Pora was going to do to its opposition.

> Plunging into the crowd of Yushchenko [the candidate favored by the West] supporters ... I met two members of Una-Unso, a neo-Nazi party whose emblem is a swastika. They were unembarrassed about their allegiance, perhaps because last year Yushchenko ... stood up for the

> Socialist party newspaper ... after it ran an anti-Semitic article claiming
> that Jews had invaded Ukraine alongside the *Wehrmacht* in 1941.[125]

Once again, a neo-Nazi party is being presented to Westerners as "freedom fighters." It worked in Croatia, and it would work again in the Western Ukraine, which was sympathetic to the Nazis during WWII. And the same tactics are used. Just a month before Mr. Laughland's article was written, Yushchenko's ally, Alexander Moroz, commented on the allegation that Jews had invaded the Ukraine alongside the *Wehrmacht* in 1941. "I personally think the argument ... citing 400,000 Jews in the SS is incorrect, but I am not in a position to know the facts."[126]

The leaders of the "Orange Revolution" in Ukraine have publicly acknowledged their debt to the 2000 "revolution" in Serbia, which led to the fall of Slobodan Milošević. In Belgrade, Otpor activist Alexandar Maric, who heads the "Centre for Non-Violent Resistance," now trains activists and "exports the Belgrade revolution worldwide." His clients include opponents of Hugo Chavez (!) in Venezuela, as well as the Ukraine. However, reports by Amnesty International and other organizations demonstrate that the situation with respect to human rights and democracy has actually gotten worse than it was during the "autocratic" regimes that had been toppled.[127]

There is no doubt that the mainstream media's representation of these events is false, and is damaging our own democratic system to the point where it simply cannot function. The mainstream media continues to market political interventions in foreign countries as "bringing democracy to the world" instead of exploitation and theft greased with bribery.

John Perkins authored *Confessions of an Economic Hit Man* (Barrett Koehler, 2004), in which he discusses his job at the Chas. T. Main consulting firm in Boston, where he was recruited by the NSA (National Security Agency). He was persuaded to become an economic hitman. His job was to convince the governments of third-world countries to make deals for huge loans with western banks to develop infrastructure projects.

> And a condition of the loan was that a large share of the money went
> back to the big construction companies in the USA — the Bechtels
> and Halliburtons.

> The loans would plunge the countries into debts that would be impossible to pay off.[128]

This is precisely what is going on in Serbia and in the Ukraine. And Germany continues spreading its influence in Eastern Europe.

Nazi Germany's dictatorship is being rehabilitated in countries that were either its allies or had been occupied by it during WWII. In addition to Croatia's elaborate re-appraisal of its Nazi puppet state, Poland has been subjected to the ministrations of the "Association for the Care of German War Graves," which has spent millions of dollars honoring German soldiers, including members of the SS, who had undertaken the destruction of the Warsaw Ghetto, including SS Gruppenfuehrer Jurgen Stroop, who was executed after the war for the crimes he committed while putting down the Warsaw Uprising. In 1991, Polish soldiers had to stand as honor guards during the inauguration of the memorial. Stoop's name was finally removed from a granite block that held the names of 362 *Wehrmacht* and SS soldiers (who had died there) when the Association could no longer cope with the scandal.[129] The "reconciliation" follows the same pattern outlined earlier. The remains of the "criminals" are mixed with the remains of the "victims" and are thus put on the same moral footing.

The Aftermath

In November 2004, the Norwegian News Agency ran a story that had already been sitting on the shelf for at least a year. Two demographers, researchers for the ICTY, conducted a study that indicated that a little over 102,000 people died in the Bosnian War.

> The results were presented at a conference for population experts, demographists, in Norway one year ago, but they have not been publicly known.[130]

The most common figure quoted in the mainstream media had been 250,000. The 102,000 deaths were closely divided between military and civilian deaths (47,360 to 55,251), and each ethnic group comprised roughly a third of the total number. So, the Bosnian Muslims were not the principal victims, after all.

Meanwhile, at The Hague Tribunal, Naser Orić has pleaded not guilty to the "cruel treatment and murder" of Serbian civilians and the "wanton destruction and plunder of at least 50 Serbian villages around Srebrenica." Orić's defense counsel depicted Srebrenica as a place where genocide, siege, starvation and disease reigned, and further claimed that the only way out of the desperate situation was to raid nearby Serbian villages to steal food and livestock. Mr. Orić's defense counsel should pick up a copy of Sefer Halilović's book, *Lukava strategija*, which discusses the plunder of Serbian villages for food stores as a deliberate military strategy (*see* p. 260). As was demonstrated earlier, there was plenty of food in Srebrenica and no one starved to death in Bosnia for the duration of the war.

> Oric's defense states that "this is the first time in history that a representative of a people under siege and facing genocide has been indicted by an international tribunal for crimes allegedly committed against the besieging foe."[131]

This is a classic example of the audacity of a man who kills his parents, and then seeks clemency because he's an orphan.

It is an undisputed fact that a certain number of Bosnian Muslims lost their lives on a trek from Srebrenica to Tuzla. The mainstream media has turned a military retreat into a true crime drama, where thousands of innocent and unarmed "men and boys" died, but in fact a large number of those who did die belonged to the Bosnian Muslim 28th Division. They could not have been described as non-combatants, much less as simply "men and boys." A certain number of civilians and less than 50 young men under the age of 18 joined the Bosnian Muslim soldiers in order to fight their way out of Srebrenica. Various sources reported that between 4,000 and 6,000 Bosnian troops arrived in Tuzla in the days following the fall of Srebrenica, while others "fell prey to firefights, artillery, landmines, exhaustion and starvation (it's a 50-mile hike over bad terrain)."[132] Mr. Malic observed that it is true that some of these soldiers, after having been captured, were summarily executed by Bosnian Serb forces. The contention arises over allegations of the number of summary executions. Specialists in forensic medicine, who are supposed to determine the cause of death, have been shut out of the media, as in the case of Helen Ranta.[133] The Bosnian Serbs never contested the fact that their forces killed large numbers of Muslims in combat. They are, instead, fighting groundless allegations that they killed 8,000 civilians as part of a program of genocide.

Mr. Malic lucidly explained that the Muslims, on the one hand, aided by the tidal wave of Western media allegations, have come to regard themselves as innocent victims of "genocide" and "Serbian aggression," which reinforces their prejudice against Serbs as well as their belief in Izetbegović's agenda for the creation of a Muslim state in Europe; the Serbs, on the other hand, have been subjected to more than a decade of systematic demonization that vilified every aspect of their culture, history, national aspirations, which cast them in the role of fascist criminals. Nebojsa Malic concluded that is why the Serbs are, therefore, disinclined to take responsibility for atrocities they may have committed, simply because such an admission would lend credence to the sustained campaign of demonization that is still being conducted against them that casts them one and all in the role of subhuman criminals and that dogmatically holds the Serbian people exclusively and collectively responsible for the Balkan Wars of Succession. Meanwhile, inhabitants of the New World Order are being indoctrinated by a plethora of social engineering campaigns to believe that the successive wars the West waged for the profits of multinational corporations are actually "liberating" the world.

> The only truth about Srebrenica that no one can contest is that war is a crime against humanity. Trying to present such state-organized murder as a fight against "evil" by putting enemies on trial for "war crimes" is simply an attempt to mask that fact.[134]

But the pressure keeps growing. The U.S., now comfortable with issuing ultimatums, threatened to block aid to Serbia unless Ratko Mladić is captured and delivered to The Hague. The ultimatum is known as U.S. Senate bill number S.1426, and it authorizes payments to Serbia beyond March 2004 only if Serbia is "cooperating with the International Criminal Tribunal for the Former Yugoslavia." Passage of the bill would have dire consequences because the IMF and The World Bank (both U.S.-controlled institutions) would probably follow suit. Senator Patrick Leahy, the senior Democrat on the Senate's powerful appropriations committee, said:

"It is inexcusable that Ratko Mladić, who perhaps more than anyone besides Slobodan Milosevic is responsible for the slaughter of thousands of innocent people, has not been apprehended," he said. "Under my amendment, U.S. aid to Serbia next year would be withheld until the Serbian authorities turn him over to the Hague prosecutor."[135]

Secretary of State Colin Powell has withheld $16 million in assistance from Serbia and Montenegro in 2004 because of failure "to cooperate with the international war crimes tribunal in the Netherlands." And Powell is going to withhold $10 million in assistance in 2005 for the same reason.

"We call on the authorities in Belgrade to cooperate fully with the tribunal by arresting and transferring fugitive indictees, particularly Ratko Mladić, to face justice in The Hague," Boucher said.[136]

The U.S. ultimately imposed new sanctions against Serbia, and withheld $10 million in aid and withdrew advisors who were "helping to reform" the economic system. And the sanctions will continue until such a time as Serbia turns over war crimes suspect Ratko Mladić to The Hague Tribunal. But Ratko Mladić is not the real issue; the systematic destruction of Serbia is. The U.S-NATO-led bombardment caused $30 billion in damage to Serbia's infrastructure. Ten million dollars is nothing: it is merely money that will be used to reward key cooperative officials.

Even putting aside Serbia's claim that it has no idea where Mladić is, what's the big deal? No Islamic nation has turned over Osama bin Laden or his top lieutenant, either, but aid is still flowing to that part of the world. Serbs, who tried to stop radical Islam, should be treated as well as countries that spawn those who embrace it.[137]

And even if Mladić were handed over, then there would be further sanctions because Karadžić would still be free. And if Karadžić and Mladić were both handed over to the Tribunal, then new demands would be made. There is no end in sight for the continuing demonization, harassment and destruction of the Serbian people.

And The Hague keeps convicting Serbs for the Phantom Massacre. A former Bosnian Serb army commander was sentenced to 17 years in prison by the War Crimes Tribunal in The Hague. Dragan Obrenovic pleaded guilty to one count of crimes against humanity. The plea bargain resulted in the dismissal of five other counts. Obrenovic was chief of staff of the Zvornik Brigade of the Bosnian Serb Army, and was judged to have been aware of the alleged murders when Srebrenica fell. He was also judged to have failed to prevent his subordinates from taking part in it, as well as for his failure to have punish the alleged perpetrators.[138]

In June 2004, the wire services carried the poignant story of a group of Srebrenica widows. Their husbands were once again described as "victims of the worst massacre since WWII." They asked Carla del Ponte, the UN war crimes tribunal's top prosecutor, during her visit to the Potoćari Memorial to create a unit of volunteers to hunt down Karadžić and Mladić.

> "Make them arrest the perpetrators! Speed it up, Carla," the nervous widows yelled as Del Ponte walked between the graves.[139]

Only in closing did the article reveal that there were only 50 widows and mothers of the victims. Where did all the other widows and mothers go?

In contrast, the Pentagon announced in 2004 that the U.S. military began withdrawing small numbers of troops from two U.N. peacekeeping operations in Kosovo and Africa because they are no longer exempt from prosecution in the International Criminal Court. Ninety four countries ratified the 1998 treaty creating the ICC, which is bitterly opposed by Washington. "The U.S. makes the claim that the ICC leaves U.S. military and civilian government officials open to frivolous and politically-inspired charges in countries that recognize the court."[140] Yet frivolous and politically-inspired prosecutions of Serbs continue unabated.

Resistance

Democracy, as it was conceived in America, is founded on the written word. Citizens vote for candidates to represent them on the basis of the positions they take on issues. These representatives write laws, which are then interpreted and applied. Multiple points of view are supposed to be presented by the print media. Not every point of view on a certain issue is correct, so bad positions are weeded out from the good ones by analysis and debate. And when matters are taken to court, they are subjected to adversarial disputation before a judge. In a television driven "democracy," impressions and perceptions are created which often have no bearing on an issue. Impressions and perceptions cannot be debated for they are delivered by candidates, newscasters and pundits in sound bytes. The postmodern debate is often about conflicting "impressions," which never even touch upon objective truth, because "objective truth" does not exist.

> There's an old saying that when the facts are against you, argue the law. But the Bushies have gone one better: when the facts are against them, they argue the very existence of facts.[141]

Ms. Huffington argues persuasively that Bush, Cheney, and Rumsfeld are postmodernists, despite their claims to moral absolutism. She quoted Donald Rumsfeld at his tautological best:

> As we know, there are known knowns. There are things we know we know. We also know there are known unknowns. That is to say we know there are some things we don't know. But there are also unknown unknowns, the ones we don't know we don't know.

And there are no more good or bad ideas; instead there is a "marketplace of ideas," where ideas are bought and sold. The most popular and profitable among them gain predominance, and become the "best" ideas without ever having been subjected to scrutiny or analysis.

> The Pentagon is engaged in bitter, high-level debate over how far it can and should go in managing or manipulating information to influence opinion abroad, senior Defense Department civilians and military officers say.[142]

Such missions would take propaganda techniques that have been approved for battlefield use and apply them to covert propaganda campaigns targeting neutral or even allied nations. Critics of the proposal maintain that such efforts would create a credibility gap like the one that poisoned political discourse during the Vietnam War. So we cannot rely on the mainstream media or the government for a straightforward account of national and international events, much less a cogent analyses of them.

The antidote is reading, which opens the world and gives color and shade to thought. Reading allows us to compare what a certain public figure said twenty years ago or last week with what they say today. Reading provides a context for issues by finding historical precedents and placing ideas in a context, because ideas are bodiless and apparitional and do not come to life until they have people who believe in and animate them. Lastly, reading allows us to make informed judgments that are essential to the democratic process.

> [T]he nation is still caught in a tide of indifference when it comes to literature. That is the sobering profile of a new survey ... describes a precipitous downward trend in book consumption by Americans and a particular decline in the reading of fiction, poetry and drama.[143]

The survey, called "Reading at Risk," was taken by the National Endowment for the Arts. It revealed that that less than half of Americans over eighteen now read novels, short stories, plays or poetry; it also found that that the "book market" has shrunk; and the study disclosed that the rate at which the country is losing readers, especially young readers, is accelerating. Sadly, the study concludes that the downward spiral cuts across all demographic areas.

The study also found a strong correlation between readers and social engagement, which is not surprising; however, the electronic media is causing a decline in cultural and civic participation. James Shapiro, a professor of English at Columbia University, remarked that:

> A culture gets what it pays for, and if we think democracy depends on people who read, write, think and reflect — which is what literature advances — then we have to invest in what it takes to promote that.

That is true, but it seems unlikely that we will reverse the effects of electronic media any time soon. Americans are working more than ever and making less than ever. We often hold down two jobs or more to make ends meet. Real earnings are falling, and the leisure time that computers had once promised for all Americans in the 1960s and 1970s has failed to materialized. In such circumstances, it seems unlikely that most Americans will have the time to "read, write, think and reflect." Thus we are less able to consider our government's actions and the vulnerabilities, such as radical Islamic terrorism, to which our leaders have exposed us.

> "If a nation, in a state of civilization, expects to be [both] ignorant and free, it expects what never has been and never will be." Folks, we are ignorant, and therefore, not free. We have swallowed lies that rival Goebbels'....[144]

Europe and Islam: The Shape of Things to Come

An Iranian filmmaker, Mohammadreza Arab, produced a documentary called "Along the Sava" that depicts "neighboring countries which indicate connections with Iranian culture, but it is astonishing when it is observed in the Balkans in the heart of Europe." The filmmaker says:

> "Everything looks somehow Eastern and you don't feel alienated from society when you hear the sound of the azan (prayer call)," he added.[145]

The documentary is composed of thirteen twenty-six minute episodes being broadcast on Islamic Republic of Iran Broadcasting Channel 1. It features Sarajevo's Gazi Husreff-Bey Library, and explores the architectural style of mosques and bazaars that bear traces of Iranian cultural influences. The filmmaker added that he was in the former Yugoslavia in 1993 during the war as a photojournalist and filmmaker. The documentary apparently ignores Christians (i.e., Serbs) along the Sava, and portends greater and more unwelcome Iranian involvement in the former Yugoslavia.

The Turkish Undersecretary of Culture and Tourism, Mustafa Isen, signed an agreement with the UNMIK to provide for greater cultural cooperation between Turkey and Kosovo. The agreement includes the restoration and renewal of cultural sites such as the Sinan Pasa Mosque in Prizren, and the Mehmet the Conqueror Mosque in Priština, as well as the Sultan Murat Tomb.[146] Turkey, of course, is not going to aid in the reconstruction of the thirty-five Serbian Orthodox churches that were destroyed in the March 2004 pogrom, nor the 100 others destroyed during the 1999 Kosovo War.

Going from "cultural appreciation" to threats of violence is not a great leap for Islamists. The Turkish Prime Minister, Recep Tayyip Erdogan, sensing opposition to the Islamization of Europe, warned European Union leaders that they will suffer continued and escalating violence from Islamic extremists if the EU rejects Turkey as a member and defines itself as a Christian community.[147] What is Europe if not a Christian community?

Tensions are rising in Europe between Christians and Muslims. Muslims in Britain are experiencing more incidents of Islamophobia and discrimination. Analysts warned that large numbers of British Muslims, young men in particular, are being marginalized by the inequalities they suffer compared with other groups. Eighty percent said that they had suffered Islamophobia.[148] Most Muslims, however, emphasize that their faith is more important than their ethnicity.

> The high commissioner of Pakistan urged British Muslims to do more to fit into society. Dr. Maleeha Lodhi said better integration would help to "beat the extremists" — in terms of both racism towards Muslims and Islamic fundamentalism. "You can integrate without assimilating, so you are part of British society," she said.[149]

How does one integrate without assimilating? Britons, like Americans, have come to regard citizenship as a matter of shared values realized in the context of democracy and freedom of speech. Why can't one assimilate into that? On the other hand, the practice of Christianity is persecuted in Pakistan, where a number of churches have been bombed over the last several years. The practice of Christianity is absolutely forbidden in Saudi Arabia. One cannot even bring a Bible into the country. Iran actively persecutes its few remaining Jews.

French analyst Gilles Kepel thinks that Bin Laden's holy war, as originally conceived, is failing, but the jihad is far from over and the battlefield is now shifting to Europe. Mr. Kepel contends that the jihad is entering a new phase. The first phase consisted of revolts in Muslim countries aimed at toppling pro-Western "apostate" regimes, what al-Qaeda calls the "nearby enemy." The second phase occurred in the 1992, when Islamic militants began using global terrorism to advance their goals. The third phase, Mr. Kepel argues, is Muslim minority populations in European countries.

> "The most important battle in the war for Muslim minds during the next decade will be fought ... in communities of believers on the outskirts of London, Paris and other European cities," he writes. The challenge for Europe is thus how to best integrate these Muslim populations. The terrorists' challenge is to find fresh converts to jihad.[150]

The Madrid bombings and the assassination of Dutch filmmaker Theo van Gogh fit Mr. Kepel's theory. Longtime Muslim residents who had turned to Islamic fundamentalism participated in both attacks. The Madrid bombings brought down the Spanish government. In the Netherlands, the retaliatory violence smashed the liberal tradition of Dutch tolerance. The "clash of civilizations" has arrived in northern Europe. On March 30, 2004, British police arrested eight suspects after they discovered more than half a ton of ammonium nitrate fertilizer, the ingredient used in the Oklahoma bombing of the Alfred P. Murrah Federal Building in 1995 that killed 168 people. The planned attack was conceived abroad, but it was supposed to be executed by U.K. subjects.

> "That is something that is deeply worrying to us," Clark [deputy police commissioner who serves as Britain's anti-terror chief] said.[151]

Despite the arrest of Abu-Hamza al-Masri, the firebrand preacher at London's Finsbury Park mosque where Richard Reid, the convicted shoe-bomber, was a member, other clerics continue to test the limits of British tolerance by openly supporting jihad and al-Qaeda. One cleric bragged of recruiting young Muslim men to fulfill "religious obligations" by doing three months "military training" in Afghanistan, Chechnya and the Balkans. The Syrian-born cleric, Bakri, claims to be protected by the "covenant of security," which leaves him alone as long as he does not sanction attacks on British soil.[152]

Khalid Kelly is an Irishman who converted to Islam. He had been working in Saudi Arabia, where he grew bored and began to distill his own alcohol for personal consumption. He was arrested, and spent eight months in prison, where he found Islam. He now acts as a spokesman for London Islamists.

> "George Bush said you are with us or with the terrorists — we have no problem being called terrorists," he says. "When you call us extremists, it's OK because we are all against all the pornography, drinking, homosexuality, pedophilia out there. When you call us fundamentalists, it's OK because we stick fundamentally to our beliefs."[153]

Can Mr. Kelly explain why Sir Richard Burton investigated and closed the houses of prostitution in Pakistan that were staffed by young boys? or can he explain the Bosnian Muslims' fondness for *rakija* (i.e., brandy)? or further, can he explain the pornography of death, such as torture and beheadings, that Islamists openly market in front of mosques in Sarajevo? But we really ought to get used to Mr. Kelly: he is the unwelcome face of the future. In time, such Western converts, zealots, will inflict many such simplistic holier-than-thou harangues on us.

Meanwhile, a new nervous splendor has seized Vienna. The Turks laid siege to the city for sixty-one days in 1683, and the city was saved only because the Polish king, John III, answered an appeal to raise an army and rescue the city. The Viennese are not delighted with the prospect of Turkey joining the European Union. One Viennese social worker spoke of a Turkish man with whom he was acquainted, who had two wives who did not speak German, and whom he physically abused. The Turkish man in question also had two sons who were terrified of him.

> They're just different from us. We're Christians. They're Muslims. And these Muslims are getting more and more extreme. It's time to make a choice. I'm against it.[154]

Now will this Viennese social worker consider for a moment how his country's animosity to Serbia created the unhappy situation in his own country?

During his last days in office, the Dutch European Commissioner, Frits Bolkestein, openly warned of the Islamization of Europe in case Turkey joined Europe. "The relief of Vienna in 1683 will have been in vain," he said.[155] Valéry Giscard d'Estaing, one of the framers of the European constitution, said in 2003 that Turkish membership would mean the "end of the EU." He went on to say that Turkey was not a European country" and that it had a "different culture, a different approach, and a different way of life."[156]

The Italians are also responding to Turkey's desire to join the EU. Roberto Castelli, Italian Minister of Justice, remarked that regardless of who thought that Turkey was a gateway for democracy in the Islamic world, Italians have to be careful because allowing enormous numbers of Muslims to enter Europe would give them a chance to become a majority in Italy.

> When I hear that we should [conduct a] dialogue with moderate Muslims I think they are moderate just when they are in minority, when they become majority, as it happened in Kosovo, Christians are obliged to live as prisoners, in fenced areas....[157]

There is a historical precedent for the current onslaught against Europe. In 2001, Pope John Paul II apologized for the Roman Catholic involvement in the sack of Constantinople nearly 800 years after it took place. In November 2004, the Vatican returned the relics of St. John Chysostomos and St. Gregory Nazianzen, Orthodox Saints and Archbishops of Constantinople.

> The Franks did not understand that New Rome, the Orthodox
> Constantinople, was the guardian and protector of the West. The
> treachery of the Crusaders in 1204 opened the way for the Ottoman
> onslaught against Europe that did not stop until it reached Vienna in
> 1683. And today, the rampant Serbophobia ... reflects the same folly
> on a much larger scale.[158]

The murder of Dutch filmmaker Theo van Gogh in broad day-light shocked the Dutch. Many called it their country's first terror-ist attack. Mohammed Bouyeri, 26, shot van Gogh as many as 20 times, then repeatedly stabbed him and slit his throat "before pin-ning to his chest with a knife a five-page text that called for Muslims to rise up against 'infidels'."[159] Van Gogh had made a film called "Submission" that severely criticized the treatment of women in Islamic fundamentalist societies. Van Gogh character-ized himself as a court jester who routinely offended Muslims, Christians and Jews. He reserved his most pungent criticism, however, for Muslims, and he "often used vulgar references to bestiality when referring to Muslims."[160]

The Dutch felt that the murder of Pym Fortuyn, a popular politician who called for an end to immigration, was a rare and isolated instance. Now, however, according to a Dutch psycholo-gist, "People are more drastic in what they say.... They want all the radicals expelled from the country. And to tell you the truth, I can sympathize with that view."[161] The murders of Fortuyn and van Gogh have unleashed frustration that has been repressed for decades because of the Netherlands' failure to assimilate a large portion of its immigrant Muslim population. On the one hand, Moroccans condemned the van Gogh murder, but complained of anti-Muslim feelings and discrimination at work; on the other hand, the native Dutch say they are concerned about whether they are able to speak openly about their feelings about Islam and its place in society because journalists who have broached the sub-ject have received death threats.

"The jihad has come to the Netherlands."[162] That was the opin-ion rendered by Jozias van Aartsen, a leading Dutch Christian Democrat after van Gogh's murder. Attacks on mosques and Muslim schools followed the murder, which were answered with attacks on churches. The question becomes: to what extent should secular western societies tolerate the intolerant? For decades, the Dutch defended the rights and cultures of ever growing numbers of Muslim immigrants. Any other response was feared to be a signal of official racism, however, now both multiculturalism and tolerant secularism are under attack.

Ayaan Hirsi Ali, a Somali immigrant and former Muslim and liberal member of the Dutch Parliament who worked on "Submission" with van Gogh, has demanded that the Dutch insist on the superiority of western liberal values to Islam.

Geert Wilders, a renegade member of the Dutch parliament, has formed a new party that is gaining popularity because of its attacks on Islam. He called for a five-year halt to non-Western immigration after van Gogh's murder. Wilders said that he feared Dutch society would lose its norms and values if Islamic immigration continued unabated, and that he would expel Islamic radicals.

> The Netherlands has been too tolerant to intolerant people for too long…. We should not import a retarded political Islamic society to our country. There is nothing to be ashamed of to say this…. If in a mosque there is recruitment for jihad, it's not a house of prayer, it's a house of war. If it's not a house of prayer, it should be closed down.[163]

Geert Wilders now travels with an escort of two policemen wherever he goes ever since police uncovered a network of radical Muslims who had plans to assassinate Mr. Wilders and other "enemies of Islam," and who promised 72 virgins in paradise to any Muslim who beheaded him. Mr. Wilders travels from one safe house to another in a convoy of armored cars.

> "My life has changed completely. I am sleeping very badly…." he said. "Even though I have this protection, I am afraid. Even when I am on the floor of the parliament, I don't feel comfortable."[164]

Mr. Wilders is correct to take the threats seriously. Mohammed Bouyeri, 27, the Dutch-Moroccan who is accused of murdering Theo van Gogh,

> limped into Amsterdam's high-security court yesterday with a Koran under his arm and insisted on his right not to be defended because he does not recognise the authority of the court.[165]

He was sentenced to life imprisonment shortly thereafter.

In France, Nicolas Sarkozy, the current finance minister, stated recently that "whether I like it or not, Islam is the second biggest religion in France. So you've got to integrate it by making it more French."[166] Nevertheless, the French monitor about 1,500 mosques around the country, and the new interior minister, Dominique de Villepin, has signed agreements with Britain, Germany, Italy and Spain to exchange information on Islamic radicals who attend training camps.[167]

Germany has also instituted a new get tough policy with Islamic radicals, and has shown little sympathy to Islamic radicals who are taking advantage of legal loopholes to stay in Germany. "Militant Islamism is only a tiny force in Europe," wrote the *Frankfurter Allgemeine Zeitung*, "yet it is dangerous because many societies on this continent have elevated their defencelessness into a virtue.... Yet the risk is that, rather than the intolerant learning tolerance, the tolerant become intolerant too."[168]

And yet there are fervent globalists who believe that Turkey must become a member of the EU despite popular opposition in France, Germany, Italy and Austria, where people are convinced that Turkey is too poor and too Muslim; and that it would flood the EU with immigrants. Globalists contend that such objections are based on racial prejudice and the "deeply reactionary" belief that Europe is a Christian entity that is struggling against Muslim hordes from the east. The globalists also remind us that up to the early twentieth century, the Ottoman Empire ruled large parts of modern-day Greece, Rumania, Serbia, Albania and Macedonia.

"Remember: the Ottomans were called the sick man of Europe, not the sick man of Asia," Turkish Premier Recep Tayyip Erdogan told a rally in Brussels on Friday.[169]

And once Turkey was dispossessed of its European holdings, it was free to remain the "sick man of Asia."

Globalists contend that there are already 15 million Muslims living in the EU, and that Albania, Macedonia and Bosnia-Herzegovina will join the EU in the next decade, compounding the number. They allege that European reactionaries and U.S. conservatives are wrong to characterize Islam and democracy as irreconcilable and that a "clash of civilizations" is emerging between the Christian West and the Muslim East.

The very existence of Turkey, a modern secular, democratic state for most of the last century, surely debunks this myth.[170]

Has the writer of this article read that Greek Orthodox churches had been bombed once again in Istanbul in 2004, or that Christian Serbs have been expelled from lands that they had inhabited for a millennium in order to recreate the green highway from Istanbul to Vienna? The Serbian resistance to the Ottomans in the Battle of Kosovo was written up in one of the earliest books ever published, Gutenberg's *Türkenkalender* (1454), which warned of the imminent danger of a Turkish invasion after the fall of Constantinople in 1453. Serbia vanished from the consciousness of the West during the Ottoman occupation. It was known as "Serbistan." Have the globalists ever heard of Englandistan, Frankistan, Germanistan and Amerikastan?

It comes down to one simple proposition: unless the West is able defend itself, Islam will continue to infiltrate it until such a time as it is strong enough to destroy it. The violent message of the Koran poses an insoluble problem for Muslims.

> We cannot solve it for them, and we should not be asked to deem the problem solved by pretending that the Koran is a pacifist tract. Humans are perfectly capable of reinterpreting scripture when necessary, but until Muslims themselves renounce the ideals of jihad, terror, tax and subjugation we must have the guts to call a religion of war by its right name.[171]

Yet apologists for Islam would have us believe otherwise. Here is a typical example: "Islam is tolerant of other faiths. Like America, Islam has a history of respecting other religions."[172] Srdja Trifkovic reminds us of the sufferings of Greeks, Serbs, Jews, Armenians, Chaldeans, Egyptian Christians, Hindus, Buddhists and countless others who have suffered blows from the Prophet's sword. Islam is not "only" a religion; it is a complete way of life and an all-embracing social, political and legal system that destroys neighboring civilizations and co-opts the surviving remnants into it.

> The West is yet to learn, fully, the lesson that the Serbs were forced to learn six centuries ago: that Islam is a collective psychosis seeking to become global, and any attempt to compromise with madness is to become part of the madness oneself. The quarrel is not of our choosing, and those who submit to that faith must solve the problem they set themselves. Until they explicitly and permanently renounce jihad, Serbs and Westerners would be well advised not to allow their differences — real and complex as they are — to prevent them from acting together before it is too late.[173]

Michael Sheuer is pessimistic about our chances for survival:

> I have long experience analyzing and attacking Bin Laden and Islamists. I believe they are a growing threat to the United States — there is no greater threat — and that we are being defeated not because the evidence of the threat is unavailable but because we refuse to accept it at face value and without Americanizing the data. This must change, or our way of life will be unrecognizably altered.[174]

Osama bin Laden delivered a videotaped speech on October 30, 2004, just before the U.S. presidential election. He praised Allah who permitted the injured party "to retaliate against the oppressor in kind." He said that "security is an indispensable pillar of human life and that free men do not forfeit their security, contrary to Bush's claim that we hate freedom." He claimed that those who hate freedom "don't possess defiant spirits like those of the 19 — may Allah have mercy on them." He characterized himself and his followers as free men who "want to restore freedom to our nation, just as you lay waste to our nation. So shall we lay waste to yours." He referred to al-Qaeda's extensive experience in guerrilla warfare and the war of attrition against "tyrannical superpowers." Along with mujahideen, he "bled Russia for 10 years, until it went bankrupt and was forced to withdraw in defeat." Then he came to his point. He promised to continue "this policy in bleeding America to the point of bankruptcy."

> And it was to these sorts of notions and their like that the British diplomat and others were referring in their lectures at the Royal Institute of International Affairs. [When they pointed out that] for example, al-Qaida spent $500,000 on the event, while America, in the incident and its aftermath, lost — according to the lowest estimate — more than $500 billion.[175]

The Release of the Execution Video of Six Bosnian Muslims, The Ten-Year Anniversary of the Fall of Srebrenica, and The London Terror Bombings

Anyone involved in event planning, ranging from private birthday parties to national celebrations, is aware of the significance of anniversaries: the most important are the first, the tenth, the fiftieth and the hundredth. Such commemorations carve a date and its events into the collective memory. So it was with the fall of Srebrenica on July 11, 1995.

The global media was going to use the anniversary to memorialize the Bosnian Muslims as "victims" and excoriate the Serbs as villains. The first salvo came in March 2005 when Paddy Ashdown ordered an investigation of 900 Bosnian Serbian state employees for suspected roles in the Srebrenica "massacre." Those who were found to have been involved would be suspended from their posts.[176]

The Mighty Wurlitzer did not play the opening notes of its Srebrenica themesong until June 1, during the testimony of General Obrad Stevanović at President Milošević's show-trial in The Hague. The prosecution of President Milošević was going badly because it has still not managed to link him, as titular head of the police forces, to the alleged massacre.

> "...there is simply no evidence to back the genocide charge [against Milosevic]" despite the fact that "prosecutors have spent months trying to prove otherwise...."[177]

The prosecution concluded its case on the Bosnian War in 2004, and had moved on to Kosovo. On June 1, the line of questioning pursued by Prosecutor Nice concerned two members of a paramilitary group called the "Skorpions" who had been charged with the murder of 19 Albanian civilians in Podujevo in Kosovo. The Skorpions were established in 1992 to fight in Bosnia as mercenaries. Some members of the Skorpions later volunteered to go to Kosovo, where they were under Serbian Interior Ministry ("MUP") command in 1999. Prosecutor Nice was trying to prove, by presenting evidence that two members of the Skorpions who volunteered to go to Kosovo in 1999, that they were also under MUP command in 1995, which is farfetched. If this were true, the Skorpions could then be linked to President Milošević by chain of command. Of the two who were found guilty of murdering Albanian civilians, one was in prison (having been convicted on evidence submitted by Natasa Kandic), and the other was fighting extradition in Canada. General Stevanović confirmed that they were not working for the MUP in Bosnia.

Prosecutor Nice then played an eight minute excerpt from a ten-year-old, two-hour-long amateur video and provided his own rambling commentary as voice-over. The video begins with a Serbian Orthodox priest blessing members of the Skorpions. Then there are shots of the Skorpions in Pale boarding busses.

Next comes a shot of apparently six Bosnian Muslim men being led out of the back a truck at another location, who are forced to lay down on the roadside; then they are told to get up. They are finally led to a field where three of them appear to be shot, and the remaining three carry away their bodies.

Media commentators called the video a "smoking gun," 'incontrovertible," "irrefutable," and "uncontestable" proof that the alleged Srebrenica massacre had occurred.

> While the number of those killed represents a tiny proportion of those who died in July 1995, the video is being seen as irrefutable evidence that Serbia's police forces, and not just Bosnian Serb forces, took part in the massacre, evidence that challenges the commonly held view among Serbs that the atrocity never took place.[178]

Tim Judah frequently writes for IWPR (a George Soros funded 'news' source) and is the author of a biased book called *The Serbs*, which can only be compared to a Monty Python version of Serbian history. Mr. Judah pointed out that the executions in the video took place in the village of Trnovo, "which lies 30 minutes' drive east of Sarajevo." And he added that: "For the Serbian authorities, a psychological barrier has been smashed. Pressure is now mounting on them to arrest at least Mladić, who is believed to be in Serbia."[179] However, it must be noted that:

> Prosecutors obtained the videotape only recently and they cannot enter it into evidence until they reopen the case and show the provenance and authenticity of the images. Mr. Milosevic said the film had been tampered with.[180]

Jared Israel of The Emperor's New Clothes, who did so much to unmask the false "concentration camp" video (produced by ITN reporter Penny Marshall) that featured Fikret Alic, an emaciated man, apparently standing behind a barbed wire fence. Mr. Israel helped prove that it was the camera crew that was filming from the fenced-in area, and that Mr. Alic was emaciated because he suffered from tuberculosis. It was not a concentration camp at all, but a refugee center (*see* www.tenc.net). Mr. Israel rightly questioned the judicial rules governing the introduction of the video as evidence as compared to routine legal procedures in the U.S. and Canada.

> These rules are not petty technicalities; they are meant to guarantee the authenticity of raw video footage, and to prevent doctoring of this footage, precisely because it is so easy to do.[181]

The prosecution was apparently desperate to introduce the tape in time for the tenth anniversary of Srebrenica. An attorney aiding President Milošević, remarked:

> This is clearly part of a media campaign. We think the film was designed to shock the public, not to prove something.[182]

Steven Kay, President Milošević's court appointed attorney, immediately objected to the presentation of the video on the grounds that: 1) there was no legal basis to introduce the video footage; 2) it was sensationalist in nature; and 3) the witness (General Stevanović) had not been asked any questions about the contents of the tape. Mr. Kay also emphasized that the existence of the video had been withheld from the defense, yet, it was being made available to the public.[183]

Zvonimir Trajković, a Serbian journalist who had helped evacuate civilians from Srebrenica, questioned why a ten-year-old video was being shown just now. He treats the ubiquitous presence of the execution video of six Muslims in the media as part of an organized campaign before the negotiations on Kosovo in order to weaken Serbia's negotiating position. Furthermore, the video did not make anybody "face the truth" because the crime shown in the video was committed in Trnovo, which is 170 kilometers from Srebrenica, about a four hour drive through mountain roads in bad repair—not the thirty-minute drive Mr. Judah cited earlier. Linking that crime with Srebrenica, he states, is intended to refresh the myth about Srebrenica Muslims on the eve of the tenth anniversary of the fall of the town, where President Tadic was going to appear and issue a full apology.

> It is the continuation of the propaganda war, which is aimed at representing to the world that the Serbs are a genocidal nation. Against such a nation, all is justifiable, including the bombing of 1999. Such a nation does not deserve to retain Kosovo in its state, and the hands of our "statesmen" will be tied because they are thought to represent the genocidal people in this particular international negotiation.[184]

Within days of the video's release, several men who had appeared in it were arrested, but the efficient action of the Serbian police and the apprehension of the suspects were ignored. It was never the point.

We Americans must know how the Serbs feel. Let us pause and reflect for a moment. We had an atrocity video of our own broadcast in November 2004 that was professionally photographed. During the attack on Falluja, U.S. Marines entered a mosque where there were some wounded Iraqis. One Marine is shown entering the mosque.

> As the cameraman follows, a marine says: "These are the two wounded that they never picked up." Another marine is heard shouting: "He's faking he's dead."
>
> Another shouts: "He's breathing." Gunfire rings out and a marine says: "He's dead now."[185]

The networks did not want to broadcast the entire tape; they claimed that it was too graphic. The footage was blacked out by U.S. networks the moment the shots were fired. What could be more graphic than the actual killing? It turns out that the Marine in question reportedly performed a little victory dance, similar to the one performed by football players after a touchdown is scored, after the killing.

Military officials were quick to point out that some insurgents had been known to attack U.S. soldiers after pretending to be dead. A U.S. Marine Corps spokesman at the Pentagon told reporters that the Naval Criminal Investigation Service was conducting an investigation into the matter for "possible law of war violations" (i.e., a studied rephrasing of the "war crimes") but "they did not want to implicate anybody ahead of that." He also cautioned people from overreacting to the tape. "I wouldn't jump to any conclusions," he said. "We don't know all the facts here."[186]

Six months later, when most people had forgotten about the incident, the U.S. Marine Corps simply announced that it would not prosecute the unidentified Marine for his actions.[187]

Now, The Hague Tribunal does not treat all atrocity videos equally. Everything hinges on the mysterious process of "authentication." The video of the execution of six Bosnian Muslims was quickly released, however, the mujahideen videos made by Doris Gluck's husband (*see* p. 341) among them "The Martyrs of Bosnia" video, have never been "authenticated."

> The quick authentication of a video that consigns Muslim victimology is in a stark contrast to Hague's procrastination in authenticating videos that depict Muslim savagery and grotesque mutilations of non-Muslims. At issue is not just the beheading of a Serbian POW Rade Rogic that was immediately circulated across the web, but also a host

of other videos, produced by Muslims themselves in order to authenticate their jihad in Bosnia.

According to the court proceedings of the Hague prosecutors, however, The Martyrs of Bosnia video is an unauthenticated item therefore inadmissible in the Court.[188]

And it seems that Naser Orić's video of the murders of hundreds of Serbian villagers from the Srebrenica area have never been authenticated, even though these videotapes had been submitted nearly a decade ago. As in show business, it's all in the timing, especially with respect to the video of the six Bosnian Muslims. Had the video been released at any other time:

it would certainly have had less political significance than it does now.

The problem for Serbia, however, is that the Scorpions affair exploded just weeks before the ... commemoration.... The event will be a major political and media event and dignitaries from both the region and around the world have been invited to attend.[189]

The foreign owners of the "independent" Serbian media have meanwhile made sure that Serbs are bombarded with messages about their own criminality and guilt.

In my country today it is almost illegal to say that we are right. Sometimes when I wake up, I believe that I live in Albania or Croatia. Even our own media are anti-Serbic! Only few media are free to comment anything, others are under democratic censorship....[190]

Besides turning off the TV whenever Natasa Kandic appeared on one of the Soros-controlled television stations, Serbs reacted to the billboard campaign that plastered "Don't Forget Srebrenica" ads from one end of Serbia to another.

Most signs where defaced in a matter of hours. The few comments I heard are questions about the 3200 Serbs tortured and killed, men, women, children, young and old. Between 1993, and 1995. No U.N., NATO, action to stop Oric or other Moslem troops. No media out cry. The Moslem killers could move freely in and out of the so called safe zone. I read one U.N. report which describe[s] [the] attacks on the Serbians as minor.[191]

"Seven days after the video it was as if nothing had happened," said Miroslav Sutić of Partner MS polling agency.[192]

In what was called a "defiant gesture," Serbs gathered to commemorate the Serbian victims of the Yugoslav wars days before the anniversary of the fall of Srebrenica.

> "We are in an absurd situation where no one talks about crimes against Serbs. We offered this film to TV stations but they refused to show it, while they looped film about Srebrenica day in and day out," said Tomislav Nikolic, leader of the Serbian Radical Party.[193]

Nikolic was referring to a documentary called "The Truth," which depicted, among other things, the killing of Rade Rogic, a father of two who was killed by mujahideen on September 16, 1995. The video showed that Rogic had been forced to kneel before Muslim soldiers who forced him to repeat "Allahu Akhbar" before they slashed his throat and beheaded him. The SRS (Srpska Radikalna Strana, "The Serbian Radical Party") video showed Bosnian Muslim soldiers demolishing a Serbian Orthodox church and spraying a cross and an icon of Christ with automatic gunfire.

> Acting SRS leader, Tomislav Nikolic, said … "I'm sorry that we had to demonstrate in this manner how senseless it is to blame only one nationality for crimes committed in a civil war." … He offered to hand the video material to the Hague war crimes tribunal for the former Yugoslavia and to the Serbian government, should they request this.[194]

The Serbian Radical Party went on to torpedo a draft declaration that condemned the alleged Srebrenica massacre. The Radicals would only agree to a sweeping condemnation of all war crimes from the 1990s Balkan wars, including those carried out against Serbs, which is an eminently reasonable position to take.[195]

Most Serbs were not fooled. A polling agency reported that the video of Serb paramilitaries executing Muslim captives "had produced short-lived condemnation when it was broadcast in early June, but had not made a lasting impression."[196]

Despite the spirited Serbian defense, the stage was now set for a media saturation campaign: the execution video of six Bosnian Muslims would be a commercial to promote the alleged Srebrenica massacre of "7,000 men and boys," which would in turn promote the arrest of General Mladić and Radovan Karadžić, which would in turn boost U.S. influence (or hegemony) in the Balkans, while collectively demonizing the Serbs, blaming them for everything that happened in the 1990s, and making them an object of universal scorn. As others have remarked, not even the

Germans were treated this badly after WWII. But the Serbs are not Germans.

Commentators took the opportunity to sermonize on the meaning of "Srebrenica." Roger Cohen is representative of many others:

> But the first real dent in the crippling Serbian denial of their crimes was made this month with the showing of a video of the execution of six — yes, six — of the more than 7,000 Muslims killed at Srebrenica in July, 1995.
>
> For once the ironclad Serbian self-image of perennial victim was breached.[197]

A few days later, U.S. Undersecretary of State Nicholas Burns told Koštunica and Tadić that they had a "major anniversary" on their hands, that they had to "atone" for these crimes by capturing Mladić before the anniversary, and that they had to repent![198] It just goes to show that the Devil himself can quote Scripture for his own ends.

But Mr. Burns was soon to face a new set of problems. On July 5, days before the commemoration, 35 kg. of explosives was found near the Potoćari Memorial Center in Srebrenica. Sabahudin Salihović, close friend of Naser Orić (!), was arrested.[199] The office of Paddy Ashdown disingenuously said it was too early to say whether the explosives were intended to cause casualties or simply to generate "negative publicity" before the Srebrenica anniversary. It made no comment on who might be behind the plot, but said it would "look with great suspicion at those who might speculatively blame someone else." Mr. Salihovic was quickly released. Why? Was he an intelligence asset?

Two days later on July 7, four suicide bombers, U.K.-born Muslims, set off four bombs, three in the subway and one on a double decker bus, killing fifty and wounding five hundred. There were obvious similarities to the Madrid bombings.

> According to Christophe Chaboud, the new commandant of the anti-terrorist unit of France UCLAT, a unit of the French criminal police which specializes in the fight against terrorism, said that the explosives used in the London terrorist bombings on July 7, 2005 were of military derivation and had come to the UK from Kosovo.
>
> Similarly, British Military and defense analyst Paul Beaver said that "a part of the investigation dealing with the London blasts is aimed at

links between radical Islamists in Bosnia and Kosovo with international terrorist groups." Beaver says that the KLA and Muslim federations developed close links with the criminal mafias in Albania.[200]

No one in the mainstream media bothered to link the London terror bombings to the Srebrenica commemoration: the West was commemorating the opening of Europe to Islamic fundamentalism via the Green Highway, and it was commemorating fallen al-Qaeda holy warriors who died in battle against General Mladić's troops. In fact, the mainstream media was selling nothing short of a death wish for Western Civilization.

Richard Holbrooke, former U.S. ambassador to the United Nations, who was the chief architect of the Dayton peace agreement, tried to set the tone. He simply ignored the London bombings. He attempted to head off any objections to U.S. policy in the very first paragraph of his article in which he invited Americans to "go to a really horrible place—one whose name has become synonymous with genocide and Western failure. Go to Srebrenica." He even tried his hand at novelistic descriptions of the ceremony: a valley of evil, leaden skies, muddy fields, etc. And if anyone had any doubts about Clinton's conduct in the war, he said:

> .... It was a classic commander-in-chief decision, made alone, without congressional support and with only reluctant backing from the Pentagon. But it worked: Without American military intervention, Bosnia would not have survived.[201]

That was an elegant way of saying that there was no domestic support in the U.S. for the war and that there was no congressional or Pentagon support. Clinton forced it through with Holbrooke as an act of imperial despotism. He was also reassuring us that no one in the Clinton administration was aiding and abetting Muslim fundamentalist terrorism. The subtext Holbrooke uses is that the Bosnian Muslims are "our" Muslims, whom we defended, and Muslims throughout the ought to be grateful to us.

Other commentators weighed in too. "Blood on their Hands" *Time Europe*, by Andrew Purvis, June, 13, 2005 transforms the paramilitaries in the atrocity video into Serbian soldiers and emphasizes the role of the Serbian priest in blessing the troops before they go out to kill Muslims. "Remember the Balkans," by Helle Dale,

The Washington Times, June 29, 2005, compares the Serbs to Nazis who cannot come to terms with their crimes, and calls them a "nation in denial about war crimes committed in its name." The article then segues into a discussion of independence for Kosovo. "The Truth Must Come Out" by Ed MacKenzie, *The Guardian* (UK), July 11, 2005, lionizes Natasa Kandic, the "human rights activist," and refers to her as "a hip older woman" and treats the video as "horrific and incontrovertible proof of Serbia's role in the massacre." "Srebrenica, an Obligation Unfulfilled" (Editorial, *The New York Times*, July 15, 2005) pits the "genocide" against the incompetence of NATO peacekeepers as the basis of U.S. intervention, and makes a renewed call for the arrest of Radovan Karadžić and Ratko Mladić. "Unfinished Balkan Business" by Nicholas Burns, *The Washington Post*, July 10, 2005, emphasizes the need for U.S. and NATO to remain in Bosnia. He too turns the subject to Kosovo's independence at the end of his article. His point is that the Serbs are unfit to govern Kosovo, therefore, it must be granted independence.

The U.S. House of Representatives joined in the fracas, too. It adopted a resolution demanding that Radovan Karadžić and Ratko Mladić, who were deemed to be principally responsible for the alleged Srebrenica massacre, be brought to justice. The resolution was not binding, but was expected to place additional pressure on Belgrade to meet all its obligations to the Hague Tribunal.[202]

It is worth recalling the words of Fred Hampton, the slain leader of the Black Panther Party, who memorably remarked: "We get answers that don't answer; explanations that don't explain; and conclusions that don't conclude." His words ring true today in a different context, whether it be in the broader world fixed information and discourse as exemplified by the current war in Iraq, or whether it be Srebrenica. The one sentence from the Downing Street Memo says it all: "But the intelligence and facts were being fixed around the policy."

Meanwhile, there was another media event leading up to the anniversary: Bosnian Muslims were retracing the steps of those killed in 1995. David Rohde wrote the article.

> About 500 Bosnian Muslim men set out on foot at 7:30 a.m. Sunday from this quiet farming village in eastern Bosnia on the third and final day of their re-enactment of the "march of death" a decade ago this week.[203]

Fifty thousand people were expected to attend the commemoration of the Muslim victims of Srebrenica in Potoćari but only an estimated 30,000 showed up. Another 600 bodies were buried there that day, bringing the total to 1,800. Here is how David Rohde characterized it.

> American and European leaders attending a ceremony ... promised that two Bosnian Serb leaders indicted for the killings would be brought to justice. But among the 30,000 Bosnian Muslims who gathered here today, relatives of the dead and others dismissed the promises as empty.[204]

Edward S. Hermann co-authored "Manufacturing Consent" with Noam Chomsky. He knows a thing or two about media manipulation and propaganda. In "Propaganda System Number One," he remarked that: "Under these conditions, remarkable structures of disinformation can be built, institutionalized, and remain parts of historic memory even in the face of ex post [facto] confutations, which are kept out of sight."[205]

Natasa Kandic, the Executive Director of The Humanitarian Law Center ("HLC"), is one such institutional factor in sustaining permanent structures of disinformation. She is often referred to by Serbs, as well as by knowledgeable Americans, as a paid traitor. She fully supports each and every imperial diktat made by the U.S. on the Serbian government, and she tries to come up with evidence of "war crimes" to support a policy of total submission to U.S. demands. Ms. Kandic has also given her full support to the ICTY and its task of exonerating U.S. and NATO aggression against Yugoslavia and criminalizing the victims of such aggression. She continues the NATO propaganda war long after the war is over.

> The HLC was created in 1992 by Natasa Kandic, its present Executive Director. It has been funded by George Soros as well as the National Endowment for Democracy and this year the Ford Foundation provided HLC with a $80,000 grant.[206]

The National Endowment for Democracy was established in 1981 to take over certain propaganda functions once controlled by the CIA. It is worth noting that Wesley Clark, Richard

Holbrooke, and Francis Fukuyama, author of the fanciful anti-Communist screed, *The End of History*, have served on its board of directors.

But those who have lionized Ms. Kandic have not scrutinized her credibility. She broke the bogus story about the refrigerator truck that was allegedly filled with the corpses of Albanian civilians from Kosovo that had been dumped in the Danube in April 1999. She based her fabrication on an incident that had been written up in a local Serbian police journal about a refrigerated trailer truck that had been lifted out of the Danube near Kladovo, at the border with Romania, that contained the bodies of dead Kurds. Even though Kandic's story was a hoax, it served U.S. and NATO political demands: NATO was at the time demanding the transfer of President Milošević to the ICTY, and NATO needed the bodies as evidence to prove its charge of crimes against humanity against President Milošević.

Natasa Kandic was also the source for a 1999 *USA Today* article which concerned "ethnic cleansing" in Kosovo. Jack Kelley, the correspondent who wrote the article, cited a three-ring notebook with a black vinyl cover that contained a direct order "typed on army stationery and stamped by the Supreme Defense Council of the Yugoslav Army Headquarters in Belgrade, which is headed by Milosevic." The order, which Mr. Kelley said was typed in Cyrillic, read: "The aim of the military activity should be to cleanse Cusk and the surrounding villages and terrain." In other words, it appears that Mr. Kelley does not read Serbian, so someone had to show him the document and explain to him what it meant.

The New York Times published an article that commented on Jack Kelley's resignation after *USA Today* conducted an in-house investigation to determine "whether Kelley might have embellished or fabricated stories."[207] Mr. Kelley at first declined to identify the individual who showed him the notebook.

> He added that United Nations investigators considered this "the strongest and most direct evidence linking the government of Yugoslav President Slobodan Milosevic to 'ethnic cleansing' in Kosovo."[208]

The UN investigators couldn't help Mr. Kelley's credibility when he had to answer to his editors. He finally claimed his source was a "human rights advocate," and then caved in and revealed Natasa Kandic to be the person who showed him the damning document in the three-ring notebook. Ms. Kandic, however, could not save either Mr. Kelley's credibility or his job by producing the document in question—because it never existed to begin with.

That's two strikes against Natasa Kandic. And I omitted to mention that this "human rights" activist physically attacked an elderly Serbian refugee who questioned her motives at a rally in Belgrade in 2004. The renowned "human rights activist" struck an old man in the face for disputing her judgment!

Jared Israel, in a second article on the execution video, asks why powerful institutions would attempt such a frame up?

> Answer: because the Srebrenica story has had a huge effect on world politics. *Srebrenica depicts Muslims as supposed victims of supposedly racist Serbian Orthodox Christians, creating the impression that Muslim violence constitutes revenge. The Srebrenica story has weakened opposition to political Islam around the world. Political Islam, once widely perceived as the most intolerant and repressive force on earth, is now widely perceived as an understandable response to repression and intolerance.*
>
> (…)
>
> *One might call this the "Srebrenica effect,"* and it is, I believe, an important component of the Western establishment's political strategy for controlling political thinking in the post-cold war world.[209] [Emphasis added.]

Mr. Israel also believes the execution video is a fake. If anyone has seen the two-and-one-half minute excerpt of the video that was made available to the public on the internet, a number of inconsistencies immediately become apparent. First of all, the opening shot that features the Orthodox priest blessing the soldiers has a date stamp that reads June 25-26, 1995; however, the remaining footage has no date stamp. Furthermore, aside from the opening scene where the soldiers receive the priest's blessing, it is difficult to identify anyone who appears later in the video, which leads the present writer to suppose that the only members of the Skorpions who were arrested were those who attended the blessing. Finally, the execution scenes themselves seem to deliberately keep the faces of the executioners out of frame, and strangely, there is no blood after the alleged victims have been executed. The three remaining Muslim prisoners actually help lift the bodies of those who had been shot. No blood or wounds can be seen. It is worth adding that the photographic quality varies, too. A trained eye would question whether the footage had been shot with the same camera, the same stock, or by the same person. It's vintage Natasa Kandic: it raises more questions than it answers, and in this case, it answers no questions about Srebrenica at all. No more than the freezer truck story or the putative "ethnic cleansing" orders in the three-ring binder answered about Kosovo.

The execution video of the six Bosnian Muslims is Ms. Kandic's third attempt for a grand publicity stunt. Apart from the anti-Serbian propaganda points scored by the video, the bottom line is that the ICTY Prosecution must prove several things for the video to have any relevance to the trial of President Milošević. First, it is of critical importance that the person who filmed it is identified, and that a "chain of custody" is established that explains who had the tape in their possession from the time it was shot until its presentation in the ICTY in order to prove that the tape was not tampered with. Secondly, the Prosecution has to prove that the victims were indeed Muslims from Srebrenica, that the perpetrators were in fact members of the Skorpions, and finally, that the Skorpions were under MUP control. Judging from Ms. Kandic's track record, it won't happen.

Meanwhile, Television B92 in Serbia, which is funded by George Soros, was running the video of the executions nonstop. Mr. Soros also controls *Vreme*, a weekly news magazine, as well as several daily newspapers. Neil Clark remarked in the *New Statesman* magazine that Soros considers a society to be 'open' if it allows him and his business partners to make money. The designation 'open' has nothing to do with human rights and freedom. Soros has profited in each and every county he has cracked 'open'. He invested $50 million in Kosovo in order to seize control of the Trepca mines, where there are untold resources in gold, silver and lead, and enough lignite coal to keep Europe running for a hundred years. The Trepca mines are an asset estimated to be worth at least $5 billion.

> He thus copied a pattern he has deployed to great effect over the whole of eastern Europe: of advocating 'shock therapy' and 'economic reform,' then swooping in with his associates to buy valuable state assets at knockdown prices.[210]

George Soros has also made significant contributions to funding the ICTY itself. He also contributes funding to the Coalition for International Justice (CIJ), which lends its support to the ICTY and provides it with much of its legal staff. Furthermore, the ICTY also has arrangements for obtaining evidence through the Open Society Foundation, which is also funded by Mr. Soros. If that were not enough, Mr. Soros' generosity extends to Human Rights Watch, which is fond of highlighting alleged Serbian atrocities. And Mr. Soros also funded the UN's Commission of Experts to Investigate War Crimes in the Former Yugoslavia, which was chaired by De Paul University's Charif Bassiouni. He collected 65,000 pages of "evidence" of war crimes committed by Serbs—but not those committed by any other party in the civil war. Mr. Bassiouni also defended Mohamed Sacirbey against charges of embezzlement (*see* p. 331). Mr. Soros has laid out a hall of mirrors in his financial labyrinth: whichever way one turns, one keeps running into George Soros.

The release of the video was timed to coincide with a conference on Srebrenica that had been organized by Natasa Kandic. But it backfired.

> Ever since the video of the crime committed by the "Skorpions" was broadcast, we have witnessed a unique Olympiad featuring NGO profiteers. Natasa Kandic & Co. barely managed to get from an exhibition about Srebrenica at B92 studios, and then take their seats on a tribunal about Srebrenica, and then they run off to a conference on Srebrenica, from which they rush off to a debate on Srebrenica, and then after that they go to a forum on Srebrenica, after which they attend a rally on Srebrenica. Meanwhile, they have been regularly making statements to foreign media—which treats them as latter day pillars of democracy and freedom of thought—about their "roles as martyrs" in revealing the "truth about Srebrenica."
>
> (…)
>
> The hysterical "All Serbs Are Guilty for Srebrenica" campaign will finally force us think: "We've had it with the "truth about Srebrenica." An action causes a reaction.[211]

Mr. Zarković, the author of the above quotation, went on to state that Americans will never apologize for Hiroshima and Nagasaki, not to mention Iraq, the genocide of Native Americans, or the deaths caused by the U.S. bombardment of Serbia in 1999. The Croats will never apologize for Jasenovac or for Operations Flash and Storm. And he is firmly convinced that the Bosnian Muslims will never apologize for the mass murders of Serbs in Sarajevo and in the areas surrounding Srebrenica.

> We Serbs, however, instead of having learned a thing or two from the Americans, the English, the Croats and the Bosniaks, keep hollering about crimes "committed in our name." Then, as a matter of due course, the US Senate passes a special resolution that brands us as the sole perpetrators of a crime that took place ten years earlier. It's quite possible that the two are linked: if you holler about war crimes "committed in your name," then the US Senate will hit back at you. It's a question of action and reaction. [212]

Boris Tadić's apology for the deaths of "the innocent victims" of Srebrenica at the ten-year commemoration theoretically excludes the victims who are not innocent. Yet his apology brought him nothing but scorn and condemnation. Just a few weeks later, Tadić asked the Croatians to apologize for Operation Storm and for the atrocities Croatian troops had committed. Tadić said the atrocities were an "organized crime," and urged Croatian leaders to apologize for the crimes, just as he had apologized for Srebrenica. Stipe Mesić gave him a tart reply: the "war crime committed in Srebrenica cannot be justified nor relativized by pointing to the (1995) crimes that were excesses." He said that he apologized for Croat crimes long ago, "and there's nothing to add to it."[213]

But things were no easier for Mesić during the celebrations Croatia held in Knin to mark the tenth anniversary of Operation Storm. Mesić, during his speech, made a slight reference to tolerance between ethnic groups.

> The crowd wasn't in a mood for tolerance, however, and responded to Mesic's words with cries of "Tzigan! Tzigan," a derogatory word for Roma. Neo-nazis in the crowd started to call out "Ante! Ante!" both in honor of Ante Gotovina ... as well as Ante Pavelic....[214]

Another commentator, Zvonimir Trajković, who was quoted earlier, was outraged by the fact that the bodies of civilians as well as Muslim soldiers, who died over the course of three years, were all being treated as genocide victims. He pointed out that the investigations of Serbian victims were halted by orders from The Hague Tribunal in the middle of 1997. He also discussed the case of Žepa, which fell just days after Srebrenica. The operation was run by the same Serbian officers and soldiers that took Srebrenica. There was no massacre there. He sardonically suggests that

> Perhaps the Muslims from Zepa were more likeable … and for that reason they transferred them safely to Serbia without killing anybody.[215]

Mr. Trajković also thought that the video would be used to brand the Republika Srpska as a product of genocide, and to argue that it should be dismantled. He goes on to skewer the irresponsibility of Serbian politicians and the present government. He argues that "our tragedy is not Srebrenica." It is instead

> the existing puppet government that does not try to fight for the truth, to defend national dignity and Serb interests. Our tragedy is the fact that our state politics is in the hands of Natasa Kandic and the band of other foreign hirelings, because our President apologizes under orders from the West without caring about possible consequences for the state and the nation.[216]

Mr. Trajkovic concludes:

> For the Serbian people it would be ideal if the whole truth could be presented. We the Serbs, for the sake of the truth, have an obligation to respond fiercely to the lies and false constructions because it is the only way for our nation to undergo a real catharsis. *It is a crime to kill one man, to say nothing of the cold-blooded killing of six fellows. However, such crimes are acts of ill-minded individuals who have first names and family names and who should be tried in a court, without any doubt.* In the recent civil and religious clashes in these areas there were various awful crimes on all sides. We should not create epopees from some of them and forget the others as if that they had never happened.[217] [Emphasis added.]

Milivoje Ivanišević, president of the Belgrade Center for Researching Crimes against Serbs, determined that 3,227 Serbs had been killed or died as a result of torture in the Srebrenica area between 1992 and 1995. This figure stands opposed to the 1,800 identified Bosnian Muslims, largely soldiers, who are buried in Potoćari. He emphasized that these were not the final figures. The evidence included photographs, eyewitness testimony, statements from relatives, municipal death certificates, data on cemetery plots, and priests' diaries.[218] Thus, more Serbs lie dead and buried in Srebrenica than Bosnian Muslims do.

Professor Raymond Kent brought up an interesting point with respect Muslim claims about the number of dead:

> In a single military battle, Mladic defeated the U.S.-trained Bosnian Muslims elite Vth Army Corps. It lost some 10,000 men in it. Their bodies have not been found at the battle ground and the Serb Army had no stake in seeking to hide them since they were casualties of a military confrontation. Professor J.P. Maher, from Chicago, asked the salient question at a panel meeting on the Berkeley Campus of the University of California—"where are the bodies?" A logical follow-up might ask to what political use might these bodies have been put?[219]

(*See* "To The Hague with Gen. Galvin; Gen. Mladic to West Point, by T.W. ("Bill") Carr on p. 516 in the Appendices.)

And when the Serbs mourned their dead to mark the tenth anniversary of Srebrenica, not one foreign official attended the Serbian commemoration despite the invitations that had been given.[220]

Nearly all of the articles from the Western mainstream media repeated old media lies. First and foremost was the media lie that 200,000 or 250,000 people had been killed during the Bosnian War when the actual figure is closer to 100,000, as established by Norwegian demographers (*see* p. 346).

Old false witnesses were trotted out to bear false testimony once again. Mevludin Orić, Naser Orić's cousin, was among them. He claimed that he had lain for hours under a pile of corpses while Bosnian Serb soldiers killed thousands of his fellow Muslims in the fields around Srebrenica. "'How is it possible they still can't arrest him [i.e., Mladić]? Ten years is a long time.... Like Bosnia is as big as America and they can't find him,' the skinny 35-year-old told Reuters."[221]

Orić even claims to have seen General Mladić peer through the door of a school gym where Orić was allegedly kept before the executions began.

> "People whispered: look, it's Mladic. There he stood with his bodyguards, looking over the gym, laughing," Oric recalls.[222]

Has anyone though to ask Mevludin Orić why General Mladić, a military commander, needed body guards? In any case, contrast Mr. Orić's statements with those of Samir Fehtić, a Bosnian Muslim soldier serving in the 28th Division, who really was in Srebrenica.

> After the fall of Srebrenica I found myself a prisoner. They treated us very correctly and humanely. One day the commander, General Mladic, came personally and asked us if we were being mistreated, and whether we had water and food. He said that all those of us who were not criminals and murders would be released. He forbade all of his people from mistreating us.... Somewhat later I was released and managed to leave and join my family abroad...[223]

Retired major-general Lewis MacKenzie was the first commander of UN peacekeeping forces in Sarajevo. He published an article — the only one that appeared in a mainstream newspaper — that questioned the alleged massacre. He stated that what happened in Srebrenica was "debatable only in scale." He also questioned whether "genocide" ever took place.

> It's a distasteful point, but it has to be said that, if you're committing genocide, you don't let the women go since they are key to perpetuating the very group you are trying to eliminate.[224]

General MacKenzie also cited that The Hague's own evidence put into question the veracity of claims of "up to 8,000" Bosnian Muslims massacred. The "up to 8,000" figure includes 5,000 who were listed as missing, and the 1,800 bodies that have been identified and buried include those killed during three years of fighting in the area. "The math just doesn't support the scale of 8,000 killed."

General MacKenzie was the only commentator who noted that Naser Orić was responsible for killing as many Serbian civilians in the area surrounding Srebrenica as the Bosnian Serb army was for the deaths of Bosnian Muslims in Srebrenica.

> Two wrongs never made a right, but those moments in history that shame us all because of our indifference should not be viewed in isolation without the context that created them.[225]

Prof. Cees Wiebes (*see* p. 179-80), appeared on a BBC radio program called "The Real Slobodan Milosevic." Prof. Wiebes, being Dutch, shed some light on the operations of The Hague Tribunal. He, of course, rejected the portrayal of the Bosnian

Muslims as Good Guys and the Serbs as Villains. Even though The Hague Tribunal flies in all manner of experts to testify against the Serbs, no one is calling Prof. Wiebes, even though he is among the dozen or so people in Amsterdam who did the most exhaustive research on Srebrenica and the Bosnian War.

> We were never invited in The Hague—we're just living around the corner—and why? What I heard from good sources at the tribunal is that [the Chief Prosecutor] Ms. Del Ponte thinks we are too "nuanced," we are not seeing things in black and white, and good military experts in our team were never consulted.[226]

Thus, the media campaign is social engineering from government sponsored behaviorists who "forge" a consensus by the strict repetition of media lies. As Mr. Hermann remarked earlier: "Under these conditions, remarkable structures of disinformation can be built, institutionalized, and remain parts of historic memory even in the face of ex post [facto] confutations, which are kept out of sight."

> It is pure boilerplate, but with a very clear purpose: to associate in the minds of the audience the "genocide" in Srebrenica with World War Two and, more specifically, the Serbs with the Nazis.
>
> (…)
>
> It is a neat little redesign of reality, with a built-in emotional shield against sound judgment.[227]

Nebojsa Malic also pointed out elsewhere that:

> This isn't a debate about the numbers of Jews, Slavs and Roma murdered in Nazi concentration camps, however much the Srebrenica genocide industry seeks to make that parallel. With the Nazis, one has the books, speeches, orders, structures, organization... a mountain of evidence pointing to genocidal intent before numbers even come into consideration.[228]

But as far as Srebrenica is concerned, the "8,000 men and boys" mantra is repeated, along with the epithet, "the worst massacre since WWII" to forge a comparison between the Serbs and the Nazis. As Gen. MacKenzie remarked earlier, "the math just doesn't support the scale of 8,000 killed."

And all of this is taking its toll on Serbs, many of whom are weary of their pariah status and want to be readmitted to the world of self-respecting nations. And these Serbs are willing to see their government fulfill any Western demand so that they can consign the Balkan Wars of Succession to history and move on with their lives.

> To that end, many Serbs alternate between practicing self-censorship (it's politically incorrect in Serbia today to defend or explain Serb actions of the 90s), and self-deception, wherein Serbs manage to convince themselves that the world is right and they were the bad guys of the 1990s, themselves chiefly to blame for the civil wars that destroyed their country. In other words, the Serbs are betraying their own history.[229]

As Julia Gorin goes on to point out in this article, we're going get an earful of the Official Truth about Srebrenica, but not a peep about Bosnian charities being shut down for financing terrorism, or Sanel Sjekirica,[230] the Bosnian Muslim who engineered the Madrid bombing, or the six Algerian-born mujahideens (who took Bosnian citizenship) who are being held in Guantanamo for plotting to bomb the U.S. and British embassies in Sarajevo, or about the Bosnian embassy issuing bin Laden and his lieutenants passports, or about the suicide bombers in Iraq who have been trained in Bosnia. Europeans are just finding out what the Green Highway holds in store for them.

And we won't be hearing much about Egyptian Mohamed el-Amir, the father of Mohamed Atta, who hijacked the first plane that crashed into the World Trade Center. He said in a recent interview that there was a double standard applied to the victims of the London bombing and the victims of U.S./U.K. aggression in the Islamic world. This is undoubtedly true, however, he added that he had no regrets about the London bombings, and insisted that there were more terrorist attacks to come. He prophesied a fifty-year religious war that would produce many more holy warriors like his son, and vowed that he would do everything he could to encourage more such attacks.

> [H]e declared that terror cells around the world were a "nuclear bomb that has now been activated and is ticking." Cursing in Arabic, el-Amir also denounced Arab leaders and Muslims who condemned the London attacks as being traitors and non-Muslims.[231]

The Bosnian War is not over yet by any means. At the commemoration for the tenth anniversary for the fall of Srebrenica, Bosnian Muslims marched wearing T-shirts bearing a photo of Naser Orić, with the slogan "Is self-defense a crime?"

... They chanted "Long live the Republic of Bosnia-Herzegovina" — the name under which the Muslim-dominated government declared independence in 1992—and "Death to the Serb Republic"![232]

Did Washington Use the Same Tactics against the American People that Sarajevo Used against Its Own Citizens?

It is almost certain that U.S. intelligence services had some involvement in the Markale market place and the Vasa Miskin breadline massacres in Sarajevo. Both of these blasts were blamed on the Serbs, despite the fact that they vigorously denied any involvement in them. Besides that, a majority of the victims in both cases were ethnic Serbs—not Muslims. The Bosnian Serbs always claimed that the Izetbegović government had ordered the bombing of its own people in order to win Western sympathy and gain Western intervention. In fact, sanctions were put in place against Serbia mere days after the Vasa Miskin breadline bombing in 1992, and the Bosnian Serbs were subjected to aerial bombardment days after the Markale green market bombing in 1995. The bombings produced the desired effect of changing public opinion to meet the requirements of the U.S. and NATO actions against Serbia. *Cui bono*?

Many U.S. citizens are likewise skeptical about the claims of the 9/11 Commission. Michael Rupert of fromthewilderness.com, among others, has explored the subject extensively. The first and foremost question is whether or not the Bush II Regime engineered 9/11. For example:

Bush was *reading to 2nd graders* for the duration of the crisis.

Similarly, Rumsfeld was passively watching the attacks on TV.

Washington D.C. *was not protected by fighter jets until 10:05 a.m.*, though at 8:20 a.m., it was known that there were multiple hijackings.

The Air Force had 5 war games that morning: One was a live-fly hijack exercise; another inserted false blips onto FAA screens; another involved a mock airplane crash into a military headquarters building outside of Washington.

At least 36 very specific warnings from FBI field agents about the attacks were ignored or blocked by their bosses in Washington.

And the question of *who stood to gain*: It enabled the Bush regime to conquer Afghanistan and Iraq, to spend hundreds of billions more for

> war, to have a perpetual war, to acquire the oil, and to begin *the steady march to despotism.*[233]

Sam Gardiner taught strategy and military operations at the National War College, Air War College, and Naval War College. He has appeared frequently on NewsHour with Jim Lehrer, BBC radio and television. He wrote an article called "The Enemy Is US," examining how "the Bush administration used disinformation and psychological warfare—weapons usually used against the enemy—against the American public in order to support the war in Iraq."[234] These were techniques that the planners had learned from marketing political campaigns. The "big lie" technique was used to advance the terrorism thesis. The Bush administration's goal was to set forth enough arguments that linked Iraq to terrorism and bin Laden that the American people would be convinced that Saddam Hussein was behind the 9/11 attacks.

> They used a technique called the excluded middle. Iraq supports terrorists. The attacks were by terrorists. Iraq must been behind the 9/11 attacks.[235]

Lastly, Mr. Gardiner touched upon the failure of democratic institutions, namely the press, to counter such efforts. Washington did not trust Americans to make the "right" decision, so it made the decision for them. The tragic irony is that if the American people had known the truth, they would not have chosen to go to war. Mr. Gardiner warned:

> [A]s I said in my paper, if you think this was bad, wait until the next war. They will be even better at manipulating the story.[236]

John Loftus presented startling evidence on the July 29 edition of Fox News Channel's Day Side program that the mastermind of the 7/7 and 7/21 London Bombings, Haroon Rashid Aswat, is a double agent working for MI6, British Intelligence. He was taken on by British Intelligence to help recruit Muslim fighters to go to Kosovo in the late 1990s. In return, Aswat was the beneficiary of a hands-off policy that thwarted his arrest on many occasions. The U.S. Justice Department in Seattle tried to arrest Aswat in 1999 for trying to set up a terrorist training school in Oregon. Then Justice Department headquarters "ordered the Seattle prosecutors not to touch Aswat." He left the U.K. on July 6, the day before the London bombing, and fled to Pakistan, where he was arrested, and then released twenty-four hours later. It ought to be clear by now that al Qaeda owes its existence to the secret services of the U.S. and Great Britain.[237]

Needless to say, the 9/11 hijackers now appear likely to have been intelligence assets shielded by the CIA, if not also by MI6, who were acting as double agents, just as Mr. Aswat was.

> The Sept. 11 commission will investigate a claim that U.S. defense intelligence officials identified ringleader Mohammed Atta and three other hijackers as a likely part of an al-Qaeda cell more than a year before the hijackings but didn't forward the information to law enforcement.[238]

One should not be surprised if the top secret documents Sandy Berger stuffed into his ample trousers proved these allegations to be true.

Positions Taken
by UK Muslims after the London Bombings

Muslims were reasserting themselves in the U.K. after the London Bombings. Two competing points of view in Britain's Muslim community came to the foreground: those who advocated violence against the West, and those who wish to co-exist peacefully in Britain's secular society. One Muslim man, who wished to remain anonymous, was quoted as saying:

> "We don't need to fight. We are taking over!" he said. "We are here to bring civilization to the West. England does not belong to the English people, it belongs to God."[239]

A moderate Muslim, said of the bombings:

> "It's not a surprise but I am still shocked," he said. "How can they do this? London is a city for all the world. This is not Islam."[240]

Perhaps it is Islam, after all. Radical Muslims have already begun Islamizing British cities in a bid to increase their political power. Muslim groups in Glasgow petitioned the City Council to prevent an Italian restaurant from serving alcohol to patrons seated at sidewalk tables. Hospitals in Leicester are considering banning Bibles from hospital wards to "avoid offending Muslim patients." A group called Muslims Against Advertising have begun painting over billboards they found "offensive to Islam." Their targets are "ads for jeans, perfume, and lingerie."[241]

But it will not end there. Educated U.K. Muslims have begun to embrace militant Islamic movements, such as Hizb ut-Tahrir (the Party of Liberation).

> The party's stated goal is to rebuild the Caliphate—the Muslim state dissolved with the fall of the Ottoman Empire—to displace corrupt dictators in the Muslim world, and to instill Islamic mores and Islamize almost every aspect of daily life.[242]

Both men who were interviewed for this article referred to Bosnia (i.e., Srebrenica) and the Persian Gulf War as the "spark" for their activism.

By early August 2005, Tony Blair indicated that he intended to ban Hizb ut-Tahrir. Hizb ut-Tahrir officials shot back that the U.K. government's proposals were part of an "anti-Islamic" agenda and could "trigger civil unrest," because there were warnings that the U.K.'s worsening Christian-Muslim relations could lead to a repeat of the inner-city riots of the 1980s. Many analysts think that Hizb ut-Tahrir's fundamentalist views aided the radicalization of young British Muslims.

> The National Union of Students banned Hizb ut-Tahrir from campuses in 1995 after its speeches, leafleting and methods in a number of universities caused worry and distress. Leaflets called for Muslims to 'exterminate' the Jewish authorities in Israel.[243]

Shiv Malik, who had exclusive access to Hizb ut-Tahrir's inner circle, spent two months investigating Britain's largest radical Islamic group. Zeyno Baran, the Nixon Centre's director of International Security and Energy Programmes, warned Malik that

> Hizb produced thousands of manipulated brains, which then 'graduate' from Hizb and become members of groups like al-Qa'ida.... Even if Hizb does not itself engage in terrorist acts, because of the ideology it provides, it acts like a conveyor belt for terrorists.[244]

Hizb ut-Tahrir has urged members of the Muslim community not to vote in recent U.K. general elections because "they would be participating in a society run by kaffirs or non-believers." It routinely promulgates separatist positions and sends an anti-assimilation message, which, until recently, was dispensed with a strong dose of anti-Semitism. Germany banned the group in 2003 for precisely this reason.

Hizb ut-Tahrir's simple, childlike answers to complex problems is directed to millions of Muslims through the internet, pamphlets and clandestine schools. Ms. Baran refers to it as a "war of ideologies, and the terrorist acts are the tip of the iceberg."

Even though Hizb ut-Tahrir has urged Muslims to "'extermi-nate' the Jewish authorities of Israel," Imran Waheed, a spokesman for Hizb, had the brassbound nerve to describe the party as having a "fifty-year history of non-violence," and that banning it would lead to many question whether or not "freedom of speech" still exists.

In fact, the former leader of Hizb, Omar Bakri Mohammed, had to resign from the organization after he referred to John Major as a "legitimate target" during Gulf War I. Then the Jordanian leadership of Hizb decided to clean up its image, and sent Bakri establish al-Muhajiroun (*see* pp. 191, 196).

The U.S. Justice Department arrested members of the New York branch of Al-Muhajiroun in 2003. They found plans to blow up two different subway stations in New York City. The remainder of the group is under surveillance.

> But the US was used by Al-Muhajiroun for training of people to send to Kosovo. ....[T]he leaders all worked for British intelligence in Kosovo. ...British intelligence actually hired some Al-Qaeda guys to help defend Muslim rights in Albania and Kosovo. That's when Al-Muhajiroun got started.[245]

In fact, Omar Bakri skipped town rather than face treason charges for the moral support he lent to the London bombers. He caused a scandal when he remarked that he would not advise the police if he had knowledge of an impending bomb attack in the U.K. Mr. Bakri was one of three Islamic fundamentalist clerics who was going to be investigated by Crown Prosecution Service lawyers and police. Anjem Choudray, Mr. Bakri's spokesman, gave a spectacularly lame excuse for his master's sudden departure. He told Channel 4 News that Mr. Bakri had been "demonized for many years" in the UK. Besides that,

> It's an obligation on Muslims that if they can't fulfill their Islamic duties in a certain place then they need to ... emigrate to a place where they can, where their lives and their religion is protected." Defending Mr. Bakri's comments, he said it was an "Islamic duty" to protect Muslims from non-Muslim authorities even if they were oppressors.[246]

To cap it all off, Dr. Mohammed Naseem, chairman of Birmingham Central Mosque, said that there were "'similarities' between new powers to tackle Islamist extremism and Hitler's demonisation of the Jews." He made this remark in response to anti-terrorism proposals made by the British government.

> He [Hitler] was democratically elected and gradually he created a bogey identity, that is, the Jewish people, and posed to the Germans that they were a threat to the country.
>
> On that basis, he started a process of elimination of Jewish people.
>
> I see the similarities. Everything moves step by step. I am saying these are dangerous times and we must take note of this.[247]

One has to admire the hutzpah Mr. Naseem displays here: Muslims are the "new" Jews. But he is simply amplifying a perception that James Harff of Ruder-Finn first expostulated: Serbs=Nazis, therefore Bosnian Muslims=Jews. Now it has come home to roost.

The pattern of home-grown Islamic fundamentalism in Europe, the question of integrating Europe's communities into the mainstream has become an urgent question in response to a rising tide of Islamophobia. A recent poll indicated that:

> A large majority of people polled in countries such as Britain, France, Germany, Spain and the Netherlands believe Muslims coming into their country want to be distinct from the broader society rather than adopt their new country's customs.[248]

A majority of the Europeans surveyed responded that there was a growing sense of Islamic identity in Muslim communities, and thought this was not a good sign for their respective countries. Yet this pleases the fundamentalists. Amin al-Husseini would have been proud of his disciples. His pioneering policies in creating divisiveness have polarized Muslims, Christians, Jews and secularists. There is no more credible middle ground left for Muslims in the face of the skyrocketing hate-crimes committed against them in the U.K. One is either a Muslim or not. Christians, Jews and secularists are left divided among themselves to argue about to what extent they may uphold a "free," "multi-cultural" and "multi-confessional" society. Liberals urge us to regard the attackers simply as criminals, which they most certainly are. However, religion is at the bottom of it, because: 1) Islam rewards terrorists for suicide attacks (they become *šehit*s); 2) such attacks contribute to the re-establishment of the world caliphate; and 3) such attacks put U.K./U.S. imperialist ambitions at risk.

Bin Laden's formula for bankrupting the West is working. The London bombers probably spent less than $50,000 to carry out the attacks; however, the losses in revenue due to government compensation for the victims (as well as compensation allegedly offered to the parents of Brazilian Jean Charles de Menezes, who was ignominiously gunned down by London police on July 22, 2005), the money lost in hotel bookings, lost ticket sales on the London Underground, losses to London restaurants, money spent on extra policing, revenues lost from London tourism, and lost revenue from London retailers was estimated to amount to nearly $2 billion. Bin Laden's formula is holding fast.[249]

One has to look to Serbia for a successful model for Muslim-Christian relations. Serbia is the only multicultural and multi-confessional society left in the Balkans. The only other alternative for the West is the Spanish solution of 1492, the Inquisition, which, by its own reprehensible nature, disqualifies itself.

> What would happen if 2/3 of Serbia's Muslims were considering emigrating to another country, fearing Christian Serbs?
>
> (…)
>
> Only, the Muslims who are considering emigration and fear of assault and humiliation don't live in Serbia, but in the UK! They fear not Serbs, but those very same Brits who so conscientiously care for Muslims in Bosnia and Kosovo. Of course, the British will never be collectively blamed, let alone punished, for these assaults on their fellow Muslim citizens. The people to pay the price will again be—the Serbs![250]

For this reason, the article concludes, London and Washington are still keeping the presence of al-Qaeda and mujahideen in Bosnia and Kosovo a secret. They have a whipping boy, Serbia, to show the Muslim world how much they really care about them.

The Sixtieth Anniversary of the Closing of the Jasenovac Concentration Camp

There was another anniversary besides the fall of Srebrenica. On the one hand, Western media commemorated the sixtieth anniversary of the liberation of Auschwitz, the largest WWII concentration camp; on the other hand, the Western media turned its back on reporting any aspect of the commemorations marking the shutting down of the Jasenovac concentration camp, and the heroic break out of several hundred of its inmates. Christopher

Deliso noted that Google listed 59,000 entries for "January's Auschwitz memorial—even though it ignored Sunday's memorial for the largest of Croatia's wartime concentration camps."[251] Only three Western sources mentioned the Jasenovac commemoration, even though it was not held in some remote Bosnian town, but in New York City and was attended by worldwide Jewish groups.

> It was organized by the Jasenovac Research Institute, which recently petitioned the Croatian government to give reparations to Jewish survivors of Jasenovac, as the German government has done. In a circular letter of 25 February to the EU Presidency, JRI National Coordinator Barry Lituchy wrote:

> "...Croatia's refusal to come to terms with its past crimes is in direct contravention of the laws and practices of the European Union. To allow Croatia entry in to the European Union without forcing it to resolve its longstanding disputes with its own Holocaust victims would constitute both an in insult and an injury to these victims as well as a travesty of immense proportions.

> To allow Croatia's entry under such conditions would inevitably harm and undermine the reputation and stature of the E.U., for these are claims that will never go away or be forgotten. They must be settled legally and it is yours and the European Union's responsibility to recognize this beforehand. I feel certain you will agree."[252]

Barry Lituchy has done more than anyone else in order to gain official recognition of the Jasenovac concentration camp and what happened there. Mr. Lituchy is responsible for the first public monument ever devoted to the Jasenovac concentration camp outside of the former Yugoslavia, which was unveiled at the ceremonies marking the sixtieth anniversary of the end of the Holocaust. Mr. Lituchy's efforts also resulted in New York Mayor Michael Bloomberg proclaiming April 17, 2005 to be Jasenovac Commemoration Day in New York City.

> Some two hundred people attended the ceremony in Brooklyn, including U.S. Congressman Anthony Weiner, New York City Ombudsman Ralph Perfetto, Radio Commentator Barry Farber, eight Survivors and Jewish Partisan fighters from Yugoslavia, and diplomats representing three countries: Israel, Serbia & Montenegro, and Bosnia & Herzegovina.

> (...)

> At the ceremony John Ranz, Buchenwald Survivor, wartime Partisan and JRI Director, noted that it was "an historic day ... for from this

day forward Serbian and Roma victims of the Holocaust shall forever be remembered with their fellow Jewish brothers and sisters with whom they shared the same fate, and the same graves." The monument was established through the efforts of the Jasenovac Research Institute which has organized the annual Jasenovac Day Commemoration at the park for the past four years.

(…)

On behalf of the Survivors and victims' families, JRI Founder Barry Lituchy thanked the Mayor, Congressman Weiner, and New York Ombudsman Ralph Perfetto for their help in obtaining the monument. Holocaust Park founders Pauline and Ira Bilus warmly welcomed the participation and inclusion of Jasenovac on an equal footing with Auschwitz, Dachau and Buchenwald. A letter from U.S. Holocaust Memorial Museum Chairman Fred Zeidman did the same….

Religious services were conducted by Father Djokan Majstorovic of St. Sava's Serbian Orthodox Church in New York who also blessed the monument. After Father Djokan, Rabbi Dr. Ephraim Issac, a member of the JRI Advisory Board and head of the Department of Semitic Studies at Princeton University, also said Kaddish for the victims…. Elisa Gutman lit a candle in the memory of her father killed at Jasenovac while Ana Beck lit another in memory of the Jews from other parts of Yugoslavia killed by German, Croatian, Muslim and Albanian fascists.

Anna Beck spoke movingly prior to the candle lighting of how she personally witnessed the mass murder of Jews and Serbs on the frozen Danube in Novi Sad in January 1942. Ricki Danon Soltan and Michael Danon recalled how they survived, while their fathers were murdered in Jasenovac along with many other members of their family. Alexander Mosic spoke on behalf of fellow Jewish Partisans and Survivors from former Yugoslavia. Survivor Eva Deutsch Costabel recalled how members of her family were killed by the Ustashe.

The Ambassador of Bosnia and Herzegovina to the U.S., H.E. Igor Davidovic, spoke movingly about the murder of his grandfather at Jasenovac. Dan Kapper, representing the State of Israel, warmly congratulated the JRI and all participants for the establishment of the Jasenovac monument and reminded all of the dire need to strengthen our remembrance activities in he face of growing threats from anti-Semitism, racism and neo-Nazism….

JRI Founder Barry Lituchy reminded the participants that justice and recognition for the victims of the Holocaust in Yugoslavia has not come without hard struggle: "The lessons of the Holocaust were bitterly learned and on this day we must remind ourselves of them as we honor the victims. The victims speak to us still, reminding us "Da Se

Ne Zaboravi!" ("So that you may never forget!") On April 17th we did not forget—we honored our martyrs in a manner they long deserved, with a permanent monument, forever."[253]

Serbs and Americans

As much of this book has been devoted to General Mladić as to a systematic review of one spectacular miscalculation after another by American leaders, be they Democrats or Republicans. The New World Order is based on a crime whose guilt will never be expiated.

America is no longer a republic but an empire, and its adventures abroad in search of world domination will end badly because the empire will surely come crashing down one day, as all other empires have. Only the date and the time have to be set. We shall be set free the day when America retracts to its continental borders and once again preoccupies itself with Americans and Americana.

The United States and the EU ought to find their soul, and behave correctly in the former Yugoslavia by withdrawing their armed forces, their NGOs, their regional corporate headquarters, their globalist bureaucrats and advisors, and by paying just war reparations to the Serbs, as well as to others whom they have injured: the people who still call themselves Yugoslavs, moderate Muslims, Croats, Albanians and others. The 1999 bombardment of Serbia caused $30 billion worth of damage to the country. That does not even take into consideration the extensive damage caused by NATO bombardment in Bosnia in 1995. Treble damages are calculated because it was an act of illegal aggression, a crime, a mistake, an error in judgment arising from *hubris*. Therefore, the U.S. and NATO countries are obliged pay Serbia at least $90 billion in reparations, and leave.

Even so, that is not really very much money considering the $500 billion in damages we suffered from the 9/11 attacks, as cited by Mr. bin Laden above. Our leaders, in their infinite wisdom, sacrificed a pawn only to lose their queen a few moves later. We can now look forward to paying out $500 billion periodically until al-Qaeda bleeds us white as it did Russia. And it will only end after we have spent our last $500 billion. So, $90 billion in reparations is really a frugal and elegant solution. Western civilization would realize extraordinary benefits by having Serbia play its historic role as the bulwark against radical Islam: al-Qaeda would lose its forward base in Europe; the green highway would hit a dead end; and Europe would be safer from terrorist attacks, as would America. But it may be too late to ask the Serbs to resume their historic role.

> I am convinced that the actual leadership (from the arrival of DOS to power in Serbia in 2000) has destroyed our army in order to create some kind of antiterrorist army phalanxes that will instead of NATO soldiers die in different war hot spots in the world. It is even heard that Serbs, since they have nothing to offer the EU besides the fight against terrorism, and it is admitted that they were successful in this fight (but remember where are now Serb generals), they should therefore be the dam against the invasion of Muslim terrorism into clean, tidy, rich, catholic and protestant Europe. If Serbs are crazy, like their government is perfidious, only then should they defend again the Christian West. Because of this they had been already decimated. Remember Serbian history and Kosovo Field tragedy and other Serbian fights against the expansion of Muslim Ottoman Empire toward Western Europe.... Serbs are not guilty for the fact that the Balkan is the natural bridge for expansion of Muslim terrorism toward "developed, democratic" rich EU, and the must not pick up the chestnuts from the fire for the EU.[254]

Recently, an uproar arose over $520. That is the amount of Ratko Mladić's pension. A member of his family, probably his son, picked up the check every month. Carla del Ponte seized the occasion to charge that elements of the Serbian army were sheltering Mladić. Boris Tadić, who is described as Serbia's pro-Western president, had to make a statement emphasizing that Mladić's family was entitled to the money under Serbian law; however, paying the pension did not mean that Belgrade authorities had any idea of his whereabouts.[255]

NATO-led "peacekeepers" inflicted one final indignity by raiding General Mladić's mother's house after she died. The operation was conducted by Italian carabinieri, but they did not find General Mladić. An SFOR spokesman told BBC News that Mrs. Mladić's remains were not in the house at the time of the raid. SRNA (the Bosnian Serb news agency) reported that troops spent one and one-half hours searching the village of Kasindol. They were backed up by four helicopters, combat vehicles and dogs.

NATO helicopters were even circling Mrs. Mladić's house when she died. "S-FOR regretted the timing of the raid ... and was aware that it could be seen as in poor taste." One has to admire the judicious use of the subjunctive in the preceding sentence, along with the dulcifying phrase, "poor taste." It was, instead, the defilement of a burial ceremony by harassing and threatening a bereaved family. We call ourselves "humans," which derives from the Latin word *humus*, which means *earth*. We are humans not because we come from the earth, but because only we bury our dead in the earth. This is what distinguishes us from animals. SFOR's actions must be seen in this light. They are inhuman. The SFOR spokesman concluded: "However, it's more important for the people of Bosnia-Herzegovina that we carry out our mandate."[256]

Much more recently, a team of NATO and EUFOR soldiers searched the house of Milica Avram, sister of General Ratko Mladić.

> "Soldiers in black uniform entered the house around 1000 [0900 gmt] without any search warrant. They frightened our two-year old grandchild and during the search, which lasted over one hour, held us at gun-point," Milica's husband and owner of the house in the Vojkovici suburb, Radivoje Avram, told SRNA.[257]

A computer, family photo albums and memorabilia were taken. Avram said that his family had been harassed by occupation soldiers earlier during the funeral of his mother-in-law, Mladić's mother. Derek Chappell, spokesman for NATO HQ in Sarajevo, had this to say:

> Support for war crimes suspects is a threat to progress in Bosnia-Herzegovina. That support is illegal and immoral and represents a direct challenge to the rule of law.[258]

Unless Mladić is caught, new sanctions will be introduced, The Hague Tribunal will effect new kidnappings of Serbian "suspects," and we shall witness a continuing cavalcade of self-congratulatory headlines: *NATO Warns Karadžić and Mladić*; *Massacre Suspect Dines in the Shadow of War Crimes Officials*; *U.S. to World's Newest Nation — Capture 'Mad' Balkan General*; *Raid on Mladić Dead Mother's House*; *Fugitive Mladić Has Disappeared from Serbia*; *Police Source Says, Hide in Plain Sight*; *US Plays Aid*

Card to Fix War Crimes Exemption; *Yugoslavia Risks U.S. Aid if Mladić Stays Free*; *Serbia Appeals for Help in Search of War Crimes Fugitive Mladić*; *Report Says Mladić 'Escaped from Serbia Last Month'*; *War Crimes Fugitive Mladić Urged to Surrender*; *War Crimes Suspect Mladić not in Serbia — Officials*; *NATO Chief Says Belgrade 'Obliged' to Arrest, Hand over Mladić*; *Serb Police Launch Mladić Search — PM*; *Mladić a 'Priority' for Serbia*; and *Serbs See Elusive Mladić as Hague's Real Target*.

"Capturing Mladić" might as well have been a Summer 2005 replacement series. Even though Mladić has not been seen or heard from in four years, he dominated the headlines. As mentioned earlier, the ICTY is supposed to wind down its operations by 2008, so time is running out for Carla Del Ponte.

> "I need Karadzic and Mladic in The Hague before 11 July to be able to participate in the commemoration of Srebrenica," said Hague Prosecutor Carla Del Ponte.[259]

Del Ponte was so embarrassed about Mladić not having been captured that she cannot show her face at the commemoration without a feather in her cap. Failing that:

> She knew that a picture, and much more a video, are worth thousands of pages of even the most graphic atrocity descriptions in today's visuals-driven popular imagination.[260]

But Serbian support for General Mladić remains strong. As early as March 2005, posters appeared in Belgrade that depicted Mladic saluting in full military uniform. The posters bore the words: "(Mladić) for Chief of Staff."[261] The posters also bore the date 1389, marking the date of the Battle of Kosovo.

Soon after the release of the video of the execution of the six Bosnian Muslims, the media issued a series of reports about General Mladić's imminent capture. Here is a sampling: "Serb Govt Denies Negotiating with War Crimes Suspect," June 8, 2005, *AP*; "Mladic 'Will soon Be in Custody'," *BBC News*, June 9, 2005; "War Crimes Suspect Mladic Found: Report," June 10, 2005, *AP*; this last article was contradicted later that same day by "Serbian Police Chief: Mladic Not Found; Search Underway," June 10, 2005, *AP* (which actually admitted that there was a dilemma regarding how to conduct the operation so that there would be no casualties and so that Mladić would be captured alive); "U.S. Lifts Aid Ban on Serbia, Urges Arrest of Top War Crimes Fugitive," *AP*, June 10, 2005 ("[Nicholas] Burns … cannot imagine a more appropriate initiative than to see Gen. Mladic in The Hague for the massacre's tenth anniversary"); "Serbs Hunting Mladic Fear Shoot-Out or Suicide," by Vesna Peric Zimonjic, *The Independent* (UK), June 11, 2005 (sources close to Mladić said that they doubted that he would surrender. "He'd rather kill himself—negotiations are out of the question"); and "Accused Serb Commander Said Unlikely to Surrender," by Jovana Gec, *AP*, June 11, 2005:

> But in a sign of continued support for Mladic among nationalists in Serbia, graffiti praising the fugitive general appeared in Belgrade on buildings along the main road reading "Mladic Our Hero" and "Srebrenica Liberation".

Then came one of the most preposterous stories: "Mladic 'Will Surrender' to UN War Crimes Tribunal," by Ian Bruce, *The Herald* (UK), June 15, 2005

> A NATO source said: "He is seeking cast-iron assurances over the financial security and physical safety of his family if he surrenders. "With the amount of financial leverage being exerted by the U.S., it is only a matter of time before he is taken by force. He is running out of options."

Then a deal was reportedly struck, according to "Mladic Puts Price on His Own Head," by Eve-Ann Prentice and Tom Walker, timesonline.co.uk, June 19, 2005.

> One of Europe's most wanted war crimes suspects, General Ratko Mladic, has struck a deal for $5m (£2.75m) "compensation" if he gives himself up before the 10th anniversary of the Srebrenica massacre in Bosnia — which was carried out by his forces.
>
> (…)
>
> Tomislav Nikolic … urged Mladic to commit suicide rather than give himself up.

The "capturing Mladić" frenzy turned out to be manufactured news for public consumption. All of these stories were built around Dragan Pecanac, chief of staff in Mladić's cabinet in the Republika Srpska Army Command during the Bosnian war. Mr. Pecanac moved to Belgrade after the war, where he runs a security agency. Even though Mladić cut off Pecanac in 1999, and has not spoken to him since, Pecanac, notwithstanding his ignorance of Mladić's whereabouts, offered his good offices for Mladić's surrender. No one who was acquainted with Mladić ever believed for a moment that he would surrender. In fact, foreign diplomats in Belgrade hold the same opinion. "As soon as he learned that somebody was negotiating about surrender, Mladić would refuse to have anything to do with them any more."[262]

There is still a $5 million bounty riding on his head, and well-equipped mercenaries have been spotted in the triangle between western Serbia, northern Montenegro and eastern Bosnia. The bounty-hunters will have their work cut out for them.

> "I would die to protect him," Zeakovic said. "Mladic is our icon. I keep his portrait right next to the icon of St. Nicholas, my patron saint. Whoever touches him will pay dearly."
>
> (...)
>
> He dismissed reports that the fugitive general has left Balkans and possibly fled to Russia. "He would never abandon his people. He is here. High in the mountains, like an eagle."[263]

Then there was a report that the Serbian secret service knew where Ratko Mladić was, and had been shadowing him for over a month.[264] Finally, sobriety set in the week before the anniversary of the fall of Srebrenica. "We must be serious, their arrest is impossible by Monday," said Gen. Dragomir Adnan, the Bosnian Serb intelligence chief. Even so, British Maj. Gen. David Leakey said that "the net is closing in" on Mladić. "It's a bit like getting Osama bin Laden,"[265] he said, succinctly conveying the depth of his own ignorance.

But Serbs remain united in the belief that Mladić should not go to The Hague. A recent poll suggested that 90% of Serbs oppose Mladić's extradition.[266]

* * *

I have exceeded my intended length for this chapter, just as the repercussions of General Mladić's tragedy have had farther-reaching effects than his original error in judgment.

There will be no peace in Bosnia until the Bosnian Muslim perpetrators of the Bosnian catastrophe are brought to justice for their crimes. It is too late for Alija Izetbegović, who conveniently died before the ICTY could issue an indictment. On one occasion, Carla Del Ponte remarked that if Izetbegović (and Tudjman) were alive, they would have been indicted. It begs the question, why did they sit on the indictments for nearly a decade? It is not, however, too late for Ejup Ganić, Rusmir Mahmutcehajić, Omer Behman, Haris Silajdžić and others. The price for their Islamic fanaticism has been paid over several times in Bosnia by the Serbs, whereas we in the U.S. are just beginning to pay the price for having supported Islamic fundamentalism.

It is too late for Franjo Tudjman and Gojko Sušak, who also died before the ICTY could issue an indictment. And it is too late for Robin Cook. But it is not too late for Stipe Mesić, Dinko Šakić, Marko Perković-Thompson, Klaus Kinkel, Helmut Kohl, Margaret Thatcher, Tony Blair and a host of others.

Here in United States, we ought to prosecute Bill Clinton, Madeleine Albright, Richard Holbrooke, Sandy Berger, Anthony Lake, Warren Christopher and their minions for the crimes they have committed, but I doubt that it will ever happen. I leave it to others to indict the current administration, whose shortcomings and transgressions are well known.

Richard Holbrooke admitted in his book, *To End a War* (Modern Library, 1999), that he used Milošević to manipulate the Bosnian Serbs.

> [H]e reveals enough information on himself to be hauled to the Hague for any real justice and calls the history the Serbs tried to tell him "historical bullshit." It's hard to imagine someone so arrogant, yet Clinton must be held accountable for allowing such an ignoramus to represent the American people.[267]

Holbrooke's scornful dismissal of Serbian history must be taken as attempted censorship, in this case animated by a vulgar populist streak. History is not over; it follows us like a ghost; it is a nightmare from which no one ever awakens. Surely, enough has been revealed here to make Richard Holbrooke eat his words. But the pleasure of beholding Mr. Holbrooke degust and ingurgitate his own words will not make America whole again, nor will it heal the damage done to Serbia. Instead, Holbrooke eating his own words stands as a luminous image of our plight.

In closing, I want to say that I had the privilege of meeting a soldier who fought with General Mladić. According to an anecdote he related, Mladić wanted to go from Romanija to Novi Sarajevo, where the Serbs were holding a picnic. Mladić wanted to dance the *kolo*. His fellow soldiers advised him not to go because the road was not secure, and there was a chance that he could be captured by Muslims.

"If you see the Muslims stop me on the way, just fire on us with mortars, and take us all out. Don't let them take me alive."

The sentiment General Mladić was expressing is one that we Americans are familiar with: "Give me liberty, or give me death."

And Mladić danced the *kolo* in Serbian Sarajevo.

By sharing this anecdote, I mean to impart courage to my fellow Americans, because difficult times lie ahead. We have been misled, impoverished, and deprived of our civil rights by our own leaders, who have consistently treated the American people as their enemy; and now we face the new dilemma of having these same leaders promise to lead us out of the difficulties in which they themselves first embroiled us.

The tragic theatre reminds us that unethical means to achieve a worthy goal are likely to end in self destruction. Raw power defies criticism and institutional restraint. And casting one's self as the good guy in the fight against evil is so alluring that one wants to keep playing the role over and over again, even after circumstances have changed, indeed, even after one finds one's self in an entirely different play.[268]

There is yet one more latent tragedy that has not been touched upon. Years of television, social engineering, and pop culture have purged Americans of civil disobedience, and have turned us into a nation of sheep. As we drift ever closer to a police state, Americans are being subjected to greater pressures than ever before to conform and express homogenous opinions.

> Here's a new slogan for the zeitgeist: stay quiet and you'll be OK. This was the message, according to the tapes released last week, that Muhammad Atta gave to the passengers on the ill-fated airplane that he and his fellow terrorists had commandeered.[269]

The Americans in that plane stayed quiet, but if others do so, the global jihad will continue to advance on all fronts: in Bosnia and Kosovo, in Iraq and Afghanistan, and from Israel to Indonesia, and from Western Europe to the U.S.

> and if you think we will not feel its impact here, just remember where Atta was when he said those words, and what happened next.[270]

Now think, instead, of the passengers of United Airlines Flight 93 who did not stay quiet, who rose to fight the hijackers. They were good old Americans who smoked and drank and swore and had guts. They stood up to a handful of pugs who thought they could hijack a plane, and they went down fighting rather than let the hijackers have their way. The passengers of Flight 93 stood up for themselves and they prevented an even greater catastrophe from occurring. They are heroes who will inspire us to stand up to not only a burley terrorist with a box cutter, but to stand up to our own home-grown terrorists who have gutted American industry and have urged the U.S. armed forces to burglarize foreign countries for profit. Todd Beemer, Thomas Burnett, Jr., and Jeremy Glick were among the leaders of the passenger revolt on Flight 93. They came to know the unthinkable after they were tipped off on their cell phones of the other three flights that had been hijacked. They digested the news, took a vote among the passengers, and acted. Now, perhaps, Americans can appreciate what Kosovo means to the Serbs. The Serbs, instead of being one hundred years behind the United States, are perhaps six hundred years ahead. Seventy seven thousand Serbs died on St. Vitus Day fighting an Islamic invasion because they believed in their cause and wanted to preserve their way of life. They saved Europe from a Muslim invasion, and got nothing for it except for the privilege of surviving and calling themselves Serbs. "War is a racket," said Gen. Smedley Butler, but fighting for your survival is not.

Ratko Mladić's tragic story is vast in scope: the untimely death of his father; betrayal by his fellow countrymen; the call to arms against the same fascist forces his father had fought and died fighting against; his heroic defiance of the great powers; the glimmers of victory; defeat at the hands of incomparably more powerful global forces; and finally, living out his last days as a fugitive in his own country, facing life in the shadow of death and disaster. Mladić, after having confronted the inexorable workings of fate, achieves unexpected grandeur and dignity in such extreme circumstances. One may, once having followed the arc of his tragedy, feel ennobled and chastened by his experience.

Americans can now fully appreciate Marko Kraljević, and his spirited response to the Sultan's decree:

Sultan Suleiman issued a decree:
Drinking wine during Ramadan was forbidden,
Wearing a green tunic was forbidden,
Carrying a tempered sword was forbidden,
Dancing kolos with women was forbidden,
But Marko danced the kolo with women,
And Marko girded his tempered sword,
And Marko dressed in tunics green
And Marko drank wine during Ramadan.
And he forced *hodja*s and *hadji*s
To join him in cup after cup of wine.[271]

This is how the defiant Serbian spirit halted Islamic incursions into Europe.[272] I invite Americans and Europeans, Christians and Jews, secularists and the religiously minded, Democrats and Republicans, the rich and the poor, black and white, native born and foreign born, optimists and pessimists, and the high and the low to convene, unite and drink wine with Marko during Ramadan.

ENDNOTES

[1] *See* "Clinton-Approved Iranian Arms Transfers Help Turn Bosnia into a Militant Islamic Base," United States Republican Policy Committee, 1/16/97, senate.gov. The policy paper is available on the web, and it is recommended to read the report in its entirety for the full dimensions of the Clinton administration's involvement with Islamic fundamentalism.

[2] "No Defense for Sandy Berger," *The Madison Capital Times* (WI), posted on commondreams.org, 7/23/04.

[3] "Clinton Aide Investigated for Taking Classified Memos," *MSNBC News,* 7/20/04.

[4] "Bush Aides Block Clinton's Papers from 9/11 Panel," by Philip Shenon and David E. Sanger, *The New York Times*, 4/1/04.

[5] "Secrets and Lies Becoming Commonplace," by Walter Cronkite, 4/5/04, commondreams.org.

[6] "Richard A. Clarke, A Liar," by Srdja Trifkovic, chroniclesmagazine.org, 4/2/04.

[7] "CIA Official Challenges Agency on Terrorism," by Josh Meyer, *Los Angeles Times*, 11/9/04, www.commondreams.org.

[8] *Ibid.*

[9] These questions were suggested by Alida Weber's article, "Why Aren't They Asking the Balkans Questions at the 9-11 Hearings?" 4/19/04, www. serbianna.com.

[10] "You Are Only Allowed to See Bosnia in Black and White," by Brendan O'Neill, 1/23/04, spiked-online.com.

[11] "In Rebuilt Bosnia, No Terror Toehold," by Colin Woodard, *Christian Science Monitor*, 3/24/04.

[12] *Ibid.*

[13] "Leader of Bosnia's Islamic Community Speaks Out,"by Patrick Moore, *Radio Fee Europe* (rferl.org) 4/23/04.

[14] "Reis Ceric's Call to War," by Igor Gajic, *Reporter*, Banja Luka (Republika Srpska), May 23, 2001.

[15] *Ibid.*

[16] *Gorski vijenac,* see http://www.njegos.org/petrovics/mwreath.htm for the unabridged Internet edition in English. Petar II Petrović Njegoš (1813-1851) is one of the greatest Serbian poets. *Gorski vijenac* ("The Mountain Wreath") is his epic masterpiece, and it has been banned in Bosnia. The epic poem presents the Serbs on the verge of extinction in Montenegro as they face a Muslim invasion. Njegoš' ancestor, a Prince-Bishop of Montenegro, faces the stark choice between extermination and all out war, so he grimly convenes the remaining Serbs and calls for the slaughter of the converts to Islam.

[17] "Reis Ceric's Call to War," by Igor Gajic, *Reporter*, Banja Luka (Republika Srpska), *op. cit.*

[18] "Leader of Bosnia's Islamic Community Speaks Out," by Patrick Moore, *Radio Fee Europe* (rferl.org), *op. cit.*

[19] "Bosnian Serb Ex-Camp Inmates' Body Condemns Islamic Leader's Religious Comments," *SRNA*, 8/11/04.

[20] "Calls for Discontinuation of Republika Srpska May Endanger Peace," *SRNA*, 6/13/04.

[21] "Bosnian Muslim Poet's call for 'Islamic' Revival Leads to Protests," *BBC Monitoring*, 1/17/05).

[22] *Ibid.*

[23] "Cardinal Etchegaray and Mufti Receive UNESCO Peace Prize," zenith.org, 9/22/04.

[24] "U.S., European Intelligence Agencies Hunt for Terrorists in Bosnia, *AP* 6/26/04.

[25] "U.S., European Agencies Use Rewards, Informants in Hunt for Terrorists in Bosnia," *AP*, 6/28/04.

[26] "Muslims in Greater Europe," by Nabil Shebaib, islamonline.net, 7/1/04.

[27] "Islam: The Next American Religion?" by Michael Wolfe, 2/4/04, aljazeerah.info.

[28] UPI 9/20/2000.

[29] *Ibid.*

30 "Siege Heil: The Bush-Rove-Schwarzenegger Nazi Nexus and the Destabilization of California," by Bob Fitrakis and Harvey Wasserman, *Free Press* (Columbus, Ohio), 10/6/03.

31 *Ibid.*

32 *Ibid.*

33 "When Are Nazi Comparisons Deplorable? For Fox News, Only When Republicans are the Target," *Fairness and Accuracy in Reporting*, 1/16/04.

34 *Ibid.*

35 The following discussion of the similarities of NATO's media/PR campaign against Serbia to Nazi tactics is drawn from "The Public Relations of Modern Warfare: Will the Real Nazis Please Stand Up!" by Susan Bryce, *New Dawn Magazine* (www.newdawnmagazine.com.au) September/ October, Issue 56, 1999. This excellent article deserves to be read in its entirety, and is available on the web.

36 "When All Else Fails, Reach for the Hammer," by Bruce Ramsey, seattletimes.com, 3/26/03.

37 "US's 'Iron Hammer' Code Name 1st Used by Nazis," *Reuters*, 11/18/03.

38 The following quotations from *Mein Kampf*, as well as the key points of Hitler's propaganda theory, are drawn from "Will the Real Nazis Please Stand Up! The Public Relations of Modern Warfare," by Susan Bryce, *New Dawn Magazine* (www.newdawnmagazine.com.au) September/October, Issue 56.

39 *Ibid.*

40 *Liar's Poker: The Great Powers, Yugoslavia and the Wars of the Future*, by Michel Collon, p. 35, *op. cit.*

41 "Will the Real Nazis Please Stand Up!, The Public Relations of Modern Warfare," by Susan Bryce, *New Dawn Magazine*, *op. cit.*

42 *Ibid.*

43 "US Is Bigger Threat than Terror," *BBC News*, electronic edition, 04/09/04.

44 "A Kind of Fascism is Replacing Our Democracy," by Sheldon S. Wolin, *Long Island Newsday*, 7/18/03.

45 *See* "Muslim Brotherhood, Nazis and Al Qaeda," a speech by John Loftus, *Jewish Community News*, 8/25/04.

46 *Ibid.*

47 *Ibid.*

48 "U.S. Court Examines Case against Vatican on Nazi Gold," by Adam Taner, *Reuters*, 10/7/04.

49 *Ibid.*

50 "Holbrooke Brands Bosnian Serb Nationalist Party 'Nazis'," *SRNA*, Beta, 10/3//03.

51 *Les Guerriers de la paix*, Grosset, *op. cit.*

[52] See *Liar's Poker: The Great Powers, Yugoslavia and the Wars of the Future*" by Michel Collon, IAC: New York, 2002, pp. 34-35.

[53] "Seeing Islam Through a Lens of US Hubris," by Anonymous, *LA Times*, 7/2/04.

[54] "The Changing Face of War: Into the Fourth Generation," by William S. Lind et al., *Marine Corps Gazette*, (October 1989), pp. 22-26. Quoted from "The Truth about Terrorism," by Jonathan Raban, *The New York Review of Books*, Volume 52, Number 1, 1/13/05.

[55] "Give the Chechens a Land of Their Own," *The New York Times*, 9/9/04.

[56] *Commentary*, September 2004, pp. 17-54.

[57] "Kerry invites Thaci to Convention," Stella L. Jatras, 8/10/04.

[58] Kosovo is and always has been the proper name for the Serbian region; "Kosova" is a deliberate Albanian mispronunciation of it.

[59] "Which Shoe? Which Foot?", by William J. Hutton, *op. cit.*

[60] "Suspected Terror Fund-Raiser Attend Event for Kerry," worldnetdaily.com, 10/25/04.

[61] *SRNA*, 12/24/04.

[62] "Echoes of Yugoslavia," by Julia Gorin, nationalreview.com, 2/26/04.

[63] "Hostage 'Beheaded on Video'," by Niko Price, *The Sunday Times*, 5/11/04.

[64] "The Pictures They Don't Want You to See," *Living Marxism* (UK), Issue 53, March 1993.

[65] *Ibid.*

[66] "Sarajevo Massacre Remembered," by Jim Fish, *BBC*, 02/20/04.

[67] *Balkan Odyssey*, by David Owen, New York, 1995, p. 260-262.

[68] "Sarajevo Massacre Remembered," by Jim Fish, *BBC*, *op. cit.*

[69] "Wesley Clark's Ties to Muslim Terrorists," by Cliff Kincaid, 09/17/03, *Accuracy in Media*, aim.org.

[70] *Ibid.*

[71] *Ibid.*

[72] "Ex-CIA Official: We Will Lose Terror War," by Krishnadev Calamur, *UPI*, 12/5/04.

[73] "The Truth about Terrorism," by Jonathan Raban, *The New York Review of Books*, Volume 52, Number 1, 1/13/05.

[74] "After Madrid, Terror Leader's 'Balkan Map' Worries Italy," by Christopher Deliso, 3/28/04, balkanalysis.com.

[75] "Holiday in Bosnia, Ashdown Urges," *BBC News*, 5/20/04.

[76] "Tourists Flock to Bosnia War Tours," by Nick Hawton, *BBC*, 6/11/04.

[77] "Muslim Beheading Videos from Chechnya, Afghanistan Sold in Bosnian Capital," *BBC Monitoring*, 1/19/05.

[78] "Analysis of Islamic Extremists Presence in Ex-Yugoslavia," *FoNet*, 5/26/04.

79 *Ibid.*

80 "The Carcass of Yugoslavia — A Letter from Belgrade," *Free Nations* (UK), 12/15/04.

81 "Chronicles Intelligence Assessment: Balkan Muslims Fit for Al-Qaeda Recruits, *Makfax*, 11/30/2004.

82 "Bosnia Arrests Pakistani for Threatening Prosecutors," dailytimes.com.pk (Pakistan), 11/22/04

83 "Bosnians Threaten Life of US Prosecutor," *AP*, 11/18/04.

84 "Bosnians Say NATO Brought 'Angel of Death'," by Ekram Tinjak et al., *IWPR*, 11/18/04.

85 *Ibid.*

86 "Leaders in Bosnia Are Said to Steal up to $1 Billion," by Chris Hedges, *The New York Times*, 8/17/99.

87 *Ibid.*

88 "Ex-Bosnian Ambassador Out on Bail," by Richard Roth and Dana Garrett, cnn.com, 7/27/04.

89 "Former Al-Qa'idah Member Writes Book on Experiences from Bosnia Prison," *BBC Monitoring*, 11/8/04, source: *BHTV1*, Sarajevo (11/4/04).

90 "Attempt on Life of al-Qaeda Informant in Bosnian Prison," *Defense & Foreign Affairs Special Analysis*, 2/21/05.

91 "PM Seeks Release of Six Bosnians Detained in Guantanomo," *AP*, 2/2/05.

92 "Madrid Bombers Trained at Bosnia-Based Al Qaeda Camps," Sofia News Agency, novinite.com, 5/10/05.

93 "Bosnian Serb police chief says Madrid terrorists trained in Bosnia," *BBC Monitoring Europe (Political)* — May 10, 2005, Tuesday, Text of report in English by Bosnian news agency Onasa web site.

94 "Islamic Terrorists Being Recruited In Bosnia, Kosovo — Serbian Analyst," *BBC Monitoring International Reports* — April 29, 2005 (Text of report by Belgrade-based private BKTV on 28 April).

95 "Ashdown Tells Bosnian Serb Police Chief To Retract Terrorism Allegations," *BBC Monitoring International Reports* — June 3, 2005 (Text of report in English by Croatian news agency HINA).

96 "State Department Recommends and Grants Agreement on Questionable Bosnian Ambassador Appointment," Congressional Record (House); Pg. H4712 – June 17, 2005.

97 "Bush Says US is in Iraq Because of 9/11 Attacks on US," *Agence France Press*, 6/19/05.

98 "Rove Criticizes Liberals on 9/11, by Patrick D. Healy," *The New York Times*, 6/23/05.

99 "CIA Chief Gave Bosnia List of 900 Al-Qa'idah Members — Analyst," *BBC Monitoring*, June 28, 2005, text of report by Bosnian Serb news agency SRNA.

[100] "Sanader condemns 'Croatia's Auschwitz'," *AFP*, 3/17/004.

[101] *Ibid.*

[102] "Croatia Seeks Return of La Guardia Hijacker," by Joseph Fried, *The New York Times*, 12/8/02.

[103] "Tours Are Returning to Shrine in Bosnia," by Jean Allen, South Florida Sun-Sentinel (posted on Kansas.com), 8/29/04.

[104] *See* "The Patron Saint of Genocide: Archbishop Stepinac and the Independent State of Croatia," by Bill Stouffer, www.pavelicpapers.com, *op. cit.*

[105] "Controversial Cardinal Beatified," *BBC News*, 10/3/98.

[106] "Pope Urges Forgiveness for Crimes Committed by Catholics on Visit to Bosnia," AFP, 06/23/03.

[107] *Ibid.*

[108] "Pope's Bosnian Visit Whitewashes Croatia's Clerical-Nazi Past", *Emperor's Clothes*, 06/22/03, tenc.net.

[109] "The Pope Says Sorry for Friar Satan," by Harry de Quetteville, *Telegraph* (UK), 6/23/03.

[110] "Email," by Julia Pascal, *The Guardian* (UK), 7/14/03.

[111] *Ibid.*

[112] *Ibid.*

[113] "One Third of Bosnians Ready to Leave Country for Good: Poll," *AFP*, 4/26/03.

[114] "Rewriting History," by Aleksandra Priestfield, June 5, 2000, swans.com.

[115] *Ibid.*

[116] "Ashdown Moves to Abolish Defense Ministries of Republika Srpska and Muslim Croat Federation," *Defense & Foreign Affairs Daily*, 1/18/05.

[117] *Ibid.*

[118] "Montenegro Police Arrest Karadžić's Brother," isn.ethz.ch, 9/11/04.

[119] "Press Anger at Karadzic Raid," *BBC News*, 4/2/04.

[120] "Media Blitz over Bosnian Suspects," *BBC News*, 4/6/04.

[121] "The Fear Born of a Much Too Personal Look at Jihad," by Richard Bernstein, *The New York Times*, 11/29/04.

[122] "Serb Assassin Who Triggered WWI — Hero or Terrorist?", *AFP*, 7/25/04.

[123] *Ibid.*

[124] The website hosting this anonymous parody has vanished, but it was quoted in its entirety in "It Was A Good Day To Die: Alija Izetbegovic," by Alexandra Priestfield, Swans.com, 11/3/03.

[125] "The West Closes Its Eyes to the Truth in Ukraine," by John Laughland, *The Age*, 11/30/04.

[126] *Ibid.*

[127] "What US-Backed 'Democracy Movements' Have Produced in Serbia and Georgia," by Justus Leicht, wsws.org, 12/10/04.

[128] "Smedley Butler, Meet John Perkins," by Rossell Mokhiber and Robert Weissman, commondreams.org.

[129] "Honouring Nazi Collaborators throughout Europe," *Free Nations*, 9/16/04.

[130] "102,000 Killed in Bosnia," by Kjell Arild Nilsen, *NTB* (Norwegian News Agency), 11/14/04. Nebojsa Malic of antiwar.com found this article and discussed it in http://grayfalcon.blogspot.com/2004/11/bosnia-death-toll-revealed.html.

[131] "Naser Oric: Srebrenica Defender Turned Defendant," by Asim Beslija, *Transitions Online* (tol.cz), 12/1/04.

[132] "Srebrenica Revisited: Reports, Confessions and the Elusive Truth," by Nebojsa Malic, antiwar.com, *op. cit.*

[133] Helen Ranta is the Finnish forensic specialist who performed the autopsies on the Albanians who were killed in Račak. Her report was heavily redacted in early 1999 in order to provide a pretext for the Kosovo War. In 2003, she publicly stated that her findings had been manipulated in order to start the war. It is another case of delayed revelations regarding a disputed event that had no impact on subsequent interpretations.

[134] "Srebrenica Revisited: Reports, Confessions and the Elusive Truth," by Nebojsa Malic, antiwar.com, *op. cit.*

[135] "US Likely to Set Ultimatum Over Mladic," by Chris Stephen, *IWPR*, (10/16/03).

[136] "Aid to Serbia and Montenegro Withheld," *AP*, 1/13/05.

[137] "Balkans: Meaningless Gesture," Jacksonville.com, 4/20/04.

[138] "Srebrenica Sentencing," *The New York Times*, 12/11/03.

[139] "Massacre Widows Demand Karadzic's Arrest," *The Scotsman* (UK), 6/2/04.

[140] "U.S. Removes Peacekeepers Over War Crimes Court," by Charles Adlinger, *Reuters*, 7/1/04.

[141] "Pentagon Weighs Use of Deception in a Broad Arena," by Thom Shanker and Eric Schmitt, *The New York Times*, 12/13/04.

[142] "The Know-Nothings," by Arianna Huffington, HuffingtonPost.com, 8/3/05.

[143] "Fewer Noses Stuck in Books in America, Survey Finds," by Bruce Weber, *The New York Times*, 7/8/04.

[144] "When Ignorance Kills: The Clinton Administration and Al-Qaeda in the Balkans, W.H. Schindley, serbianunity.net, 11/1/04.

[145] "Along the Sava Finds Links between Iran and the Balkans," mehrnews.com, 1/4/05.

[146] "Kosovo Embraces Islamic Treasures," zaman.org (Turkey), 2/29/04.

[147] "Turkish Leader Warns of Terror Wave if EU Rejects Membership," by Suna Erdem, timesonline.co.uk, 12/13/04.

[148] "Islamophobia Makes British Muslims Feel Increasingly 'Isolated' in their Own Country," by Maxine Frith, *The Independent* (UK) electronic edition, 11/22/04.

[149] *Ibid.*

[150] "Islamists Shift Focus to Europe as Jihad Enters Third Phase," by Simon Tisdall, *The Guardian* (UK), 11/18/04.

[151] "Militant Muslims Find Haven in 'Londonistan'," by Lynne O'Donnell, sfgate.com, 7/24/04.

[152] *Ibid.*

[153] *Ibid.*

[154] "In 1683 Turkey Was the Invader. In 2004 Much of Europe Still Sees It that Way," by Ian Traynor, *The Guardian* (UK), 9/22/04.

[155] "EU-Turkish Engagement: A Must for Stability of the Region," by K. Gajendra Singh, aljazeerah.info, 9/30/04.

[156] "Turkey in Europe," Monday Morning (Lebanon), 12/16/02.

[157] "Turkey: Castelli, Italy Could Become a New Kosovo," Agenzia Giornalistica Italiana, 10/20/04.

[158] "Islam and the West: The Threat, The Defense," Srdja Trifkovic interview with Al Kresta on Ave Maria Radio, 10/14/04.

[159] "Murder Fuels Fears among Dutch," by Thomas Fuller, *International Herald Tribune*, 11/8/04.

[160] *Ibid.*

[161] *Ibid.*

[162] "After Van Gogh," economist.com, 11/11/04.

[163] "Popular Dutch Lawmaker Urges Halt to non-Western Immigrants, Shutting down Radical Mosques," by Antony Deutsch, *AP*, 11/19/04.

[164] "Death Threats Force Controversial Dutch MP Underground," by Anthony Browne, timesonline.com, 11/20/04.

[165] "Islamist Accused of Killing Director Offers No Defense," by Anthony Browne, *The Times* (UK), 7/12/05.

[166] "After Van Gogh," economist.com, 11/11/04, *op cit.*

[167] *Ibid.*

[168] *Ibid.*

[169] "Commentary: Why EU Should Say Yes to Turks," by Gareth Harding, wpherald.com, 12/13/04.

[170] *Ibid.*

[171] "Jihad, Then and Now," Pt. I & II, by Srdja Trifkovic, Islam, the West, and the Serbs, *op. cit.*

172 "Islam: The Next American Religion?" by Michael Wolfe, 2/4/04, aljazeerah.info, *op. cit.*

173 "Jihad, Then and Now," Pt. I & II, by Srdja Trifkovic, Islam, the West, and the Serbs, *op. cit.*

174 "Seeing Islam Through a Lens of US Hubris," by Michael Sheuer, Los Angeles Times, 7/2/04.

175 "Full Transcript of bin Laden's Speech," aljazeera.net, 11/1/04.

176 "900 Bosnian Serbs to Be Probed over Srebrenica," by Olga Ninkovic, *Reuters*, 3/31/05.

177 "Milosevic: 'No Link to Genocide Found'," by Chris Stephen, *The Observer* (UK), 10/10/04.

178 "Video of Serbs in Srebrenica Massacre Leads to Arrests," *The New York Times*, by Nicholas Wood, 6/3/05.

179 "How Video That Put Serbia In Dock Was Brought To Light: Srebrenica Massacre Tape Has At Last Forced Belgrade to Face Up to Its War Atrocities," Tim Judah In Sarajevo And Daniel Sunter In Belgrade, *The Observer* (UK), 6/5/05.

180 "Prison Changes Milosevic, but Not His Version of Events," by Marlise Simons, *The New York Times*, 6/24/05.

181 "Evidence that the Supposed Srebrenica Execution Video is a Lie, Part I," by Jared Israel, *Emperor's Clothes*, tenc.net, 6/24/05.

182 "Prison Changes Milosevic, but Not His Version of Events," by Marlise Simons, The New York Times, *op. cit.*

183 "Chilling Video Footage Shown of Purported Execution of Srebrenica Muslims by 'Scorpions' Paramilitary Unit — Allegedly Under Serbian MUP Command, International Criminal Tribunal for Yugoslavia (ICTY), Milosevic Trial — The Hague," 01 June 2005, submitted by Edgar Chen, Coalition for International Justice, www.cij.org.

184 "Srebrenitsa, Lies and media games — I Was Evacuating Civilians from Srebrenitsa," *Cirque Minime*, by Zvonimir Trajkovic, (Text of report by Belgrade-based *Ogledalo*, 6/22/05).

185 "Video Captures Marine Killing Unarmed Fighter," by Thomas Ricks, *Washington Post*, 11/17/04.

186 *Ibid.*

187 "No Court-Martial for Marine Taped Killing Unarmed Iraqi," Day to Day, 5/10/05.

188 Hague's Politics of Massacres, By M. Bozinovich, serbianna.com, 6/23/05.

189 "Massacre Video Sparks Balkan Confusion," by Tim Judah, *ISN Security Watch* (Zurich) 6/21/05.

190 "Serbs, Lies, and Videotape," by Julia Gorin, 6/17/05, FrontPageMagazine.com

[191] "Telling the Serbian Side of the Story," Mary Mostert, 714/05, posted on serbianunity.net.

[192] "Survey Shows Serbs not Ready to Face War Crimes Yet," *Reuters*, 7/4/05.

[190] "Hardline Serbs Defiant before Srebrenica Memorial," by Douglas Hamilton, *Reuters*, 7/9/05.

[193] "Balkans: After Shock Srebrenica Video, Serbs Hit Back on War Crimes," adnki.com, 6/17/05.

[194] "Serbian Lawmakers Fail to Agree on Draft Declaration Condemning Srebrenica Massacre," *AP*, 6/14/05.

[195] "Survey Shows Serbs not Ready to Face War Crimes Yet," *Reuters*, 7/4/05.

[196] "Globalist: Crack in Serb Armor gives U.S. an Opening," by Roger Cohen, *International Herald Tribune*, 6/25/05.

[197] "US Tells Tadic and Kostunica to Repent," *B92 News* (S-M), 6/27/05.

[198] "Bosnian Muslim Arrested for Planting Explosives at Srebrenica Memorial," *FoNet*, 7/6/05.

[199] " Srebrenica: Police Hunt Bomb Plot Suspects," *Aki*, 7/6/05.

[200] "The Brooklyn-Kosovo-London Connection," by M. Bozinovich, Serbianna.com, 8/8/05.

[201] "Efforts in Bosnia Must Be Continued," by "Richard Holbrooke, The Washington Post, 7/20/05.

[202] "US Congress Addresses Srebrenica," see.oneworld.net (B92), 6/30/05.

[203] "Bosnian Muslims Retrace Steps of Those Killed in 1995," by David Rohde, *The New York Times*, July 11,2005

[204] "In Bosnia, World Leaders Apologize for Massacre," by David Rohde, *The New York Times*, 7/12/05.

[205] "Natasa Kandic & the Propaganda War," by Ian Johnson, June 17, 2005, http://cirqueminime.blogcollective.com/blog/_archives/2005/6/17/947793.html, posted on serbianna.com.

[206] *Ibid.*

[207] *The New York Times*, January 26, 2004.

[208] *Ibid.*

[209] "Evidence that the Supposed Srebrenica Execution Video is a Lie, Part II," by Jared Israel, July 2, 2005, *Emperor's Clothes*, tenc.net.

[210] Quoted from "Natasa Kandic & the Propaganda War," by Ian Johnson, June 17, 2005, http://cirqueminime.blogcollective.com/blog/_archives/2005/6/17/947793.html, posted on Serbianna.com.

[211] "Srebrenica i reakcija," by Miodrag Zarkovic, *Glas javnosti* (S-M), 29 June, 2005.

[212] *Ibid.*

213 "Croatian Leaders Blast Serbia's President Statement on 1995 Crimes against Serbs," *AP*, 8/1/05.

214 "Croatia: Neo-Nazis Celebrating Ethnic Victory of Balkan Wars," dzeno.cz, 8/10/05.

215 "Srebrenitsa, Lies and Media Games — I Was Evacuating Civilians from Srebrenitsa," Cirque Minime, by Zvonimir Trajkovic, (Text of report by Belgrade-based *Ogledalo*, June 22, 2005).

216 *Ibid.*

217 *Ibid.*

218 "Serbian Researchers Say More Than 3,000 Serbs Killed in Wartime Srebrenica," BBC Monitoring International Reports — June 14, 2005, Text of report by Bosnian Serb news agency SRNA.

219 "Poisonous Trees and Decaying Forest: The Civilized World and Anti-Serb Racism: 1991-2005," by Raymond K. Kent, June 2005, apisgroup.org.

220 "Serbs Mourn Their Dead around Srebrenica to Mark 10th Anniversary," by Dusan Stojanovic, AP, 7/12/05.

221 "Srebrenica Massacre Survivor Hid under Corpses," by Daria Sito-Sucic, Reuters, 7/10/05.

222 *Ibid.*

223 "Srebrenica: Genocide — Against the Truth or Comrade Naser Rides at the Head of the Column," by Slavisa Sabljic, *Puls* magazine, Banja Luka, Republika Srpska Issue 4, June 11, 2004, pp. 8-13.

224 "The Real Story behind Srebrenica," by Lewis Mackenzie, *The Globe and The Mail* (Canada), 7/14/05.

225 *Ibid.*

226 "Srebrenica and the Neocolonial Community," ZNet Blogs, 6/27/05, posted by David Peterson.

227 "Silver City: Srebrenica, 10 Years Later," by Nebojsa Malic, July 7, 2005, antiwar.com.

228 "Fuzzy Math and "Genocide", Nebojsa Malic, antiwar.com, 7/13/05.

229 "Serbs, Lies, and Videotape," by Julia Gorin, FrontPageMagazine.com, 6/17/05.

230 "London Bombings: More Balkans Blow-Back," by William Norman Grigg, 8/1/05, thenewamerican.com.

231 "Father of 9/11 Hijacker wars of 50-Year War," *Daily Mail* (UK), 7/20/05.

232 "Bosnian War a Long Way from Over," Gray Falcon/Nebojsa Malic, 7/15/05, serbianunity.net.

233 These well known points were drawn from a flyer advertising *Films for Peace and Freedom*, which "presents Sunday Night Films at St. Mark's in

the Bowery, 2nd Ave & 10th St., Sunday June 5, 6:00 p.m.-10:00 p.m., "Confronting the Evidence: A Call to Re-Open the 9-11 Investigation" (2005, 90 minutes. Discussion follows.)"

234 "The War Before the War, An interview with Col. Sam Gardiner (ret.)," by Kevin B. Zeese, 7/23/05, antiwar.com.

235 *Ibid.*

236 *Ibid.*

237 "Terror Expert: 7/7 Mastermind Was Working for British Intelligence, Group was Used by Brits in Kosovo in the Late 90s," by Steve Watson/Infowars, 8/2/05, inforwars.net.

238 *Ibid.*

239 "A Defiant Islam Rises among Young Britons," by James Brandon, *The Christian Science Monitor*, 7/11/05.

240 *Ibid.*

241 *Ibid.*

242 "Anger Burns on the Fringe of Britain's Muslims," by Hassan M. Fattah, *The New York Times*, 7/16/05.

243 "Islamic Radicals Warn of City Riots," by Mark Townsend, *Observer* (UK), 8/7/05.

244 "The Radical Islamic Group that Acts as 'Conveyor Belt' for Terror," by Shiv Malik, *The Independent* (UK), 8/7/05.

245 "Terror Expert: 7/7 Mastermind Was Working for British Intelligence, Group was Used by Brits in Kosovo in the Late 90s," by Steve Watson/Infowars, *op. cit.*

246 "Radical Cleric Flees Britain after Threat of Treason Trial," by Nigel Morris, *The Independent*, 8/9/05.

247 "Mosque Chairman Sparks Fresh Row," *BBC News*, 8/6/05.

248 "Muslim's Integration in Europe Is Urgent Challenge," by Roula Khalaf, *Financial Times*, 7/14/05.

249 "The Radical Islamic Group that Acts as 'Conveyor Belt' for Terror," by Shiv Malik, The Independent (UK), *op. cit.*

250 "War of Values," *Vecernje Novosti*, July 20, 2005, posted as "The Whipping Boy," by Gray Falcon, http://grayfalcon.blogspot.com.

251 "Western Media Ignores Serb, US Memorials of Jasenovac Death Camp," Posted on Wednesday, April 20, 2005, by Christoper Deliso.

252 *Ibid.*

253 "First Monument to Jasenovac Victims in New York Holocaust Park," American Srbobran, May 18, 2005.

254 "Terror and Serbian Dam," by Spomenka Deretic, 5/10/05, www.serbia-nunity.net.

255 "Report: Mladic Gets $520-A-Month Serb Army Pension, *Reuters*, 12/7/04.

256 "Raid on Mladic Dead Mother's House," *BBC*, 8/14/03.

257 "Nato Soldiers Search Home of Mladic's Sister in Bosnia, *BBC Monitoring*, 3/10/05.

258 *Ibid.*

259 "Del Ponte's Showmanship Might Be Sickening, But It Has Ramifications for the US," by Christopher Deliso, balkanalysis.com, 6/4/05.

260 *Ibid.*

261 "Posters Call for Mladic Return in Central Belgrade," *Reuters*, 3/7/05.

262 "Serbia: 'Source' Says Mladic Gave Orders to Be Killed if Situation 'Desperate'," BBC Monitoring, 6/20/05.

263 "With Mladic at Large, Bosnian Serbs Remain Loyal to Their Wartime Commander," *AP*, 6/27/05.

264 "Serb secret services shadowing Mladic—Report," *Reuters*, 6/29/05.

265 "Official: Net Closes in on Bosnia Suspects," by Dusan Stojanovic, *AP*, 6/10/05.

266 "Serbian Poll Suggests 90 per cent of Viewers Oppose Mladic's Extradition," *BBC Worldwide Monitoring*, 2/7/03.

267 "When Ignorance Kills: The Clinton Administration and Al-Qaeda in the Balkans," W.H. Schindley, serbianunity.net, 11/1/04.

268 "Journalism and the CIA: The Mighty Wurlitzer," by Daniel Brandt, NameBase NewsLine, *op. cit.*

269 "Stay Quiet and You'll Be OK," by Robert Spencer, frontpagemagazine.com, 6/23/04.

270 *Ibid.*

271 "Marko Drinks Wine in Ramadan" or "Marko Pije uz Ramazan Vino," anonymous ballad.

272 This closing paragraph, its sentiments and the citation of the preceding verses are based on the conclusion reached in "Facing the Muslim Threat," by Thomas Fleming, 9/02/03 (a lecture given at Matica Srpska in Novi Sad, Serbia, September 11, 2003, at a Conference on Islam and the West organized by The Rockford Institute).

RATKO MLADIĆ IN CLOSE UP
Interviews and Speeches

General Mladić's interviews and speeches have been arranged in chronological order to present his thoughts on and reactions to the war in a manner consistent with their development.

What the Bosnian Serbs Want

NIN (Belgrade) on February 13, 1993

General, Sir, was this war inevitable?

To tell you the truth, I often ask myself the same question. I can categorically affirm that the war was not initiated by the will or the desire of the Serbian people. The Serbs did not want war, I am convinced of it. I can even believe that a majority of the other ethnic groups did not want it, either. It simply arrived as unexpectedly as an ill wind. It was brought about by certain forces that had planned the break-up of Yugoslavia, centers of power outside the former Yugoslavia, because Yugoslavia got in their way.

But those who planned this war found allies in Yugoslavia!

Unfortunately, they did. The war was inevitable precisely because the tissue holding together the former Yugoslavia was diseased. While we were lulled to sleep by the laurels of eternal peace, many others were preparing for brutal settling of scores.

You have said many times that the plans for the break-up of Yugoslavia were made outside the borders of the former and the present Yugoslavia. Can you tell us more about this scenario for war?

It is no longer a secret. And it has been well researched. Over the last ten, twenty years, several military academies belonging to superpower nations have worked out detailed plans, and even exercised peacetime war-games in our territories, from Kosovo on. It was all pretty well camouflaged. They concentrated their attention here and worked out a detailed plan for the break-up of Yugoslavia. Unfortunately, events are still unfolding according to that scenario. It is still in progress and it is not going to stop.

If Serbs in the Serbian Republic of Krajina and the Republika Srpska had not resisted the 'New World Order', do you believe that war would have broken out in Serbia and Montenegro anyway?

The great powers that planned the break-up of Yugoslavia and participated in it were astonished by the resistance of the Serbian population of the Serbian Republic of Krajina and the Republika Srpska. What is happening now holds dangerous repercussions for the rest of the world, which is living in peace. Many countries participated, directly or indirectly, in the war that broke out in the former Yugoslavia. Even some great powers.... During the negotiations in Geneva, I took notice of the concern expressed by ordinary people on account of what was happening to us here. People were afraid. They viewed the current situation here with cold realism. The warfare that befell us could easily have spread to their own countries, especially when it came to some kind of foreign military intervention in our territories.

What if by some chance military intervention does occur? How will the Serbs reply?

The question of intervention was mentioned often, unfortunately, even during the negotiations in Geneva. It is really possible, because the international community is using pressure tactics on all sides in the conflict, especially on the Serbian side, to accept the proffered solutions. We will indeed do everything we can to solve the crisis by political negotiations in a peaceful manner, so that the solutions will not come at the expense of any ethnic group in the former Bosnia-Herzegovina; however, we let the co-presidents of the conference at the Geneva negotiations know in no uncertain terms that several conditions have to be met if they want to solve the situation in the former Bosnia-Herzegovina fairly.

What are those conditions?

First of all, the terms of UN Security Council Resolution 787 must be brought into effect, namely, the unconditional withdrawal of Croatian armed forces from the territories of the former Bosnia-Herzegovina. Their armed forces have absolutely no reason to be there. They caused the war.

The next condition is to dismantle any contracts or agreements between Tudjman's and Izetbegović's governments about fighting an allied war against the Serbian people.... The next condition is that Alija Izetbegović must annul his decision to announce a state of war and he must annul his declaration of war against the Serbian people. Only when such circumstances have been achieved will conditions for real peace negotiations exist, and bring together the three sides of the conflict: the Republika Srpska, the Croatian union, which they call Herzeg-Bosna, and the Muslim part of the former Bosnia-Herzegovina.

Now, we have a foreign power here, the internationally recognized state of Croatia, which is the aggressor in this region.

You mentioned Geneva, where you participated as an official representative of the Army of the Republika Srpska. Were you pressured to accept the constitutional order in Bosnia-Herzegovina and the proposed maps that were presented to you?

So far, I have not had any such experiences. But I was surprised that the co-chairmen decisively emphasized results that could occur if one did not act in this or that fashion. Their method itself is a subject ripe for discussion. For example, they bring in documents that were drawn up without Serbian representatives and the documents are offered as a done deal. It was very difficult to change any of the terms set forth. They did not accept the facts or the real situation as it was, is or will be. That is specific pressure.

Being the commander of a powerful army, which has been designated in some international circles as the major obstacle for the realization of their plans for our territories, I am interested in knowing if they applied any pressure to you personally.

Our delegation, headed by Dr. Radovan Karadžić, has a united platform. We are persistent, and we will see it to the end, since we are responsible to our people, so that we realize the adopted policy. We start such negotiations with the interests of the Serbian people and with the official documents of the Parliament of the Republika Srpska. Parliamentary resolutions, which cannot be renounced, form the platform.

At the previous round of talks, co-chairman General Satish Nambijar expressed, in clear but lofty tones that become such high-ranking diplomats, preliminary expositions to a military group regarding what eventually could be expected if the Vance-Owen Plan for the resolution of the crisis in Bosnia-Herzegovina is not accepted. However, we cannot proceed at the expense of either our people or our own interests. We made it clear to them. In the end, nothing happened to those who broke up Yugoslavia, even though Yugoslavia was one of the founding signatories of the League of Nations as well as of the United Nations. If

Yugoslavia could be smashed to pieces, and broken up into small countries, erased as if it had never existed — why could this not be done, following the same principles, in the case of Bosnia-Herzegovina? The Serbian people in the territory of former Bosnia-Herzegovina do not ask for anything more than what other nations in the former Yugoslavia have already received, the right to their own statehood.

In spite of all that, various international organizations have blamed the Serbs as the principal culprits for the war in the former Bosnia-Herzegovina.

That is true. And we are largely culpable for it. We are guilty because we did not know the world that surrounded us well enough.... It is often said that the Croats won the media war. They still have not won that war. Strictly directed, a media war forms and orients a nation. They simply show their people only the 'truths' that they are interested in seeing. It is no secret that Croatia invested huge sums of money in propaganda. Kuwait invested about $13 million in public relations during its war with Iraq, while Croatia spent more than twice that sum, investing more than $30 million, so that the goals of Franjo Tudjman and his extreme right-wing party, the HDZ, were reported favorably in the press. We did not, however, invest in propaganda. We are not interested in fabricated truths.

I watched various channels of Western European television during my visit to Geneva. They follow a strictly formatted scheme. At the beginning of their news programs, they show that everything is going very well in their own country. And when they want to show scenes of underdevelopment, as if from a primitive society, then they go to the Balkans or to the Asian part of the continent, where they find evidence of the worst misery and poverty. Extreme poverty also exists in the West, but it is not shown. The West understands that the human mind has a limited capacity, and that they can shape it as if it were well-kneaded dough. Various organizations, which accept money for their services, work according to the same system, fabricating loathsome lies about the Serbian people, the Serbian army, and they are demonizing us. But these are short-range volleys.

A hue and cry has been raised against Serbs because of the positions they hold around Sarajevo.

The Serbs are not holding anything that does not belong to them. Furthermore, we do not hold everything that belongs to us in and around Sarajevo. The Serbs made the greatest investment in Sarajevo because it was built on Serbian territory.

The bombardment of Sarajevo is frequently mentioned. And when the subject is brought up, it is usually thought that Serbs are doing the bombardment!

The world was not at all astounded by scenes of the killing of soldiers, the killing of Serbian wedding guests, the destruction of Serbian houses, and the killing of Serbs. When innocent soldiers from the columns of the former Second Army floated in the Miljačka River for days or when their bodies were scattered along sidewalks, the world was not horrified. The world was also not horrified when Alija's warriors, led by Juka Prazina and other criminals, launched rocket attacks against a military hospital and barracks. But when Serbian people were obliged to answer with appropriate measures, they were then quickly proclaimed the guilty party and satanized. Many Muslim atrocities are even today attributed to the Serbs by Western television and the press. Let's just recall the staged scenes that took place on Vasa Miškin Street or the terrible images of what took place on Dobrovoljačka Street, where even UNPROFOR vehicles were used.

There are many Serbs left in Sarajevo. What is happening to them?

They are twentieth-century martyrs. The Serbian population of Sarajevo has been exposed to the most brutal actions of Izetbegović's army. Many are barely surviving thanks to the mercy shown by good Muslim neighbors (some protect certain families). Many families, however, have disappeared forever. Only those who managed to get out of Sarajevo are able to give a truthful account of the tragedy they survived. Many of them are surviving marginally. According to the facts we have at our disposal, a small, almost symbolic portion of the total humanitarian aid that gets into Sarajevo, about 10%, is delivered to the Serbian population, even though they are now by all accounts the majority because Croats, Jews, Slovenes and large numbers of Muslims have left. The Serbs and Alija's 'Green Berets' were unfortunately the only ones who remained. Over there, Serbs are being tortured in private jails, and our women, sisters and mothers are being raped. Serbs are either killed or they leave [Sarajevo] as corpses and skeletons. They have been left without properties for which they had worked for decades, for centuries. Everything their ancestors and their descendants had created has been destroyed, seized or pillaged.

What is your evaluation of UNPROFOR's position?

First we have to say that most officers and soldiers of UNPROFOR are performing their duties credibly and honestly in accordance with the mandate with which they have been charged. Unfortunately, there have been cases of a few individual soldiers who have abused their positions by helping Alija's army.

How?

In many different ways. Some have become a private taxi service for Alija's officials, taking them by the hand from the airport to Sarajevo, Zagreb or other places. But, in the end, we have to say that UNPROFOR's forces are the forces of peace. But by the same token, it has to be taken into consideration that, regardless of the presence of the forces of peace, Alija's military has managed to get quite a bit of ammunition, gasoline, and other material to wage the war. They never had the capability of producing ammunition in Sarajevo, nor do they have it now, but they are still fighting and more fiercely than before. With each passing day they have more ammunition. I don't want to say that UNPROFOR is giving it to them. If certain individuals are doing that, it does not mean that UNPROFOR is doing it officially. But Alija's military gets everything it needs from various humanitarian convoys, especially those organized by Merhamet and Caritas.

Is this an isolated case restricted to Sarajevo?

No. Humanitarian convoys also armed Goražde. Ammunition was smuggled to Muslim units in Srebrenica in humanitarian convoys. Not to mention that huge quantities of military supplies were shipped to Alija's military in Cazin Krajina through humanitarian convoys and by other means as well, especially by air. Arms, ammunition and other necessary supplies came legally in convoys from Croatia, through Western Herzegovina, into Central Bosnia. The flow of arms has been reduced somewhat by the most recent clashes between Muslims and Croats around Gornji Vakuf, Konjić, Mostar, Prozor and Bugojno.

You mentioned Goražde. There have been different comments in the media about the withdrawal of the Army of the Republika Srpska from its positions around the city. What is the truth?
It's best for the people of Goražde to speak the truth. The Army of the Republika Srpska has not withdrawn from Goražde. Only those who lost spirit at a certain moment withdrew.

One Serbian soldier, several of whose family members had been killed by mujahideen, recently killed the Vice President of the Muslim government, Hakija Turlajić, who was supposed to 'officially' greet sixty Turkish officers. Turlajić was in an UNPROFOR vehicle!

Yes, I think one the officers from the French battalion contributed a great deal to this unpleasant event. I do not know the reason why nor who gave approval to it, but he drove Mr. Turlajić to a meeting with Turkish mercenaries. In any case, individual acts of violence must be condemned. That incident took place before the second round of talks in Geneva, and it greatly worsened our negotiating position. But we have to understand that just a few days before, this young man's family had been brutally murdered by Muslim soldiers. He was probably in the throes of a nervous breakdown, and when Mr. Turlajić insulted him, he decided to carry out such a drastic act. The judicial body of the Army of the Republika Srpska is now examining the case, and I think it will establish all the facts.

Large numbers of mujahideen have arrived in Bosnia. Is their exact number known?
The people who hired them probably know. They come every day. The estimate is that there are around ten thousand of them.

The Americans, the Croats, and the Muslims have declared you to be a war criminal. Are you concerned about it?
I would be worried if in America or France a list were to be published of war criminals who committed war crimes in Dien Bien Fu, in Vietnam, in Cambodia and elsewhere. I did not go to fight a war either in Vietnam or in Okinawa. I instead defended my people because it is my duty and obligation as an officer.

Regarding the fact that the Muslims and the Croats have declared me a war criminal, they don't even deserve a penny for their thoughts.

Some people are accusing you of trying to create a Greater Serbia. Among them is co-chairman of the Conference on Yugoslavia, the British diplomat, Lord David Owen.

At this moment, our fundamental interest is to protect our people from extermination and from expulsion from their own homes, and to create conditions for a life of peace and prosperity. And it is the people's will and their democratic right to decide whom they will join and in what kind of alliances they will participate. In the end, I have to tell you we are not very interested in presenting ourselves as some small units of the Serbian nation. It would be very good if the Serbs, as a whole, had a united national program, and presented it to the world. And not only that, I think that the time has come to broaden our platform of ties. Islamic countries have held Islamic conferences and gatherings for decades. No one criticizes them. Western countries have joined various alliances and unions and no one criticizes them. And why, for instance, should Orthodox countries not be able to form their own assemblies, where we could clearly present what we want, define our place in the world, and explain our vision of the contemporary world.

General Mladic's Speech on the Vance-Owen Peace Plan

Athens, May 1993

Low-Flying Aircraft over the Vance-Owen Map

....Gentlemen, this is the real situation as of yesterday at noon in the former Bosnia-Herzegovina. This is the result of a war imposed on the Serbian people, which is not limited to the former Bosnia-Herzegovina.... This is a map of the Vance-Owen Plan. As a soldier, I wish to say to all of our guests that we are making a fateful decision for our nation in very complicated circumstances at a moment when some of the most sophisticated aircraft of the air forces of Western countries are flying directly overhead, making a show of force. Gentlemen, they are not simply making a show of force, but at this very moment they are using force against us. American, English, and French aircraft, guided by German experts from AWACS[1] are flying close to the ground over our villages and cities. Our nation has never been under such pressure. Our nation has never been attacked a greater force, and our nation has never been imperiled by a more dangerous enemy. The most sophisticated weapons that the human mind has created are attacking our people. Our people are being attacked by neighbors from apartment buildings, friends from school and work, who were fellow citizens until just recently, although we were not prepared to fight such a war, nor could we have dreamed that we would have such an enemy.

The Serbian Nation Is Breathing through a Straw

This is a civil and religious war, in which we [i.e., the Serbs] have been driven onto wind-swept plains and proclaimed to be "criminals" before the world. And the world, the international community, did not condemn the inhumane and brutal acts of Slovene and Croat secessionists in olive-gray uniforms who killed innocent children without asking if they were Serbian or not. The world did not impose sanctions when JNA soldiers went for months without food, water and electricity in blockaded bases. The world kept quiet about the fact that the Croats and Muslims had been preparing this war for decades. And it is not true that they are unarmed. They are better armed than all the armies present here, including our own, because they possess the most sophisticated weapons in infantry, artillery and rocketry. And if they did not obtain them before this war, the fact that they have nine munitions factories in territories under the control of the Muslim-Croat coalition in the Neretva and Bosnia valleys is more than enough compensation.

All of the factories that manufacture these deadly weapons, ammunition, planes and tanks are in their hands, from Slavonski Brod to Grude. The Serbian people have nothing. We soldiers are concerned because the international community turned Srebrenica into a stage where their script was performed for the entire world to see. The Muslim population of Srebrenica could fit into a couple of apartment buildings, while Serbs are blockaded from Sarajevo to Zenica, and through Tuzla and Mostar to Livno, etc.

Each humanitarian organization made appeals to supply Srebranica with water, but they paid no attention to us when we informed them that the Serbs were without electricity, water, and the ability to produce food. They blockaded us so that we cannot import either medicine or gas for agricultural purposes. That is why we soldiers see a manifold danger.

I'll give you the facts, as a soldier does, not to influence you but to present the dangers and the consequences; and it will be up to you to make decisions in the interest of the people. There was a state of war between the Croats and the Muslims until they signed up to a mutually agreeable plan.

The Regional borders that were proposed by the Vance-Owen Plan.

They formed a coalition and Franjo Tudjman welcomed Alija Izetbegović with an honor guard. They held many meetings in Zagreb that were reported in the world media. Both declared war against the Serbian people, not only in the former Bosnia-Herzegovina, but they also made a common declaration about military actions against our nation in general. Alija Izetbegović went a step further and declared war against Serbia, Montenegro and the JNA. Such monstrous decisions, which have produced so much bloodshed, have not been rescinded to this very day. And we don't expect them to be rescinded in the future. But we did expect the international community to condemn such criminal acts.

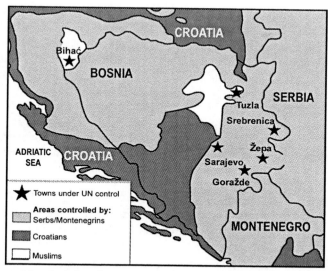

Map depicting the situation in Bosnia at the end of May 1993.

Gentlemen, there is no Serbian soldier in the Army of the Republika Srpska outside the borders of the former Bosnia-Herzegovina; we are in our own territory here. Prime Minister Mitzotakis, I'm referring to you and President Ćosić. The Serbian nation has been breathing through a straw for an entire year, without electricity, water and production. Ozren, a heroic city, harbors more than 100,000 Serbs who have escaped from cities in the Tuzla Basin, Zenica, Vareš, etc., right in the middle of Bosnia. Our representatives in Parliament don't even know about our misery and suffering because they have no way of getting there. Two very old Serbian monasteries are to be found there, Tumare, and Petrovo Selo and Vozuća, our shrines. In the Neretva River Valley, there are Serbian monasteries that pre-date the Battle of Kosovo, like the monasteries of Kolani and Krk in the Serbian Republic of Krajina. Unfortunately, it was flooded and submerged by an artificial lake when the Peruca Dam was built. The greatest shrines of the modern history of our nation are to be found in the village of Prebilovci in the Neretva River Valley. The mortal remains of only a portion of the Serbs massacred in Western Herzegovina and the Neretva Valley during WWII are to be found there.

Look at who inherited our shrines. The Croats are in Province 8, and the Muslims are in Provinces 5 and 9. This is a book that was given to me as a gift by the historian, Ante Valenta, a Croat from Vitez, during the negotiations with our presidents on my second visit to Geneva. It is titled 'The Division of Bosnia and Struggle for Integrity', published in 1991. On page 37 is a map almost identical to the Vance-Owen map. It omits the former Trebinje County, an area conquered by the Croats, which was legalized by the Vance-Owen Plan. I was a participant in the events surrounding Knin. I was a corps commander there and discharged many command responsibilities before this war. I fought side by side with these people.

There is a village called Siritovci near Drniš, nestled in a triangle formed by the rivers Čikola and Krka, where there is a new burial pit that contains the bodies of Serbian fighters and civilians, which was created after the departure of myself and other officers from these territories that were handed over to UNPROFOR to be protected. A Kenyan battalion was stationed there, along with 58 soldiers of the Serbian Republic of Krajina, actually police officers, who were killed and thrown into a pit. Who was charged with that crime? Croatia attacked the Pink Zones around Benkovac and Obrovac in January of this year, and killed about 800 Serbian civilians. An expeditionary battalion of French Foreign Legionnaires fled their positions there. Did the international community condemn the Croatian aggression? Did the French punish the soldiers and officers who left Serbian people unprotected and exposed them to slaughter? Gentlemen, they did not, and that is why we do not want Pink Zones, and we do not want foreign mercenaries protecting us.

We have protected our own people, and we have every right to protect them in the future. We do not have a single soldier in Croatian territory, and there is not a single unit of ours in any European country, much less in America.

We have two military airports in Banja Luka. After the passage of Security Council Resolution 781, UN observers were stationed on the airfields. The Security Council members knew that we honored the resolution and that we did not fly out of there, because UN observers were on duty twenty-four hours a day. This is in addition to NATO rigorously controlling the planes that fly over our air space.

Prime Minister Mitzotakis, there are no planes flying over this area because of this conference, but they are flying over Srebrenica. The international community legitimized the American operation 'Parachute', which airdropped food and supplies to the Muslims. Photographs that we allowed to be published show that they are better fed than we are. President Clinton's announcement that the operation would provide help to all of the people in this region was given great media coverage. I even asked an UNPROFOR officer to have some countries drop empty boxes to the Serbs so that I could help the people of Bihać, where the Muslims had slaughtered more than 1,350 Serbs, including the frail, woman, children and the elderly, the innocent victims.

The Debt Owed to the Serbs
by the Federal Republic of Yugoslavia

Prime Minister Mitzotakis, this is the village of Tregar, which is right on the border with Serbia. I witnessed an unimaginable scene there in June. I must call this to your attention because presidents Milošević and Ćosić, as well as the other representatives, are attending this meeting. Muslims destroyed the village of Tregar, and it went down in flames while Serbian children on the other side of the Drina were playing soccer. We are Serbs. Now judge for yourselves whether or not the pressures and sanctions used against this part of the Serbian nation are justified. I disagree with any representative who accuses any of our own people, especially our guests. We will never be able to repay the Serbs, the Montenegrins and the Greeks, especially the Serbs from Serbia and Montenegro, because they took in the frail, and women and children who were expelled from towns and villages that the Muslims and Croats had conquered. Because they treated our wounded and because they provided us with humanitarian aid.

Please try to comprehend: a humanitarian convoy, led by Father Filaret and organized by the Serbian Orthodox Church, was attacked at the airport in the presence of UNPROFOR troops, right on Serbian land that we had ceded for humanitarian aid, even though UNPROFOR had been advised of this mission in advance. Four drivers were wounded. Please try to comprehend that the Muslims in Cazin Krajina, Sarajevo, Srebrenica, Žepa and Goražde are at this moment being armed by *Caritas* and *Merhamet*.[2] Unfortunately, their clandestine armament is still going on because now they are using convoys provided by UNPROFOR. This was the case in Sarajevo, where ammunition was hidden in the false bottoms of containers. Ever since May, Sarajevo looks like this: there are no natural reserves of oil there, nor are there any Arab or German ammunition or weapons manufactured there, either. But Muslim Sarajevo's firepower is stronger and more intense now than it was at the beginning of the war.

Next, in the Neretva River Valley, in the upper part of Vrbaš stream, and in the Bosnia River Valley, I have to say that a mutual genocide of Croats against Muslims and vice-versa has been hidden from the international public. I must also inform you that I ordered the evacuation and rescue of the frail, and women and children (and even the wounded) from both opposing sides. From the area of Srebrenica, we allowed the UNHCR to evacuate 12,500 Muslim women, children and elderly, and 498 of their wounded, among them many who should have been tried for war crimes committed against the Serbian people. I am proud to belong to an army that allowed an enemy who refused to treat our own wounded in their hospitals, and that my army allowed UN helicopters to evacuate them to Tuzla.

This Is Our Land

Gentlemen, we do not want war. We did not want war in the past, and we do not want war now. I'm not here to declare a war. This war was imposed on us, and we had to defend ourselves. We are fed up with war. Not because we are exhausted, but because we saw the many horrors of war, and I will share just one of these horrors with you. I happened to be in the village of Drinjača when a UNHCR convoy of about ten to fifteen trucks was transporting about 850 Muslim women and children. The convoy stalled when two policemen could not stop the mother of an eleven-year-old boy, Slobodan Stojanović, from blocking the road. It was reported that a Muslim woman, Kosovka Mula from Vlasenica, forced the eleven-year-old to dig his own grave in the village of Kasaba, and then she killed him in the most brutal way, first by cutting off his fingers, not to mention other acts of heinousness. I'm advising you of this so that you understand that we have been attacked by the most terrible of enemies, because we were not expecting it. We do not want a militarily solution to the war in Bosnia-Herzegovina. A military solution can be catastrophic, much worse than the catastrophes that have already struck the former Yugoslavia. We do not want to draw other nations into these troubles. We want to contribute to finding a peaceful political solution that is acceptable and not made at the expense of any nation. Representatives of the Vatican and others who planned the break-up of Yugoslavia drew this map. Our leadership, the supreme military command, and I personally were not unaware of these plans. Such plans also existed east of our regions, and that was why we could not take them for granted. This region is not Croatian land. Maps of this region show that Serbs have been paying taxes here for four hundred years.

I saw another of the horrors of this war in the former Bosanski Brod. After the liberation of the city, I found more than 2,000 complete sets of men's, women's and children's clothing whose owners were missing. Of all the reporters who were there, only a Japanese journalist videotaped it, and the story never appeared anywhere in the media. In 1991, 4,140 Muslims, 11,844 Serbs and 3,609 Yugoslavs (the majority of whom were, as a rule, Serbs) lived in Bosanski Brod. If, as we know, there were 13,923 Croats, then it is clear that the Serbs were in the majority, most of whom lived in Derventa, Modrica, and Samac. Croats formed a majority in Orasje, but we are not seeking to make it ours. This is Serbian soil, and it must not be a corridor. If we were to go through Orasje, that would be a corridor, because it is theirs. We do not want their land, but we are not going to give up our own land.

Gentlemen, this area of Herzegovina in the Neretva Valley was not seized by Muslims and Croats from Bosnia. This area was seized by Croatian armed forces, concentrating first on the Konavle region, which was under the protection of UN forces, after the withdrawal of the JNA to the territory of the FRY. Thirty-eight Serbian villages were completely razed, as was Prebilovci, where lay the mortal remains of our martyrs from WWII. Croatia united the Croatian people in Međugorje by claiming that the Virgin Mary appeared on a hill.[3] Roman Catholic monks and Ustashi emigrants, whose fathers committed crimes against and exterminated the Serbian people in Western Herzegovina and other regions, have gathered in Međugorje for decades from all over the world. From the hilltop where the Virgin Mary appears, you can see nine burial pits in which the Ustashi threw Serbs, and each contains at least 1,000 unfortunate victims. We did not recognize the fact that wars have taken away those who could relate their view of the war, because those Serbs who could tell that story have been thrown into burial pits *en masse*, and that is our misfortune as a nation. That is why our goal is not to defeat the Croats and the Muslims. Our goal is to save our own people, and not to allow them to be thrown into burial pits. In any case, UNPROFOR cannot defend itself in the former Bosnia-Herzegovina without the cooperation of the leadership of the Republika Srpska.

I Don't Want to Influence the Decision of the Representatives

America is a great power. We cannot go poking a finger in America's eye. And the NATO alliance is even larger, and much less can it be provoked, but I can assure you that they cannot poke us in the eye, either.

We relinquished control of the Sarajevo airport, which was on our territory, and I personally withdrew our brigades. Tons of humanitarian aid arrived every day, but we had no evidence that it ever reached Serbian prisoners, who numbered between 70,000 and 100,000 in Sarajevo alone. And we know even less about the situation in other cities under Croat control. I disagreed with those who were saying, "You are the winners!" We are not interested in being the winners. Our goal is not to defeat the Muslims and the Croats. Our goal is to rescue our people who are blockaded in Sarajevo, Tuzla, Zenica, and Mostar, and all the way to Zagreb. Serbs are not human beings in Zagreb: they are considered fit to be killed. In Tomislavgrad, actually the village of Rascani, Serbs were first blockaded, then robbed, and then finally killed. There were more than 4,000 Serbs in the villages of Gornji Guber, Donji Guber in the Livno area, and Zasinje. Few escaped by fleeing to our territory. No one asked if they had food, water or electricity. I wonder why Mr.

Bosiljčić and the gentlemen from Ilidža did not criticize me, even though they had every right to do so. Since we ceded the Sarajevo airport, not one wounded Serb has been evacuated or saved, because we have to give a 13-hour evacuation notice in order to receive qualified medical care. Our blood supplies have always been low, so it was hard to transport the wounded. UNPROFOR did not evacuate a single wounded Serb, and UNPROFOR thus became logistical support at different times for Izetbegović, Tudjman, and Boban. And a certain English General Stuart was boasting about how he and his battalion were evacuating the dead and the wounded under fire. When did he ever evacuate a dead or wounded Serb? Gentlemen, he never did, and we are not asking him to do so. They don't have a mandate to take such action. They have a mandate to protect only the Serbs in the Pink Zones. But they did not protect them. They did not have a mandate to enter Srebrenica at all costs. But they entered Srebrenica anyway. We let them go through not because we were afraid of international intervention — our people are not afraid of intervention, because this is total war, because the enemy shows no mercy to either the frail or to children. They massacre whomever they catch in the most brutal fashion. UNPROFOR evacuated thousands of Muslims, but Serbs are still imprisoned and cannot rely on their help. In central Bosnia they offer medical services to both sides. How can one then explain to our people that UNPROFOR will protect them? Believe me, no one with any common sense would believe it. The Vance-Owen Plan proposes progressive demilitarization in these regions, but the first step is to disarm the Army of the Republika Srpska by using the same principles applied to disarm the Army of the Serbian Republic of Krajina. And I ask you to inform yourselves or to allow me to inform you in your free time of the dreadful consequences of the actions taken at the Maslenica Bridge, at the Zemunik Airport or at the juncture of the rivers Krka and Čikola.

Thank you for your consideration. I did not call this to your attention to influence your decision. The Army of the Republika Srpska and our people know that our representatives will do everything in their power to protect our own people.

Nato Aircraft Drop Weapons and Gas To Muslims

by Jose Manuel Aria
Cambio 16 (Madrid), November 5, 1993

The fifty-year-old former JNA General and present Supreme Military Commander of the Bosnian Serbs, Ratko Mladić, is a charismatic figure for his own countrymen, but reviled by Muslims and Croats.

He is not a man who forgets, and he still has a score to settle with his enemies....

"Our present enemies were also the enemies of our fathers and grandfathers," emphasized General Mladić, referring to WWI and WWII. He thinks the same of Croats and Muslims ... and Germans. In his judgment, the German government had an indisputably large responsibility for everything that happened in the former Yugoslavia. He even thinks that the Muslims will not sign on to the peace plan because they are simply "tools in the hands of their masters."

Q: When you say masters, what countries are you thinking about?

A: Germany is leading one block, and Turkey is leading another Islamic block. The Germans want to reach eastwards and Turks want to get into Western Europe. As an Islamic fundamentalist, Izetbegović believed that he had found the middle road and that he could unite both of those two interests in Bosnia. All of the wrongs that Serbs suffer today, as in the past, stem from Germany. The appetites of German leaders grew after reunification, and they used disputes between Europe and the U.S. [to achieve their own goals].

Q: What, in your opinion, presents an opportunity to end the war in Bosnia?

A: It is a solution by peaceful means. The international community must stop the killing and the suffering experienced by all nations in the Balkans, not simply Bosnia. In any case, they must be conscious of their own mistakes, because Yugoslavia, an internationally recognized country that was one of the founding members of the UN, cannot collapse in this fashion. The paradox is that the Serbs, who comprised 50% of the population of Yugoslavia, do not exist on paper and do not have their own country. The Slovenians, who are fewer in number than the Serbs in Bosnia, have their own country for the first time in history, and for the first time since the word "country" has existed, the Serbs do not have one.

Q: Therefore, at minimum, you propose an ethnic state, and at the maximum, a Greater Serbia or "all Serbs in one country."

A: We don't want an ethnic state. Thousands of Muslims and Croats live peacefully in Serbia. Isn't it logical that all Serbs would want to live together? We are not responsible for the negative opinion that the world has about Serbs. A few democratic European countries are responsible for deciding to destroy our country by means of the media. CNN searches for the topics that Americans are interested in. Is killing Somalis or what Yeltsin is doing really democracy? But I have to admit that CNN is more accurate than some European TV networks.

Q: What kind of military operations are you planning this winter?

A: I think that our military operations in this war, which was imposed on us, are over. We wanted peace from the outset because we were defending our families, our children and our land. The Croats and Muslims, however, wanted the war.

Q: Why did they want a war?

A: Croats wanted to create a Greater Croatia along the Drina River. They deceived the Muslims: they promised them a Muslim State in Bosnia on the condition that they eliminated the Serbs. Since they couldn't throw us out of Krajina and Bosnia, they are now waging a war among themselves. That is absurd. At this very moment, there are 90,000 Croatian soldiers in Bosnia-Herzegovina.

Q: Where are the interests of the Muslims?

A: Alija Izetbegović, a hardcore fundamentalist, neglected one significant fact: the inability to impose the Koran on Muslims who have European customs and habits. Bosnia is not Iran, nor is Sarajevo Teheran.

Q: Are you winning [the war] because you had better weapons?

A: To a certain extent. We had only our own weapons. The Muslims and Croats received weapons from Austria, Germany,

Turkey, Argentina, Czechoslovakia and other countries in spite of the embargo.

Q: Where did these weapons arrive?

A: Weapons arrived through Rijeka, Ploče, Split and Šibenik until conflicts erupted between the Muslims and Croats. They also came through Slovenia and Hungary. The Slovenian Prime Minister was even involved in such business.

Q: A U.S. Senate Commission prepared a report about Croatia smuggling nuclear materials.

A: This is a great danger for the entire world. Croatia developed a network for smuggling nuclear material out of the republics of the former Soviet Union. Its final destination was Turkey. In any case, some of this nuclear material ended up in the Islamic world.

Q: That happened about two years ago, when the news was reported?

A: I assure you that the smuggling of nuclear material is still going on. The "Ruper Bošković" Research Institute near Zagreb has raw material for producing its own bomb. The appropriate technical and scientific means are available to them and they are working on it at full speed.

Q: Aren't you overemphasizing the role of Germany and Turkey in this conflict?

A: They want to revitalize German Fascism because they believe that they have to rule Europe. In order to achieve this, they must crush the Serbs because we are in the center of Europe. I assure you that a war in the Balkans would endanger both the Scandinavian and Iberian peninsulas, as well.

Q: And the Turks?

A: Fundamentalism has reached as far as Paris. South of Spain, at the very doorstep of Europe, there are 150 million Muslims who can't live off their own land and they must expand. In fifty years time, there will be three times as many Muslims as there are today. They will penetrate Europe through the Dardanelles, southern Bulgaria, Albania and Bosnia-Herzegovina. They call that entry the Green Highway (*Zelena Transversala*, or "Zetra"). They defined the Green Highway at the Winter Olympic Games in 1984. Eight years later, we found out what the word "Zetra" meant.[4]

Q: Are you satisfied with the role UNPROFOR is playing?

A: UNPROFOR forces form the core of the Croat and Muslim logistical forces. Besides that, they provide a taxi and limousine service for Izetbegović and Tudjman.

Q: That is a very harsh accusation, General, Sir. Do you have proof?

A: At the recent assembly of the Bosnian Government in Sarajevo, Muslims arrived from seven different enclaves because UNPROFOR provided them with helicopter transport. Besides that, where were they getting fuel? Sarajevo does not have a munitions factory, but it is loaded with German, Austrian, Argentinean and South African ammunition. They must be getting weapons and ammunition all the time through international organizations as well as through UNPROFOR.

Q: Can you prove that?

A: We already proved it last year when we discovered that a French battalion was smuggling weapons. I'll tell you something else: some organizations, even UNPROFOR, supply Muslims in Žepa, Goražde and Sarajevo with German deutsche marks.

Q: You mean to say that international forces aren't neutral?

A: After a year and half of war, where is Bosnia getting its weapons and oil? NATO aircraft are dropping weapons and oil.

Q: Are you sure of it?

A: We seized Milan and Fagot rocket launchers, as well as other material. We showed it to the foreign press, but they did not publish any reports about it at all.

Q: Why have the Muslims from Bihać split with the Muslims from Sarajevo?

A: Abdić is not a fundamentalist, but a reasonable man who understands that they have to live in peace with the Serbs. If they had asked him about it, they would not have started the war. If it were up to me personally, I would not have anything against Bihać being a state.

Q: Of course, because it weakens Alija Izetbegović's position.

A: Nothing will happen as long as Izetbegović is weak. If he had not had outside support, we would have eliminated him from the political scene within a month's time. He has no control over his own forces and soon they will go to Zenica, Mostar and Travnik. His people are divided into eight enclaves. Only Islamic countries are offering him financial support.

Q: Many crimes have been committed in this war. Have you punished the perpetrators?

A: It is hard to control a person who has lost his whole family and all of his property. We have taken strick measures against all forms of criminal behavior and we have punished them severely.

Q: And the rape of Muslim women?

A: It was made-up by the foreign press. Representatives from all [major] international organizations visited our camps and they did not find one single Muslim or Croat woman who had been raped. We are not fighting against the Muslim or the Croat people but against their extremist and fascist leaders. I evacuated 12,000 women and children from Srebrenica. We pulled almost 30,000 [Croatian] civilians [fleeing the Muslims] from Travnik, Vareš and Bugojno. We released soldiers who surrendered their weapons. I allowed the evacuation of wounded soldiers from many villages, about 200 of them from Žepa alone. They were transported by UNPROFOR helicopters. The other side, however, did not allow Serbian civilians to leave Tuzla, Zenica or Sarajevo. We fight on the battlefield. We don't hide behind civilians. They spread monstrous lies through their own propaganda machinery and through the foreign press.

Q: Do you still have prison camps?

A: Yes. We still have a couple of such camps, but only for prisoners of war.

Q: Can you tell us where these camps are?

A: They are in Foča, Sarajevo and Bijeljina. Each prisoner is registered with the Red Cross.

Q: How many people have died in the war in Bosnia-Herzegovina?

A: I only have data about Serbs, but I will not tell them to you because it is not known how many have been killed in villages that are in Muslim and Croat hands. I fear that the number is huge. 230,000 Serbs used to live in Sarajevo and we don't know how many are left. It's the same in Zenica, Travnik and Vitez. We don't know how many of them survived. The international community wanted to decapitate the Serbs and leave them without a state. They will never succeed. We have to do everything in our power to stop this war so that the peoples in this conflict can talk about peace.

Q: Weapons must first be laid down to achieve peace.

A: No. First the production of weapons must be stopped. Americans can't arm themselves to the teeth and disarm others. They want to disarm the Somali people, who are dying, and they want to disarm the Serbian people who are being attacked by the entire world.

Q: UN forces can protect you.

A: Do you really believe that I would leave the fate of my people to a Colonel [May], who is guilty of a massacre at the Zemunik Airport near Maslenica or to the Colonel who was responsible for the massacre in Divoselo? To which UN General will we have to leave the defense of the Serbian nation? Thank you, we can defend ourselves alone.

Q: Excuse me, General, you cannot put all the blue helmets in the same basket. Spanish officers and soldiers have offered help to everybody in Bosnia.

A: You are right. Officers from Sweden, Spain, Egypt and Nepal are upright. I would say that the Spanish public has not been informed about how Spanish soldiers died when their vehicle fell into the Neretva.

Q: How so?

A: It was a trap prepared by the Croats. All the Spanish soldiers were killed by Muslims or Croats. The Serbs never fired a single bullet at a Spanish soldier. Every UNPROFOR soldier and officer knows very well that it is not in the interest of Serbs to fire on them. Why must a young Spanish man die in a conflict between Serbs, Muslims and Croats? They accuse the Serbs of these attacks because they need NATO intervention. You see, I have enough military power to defeat the Croats and the Muslims.

Q: Why don't you stop the siege of Sarajevo?

A: Excuse me, but I have to correct you. We are not holding Sarajevo under siege. We are keeping the peace in the part of Sarajevo that is Serbian. But there is the part that we do not control. My house is located in the center of Sarajevo on a hill where a TV transmitter is located. I could take it but I let them have it, because I want them to feel ashamed. My house was among the first to be burned down. There, 300 innocent Serbs were the first to die. [*See* "Pofalići" in the Appendices.] Let the world know about it.

Q: In other words, Sarajevo is going to remain under siege?

A: I repeat, we are holding only what we consider to be ours. I admit that the Muslims and the Croats are not having an easy time. But it will be even worse if they still want to continue the war. Neither General Mladić nor the Serb Army nor Doctor Karadžić will be responsible. Those who started the war will be responsible. They got what they asked for. And if they continue, it will get even worse for them. I can guarantee you that.

Q: What do you think about international humanitarian aid?

A: The best humanitarian aid of all would be for the war to end. Instead of spending millions of dollars on humanitarian flights and convoys and risking the lives of innocent Spaniards, Nepalese and others, that money should be invested in the reconstruction of the country and should provide for the relocation of the population. Certainly no Serb would want to live in Zenica, Tuzla, Livno, Split or Zagreb. None of the Muslims want to stay in Srebrenica or Goražde. Why not allow normal and peaceful transfers of populations? Why not organize the exchange of properties and an equal division of international aid to provide normal living conditions? We are not asking for anyone to pity us. We don't want foreign journalists, statesmen or soldiers to pity us, either. We will have our own government, a state that is chosen by the Serbian people, and not one that is imposed on us by Germany or some Islamic country. We ask you to make it easier to protect the peace so that we can trade with whole world and so that we can live with Croats and Muslims and maintain good, neighborly relations. God forbid that we should now have to live in the same country as they do!

Q: Did Yugoslavia, which is currently under pressure from the international embargo, demand that you to relent?

A: It is not an embargo but a crime! It is a crime against infants and the elderly, who are dying as well as civilians because we can't import medicines, medical supplies, food, oil.... It is an injustice committed by the international community.

Q: But the embargo doesn't effect Bosnian Serbs?

A: Yes, Bosnian territory is not under embargo. But we can't import anything because we are Serbs. On the other side of the same territory, which is controlled by the other sides, NATO planes bring ammunition, weapons and oil every night while F-16 and F-18 jet fighters fly over our territories every day. What are American planes doing flying over my village? Did one of my soldiers or officers go to Germany or America? Where do they get the right to threaten my country? The Germans killed my father. But I never killed any Germans. The Germans killed almost one and half million Serbs during the Second World War. Has any Serb gone to Germany to kill Germans?

Q: One last question, General: Will the Bosnian Serb Army come to the aid of the Krajina Serbs if they request such aid?

A: Of course. I wouldn't hesitate a second. They are my people. Wouldn't you protect Spaniards from Palma de Majorica? What would you do if the international community was to recognize Catalonia, and if I were to send food, weapons, oil ... to Catalonians, and banned the import of the same goods to Spaniards! I was in Gibraltar and I know it is a bone caught in your throat because it is Spanish territory but it does not belong to Spain.

Q: Is peace in Bosnia near at hand?

A: Peace is still far away, because the Croat and Muslim governments do not want peace, just like their mentor governments. The people want peace. We want peace to reveal the brutality of the international community, which does not allow us to even import baby food while it supplies our enemies with oil and weapons.

I'm Waging War
but I'm Dreaming of Peace

Gaspari di Sclafani interviews General Ratko Mladić
in Han Pijesak
Gente, Milan, January 1994

We journeyed through the former Yugoslavia, which had been torn apart by warfare, to an area near Sarajevo to meet with General Ratko Mladić, commander of the Bosnian Serb Army, who is one of the most frequently discussed figures in this war. "War is a terrible thing," he said, "but we were compelled to take up arms. We have to protect ourselves from Islamic expansion toward the West. Many lies about us have been widely spread."

The Western press considers him to be an executioner, a war criminal. The brunt of the responsibility for the cruelty committed in Bosnia against the Muslims has been ascribed to him. He is considered to be an instigator of rapes, slaughters and massacres.

But for the Bosnian Serbs he is a true hero, a symbol. Without a doubt he is one of the most redoubtable personalities in this war. That is why we are discussing General Mladić....

To meet General Mladić and to interview him is not at all an easy thing to do.... He takes part in battles. He has no permanent base. He is always moving from one place to another. And he harbors absolutely no sympathy for Western journalists.

In any case, we succeeded in arranging a meeting with him, thanks to the efforts of a journalist for the Belgrade daily, *Politika*, who knew Mladić quite well and was trusted by him.

The meeting took place in the Bosnian mountains, in the village of Han Pijesak, on the road between Zvornik and Sarajevo.

Traveling by car to Han Pijesak, we passed through areas of indescribable beauty. The sun illuminated the surrounding white-capped mountains. But signs of war quickly appeared: first we came upon two houses in ruins, then others, until we then saw an entire village half destroyed. The only vehicles that could be seen on the road were military. Every few kilometers we came upon some village that always had a roadblock. Armed policemen and soldiers inspected our documents and asked questions, but they were friendly.

We reached Han Pijesak well before the scheduled meeting. We were escorted to an old hotel, which now served as barracks. Two colonels gave us a warm welcome, which in no way suggested the ambience of war. They led us to the top floor, where the commander's office was located.

Humanitarian Aid

It was a small room dominated by a desk with numerous neatly organized documents on it. There was a book there, too: *Titove ljubavi* ("Tito's Love Affairs") by Filip Radulović. Above the desk was a mirror covered by the heraldic shield of the Republika Srpska and the Bosnian Serb tricolor flag. Opposite the desk was a color television set, and in a corner was a cabinet on which an icon rested between two Serbian flags. "That's St. Sava, our patron saint," one of those present informed us.

While waiting for General Mladić, we were offered *šljivovica*, the national liquor, and shown "trophies."

First, an ancient rifle, made out of a pipe.

"It belonged to a Muslim," joked one of the colonels.

Then they showed us a large box in which there was a "mess kit" taken from the Italian army during WWII.

"And we confiscated this from a Muslim, too," they explained. They carefully observed our reactions. The telephone was ringing constantly.

A general entered, but it was not Mladić. It was his representative, Đorđe Đukić.

"General Mladić will be right here," he said.

One of the soldiers hastily concealed "Tito's Love Affairs" beneath a pile of documents.

At last, General Mladić arrived at about 1 p.m. with several other officers. He is not that tall, about 5'10", but he certainly left a strong impression. He was even wearing camouflaged fatigues.

We regarded him with curiosity and suspicion. He greeted us politely, apologized for the setting, and took a seat behind the desk, ready to answer our questions.

"Many people in Italy don't understand this war," we began. "Specifically, they don't understand what is taking place in Bosnia, in Sarajevo. Serbs are fighting against Serbs. Religion is the only thing separating you: you, the Orthodox, on the one hand, and the Muslims on the other. Can you explain why this struggle assumed such a brutal character?"

"It is not easy to explain what is going on here," answered General Mladić. "First of all, my people, the Serbian people, have always been against the war. War is a terrible thing. A war should be waged against war. But we were forced to take up arms. Principally, our history compelled us, but Christian Europe has underestimated the danger that Islam presents. Our misfortune lies in the fact that we are the center of various interests whose goal is the destabilization of Europe. We were forced to create a bulwark to protect ourselves from Islamic expansion toward the West. Besides the enemies we are fighting in Bosnia, there is the entire Muslim world, whose leader is Turkey. All things considered, it is paradoxical that Christian Europe is aiding the creation of an Islamic state in the Balkans. Specifically, France and Germany are providing the necessary support. France is doing this in order to defend its own interests in Algeria and other Arab countries, to whom they sell more than a billion dollars worth of arms. And Germany wants to extend its influence to the Middle East as well as to the Balkans. Germany is taking advantage of the Bosnian Muslims just as it once had exploited the Ustashi of Ante Pavelić during World War II."

General Mladić shook his head in protest. "I ask myself," he said, "if France indeed wants to create a Muslim state in Europe, is it because France wants to make it impossible for them to create a Muslim state in Paris or Britain?"

The others laughed.

"What do you think of the role of the United States?" we asked.

"America does not want a unified Europe," he explained. "They agreed to the unification of the two Germanies precisely because it would easily destabilize our continent, and to stir up more trouble. But America has underestimated numerous factors. For example, it did not foresee that a war in the Balkans would call into question not only European peace but world peace as well."

"Do you know that the Western press is describing you as cruel and bloodthirsty? They call you an 'executioner'. What do you have to say about that?"

"Thank you for asking that question," he said. "We stand accused of having started this war and of waging a war in foreign territories. We stand accused of simply being an imperialistic nation. But that is not the case. The war we are waging is a defensive war. We are defending our women, our children, our homes and our territories. Unfortunately, almost all of the countries of the West are on the side of our enemies. They are abusing news services and spreading lies. In reality, the one 'accusation' that can stand against me is that I am a patriot who is fighting for his people. I don't have to reproach myself for it. If you saw some strangers killing your men on a bridge over the Korana River on September 21, 1991 in Croatia, you would have acted just as I did if you had been there."

"The world did nothing to lighten the burden of Serbian soldiers, who were trapped in Slovenian and Croatian barracks, held without food, water or electricity. On the other hand, they reacted angrily — and they were right to do so — when they saw the massacre committed against people who were standing in a breadline on Vasa Miškin Street in Sarajevo. The Serbs did not commit that massacre, but Alija Izetbegović, the Muslim leader, did, who paid foreigners to massacre his own people so that he could blame the Serbs. Not even Agatha Christie would have been capable of imagining such a shocking story. In any case, I am convinced that one day the truth will come out. I would like to emphasize that the Serbian army always helped Croatian and Muslim civilians. For example, we gave our approval for humanitarian aid to reach them through our territory. And that is not all. During the battles around Zenica, we evacuated thousands of Croatian civilians, and 904 soldiers whom the Muslims had driven out. From Vareš and central Bosnia, 15,000 Croatian soldiers reached us, whom we received and sheltered as if they were our own. We gave our approval to the evacuation of 12,000 Muslim women and children from Srebrenica. We even gave our approval to the UN, during some of the most brutal battles, to evacuate hundreds of soldiers who had previously massacred our own people. We enabled the UN peacekeepers and the International Red Cross to evacuate more than 200 wounded from Žepa. Tell me where the Croatians or the Muslims helped our people and our soldiers? Give me at least one example."

"The Western press always neglects these things," added the infuriated General. "And not only that: they kept harping about Serbian concentration camps, but why didn't they ever show pictures of the piles of Serbian and Muslim corpses who were killed by the Croatians in western Herzegovina? Why isn't the world informed about the shocking situation of Serbs who have remained in Sarajevo, Zenica, Mostar, Tuzla, Srebrenica and Zagreb? Even before the war had started, the Croatians destroyed Serbian homes in Zadar and Zagreb. Why was everyone silent then?"

"Many things are said about us that are simply not true," added the General. "Even the UN Security Council turned against us on the basis of dangerous, deceitful information, and introduced unprecedented sanctions against the Serbian people. The UN made the maximum effort to aid the Croatians and the Muslims. All humanitarian aid, even the aid dropped by planes, goes to them, and the UN even takes unfortunate advantage of Italian airfields, like the one in Ancona. Perhaps the Italians aren't even aware of it. But our people's blood has been shed for three years already, and we aren't even capable of outfitting field doctors or providing necessary drugs. There is no food. We can't even till the land, because we can't import enough gasoline for farm machinery. In contrast, the Croatians and the Muslims have at their disposal even arms, which are brought in clandestinely from Pula, Rijeka and Split. Every day arms reach our enemies either by sea or by air. In any case, it is never too late for things to change. This is an appeal I am making to Italy. The Italian and Serbian peoples are remarkably similar. Even our past destinies have been identical. In 1943, during the Second World War, the Italians gave the Serbs a great deal of aid...."

"Mali"

"I was born in a small village near the Neretva, and I survived thanks to one of two Italian soldiers from the Murgia Division. At that time, they were among other prisoners the Germans held who were placed in several nearby factories. That particular soldier was lodged in our house, along with eleven other Italian soldiers. They stayed for six months. My mother and father were so sick that they were barely able to move. And I was sick too. I would have died if that good soldier had not made an effort to feed me day after day, healing me with herbs and making me soup from grasses he managed to find."

"Do you remember the name of that Italian soldier?" we asked.

"Unfortunately, no," answered General Mladić. "But I remember that he called me 'Mali'."[5]

We returned to the war. "What is the ratio of forces between your side and the Muslims?"

"It is difficult to say. This is a civil war. And I repeat that we must not forget who is supporting the Muslims."

"Is it possible to stop the conflict?"

"If anybody had bothered asking the Serbs, this war never would have started. I repeat that we were forced to fight. Even now we are prepared to sign a peace agreement and resolve all existing problems in a peaceful manner. But the war cannot come to an end because neither the Croatians nor the Muslims want peace, nor do those who are lending them support."

"Aren't you troubled by the constant threat of NATO bombardment?"

"We receive threats of military intervention and bombardment every single day. We know that we are defending ourselves. How? Go ask the Croats and the Muslims. We aren't afraid, even if they approve sending a million-man fighting force against us. And I don't know how many mothers should have to send their sons here to die defending the borders that Tito's politicians drew up."

"Earlier, you said that it was not possible to end the war because of the policy followed by your enemies. But, if the war continues, doesn't it run the risk of spreading outside of the borders of Bosnia?"

"That will happen. I'm one hundred percent sure. And further-more — a million percent. If this war is not ended in time, it will surely spread throughout the entire world. Do not forget that the Balkans are the crossroads of Europe, Asia and Africa. And remember that today they are killing our children with weapons that come from German and French factories. But be careful, because if the war does not end, it will be a matter of concern for your children as well! You Italians should have been the first to be concerned. You remember the saying, that if a fire breaks out at your neighbor's house, it's always better to help him put out the blaze before it spreads and consumes your own house as well."

General Mladić was interrupted by a phone call for the hundredth time. He came back to finish his story.

"There will not be a single safe place on the entire planet if this war spreads beyond these borders," he warned us.

That was the end of the official interview.

General Mladić then invited us to join him and his men for dinner in a chilly ground-floor dining room. Smoked meat, cucumbers and cheese or mashed potatoes and meat. This was not a *de luxe* meal by any means. And our feet froze. In any case, thanks to the *rakija*, which was freely served, the atmosphere improved.

Our conversation returned to the cruelty of this war.

"Cruelty? No one knows what war is until they take part in it."

Then he spoke about Italy.

"Every Italian hospital has beds reserved for four or five Muslim children. How many beds are reserved for Serbian children? Why are you aiding the Muslims, but not us? Is it really possible that we have not even received a sack of potatoes from you, who have always been our friends?"

Mladić added, as if finishing his thought, "You even gave up all claims to Istria. But Istria is not Croatia; it has always belonged to Italy. It must be returned to Italy."

"I know Italy. I admire your country and its museums, artistry and traditions."

He smiled: "And you're good in sports, too: soccer and basketball. I was in Italy only once, back in 1979, when I graduated from the military academy. I was in Livorno, Pisa and Genoa. Later I went to Libya and visited Tripoli. What a difference!"

General Mladić, now relaxed, indulged in recollections.

"In Livorno, I wanted to buy a pair of shoes. I went into a store where there was an enormous selection. But shoe sizes differ in Italy and Serbia. I tried on one pair, and then a second, and then finally a third. None of them were any good for me. But I couldn't leave without buying anything. I finally settled on a pair that was tight. Later, I gave them to a friend. I remember an incident in Pisa. I was in uniform, and in the beginning everyone was looking at me as if they couldn't believe it. They thought that I was a Russian officer. That was in the days of the Red Army, and the Italians didn't really love the Russians very much at that time. Once they found out that I wasn't a Russian, but a Yugoslav, they started treating me nicely. My friends and I wanted to visit the leaning tower of Pisa, but we didn't have any lire. One young lady saw our dilemma and bought all of us tickets. She even offered to keep us company. The Italians are really extraordinary people!"

General Mladić did not satisfy our request to continue his story.

"You have a marvelous country," he said.

In any case, he did tell one more story: "During my stay in Italy, I was newly married and I really missed my wife. I sent her a letter from the ship and I put it in an envelope and addressed it to her. And I put the envelope, along with ten dollars and ten cigarettes, in a bottle. The money and the cigarettes were a reward for the one who found the bottle and sent my message of love to her. I flung the bottle into the sea as we were passing through the *Stretto di Messina*. My wife actually got the letter after some time. Not only the letter, but the money and cigarettes, too."

The end of dinner signaled the end of our conversation as well. We took leave of General Mladić, who left us with a twofold impression: he was a genuine soldier: strong, decisive and perhaps even merciless to his enemies, but a man who was free to laugh and be moved by emotion.

The message which General Ratko Mladić sends to the readers of *Gente*: "I hope that the truth will soon be discovered for the benefit of one and all, especially the Serbian people."

Symbol of Serbian Resistance

The following excerpts are taken from Jovan Janjić's interview with General Mladić, which was published as a five part series in NIN over January/February 1994.

General Ratko Mladić is the symbol of Serbian resistance in the war in the Republika Srpska Krajina and in the Republika Srpska. Mladić is not an officer who wears polished epaulettes. Most of them can't even be seen because they are caked with mud, since he spends most of his time on the front lines. His life has been in danger who knows how many times, but it looks as though he doesn't care. He says: "Why is my life more valuable than that of any other soldier fighting in the trenches?!" For this reason, and because of his bravery, his knowledge and courtesy, soldiers praise him to high heaven, emphasizing that they would go to war simply for him. Legends about him have arisen, and even though Mladić is egocentric in his job (with good reason), he replies: "I am not any kind of legend at all. I am simply an ordinary man defending my nation." He confers all the praise that he receives on his soldiers. He asks journalists to devote as much of their attention as they can to the soldiers: "I don't like talking to journalists, because I cannot emphasize all of the merits of every soldier. Can you imagine the conditions this winter? Each and every soldier is being showered with snow and rain and a hail of enemy gunfire. The enemy doesn't just go after us with just rifles and guns, but with weaponry they have received from all over the world ..."

How did you become a general?

In war and in greatly troubled times. My career as an officer began in Skoplje, where I arrived on November 4, 1965 to serve as the commander of an automatic weapons squadron in the regiment. By November 7, we had already commenced military maneuvers called "Autumn 65." Books could be written about these first days, because I was younger than everyone else in the unit I commanded. Somehow I managed to fit in. My first encounters with the difficulties of a soldier's life began during those maneuvers, which were attended by the then-Defense Secretary, Ivan Gošnjak. The maneuvers were difficult, but they had to be because even the most difficult days could not be compared with the easiest day of a war. That was how I began as a second-lieutenant and went though all of the ranks, including the rank of Brigade Commander. Then from 1989 to 1991, I served as the Head of the Department of Education in the then-Third Army Area in Skoplje, so from January 14 until June 26, 1991, I was one of the assistants to the Commander of the Priština Corps.

On June 26, while I was visiting a guardhouse in Morina during an inspection of the Yugoslav-Albanian border, the Commander of the Third Army called me on the phone. He informed me about a decision by the Supreme Command that I was to go on duty in Knin, and he asked me what I thought about it. I said I had nothing to think about; I had already decided to do it. He thanked me, but also warned me to go in a lower-ranking position than I currently held. But I did not interpret it as a demotion but as confidence that I could contribute to the prevention of war in those difficult and complicated times. At that time, fires were burning around military bases and guardhouses on the border in Slovenia. A brutal war was being waged against the JNA, water and electricity were turned off; innocent soldiers were killed in passing. It was the maximum humiliation that the army and the state could have received. So, that was how I took a seat in a helicopter on June 29, and went to Knin."

Mladić was said to be an unruly officer, even during the "Communist" era, while he was serving in Macedonia. In particular, he was the target of the then-Macedonian generals' lobby because he opposed decentralization, which was seasoned with anti-Serbian sentiments of growing proportions. He caused a genuine avalanche of fury after he arrived in Knin, when this city was the center of Serbian resistance. They (chiefly Croats) proclaimed him to be a war criminal of the first rank, but the Serbs turned him into a mythic figure. Mladić answers briefly, as if it did not matter to him: "I don't feel like that. I'm just defending my country."

His greatest "sin" was standing in defense of the Serbian nation and mobilizing it. Although he had difficulty understanding that there was no more common life to be had with yesterday's "brothers," and that a horrifying war was coming, Mladić warned soon after his arrival in Knin that: "Silence and passivity will not turn butchers and murderers into delicate creatures. Those who do not understand that the time has come to be or not to be, will go to the dung heap of history. Now is the time for all honest people to realize the danger that threatens us; many innocent people will perish in this vortex. The evil that has been visited upon us from elsewhere or resurrected on our own soil should be opposed with all the means at our disposal…"

In 1945, when he was only two years old, the Ustashi killed Mladić's father in the village of Sunj, which is in the area where Ante Pavelić was born. That is why he avoids using the word "Ustashi."[6] His mother, Stana (who lives in Pale), is in her eighties and she organized women from the Kalinovik area to take part in the struggle in this war as she had in the previous one. Ratko's brother was always in the trenches on the front lines. His wife, Bosa, is a great source of moral support for her general-husband, because she understands all of his difficulties and responsibilities; she cares for their son and daughter, and is involved in their education…. The big common house, where Ratko Mladić and his brother had spacious and luxuriously furnished apartments in the Sarajevo suburb of Pofalići, was the first one blown up when the war broke out in Sarajevo…

"I was never a 'disobedient' officer, but one who used his own mind to think…. By the end of July 1991, I was the titular commander of the Knin Corps in the General Headquarters of the JNA, where plans were being drawn up about what to do in case of aggressive behavior on the part of Slovenia and Croatia. At one meeting of analysts, I expressed my own observations and judgments. Actually, it was the observations and judgments made by the Knin Corps. I spoke in favor of performing appropriate tasks in this area to improve situation and to put forces of the then-*Zbor narodne garde* (The People Guard Corps)[7] in a position to surrender their weapons. But unfortunately, this concept was not accepted, which later resulted in horrible battles in areas of the Republika Srpska Krajina and in areas of the former B-H. Because military depots and storehouses came into the reach of many who should not even have seen mere pictures of weapons."

What was the hardest part about being in Knin?

Nothing was easy, either in Knin or in the former B-H. I am anticipating my third year of war in the trenches with the people and with the army. It was difficult to objectively grasp that this situation arose in the country and its Army. It was difficult to change people's understanding of things. There was no clear concept, no political attitude, no platform or position in which you could find support and from which you could act. It was very hard, for instance, to rely on what was coming from the highest level of state and military leadership because it was reacting, for the most part, to events. All of these measures were not enough to change the course of the ship. I was hit hard by the misfortune that struck the people, as well as by the misfortune that struck colleagues of mine who were blockaded in garrisons. I was hardest hit by the following situation: I learned about the brutal manner in which Croat authorities settled scores with members of Naval Area command center in Zrnovnica near Split, where 164 officers and soldiers were trapped in an underground facility. Instead of sending them proper provisions, they sent them dog food....

In one analysis that appeared in *The Guardian* (U.K.), Mladić was presented as a "moving force" who stood behind the Serbian military campaign in Bosnia. [*The New York Times*] presented him as the "Serb who calls the shots." And one diplomat, after meeting with Mladić, said that he was impressed with his almost encyclopedic knowledge of all the military maneuvers, victims and losses in his area. This confirms, among other things, the other aspect of General Mladić, to which his assistants testify, that the hardest news for him to take is learning about a new victim.

General Ratko Mladić is not only a great military leader and strategist who follows a clear objective for his soldiers, but oftentimes he is a real parent who shows understanding for the misfortunes and the problems of each and every one of his soldiers.

His present life is almost no different than the life of any soldier on the front lines. And how could it be any different when he is on the front lines himself, where shooting and killing are going on? A young soldier died in his arms from wounds he had sustained. This seldom happens to generals. Only a general like Mladić, after this incident in Žitnić, could say as bitterly as any parent: "Oh, God, why didn't you hit me with that piece of shrapnel instead of this child?!"

Your incursions behind Croat lines, as well as those of Colonel Lisica, often seemed to be pure exhibitionism...

For instance, there may be military actions taking place, while Lisica and I have to go to the village of Prokljan. As we pass through the village of Vaćani, where we find enemy forces, I tell Lisica that we shouldn't go through Bribir and Kistanje, but through Gorica to visit our unit in Bratiškovci, and then to Knin. There was a severe clash with the Croats in the village of Gorica because they captured a Krajina policemen named Lalović. Lisica says: 'Man, how are we going to go through Gorica when you know they've got a check-point there along with their own positions?!' Lisica is, otherwise, a brave man. Lisica is pretty harsh with them; he would have fought them right away. Anyway, we decide to take that route. We reached their check point in Gorica. I say to these soldiers: "Come on, get that thing out of the way, let us get through!" They were probably surprised by our insolence, so they moved the traffic barrier out of the way, and so we continued on our way without any problems ... By the time they figured out what had happened, we were long gone....

How were you named Commander of the General Headquarters of the Army of the Republika Srpska?

In beginning of May 1992, a few days after the attack on Second Army Area column in Sarajevo, I was in Belgrade to receive orders from the then-Chief of Staff, General Blagoje Adžić. At the time General Veljko Kadijević had resigned from his duties as Federal Defense Secretary, so Adžić was named as acting Federal Secretary of Defense. He called me to Belgrade to exchange views and to discuss changes in the situation. Our meeting was very constructive, and it lasted for more than an hour. I received certain orders and took a plane to Udbina. A waiting car took me to Knin. Just I walked into the Knin Corps

Command Center, the secretary handed me a telephone with General Adžić on the line, who ordered me to immediately transfer my orders and return to Belgrade right away, and that I was to travel to Sarajevo from there, where I was going to get new orders from General Milutin Kukanjac, the then-Commander of the Second Military Area, whose headquarters were in Sarajevo. It was a big surprise for me, a shock.

I was not expecting this. I did not suspect that the Command of the Second Area was going to be massacred on Dobrovoljačka Street during its retreat from Sarajevo. But it happened. Actually, in some way, I had expected as much. At this time my Ninth Corps (Knin), the Fourth, Fifth, Tenth and Seventeenth Corps were in the Second Military Area. On one occasion, when General Kukanjac came to see us after visiting the positions of my Corps near Drniš, he asked me for recommendations, based on my previous military experience, that I might have. I asked him as I was taking off my windbreaker: 'Excuse me, is your Command Center still in Thessaloniki?' He was surprised, and exclaimed: "What do you mean by *Thessaloniki*?" I replied: "There, in Baščaršija." He said: "Sure it's there. You don't expect it to be in your Kalinovik, do you?!" Then I told him: "First order General Praščević (Chief of Staff of the Second Military Area) to clear out of there and if you listen to me...." Unfortunately, he did not know what I was talking about. Not long afterwards, it was too late.

I was ordered to take over the duties of the Chief of Staff in the Second Military Area, however, I assumed the duties of Commander as well because Generals Kukanjac and Stanković had to go to Belgrade. I took over these duties at the new location of the Second Military Area. I found a very complex situation with a large number of traumatized people. Many men from these units did not know anything about their loved ones. There were more than a dozen officers in that unit, and some of them had spent their entire careers in Sarajevo. Many of them had left entire families and property behind, but they saved the Army and its property. Unfortunately, many of these men were never reunited with their families. Many families died. These events in Sarajevo certainly suggested the beginning of very brutal war in the region of the former B-H, because events were unfolding expressly in that direction. All the events followed the same screenplay, beginning with attacks on border posts in Slovenia to the tragedy of the Command of the Second Military Area. The attacks on Serbian wedding guests in Baščaršija on March 1, 1992 must certainly be taken into account, as well as other attacks on innocent people.

Unfortunately, in all of these events, from [the secession of] Slovenia to the acceleration of war in the former B-H, the Western media, the Slovenes, the Croatians and the Muslims played tragic roles and contributed to inflaming civil war. They fanned the flames of war by sensationalizing certain episodes. They blew things so much out of proportion (in order to cultivate hatred among Muslims and Croats for Serbs and the JNA) that no one can remember anything like it. Not even Goebbels' propaganda machine was able to create such effects.... When I took over the duties of the Second Military Area, I made it my goal to gather people and form a Command Center and General Headquarters, with some of the survivors of the Second Military Area, and with others who came with me from Knin, and with still others who were born in B-H.

We formed the General Headquarters of the Serbian Army right away. It was immediately clear to me that this was going to be a significant historical event. Even by then I had learned from some unconfirmed sources that the decision was made to withdraw the JNA from the territory of B-H. That left me deeply shaken. I could not believe that they would leave empty-handed people in such misfortune to fend for themselves. Events overtook each other, each one successively more tragic, and each one a defeat for the destiny of the people.

As soon as the decision was made to withdraw the JNA from the territory of B-H on May 19, 1992, we gathered the highest ranking political and military leaders, and made the decision to form the Serbian Army and its General Headquarters. It was formed at a session of Parliament in Banja Luka on May 11 and 12. I went to Banja Luka and met with the President, Dr. Radovan Karadžić, and with representatives. They informed me that the decision had been made that I was to take over the duties of Commander. The speedy withdrawal of the JNA soon followed. It was a long and exhausting battle which required the maximum physical and mental effort to withdraw military academies from Sarajevo and military bases from all across B-H, to rescue the civilian population, to create the General Headquarters of the Army of Republika Srpska, and fierce fighting was still going on....

Borders Are Drawn with Blood

Der Spiegel, Hamburg, November 7, 1994

©1994 Der Spiegel. Reprinted with permission of the publisher.

Q: General, sir, the Muslims are making advances. Do you fear that the Bosnian Serbs will be defeated?

A: The Muslims are well armed thanks to Western support, as well as to the former Yugoslav munitions factories that remain within Bosnian Muslim territory. We won't lose anything at all, but we will in fact retake territories that the Muslims have occupied — and along with that, as punishment, many more areas.

Q: Before that, are you going to order an offensive against UN-declared safe areas?

A: That has not yet been decided. The UN is supporting the Muslims in safe areas and is delivering arms to them. The blue helmets [UN peacekeepers] are nothing more than a striptease act, and they are goading the Muslims on. Why are the Western powers keeping silent about the number of airplanes, for instance, from Turkey or Germany that have been shot down — airplanes that were clandestinely delivering arms and munitions to the Muslims?

Q: The leader of the Bosnian Serbs, Karadžić, was the first to acknowledge weakness. The high command has announced a state of war — is that a measure you were forced to take or have your compatriots grown weary since you are unable to find volunteers for the front?

A: We have enough soldiers and enough tanks to defeat the Muslims by and large. But we will not do that. By declaring a state of war, we only wish to warn the world not to push us into an all-out war.

Q: But you alone are guilty of its escalation. Up until now, you rejected all peace plans.

A: Fruitless meetings have been taking place one after the other for three years already. We are, at this moment, interested in peace. But it must be agreed between the three parties engaged in the conflict. First, this truce must be withdrawn. We don't acknowledge diktats from abroad.

Q: Are you prepared to give up territories you have already taken possession of? And how much?

A: Don't raise my blood pressure. Earlier, all of Bosnia was Serbian. But, after the Second World War, the Muslims inflated themselves like a balloon. Today, we hold 73.8% of Bosnia; that is our living space, and we are defending it. In spite of that, we have generously given up the remaining 26.2%. To me, it is the same whether the Muslims and the Croats establish an Eskimo government in those areas or launch themselves into outer space with rockets.

Q: But Karadžić has agreed to negotiate Serbian-held areas. Would you oppose him if he were to give up territory?

A: We leave negotiations about percentages to the politicians. I am a general. Not one decision will be reached without the participation of the people. Unfortunately, borders have always been drawn in blood. If the Muslims continue the war, they will lose everything. Then you Germans can take them in, if you love them so much.

Q: Germany continues to be, for you, it seems, the principal culprit responsible for the war in the former Yugoslavia?

A: No, but an accomplice. After all, I have a positive opinion of Germans: in no way do I consider the present generation answerable to the crimes of the past. But Germany, as a great power, cannot blindly bind itself to the Croats and the Muslims. When the Croatians sang *Danke Deutschland*, it raised the hair on the heads of many Germans who are conscious of history. And that guy Koschnik from Mostar came over here to Pale and threatened us with NATO bombardment if we were to defend ourselves from Muslims in Mostar. We require a bit more understanding from the side of the Germans.

Q: Why?

A: German neutrality is important to find a peaceful solution. Why doesn't at least one German general come to the scene of the crime and confirm how dangerous the new escalation of this war is? I can guarantee his safety; not a hair on his head will be harmed.

Q: Your own brothers in Serbia have left you in a lurch. President Milošević is furious because you haven't signed the peace agreement.

A: Our goal was and is the unification of all Serbian lands, from Knin across Banja Luka and Sarajevo to Belgrade. What has been permitted to the German people — to live in a single state — cannot be denied to the Serbs. We will not permit a peace treaty to break us up into three parts.

Q: How much more time will it take before the sanctions on Belgrade will take effect and destroy your war machine?

A: A very long time. The world has instituted terrible and criminal sanctions against Serbia, and has forced the Serbian leadership to ... punish us. But the Serbian people on both sides of the Drina are united, and one day we will render our judgment.

Q: What will you do if President Milošević recognizes — as the UN is now demanding — Bosnia-Herzegovina as a sovereign nation?

A: That would be fatal, a fatal error with unforeseen consequences.

Q: In Serbia, many people believe that the Yugoslav army is not standing convincingly outside of Milošević's course in connection with the Bosnian crisis. At least one fourth of the officer corps is allegedly prepared to immediately engage on the side of their Bosnian compatriots in the case of a NATO attack.

A: We are sufficiently strong. We don't need any help, and we don't need men from Belgrade. But NATO has to finally get it through their heads that aerial bombardment alone has not yet won a single war. It will be decided by ground troops. But, just like Germany, the United States cannot even dream of allowing their sons to die for the Muslims. American generals have confirmed that for me right here.

Q: Aren't you afraid that one day you will have to go before the International Tribunal for War Crimes in The Hague? Even a part of the Serbian press describes you as a brutal cynic who is responsible for atrocities committed by the Serbian army.

A: I don't have time to spend with paid hacks. When American generals who have served in Vietnam or British officers who wrecked havoc on the Falkland Islands voluntarily come before the War Crimes Tribunal, then I too will come voluntarily to the

Hague. They waged wars in foreign countries — I defended my people, those who remain of our ancestors. I have not in any single act of war broken the rules of the Geneva Convention. Crimes must be pursued wherever they take place — but the West must not impose a judgment by force on the Balkans.

Nato Is Risking an Even More Dangerous War

by Sergei Sidorov, *Krasnaya Zvezda (Red Star)*, Moscow, 12/21/94

Q: General, Sir, please comment on the events that have taken place in Bosnia over the past few weeks.

A: I want to remind you that in Geneva last summer we proposed a halt to all acts of war for one year in order to activate a political dialogue. The Muslims, whose leader is Izetbegović, would not agree. Then we proposed a six-month cease-fire, and then a four-month cease-fire. In the end, we agreed to a one-month truce. However, the Muslims violated the cease-fire. Twenty days after that document was signed, they commenced operations in the area of Sarajevo. They were probably expecting that captured territory would be turned into a "safe area," and that all the rest — i.e., the Republika Srpska — would be turned into territories where they could share power through a NATO treaty.

Aside from that, Izetbegović's army was seriously counting on NATO airpower. Particularly indicative of that was the offensive launched by the Fifth [Bosnian Army Corps] from "safe areas" in Western Bosnia. They took advantage of their "protected status" to arm themselves and achieve offensive potential by means of a humanitarian convoy. Afterwards, by synchronizing their actions with the attack of the Muslim-Croat Federation in central Bosnia, they insolently penetrated and seized a recognized part of Serbian territory. We were compelled to reply sharply. Prior to that, the aim of our operation was not the Muslim people in Cazinska Krajina [western Bosnia], but was in fact the Fifth Army. When Dudaković [Commander of the Fifth Army], began suffering defeats, NATO airpower rushed to his aid. One hundred and twenty seven aircraft participated in three days of armed assaults. The attacks were carried out not only on our positions but on civilian targets as well, and with the most destructive means available to them. There were victims among the civilian population.

Q: From your point of view, where do the United States and Western Europe diverge on the question of Bosnia?

A: I think that this war has shown the untenable conclusions reached by those in Western Europe who consider it indispensable to preserve the powerful NATO alliance. The North Atlantic Treaty was created with the aim of protecting the territories of their member countries. However, NATO has, in the Yugoslav conflict, gone out of the framework of that mission and has shown its true face. That is not a defensive organization, but an offensive component of a strategy to widen their sphere of influence. Now, according to my reasoning, Western Europeans realize that they are threatened by the danger of being sucked in, through the Bosnian conflict, into a war far more dangerous than this one. It is possible that the difficult times, which Europe is experiencing, offer Americans an argument in favor of preserving their leadership of NATO, and that means control of the dangerous rivalries that are being unified.

Q: It is known that the United States recently stated that, if it had to choose between rescuing an American client-state like Bosnia and rescuing the NATO alliance, they will come to the side of the latter. That is, in fact, a backhanded compliment intended for you.

A: NATO gave itself a knockout punch. It resembles an overripe pear and it is only a question of time before it falls. After the Warsaw Pact had ended, the original reasons for the existence of NATO vanished. Russia has undertaken a peaceful orientation in international affairs, which also pulls the rug out from underneath NATO; however, another problem exists. Germany, for example, by taking advantage of disagreements between the United States and one part of the Western European countries, is continuing to spread its influence to the south, the south east, and the east. In Bonn, they are once again meditating on the geopolitical triad of Berlin-Belgrade-Baghdad. The United States, by aiding and building up Turkey, as with some other Islamic regimes, gravitates toward guaranteeing their interests and position in the Balkans. But that is contradictory to European desires. European interests suit peaceful concepts. War is not in its interest, neither here nor, for example, in Belgium. The European Union should have made a greater effort to restrain the NATO alliance during the Bosnian crisis, because the United States has been able to impose, precisely by means of NATO, its presence in the Balkans at Europe's expense.

Q: It seems to me that the West was concerned about the fact that, as a result of the quick military victories of the Serbs, as the best organized and the best armed side, the interests of the Croatians and the Muslims were endangered.

A: We never tried to inflict defeat on our enemies. Even though we could have done it, and we still can do it. We did not go to war against the entire Croatian or Muslim people. I will give you an example. In 1993, during the war between the Croats and the Muslims, when the Croatian population of central Bosnia was threatened with extinction, the Serbian people and its army helped them. We accepted them in our territory, and afterwards we transferred them, with the exception of armed military formations, to Herzeg-Bosna (a Croatian-held part of Bosnia and Herzegovina) and even to Croatia. In the vicinity of Vareš, we accepted over 30,000 Croatian refugees and over 700 of their soldiers and officers; in the Žepa region, 12,500 refugees and 903 soldiers; in the area of Bugojno, 6,000 refugees and 604 soldiers and officers.

Let me call your attention to the difference between us and the Croatians in the eyes of the world. We transferred them across Kupres and Livno. But they attacked us, not a full year later, with the goal of conquering Serbian territory. And, regrettably, they succeeded in taking the city of Kupres and the surrounding plateaux. In a similar manner, in 1993, we even helped Muslims to survive the tragedy in Mostar. And thanks to our help, they survived in Mostar.

Therefore, returning to the intentions of the Serbian side, I wish to emphasize that we stand where we stood before. We want the Muslims and the Croatians to rule their own territories. We don't need their homes, their roads, their bridges, nothing that belongs to them. But, by the same token, we don't want to give them what belongs to us. According to records of land ownership in the former Bosnia and Herzegovina, the Serbs own 70% of the land outright, which is approximately the amount of territory that they control today. And we only want our private property rights honored just as they would be honored in the West.

Q: Is it possible that the three sides in the Bosnian conflict could find a solution on their own, without the help of outsiders?

A: I think that is possible. The war would have been over a long time ago if there hadn't been any outside intervention and if there had been a ban on arms sales to all three warring parties, and not just Serbia. We could certainly find a solution, once the United Nations starts to treat all three sides in the conflict equally, and extends the opportunity for the three sides to come to an agreement among themselves. No peace plan imposed by outside powers will ever work. The warring parties must work out a peace among themselves.

Q: One commonly observes talks among the three warring parties — the Bosnian Serbs, the Croatians and the Muslims. Now it seems to be about two sides, doesn't it? The Muslim-Croat Federation and the Bosnian Serbs.

A: Exactly. Beginning in 1992, when Croatia carried out its aggression in Bosnia and Herzegovina, one continually found Croatian regular troops here. And today in Glamoč, and elsewhere, you will find Croatian troops: ... the 113th Brigade from Šibenik and the Fourth Elite Guard from Split, and a large number of special Croatian armed forces and the [Croatian] Ministry of Internal Affairs. With regard to that, one of the sides in the struggle is Croatia and its army. It started a war here with the intention of creating a Greater Croatia, taking advantage of, as it did in the Second World War, the Muslims so that they could extend their holdings to the Drina. Germany, Austria, the United States, and later other Muslim countries accepted Croatia's plans through the agency of the Bosnian Muslims.

The other side is the Muslims and their patrons. Before that, a word about the Muslim, Alija Izetbegović, is called for. He represents a current of fundamentalism, which Iran, Saudi Arabia, Pakistan and other Islamic countries are supporting.

The next side is the HVO [i.e., *Hrvatska Vjeće Odbrane*, The Croatian Defense Council]. That is the army of the former Herzeg-Bosna. They are supported by the same powers that stand behind Croatia.

The independent factor at this moment is the power of the federation. An agreement for its creation was signed in Washington by Croatian and Muslim representatives. For now, that federation exists only on paper; however, they invested serious effort in the goal of creating a united Muslim-Croat federation and a Croatian regular army in Kupres.

Another warring party is the Muslim army of Fikret Abdić. It has rather powerful military potential. In fierce fighting with the Fifth [Bosnian Government] Corps, Abdić succeeded in holding a part of his territory in Cazinska Krajina, consolidating and reorganizing the army which was loyal to him, and afterwards undertook successful operations. All through these operations he is gradually restoring lost territories and will most likely prove to be the decisive strength that will defeat the Fifth Corps. Abdić's Muslims find themselves in the same place in relation to Izetbegović, as do the Serbs, because of the fact that Izetbegović did not wage war only against Croatians and Serbs, but against his own people. Abdić has far fewer troops than Izetbegović. But many more Muslims voted for Abdić than for Izetbegović[8] in the first democratic elections in Bosnia, which were held before the war.

And finally, the Serbian community is a warring party in Bosnia-Herzegovina. All the warring parties started wars with us, except for Abdić's, which acted from the very beginning from a position identical to ours — to find a solution to the Bosnian problem, not on the battlefield but at the negotiating table.

We have always been in favor of a political dialogue. In order for the negotiations to be concrete, we have proposed and continue to propose a meeting between commanders of the warring parties, to sign an agreement for a final and lasting settlement of the war. In the future, all disputed questions must be resolved by the consideration of legal interests applied absolutely to all three sides. For example, the international organizations, including the UN, have been supporting Izetbegović's Muslims and the Croats. We have nothing against that; however, the other warring parties, including the Muslims of Fikret Abdić and the Serbian side, must as well be represented. Our delegation proposed such access to resolving the Bosnian crisis during recent contacts with the leadership of the UN; however, Izetbegović's representatives unfortunately reacted negatively to the proposal. That means that they were in favor of a war and a military solution from the beginning.

Q: The war in Bosnia is extremely unusual. It contains many aspects that invite new analyses by military experts. What formulations have you made about its character?

A: This is an extremely serious civil and international war, but for us, at the same time, it is also a war of national liberation, which has been conducted under conditions of massive outside involvement as well as NATO's strategy to manufacture a crisis. Up until now, they have used everything against us except nuclear weapons and their fleet of submarines.

As far as the mechanism of interference is concerned, it does, indeed, deserve to be written up in textbooks that teach the "required platform" for causing crises [in foreign countries]. A terrific number of governmental and non-governmental agencies have arrived in the territory of the former Federal Socialist Republic of Yugoslavia, committees and things like that, from the UN High Commissioner for Refugees to contingents of "blue helmets." They have, in fact, created a procurement-rearguard structure for the Muslim-Croat forces, which performs numerous favors for them, from building roads and bridges to cleaning city sewers. You just keep fighting!

On the other hand, thanks to the UN Security Council, a whole series of anti-Serbian resolutions have been adopted. They not only forbid us to defend ourselves with the means at our disposal, but also at the same time threaten to use the combined NATO air force to lend air support to Muslim-Croat operations. The resolutions for creating "safe areas" for Muslims have the same goal. What kind of safe havens are these if they serve as platforms for the resumption of warlike acts against the Serbian people? If I haven't provided enough examples, I can enumerate more of them.

Q: Indeed, all of this reminds one of George Orwell: Peace Is War; Truth Is a Lie...

A: And consider this. Compare me, for example, with General Rose or De La Presle, who command UN forces. We are all about the same age. I'm fifty-one. This war is the first in my career and I am waging it for all the people in this land with whom I was born and raised. Now count how many military campaigns my contemporaries have led and where. Now, after Vietnam, Africa, the Falkland Islands and the like, they can put blue berets on their heads and call themselves peacekeepers, but I, because I am defending all of my people from biological extermination, must be treated almost like a war criminal.

We Are Defending Our Pride and Honor, The Holy Crucifix and Freedom:
General Ratko Mladic's *Vidovdan*[9] Address (1995)
Oslobodjenje (Serbian)

The Army of the Republika Srpska celebrated its slava, Vidovdan, in Bijeljina in 1995. Representatives of state, political and military institutions attended, including President of the Republika Srpska, Dr. Radovan Karadžić, who awarded medals to units of the ARS, and General Ratko Mladić, who delivered the following speech.

The Divine Liturgy was conducted in the Hram Svetog Velikomučenika Georgija (the Church of George the Martyr) in Bijeljina by the Bishop of Zvornik and Tuzla, Vasilije. Crowds gathered to light candles for the souls of all Serbian victims from the Battle of Kosovo to the present day.

We are now celebrating *Vidovdan*, our Army's *slava*, for the fourth consecutive year in a state of war. It is a return to our ancient history and traditions. It calls to mind illustrious moments in Serbian history from the Battle of Kosovo to the present day. Thanks to the generous help of our mother countries, Serbia and Montenegro, we created a Republic during three difficult years of trial by warfare. The Serbian people have been forced once again, as they have been so many times in their history, to fight for their right to live, to fight for their very existence, and to fight for freedom, independence and the Orthodox faith. We are waging war for the fifth time this century to defend our centuries-old hearths; it is a war that was imposed on us by an Islamic-Western alliance. They imposed this destiny on our nation; we did not choose it alone. We were compelled to act. We defended our pride and honor, the holy crucifix and freedom throughout all these wars. All our values have been jeopardized countless times. It is precisely because of our dignity and honor, that we survived these catastrophes and battles, that [the Islamic-Western Alliance] wants to exterminate us once and for all. This is what they want today as well. And *Vidovdan*, a landmark in Serbian history, has great significance and is surrounded by the aura of legend; it is the gift and the imagination of the Serbian nation, and its shrine. *Vidovdan* is, by knowledge and tradition, an emblem of Serbian tragedy and glory. Tragic because it expresses the disunity and the decline of Serbian greatness, and glory because of the indomitable defiance of Serbian chevaliers, who, although they had fallen in battle, stopped the great Arabic flood that threatened to sink not only our nation but Europe as well. The tragedy of *Vidovdan* makes us one of the distinguished nations of the world community. We belong to the world community, even though our nation is set apart by virtue of *Vidovdan*. Nevertheless, we preserve something of our history, which inspires us to resist the uncivilized and anti-human creations of the contemporary world. Precisely for that reason, in addition to those who perished on *Vidovdan*, we celebrate our own victory and enthusiasm, which others cannot understand, nor will they ever understand ... our pride and resistance today. *Vidovdan*, as the cornerstone of our history, demonstrates in essence, our moral scope, and significance, in other words what kind of people the Serbs are. We Serbs have simply been compelled to go to war because we do not wish to trample our pride, our dignity and all the *Vidovdan*s that we survived up until now. *Vidovdan*, as the foundation of our history, disposes us to resist conquest, such as has been set on the stage of today's world. To many it seems superfluous and incomprehensible. But we are not putting the world on notice about our history in order for them to understand us; instead, we do not want the world to jeopardize us, conquer us out of sheer incomprehension. They will never be able to conquer us, regardless of the means by which they try to do so, whether they are military, political or others, more or less concealed and sordid. But we understand the world, so the often-repeated statement that there is no communication between us and the rest of the world is false. It is simply a lie, because the Serbs will not accept false and alien values. The Serbs will not renounce their national values, even though our enemies have tried to separate us from them countless times throughout history. Whenever they could not do so peacefully, they tried forcefully. The enemy unfortunately has reappeared because of our resolve and determination to be ourselves in our own land. For that reason, only Serbs seem to understand the great importance of *Vidovdan*. I feel that many theorists tried to come to a point where they could understand Serbian history, culture, and politics and with it, our nation. Few have succeeded. Even today, great mistakes are being made in analyses that forecast how the Serbian people will act in this historic moment. Something more than six centuries divides us from the day when Prince Lazar died on the plain of Kosovo in battle against the Turks. According to tradition, Prince Lazar and his army took the sacrament and bowed reverentially to the heavenly kingdom, defending their homeland, and the faith, freedom and honor of the Serbian nation. It is logical and natural for us to call to mind the illustrious name of the Serbian people. We understand the essence of this sacrifice and draw historic lessons from it. Today, we are creating a victorious army, and Prince Lazar's sacrifice has not been turned into a blind cult. We are neither kamikazes nor blind slaves who deceive their own people with insane sacrifices. We care for each and every one of our people and for that reason we have a great advantage over our enemy. Everything that we do in the name of *Vidovdan*'s values, honor, faith and freedom, must be done wisely and knowledgeably. We know well that the war is not the only means by which these values have been created. But if these values are fundamentally jeopardized, as is the case today, then the war, which outsiders have forced upon us, is the only way to protect and to defend these values. We understand each obstacle [placed before us] to be unjust and compulsion by force. This is clear to us and understandable to the rest of the world. Only those who wish to exterminate us refuse to recognize our true and irrefutable arguments. We have the right, as every other nation on earth, to live on our own land in a single country. And that right has been denied only to us Serbs. They want to tear Serbian state territory asunder into statelets, which they will then proclaim to be [territories belonging to] national minorities. It is clear to us that this is done only to nations designated for destruction. Germany did in 1941 what those today wish to do by cutting along the same seams, but by using other means with the aid of other mentors. These world powers want to dilute, divide and weaken our united strength. In this fashion, another great mistake is being made. All of the former Yugoslav territories have been given statehood and recognition. No one gave a state to the Serbs; they already had one. Unfortunately, not one single Serbian state is recognized today. It is best to be recognized by unification in one single country. That is the only way the Serbian people's sense of justice will be satisfied. The entire world has the right to self-defense, as do the territories of the former Yugoslavia, and these territories have even received [foreign] aid to do so, but only the Serbs have been denied the right to self-determination. It looks as though they would like to exterminate us. Peacekeeping forces that should have been assigned to maintaining peace were brought here to impose peace by force at the expense of our nation. They should be neutral but they behave in a biased fashion, protecting, aiding, supporting and urging our enemies on, not only by political means but by military means as well. The greatest paradox is that the UN supports a military alliance whose actions and military involvement is carried out under the aegis of the UN Security Council. Roads are opening for one and all, allowing and providing for uninterrupted communication between their peoples and the rest of the world. The imposition of blockades, embargoes, and even the interruption of communications between our own people is reserved only for the Serbs. Its purpose is to weaken Serbian resistance and Serbian decisiveness to prevail. This war was imposed on the Serbian people, a war of defense and liberation, and even though we were not prepared for it, we rose to the occasion. The wounds and the burial pits of the past, painful and difficult memories, deepen the feelings of jeopardy and the need for a decisive battle for survival. The Serbian people organized themselves to fight, and created their own army, which, together with them, prevented well-planned preparations for genocide, and protected the greatest part of historic Serbian territories, and liberated most of the occupied areas and created the prerequisites for Serbs to finally create a united country. All that we have created, and the many lives that have been lost, compel us to keep the memory of their bravery and heroism alive, obliging our further efforts and glorious battles to be waged by our Army for the defense of our people and the creation of the Republika Srpska. Throughout the trials of war, our army grew into a redoubtable military force, gained tremendous battlefield experience, and is ever ready to defend the results it has achieved, and so successfully bring the war to its conclusion. The soldiers and officers, and the army as a whole, have so far shown the highest level of patriotism and readiness for victory in crushing the newest Muslim-Croat offensives, and have displayed heroism *en masse*. They are conscious of the fact that, besides many problems, they have to wage this war and conclude it with victory and with a just peace. The Serbian nation, ever since it was founded, has not had a more difficult, complicated and dangerous war against a stronger, better equipped, and better supported enemy armed with the most advanced technology and weaponry. Even though we have been exposed to numerous incidents of blackmail, trials by fire, and pressures, we will endure and emerge as victors. Efforts are being made so that all our resources will have a greater function in the war, so that we can rationally use all the forces available to our people and society.

I would like to take this opportunity on behalf of all the members of the army, who bear in the most direct fashion the burden of war for the Serbian nation, here and in general, to express gratitude for the tremendous support that Serbian patriots and sympathizers have provided for our just, defensive battle for liberation.

The next phase is very important, and it could have crucial bearing on the outcome of this war. The Army of the Republika Srpska and forces of the Interior Ministry will do everything in their power to ... preserve Serbian territory, its people and country, and to try to obtain the earliest possible peace built on just foundations. During this difficult period, we expect the consolidation of Serbian unity. The results we have achieved, as well as the victims fallen in our struggle, will not allow anyone the right to weaken our fighting power or our right to behave according to our own best interests. We must dedicate ourselves one and all to the struggle and give everything we have. Only by being united and certain of the justice of our struggle will we achieve a just peace. In that sense, I hope we can work together, because all the sacrifices from the Battle of Kosovo to the present day oblige us to do so. Then the world will understand our struggle and will understand the war, which they have imposed on us. With faith in our unity and victory, it is my hope that the Serbian people will await the next *Vidovdan*, a great holiday, in freedom, peace and in a united Serbian nation.

Long live the Republika Srpska!

Excerpts from
General Mladic's Remarks
Following the Croatian "Operation Storm"

Over the course of August 2-5, 1995, the Croatian army drove 250,000 Serbs out of Krajina. An estimated 4,000 to 7,500 civilians were killed in the matter of a few days.

For the third time this century the baneful shadows of killings, genocide and exodus hang over the Serbian people, and it is in many ways probably the most tragic manifestation in its history. And the Serbs did not start this war any more than they did the others. They were dragged into this war against their will.

.... I must tell you that the Serbian people have lived in these areas for more than a thousand years and the real estate registry indicates they own 64% of the land; accordingly, the Serbs are the true owners of a large part of the former B-H. Bearing that in mind, the international community must be on the same terms with all three sides in this struggle with respect to their self-determination.

.... The international community, according to the Vance Plan, provided guarantees for the security of the Serbian people in the RSK, but that promise was not fulfilled. We witnessed the regular armed forces of Croatia provoke the greatest single act of ethnic cleansing in this century in Europe. It was committed against the Serbian people, and certain members of the international community lent support to Croatia and its aims.

In the course of a single year, about 700,000 Serbs were driven from areas where they had lived for a thousand years, and all their properties were plundered or burned. At the same time, members of the Croatian armed forces committed crimes *en masse* throughout the RSK, where nothing is known about the fate of some 10,000 Serbs. It is strange that the democratic world sees all of this, but makes an effort to shut its eyes to the crimes committed by the Croatian armed forces.

.... Fifty thousand soldiers participated in the aggression against the Republika Srpska. These forces were composed of a broad coalition of Croatian defense forces as well as the armed forces of the Muslim-Croat Federation, which does not exist except on paper. The armed aggression of Croat forces resulted in the deaths of 5,000 civilians, while 125,000 were driven from their centuries-old homes right before the eyes of world public opinion. It is noteworthy to add that Grahovo, Glamoč and Drvar were townships in the former Yugoslavia that each had a majority Serbian population that composed ninety percent or more of the population. A majority of these people were relocating for the second and third times over the course of the war.... There are about 300,000 of them in RSK, not counting those from the RSK who have decided to stay here in the RS.

.... One part of UNPROFOR, but chiefly Islamic countries, and the NATO air force, launched armed military action against the Serbian people over the last month, and have undertaken criminal attacks against military and civilian targets. International public opinion could have confirmed the barbaric destruction at the crime scenes, especially the telecommunication systems of Serbian radio and television (Kožara, Svinjar, Bečanj, Majevica, Trovrh, Nevesinje and several smaller transmitters), hospitals (Serbian Sarajevo, Ozren), radio stations (Sokolac, Prnjavor, Doboj, Ozren, Lukavica, Srbinje), water reservoirs (Sarajevo, Han Pijesak, Kalinovik, Nevesinje), PTT [i.e., the government postal, telephone and telegraph services] transmitters (Kozara, Ciganište, Kula, Trovrh, Nevesinje, Han Pijesak, Majevica, Serbian Sarajevo), cattle farms and agricultural properties (Romanija, Han Pijesak, Srbinje, Kalinovik, Jahorina, Doboj) refugee centers in Han Pijesak and Višegrad, numerous factories, bridges, all four bridges on the Drina at Srbinja, electrical substations and 110 kilovolt long-distance power lines in Višegrad....

NATO Rapid Reaction forces have long participated in attacks on the settlements in Serbian Sarajevo. I warned Generals Smith and Janvier that we did not attack UNPROFOR forces nor did we have reason to, but that didn't count. It is well known that Rapid

Reaction forces came to B-H to protect UNPROFOR forces. I would like to remind you that not one single member of the peace-keeping forces was killed because of Serbian actions. At the same time, a fierce artillery attack was launched by the Rapid Reaction Forces, during which some 450 mortar volleys were launched, incurring terrific material damage, killing 17 and wounding 46 civilians. Ten patients were killed over the course of two attacks on the Žica hospital in Blažuj.

Some 3,200 aircraft participated in NATO's barbarous attacks on the Republika Srpska, dropping more than 10,000 tons of explosive material, killing about one hundred civilians and wounding more than two hundred. Citing only the instance of Srbinje, two children were killed near a bridge while five children were seriously wounded and taken to VMA [the military hospital] in Belgrade. Enormous physical damage was inflicted which runs in the billions of dollars....

In addition to the massive air strikes against civilian and military targets, NATO made daily surveillance runs, photographed positions of ARS units, and provided this intelligence to the Croatian and Muslim armies. NATO has become an aggressor by taking such action, because it has taken one side in this conflict.

From the evidence we have, the sustained massive air strikes by NATO forces, the U.S. and other Western countries permitted Croatia to turn to open aggression against the RS, while the forces of the Muslim-Croat coalition in the former B-H began a new offensive in nearly all theatres of operation. The Great Powers use such tactics to prevent the quick resolution of a conflict and the return of peace, but this most recent eruption of military action threatens a new and greater escalation of the conflict. At the same time, we have information that within the ranks of the Muslim and Croatian armies, there are more than one hundred generals and high-ranking Pentagon officers, the CIA, as well as members of other western secret services who are training their units and preparing the offensive for them. It is not even worth mentioning the violations of the arms and equipment embargo on this occasion, because it never really mattered for the Muslims and the Croatian side, since they have been continually receiving large quantities of military equipment and state-of-the-art weaponry from all sides, which one can see in military inspections in Zagreb, Bihać and Zenica.

The world's largest public relations firms are participating in a media war against our people. It is well known that we have been judged to be the criminals for the Markale marketplace bombing, and for numerous other crimes, even though it was later shown that Serbs had not perpetrated these crimes.

I warned Commander Janvier in a timely fashion that the most recent massacre — Markale II, which served as the pretext for NATO air attacks, was stage-directed against the Serbs because the Muslims had committed the atrocity, but he replied that he was not competent to order an investigation and halt the planned attack. That confirms that NATO forces are beyond the control of the UN and that nothing can rein in their behavior. Western diplomats have used media pressure and the demonization of the Serbian people as a pretext to introduce harsh punitive measures by the international community against the Serbian people. Numerous global public relations firms have accepted statements and information from the Muslim and Croatian sides in global centers of power, and have prepared media actions in advance to launch accusations against the Serbs and in this fashion guarantee an anti-Serbian posture.

....Where is the international community today? Where are the humanitarian organizations to witness the greatest exodus of Serbs ever to have taken place? There are nearly half a million homeless, resulting from the ethnic cleansing Serbs from Serbian regions by the Croatian and Muslim authorities.

Public opinion was alerted when the Croats laid in wait and torched an overcrowded busload of Serbs from Srbobran, which was in transit to Jajce. More than seventy women, children and the elderly died on that bus.

....The Serbs have recommended peaceful solutions from the beginning, but the horsemen of the apocalypse of war did not allow it, and they did not accept it....

Answer to The Hague

NIN (Belgrade), March 1996

"I think that the war is over here. It would be a real catastrophe if it were to continue, not just for peace in these areas, but on a much wider scale. We will do everything to keep peace alive. There are negotiations sponsored by the OSCE underway in Vienna about creating trust among the warring sides, reducing tensions, and military capability and arms control, which is a good sign.

"But we are concerned because American leaders indicate that they will arm and train a Muslim-Croat army and that they have already appointed some so-called "private agencies"[10] [to undertake this task] and it is a well known fact that this agency works with the current staff of military experts in NATO. Peace is necessary not only for the Serbian people, but also for all the people who were at war with us, because many are tired of it. I think that, at the end of this century, we and the international community have to learn a lesson from this war and let it perhaps be the last one.

"We created the Republika Srpska and now it is necessary to ... let reason guide us. My heart was broken when I saw the Republika Srpska Krajina disappear. Then the counties in the western part of our Republic disappeared one after the other. If we had been all together, from Belgrade to Banja Luka, we would now be loading cannons and supplying our military instead of participating in elections for peace, and the result would probably be different."

The war in the territories of the former B-H is a very specific case, judging by the engagement of military forces, military actions and relations with the international community. Many people participated in different ways in this war, and are now quite wisely washing their hands of it. What is your comment on all that has happened?

It cannot be said that humane and inhumane wars exist. All wars are generally inhumane, except defensive wars. This war was imposed not only on the Serbs but also on the Muslim and Croat people. Unfortunately, the Muslims and Croats (who are merely toy soldiers that the great powers moved) declared war on us, and it is a fact that they waged war not for their own interests but for those of the Great Powers.

This is probably one of the most inhumane wars ever waged on our planet in recent memory. The Great Powers wanted to settle their interests in the Balkans and they swam in murky waters to help the Muslim and Croat sides. On one hand, Islamic countries endeavored to use the war for the expansion of Islam toward Europe and for the Islamization of the Balkans and Europe. They accomplished this with humanitarian aid and by arming the Muslims, and with terrific financial support from America and some Western European countries, which financed weapons purchases and paid off the media, enabling them to obtain diplomatic, political, economic and all other kind of aid for their protégés.

Some European countries, first of all Germany, endeavored to use this time and this war for their own interests. For them, the Croats were the vanguard for the realization of their goals. America played a negative role in this war. It even forced some of its allies to bomb the Serbs for the benefit of the Croats and the Muslims. Imagine one small country like Holland, which dumped its own deadly bombs on the Serbian population, taking orders from America and NATO! The question is raised — why did it happen that way? America skillfully exploited the Gulf War, the war here, and the war in Chechnya, and is trying to put Orthodoxy and Islam on a collision course. We must be conscious of the fact that Orthodoxy must not fall into such a trap.

At the same time, the international community has been marginalized, especially the UN, in a completely humiliating fashion, which has behaved, over the last few years, just as one lady getting on in years[11] has dictated them to behave."

Now that the fighting has ended and the implementation of the Peace Agreement is going according to plan, can you give an evaluation of the course it is taking?

We really suffered a lot during this war. We neither won nor lost, which is perhaps a tragedy. Such politics were imposed on us because the war was not ended by military means. Obviously, international factors emphasized the outcome of such a war. At the same time, Western countries, led by America, always stepped in on the side of the Muslims and Croats at critical moments and helped them survive defeat, so that we could not, taking into consideration that we were under a total blockade and alone, do something more than what we did.

The Croats were defeated in the war in 1991, and if the international community had not come to their aid at that moment, and if the UN had not been abused, they would not even have thought of continuing the war. The same thing took place in the war in the former B-H. The international community always leapt to the aid of the Muslims and Croats, whether to issue ultimatums not to take Sarajevo, Bihać or Goražde, or ultimatums to surrender mounts Igman and Bjelašnica to UNPROFOR forces that would later turn this area over to the Croats and the Muslims.

You have said that this was an inhumane war and that many aided the Muslims and Croats. Isn't this the reason you have been branded as a war criminal [by the ICTY, which] ... seeks your arrest and trial?

The Serbs were proclaimed guilty for everything that happened, from the beginning of the war to the time of the Dayton agreement. From the point of view of the Great Powers who started this war, we are the sole perpetrators, while they rub their own bloody hands with relish over the common calamity. The Germans want everybody to forget the atrocities they committed during the First and Second World Wars; they fabricate atrocities supposedly committed by our side, and lead anti-Serbian campaigns. We have lost, however, the Republika Srpska Krajina and almost one third of the Republika Srpska in this war, which are centuries old Serbian territories. We are the greatest victim of this war.

The Americans have their own calculated interests. They want the world, by means of this war, to forget about their crimes in Hiroshima, Nagasaki, Vietnam, Cambodia, the Gulf, etc. It is a fact that we defended our own land not just against Muslims and Croats, but also against the German volunteers who served in the Croatian army — mujahideen from Islamic countries — and against the Americans who not only bombed us but also planned military operations for the Muslims and Croats. And their so-called 'retired generals,' like General Galvin, prepared their army. Imagine how many generals, colonels and other military experts served in their ranks [i.e., with the Muslims and Croats].

There is no greater shame for Serbs than to have been bombed by a country as small as Holland. I don't know, but who could the Dutch attack on her own? Not even Denmark. And they dared to bomb the Serbs. That miserable Van den Broek [the Dutch Foreign Minister in 1991] committed atrocities and contributed immeasurably to the disintegration of the former Yugoslavia.

What, in your opinion, influenced the worldwide anti-Serbian media campaign?

In most of the Western media, truth that has been paid for is funneled through TV, the press and radio. Fabrications and untruths were financed by oil magnates from Islamic countries; and certain foreign media spread monstrous lies about the Serbian people, about certain individuals and about me, personally — a person wouldn't believe it! And to top it all off, they reported my death several times.

Certain Western media had positioned themselves well in advance wherever Muslims had prepared diversionary attacks on their own people, such as in the Muslim cemetery, Vasa Miškin Street, Markale, and others, and they portrayed these as Serbian atrocities and demanded that the Serbs be punished. Now it is known that these incidents involved media lies, frame-ups, and the handiwork of the Muslims and a few Western intelligence agencies. Even though everything is known today, the Serbs were nevertheless severely punished, and nothing happened to any one [of the actual perpetrators].

Even though the Great Powers attacked us — not in a sense that applies to Croats and Muslims, because they are non-entities as military powers, but NATO and some Western powers — we did not truckle, we remained upright and dignified, as we always have in our history. We did not try to suck up to the stronger party, as the Croats behaved toward Austro-Hungary, and so became their stable boys,[12] or the way Muslims and Croats acted in concert with Hitler in the Second World War, as blind servants of fascism. Imagine a powerful America and some Western powers, our nation's allies in past wars, who in this war are allied to those whom they had fought in the Second World War.

General, Sir, why was there such a high level of foreign involvement in the armed conflict in the former Yugoslavia? What were their real intentions?

Plenty of them were meddling [i.e., in the affairs of the former FRY], and the face of the international community as presented by the facade of the UN, collapsed after all this happened. It should be said that there were honest individuals among them who attempted to present things realistically. However, it was probably unsuitable for those who wanted to marginalize the UN and put them in the back seat with regard to [emerging] historical events. Some Western countries are a disappointment to me and to my nation because they have been knocked down to the level of servants. I cannot at all comprehend how our fathers and grandfathers fought in the same trenches with the French, the English and the Americans, and how we waged wars against the same evil in the First and Second World Wars, and to see how they are behaving toward us today.

It is incomprehensible that the Americans, on the one hand, are fighting Iranian fundamentalism and want to topple Teheran in Asia, while, on the other hand, they are supporting the fundamentalism of Alija Izetbegović and are creating a Teheran in Europe. The entire international community, at least in the Western hemisphere, was united in the Gulf War and relentlessly bombed Baghdad, which is several thousand years old, under the pretext of fighting Islamic fundamentalism. In the coming years, there will be 500,000 to 600,000 Muslims from Islamic countries in Sarajevo. Who knows what will happen there?

Now there is peace. After signing the Dayton Accords, the Serbian people in the Serbian part of Sarajevo voted by referendum that they do not want to remain part of the Muslim-Croat Federation. The international community did nothing to listen to the democratically elected leaders of the people but answered to the orders of the Great Powers. Now, together with IFOR, ARK and international police forces, they regard what is happening to the Serbian population with indifference and are not offering any help at all.

During the war, you met with many international representatives, UNPROFOR commanders and humanitarian organizations. To what degree were they biased?

There are numerous examples of extremely biased behavior by representatives of international organizations in this war, but I will call your attention to only the most recent examples. His Excellency Carl Bildt, along with experts on international politics and IFOR, brought Muslim policemen to Vogošča and Ilijaš and established their authority, and Bildt was present during uncivilized acts of taking down the Serbian flag and throwing it to the ground, and did not condemn it. On the other hand, not one international official followed the return of the Serbian population to Mrkonjić Grad and Šipovo, aside from some low-level officials and IFOR officers.

UNHCR representatives have been stampeding over the last few days to make contracts with Alija Izetbegović to replace windows on buildings in Sarajevo, and the French contingent of IFOR is using helicopters to airlift high-voltage lines to Muslims, and build bridges for them, but not one of them even thought of repairing bridges that they destroyed during the bombardment of Serbian territory, especially the bridges on the Drina. At the same time, hundreds of IFOR vehicles escort Muslims to Goražde through the territory of the Republika Srpska by way of Sokolac and Rogatica, but the IFOR and ARK generals deny all of our requests when we ask them to open lines of communication for the passage of the Serbian population through Goražde from Višegrad for Srbinje or Čajniče, and vice versa.

I must say that there are political elements in the international community and humanitarian aid organizations that behave uprightly and honestly. There are straightforward relations with some national contingents in IFOR and ARK, first of all with the Spaniards, Greeks, Russians and others, but there is a great deal of provocative behavior arising not just from individuals but entire ARK or IFOR units, and extremely arrogant behavior by some officers. They conduct brutal raids on factories and camps and are always looking for violations on our side.

There are cases of soldiers and officers from some countries within ARK or IFOR who are forcibly handing out propaganda to our children, carrying out raids, hunting for President Karadžić and General Mladić, controlling the movement of the population at some checkpoints, conducting surveys among the population to find out where they took part in the fighting. They have no right to do that. The Great Powers are now making up all sorts of mass graves of Muslims and are running around all over to find them....

There were many difficult moments in this war. How do you feel about the exodus of the Serbian population from Sarajevo?

The continuing attempt by the international community to throw us in the same basket as the Muslims and Croats after such a bloody war is pure nonsense. The mass exodus of Serbs from Sarajevo is the strongest example. These people simply do not want to live under the rule of those who once slaughtered Serbs during the First and Second World Wars, as well as in this war.

These people simply do not want to serve either Alija Izetbegović or Franjo Tudjman. They did not fight for that. That spells defeat for the international community. They failed the test because that peace agreement caused an exodus of the Serbian people. We did not lose Sarajevo during the war; we lost it on the negotiating table in peacetime.

We were under a blockade until a few days ago. We don't have the fuel to help these people. They are our soldiers, our nation, and our children. The international community, for example, provided fuel and supplies to evacuate Muslims from Srebrenica and Žepa Croats from Žepča, Vlašić, Kupres, etc. They provided everything: tents, housing, food but they are putting pressure on us not to move.

Why are IFOR commanders refusing to meet with you, even though you are still Commander of the Supreme Headquarters of the Army of the Republika Srpska?

They can avoid me as much as they want — Generals Smith, Walker and Joulwan are the representatives of great world armies — but the people are fleeing from them. These people are coming to me, Ratko Mladić, whom these generals want to crucify.

Imagine the situation that takes place when officers and IFOR soldiers take a poll among refuges from Sarajevo who sacrificed their homes, their property and everything that they and their ancestors had worked for over centuries, and are running away to save their own lives. It is unheard of. Never in any war has any nation exhumed the remains of their own dead, centuries old or recent, and moved them to another area. Imagine what kind of situation it is when you meet a freezing mother carrying the bones of her own son, who was killed in 1992. The elderly women gathered the bones of her son in some plastic bag, carrying them on her back to rebury them on Serbian land, so that Muslim extremists would not take revenge on the dead.

The international community doesn't see the tears of Serbian mothers. Never in my life have I seen such horrific and touching scenes, to dig up and remove human remains. The Serbian people are moving one- and two-hundred-year-old graves from Sarajevo to other territories. Is this the democratic world order that is offering us well being? Are these the results of NATO expansion?

Serbian people have proclaimed you to be a hero.

Everything that I did in my life I did not do [merely] to please people. Everything I did was motivated by my personal beliefs and by interest in my nation. And in this war I attempted, through personal example, to protect the lives of our people, soldiers and officers, and not to think about my own life. My nation was my army and I am a small part of that army. All honors go to the Serbian soldier.

My life was in danger many times during the war. I was wounded, as were my fellow soldiers, but we prevailed. But I did not think about my own life during the war, or before the war, nor do I think about it now after the war. Every one who is born must die; God and nature have decreed it so. Despite all the efforts of medicine and its great achievements, nature cannot be stopped. It is natural that everyone has to die. Immortal people do not exist in a physical sense, but there are people who are immortal because of the things they did during their lives.

I was never intoxicated by thoughts of greatness or by ecstasies of glory with the thought of being immortal. I had my own approach to life. It was never important to me how long or how well I was going to live, but what I was going to give to my nation. And if I, in the course of my life, was able to give something in these difficult times to my nation, and insure its survival, then I would be happy and satisfied.

During the war, you continuously spoke in favor of honoring the Geneva Convention, and of your support of humane treatment for the enemy from the Army of the Republika Srpska. Any comment?

We are the only nation and the only army that offered a helping hand to our enemies when it was most difficult for them. During the war between Croats and Muslims, we allowed weaker Croat forces to withdraw the Croatian population of Žepča, Travnik, Bugojno, and Vareš through our territory, even though the forces were armed. We accepted more than 1,000 of their officers and soldiers and 30,000 civilians from the region of Žepča and Zenica. We hospitalized hundreds of their wounded and we allowed supplies to reach their population through our territory, because we considered them to be human beings. We accepted more than 600 of their soldiers and officers and more than 6,500 civilians from Bugojno at Kupres, and more than 20,000 civilians and who knows how many soldiers from the region of Vareš, and 1,000 soldiers and more than 20,000 civil-

ians from Travnik.... We transferred them safely to their territory —
so that they could treacherously attack us a couple of months later
with these same Muslims, when things were the most difficult for us!
The Croatians of Herzeg-Bosnia and Croatia were not grateful for
such help, but on the contrary, they displayed unprecedented hatred
and fury towards Serbs in the Krajina in the final battle.

If we had wanted it so, none of the Muslims of Srebrenica and
Žepa would have made it out. They were in a hopeless situation. We
evacuated them in the presence of UNPROFOR from Srebrenica
and Žepa through our territory in central Bosnia. In both cases, you
will ask yourself, why? Because the Serbian people are proud as a
nation and because, first of all, I'm a human being [first] and then an
officer and a general. Not for a second, not to mention days, did I
wage war against civilians, either Croat or Muslim.

I waged war against hordes of Muslim bandits under the leadership of Alija Izetbegović, and against hordes of fascist Croats
headed by Franjo Tudjman, who are worse than the worst fascists
in World War II. We waged this war to defend ourselves. I did as
much as I could, but they want to humiliate everyone, and rub
everyone's face in the dirt at all cost, including that of the Serbs.

What does The Hague Tribunal mean to you?

It's a parapolitical court. It is not a court of justice, but a court
of politics. If it were a court of justice, it would have first tried
those who declared this war and those who began this war — the
Croats and the Muslims. We proclaimed a state of war only at the
end of last year, first in part, and later the whole territory of the
Republic. Why has this court been reserved for Serbian politicians
and generals, as if we had waged the war with aliens from another planet? Why isn't there any room for Tudjman and Alija and
their generals? Why is there no room for the international powers
that cooked up this war? What about the generals who bombed
Serbian civilians, Serbian positions and our people, killing the
weakest of them? Yes, of course, now they are playing the role of
peacekeeping forces with ARK and IFOR. In the end, this court
legalized terrorism. The tribunal legalizes Muslim kidnappings of
our officers, General Đukić, Colonel Krsmanović and other soldiers, and then they take them in The Hague, proclaiming them to
be witnesses, and emphasizing that they will keep them in prison
until they start talking. This kind of behavior and the imprison-

ment of witnesses did not even exist in the Stone Age, not to mention today's civilization.

I would have been stricken by bad conscience if I had waged the war in someone else's land, in other country, or if I were to have invaded some other country. Throughout the entire war, I defended my nation on its own Serbian land. It was my duty to do so, an obligation and the highest honor. That is why I'm an officer, to place myself at my nation's disposal during the most difficult times.

Did war crimes take place that would justify the creation of The Hague Tribunal? And, why does the West insist that it is necessary?

Every war, by nature, is a crime, but that does not mean that everyone who takes part in it is a criminal. We defended our land and our people. War was declared against us. All of those who started this war against us and those who supported them committed crimes against us. The international community committed a crime by going easy on the break-up of Yugoslavia, one of the founding nations of the UN, and a loyal member for more than fifty years.

I'm absolutely sure that no one — neither an individual nor a unit — had permission to do anything outside of the international laws governing warfare. Our nation fought righteously, honestly and bravely. The army exchanged each and every Muslim and Croat prisoner early or simply released them, as we just now did, although the Muslims and Croats are still holding a mass of Serbian civilians, soldiers and officers in their prisons.

The Army of the Republika Srpska did not take part in any crimes, and it did not commit any crimes. We waged the war in compliance with provisions of the international laws governing warfare. For instance, many have manipulated the facts concerning Srebrenica, Žepa, Goražde, Sarajevo, the French pilots, etc. We treated Muslim civilians in a manner befitting a civilized people, and we transferred them with our own buses in the presence of international forces. UNPROFOR soldiers and officers were in every bus. They provided fuel, and they gassed up the trucks and buses for transport with their own tankers. And now it doesn't even occur to these generals, like Walker, Smith and others, to provide fuel for the Serbs in Sarajevo, to help our tormented people who don't want to stay in the Muslim-Croat Federation.

The Hague Tribunal was created in order to cast Hiroshima and Nagasaki, Auschwitz, Dachau and Jasenovac, Cambodia, the Falklands, and the Gulf War into oblivion to thereby make the Serbs the black sheep of the planet until the next brutal war that is dreamed up by the same persons who wrote the screenplay for this one. And this war was not dreamed up here or in Serbia, but far away.

For example, the Croatian Defense Minister is Gojko Sušak, a foreign citizen of an overseas country. And he, who came to attack our people, is not criminal, while I should be considered a criminal because I defended my nation from such a criminal and his supporters, who, for his own interest and on his command even bombed powerful NATO forces.

According to such criteria, I should be put on trial along with our political leadership and the Serbian nation — but those who prepared bombs in Aviano, Cesenna, and on aircraft carriers and then dumped them on our children should not be tried. This is not international law. Maybe this court was created to provide someone with a victory in upcoming elections in one of those gardens of democracy in the West. This court is located in The Hague, but no Serbian plane ever bombed The Hague or Holland, and no Serbian plane ever will. On the contrary, their bombers and officers came here to show us their skills. And now they should be free to walk around and explain democracy to our people, and to generals of the Serbian army like Đukić, who should be taken to The Hague with Mladić leading them all to be tried and crucified just as Samson was, to entertain the world for the next year or two, while the Great Powers think up something tastier for their audience. They would like to tie up our generals and take them to The Hague, and have their own generals swagger through the Republika Srpska to offer Serbian children "democracy" posters and propaganda material.

NATO is looking for you. They put your picture on a wanted poster, just like the ones in old Westerns. Is there any chance that they will catch you?

They have to understand the fact that I'm valuable and that the people will protect me. My good name, my honesty and my personal sacrifice in this war protect me. It is not my intention to play peek-a-boo with NATO forces in the former B-H.

Some people have to realize that conditions must be created to heal the immeasurably deep wounds created by this war, but instead they are forming whole CIA teams to find out where I go and what I do; and they are coming up with various plans. They want to execute these plans and arrest me. But I think they learned something from Aidid in Somalia. They would be better off offering a hand to strengthen the peace — not to create further problems and complications. Recently, their generals, politicians and journalists have been making assertions that I am threatening them. I am not threatening them; and I was not in a position to deny the many lies that journalists printed. On the contrary, they are constantly threatening me and weaving a net around me. The message for them is simple: they came here as a military power that was going to guarantee peace, but the Serbian people fled from them in Konjic, Serbian Sarajevo and from other Serbian areas.

What kind of a country will the Serbs create in the former B-H?

We'll create the country that the Serbs want to have created. We will be the heads of our own household. We're not asking the international community to help us, but we don't want them to oppress us. We did not want to be enslaved by the Ottoman Empire nor by Austro-Hungary nor by Hitler, and we don't want to be enslaved by the "new world order," which bombs and shells entire nations with tanks and planes, with napalm and radioactive cluster bombs. We want to live freely and peacefully on our own land, and we won't bother anyone, as long as no one bothers us.

The best thing to do is to understand that whatever happened, happened, and to look to the future and build peace in this region, restoring confidence among peoples and among ourselves. The new Serbian democratic state should devote special attention to soldiers, families of lost soldiers and disabled war veterans who made the greatest contribution to the creation of the Republika Srpska. With the peace agreement now in place, the conditions have been created for the unification of the Serbian people in one state, and the way that process unfolds will be decided by the true representatives of our people.

If we are wise and united in purpose from Una to Timok, and from Subotica to Boka ... we can restore many of our areas. We're on our own land. As long as we are united and one idea leads us — to be on our own land — we will succeed. In this war we were disunited and isolated, except for fraternal aid from

Serbia and Montenegro, who healed the wounds of our children. I want to take this occasion to express my sincere gratitude.

What are your political ambitions, and for how long will you be heading the Army of the Republika Srpska?

I never found politics attractive, and I never had any military ambitions, not to mention political ones. I was always inclined to be an ordinary man.

Others will decide how long I will lead the army. I will probably stay as long as my country needs me. I'm not in favor of people and authorities becoming fixtures, either in peace or during wartime. I'm more in favor of giving chances to young people at the right time, but we did what we did. Let them go further.

I was not prepared to and I did not obey some of the diktats issued by the West — such as being nominated a counselor of the President of the Republic, to be replaced by the diktat of some foreign intelligence circles, because they did not appoint me to my position, so they cannot replace me.... And finally, in the opinion of my colleagues and of the army that I command, I am still necessary and should continue to serve — or at least give advice if nothing else.

Some People Would Betray the People through the Army

The Western media falsely reported that General Mladić had fallen seriously ill, but even so he still could not be brought to The Hague Tribunal for trial. General Mladić's reply appeared in Sprska Vojska, *June 26, 1996:*

Dayton achieved its goals — it imposed peace in this region, but the Serbian people have paid the largest price for this peace. In any case, given some thought, one has to give peace a chance, despite the militant outbursts made by numerous Muslim leaders in the ruling coalition with Alija Izetbegović, despite the actions of Islamic countries, and, unfortunately, despite the U.S., which has been continually arming the Muslims: such things can be a genuine threat to peace.

The military aspect of the agreement was, executed from our side without any difficulty. We have made great efforts together with IFOR to bilaterally execute the orders given to us.

Our people were drawn into this war. The Serbian people neither wanted nor desired this war. The Muslims and the Croats, on the contrary, wanted this war. The Serbs had their statehood during the first and second Yugoslavias, and the Croatians and the Muslims lived well in Yugoslavia in the inter-war period. They did not want Yugoslavia to exist any longer, and they seceded violently and destroyed it. The whole of the Serbian people, especially in B-H and Croatia, wanted to live in Yugoslavia.

The Republika Srpska is the result of this war. Indeed, there are different appetites, political and otherwise; however, I consider the Serbian people to be united as a whole. We have the same faith, the same language, the same territory.... And, if the unification of Croatia and of the Muslim areas can be allowed, then why should it be troublesome for the international community to acknowledge the right of the Serbian people on both sides of the Drina to be united? The attempt made by some international forces to once again throw Serbs, Croats and Muslims into the same basket is counterproductive. The history of the twentieth century has demonstrated that. Such an entity could not survive on Yugoslav territory, so why are they expecting it to thrive in a mini-state like Bosnia? Let nature instruct us: eagles do not fly in formation with crows. Each is born in its own nest and flies with its own flock. In this fashion, the Serbian people desire to live with their own.

The Hague Tribunal is a political court that imposes the will of others. The Great Powers must know that it is no sin to defend one's own people. On the contrary, it is the greatest honor [a soldier may have]! We did not wage a war of conquest, such as the world media described and crammed down the throat of its respective populations. We merely defended what belonged to us. The upshot is that they were able to take things away from us in Dayton that they were unable to take during the war. In the same manner, perhaps there are a few pilots — officers who bombed the Serbian people — who should be put on trial in The Hague Tribunal, but they want to put the Serbian people on trial, instead. You can't put pilots on trial in The Hague. It is alleged that I should be tried, I who had to defend myself from aerial bombardments by American, English and other aircraft, and from Muslim mujahideen and Croatians — is there a court of law for them? They [i.e., NATO] bombed our people, our churches, and now they say it was a "blunder." It is their right to do so. [But] I acknowledge only the judgment of my own people. The moment The Hague indicted me, it meant that I was in the right. It's obvious that they are trying people on the principle of the Ottoman sultans: the *kadija*[13] indicts you, then the *kadija* tries you. They will indict anyone whom Albright tells them to indict; however, I am not in the least concerned.

The army belongs to its people and cannot be a political instrument in a multiparty system or a unique [political] party in itself. I am a part of this army and this people and I am against the army being turned into a political party. The army must not be manipulated or abused, and must not be an instrument to help anyone who wants to bridle and mount the people. A normal atmosphere must be created in which the people can freely choose their representatives, and the people will choose, not according to how pretty they are, but according to what they have to offer.

The atmosphere now is such that certain leaders want the people and the army to follow them. I would not be surprised if pyramids, like those of Cheops, were to be once again erected in the Balkans, where certain leaders would like to be mummified, so that they would remain eternally in this world as well as the next.... Politicians want to be some kind of axis around which the world turns, including the people and the state. My colleagues judge me to have been much more correct in my relations toward politicians individually than they have ever collectively been toward me.

The Serbian people from the far side of the Drina have invested the maximum effort to help their brothers on this side of the Drina, and we must be grateful for that. The Serbian people were not able to go against the Great Powers alone, especially without a united national program, and not to mention an Orthodox Christian program. I am awaiting the results of the understanding that all interested parties have come to; I am awaiting the results of equal relations with respect to the Dayton Peace Accords; and I await the prosperity of the Serbian people, which I also wish for the other peoples living in our region.

General Mladic's Vidovdan Greetings (1996)

Officers, non-commissioned officers, soldiers and employees of the Army of the Republika Srpska, *Vidovdan* is the *slava* of the Army of the Republika Srpska, and I extend my greetings to the Serbian people, to Orthodox priests and to the institutions of authority on the occasion of this great spiritual and state holiday.

The Army of the Republika Srpska, the Serbian people, the Orthodox clergy and the Republika Srpska on Vidovdan 1996 are for the first time celebrating this holiday in peace and in freedom, preserving and fostering our beautiful traditions and customs with the dignity befitting them, and continuing the memory of illustrious moments in our history. Peace, national and spiritual, dignity and merit, and the Republika Srpska are the results of the four-year-long struggle of the Serbian people, its army, and its bold and heroic leadership that found itself in unequal relations with the Great Powers as well as with numerous enemies. The Serbian people and its army brilliantly disentangled themselves from invasion by the Muslim army, defended itself from Croatian paramilitary formations and from the army of the Croatian Republic, all of whom are now protected by one of the most powerful military organizations in the world, NATO, with political, diplomatic, and psychological propaganda and with the material support of the Great Powers to an extent never before seen, who have spun their plans for a "New World Order" while we, at the same time, were left without either friends or allies and without aid of any sort, excepting our brothers from the Federal Republic of Yugoslavia and some virtuous exceptions from around the world. The truth, which we understood and for which we fought, is the truth: we wanted nothing more, but nothing less than what our enemies have received — the right to self-determination and statehood and no Great Power has been able to disparage the ideas in which we believed and still believe.

In this lopsided battle, the Army of the Republika Srpska achieved brilliant results for you, and rendered to the dead due respect. The peace that the people of the Republika Srpska now have is unstable and unsure, because our enemies, who are being aided by the Great Powers, have not achieved their goals, nor have the Great Powers. For that reason, in the coming period, we must dedicate our knowledge and experience, ... effort and self-sacrifice ... to direct the training and preparation of senior officers and commanders of units and soldiers for the successful execution of orders for the defense of the freedom and integrity of the Republika Srpska and the interests of the Serbian people.

May the execution of these peacetime orders fill you with the spirit of Vidovdan, the Orthodox faith and the spirit of St. Sava, so that the confidence and fellowship, experience and tradition of our units bring results from this four-year-long war.

Sretna slava to one and all, let your reason lead you and your conscience prompt you, with the desire that Vidovdans of the future be celebrated with greater contentment, happiness and wealth in a strong, powerful, peaceful and united Serbian state.

ENDNOTES

1 *AWACS*, Airborne Warning and Control Systems.

2 *Caritas and Merhamet*, Roman Catholic and Muslim charitable organizations, respectively, that smuggled arms into Bosnia. Regarding Caritas' involvement in arms smuggling, <u>see</u> *Liar's Poker*, by Michel Collon (2002).

3 This is a reference to Medjugorje, which the Croats used to raise money and gain sympathy for independence. See *The Medjugorje Deception: Queen of Peace, Ethnic Cleansing and Ruined Lives*, by Michael Jones, Fidelity Press, South Bend, IN: 1998)

4 *Zetra* was the name given to the Olympic stadium built in Sarajevo.

5 *Mali*, (Serbian) the little fellow.

6 *why he avoids using the word "Ustashi,"* in Serbian culture, one does not mention an enemy by name.

7 *Zbor narodne garde* (The People Guard Corps), a Croatian militia, which was an illegal military formation, active in operations against Serbs.

8 More Muslims voted for Abdić than than for Izetbegović, Izetbegović lost the Bosnian presidential election to Fikret Abdić: Abdić 1,010,618 votes to Izetbegović's 847,386. Izetbegović reportedly made Abdić "an offer he couldn't refuse," and Abdić ceded the election to him. Moderate Bosnian Muslims continued to support Abdić, whose forces joined Serbs in their fight against Izetbegović fundamentalist fanatics.

9 *Vidovdan*, i.e., St. Vitus Day (June 28), an important holiday for Serbs that marks the date of the Battle of Kosovo in 1389.

10 The General is referring to corporate entities like MPRI (Military Personnel and Resources, Inc.) that supply ex-U.S. generals and other mercenaries to client states approved by the U.S. State Department.

11 *one lady getting on in years*, i.e., U.S. Secretary of State Madeleine Albright.

12 *stable boys*, refers to Lipica, close to the Italian border, where there is a stud farm that breeds Lipizzaner horses for the Spanish Riding School in Vienna. Archduke Charles of Austria, then ruler of Carnolia, Istria and Trieste, established the stud farm in 1580.

13 *kadija* (Arabic), a Muslim judge who renders decisions on sharia law. The kadija acted as both judge and jury.

General Ratko Mladić on the front lines in Bosnia.

2

Ante Pavelić, war criminal and fascist leader of the Independent State of Croatia ("NDH") during WWII. He was one of the assassins of King Aleksandar of Yugoslavia and French Prime Minister Barthou in 1934. He passed a decree on April 30, 1941 declaring Croats to be Aryans.

3

Andrija Artuković, Minister of Internal Affairs of the NDH during WWII. He issued an order banning "Serbs, Jews, Gypsies and dogs" from entering parks, restaurants and from using public transportation in Zagreb. He found refuge in the U.S. in 1947. See pp. 201, 214, 235.

4

5

Fr. Miroslav Filipović-Majstorović (AKA Fr. Satan), war criminal: as a Franciscan (left), and as an Ustashi officer (right). He admitted that he personally oversaw the extermination of 30,000 inmates of the Jasenovac Concentration Camp. Croatian nationalists are now seeking his rehabilitation by claiming that his trial was unfair.

5

nternational Fascist links. Amin al-Husseini, the Grand Mufti of Jerusalem (middle), the principal organizer of the bloodthirsty SS "Handžar" Division in Bosnia officially meets representatives of the NDH (The Independent State of Croatia). On he right is Mile Budak (see pp. 227-229). Al-Husseini worked closely with Hitler to exterminate European Jews. He recruited Muslim troops for the Nazis from Bosnia, Kosovo and Chechnya. Alija Izetbegović, one of his Bosnian disciples, applied many of al-Husseini's techniques, such as attacks on moderate Muslims, to the Bosnian conflict.

6

Croatian Archbishop and Military Vicar Aloizije Stepinac (far right) is here taking part in the funeral services of the Ustashi criminal Marko Dosen. Despite well documented evidence of Stepinac' involvement in the genocide of the Serbs in Croatia during WWII, Pope John Paul II beatified his remains in 1998. It will apparently be left o a future Pope to elevate the Archbishop of genocide to official sainthood. *See* p. 337

7

Part of the Jasenovac complex of concentration camps where 750,000 Serbs, 75,000 Jews, and 50,000 Roma perished. The Jasenovac concentration camp was fully operational six months before the German concentration camps were opened. As the war drew to a close, the Ustashi blew up the camp and killed most of the remaining inmates in order to destroy evidence of their crimes. Tito demolished the crematorium (below) and the remaining buildings in 1948. Franjo Tudjman claimed in his book, The Wasteland of History, that "about 60,000 perished in all the camps and prisons." According to Tudjman, only 30,000 victims died in Jasenovac. The Croatian government is still trying to bury the past by creating a new Jasenovac Memorial that would mix the remains of the victims with their murderers, putting them on the same moral footing, in order to rehabilitate the current Croatian state.

8

The furnace complex in Jasenovac, designed by the engineer Hinko Piceli, where victims were burned.

9

Ustashi escorting Serbs from Kozara to a concentration camp on the Prijedor-Bosanska Dubica road, July 1942. Kurt Waldheim, later UN Secretary General and President of Austria, was one of the Nazi's commanding officers in the Kozara Operation. Approximately 68,600 Serbian Orthodox civilians, including 23,800 children from the Kozara region were driven from their homes and resettled in concentration camps, where most of them perished. Arnold Schwarzenegger, Governor of California, is a personal friend of Mr. Waldheim. He dismissed the charges against "Kurt" as "Nazi stuff." *See* p. 312.

10

Serbs who were hung *en masse* in a village at the foot of Mt. Kozara in July 1942 during an attack by the Nazi troops, Ustashi and Domobrans (Croatian Home Guardsmen). As in many other cases, the victims were forced to raise their own

11

A killing field in the Mt. Kozara region, where Ustashi are shooting men, women and children, finishing off all those who still showed any sign of life (June-July 1942).

12

Ustashi commanded by Max Luburić decapitating a Serb with a hatchet in Gradina, near Jasenovac (1942). The Ustashi left behind an extensive photographic record of the atrocities they committed. They used knives, mallets and hatchets to execute victims. Even the Nazis were disgusted by their tactics.

The victims of Jasenovac often washed up on the banks of the Sava River. The Ustashi routinely threw the bodies of their victims into the river, whose current would carry the bodies down to Belgrade. On one occasion, the Ustashi killed an entire Serbian wedding party, then affixed them to seats on a boat that was sent floating down the Sava River; it arrived in Belgrade as a gruesome message. Mr. Perković-Thompson, the Ustashi folk singer, celebrates scenes such as this one in his songs: "The Neretva flows on and takes [the Serbs] to the blue Adriatic." *See* p. 232.

13

14

Halil Abaz Aziz, a mujahideen fighter from Saudi Arabia, holding the decapitated head of a Serbian soldier, Nenad Petković (age 23), pointing it toward his headless body, which had been bound to a tree on the right. The unprocessed film containing these photos was found on the body of Aziz, who was himself killed in a firefight in August 1992, during clashes with the Serbian Army near Teslić. The British government banned a photography exhibition in January 1993, which contained these and other pictures of atrocities. Bojana Isaković, the organizer of the exhibition, "Genocide Against the Serbs," said: "It is understandable that the Americans and the Europeans don't want to show our pictures to their people — because they are the authors of these pictures." *See* "The Pictures They Don't Want You to See, LM Archives, www.informinc.co.uk for a fuller treatment.

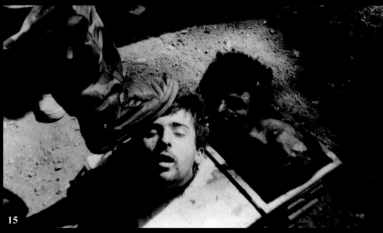

15

Aziz's foot on the heads of slain Serbs. The dead men are Brane Đurić (age 40) from Jasenova near Teslić; Blagoje Blagojević (age 44) who was employed by the Graditelj Company in Teslić; and Nenad Petković (age 23), a volunteer soldier from Belgrade.

President Radovan Karadžić and General Ratko Mladić conferring at the height of the Bosnian War. The West charged Mladić with encircling and laying siege to Sarajevo; he retorted that he was defending the Serbian residents of Sarajevo, who lived largely in the suburbs surrounding the city. Muslim forces set up mobile mortar positions in various residential neighborhoods from which they shelled Serbian neighborhoods in order to provoke return fire, which was part of the Muslim scheme to gain Western support. Most news reports focused on the damage to Sarajevo and its cultural monuments. Western journalists did not see the extensive damage to suburbs like Ilidža until after it had been handed over to the Muslims, and then ignored it in their reports.

16

17

18

"The Trial of a Serb Whose Heart Has Been Torn Out: Mladić and Karadžić Stand Accused by the Hague Tribunal," a painting by Milić of Mačva, executed at the Painters' Colony, Pale 1996. Milić of Mačva: "Mladić, however, long ago demonstrated a great attachment to the Serbian Orthodox Church and to Serbdom in general. That is why he is the target of Western 'democrats' who style themselves as defenders of Islam. He was thoughtlessly proclaimed to be a 'first-class war criminal' because he prevented an all out slaughter of Serbs throughout the former Croatia and Bosnia."

19

Left to Right: French General Morillon, French General De La Presle, and the painter Milić of Mačva and General Mladić. *See* pages 286-289 for General Morillon's testimony about the alleged Srebrenica massacre.

Mrkonjić Grad, a small town in south west Bosnia near Croatia Krajgna region. A report of Ustashi massacres of Serbs during WWII. In March 1996, I took a Bosnian Serb prosecutor and a camera crew from Court TV to the site of a mass grave containing the bodies of at least 185 Serb civilians," Nick Kostich recalled to *The New*

20

American. "The bodies were not those of military personnel. They were civilians including people as much as 80 years old." The shocking discovery had little impact on the media. *The New York Times* published one photograph of the massacre site without an accompanying story. There have still been no indictments, despite the fact that an investigator from the ICTY's office of the prosecutor visited the site.

One of the reasons the media ignored the atrocity in Mrkonjić Grad is that the Croatian army unit accused of the massacre was probably trained and equipped by MPRI, Inc., a privately owned U.S. firm that supplies mercenaries to client regimes. *See* "Selective 'Justice' Turns Blind Eye to Croatian Atrocities, by William Norman Grigg, The New American, Vol. 13, No. 21, October 13, 1997.

21

This scene was broadcast around the world. It was purported to show a grieving Muslim woman who had lost her son; however, the woman, was, in fact, Dobrila Prodanović, Serbian woman and the skull is of her son, Živan (1966-1992), who was killed along with many others in the Serbian village of Ratkovici by Muslims from

the funeral of Gen-
eral Djordje Djukić
in Belgrade. Thous-
ands of ordinary citi-
zens attended the
funeral, as did Gen-
eral Mladić, who is
pictured below.

22

General Djukić was kidnapped with Colonel
Aleksa Krsmanović and remanded illegally to The
Hague Tribunal.

Dr. Slobodan Ivkovic, who looked after Djordje
Djukić during his last days, said that 'inadequate
treatment and therapy during his time in [the War
Crimes Tribunal] prison and hospital brought on a
sudden deterioration in the General's health' and
added at General Djukić received salted, greasy
food which 'third and fourth year medial students
know that patients operated on for cancer of pancreas must not eat." *Nasa Borba*, Feb. 9, 1996. *See*
Unjust from the Start: The War Crimes Tribunal
vs. General Djorde Djukić," by Dr. Kosta Cavoski
in the Appendices on p. 592.

23

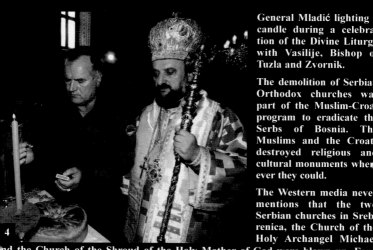

4

General Mladić lighting
candle during a celebra-
tion of the Divine Liturg
with Vasilije, Bishop o
Tuzla and Zvornik.

The demolition of Serbia
Orthodox churches wa
part of the Muslim-Croat
program to eradicate th
Serbs of Bosnia. Th
Muslims and the Croat
destroyed religious an
cultural monuments when
ever they could.

The Western media neve
mentions that the two
Serbian churches in Sreb
renica, the Church of th
Holy Archangel Michae
and the Church of the Shroud of the Holy Mother of God were blown up. Fou
Serbian Orthodox churches in Sarajevo were plundered and damaged, including th
old Serbian Orthodox Church of the Holy Archangels Michael and Gabriel, whic

Photo Credits

Photographer unknown.

3–5   *The Crimes of the Fascist Occupants and their Collaborators against Jews in Yugoslavia*, by Zdenko Löwenthal, Federation of Jewish Communities of the FPRY. Belgrade: 1957; reissued by Danko R. Vasović in 2005 in conjunction with the Jasenovac Research Institute.

6   Yugoslav Cinematek.

7–8   *The Crimes of the Fascist Occupants and their Collaborators against Jews in Yugoslavia*, by Zdenko Löwenthal, op. cit.

9–13   *Genocide of the Serbs of Bosnian Krayina*, 1941–1945, by Branko J. Bokan. Evropsko Slovo: Belgrade, 1996.

14–15   From "Genocide against the Serbs," a photography exhibition curated by Bojana Isaković in 1992.

16–17   Mile Rajić, photographer.

18–20   Photographer unknown.

21   Report about Case Srebrenica (The First Part), by Drarko Trifunović. Documentation Centre of Republic Srpska Bureau of Government of RS for Relation with ICTY: Banja Luka, 2002.

22–24   Photographer unknown.

APPENDICES
I. KEY WESTERN ARTICLES AND A PAPER

Serbian General Who Calls the Shots: Determined and Calling West's Bluff

by Roger Cohen, *The New York Times*, April 17, 1994

ZAGREB, Croatia—Beguiling and brutal by turns, Gen. Ratko Mladić, the commander of the Bosnian Serbs, has called the West's bluff yet again.

Western officials have speculated widely on the influence, and even the mental stability, of this blunt, explosive and passionate soldier, but his abrupt and devastating assault on the Muslim enclave of Goražde in eastern Bosnia suggests that the United States and its allies have not come to terms with the general's decisive role.

For to underestimate Mladić is to risk underrating the depth of Serbian passion aroused by the war and, thus, the complexity of making peace.

His life story personifies the themes, fears and demons that have haunted Serbian history.

Mladić, 51, a former Yugoslav army officer who likes to lead from the front, has emerged as the orchestrator of Serbian tactics in Bosnia and the wild card in the quest for peace in the Balkans.

The sustained Goražde attack — remarkable for its effrontery under the nose of NATO planes — betrayed two qualities of Mladić that have characterized the Bosnian war since its outset: ruthlessness and an uncanny sense of timing.

"Mladić has a clear military aim: the consolidation of Serb-held territories in Bosnia, the eradication of Muslim enclaves within them such as Goražde, and the severance of any possible military links between Muslims in Bosnia and those in the Sandžak area of Serbia," said Paul Beaver, a defense expert at Jane's Information Group.

"The attack on Goražde, a strategic enclave on the road between Sarajevo and the Sandžak, was perfectly consistent with this strategy."

But coming just as U.S.-led negotiations were moving forward briskly, the onslaught surprised American officials, upset the plans of Charles Redman, the special American envoy, and pushed the diplomatic process back to somewhere near square one.

How far the Mladić strategy is shared by other leading Serbs, including President Slobodan Milošević of Serbia, and Radovan Karadžić, the Bosnian Serb political leader, is a matter of some dispute among Western diplomats and officials.

Some see more readiness to make concessions in Milošević — whose cool, sullen manner contrasts vividly with that of the extrovert general — and in Karadžić.

They tend to dismiss Mladić, whose 23-year-old daughter, Ana, committed suicide in Belgrade last month, as an increasingly unbalanced figure who will eventually be reined in.

"One has to speculate on the mental stability of Mladić at this point, especially after his daughter's suicide," said an American official who follows the conflict closely.

Pariah as Patriot: Ratko Mladic

David Binder, *The New York Times*, September 4, 1994

The Bosnian Serb commander has been called a war criminal. He doesn't see it that way. He is a child of war and now a man of war. His eyes are a piercing light blue, his hair close cropped and steel gray, his face as wide as a shovel. Seated at a conference table, Gen. Ratko Mladić talks in a husky baritone about the war in Bosnia and Herzegovina that has left several hundred thousand dead or missing and driven a million people from their homes.

We are in a small stuccoed building in the ski resort town of Pale. Perched on a bluff amid red pines, the building commands a spectacular view of the mountains above Sarajevo. Here the Bosnian Serbs have established the presidency of their self-proclaimed rebel state, the Republika Srpska, or Republic of Serbians. In peacetime the building was a psychiatric sanitarium.

Mladić (pronounced Mlah-ditch) commands the Bosnian Serbs who seized, and for the last two years have held, more than 70 percent of a disputed territory about the size of West Virginia. Although atrocities have been committed by all sides in the Bosnian conflict, the Serbs have been held accountable for widespread systematic barbarities, including death camps, on a scale not seen in Europe since the Nazi era. Two years ago Lawrence S. Eagleburger, then Secretary of State, included Mladić in a list of Serb leaders with "political and command responsibility for crimes against humanity" who should be held to account "under international law." Last year, Senator Dennis DeConcini, co-chairman of the Commission on Security and Cooperation in Europe, said that troops under Mladić's control "are responsible for many of the atrocities we hear about in Bosnia and Herzegovina, including the continuing siege of Sarajevo, which isolates and strangles the city's more than 300,000 remaining residents."

Asked point-blank about Serb atrocities committed against Muslims, Mladić responds: "I don't see it that way. I did what everyone else has done to defend my own people. That is our patriotic duty." Unruffled, he continues: "It would be true to say of me that I had horns on my head if I had invaded Vietnam, Cambodia or the Falkland Islands. I did not go to the Gulf or Somalia. I was defending my own home. In fact, my house was one of the first to be burned down." In May 1992, a month after Serb rebels declared war on the Bosnian Government by shelling Sarajevo, Mladić watched the house he shared with his brother in the Sarajevo borough of Pofalići go up in flames.

Questioned about the two-year pounding of Sarajevo by heavy Serb guns and other acts of brute aggression against Bosnian civilians by Serb forces, Mladić lists brutalities committed by the other side. "Croats in March 1992 began a war of terror against Serb civilians from the Kupres Plateau up to Doboj," he says. (War in Croatia between the Serbs and the Croats broke out in 1991.) "They began a policy of genocide against Serbs in Šamac, Modrica and Derventa, the Neretva valley up to Mostar. In June and July, Muslims burned down more than 100 Serbian villages along the Drina."

By the time Mladić was made commander of the Serbian army in Bosnia in May 1992, Serbian militias — capitalizing on their overwhelming military superiority — had already conducted a vast "ethnic cleansing" campaign, driving hundreds of thousands of Muslims from their homelands over a seven-week period. Mladić was not given full authority over the widely scattered militias until a year ago, but the "cleansing" operations have gone on. His role in the subsequent actions is not clear.

An officer who served with Mladić at the front recalls that Mladić prevented his soldiers from executing Muslim prisoners of war, once during Serb offensives on Mount Igman, south of Sarajevo, in the summer of 1993, and again at Majevica, near Tuzla, last spring. According to a recently released Croat P.O.W., after Mladić's visit to a prison in a Serb-held area of Sarajevo last March, conditions for the 430 Muslim and Croat prisoners of war "improved greatly."

Of late, Mladić has been under attack not only in Washington but also in Belgrade. The latest international peace plan for Bosnia calls on Mladić and the other Bosnian Serb leaders to give up control of a third of the territory they have seized. The plan has been accepted by the Muslim-dominated Bosnian Government and Bosnia's Croats, but the Bosnian Serbs have rejected it. In response, the international community early last month issued renewed threats of harsher economic sanctions against Yugoslavia (now comprising Serbia and Montenegro), until then the Bosnian Serbs' sole supporter. Faced with such threats against Belgrade, Slobodan Milošević, President of Serbia, warned Mladić and the Bosnian Serb leader Radovan Karadžić that rejection of the peace plan would result in a severing of political and economic ties. The general's retort was to the point: "If you do that, I'll bring the war to your doorstep." Announcing the cutoff of links to the rebels on Aug. 4, Milošević described the Bosnian Serb leaders as "war profiteers" who were "insane with political ambition and greed."

Mladić's first name, Ratko, is a diminutive of Ratimir (War or Peace) or Ratislav (War of Slavs).[1] Ratko is a name typically given a male baby in wartime. The general, 51, refuses to be identified in any way with the Republic of Bosnia and Herzegovina, created in April 1992 as an independent and multi-ethnic state and recognized by the United States and the European Community.

---

[1] Both translations are wrong. The name "Ratimir" does not mean "war or peace" but could be could be construed as "war and peace," which makes no literal sense. "Mir" and "slav" are merely suffixes that signify a proper name, and they are unrelated to either "peace" or "Slavs." These endings are common, as in Radomir, Slavomir, Branimir, Vladimir, etc., just as in the case of Milisav, Branislav, Prvoslav.

"I was born in what was called Old Herzegovina," he says, referring to a strip of mostly mountainous territory that was an ancient Serbian dukedom. "Bosnia and Herzegovina was an artificial creation of the Communist system and before that in the Austrian Empire. We Serbs reject the term 'Bosnia'. We are Serbs and we know who we are."

Yet being a Serb did not play a critical role in Mladić's life until he was 48. In the 1991 Yugoslav census, the last before the old federation collapsed, he listed his nationality as Yugoslav, not Serb. He was in many respects a quintessential Yugoslav, born of parents who had joined the Communist-led partisans to fight German invaders and their Croatian henchmen, the Ustasha.

The mottoes of the partisans of Josip Broz Tito were "Death to Fascism! Freedom to the People!" and "Brotherhood and Unity!" Mladić's father, Neđa, died fighting the Fascist Croatian Ustasha in 1945. Other Serbian partisans died in combat against Muslim Ustasha, still others against Serbian royalists called Chetniks. Of the 1.7 million Yugoslavs killed during World War II, 1 million were the victims of the civil war that raged within the larger conflict.

Tito constructed his Yugoslavia as a delicately balanced mechanism designed to prevent a resumption of the ethnic slaughter among the South Slavs. Until his death in 1980, his party, the League of Communists of Yugoslavia, and the Yugoslav People's Army held the federation together. In its ability to be independent of the Soviet Union, its relative openness and material wealth (made possible by generous Western loans), Yugoslavia was the envy of Eastern Europe. But after Tito's death the country gradually unraveled. The party disintegrated in 1990, the army in 1991.

At 15, Ratko Mladić completed studies at an army school on the outskirts of Belgrade. He graduated from the nation's military academy in 1965 and joined the Communist Party. His initial postings in Europe's fourth largest army were in Macedonia, where he commanded a platoon, then a tank battalion, then a brigade. In January 1991, with the clouds of civil war already gathering, he was promoted to deputy commander of the army corps in the province of Kosovo, where the population is more than 90 percent Albanian.

Six months later, as the federation of six republics crumbled amid the secessions of Croatia and Slovenia, Mladić received a call from the high command in Belgrade. Could he make his way north to Croatia where fighting had broken out between Croatian militias and the Yugoslav army: "They asked me what I thought," he recalls. "I said I didn't have to think about it — just about the means to do it." He left three days later by helicopter for Knin, the center of a Serbian uprising in the Krajina region against the breakaway Croatian nationalist authority. There he was soon given command of the army corps, with the rank of colonel.

Like many of his fellow officers, Mladić was still devoted to the preservation of a federal and multi-ethnic Yugoslavia. Both Croatia and Slovenia had declared but not yet achieved independence. Bosnia and Herzegovina — a miniature Yugoslavia in its mixture of Slavic Muslims, Serbs and Croats — teetered between continued association with the federation and some degree of independence. "At the time, I never considered that we couldn't have a common life," Mladić says. "We are all still captivated by that united life. But a man is formed by the events he undergoes."

A gradual transformation of Mladić's vocabulary can be seen in a seven-part interview that appeared early this year in the Belgrade weekly *Nin*. In the early sections, he speaks of Croats as Croats. But when he talks about his battles with the Croats in 1991-92 he refers atavistically to them as Ustasha.

What Mladić found in Krajina was a military man's nightmare. Army command was breaking down as senior officers suddenly reverted to their Croatian or Slovenian origin, wavered or went over to the other side. A hastily formed Croatian national guard fought hastily assembled Serbian militia. Civilians were uprooted amid atrocities in villages of mixed populations. Army garrisons were blockaded.

Mladić's first question was: "Who is the enemy?" His answer to himself and his troops: "First, the enemy is anyone who shoots at our soldiers, cuts off their water and electricity, provokes, blockades."

In the Croat-Serb fighting of 1991, Mladić moved with a combination of audacity and guile that astonished his opponents. Before new uniforms and insignia made the various sides distinguishable, he traveled across the lines in mufti, using identification papers of Croat officers he had known. Once, when he was posing as Col. Stjepan Fazlija, a Croatian militiaman spotted his large ring and stopped him, saying, "You're not Stjepan. You're Col. Ratko Mladić. You're dangerous. We should liquidate you."

"I was uncomfortable," Mladić recalls. He flashed an identity card belonging to Fazlija and persuaded the militiaman he was the Croat. "I told him Mladić was really dangerous and ought to be liquidated."

Then, in August 1991, Mladić led troops to liberate a Serb army barracks near Vrlika. The road was blocked by a bus rigged with more than 70 pounds of explosives. An engineering unit was unable to defuse the bombs. But Mladić, watched by reporters and cameramen, entered the bus and cut the detonator wires.

He was promoted to general in April 1992 after he successfully — and ruthlessly, said his critics — consolidated Serbian positions in Krajina. Soon, thereafter, Bosnia and Herzegovina declared its independence and Bosnian Serb leaders searched for a commander to prosecute their war aims. Nikola Koljević, the Shakespeare scholar turned politician who is vice president of the self-declared Bosnian Serb republic, remembers: "We didn't know Mladić. But then we read about him in a Croatian newspaper that said, 'Mladić is no social worker.' We decided, That's the guy we need." In May 1992, Mladić was transferred from the Yugoslav army to the newly constituted Bosnian Serb forces.

By his own account, Ratko Mladić is a student of Hannibal, Alexander the Great and Carl von Clausewitz. But over the last three years, in battle after battle, he has shown his belief in the doctrine of concentrated force espoused by Neiz Guderian, the German panzer general: *Klotzen, nicht Kleckern*! — "Smash! Don't sprinkle!" Mladić's commands to his artillery units around Sarajevo included: "Roast!" "Pound them senseless!" (Some would argue that what the Bosnian Serbs have been doing from the hills around Sarajevo hardly involves military skill and is tantamount to shooting at sitting ducks.)

"The dominant shape of armed conflict for me is attack," says Mladić. "I have an offensive character, and that's acceptable to the high command of the army of the Republic of Serbians." In mid-June, a Bosnian Government offensive cracked Serbian lines on the southern slopes of Mount Ozren. It was an effort by Bosnian forces to secure a vital road link between Sarajevo and

Tuzla, a Muslim majority enclave. But in a sudden pincer movement the Serbs retook the salient, killing — according to United
Nations officials — close to 1,000 Government troops.

Mladić eats and sleeps among his soldiers, whom he often
leads into battle in an armored vehicle. Initially he toured his
nearly 800 miles of front lines by helicopter, but that stopped last
year in compliance with a flight ban imposed by the United
Nations. "I like to go on foot," he says. "On foot, soldiers are at
their best." In his underground headquarters about 40 miles
northeast of Sarajevo, he sleeps on an army cot.

Mladić can be hotheaded. Last year, when the United States
and the European Community proposed air strikes against
Serbian positions, he threatened to unleash terrorist bombers on
Washington and London. Radovan Karadžić, president of the
self-proclaimed Republic of Serbians, sharply reprimanded him
for his "idiotic and irresponsible statement."

On March 11, Gajo Petković, the retired editor of the monthly
magazine *People's Army*, wrote a blistering attack on Mladić in a
Belgrade magazine. Calling the general "conceited," a "cynic and
a sadist," and accusing him of being "carried away by rage and
brutality," Petković asserted Mladić had "undoubted responsibility for the crimes of members of the army he led." That night,
Petković wrote in a subsequent article, Mladić called him from
Pale and threatened him: "You'll get yours soon. You'll remember who Ratko Mladić is." Mladić denies having made the threat.

That was not the end of the episode. On March 24, Mladić's
daughter, Ana, a 23-year-old medical student, committed suicide
in Belgrade. Her friends said it was because she had become dis-
traught after reading the Petković attack on her father.

With his wife, Božana, and their son — both of whom live in
Pale — Mladić went to Belgrade to attend the funeral at the
Serbian Orthodox Church in the Topčider Cemetery. Brought up as
a Communist and atheist, Mladić placed coins in front of an icon;
at the graveside, he kissed a candle, lit it and crossed himself.

Ratko Mladić is serving a self-proclaimed state that aims eventually to merge with a larger Serbia. Until Aug. 4, when
Milošević imposed his embargo against the Bosnian Serbs, Pale
drew oil and gasoline from Serbia. (Officials in Pale now say
they have enough fuel reserves to wage a full-scale war for four

months.) Bosnian Serb army uniforms have a Velcro patch on the breast pocket so that the Srpska Republic coat of arms can be attached or removed.

Whether or not their self-styled republic is transitory, the Bosnian Serbs are determined to have their way in the Bosnian conflict. On a recent day, fighters along the front lines facing Goražde, Sarajevo and the region north of Tuzla were openly defiant. In a log-lined bunker called Little Paradise, a machine-gunner named Dule echoed Mladić when he gave his reason for going to battle: "We're defending our homes."

Every few minutes dum-dum bullets from Muslim snipers popped in the elm branches above the bunker — high-velocity 5.56-millimeter rounds that are the latest in infantry warfare. This day, the Serbs did not fire back. Then came a shout from a Muslim trench: "Hey, Čedo" — a diminutive for Serb nationalists. Dule yelled back: "What do you want, *Komšija?*" *Komšija* means "neighbor." This is, after all, a war of neighbors.

There are other surprises at the front. Women are part of the combat units, as are volunteers from Russia, Greece, the United States and Canada. And the Bosnian Serbs have developed new weapons, they say, Mladić calls one of them "the needle" — a state-of-the-art, adapted form of surface to air missile that lets the heat-seeking guidance system distinguish between an attack plane's jet engines and the flares it drops for decoys. The missile was used to down a British fighter-bomber during the heavy fighting around Goražde in April.

More often than not, Mladić has accepted the political lines laid down initially by his superiors in Belgrade and subsequently in Pale. In 1991 he was ordered not to seize the coastal cities of Zadar and Šibenik, which would have split Croatia, although he claims his forces could have done it in a matter of hours then and "in a day or two" now. Similarly, in spring 1993, he bowed to higher authorities fearful of Western military intervention and refrained from seizing the Muslim enclaves of Srebrenica and Žepa along the Drina valley. He stepped back again from Goražde in April.

But cede to the Muslims land his 80,000 troops conquered? "I would never order my units to retreat," he says emphatically. "I wouldn't do it if I had one million lives and had to lose them all.

Only an army that is defeated retreats."

That same conviction motivated him to defy Karadžić and the entire international community in May 1993 when he opposed the Vance-Owen peace plan for ending the Bosnian conflict. The general's 45-minute speech (*see* p. 422) persuaded the Bosnian Serbs' assembly in Pale to reject that plan. Now, with Pale politicians unable to accept the latest peace plan, with President Clinton giving them until Oct. 15 to accept it or face a lifting of the arms embargo against the Bosnian Government, which is eager to regain more territory, prolonged war is virtually guaranteed.

This would almost certainly mean renewed fighting by the Bosnian Serbs and possibly a full-scale attack on Sarajevo. (The Serbian bombardment of the capital ended in February when a NATO ultimatum forced the withdrawal of heavy weaponry to points beyond a 12.4-mile radius of the city.) Heavy fighting could prompt large-scale air strikes by NATO planes, a lifting of the arms embargo on the Bosnian Muslim forces and the withdrawal of United Nations peacekeepers from Bosnia.

"Our commitment to peace is not a sign of weakness," says Mladić. "We have shown who we are and what we are. We take measures not to be surprised. I'm ready for them anywhere."

Mladić — Man of the Year

by Robert Block, *The Independent on Sunday* (London), December 18, 1994
Copyright © 1994 by The Independent (UK). Reprinted with permission.

General Ratko Mladić will certainly have cause to remember 1994. It was the year in which his daughter Ana, a 23-year-old medical student, committed suicide following a spate of press criticism of her father in Belgrade. It was the year in which relations between Mladić's erstwhile patron, President Slobodan Milošević of Serbia, and the Bosnian Serb leadership broke down because the Bosnian Serbs rejected a peace plan that would have forced them to withdraw from land they had conquered.

It was also the year in which the Bosnian Serbs triumphantly defied world opinion, pulling off a string of political and military successes while the direst threats of NATO, the European

Union and the United Nations evaporated amid a frenzy of international buck-passing. The credit-or blame-for this belongs largely to Ratko Mladić.

When the leaders of the Western world threatened to rain punishment from the skies, he called their bluff and pounded towns such as Goražde, Maglaj and Bihać at his leisure and with impunity. Radovan Karadžić may be president and spokesman of the self-declared Bosnian Serb Republic, but Western diplomats and generals who have faced both men across the bargaining table say that Mladić is tougher, and that Karadžić is nervous about agreeing to anything before clearing it with his burly, blue-eyed military commander.

A chess player, Mladić likes to use metaphors from the game. He boasted once that the West "will move the pieces the way I want them to move, not the way they want to move them." And in his tactic of signing cease-fires only to break them immediately we can detect the calculated risk of the grandmaster. He understands Western reluctance to get involved in Yugoslavia and he knows that it is forces on the ground that dictate events. He may horrify us, but for successfully defying all the great powers and international institutions, Ratko Mladić must force himself on to any list of contenders for Man of the Year. How is it that this Bosnian Serb from the wilds of Herzegovina, a windswept land of stones, scrub and rattlesnakes, has managed to run rings around the world? The answer may lie in a remark he made to a US reporter: "A man is formed by the events he undergoes."

....Another story relates how General Mladić, while travelling to an important meeting on Mount Jahorina in 1993, found his way blocked by a huge boulder that had fallen from a cliff moments before. There was no time to find an alternative route or to wait for a bulldozer to remove the obstacle. The general got out of his car and, like Superman, moved the rock with his bare hands. Unruffled, he arrived at Mt Jahorina in plenty of time to deliver the speech that persuaded the Bosnian Serb parliament to reject the Vance-Owen peace plan and accept international pariah status.

Such tales, which may well be apocryphal, do more than illustrate the devoted loyalty of the Serb soldiers to the man who styles himself as the Napoleon of Bosnia. They also faithfully reflect his character: his resourcefulness and his single-minded determination to let nothing and no one stand in the way of his dream of a Greater Serbia.

Mention of his undoubted charm infuriates the Bosnian Muslims. When one senior Muslim officer was asked if he found Mladić a snake or a charmer, he responded with a line from an e e cummings poem about Buffalo Bill Cody: "How do you like your blue-eyed boy mister death." Through almost four years of war, first in Croatia and then in Bosnia, his strategy has been to secure solid swaths of territory with good communications and supply lines, while crippling his enemies by chopping their holdings into isolated, scattered pockets. His troops have pursued the war in Bosnia with persistent ruthlessness, using their overwhelming superiority in arms to their advantage with often brutal consequences for Muslim communities caught in the line of fire. Two years ago, the U.S. named Mladić as a war criminal who should be held accountable under international law for his actions, but he seems not to care. His peculiar brand of Balkan chutzpah, combined with his complete dedication to the Serbian nationalist cause, has made him virtually impervious to the world outrage that his forces have stirred. "It is not a crime to defend one's people, it's a holy duty," he has said.

He is capable of breathtaking arrogance. When reports were circulating of the mass rape of Muslim women by Bosnian Serb soldiers, Mladić said he had investigated the claims and had not found one case of a Muslim woman being sexually attacked by one of his soldiers. Confronted later with the further allegation that as many as 30,000 Muslim women had been raped, he declared:

"We would all have to be supermen to do this. We would have to be sexual maniacs worthy of an entry in the Guinness Book of Records."

As to the possibility of trading captured territory for peace, he is adamant: "I would never order my units to retreat. I wouldn't do it if I had one million lives and had to lose them all. Only an army that is defeated retreats. Once the Serbian flag is flying, we never take it down."

On the Front Line:
Mladić Almighty — War And Peace

by Laura Silber, *Financial Times* (London), 12/31/94
Copyright © 1994 by Financial Times. Reprinted with permission.

When reading Bosnia's tea leaves, analysts tend to ask two questions. Where is General Ratko Mladić and what does he think?

As much as he detests western observers, the Bosnian Serb commander does not appear to have much time for local politicians either. He appears to enjoy keeping them guessing. This may be the most innocuous of his pleasures. Over the past 32 months of war, Mladić has gained a reputation for brutal genius, masterminding the Serb campaign to carve out an ethnically pure state in Bosnia-Herzegovina. His frequent disappearances have fuelled excited rumours of his death, and raised the hopes of his outmanoeuvred Bosnian Moslem and Croat foes. Even Western newspapers have jumped the gun, carrying banner headlines reporting the 'murder' of Mladić.

In his brash and crudely mischievous manner, the 52-year-old general shrugs off the reports, making impromptu appearances, usually somewhere on the front. Amid intense speculation about his split with his leadership last April, Mladić played a flamboyant chess match with his political counterpart, the Bosnian Serb leader Radovan Karadžić, on the front lines near Goražde. Mladić thumbed his nose at the outside world, which was focused on NATO air strikes against Serb targets attacking the Moslem enclave.

Nine months earlier, in flagrant defiance of a UN no-fly zone, he had flown in a helicopter touring Serbian positions on strategic heights besieging Sarajevo.

Adored by the Bosnian Serbs, especially by soldiers for his hardline stance, the short and stocky Mladić regularly visits the front lines. "We'll never hand over land for which Serb blood has been spilled," he pledges by way of explaining his refusal to meet international demands to roll back current Serb holdings from 70 to 49 percent of Bosnia.

Described by a UN official as a 'soldier's soldier', Mladić has spent long evenings over dinners and rakija, home-brewed brandy, with his UN opposite numbers in the Serb stronghold above the Bosnian capital. This camaraderie with the man who has been named by the US as a potential war criminal has stirred bitter comment in Sarajevo.

But the ruddy-faced general appears not to care. Earlier in the war he was overheard ordering his men to pound Sarajevo with the largest-calibre artillery the Serb forces had.

Personal tragedies seem only to have hardened his resolve to 'completely defeat the Muslims'. His mother was killed in the beginning of the war in a mortar attack on the outskirts of Sarajevo. [N.B., This is an error in reportage. General Mladic's mother died in 2003 of natural causes. *See* p. 411. *Editor's note*.] Last April, his beloved daughter Ana, a 23-year-old medical student, committed suicide. The Serbian commander appeared dressed in black mourning clothes during marathon negotiations aimed at defusing the crisis round Goražde.

Long before, Mladić was primed to seek revenge. The battle lines in 1991 gave him the chance to avenge his father's death in the Second World War. Born in the village of Božinovići, in traditionally Serbian south-east Bosnia-Herzegovina, Ratko was two years old when his father, a communist partisan fighting against the Croat Ustashi fascists and the Germans, was killed in an attack on the native village of the Ustashi leader, Ante Pavelić.

As soon as the Serbo-Croat war broke out in 1991, Lt-Colonel Mladić was transferred, appointed corps commander in Knin, which would be the heart of the Serb armed rebellion against Croatian independence. In this remote region, the loyal communist officer, who once vowed never to remove the red star from his cap, underwent a transformation into a Serb nationalist hero, wearing the uniform of Serbian royalist generals from the First World War.

But the cruel soldier occasionally wants to bestow what he sees as his gift of life on Muslims or Croats. "When I guarantee something it is the same as the word of the Almighty," he often says. During the mass exodus of Muslims from the eastern enclave of Srebrenica, a man of military age was discovered hiding among hundreds of hysterical Muslims jam-packed into a lorry. Mladić told the terrified man: "I will spare your life, but just remember who did it."

Bosnia's Bombers

by David Binder, *The Nation*, October 2, 1995

Reprinted with permission from the October 2, 1995 issue of The Nation

Amid the roar and blinding flashes of NATO's air-strikes against the Bosnian Serbs, the impetus for the bombing was obscured: the August 28 explosion in a narrow, enclosed market in the center of Sarajevo that killed thirty-seven people.

Within a day of that explosion, investigators for the UN. Protection Force under Lieut. Gen. Rupert Smith "concluded beyond all reasonable doubt" that the lethal mortar round had been fired from a Bosnian Serb position in the suburb of Lukavica, 1.5 to 3.5 kilometers southwest of the marketplace. On August 30, NATO's bombs began to fall.

The crucial UN report on the market massacre is classified secret, but four specialists — a Russian, a Canadian and two Americans — have raised serious doubts about its conclusion, suggesting instead that the mortar was fired not by the Serbs but by Bosnian government forces.

Similar suspicions were raised following the February 1994 mortar shell explosion that killed sixty-eight Sarajevans in the adjacent Markale marketplace. The origin of that shell was never determined officially. The UN's after-action report in 1994 (also classified) was based on separate examinations of the impact site by eleven artillery specialists over a period of nine days and ran forty-six pages. General Smith's report was based on three hours of on-the-spot investigation and covered only one page. Yet virtually nobody has questioned how the blame was assigned this time almost immediately to the Bosnian Serbs.

The Russian dissenter is Col. Andrei Demurenko, an artillery officer who commands the small Russian UN peacekeeping force in Sarajevo. On August 29, Demurenko announced that the probability of hitting a street less than thirty feet wide from one or two miles away, "the distance to the nearest Serb artillery positions," was "one to one million." Noting that no UN artillery observers heard the distinctive high-pitched whistle of a mortar shell prior to the detonation, he said he believed the fatal round had been "fired from some technical weaponry other than mortars."

On September 2, Demurenko went on television in Sarajevo, declaring the UN report "a falsification." With maps and diagrams he pointed out what he called inconsistencies and contradictions, saying, "It is absolutely unacceptable for me to consent to the arguments ... that the shelling came from the Serb side." Later a senior UN official confided to the Associated Press that the UNPROFOR command was considering disciplinary action against Demurenko.

The Canadian specialist, an officer with extensive service in Bosnia, said in a telephone interview that the UN report, which he'd seen, was "highly suspect." He cited "anomalies with the fuse" of the mortar shell recovered from the marketplace crater. Unlike the fuses of four other shells that hit Sarajevo that morning, this one, he said, "had not come from a mortar tube at all." He added that he and fellow Canadian officers in Bosnia were "convinced that the Muslim government dropped both the February 5, 1994, and the August 28, 1995, mortar shells on the Sarajevo markets."

A US Administration official who may not be identified further says, "It is impossible to see the street level" of the marketplace "from the distance and location of the Serb gun positions," meaning the Serbs would have been "shooting blind." Further, such a shot from such a distance would have had a high trajectory, he says; however, since there was no distinct whistle ... a shell could not have fallen from a very great height." Also, "the crater as shown was very shallow, while a high trajectory shell digs deep." He contends that the available evidence suggests either "the shell was fired at a very low trajectory, which means a range of a few hundred yards - therefore under government control," or "a mortar shell converted into a bomb was dropped from a nearby roof into the crowd."

A second US dissenter, a military officer, says that at least three of the five mortar rounds that hit Sarajevo in August "came from the identical firing position" on the Serb side. "But the fourth was of different origin, the one that killed people in the market."

The UN command in Sarajevo has offered a point-by-point rebuttal to these arguments. Curiously, it agrees with the dissenters on three basic points: that the fatal shell was fired at a very low trajectory; that it would have been a "one in a million" shot if it had been fired by Serbs; and that it would have been fired blindly. Nevertheless, the UN's Lieut. Col. Chris Vernon says the UN sticks by the conclusions of its inquiry.

Why would the Bosnian government kill its own people? The fact is that in the week before the marketplace killing, government forces launched heavy artillery attacks on Serb positions around Goražde and at Vogošča, north of Sarajevo, both times provoking Serb retaliatory fire. On each occasion the Muslim leadership loudly demanded NATO air attacks, but General Smith refused to call them in.

Then came Assistant Secretary Richard Holbrooke's August 27 threats that "in the next week or two, the consequences will be very adverse to the Serbian goals" and a few seconds later his warning of "more active NATO air."

Clearly the airstrikes had already been planned before Holbrooke set off for the Balkans to push President Clinton's peace plan. Only a pretext was needed. Indeed, State Department spokesman Nick Burns was talking about Serb responsibility and airstrikes before the UN report even reached New York. The first wave of US planes started bombing targets just thirty-nine hours after the marketplace explosion.

On September 5 a senior UN official with four years of experience in the Yugoslav conflict said of the marketplace killing: "It is not all that material. It's the three years and four months of Serb shelling of Sarajevo that is material. That's why the air raids started."

Once the bombing was under way, Gen. Rasim Delić, commander of Bosnian forces in Sarajevo, began picking targets — phoning Adm. W.A. Owens, vice chairman of the Joint Chiefs of Staff, daily with his wish list of sites. The Pentagon then passed these on to NATO in Naples. As one U.S. officer put it, "We have become the Muslim Air Force."

The Muslim offensive of 1995 was planned and executed by US Army General John Galvin...

To the Hague with Gen. Galvin; Gen. Mladic to West Point

by T.W. ("Bill") Carr

German and US Involvement in the Balkans: A Careful Coincidence of National Policies?

The Author is Associate Publisher, Defense and Foreign Affairs Publications, London. This text was presented at The Symposium on the Balkan War Yugoslavia: Past and Present, Chicago, 31 August - 1 September 1 1995

On May 3, 1995, the Bosnian Muslim troops launched a major offensive at 06.00 hrs. and at 10.00 hrs. NATO air strikes were made against Bosnian Serb positions ahead of the Muslim advance. The aircraft making the strikes were mainly USAF F-16 fighters supported by USAF F-111s reportedly acting in an air defense suppression role. In addition, the Bosnian Serb forces say that a small number of French, Spanish and Dutch aircraft took part in the air strikes. The air strikes ceased only after the Bosnian Serbs took UN troops hostage. Bosnian Serb intelligence says that the hostages were only handcuffed to posts for a very brief period to allow TV cameras to film footage for distribution in the West. All those involved were well treated; on Spain's national day, Spanish TV filmed their troops held hostage telephoning home to parents, wives and girlfriends. The British troops said they had been well treated and that they understood the military situation which caused their detention, however, on their way out through Serbia and since, they have not been permitted to make any comment to the media.

Unknown to the Bosnian Muslims and their US Advisers, Bosnian Serb intelligence had secured a copy of the planned Muslim offensive three days before it took place. Its main objectives were to secure Mt. Igman, to destroy a major portion of the Bosnian Serb Army and lift the siege on Sarajevo. Attacks were launched from a number of locations towards Sarajevo, including three major thrusts from Vares, Visoko and Pazaric. Another line of attack moved behind Mt. Igman across

Mt. Bjelasnica and Mt. Treskavica before one column hooked left toward Sarajevo, and a second column headed for Trnovo in an attempt to secure the road and tunnel linking Sarajevo and Kalinovik. At the same time, the Croats attacked Livno and Drvar in an attempt to drive a wedge between the Krajina Serbs and Bosnian Serbs. According to the Bosnian Serbs, it was quite clearly a two front attack coordinated by the joint Croat-Muslim Command headquarters.

At the Sarajevo battle, the Bosnian Serbs fell back to pre-pared positions giving the impression that the Muslim forces had them on the run. Indeed, at the time, some Western media reported an outstanding success had been achieved, the Serbs had been routed, and went on to speculate that this offensive, by a well-equipped Muslim army, could be a turning point in the war in favour of the Bosnian Muslim Government.

According to Bosnian Serb intelligence, the man who planned and executed the Muslim offensive was former US Army General John Galvin, recently retired, and now advising the Bosnian Muslim Government in Sarajevo. Sadly for the Muslims, they fell into a classic military ploy. The Bosnian Serbs enticed them into a large valley by retreating rapidly as the Muslim Special Forces pressed home their attack. When the valley was full of Muslim troops, the Bosnian Serbs opened up from the surrounding hills with heavy artillery, mortars and machine guns. According to one quiet spoken Bosnian Serb colonel, it was horrific. He said: "It was a slaughter. Even though I know they had come to slaughter us, I cannot be joy-ful at so many deaths which could have been avoided if only we had been allowed to remain united in Yugoslavia. In past times we lived together in peace, all of us, Serbs, Croats and Muslims.

The Americans and Germans broke up Yugoslavia, for what? Now they prolong the war, setting the Croats and Muslims together against us, planning the war for them, arming them and importing mujahedin into my country. If he wants to manipulate land, tell President Clinton to go back to Arkansas." I asked the colonel how many Bosnian Muslim troops had been killed in the May offensive.

He said: "There were two offensives, not one. It is difficult to judge how many died eventually, as the Muslim Government imposed a curfew on Sarajevo on the excuse that Serb snipers were in action, but this was to prevent the people from finding out what had happened. They set up field hospitals but I think they could not cope with all the casualties and many must have died of wounds. What I do know is that the Bosnian Muslims lost many thousands of their Special Forces who were spearheading the attack. In that one valley there must have been more than 10,000 Bosnian Muslim troops killed, and those were their best men."

He went on to say: "You know, even after such a defeat, the Muslim politicians still wanted more blood to be shed. They gave orders immediately for the Muslim units in the enclaves to launch attacks from Srebrenica, Gorazde, Tuzla and Bihac. From Srebrenica they launched three attacks in early June in which 12 Serbs were killed and many houses burnt. They made another two attacks from Srebrenica and Zepa using about 640 troops. The villages were not expecting the attack and many Serbs were killed. From

Gorazde they made two attacks towards Rogatica and burnt several Serb villages. In Gorazde the Muslims surrounded the Ukrainian UNPROFOR unit and took their weapons and Armoured Personnel Carriers. From Tuzla there were three attacks towards Majevica, and from Bihac the Muslim Special Forces made four attacks in the direction of Petrovac and one towards Novigrad."

He concluded by saying: "The Muslims wanted to provoke us into attacking the enclaves so that the Muslim Government could demand that NATO must protect the safe havens with air strikes and use the Rapid Reaction Force to fight Bosnian Serbs at Gorazde, Zepa, Srebrenica, etc. "Because the Muslims lost heavily at Sarajevo using an American strategy, I believe the Muslims expected the Americans to use NATO air strikes to punish Serbs. I don't think we have seen the end yet, we are awaiting another Muslim offensive and another staged incident by the Muslims on Muslims in order to give the Americans an excuse to send in NATO warplanes."

II. THE POFALIĆI MASSACRE

Tanjug, May 18, 1992

One of the more than 300 Serbian civilian victims of the massacre at Pofalići.

Pofalići is located in the Center Borough of Sarajevo. According to the real estate registry, most of it once belonged to Serbs. The suburb is comprised chiefly of residential homes, but it is also the location of two of Sarajevo's oldest factories, Fabrika duvana Sarajevo *(Sarajevo Tobacco Factory) and* Sarajevska Mlekara *(The Sarajevo Dairy).*

The eyewitness accounts presented in this chapter concern the Serbs of Sarajevo. They are only a handful of the testimonies collected by The Commission for Refugees in Serbia. General Mladić's family also lived in Pofalići until the war broke out.

In the last published part of an interview with General Mladić, "Symbol of Serbian Resistance," which was published as a five-part series in NIN over January/February 1994, Jovan Janjić provided the following luminous detail:

> During the first days of the war, General Ratko Mladić watched his house burning in Pofalići from Vrace. He was terribly worried because he did not know whether or not his mother, his wife, his children and his brother had managed to escape. He watched from a straight-line distance of less than a kilometer. At this moment many neighbors, Serbian civilians and soldiers who had escaped from Pofalići, surrounded him. One of them was Mladić's chauffeur from Ohrid, whose father and uncle had been killed....

Later, one of the soldiers told Mladić that he was watching on television the sixteen-year-old son of his neighbor, Hamid Duraković, bragging about how he had set fire to the General's house. He said that "all of Mladić's family had managed to escape harm, but at least his house did not!" At this moment, one of the artillerymen aimed his cannon at Hamid's house, and asked Mladić: "General, Sir, you have the honor of firing this shell!"

Mladić approached the gunsights. He had a grandstand view of his neighbor's house. But—he refused to fire!

Personal Statement 71/0038 B.O.

I worked in Sarajevo at the Sarajevska Mlekara. I lived in an apartment on Čengić Vila with my wife and children, and we had a house in Pofalići too. On May 15, 1992, we were informed that the supermarket on Orlovačka Street had been broken into and that my wife had to go to do the inventory. I stayed in the apartment.

That night Čengić Vila was bombed, and my wife could not come back home. She stayed over on Orlovačka Street. The next day, I went to work, and at 11 a.m. I learned that Dragan Vikić was going with two transports down Humska Street toward upper Pofalići. I told my wife to get out of there, thinking it was routine control of citizenry. But then I learned that Juka Prazina (*see* p. 142, fn 14) was heading toward upper Pofalići with about 3,700 men and that *Kruško*[1] was coming from Buća Potok. The attack started about 11:00 a.m. and it was horrible. We left work and went home. At about 4 p.m. my neighbors Ibrahimović and Tahirović told me that the Muslims had taken over Pofalići, and that we should go looting. I left with their mother for Pofalići to try to find my wife because I hadn't heard from her. There we found out that a horrible massacre had taken place. The bodies of slain men, women, children and animals were strewn in front of houses and along the streets.

The houses on Orlovačka Street had been put to the torch, and Humska Street was completely destroyed. It was dead. I looked for my wife. I turned corpses over with my own two hands. By my own reckoning and in my conversations with Muslims, three hundred and twelve (312) people were killed in this massacre. The surviving Serbs had to dig graves to bury the dead.

They were buried in two pits near the sign on Orlovačka Street. The remaining bodies were thrown into trucks and driven to the garbage dump in Buća Potok. I could not find my wife, and much later I learned that she managed to escape and got out of Sarajevo. Freedom of movement for us Serbs was limited. We could only go to work and come back home. Throughout this time Ismet Vrazalica, a member of the [Muslim] *Green Berets*,[2] gave me rides. Back then I brainstormed with friends to get ideas on how to get out of town, but it was impossible.

Serbs were asked over the radio to leave town in an organized manner, but those who managed to get through the various barricades to reach the collection center were arrested.

The collection centers were bus terminals in Alipašino Polje and in Dobrinja.

I was arrested because I worked in the local community in food delivery.... There were two of us Serbs. Since I worked in the Sarajevska Mlekara, I had large quantities of powdered milk and I delivered milk in our neighborhood. There were many mixed marriages in the building where I lived. One of the neighbors informed on me, saying that I gave food only to Serbs. It was an apartment building with 56 units on 31 Džemal Bijedić Street and at that time I happened to be the president of the building management council.

It became clear to me that police had put me under surveillance after inspector Branko Kuljačić (a Croat) visited me and told me to look out for myself, and that if I had any weapons, to surrender them to him because the police would not search him.

I did not have any weapons, so I was not afraid. On June 22, 1992, two inspectors came to my apartment at about 4 p.m. Later I found that both of them had been released from jail in February 1992. They told me that they had come to have a little talk with me.

I offered them drinks, they sat down, and we began to talk. It turned out that one of them knew me because I was a hiker, and we used to run into each other at hiking lodges.

All of this resembled a friendly chat. At about 6 p.m., one of them, Damir Ismailović, began searching the apartment. First they went in to the children's room, which had posters of the *Crvena Zvezda* (Red Star) soccer team tacked up on the wall. When they found school notebooks with *four interlocking esses*[3] written on it, they started to holler: "What's this? What kind of education do you call this?!" Then I got pistol whipped for the first time in my life. They cursed me and called me a *Chetnik*.[4]

They found an audiocassette with Chetnik songs that I really did not know about — the kids bought it and hid it from me. You could buy those cassettes on the street. They were sold along with audiocassettes of Muslim and Croat patriotic songs, and people bought them. I have to mention that my children were not in Sarajevo at the time. I had sent them to Bijeljina to my parents' home after the first teachers' strike, so that they could finish the school year in a normal fashion. They also found a videotape from a wedding in Rajlovac. We were shown singing an old Serbian song *Odalke si sele* on this videotape, which we all sang, Serbs and Muslims. They found that especially irritating. Then the mistreatment began. They took me to the Interior Ministry (SUP) and I had to give information about all the people who appeared in the videotape. They searched through my personal address book, and when they found the names of some Serbs from Sokolac, they accused me of being a member of a "Chetnik movement." They took me into the Republic's Interior Ministry on Sava Kovačević Street, which had been occupied by Green Berets. There I was, awaited by an inspector named Dragan, who, after introducing himself, immediately kicked me in the head. "What's your problem with Muslims? You see, I work with them."

They put my hands down flat on a table, and nailed me to the wall with bayonets that poked through my shirt. (I still have that shirt.) They interrogated me about my kids, about weapons, about what I knew about Serbs.... Since I did not answer, they told me they were sending me to the main prison facility, Čelo, to the "meat grinder."

They took me to the main prison facility where [I met] Bajramović, a military police commander and prison warden. He himself had been released [from this same prison not long ago]. I waited in front of the office because someone was being "processed" inside. Over there I met a neighbor, who spoke to me normally until they told him about the videotape. Then they roughed me up. After that they took me at about 8 p.m. to the front of the Central Prison complex on the square, where the student dormitory Mladen Stojanović is located. Rocket-propelled grenades were falling all around but fortunately none of them hit me.

They took me to the fifth floor of the Central Prison — the military section — and threw me into solitary confinement. After fifteen minutes, they handcuffed me together with Savo Jovanović, and took us back to Čelo. There they stripped us down to our underwear and took us to the ladies hair salon in the Mladen Stojanović dormitory. The humidity was terrible, but since it was dark, we did not know what it was. All we knew was that our legs and shoes were sopping wet. In the morning, we saw that it was blood. That night we spent hanging from radiator pipes on handcuffs. The next day, some guys carrying three-foot long lengths of pipe came to take us for interrogation. They got us off the radiator pipes and took us to the exit. There was a waiting truck and they began throwing us in. Since I was in good shape, I jumped in first, and avoided a heavy beating.

The other ten guys had a very hard time. They beat them with the lengths of pipe and bayonets. We did not know where they were taking us, but I saw through a crack that they were taking us to the Viktor Bubanj military base. When we arrived, I once again ran out first and again escaped a heavy beating. Seventy-four prisoners were brought to Viktor Bubanj that day. The camp started "work." We had to face a wall with our hands up. We were striped naked. The interrogation began with beatings. They hit me in the head while I was up against the wall, and I lost consciousness. That was when they killed Milorad Gligorić, the mathematics professor from Ilidža.

The guards were the professor's former students. They beat him, all the while shouting "Professor, can we get a D!?" They were beating him to death, and the man finally succumbed. Then they threw me into a cell made to hold four with eight others, and by the next day, there were fourteen of us in there.

The cell was 5'-5" x 12' (1.65 meters by 3.7 meters), about 66 square feet. There was only fourteen inches of space for each one of us. I spent four months there without being indicted, without anything. After four months, the investigating judge, Ignjac Dodig, took me out first. At the time I was not looking like myself; my weight dropped from exactly 100 kilograms to 54 kilograms.

Meanwhile, many died; some from hunger, others from beatings.

After the interrogation, they informed us that we would have defense attorneys at the trial.

Director Ramiz Avdić, a former prison counselor from Foča, took special pleasure in the maltreatment of prisoners, which did not occur daily, but by the minute. The food consisted of bread and water, and it was a thin slice of bread, 2 grams, that was no thicker than my fingernail.

Once, I took such a slice of bread and showed it to some visiting journalists. After that they broke my ribs. Two of the journalists from TV Sarajevo introduced themselves as Serbs, so I confided in them and begged them to notify my family that I was alive.

They promised to do that, but I didn't hear from my family until March 22, 1993. The same night after speaking with the journalists, the police found out about my family in Bijeljina, and called my wife on the phone. They introduced themselves as my friends, and they tried to learn from her whether or not I had any weapons, where they were hidden, etc. From her they found out about some of my friends, and these people were arrested the same night. I learned about my family for first time when the International Red Cross came to register us on February 22, 1993, eight months after my arrest. From then on, our treatment improved slightly. Until the Red Cross arrived on the scene, people were disappearing — "the darkness swallowed them up," as the saying goes. They were taken out as if they were going to be exchanged.

The International Red Cross was supposedly looking for Ognjen Kojević, who was incarcerated with us. Our captors took him for a prisoner "exchange." Trivo Guslov, Novica Ničević, Colonel Bračanović, Aleksandar Matić, and Stevo Siljegović died from hunger and beatings.... Solely responsible for their deaths was the "Doctor," actually a veterinarian, Himzo Dolac, the camp commander.

They could have saved these men with a crust of bread.... Nedeljko died from hunger just as Mišović from Stup did. The "Doctor" kicked them and told them to stop faking illness. He said that they were healthy, and that nothing was the matter with them. But these men were mere skin and bone. We were always forced to work. We were particularly mistreated on the work details by the members of the Drinska unit, which was under the command of a man named Sabanović.

Their 101st brigade was located there. We cleared rubble while being horribly mistreated.

I spent 12 months there, and I had fourteen trial appearances during that time. They kept extending my jail term. On May 15, 1993, I was sentenced in Viktor Bubanj, and remained incarcerated until June 9, 1993. They asked me to enlist in the Army of Bosnia-Herzegovina, in which case my sentence would be rescinded.

I refused. After sentencing they moved us to the Central Prison, where we thought we would be exchanged, but we knew nothing for certain. After they took Branko Rogan, we thought he had been exchanged, but I found him nine months later in the Central Prison. It was a real disappointment. The conditions in the Central Prison were somewhat better, but there were also murders. I personally know of six. Responsible for these murders was the director, Sobo, who was once a judge in Foča. Dragan Zelić allegedly hanged himself there. They killed Ostoja Soja on a work detail. I personally carried out four of the murder victims from the investigative division of the military prison on the fifth floor. All I know is that two guys were from Ilidža, and the other two I didn't know. Himzo Dolan was also there. We had more frequent visits by the ICRC, and they brought food and clothing, which was confiscated after their departure. Management first took whatever it needed, and then the back office staff helped themselves. Whatever was left was for us.

From December 16, 1993 until March 1994, they did not give us anything so we were once again terribly weakened. When we complained, Miroljub Torbica and Vojislav Čangalović forbade us to have contact with our families, so I didn't know anything about my family from that time up until my release.

Meanwhile (in February 1994) I had begun to receive some confirmations bearing a postmark from Bijeljina that they had killed my wife and two uncles in Tuzla. Then it was really hard for me. I did not know it was all a lie. They toyed with us, blackmailed us, and tried to force us to convert to Islam. All we had to do was change our first names; our surnames could stay as they were. They kept making us offers to join the Muslim Army.

I found out from the judge that they were searching for the location of weapons and ammunition, supposedly known by me, before they could set me free. I told him that I was not worth a single bullet, and that I did not want to be exchanged in that fashion. Horrible beatings followed. They pulled out my nails....

I want to say something else about the living conditions. We snatched bread from dogs and birds, and soaked it in water. This resulted in dysentery. In contrast, many of us did not have a bowel movement for thirty to forty days.

We had a terrible problem with lice. The former head of the sanitation department, Dragomir Mihajlović, was imprisoned with us. He collected lice in a small bottle to see how long they could survive with out food and air. They remained alive for thirty days. We had to just physically destroy them: we use to get disinfectant shampoo from the Red Cross, but they would take it away from us. They would give us DDT with expired dates, which had no effect at all on the lice. After registration with the Red Cross, they allowed us to take showers.

It looked like Auschwitz. We were just waiting for the time they were going to gas us (making the association was inevitable). The shower lasted for 30 to 40 seconds, while they deliberately switched the water from hot to ice cold, and so many of us were packed into the showers that we didn't even have a chance to take off our clothes.

On May 10, 1994, I was released from the Central Prison at 11 p.m. I did not understand that I was going to be exchanged, because a guard often took us out on work details at night. It was clear to me when I saw the IRC representatives in the hallway. Muratović approached from the Muslim side, and began telling us how we had to behave, and he made us an offer to stay in the city. Only one man accepted because his family was in Sarajevo. The prisoner exchange took place that morning in 8:47 a.m.

Personal Statement 71/00403 V.R.

My name is V. R. I was born in 1949 in Pofalići and I make the following statement. One of the principal goals in the plans of the Muslim leadership was to dominate the political and economic life of Bosnia-Herzegovina, and to marginalize the Serbian population wherever even the smallest opportunity presented itself in the Sarajevo area. The suburb of Pofalići was of special strategic interest for Muslim fundamentalists. A Serbian majority had always inhabited this suburb, which lies on the slopes beneath Hum Hill, until a few years before the war broke out in April 1992.

The scenario of resettling Pofalići was tied to the unified and perfidious policy of the Muslim-Croat political leadership that practically dominated all areas of social and political life over the past decade. A well organized Muslim demographic policy has been carefully promoted in the political life of Sarajevo over the last ten years, whose only goal was to expropriate property from Serbs and redistribute it, first of all, to people from the Sandžak region of Serbia, whose numbers have risen over the last ten years to 200,000. If the organized resettlement of the Albanian population, whose numbers reached 80,000 residents just before the war, is taken into consideration, then one could clearly see where such policies led. The Serbs, dispossessed landowners in areas where they had lived, as in Pofalići, for more than 500 years, could not resist the unscrupulous seizure of their properties. Every protest and complaint about each instance to the authorities, whether it were addressed to a precinct or to Sarajevo city officials, was treated as a violation of national relationships at the expense of other peoples.

In this fashion, Serbs were driven from their properties, which were seized up to their very doorstep, just to have Muslims for neighbors.... The same scenario was applied in other parts of Sarajevo where Serbs were in the majority. The hardest thing for us Serbs to bear is the fact that we were attacked by our neighbors, who had settled here from Sandžak, and who built family homes on our properties.

Instead of eternal gratitude toward their Serbian neighbors, who had less than willingly given them properties, the Sandžaklia began a bloody settling of scores with the Serbs, who never gave them any specific reason for such actions. It should be said that the Muslims had been preparing for this war for years, especially in Sarajevo, which was the object of their interest.

The war "officially" began in Sarajevo during the Muslim festival of Bajram on April 4, 1992, but the preparations had been going on for years. On the aforementioned day when the war broke out, Serbs were the "principal" guests of many Muslims. Many of those who took part in this Muslim religious holiday ended up losing their lives.

This was how the great, ambitious Muslim fundamentalist scenario began. The war that was being waged in some parts of the town came to Pofalići on May 15, when Rajko Savić was killed on 185 Orlovačka Street by his next-door neighbor, Mirsad Bungur. Mlađen Bratić, Branko Jeremić, Branko Bozalo, Vukadin Vojin, Slobodan Odzaković, Nedjo Odžaković, Savo Elez and the married couple, Mirko and Rosa Savić, were killed at the same time. Vida Bratić was killed on his own doorstep with an ax.

The murders of these Serbs was simply a warning to the other Serbian inhabitants of Pofalići. And it came true. On May 16, 1992, more than 3,000 Muslim fighters attacked two hundred Serbian families in the early morning hours, from all directions. The newly settled Sandžaklia took over the killing of Serbs.

We were surrounded on all sides. The remaining Serbian families, panic-stricken and in disarray, began to retreat toward Hum, and then toward Žuč Hill, just to save their lives, because none of them ever expected such a scenario to unfold. During the retreat, many Serbian families left weak and invalid family members behind, who were killed in the most brutal fashion shortly afterwards. The chaotic column of Serbian residents was apparently allowed to pass through to the northwestern slopes of Hum, which led to a small river, Buća Potok, which runs along the base of the Hum; from there we had to climb up a slope more than 700 yards to reach Žuč, another hill.

But during the retreat, the Serbian column was cut in the forested part of the Hum slope, where Muslim fighters, armed to the teeth, were waiting. Hemmed in from all sides, unarmed women, children and the elderly fled in all directions. Several people died on the spot.

While the Muslim fanatics, who were all jagged up on drugs, fired mercilessly on the column of Serbian civilians, *ilahija*s and *kasida*s[5] echoed throughout Hum, along with the well-known Muslim refrain, *Alahu ekber*.[6] The forested area became a grave.... Wailing and screams echoed, and calls for help that did not arrive. All those fortunate enough not to get hit by a Muslim bullet during the attack fell into a gorge that was 200 meters (220 yards) deep as they fled in panic through the forest.

The whole scenario was repeated three times because the column of Serbian refugees was allowed to enter the area of fighting three times, and three times the column was cut. There I saw how Nada Vasković was killed right after Božo Kovačević, an elderly man who never gave anyone any reason to commit a crime. The column of Serbian refugees from Pofalići, decimated by the Muslim fighters, moved toward Žuč. At first, no one could tell how many people were lost, but we took note of significant losses suffered by some families who had left their homes in panic. As the last part of the column made its way toward Žuč, the Muslim fighters set fire to Serbian properties and homes.

It was unbelievable. It was hard to watch this sad picture of more than 500 homes going up in flames. The flames rose into the sky, but none of those unfortunates had time to consider whether his home was on fire or not. The entire retreat of the decimated Serbian families from Pofalići was targeted by artillery fire on the road to Žuč, which was not forested. Some twenty or so Serbs were killed or wounded there. I want to point out that during the escape I was forced to leave my invalid father. I had to take care of my children, my mother and my wife.... When we got to Žuč, I saw what survivors remained of my relatives and neighbors.

Dozens of dead and wounded people for whom there was no help were left on the slopes of Hum and Žuč. The moans of women and children could be heard from a distance of more than 1,000 meters. The Muslim fighters moved through the forested part of Hum to finish off the wounded on the spot.

The surviving Serbs who managed to climb to the top of Žuč tearfully watched their homes and their properties, in which they had invested their whole lives and their savings, burn. As sad as it was to see hundreds of Serbian houses burn, it was at the same time a unique event that could serve poets and artists as an inspiration to depict the non-culture and the savagery of the insane Muslim *jihad* warriors. Tongues of flame rose 30 meters into the sky as Serbian properties were converted into an "ethnically clean" sheaf of smoke. The end of this catastrophe for the Serbs of Pofalići was described in broad strokes, and it would not be complete if we did not mention the names of the Sandžaklia who settled there and led the bloody operation against innocent long-time residents. First and foremost among the Muslim criminals were from the family of Sandžaklia Habib Idrizović, who settled in Pofalići fourteen years ago and brought with him six brothers, all of whom built houses on Serbian property.

Omer Gabela, a former journalist and long-time resident, assisted Idrizović in every possible way. Gabela brought a

Sarajevan TV crew to Pofalići on May 17, the day after the criminal persecution of the Serbs took place, which took video footage of imprisoned Serbs in undamaged Muslim homes, and presented a completely false picture while claiming at the same time that the Serbian families of Pofalići did not suffer.

The imprisoned Serbs gave statements under duress to Sarajevo TV, which broadcast the report of the Muslim Army's "victory" in Pofalići. Then the Serbs who gave statements to the press were killed. The elderly Stanko Pikulić, one of the long-time residents who had been forced to state that his home had not been burned, was killed. Besides Idrizović and Gabela, Arif Ljuca and his son Nusret as well as his brothers Karamović-Fadil, Dževad and Faik committed atrocities against their Serbian neighbors. Habib Idrizović, his six brothers who were his right-hand men, as well as Omer Gabela bear the greatest guilt for the destruction of the Serbian community in Pofalići. They must be prosecuted in a court of law.... The same goes for the Muslim fighters who drove Serbian families from Pofalići. Among the families driven out were those of Čangalović, Pikulić, Đukić, Bunjevac, Andrijašević, Vasković, Andrić, Trišić, Maparević, Golijan and others.

I want to emphasize that this war took several victims from my own family. My father, mother, brother, and his wife died, and one of my brothers was seriously wounded. We lost all of our property, which consisted of three houses with seven apartments.... As this short retelling comes to an end, I want to say that I omitted dozens of tragic details, and I want to say that we will never accept the fact that Serbian Pofalići belongs to the Muslims.

We, the citizens of Pofalići, want to inform all institutions of the international community about the real catastrophe that struck the Serbian inhabitants of Pofalići, and that we do not accept any presentation of facts made by Muslim television.

Personal Statement: Vesna Mijović[7]

... It was Thursday, the May 14, 1992. My mother and I went to have coffee with the Ignjatović family at about 10 o'clock, while my father went to visit the Šarović family, who lived in the same building. Milenko, Anđa, their daughter Snežana were in the Ignjatović home, along with their daughter Nada who is married to Đorđe Manojlović, a major [in the army] who was at that very moment on the front lines in Kupres. She had escaped from Igman. Slavica Ćelić and Dragica, their neighbors. On the other side of the building, where the Šarović family lived, were Blažo, Jelo, Blažo's nephew Zoran, my father Miloš and Neđo Ćelić. After we had our coffee, we discovered that we could not leave the house because of the countless grenades that were exploding all around the house (we even spent the night there) because it was the safest place to stay as far as the grenades were concerned. My brother Ranko, whose nickname is Gagi, was in the trench not far from us. I have to write something about him, kbut I could write a whole book. He is an extraordinary young man who was born in 1967: he is a true Serb, an honorable soldier, the kindest of men and most importantly he is not two-faced. He says what he thinks, and I am proud to have such a brother — not a coward. He was on the first line of barricades in Pofalići.

We had been marked. The Muslims stopped coming to our cafe, "Mali raj." They regarded us with contempt, but we were not afraid of them even though we knew they were well-armed. They had armed themselves publicly. On the day the barricades went up, a truck full of weapons made a delivery to our next-door neighbor Munib Tucak, and they handed them out right on the street. From then on, we no longer slept at my brother Rora's because of the night watch. Over the course of several days, my house was hit by eight bullets and one of them could have hit me. I left my room and the bullet hit the wall. Someone must have had me in their crosshairs because that bullet would have ended up in my temple, but luckily it didn't...

We sought refuge in the Ignjatović house in the evenings. We slept in the bathroom, the hallway, in the pantry. Rora told us to flee. Father was going with him to the trench, while we should head for Reljevo or Pale. Anywhere, as far as possible from Pofalići. But my father Blažo, Neđo, Vajo, Radoslav and Danilo Gagović did not want to go. It seems to me that they trusted their neighbors. I had finally packed two days earlier, and was ready to set out for Reljevo. I was in touch with the Savić family because they had stayed in the battle zone in Žuč. Rora urged us again to flee, and he ended up quarreling with me because I said I could not leave my father or mother, and my mother did not want to leave without my father. At 4.30 a.m. on the day before the attack, I brought my brother a change of clothing. I found Milisav Rističević on guard duty. He told me that he had taken over for Rora, who had gone to try and get some sleep because he was worried about. He had premonitions of danger, and he saw that there was no chance of saving Pofalići. I returned home, where I spent another night and day. On May 14, 1992, the first shot was fired at 3:55 p.m., and we all recognized that shot for what it was. We heard Zuhro Zijadić fire. We later found out that the bullet ended in my father's jacket. Then we heard the thousands of other shots that followed. Bullets smashed through the panges of glass in the windows, and ricocheted off the parquet floor. We finally heard people breaking in through the windows and entering our floor. They overturned furniture, and shouted "Surrender!" It was a madhouse. We were trapped.

My father, Blažo and Neđo were carrying weapons. We heard Blažo say, "Let's surrender, let's surrender." I didn't know what was going on out there. Fifteen minutes later, they were at our door and Blažo told us to open the door and surrender. We did not have anything to surrender. We didn't have any weapons or anything else to defend ourselves with. I embraced my mother. I was not afraid of those savages. I opened the door and there were indeed a great many of them. They looked like onions planted in rows, all of them armed and wearing various uniforms. Our neighbour Safet Trnka was among them.

They took my father, Zoran and Blažo away somewhere, and Neđo Ćelić managed to hide with us. Gale drove everyone out of the house where we were. He left relative of his to guard us and he went off to bring my father, Blažo and Zoran back. The women were crying, but they continued shooting. I managed to get the telephone into the pantry to call Vajo Gagović to tell him to get out (he had no idea what was going on outside), and to tell him that we had been captured and to call the Rističević family and to tell them that we had been captured and that the people in the trench had be ready and that there were a great many of them compared to the "berets" who had attacked us and to tell Rora not to come back no matter what happened to us and to go ahead. Even though they hadn't heard my phone conversation, they told me to bring the telephone out into the hallway. I did this, then the phone rang. Biljana Krakšić called us from Briješče. She was the daughter of Milenko Ignjatović, and she told us to flee, not knowing that we had already been captured. I spoke to her normally as though nothing had happened because guns were being pointed at me. Then they used the phone. At one point, Hido Baktanović, a neighbor, a little jerk, said that there had been gunfire coming from our house all day long. I steeled myself and said, "Get lost, you bum. Aren't you ashamed of lying." Alija Sakin, a boy of only 14, threw him out. Gale returned with my father Miloš, Blažo and Zoran. My father was covered with blood, and he had cuts on his face. But he spoke normally as though nothing had happened. I could not wipe off the clotted blood. Blažo did not say anything for a while, and after a few moments, he said it would be safer for us to to go to his place. So we went. I was the last to leave. Someone said, "Halt." I stopped. Neđo was in front of me, but everyone had left and I was alone. Someone asked: "Zdenka is that you?" I answered, "Yes." "Walk slowly. Don't run."

To this day I don't know who it was. I realized that Blažo had asked us to come to his place because he want-ed to see what had happened to his home and belongings. But it was horrible. They took my father, Blažo and Zoran away again for a while. Gale told me that he could do nothing more than to have them moved to the central prison and that he would leave his identity card as a guarantee for us and for them. He was soaked [in sweat]. However, the "berets" had caught enough Serbs and they did not arrest them. We returned to the Ignjatović home. Just before dawn, we saw them plundering our homes, carting our possessions away, and driving away with our cars. Alija came out at 5:00 a.m., and I went out with him and went back to my house. On the ground floor everything was overturned ... completely destroyed, and the same with the telephone and vacuum cleaner. All the windows had been smashed. The bag I packed had been completely torn apart and all my money had been stolen. I went upstairs and saw the electricity meter in the hall had been broken, and the telephone too.

I heard a thumping noise, so I didn't dare go any further. I went out into the garage. Father's "Lađa," Rora's little Fiat, my Fiat, were completely open and ready to go. The tools in the upper and lower parts of the garage had been overturned. The big van and the Volkswagen that were parked on the street were full of bullet holes. I returned to the ground floor, put on my tennis shoes and left. My mother had also gone. I took only a jacket for her. Then they started shooting at us and asked us what we were doing, and they told us that we could not take our things. They told us to run. So we ran and all of us escaped to the Serb quarter near Dom. We went without paying any attention as to whether or not they would fire on us. Here we spent the night because Neno Pikula said so. The next day my brother Rora came. We wept and he said that we should leave immediately and Neno did his part. We spent the night there, and in the morning we saw that the houses in our suburb were burning. I watched our house, the restaurant and garage [burn] with my mother. It was sad and painful. Hearing that the "berets" had moved closer, we carefully started to flee at 12:30, but there were many more of us.

The grenades fell like rain. People fell. My mother Slavica and Neđo Ćelić were running ahead of me. At one moment, I heard the whistling of mortar shells. I called to my mother to hit the ground. She didn't hear me. I threw myself over her and covered ourselves with my jacket. I heard nothing. Everything looked white. When I came to, I looked around and was shocked. There were 10-15 people lying on the ground, all of them my Serbian neighbors, but they were unrecognizable because they were covered with blood and mutilated. It was horrible. At one moment, a young man in a white jacket and jeans got up and he held a rifle in his hands. He was running and was covered with blood. I recognized him. It was Njegoš Bratić. Another boy was alive but wounded and he said "Kill me. Don't leave me." It was Boriša Šajić. We threw him a towel and four or five young men ran up to help him. We kept running and reached the Jovičić house. There were about 30 of us. We heard a voice say, "Hasim, Hasim, now let's go clear out the woods and the houses." The berets appeared in front of us and no matter where we turned, there were more berets. Some women and men suggested that we go to Gojko Pikula's basement. I did not want to. I took my mother by the hand and we headed straight for the forest. After us came Jelo Šarović, Dragica, Slavica and Neđo Ćelić, Radojko and Gagović, and Brezo, I don't known the man's name and Ljubo Vasković. Neđo and Brezo threw their weapons away. The remainder went off to the basement and later I learned that they had been captured. We went through the forest for a long time. They were firing on us from all sides. We entered a small ravine where a stream flowed. I looked at my watch and it was 2:30 p.m. Branches and earth were falling on us (the mortar shells were doing their job). A sniper was constantly firing on us. Later, I learned it was Rora who was shooting at us. He didn't know that it was us because everyone thought the Serbs had gotten out. Unfortunately they hadn't. I was wearing a silver necklace with a silver crucifix. I held it tightly and recited the "Our Father, who art in heaven" and begged God to save us. When a branch hit me on the head, I lost the crucifix. I could not find it and I will never get over my regret for having lost it.

We spent the night [in the forest] and heard the berets still plundering [homes]. We moved still farther down because we could no longer remain in raving where the stream ran. We were soaked. We crossed a meadow and hid in some bushes. We could not go any further because the berets were there. Only the bushes separated us from them. We could hear everything they said. At one moment, Neđo said, "Fellows, here we are!" Fortunately, they did not hear him. We told him to be quiet. We remained there until 6:30 a.m. We were freezing. Marijana and Slavica were trembling and stiff with cold. I warmed them up. We had to keep going. We entered another forest. Then I saw those three houses that Rora identified as landmarks. In the forest we found small boxes of ammunition and bandages soaked with blood. I knew that the Serbs were here... We reached the first house. It was empty, deserted. The other house belonged to Miro Poluga. We saw him. Radojka Gagović began to run back and said I had brought her right into the hands of the Ustashi. Neđo caught up with her, threw her to the ground and talked some sense into her. Later, she saw we were right. Miro told us how to continue. And somehow we reached Žuč....

Endnotes

[1] *Kruško*, another Sarajevo criminal who had organized a brigade for the Patriotic League.

[2] *Green Berets*, an elite group of Bosnian Muslim government soldiers.

3 *four interlocking esses*, an abbreviation for *Samo Sloga Spasi Srba*, "only unity can save the Serbs."

4 *Chetniks*, Serbian resistance fighters who remained loyal to the monarchy during WWII. Later they were unjustly accused of collaboration with the Nazis, but were later vindicated.

5 *ilahija*s and *kasida*s, holy songs and long, rhymed eulogies in Arabic or Turkish.

6 *Alahu ekber*, (Ar.) God is great.

7 *The Eradication of the Serbs in Bosnia-Herzegovina*, 1992-1993, edited by Drago Jovanović, Gordana Bundalo, Miloš Govedarica: Montreal, 1995, *op. cit.*

III. CROATIAN FASCISM AND THE VATICAN

Croatian Fascism: Back From the Grave

by A.M. Rosenthal, *The New York Times*, April 15, 1997
Copyright © 1997 by The New York Times. Reprinted with permission.

Mr. Rosenthal is the former executive editor and columnist of The New York Times. *He joined* The New York Times *in 1943, where he worked for the next fifty-six years.*

In World War II, Hitler had no executioners more willing, no ally more passionate, than the Fascists of Croatia.

They are returning, 50 years later, from what should have been their eternal grave, the defeat of Nazi Germany.

The Western allies who dug that grave with the bodies of their servicemen have the power to stop them, but do not.

Croatian Fascists, known as the Ustashe, fought alongside German troops against Serbs, Muslims and Croats trying desperately, and vainly, to block the Nazi conquest of Yugoslavia. In 1941 Hitler rewarded Croatian Fascists by carving out a Croatian state and letting them run it. They did not let him down.

The Ustashe slaughtered Serbs, Jews and non-Fascist Croats — and with such glee and such cruelty that their name became a terror and stench throughout Europe.

Croatia disappeared with Hitler's annihilation in 1945. A half-century later the West created a new Croatia, by recognizing the secession from Yugoslavia of Croatian nationalists, led by one Franjo Tudjman.

Not all were Fascists, by any means, but now the Ustashe is running in elections, brutalizing its enemies — Croat, Serb or Jew. Mr. Tudjman is giving them what they need most — presence, and the rewriting of history.

Two documents are a short course on the Ustashe. To honor the murdered and protect the future, read them.

From pages 323-328 of the *Encyclopedia of the Holocaust* (Macmillan): "More than a half million Serbs were killed, a quarter million expelled, 200,000 forced to convert to the Catholicism of the Croatian Fascists.

"Thousands were hurled from mountain tops, others were beaten to death, entire villages were burned down, women raped, people sent on death marches in the middle of winter, still others starved to death."

Jews? Ante Pavelić, the Ustashe leader, announced that the Jews would be "liquidated within a very short time." They were, most of the 40,000.

But some chosen as victims did survive. Study the picture of the children after the camps were freed. They wear only bones and tightened skin. Serbs? Jews?

The second document is a fine piece of journalism from Croatia by *The New York Times* correspondent Chris Hedges (April 12) about the rebirth of Fascism there — the bullying, the sieg-ing and heil-ing in Croatian, the whole nastiness.

Most important is the increasing work of Mr. Tudjman — a longtime Holocaust denier — to recast the Fascists as patriots and founders of the new Croatia.

This man likes to talk about how he himself fought German soldiers. Now a major political, military and financial beneficiary of the West, he permits pictures of Fascists dead and alive to be plastered around the country. He gives special status and pensions to Ustashe veterans.

He tried to get the body of the killer-chief Pavelić returned from Spain, where he had fled, and buried with honor in Zagreb — like reburying Himmler under the linden.

The family objected. So he brought back another Ustashe killer, this one alive, and made him a member of Parliament.

Western recognition of Mr. Tudjman's Croatia was pushed hardest by Germany despite warnings from Bosnian Muslims that the timing could set off war among themselves, Serbs and Croats.

Franjo Tudjman is now ours. The West cannot evade responsibility for the rebirth of Fascism in Croatia. Peter Galbraith, U.S. Ambassador to Croatia, told me he had denounced Croatian ethnic cleansing of Serbs last year, and considered the glorification of the Ustashe an insult to Croats who fought Nazis, and to American veterans of World War II.

Mr. Tudjman and his Fascist protégés brush off ambassadorial protest with insult. Would he brush off the Presidents of the U.S. and France, the British Prime Minister — or the Chancellor of Germany — if they took action to stop Croatian Fascism? Such as denouncing the Tudjman buildup of the Ustashe, then reducing Western representation to sub-ambassadorial and slashing economic help to Croatia - the whole list?

That won't change the Ustashe or improve Mr. Tudjman's sickness of body and character. But it could force him to end Fascist rehabilitation work.

Or has the West become so sick itself that it will permit Croatian Fascism to live on beyond the grave?

Fascists Reborn as Croatia's Founding Fathers

by Chris Hedges, *The New York Times*, April 12, 1997
Copyright © 1997 by The New York Times. Reprinted with permission.

SPLIT, Croatia — The old fascist marching songs were sung, a moment of silence was observed for all who died defending the fatherland, and the gathering on Thursday was reminded that it was the 57th anniversary of the founding of Croatia's Nazi-allied wartime government. Then came the most chilling words of the afternoon.

"For Home!" shouted Anto Dapic, surrounded by bodyguards in black suits and crew cuts.

"Ready!" responded the crowd of 500 supporters, their arms rising in a stiff Nazi salute.

The call and response — the Croatian equivalent of "Sieg!" "Heil!" — was the wartime greeting used by supporters of the fascist Independent State of Croatia that governed the country for most the Second World War and murdered hundreds of thousands of Jews, Serbs and Croatian resistance fighters.

On Thursday, the final day of campaigning before local elections on Sunday, supporters of Croatia's Party of Rights used the chant as a rallying cry. But the shouts of the black-shirted young men — and the indifferent reactions of passers-by — illustrated a broader aspect of this country's self-image.

President Franjo Tudjman and his Croatian Democratic Union party rose to popularity and power on the strength of its appeals to Croatians' national pride. Now, six years after the war that won Croatia its independence from Yugoslavia, Tudjman's party continues to cast the World War II fascist regime as patriots and precursors of the modern Croatian state.

The Party of Rights took only 7 percent of the vote in the last election, but it is the closest ally of Tudjman, who is reported to be suffering from cancer and who has actively participated in the campaign.

Perhaps no other country has failed as openly as Croatia to come to terms with its fascist legacy. While the French celebrate a resistance movement that was often dwarfed by the widespread collaboration with the Vichy regime, and while the Austrians often act as if the war never happened, the Croats have rehabilitated the Croatian fascist collaborators, known as the Ustashe.

The Ustashe was led by Ante Pavelić, the wartime dictator whose picture was plastered on walls in Split in preparation for the rally.

"A majority of the Croats oppose this rehabilitation," said Viktor Ivančić, editor-in-chief of the opposition weekly, *The Feral Tribune*. "But they are afraid. These neo-fascist groups, protected by the state, are ready to employ violence against their critics."

Ustashe veterans receive larger pensions than old Partisan fighters, who waged a savage fight against the German and Croatian fascist armies. Former Ustashe soldiers are invited to state celebrations, like the annual army day, while Partisan fighters are ignored. And state authorities have stood by as pro-Ustashe groups have dismantled or destroyed 2,964 of 4,073 monuments to those who died in the resistance struggle, according to veteran Partisan groups.

The identification with the quisling regime does not stop there. The Croatian currency is the kuna, the same instituted by the fascists. And the red and white checkerboard on the flag, taken from medieval Croatian emblems, previously adorned the Ustashe uniform.

The president recently proposed bringing Pavelić's remains from Spain, where he died in exile in 1959, for burial in Croatia, a move rejected by Pavelić's family. And Vinko Nikolić, an 85-year-old former high-ranking Ustashe official who fled into exile after the war, was appointed by the president to the Croatian Parliament.

The transformation is all the more noticeable because of widespread participation by many Croats in the Partisan guerrilla movement led by Josip Broz Tito, himself a Croat.

"A huge number of Croats fought the Nazis and the Ustashe," said 77-year-old Partisan veteran Milivoj Boroša, who defected in his bomber in 1942 from the Ustashe air force and dropped his pay load on a German unit during his escape to the Soviet Union. "But today those who should hold their heads in shame are national heroes."

The Partisans, who included among their ranks a young Franjo Tudjman, committed what today is viewed as an unforgivable sin. They built a united, communist Yugoslavia.

And while the Ustashe state may have been a Nazi puppet, it had as its stated aim the establishment of an independent Croatia, although it was forced by the Axis to turn over large parts of Croatia, including much of the Dalmatian coast, to the Italians.

In the current campaign, Tudjman sought to reconcile the country's wartime divisions by arguing that the fascist and anti-fascist Croatians performed equally valuable service for their country.

A general who became a historian after leaving the Yugoslav army, Tudjman is among the leaders of a revisionist school of history that has sought to counterbalance the communists' relentlessly dark view of the fascist years.

But many Croats, especially those who had relatives killed by the fascists, smolder with indignation over the glorification of a regime that slaughtered opponents with a ferocity that often shocked its Italian and German allies.

"You cannot reconcile victims and butchers," said Ognjen Kraus, the head of Zagreb's small Jewish community. "No one has the right to carry out a reconciliation in the name of those who vanished."

The climate has become so charged that those who oppose the rehabilitation of the Ustashe do not dare raise their voices.

And there have been several attacks carried out against members of the Social Democratic Party, the old communist party, currently fielding candidates for the municipal elections. Many of the black-uniformed bodyguards at the rally fought against the Serbs as members of the Croatian Liberation Forces, a brutal right-wing paramilitary unit formed by the party.

The Ustashe supporters also have a powerful ally in the Catholic Church in Croatia. The church, led during the war by Archbishop Alojzije Stepinac, was a prominent backer of the Ustashe regime. It forcibly converted tens of thousands of Orthodox Serbs and did not denounce the government's roundup and slaughter of Jews and Serbs.

During the war, Jews and Orthodox Serbs were subject to racial laws. The Serbs had to wear blue armbands with the letter "P" for "Pravoslav" — Orthodox — before being deported to death camps like Jasenovac.

After the war, many priests, rather than condemn the brutality of the fascist regime, went on to set up an underground network known as "the rat line" to smuggle former Ustashe leaders, including Pavelić, to countries like Argentina.

The church, persecuted by the communists, has now re-emerged as one of the most powerful institutions in the country, in large part because religion is the only tangible difference separating Serbs, Muslims and Croats. Several priests have enthusiastically joined the rehabilitation campaign, portraying Pavelić as a pious leader who championed Christian values.

"Ante Pavelić was a good Catholic," said Father Luka Prcela, who has held a memorial mass for the former dictator in Split for the last four years. "He went to mass daily in his own chapel. Many of the crimes alleged to have been committed by his government never happened. These stories were lies spread by the communists. He fought for a free, Catholic Croatia. We have this state today because of him."

WHAT IS THE VATICAN HIDING?
The Suppressed Chapter
of Holocaust History

by Barry Lituchy, 10 May 1998

Copyright © 1998. Reprinted with permission by the author.

Barry Lituchy, Director of the Jasenovac Research Institute (JRI, see www.jasenovac.org), teaches History at Kingsborough Community College in Brooklyn, NY. He organized the First Conference on the Jasenovac Concentration Camp at Kingsborough Community College in 1997. This article first appeared on The Internet Anti-Fascist: Wednesday, 20 May 98 Vol. 2, Number 31 (#115).

Fourteen years ago the U.S. Government de-classified the now famous "La Vista Report" of May 15, 1947, a top-secret U.S. Army Intelligence report documenting the Vatican's role in aiding the escape of numerous high-ranking Nazi war criminals, among them Ante Pavelic, fascist leader of wartime Croatia; Franz Stangel, Commander of Treblinka; Eduard Roschmann, "the Butcher of Riga"; Klaus Barbie, "the Butcher of Lyon"; SS General Walter Rauff, inventor of the mobile gas truck; Adolf Eichmann, "architect of the Holocaust"; and tens of thousands of others. Writing about the document prior to its release, internationally renowned Nazi hunter Charles R. Allen Jr. noted that in light of the revelations contained in this and other classified documents about the role of the Vatican in the Holocaust it would be logical and proper that

> "A commission of inquiry into these concerns including Jewish and Catholic scholars ought to be established to locate and examine all documentation in all relevant archives so that collectively they may determine what role both the Vatican and US Intelligence played in aiding and abetting the escape of some of history's most notorious murderers.[1]

Logical, that is, if one assumed that the Vatican truly wanted to get to the bottom of what really happened, and maybe even try to atone for some of the injustices it committed. But fourteen years after the fact, with the release of the Vatican's official statement on "the mistakes" of the Catholic Church during the Holocaust, we now can see how overly optimistic that assumption was. The "La Vista Report" was documentary evidence that opened a window on a suppressed chapter of the Holocaust: the role of the Vatican in the Holocaust. The Vatican's report "We Remember, a Reflection on the Shoah (Holocaust)," issued this past March makes it abundantly clear that the Catholic Church is determined to do all that it can to shut that window as tightly as it can, and to keep it shut forever. Forget the idea of a commission — the Vatican has no intention of opening its archives or admitting anything other than "...the errors and failures of those sons and daughters of the Church" who did not "give every possible assistance to those being persecuted, and in particular ... Jews."

Far from suggesting that the Vatican did anything wrong, the document instead tries to portray the role of the Church during the Holocaust in a mostly positive light, insisting that "many" members of the Church did "give every possible assistance" — implying that those who didn't were a minority, and going on to claim that the Vatican categorically condemned and opposed fascism and Nazism, making reference to pronouncements that at best are equivocal. It also claims that "Jewish communities and Jewish leaders expressed their thanks for all that had been done for them...," a cynical manipulation of a half-truth if there ever was one. And to top it all off the document tries to argue that fascism and genocide were incompatible with Catholic teachings: "...the work of a thoroughly neo-pagan regime. Its anti-Semitism had its roots outside of Christianity...."[2] Certainly not the view of the tens of thousands of Catholic clergy all around the world who warmly embraced fascism and joined its ranks from Berlin to Detroit (have they forgotten our own "dear" Father Coughlin?).

What all of this amounts to is a staggering lie of gigantic proportions, a total whitewash of the crimes committed by the Catholic Church and the Papacy before, during and after the Holocaust. It is worthwhile that we now review some of the media response to this deliberate falsification of history before we examine some of the facts this most recent Vatican document conveniently "forgot" to mention.

The Vatican document is the result of a sophisticated public relations campaign aimed at improving its image with both Jews and the American public by shirking responsibility for its crimes before, during and after the Holocaust while pinning all of the blame on others. This necessarily involves a deliberate falsification and suppression of the historical record. The New York Times was correct when it predicted that the document would try to put as much distance between itself and the Holocaust as possible. Even anti-Semitism is portrayed as the result of "wrong-headed Christian thinkers," not the papacy or its clergy.[3] As one CNN reporter put it, "the Pope has steered clear of blaming the church itself."[4]

Thus, the Vatican's "memory" is highly selective. The "errors" the Vatican is willing to recall are limited only to those of omission, not commission. In other words, the errors of the Church during the Holocaust are defined only as the silence or indifference of the Church in the face of crimes of genocide, a failure to speak out. The Vatican — and apparently many journalists — would like us to believe that this is the limit of wrongdoing. Defined out of the discussion are complicity in or support for these crimes — not to mention active participation in deportations, expropriations, forced conversions, and mass murder of a specific people, that is to say, genocide itself. As long as the role of the Vatican in the Holocaust is defined in this way, it safely avoids serious examination of the much worse crimes it did commit.

We shall return to these matters presently. First, some credit should be paid to those who have openly criticized the Vatican for its mendacity. To its credit CNN presented an interview with Israel's Chef Rabbi, Meir Lau, who was forthright in his condemnation of this atrociously retrograde document and who focused attention on the actual historical role of Pope Pius XII, whom he called "an accomplice to Nazi murderers."[5] There are many good reasons for this designation: Pius XII's (then Eugenio Pacelli) efforts as Papal Nuncio in Germany were central to bringing Germany's Catholic Center Party close to Nazism in the 1920's, and then to cementing the agreement between the Vatican and Hitler known as the Concordat of 1933. Pacelli's support for Hitlerism in its early stages is historical record, and preventing the disclosure of the full scope of this support is one of the reasons the Vatican will not open its archives from this period.

Indeed, Pius XII brings us to the real heart of the matter, and Pope John Paul II's response to the question of the wartime

Pope's culpability reveals the real design behind the Vatican's report. John Paul II has consistently defended Pius XII, often in a truculent manner. The current Pope has made it clear that he will do his part to uphold the doctrine of Papal infallibility. One of his speeches during a trip to Germany in 1995 even contained a passage attacking all criticisms of Pius XII as "cheap polemics."[6] This kind of attack is part of a pre-emptive strategy aimed at creating an unreceptive climate for scholarship or discussion dealing with the role of the Vatican. Once again the Church finds itself fighting to prove that the world is flat.

But more importantly it exposes the motives behind this recent report, which shares certain similarities with some interpretations of the Holocaust. By placing blame on wrong-headed individuals in the Church and denying any wrong doing by the Pope or Vatican, the Church is shifting responsibility from its leaders and from the institution itself to the rank and file followers, in effect side stepping all blame whatsoever. Thus, the Church really is completely innocent — it's the sheep, not the shepherd who are responsible! The similarities with the manner in which the ruling elites in Germany prefer to interpret the Holocaust are quite striking. In Germany, authors like Daniel Goldhagen are all the rage because books like Hitler's Willing Executioners blur responsibility for the rise of Nazism by taking the focus off of the capitalist and aristocratic elites and institutions who backed Hitler (many of which were left unscathed by the so-called de-Nazification of post-war Germany) and putting it on the popular culture and working masses instead. Not having their own Goldhagen to rely on, the Catholic Church has to hustle this cheap shell game itself.

The Vatican's Role:
A Suppressed Chapter of the Holocaust

If we consider for a moment the manner in which the phenomenon of genocide has been treated in the twentieth century by both historians and governments, in general we can say that it often has been cynically exploited for political purposes. When it suited the Western powers, they criticized the genocide of Armenians by Turkey in World War I. But after Turkey became a bulwark against the Soviet Union and a military ally, this chapter of twentieth century history was suppressed — and largely remains so to this day. Most historians in this country are still unwilling to consider the mass extermination of Native American peoples or the deaths of millions of Africans during slavery as acts of genocide, legally sanctioned by this country. At the U.S. Holocaust Museum the history of the Holocaust has been tailored to fit the political fashions of the Clinton administration and the New World Order: hence, one finds the words "Serbs" and "Russians" are altogether absent from the official record of the Holocaust, and instead are replaced in the most obscene Orwellian manner by the words "Yugoslavs" and "Soviets." A most vicious and ironic cover up, considering that the U.S. today does not even recognize the existence of these states or peoples. In all of these cases we see instances of the suppression of the history of genocide against certain peoples for clearly political purposes (not least of which is the desire to target these same peoples for future destruction). The role of the U.S. and British governments in protecting and employing Nazi and fascist mass murderers will also probably not be fully disclosed or incorporated into history books in our lifetimes.

But nowhere has the truth been hijacked and suppressed more than in regard to that one chapter of the Holocaust that historians still hesitate to confront: the Vatican's role in fascist Croatia. The story of the Holocaust in wartime Croatia is absent from many scholarly discussions of the Holocaust and from most Holocaust museums in this country. It is an odd omission considering the fact that if one defines the Holocaust from the first mass murders of civilians, then the Holocaust itself began in Croatia with the first murders of Serbs, Jews and Gypsies by the Croatian fascist regime in April 1941 — some nine months before the Wannsee Conference, more than two months before the Nazi invasion of the Soviet Union. It is like a book whose first chapter is torn out.

What then are the political reasons for the systematic and deliberate suppression of the history of the Holocaust in Croatia? There are several, and they are all connected to vital geo-political considerations of the leading Western powers. One is the leading role that Croatian fascist war criminals played in establishing the "ratline" escape routes of European fascism after the war and their enormous contributions to U.S. and British intelligence agencies during the Cold War. Another was the American and British governments' refusal to return for trial and punishment to post-war Yugoslavia Croatian war criminals in particular, thus violating the Moscow Declaration of 1943 in which they had sworn to do so. Still another was the long range goal of U.S. and Western imperialism to partition and destroy Communist Yugoslavia, a plan which depended on the support of the thousands of escaped Croatian fascists subsidized by the U.S. for decades in anticipation of this long sought goal.[7] The need to suppress such information from the public and from political discourse is obvious: a self-proclaimed moral superiority based on genocide is a fraud the whole world can see.

But all of these justifications pale in comparison to the importance placed on suppressing the truth about the Vatican's and the Catholic Church's role in the Holocaust in fascist Croatia. For in Croatia, the question of what role the Catholic Church played in the Holocaust is not limited to the relatively minor issues of whether they did or spoke out enough against it — here the question concerns the role of the Church and the Vatican in running concentration camps and in carrying out a religiously inspired genocide. Nowhere is the role of the Vatican more worthy of investigation, and nowhere has that role received less attention.

Vatican Sponsorship of Fascism

To understand the Vatican's role and motives in the Holocaust in Yugoslavia we need to understand the phenomenon of genocide as a product of modern imperialism. Genocide is a direct consequence of imperialist wars of conquest aimed at territorial expansion for economic, political and military domination. After World War I the Vatican was determined, like its fascist partners of Italy and Germany, to destroy the Yugoslav state and reconstitute in that region the power and influence the Papacy had lost with the collapse of the Austro-Hungarian empire.

The Yugoslav state emerged out of the century long struggle of the peoples of the Balkans to overcome colonial oppression. The idea of a federation of Balkan peoples had its roots in the struggles against first Turkish and then Austrian-German and other Western domination. It was born of the realism of Balkan political leaders in the nineteenth century that small nations by themselves cannot defend themselves against the great imperialist powers, but that together they might be able to do so. It was this ideal that Yugoslavia in a truncated form represented, and that German and Italian fascism were determined to annihilate.[8]

The Vatican was also determined to destroy Yugoslavia, though for its own reasons. The dismemberment of the Catholic Austro-Hungarian Empire was a catastrophe for the Catholic Church. The Vatican was no longer the supreme religious authority in Central and Eastern Europe and had lost the state foundations on which citizens owed a dual allegiance to Church and state. Its disappearance marked a sharp decline in the Church's world power and influence. Worse still was the replacement of the Austro-Hungarian Empire with states dominated by other religions in which Catholics sank to a minority status. The worst of the bunch was Yugoslavia which was ruled by a King of the Serbian Eastern Orthodox faith, a church that the Vatican viewed as a "schismatic sect." From the Vatican's point of view, this "schismatic sect" was a cancer, to be eliminated.

The Vatican had done all it could to support the Austrian and German war effort in 1914 against Serbia and considered Serbia as the "evil" behind the war. In his report of July 29, 1914 to the Austrian Foreign Minister Berchtold, the Austrian charge d'affairs to the Vatican, Count Palffy reported the views of the Vatican Secretary of State, Cardinal Marry del Val, who, speaking on behalf of then Pope Pius X

> "...expressed the hope that the monarchy would go through to the end... [and] the opinion that it is a pity that Serbia wasn't made smaller much earlier.... The Pope and the Curia see Serbia as a destructive disease which is slowly eating away at the Monarchy to its very essence and which will eventually destroy it.... Austria is and remains a Catholic state par excellence, the strongest bulwark of Christ's Church in this century. The demolition of this bulwark would mean for the Church the loss of its firmest support. It would lose its strongest defender. Therefore, for this reason, just as it is necessary for Austria, for the sake of its self-preservation to get its organism rid, if necessary by force, of the evil which is eating away at it, so it is indirectly necessary for the Church to do everything that could serve this purpose."[9]

In August 1914 the Vatican encouraged its clergy to rally the Catholic populations of Croatia and Slovenia to fight Serbia, portraying the conflict as a holy war against the very "enemy of Jesus," i.e.: the Serbs. The Bishop of Ljubljana, Anton Jeglich, called on the Slovenian soldiers

> "...to take arms and defend Catholic Austria and our Catholic imperial family from the sworn enemy of Jesus himself....let us fight the enemies of God, against the enemies of Catholic Austria, against the enemies of the Catholic Habsburg house."[10]

Combined with the Catholic fanaticism encouraged by the Vatican was the extreme racial violence expressed toward the Serbs throughout Austria-Hungary and summed up in the popular jingle of August 1914: "Alle Serben mussen sterben!"[11] This blending of Catholic fanaticism and racial violence toward the Serbs born in the last days of the Habsburg Empire and sponsored by the Vatican prefigured the later emergence of Croatian fascism. Indeed, in World War I, one out of every four male Serbs would be killed — a dress rehearsal, one might say, for the greater genocide to come.

Having lost its "strongest bulwark" with the end of the first World War, the Vatican turned to Mussolini and fascist Italy to defend it and its long range goals. Likewise, the Vatican threw its support behind Mussolini's imperialist ambitions for fascist Italy. The aims of the two Italian dictatorships were quite similar. Both were implacable enemies of the Yugoslav state seeking its destruction: the Pope wished to carve out a Catholic majority state from its northern half; Mussolini sought to annex parts of Slovenia, the Dalmatian coast, and Montenegro, along with Albania and Kosovo, so that he might "turn the Adriatic into an Italian lake."

The origins of fascism in the Balkans can be traced directly back to Mussolini and the imperialist ambitions of fascist Italy, as well as to the generous support provided to them by the Catholic Church in Croatia. It was Mussolini's fascist state that originally financed and sponsored nationalist extremist political movements in the Balkans, transforming them ideologically and organizationally into full blown genocidal, fascist parties. According to the diary of Mussolini's foreign minister Ciano, the Italian government financed Croatian fascism at the level of around 25 million lire a year in the 1920's and 1930's.[12] By 1934 Italy's investments in Croatian fascism paid handsome dividends when on October 9th King Alexander of Yugoslavia was assassinated by Croatian fascists in Marseilles, France along with the French Foreign Minister Barthou, both of them obstacles to the fascist domination of Europe.

The Vatican was kept apprised of fascist strategic planning in both Rome and Berlin through the 1930's right up to the invasion of Yugoslavia. In May 1940 the Archbishop of Zagreb, Aloysius Stepinac, was called to the Vatican for briefings on the future invasion and partition of Yugoslavia.[13] In the years immediately preceding the German and Italian invasion of Yugoslavia of April 1941, the head of the Catholic Church in Yugoslavia, Stepinac, met regularly with representatives from both the Italian foreign ministry and the illegal Ustasha terrorist organization, as Stepinac himself noted in his diary.[14] Among these visitors was the future Ustasha Minister of Education Mile Budak, a chief architect of the genocide in Croatia, who is best known for his infamous speech on the final solution for the Serbs: "We will kill a third, expel a third, and convert a third."[15]

The three nationalist movements that Italian fascism took under its wing were the Croatian, Albanian and Macedonian nationalist movements. The only one of these three that would graduate under Italian (later also German) fascist tutelage and financing, from a loose terrorist organization into a fully mature fascist movement was the Croatian Ustasha. Its success in becoming the largest and most mature of these fascist movements was in large part due to the considerable institutional support the Catholic Church in Croatia could provide — a factor altogether absent in the Albanian and Macedonian cases.

The leadership of the Church was well aware of the leading role it was expected to play in the soon to be independent, fascist Croatian state. In the years prior to 1941 the Croatian fascist movement recruited members of legal Croatian nationalist parties and from within the Yugoslav military with the help and encouragement of the Croatian Catholic Church. Not only did the Croatian Catholic clergy meet secretly in the years prior to 1941 with Italian fascist agents to help prepare for the final destruction of Yugoslavia, but they provided the Ustasha with all of the vast resources at its disposal, including its buildings and monasteries for meetings and safe-houses. The operational headquarters in which the plans for the Ustasha take-over were made was in the Franciscan monastery at Chuntich. Monasteries, parish houses, cathedrals, Franciscan high schools, seminaries, etc., throughout Croatia doubled as meeting places, recruiting centers, arms depots and staging areas for Croatian fascism and terror in the years prior to the war. We know this to be true because the Croatian fascists themselves boasted of it when they came to power in 1941 in their official publications and on the memorial plaques they affixed to these places.[16]

If the Vatican criticized Nazi Germany in the last half of the 1930's, it had less to do with fascism than with Hitler's imperialist conflicts with Mussolini over the fate of Central Europe. The Vatican's interests were more in line with those of Mussolini's: a "Pan-Danubian" confederation of Catholic states centered around Austria and Hungary as the core of a restored Catholic empire.[17] The Ustashi too favored a reconstitution of the old Habsburg empire following the destruction of Yugoslavia. But by the time Hitler annexed Austria in 1938, Mussolini had to face facts and reach a tacit agreement with Hitler over who would call the shots. Moreover, the Munich agreement in the fall of 1938 signaling the end of Czechoslovakia, and Hitler's creation of the clerical-fascist puppet state of Slovakia several months later, proved to Croatian fascists (if they had any doubts by then) that Hitler was their real fuhrer, not Mussolini. Hitler had wanted to put off the destruction of Yugoslavia until after Britain and the Soviet Union were defeated. But Mussolini's mucked up invasion of Greece forced the issue, much to the delight of the Croatian fascists — and the Catholic Church in Croatia.

It is assumed that Pius XII would have preferred Mussolini's leadership in Central Europe to Hitler's. But Hitler's creation of two semi-independent clerical fascist states out of the remnants of Czechoslovakia and Yugoslavia certainly showed a great deal of consideration for the Vatican's interests as an ally. Besides, the Vatican recognized that of the three major alternatives for Central Europe, Nazi Germany may have been a less desirable arbiter than Fascist Italy, but still a whole lot better than Soviet Russia. And in the end, faced with larger problems, Hitler granted the Italian and Croatian fascists and the Vatican most of what they wanted anyway.[18]

Why did Hitler create two independent clerical-fascist states which considered themselves vassals of the papacy? The answer to this question explains why historians hardly ever mention Slovakia and Croatia in their discussions of World War II or the Holocaust: because the Vatican was a silent partner in the Axis alliance, as well as in the Holocaust.

The Vatican's Holocaust

The Croatian Catholic Church and the Vatican were directly involved in helping the fascist regime in Croatia carry out a triple genocide against Serbs, Jews and Romas from 1941 to 1945 in every possible way. By the time they were done, they had killed one million people. The Catholic Church assisted the Croatian fascists in every aspect of their murderous rule, from open political and financial support, to serving in their military units in every phase of the war, to serving in their government, to participating in arrests, expropriations, deportations, forced conversions and mass murders of racially persecuted peoples. Catholic Priests even served as concentration camp commanders in some of the worst death camps of World War II. And it was all done with the full knowledge and support of Pope Pius XII and the Vatican.[19]

On April 10, 1941 the Independent State of Croatia was declared by Ustashi arriving in Zagreb with Nazi troops during the Nazi's invasion and dismemberment of Yugoslavia which began on April 6 and continued until the surrender of the Yugoslav government on April 17. While 30,000 were killed by the Luftwaffe in the bombing of Belgrade, Zagreb and Croatia were left untouched and the Nazis were greeted like heroes in the streets of Zagreb. Once again much of the responsibility for preparing public support for Nazism in Croatia lies with the Catholic Church, which had published articles in its publications as early as 1939 calling for an independent Croatia. In 1940 an article appeared in the official Church publication "Catholic List" praising *Mein Kampf* and adding that there was no conflict between being a good Catholic and a good Nazi.[20] Indeed, similar articles were published by innumerable Catholic clergy all over Europe in the 1930's and 1940's. Urged on by the Catholic clergy, thousands of Croatian officers and soldiers in the

Yugoslav army deserted to the Nazi-Ustasha side as did a large part of the membership of the popular Croatian Peasant Party.

While the Ustashi rode to power on the backs of the Nazi Wehrmacht, units of Ustasha soldiers fought alongside them. Among the very first armed divisions of the Ustasha army were numerous Catholic priests. The military exploits of one priest, Ilija Tomas of Klepac, were hailed in the Croatian fascist publication "Hrvatski Narod" on July 25, 1941.[21] Another Catholic publication "Nedelja" praised the military exploits of dozens of priests, especially those in monastic orders such as the Franciscan Radovan Glavas, and the priest Ivan Miletic who led Croatian fascists in joint battle with Wehrmacht forces.[22] Priests who led Catholic organizations in Croatia and Bosnia such as the "Crusaders Brotherhood" and "Catholic Action," which had tens of thousands of members, established military units within them and were used as recruiting centers for the Ustasha military.[23] These are not unique examples. The entire Catholic press in this period in Croatia was thoroughly pro-fascist, racist and supportive of the elimination of the "minorities."

The leader of the Catholic Church in Croatia, Archbishop Stepinac, fervently supported the Ustasha movement and welcomed the invading Nazi army as it entered Zagreb. On April 11th he met with Ustasha leaders and on April 12th he blessed the newly arrived Ustasha leadership in a public ceremony at his cathedral. In his Easter address of that month he compared the creation of the new fascist state to the resurrection of Christ. In his pastoral letter of April 28th he ordered the clergy and called upon all Catholic people of Croatia and Bosnia to follow their "Poglavnik" (Fuhrer) Ante Pavelic, for he had seen in Pavelic's rule "God's hand in action."[24] The pastoral letter was read over the radio and in every Catholic parish in fascist Croatia.

Stepinac met with the Croatian Fuhrer when he arrived from Italy on April 16th. That evening Stepinac held a dinner party in his residence in honor of Pavelic and the Ustasha leadership. In his diary, Stepinac described the day and admitted that Pavelic told him of his plans to "exterminate" the non-Catholic religions in Croatia. Stepinac's diary indicates that he too was prepared for an all out religious war, for he added that "If that man (Pavelic) rules Croatia for ten years.... Croatia will be a paradise on earth."[25]

There is no question that Stepinac knew of the Ustasha's plans for committing genocide even before they came to power. After Stepinac's death in 1960, Ilija Jukic, a leading member of the Croatian Peasant Party, wrote of how he had told Stepinac in March 1941 that the Pavelic-Budak group "were thinking of applying Hitler's methods to the Serbs in Croatia if they ever came to power." Stepinac disingenuously told Jukic that he would look into it.[26] But Stepinac already was resolved on an attitude of passive acceptance of genocide, as is revealed from entries in his diary, such as one from 1940 when he wrote: "... the Serbs have not learned anything... and in the end they will lose everything.... I wish them no evil because they are God's children. But if nothing can teach them a lesson, distress will."[27]

Of course, Stepinac was easily outdone in fascist criminality by other high ranking clergy, most infamously by the second highest ranking cleric in fascist Croatia, the Archbishop of Sarajevo, Ivan Sharich — called "the Hangman of Serbs" by his fellow Ustashi. Sharich had been a secret member of the Ustasha since 1934, and had been in close contact with them at least since 1931. Whereas Stepinac was willing to spare the lives of some Jews and Serbs who had converted to Catholicism, Sharich ridiculed those who did not have the stomach for total genocide, declaring it "stupid and unworthy of Christ's disciples to think that the struggle against evil could be waged in a noble way and with gloves on." Among Vatican documents that have emerged is one dealing with Sharich's personal expropriations of property belonging to Jews in Bosnia[28]

Since the Ustasha wished Croatia to be a vassal of the papacy, Catholic clergy held high positions at every level of the fascist government. In the majority of towns and villages throughout the newly created fascist state, Catholic clergy became the official Ustasha authority. A certain number of seats in the fascist "Sabor" were reserved for Bishops including Stepinac and Sharich. Pavelic included several priest-advisors and a personal confessor in his cabinet. In its inaugural radio address to the nation on April 11, 1941, the new fascist government instructed the population to apply to their local priest for further instructions, indicating again that the fascist take-over was planned in advance with the complete knowledge of the Church hierarchy.[29] When Pavelic fled the country in 1945 he turned over the reigns of state leadership to Stepinac. Thus, it truly was a clerical-fascist state in praxis as well as theory.

In its ideology, Croatian fascism combined extreme Roman Catholic fanaticism, Nazi eugenics and Croatian chauvinism, creating perhaps the most psychotic political movement of all time. Pavelic was obsessed with Croatia's racial purity on both biological and religious grounds. The Ustashi claimed that the Croats were not Slavs but rather of the "Aryan race," descendants of the Germanic Goths. However, unlike the Nazis, the Ustashi's leading racist theorists were Catholic clergy, like Dr. Ivo Guberina, a priest and leading Ustasha emigre, whose writings reconciling religious purification with racial hygiene lent a spurious scientific veneer to Ustasha propaganda.[30] Croatia had to be purified of its "foreign elements," namely Serbs, Jews and Romas. Purification for the Ustashi always meant extermination; they never hid their desire to commit genocide. In the 1930's they were already known for songs with verses like: "We shall hang Serbs on the willows" ("Serbe o verbe"), and "We shall tear their children out of their womb."[31]

The Italian and German fascists were astonished by the speed with which the Ustashi initiated their systematic policy of genocide. Already on April 18, 1941 the very first racial law, on "the Aryanization of Jewish property" was issued. Other racial laws of the Independent State of Croatia promulgated in April 1941 included laws ordering Serbs to wear blue bands on their sleeves with the letter "P" (for Orthodox), and Jews a band with the Star of David and the letter "Z" (for Jew), along with laws forbidding Serbs and Jews to walk on sidewalks and ordering the posting of signs in public places stating "No Serbs, Jews, Gypsies or Dogs Allowed!" In May 1941 laws carefully defining Serbs, Jews and Romas (as well as anti-fascist Croats) as "undesirable peoples" directed what was to be done with them: their rounding up, the dispossession of their property, and their deportation to death camps. Laws on the rounding up, dispossessing and deportation of the families of undesirables as well, including children, were issued later that same month. Racial laws regulating all aspects of society continued to be issued in the weeks and months to follow. Bound volumes of these published laws are available in the European Law Division of the Library of Congress.

The so-called Ustasha Minister of Education, Dr. Mile Budak, summarized the racial policy of Croatia in a speech on July 22, 1941 in Gospic when he said:

> "The movement of the Ustashi is based on religion. For the minorities — Serbs, Jews and Gypsies, we have three million bullets. We shall kill one part of the Serbs. We shall deport another, and the rest of them will be forced to embrace the Roman Catholic religion. Thus, our new Croatia will get rid of all Serbs in our midst in order to become one hundred percent Catholic within ten years."[32]

Meanwhile the foreign minister of fascist Croatia, Mladen Lorkovic, sent instructions to his diplomats and to the world: "... the Croatian people annihilate all foreign elements, which weaken its powers; those foreign elements are the Serbs and the Jews."[33]

How committed was the Catholic Church in Croatia to this ideology and its racial laws? As has been mentioned already, priests were among the intellectual godfathers of Croatian fascism and racism. Whereas anti-Serbian racism had roots deeply connected to the Austro-Hungarian Empire, anti-Semitism in Yugoslavia was almost entirely the product of Catholic propaganda after World War I. Official church publications in Croatia like Catholic List frequently published condemnations of Jews during the 1930's as being the source of communism, free-masonry, abortions and immorality.[34] It should not be surprising therefore that the man appointed to be President of Ustasha Central Propaganda Office (equivalent to the position held by Goebbels in Germany) was none other a priest, Father Grga Peinovic. To claim that the Catholic Church simply adapted to the fascist regime would be a whitewash of their long-standing promotion of racism. They were the very leaders responsible for articulating this ideology to the people and for the regime itself.

But there were considerable obstacles blocking the creation a pure Croat-Catholic state. The most serious of these was the fact that Croats did not even constitute a majority of the population in their own state, just 3.3 million out of around 6.7 million people. There were 2.2 million Serbs, 60,000 Jews, 700,000 Muslims, 70,000 Protestants, not to mention hundreds of thousands of Romas and other minorities. The Ustasha solution was clear: kill as many Serbs, Jews and Romas as quickly as possible — and then sort the rest out later.

The Ustasha regime wasted no time at all commencing upon their systematic policy of racial extermination of all Serbs, Jews and Romas shortly after coming to power. If we are to adjudge that the Holocaust began with the first mass murders of entire peoples, then it is clear that the Holocaust began in Croatia in April 1941. The earliest punitive actions against Serbs are believed to have taken place on the evening of April 13, 1941 in Ogulin where Pavelic stopped to make a speech on his way to Zagreb from Italy.[34] Mass killings began in earnest on April 28, 1941 as Ustasha military units were dispatched to towns and villages all across the fascist state. Thousands of Serbian men, women and children were rounded up and killed that day, their property confiscated, in cities like Vukovar and villages like Gudovac, Tuke, Brezovac, Kokochevac, Bolch. Throughout May and June hundreds of towns and villages throughout the Croatian state underwent these same terrorist operations in which Serbs, Jews and Romas were either murdered on the spot or led away to concentration camps. By the beginning of July nearly 200,000 people, the vast majority of them Serbs, already were killed.[35] As Holocaust historian Jonathan Steinberg has pointed out, the Ustashi pioneered the methods of genocidal terror and extermination only later perfected by the Nazi SS Einsatzgruppen another fact "conveniently" overlooked in conventional Holocaust studies.[36]

The Ustasha operations were carried out with incredible acts of sadism and torture. In some cases entire villages were axed to death, in others men and women were hanged, crucified, burned to death or buried alive, body parts mutilated, decapitated, infants impaled or hammered. In the Orthodox church at Glina hundreds of Serbs were lured inside only to be slaughtered. Nazi Wehrmacht units attached to the Ustasha military were so impressed by the Ustashi's methods for carrying out genocide that they established a commission to study the killings at Bjelovar, exhume the bodies, take photographs and write a report, later published under the title "Ustachenwerk bei Bjelovar."[37] However, the top Nazi and Italian military authorities were concerned that they were dealing with out of control psychopaths who would destabilize their own regime, and thus Axis control of the Balkans. They were right. The Nazi

"Plenipotentiary" in Zagreb, General Edmund Glaise von Horstenau reported back anxiously to Berlin in early June 1941 that "according to reliable reports from countless German military and civil observers during the last few weeks, in country and town, the Ustashi have gone raging mad."[38]

As the noted historian of fascism Ernest Nolte has put it, "Croatia became during the war a giant slaughterhouse." The operations continued with only brief pauses throughout 1941 and 1942, then at a slightly slower pace thereafter through 1945. No portion of territory given to Ustasha rule was untouched by this terror. In those areas where the Orthodox Serbs comprised a majority of the population, the Ustashi committed the worst atrocities. Vast areas were emptied of population and left a wasteland. Only a minority of those affected were killed immediately, the rest were rounded up for deportation to death camps.

Croatia became at this time, as Croatian historian Antun Miletic has said, "a land of concentration camps." In order to execute the state's racial laws, the Directorate for Public Security under Eugen Kvaternik was ordered by Interior Minister Andrija Artukovic to create a series of concentration camps throughout Croatia. From April to August 1941 Serbs, Jews, Romas and antifascists who were not killed outright were relocated to collection camps, such as Danica, Kerestinec, Pag, Caprag, Jadovno, Krushchica, Loborgrad, Gornja Rijeka, Djakovo, Tenj, Sisak, Jastrebarsko and the Lepoglava Prison. Some of these, like Jadovno and Djakovo were also major death camps. In other cases surviving inmates were transported for extermination to the main concentration camp system in Croatia which opened in August 1941, Jasenovac.

It was at Jasenovac that between 600,000 and 700,000 Serbs, at least 30,000 Romas and 25,000 Jews were systematically murdered between August 1941 and April 1945. Of all of the death camps during the Holocaust Jasenovac was the third largest overall in terms of victims. In terms of size it was probably the largest, spread out over 240 square kilometers (150 sq. miles) and encompassing actually a series of five major and three smaller "special" camps.[39] Jasenovac was intended to serve as "the radical solution" to Croatia's racial problem a factory of death. Indeed, it was built around a former brick factory. Its first

Commander was the notorious Maks Luburic, a man specifically sent to the Third Reich for training at various Nazi concentration camps prior to the opening of Jasenovac. Jasenovac holds a number of ghastly distinctions for its cruelty. It possessed some of the largest camps for women and children during the war — the names of some 20,000 children murdered there have been collected thus far. It was noted also for its extreme brutality every known method of murder and torture was employed there, as well as a few unknown anywhere else. There are very few examples in human history that can compare with the scale of murder, terror and barbarism conducted at Jasenovac. And yet it is not even mentioned at the U.S. Holocaust Museum in Washington, D.C. Why?

The answer lies with the Catholic Church. What was the Church's reaction to and role in all of this? How deeply involved in genocide in fascist Croatia was the Catholic Church and the Vatican? In response to the persecution of the Jews and Serbs the Croatian clergy rallied around the regime and provided endless articles and pamphlets justifying their extermination. Stepinac had the racial laws published in his own publications. Writing in response to the publication of the racial laws of April and May 1941 the Catholic weekly "Hrvatska Strazha" in its editorial of May 11, 1941 welcomed the legislation as necessary for "the survival and development of the Croatian nation."

> "Defense from Judaism, from that destructive worm, was started by the Fuhrer and Duce.... Our Poglavnik has also announced a regulation on the protection and honor and blood, and we would add, on the protection of the survival and development of the Croatian nation, and with it the Poglavnik wants to prevent the dangerous worm from eating away at the tree of our Croatian national life."[40]

Writing in response to new racial laws against the Jews the Archbishop of Sarajevo Ivan Sharich declared: "There exists limits to love. The movement for ridding the world of Jews is a movement for restoring human dignity. All mighty God stands behind this movement." The Catholic Bishops of Banja Luka and Djakovo made similar public statements. The Croatian Academic Catholic Society also published a brochure in 1941 entitled "Why Do They Persecute Jews In Germany?," explaining that Hitler was to be praised for eliminating the Jews because he was defending the German people. Hitler was merely righting the wrongs of the past.[41] By the time the Ustashi and Catholic Church were done with their work they had killed approximately 30,000 of the 40,000 Jews living in the territories of the Independent State of Croatia.[42]

Toward Serbs the rhetoric in favor racial extermination was even more severe. The Franciscan Priest Shimich stated bluntly: "All Serbs must be murdered within the shortest time. That is our program."[43] And the actions of the Catholic clergy were not limited to words. Catholic priests and members of orders were recruited into as many Ustasha military commands as possible. As with the clerical fascist state, the clerical fascist army was led by priests. Taking up arms as if in a medieval crusade, the Catholic clergy were transformed, as Carlo Falconi has said, "into thorough going butcher-leaders."[44] At the very first punitive action against Serbs at Ogulin it was the parish priest, Ivan Mikan, who addressed the Ustashi and said "Now there will be some cleaning.... Scoot you dogs (Serbs) over the Drina."[45] It was speeches such as these that gave the signal to launch massacres all across the Independent State of Croatia. Sometimes priests gave less than spiritual reasons for liquidating Serbs, such as Father Mate Mogus in Udbina who told his congregation "Look, people, at these brave Ustashi who have 16,000 bullets and who will kill 16,000 Serbs, after which we will divide among us in a brotherly manner the fields.." Meanwhile, Franciscan priests in dozens of villages attacked Serbian and Roma settlements, tortured, killed and expropriated their victims. Father Mogus explained in another sermon that "We Catholics until now have worked for Catholicism with the cross and with the book of the mass. The day has come however to work with the revolver and the machine gun.[46] The Jesuit priest Dragutin Kamber, who was also the Ustasha Commander for the district of Doboj, personally led numerous raids and ordered the execution of 300 Serbs in Doboj. Father Peric of the Gorica monastery participated in the massacres of 5,600 Serbs in Livno. Father German Castimir, the Abbot of the Guntic monastery, personally directed the massacres at Glina.[47]

The genocide of the Serbs was to be carried out in three ways: extermination, deportation and forced conversion. There were simply too many Serbs to kill them all. We have left this third part of the genocide plan, forced conversion, for last because this phase of the genocide was almost exclusively carried out by the Catholic Church itself. At his trial for war crimes in 1986 Andrija Artukovic emphasized that the management of forced conversions was entirely in the hands of Archbishop Stepinac and the church leadership.[48] In June 1941 the Ustashi created an "Office of Religious Affairs" to handle the conversion of Serbs to Catholicism. On July 18, 1941 the government decreed that the Serbian Orthodox religion had ceased to exist. By early September 1941 the government decreed the expropriation of all Orthodox Church property. Across Croatia Priests were instructed to inform the Serbian population that they had only one way out: become Catholic or die. This was the ultimatum the Catholic clergy offered to a lucky third of the Serbs in fascist Croatia.

The Ustashi kept particularly good records of this phase of genocide. One of the reasons for this is that the Ustashi were so awfully proud of their accomplishments in this regard, that they filmed dozens of such forced conversions for Croatian newsreels. Another is that each Catholic diocese published weekly and sometimes daily reports of new conversions. Children were especially targeted for conversion, especially orphans. No doubt, today there are tens of thousands of people living in Croatia, if not more, who do not know that they had Serbian or Jewish parents or grand-parents, nor what happened to them. In a letter to the Vatican dated May 8, 1944 Stepinac informed the Holy Father that to date 244,000 Orthodox Serbs had been "converted to the Church of God."[49]

As the Serbs were marked for genocide, it was desired that no trace of their cultural heritage should remain. 299 Orthodox churches were destroyed. Some 300 Orthodox priests and five bishops were murdered. As this was a clerical-fascist crusade, the Orthodox clergy were marked for especially cruel torture, usually ending with the gouging out of their eyes or other forms of bodily mutilation. In one case the eighty-one year old Bishop of Banja Luka was shod like a horse and forced to walk until he collapsed, at which point his heart was cut out and he was set on fire. In Zagreb the Orthodox Bishop was tortured until he went insane. Some 400 Orthodox priests were killed in concentration camps.[50]

The Croatian Catholic clergy saw the rise of fascism as the beginning of an international Catholic-fascist crusade that would convert the world for Catholicism and the Papacy, as the following statement in *Katholicki Tjednik* of August 31, 1941 makes clear. This was the time to destroy the enemies of Catholicism: Communism, Judaism, Eastern Orthodoxy.

> "Until now, God spoke through papal encyclicals....And? They closed their ears... Now God has decided to use other methods. He will prepare missions. European missions. World missions. They will be upheld, not by priests, but by army commanders, led by Hitler. The sermons will be heard, with the help of cannons, machine guns, tanks, and bombers. The language of these sermons will be international."[51]

The clergy had to be ready to take on a military role if that was God's will. Indeed, it had to be prepared for death and destruction. Perhaps this explains the scale of the Catholic clergy's participation in running concentration camps. The exact number of Catholic priests who worked as commanders or guards at these camps in Croatia is unknown. However, there is no question that there were hundreds, if not thousands. In a surprising number of cases Catholic priests were named commanders or staff officers of concentration camps. These appointments were reported in the Catholic press during the war. Thus, we read in *Novi List* in 1941 that Father Stepan Lukic was named camp adjutant of the Zepce concentration camp, Priest Ante Djuric Commander of all camps in the Drvar district, and Father Dragan Petranovic commander of the camp in Ogulin. The active participation of clergy in running concentration camps in Croatia was known by the German, Italian, British and American intelligence services, as well as the Vatican. The U.S. intelligence report of February 23, 1943 entitled "Massacres of Serbs in Croatia" speaks bluntly of "the bloody hands of the Catholic clergy in the camps."[52]

The scene of some of the most barbaric killings of all time was the concentration camp complex known as Jasenovac. German, Italian, British and American intelligence reports (as well as Croatian accounts) suggest that between 600,000 and 700,000 were killed there. Aside from intelligence reports, we have the testimony of survivors and of a few of the perpetrators as to the crimes committed there by the Catholic clergy. Testimony was collected by a Yugoslav War Crimes Commission and obtained during the trials of various Ustashi. A key witness was the parish priest of Jasenovac, Juraj Parshich, who along with survivors testified to the barbaric murders committed at Jasenovac by numerous priests, among whom the most infamous were Zvonko Brekalo, Pero Brzica, Anzelmo Chulina, Father Brkljanic, and the Jesuits Zvonko Lipovac and Father Cvitan. However, there was one priest who has carved out a special place for himself in the annals of sadism, barbarism and genocide. His name before the war was Vjekoslav Filipovich, a Franciscan priest who some say was excommunicated. During the war he went from wearing priestly robes to an Ustasha officer's uniform, and bore the name Miroslav Majstorovich. He directed numerous actions against Serbian villages in which he played a conspicuous part in the killings. Before one such attack in the town of Drakulic he strangled a Serbian baby in his hands. Then he went to Jasenovac where he served as Commander for four months, from September 1942 to the beginning of January 1943. At the War Crimes investigation prior to his trial, Filipovich testified that during the four months of his command "according to my own calculations between twenty and thirty thousand were liquidated in the Jasenovac."[53]

It is beyond the scope of this author's comprehension to explain the psycho-pathology of clerical-fascism. However, I do know that they killed a million with clear consciences for their belief in God, the Catholic Church and the Aryan race. This is nowhere more eloquently expressed than in the comment made by Father Srecko Peric of the Gorica Monastery who reassured his fellow Ustashi prior to a massacre by saying: "Kill all Serbs. And when you finish come here, to the Church, and I will confess you and free you from sin."[54] In other words, they were not responsible for their actions for they killed in the name of God, on behalf of God's vicar on earth, Pope Pius XII.

The Verdict: The Vatican Is Guilty of Genocide

Today Pope John Paul II claims Pius XII was innocent, the Vatican was innocent, the Church was innocent. For all these years it has kept its archives closed, claiming it has nothing to hide. But we know otherwise. Even without the Vatican's archives we have sufficient evidence to find not only Pius XII, but Pope

Paul VI (then Cardinal Montini, Pius XII's closest advisor) and the entire Vatican guilty of crimes of genocide. We cannot convict or punish them because the United States is their protector today in the same way the Habsburg Empire once was in centuries past. But we know enough of the details to reach a verdict.

We know that the Vatican met with and supported the Ustashi before they ever came to power. We know that on April 7, 1941, the day after the Nazi invasion of Yugoslavia, the British Ambassador to the Vatican, D'Arcy Osborne, implored the Pope to condemn the invasion, but that he refused to do so.[55] We know that Pius XII met with and embraced Pavelic on May 17, 1941, exactly one month to the day Pavelic arrived in Zagreb to take power, and in the very weeks in which most of the racial laws calling for a triple genocide of Serbs, Jews and Roma were being issued.

We know the Pope also met with dozens of the Ustasha leadership and blessed them all. Pavelic made another state visit in 1943, this one more friendly and loving than the first, at which point his regime had killed upwards of 400,000 people. No doubt, the Pope probably met with Pavelic after the war too when he was a wanted war criminal hiding in the Vatican before escaping with the Vatican's help to Argentina. The Vatican cannot claim that it was too far removed from events in Croatia or too poorly informed. Croatia was on the Italian border and Vatican and Ustasha officials traveled regularly back and forth. The Vatican had its ambassadorial Legate Ramiro Marcone in Zagreb throughout the war and his Secretary Guiseppe Masucci who spoke Serbo-Croatian fluently. Both of them visited concentration camps in Croatia and met directly with those most responsible for the Holocaust there: Artukovic, Kvartnik, etc. Meanwhile, the Italian military and government officials in Zagreb were protesting the Ustashi's massacres and the Italian press was writing about them regularly. We also have dozens of acknowledgments of receipt from the Vatican of detailed descriptions of the Holocaust in Croatia, including those from the very few Croatian clergy who actually did protest the genocides, like the Bishop of Mostar. His protest is incriminating on several levels: on one it shows that Pius XII knew exactly what was going on; secondly, it shows that clergy could oppose the Holocaust if they wanted to and not be punished, though almost all supported it; thirdly, it offers a sickening justification for stopping the killings, namely that more Serbs and Jews would convert to Catholicism.[56]

We know that the Vatican was very enthusiastic about the thousands of forced conversions of persecuted people who converted to Catholicism in order to stay alive and that the Vatican sent notes of encouragement to the Croatian clergy, though warning them that they should not accept conversions of adults who were not sincere. We know that the Pope personally met with Archbishop Stepinac in May 1943 to discuss the persecution of the Jews. This is in the report of the Ustasha ambassador to the Vatican, Lobkowicz, to the Croatian Foreign Ministry where it is explained that Stepinac "spoke very much ...about the crime of abortion, which was very well received in the Vatican. On the basis of these laws the archbishop partly also justified the treatment of the Jews, who were the greatest advocates and the most frequent perpetrators of such crimes."[57] We know from his diary that Stepinac was an arch anti-Semite. And we know how staunchly Pius XII defended Stepinac after the war, even after his trial and conviction for war crimes in 1946, rewarding him with the robes of a Cardinal, calling him a martyr. Indeed, every Pope since Pius XII has called Stepinac a martyr including the current Pope who hints at Stepinac's beatification, and who has worshiped at his tomb. John Paul II will travel once again to Croatia this October to celebrate the Ustasha clergy. But the only real martyrs were those who died at the hands of the Catholic gangsters. Pius XII and Stepinac as far as we know never personally murdered anyone, but what they did was far worse than any single murder: they supported a triple genocide of Serbs, Jews and Romas in fascist Croatia that cost a million lives.

We know that the Vatican aided in the escape of thousands of war criminals from Croatia and all other parts of Yugoslavia. Although Vatican representatives and Stepinac's representatives visited Jasenovac several times, they did nothing to rescue the victims. However, when it was the turn of the fascists to face defeat and punishment at the end of the war, the Vatican stepped forward to rescue every single one of the millions of fascists it could, funneling tens of thousands of fascists from Austrian POW camps to the Vatican with false International Red Cross identity papers and the like. As early as 1943 the Vatican intervened with Allied military leaders on behalf of Nazi and other fascist POWs in Italy "to exercise that mission of charity proper to the Church." Where was that mission of charity proper to the Church for the one million Serbs, Jews and Romas killed by the Church's Catholic-fascist gangsters!?[58]

It is interesting to note that the Vatican ratlines, organized by the Vatican and Croatian-Ustasha clergy, would probably have never become widely known if not for the discovery and trial of Klaus Barbie who escaped through them. Because of the Barbie trial, slowly the truth about the ratlines emerged.[59] And so too did the protection by the Vatican and U.S. and British intelligence of thousands of war criminals involved in crimes of genocide in Croatia and Serbia emerge, hidden for the entirety of the Cold War. They were hidden for two reasons: because the United States and its imperialist allies were committed to the destruction of socialist Yugoslavia and therefore did all they could to prevent the extradition for trial of any of them; and secondly because of the importance of the Catholic Church to the West in the Cold War. Indeed, this is why a war criminal could become Secretary General of the United Nations: had Kurt Waldheim committed his crimes of genocide in a non-Communist country he at least would have been exposed after the war, if not also punished. Such is the human rights record of the United States and Britain concerning crimes of genocide. But should not we who do oppose fascism and do seek justice for its victims be at least as vigilant in pursuing these criminals as the Vatican has been vigilant in protecting them?

Incredibly, details now are even leaking out of the Vatican's stealing of plundered property of murdered Serbs, Jews and Romas in Croatia.[60] This story emerged in June 1997 when a memo dated October 21, 1946 written by OSS agent Emerson Bigelow was discovered in the U.S. Treasury Department's archives stating that the Vatican was holding around $170 million worth of Ustasha gold plundered from Holocaust victims in Croatia. President Clinton personally promised a full State Department investigation and report that was to be issued in December, then January, then February, then March.... Clinton will never keep his promise because the Vatican is not only hiding the fact that it stole the property of the people it murdered, but that it shared the loot with America's allies, like Argentina, who were paid off to accept Nazi and Ustashi war criminals. Besides, the American government will never assist in the payment of war reparations to Serbs, or even Yugoslav Jews and Romas. America is currently in an undeclared war with the Serbs and with Yugoslavia. And who would pay?

This brings us back to the question with which we began: What is the Vatican hiding? Obviously, quite a lot. One might say that the answer is "simply" complicity in the murders of tens of millions of Jews, Serbs, Romas, Russians and others during the Holocaust. But this would not be sufficient, for the true answer goes far beyond this. The full answer to this question is that the Vatican is hiding its true historical identity and legacy, an identity that, were it to be widely recognized by historians, would bring the entire edifice of the Catholic Church crashing down. Indeed, the answer to this question is one that historians are not yet ready to acknowledge, for when one considers the crimes of the Vatican during the Holocaust alongside those committed during the Crusades, the Inquisition, the Counter-Reformation, and through thousands of years of anti-Jewish, anti-science, anti-democratic and anti-labor hatred, then what one must recognize is that it was not in Hitler's Nazi Reich nor in Stalin's gulags that the worst crimes against humanity of torture, oppression and murder in all of history were committed. Rather, that dubious distinction belongs to none other than the Roman Catholic Church and its "infallible" leaders, the Papacy, the most criminal institution the world has ever known.

ENDNOTES

1 Charles R. Allen, Jr., "The Vatican and the Nazis, Part II," Reform Judaism, Fall 1983, p. 33.

2 "We Remember: A Reflection on the Shoah," Commission for Religious Relations with the Jews, the Vatican, March 1998.

3 This has been a long term public relations effort. *See* "The Pope's In A Confessional and Jews Are Listening," New York Times, 30 November 1997.

4 "Vatican Expresses Sorrow over Holocaust, defends wartime Pope," *CNN*, 16 March 1998.

5 "The Vatican Releases Document on Church's Role During the Holocaust," *CNN* Transcript of Program aired 16 March 1998.

6 "The Pope's In a Confessional and Jews Are Listening," *New York Times*, 30 November 1997.

7 The story of the "ratlines" and the employment of Croatian fascists and war criminals during the Cold War by the U.S. and British governments is told in Christopher Simpson's *Blowback* (New York: Colliers, 1988) and in Mark Aarons and John Loftus, *The Unholy Trinity*, (New York: St. Martin's, 1991). The singularly shameless and criminal refusal of the U.S. and Britain to cooperate with Yugoslavia in the return of war criminals in total disregard of international treaties and laws is discussed in detail in Christopher Simpson's *The Splendid Blond Beast*, (New York: Grove Press, 1993).

8 *See* L.S. Stavrianos, *The Balkans Since 1453*, (New York: Holt Rinehart, 1961), or Mihailo Crnobrnja, The Yugoslav Drama, (Montreal: McGill, 1994).

9 Cited in Milan Bulajic, *The Role of the Vatican in the Break-Up of the Yugoslav State*, (Beograd: Struchna kniga, 1994), pp. 41-42.

10 *Ibid.*, p.38.

11 "All Serbs Must Die!" In his autobiography, Leon Trotsky (then living in Vienna) recalled the popularity of that song in the Austrian empire in 1914 and how his own son had been beaten up in the street for answering back "Hail Serbia!" *Leon Trotsky, My Life*, (New York: Pathfinder, 1970), p. 233.

12 Cited in Avro Manhattan, *The Vatican's Holocaust*, (Springfield, Mo., Ozark Books, 1988), pp. 9-17.

13 Bulajic, pp. 48-49.

14 *Ibid.*, pp. 49-50.

15 *Ibid.*, p. 59.

16 *Ibid.*, pp. 51-59.

17 Mark Aarons and John Loftus, *The Unholy Trinity*, (New York: St. Martins, 1991), pp. 3-17, 48-54, 125-127.

[18] Frank Littlefield, *Germany and Yugoslavia, 1933-1941. The German Conquest of Yugoslavia.* (New York: Columbia U. Press, 1988).

[19] One of the most widely respected scholarly studies of Vatican complicity in the Holocaust in Croatia is Carlo Falconi's *The Silence of Pius XII*, (Boston: Little, Brown and Co., 1970). Falconi believed that the Pope gave his blessings to the Ustasha in 1939. See p. 266.

[20] Falconi, p. 409, footnote 13.

[21] Bulajic, pp. 72-73.

[22] Manhattan, pp. 20-22.

[23] *Ibid.* Also Falconi, p. 271.

[24] Falconi, pp. 272-273.

[25] Bulajic, p. 74.

[26] *Ibid.*, p.59.

[27] *Ibid.*,p.47.

[28] Falconi, pp.294-296.

[29] *Ibid.*, pp. 266-272.

[30] Vladimir Dedijer, *Jasenovac — The Yugoslav Auschwitz and the Vatican*, (New York: Prometheus, 1992), pp. 136-137.

[31] Recalled in an article by Josef Matel, a Professor at Graz who served in the Wehrmacht in Yugoslavia, quoted in Lazo M. Kostic, *Holocaust in the Independent State of Croatia*, (Chicago: Liberty, 1981), p.12.

[32] Kostic, p. 272.

[33] *Ibid.*, p. 80.

[34] Manhattan, p. 62.

[35] This figure was cited by several German intelligence reports compiled by Abwehr and other Nazi officers in Croatia in July 1941. Quoted in Kostic, pp. 36-37. Carlo Falconi, who had extensive and perhaps better access to archival materials than most historians, argues that by July 1941 350,000 people had been killed by the Ustashi, Falconi, p. 291.

[36] Jonathan Steinberg, "The Roman Catholic Church and Genocide in Croatia, 1941-1945," unpublished essay marking the fiftieth anniversary of the Wannsee Conference, January 1992.

[37] Manhattan, p. 52.

[38] Jonathan Steinberg, *All or Nothing: The Axis and the Holocaust, 1941-1943*, (New York: Routledge, 1990), p. 57.

[39] German, Italian and Croatian primary sources collectively support these numbers as base figures. The works by Kostic and Bulajic cited above provide abundant information on and from these sources. The Roma historian Dragljub Ackovic argues that the number of Roma victims was much higher in Dragoljub Ackovic, Roma Suffering in Jasenovac Camp, (Belgrade: Struchna, 1995). The names of the camps (logors) within Jasenovac were

Versajev, Krapije, Ciglana, Kozhara, Stara Gradishka, Ciganski (Gypsy), Mlaka, and Jablanac. The current regime in Croatia today carries on a constant propaganda war of denial about Jasenovac and has desecrated the site itself. The Tudjman regime to date has not acknowledged that crimes of genocide were even committed by fascist Croatia during World War II and holds to the view that it represented a positive chapter in Croatian history.

40 Bulajic, pp. 129-130.

41 *Ibid.*

42 The Independent State of Croatia comprised the provinces of Croatia, Bosnia-Herzegovina, Srem, and Slavonia. In these territories there were about 40,000 Jews, out of a total of 82,242 in pre-war Yugoslavia. About 35,000 Yugoslav Jews from other parts of Yugoslavia which were under German, Italian, Bulgarian, Albanian and Hungarian rule, died, most of them in German death camps. Thus, altogether 65,525 Yugoslav Jews were killed.

43 Kostic, p. 80.

44 Falconi, p. 298.

45 Bulajic, p. 73.

46 Manhattan, pp. 61-67.

47 *Ibid.*, p. 102.

48 Bulajic, p. 88. Bulajic was present at the trial.

49 *Ibid.*, p. 99.

50 Falconi, pp. 287-293.

51 Manhattan, p. 83.

52 Bulajic, pp. 159-161.

53 Bulajic, pp. 148-161; Falconi, pp. 297-298.

54 Manhattan, p. 68.

55 Bulajic, p. 100.

56 Falconi, p. 294.

57 Bulajic, p. 115.

58 Aarons and Loftus, pp. 35-36.

59 The best account is Christopher Simpson's *Blowback*, (New York: Collier, 1988).

60 *See* "A Vow of Silence. Did Gold Stolen by Croatian Fascists Reach the Vatican?," U.S. News & World Report, March 30, 1998. The Bigelow document is listed as PG 226, Entry 183, Box 29, (copy in possession of the author).

Supplemental Articles: The Vatican and International War Crimes

1) Roger Cohen (*NY Times*), "French Catholic Church Apologizes for Silence on Holocaust," 1 Oct 97

2) Celestine Bohlen (*NY Times*), "The Pope's in a Confessional, and Jews Are Listening," 30 Nov 97

3) Gayle Young (*CNN*), "Vatican expresses sorrow over Holocaust, defends wartime pope," 16 Mar 98

4) *CNN* Transcript, "The Vatican Releases Document on Church's Role During the Holocaust," Aired March 16, 1998 - 6:13 p.m. ET

5) Edward Idris Cardinal Cassidy, Pierre Bishop Duprey, Fr. Remi Hoeckman (Vatican Information Service), "We Remember: A Reflection on the Shoah," selections from the report of the Vatican's Commission for Religious Relations with the Jews, 17 Mar 98

6) *CNN* Transcript, [Vatican Report], Aired March 17, 1998 - 4:30 a.m. ET

7) *NY Times* (Editorial), "The Vatican's Holocaust Report," 18 Mar 98
<ftp://ftp.nyct.net/pub/users/tallpaul/publish/tinaf/tinaf114.txt>

IV. THE HAGUE TRIBUNAL

War Crimes: All's Not Fair

by David Binder, *Legal Times*, April 22, 1996

David Binder has covered the Balkans for The New York Times *since 1963.*

"All's fair in love and war," the venerable English saw tells us and, looking at the performance of the international tribunal in The Hague, it could be updated to "All's fair in love and war crimes prosecutions."

Lopsidedness persisted for more than two years as the tribunal dealing with the Bosnia conflict indicted more and more Serbs on allegations of mass murder, but seemed to be uninterested in identical crimes by Croats or Bosnian Muslims in the three-sided civil war. Although this has been redressed somewhat (at this writing, 57 suspects have been indicted: 46 Serbs, eight Croats, and three Muslims) the imbalance continues, and the impression remains that The Hague method may be the judicial equivalent of "shoot first, ask questions later" — that is, "indict now, investigate later."

This impression hardened through the seizure and arrest of a general and a colonel of the Bosnian Serb army earlier this year by the forces of the Muslim-led government of Sarajevo, and through the *ex post facto* endorsement of this action by Richard J. Goldstone, the South African judge who is the outgoing chief prosecutor of the tribunal.

Under considerable pressure from the United States, the Muslims handed the two Serbs over to NATO, which swiftly delivered them to Mr. Goldstone's custody. He indicted General Djordje Djukić, the chief logistics officer, on February 29, on allegations that he took part in the siege of Sarajevo. His fellow prisoner, Colonel Aleksa Krsmanović, though unindicted, was not set free, but was returned April 3 to the very people in Sarajevo who had seized him — Serbs say "kidnapped" — in the first place, for "further investigation."

By extrapolation, this seemed to posit the Muslim government as a police force empowered to seize as a potential war criminal any Serb who ever put on a uniform in the last four years. The

Djukić-Krsmanović seizure has already proven to be a dangerous precedent that could be employed in retaliatory fashion by Bosnian Serbs against Muslims.

For a time the Muslim-Goldstone actions stalled further implementation of the peace accords agreed in Dayton and signed in Paris last year because the irate Bosnian Serbs simply broke off talks with the peacemakers. Even the U.S. government, the chief advocate of the Bosnian Muslim cause for the last four years, was displeased with this sequence of events which called into question the purpose of the Dayton-Paris accords: Was it to bring peace to the ethnically jumbled and now almost hopelessly hostile mountains and valleys of Bosnia and Herzegovina? Or was it an instrument principally for prosecuting war criminals, mainly Serbs?

World's Strangest Court

The tribunal at The Hague has to be the strangest court in the world. It has no power to enforce an order to arrest suspects. It has limited powers to investigate alleged crimes on site and a doubtful capacity to conduct fair trials. It lacks adequate funding and it has had to change chief prosecutors just as the first trials get under way.

There is no comparable institution in the short history of international law. Nuremberg, after all, was created by the victorious powers of World War II to prosecute the Nazi losers.

Rather, The Hague tribunal is primarily a political creation, pushed upon the international community by a nervous Clinton administration in May 1993, with Madeleine Albright in the lead at the United Nations, as a fig leaf to cover up the deliberately adopted impotence of the United States toward the Bosnian conflict at that time.

The court was established by the United Nations Security Council under Chapter 7, the organization's vague, all-encompassing instrument for dealing with any casus belli. This alone was unusual. In classical terms, it should have been established by convention in the General Assembly (with now more than 170 members), which would have then required accession by treaty ratification of each member. But the United States was, as usual, in a hurry and it was decided to sidestep such niceties.

Then, with a powerful — some would say predominant — injection of American funding, manpower, and technology, the court adopted rules that would not be tolerated in the United States. The accused has no right to confront his accuser. That means accusers may remain anonymous and, as the American Bar Association has noted in a critique, immune from cross-examination. In short, contrary to the American system of justice, the accused, whether Serb, Croat, or Muslim, is held guilty until proven innocent.

Nor are the rules of evidence even spelled out.

Its initial practice showed that the tribunal was virtually incapable of prosecuting Dušan Tadić, the first and, for a long time, the only (Serbian) defendant in its hands, because the interpreter hired by the court was incomprehensible.

Goldstone has been described by a senior U.N. official as "in equal measure political and judicial." His recent activities would seem to bear out the political side of that analysis. He lobbied in the press and on television in Washington, New York, and Brussels for more money and more time, threatening to quit over the former and hinting that he would like to stay on, in the limelight of The Hague, if people really wanted him.

In January he complained bitterly that he had to beg for alms every three months — $7.6 million in alms — to keep the 282-member Hague operation going. "No criminal justice organization should be dependent on handouts," he declared. Mr. Goldstone has since been replaced by Louise Arbour, a judge from Ontario, Canada. The senior U.N. official expressed the hope that "his successor might be more judicial and less political."

So what are the prospects for prosecutions now, especially after Mr. Goldstone and others have declared that their investigations and indictments would be carried up the line of command to the very tops of the Balkan war crime gangs?

We know they have done that with General Ratko Mladić and with Dr. Radovan Karadžić on the basis of their responsibility for alleged massacres of Muslims around Srebrenica last July. (Karadžić has told me and I guess others that he is prepared to go to The Hague and face the music.)

But those were easy, the Republic of the Serbians and its leaders being the pariahs the so-called civilized world has made them.

As for apprehending them, Lt. Gen. Patrick Hughes of the Defense Intelligence Agency predicted in March that "the U.S. element of IFOR [implementation force] will do that when the time comes." A few days later John Shalikashvili, chairman of the Joint Chiefs of Staff, said he was "absolutely" opposed to such an operation.

Concerning Srebrenica, the tribunal has been all over the place with its allegations of Muslim massacre victims, ranging from 8,000 down to 3,000. Characteristically, in early April, John Gerns, its representative on the scene, had plenty to say as teams of investigators probed possible massacre sites around Srebrenica and nothing to say when he went to a mass grave site in Mrkonjic Grad where the corpses of 181 Serbs massacred by Croats last summer had just been exhumed. The press also continues to be selective, rushing almost like ghouls to sites where Muslims were killed, but studiously ignoring those of murdered Serbs.

But, what about Slobodan Milosevic or Franjo Tudjman or even the Bosnian Muslim leader, Alija Izetbegovic?

If Bill Clinton was shaking hands with these men in Paris and Ambassador Richard Holbrooke changed from calling Milosevic a "Communist thug" a year ago to the Prince of Peace today, you can bet your bottom dinar that this tribunal is not going to be prosecuting them.

Nor is it likely that either Belgrade or Zagreb is going to deliver many of the most prominent indicted men to that spiffy former insurance company building in The Hague.

For that matter, not even the funding of the tribunal is certain, for all the moralistic bombast of the Clintons, Albrights, and Holbrookes, especially in a budget-conscious election year in America.

Moreover, there is a debate under way in the United States about whether The Hague tribunal might set a dangerous precedent for creation of a permanent international criminal justice system, posing the issue of infringement on U.S. sovereignty. The argument pits conservatives against liberals (personified by the World Federalists, who have long lobbied for such a global criminal justice institution). That debate is not likely to be settled in favor of the Goldstones of this world, unless Ambassador Albright prevails with the idea that, as a permanent Security

Council member, the United States could simply veto any procedures against Americans charged with war crimes — a kind of "not in my backyard" on a global level.

Declaration of the First Open Session of the Committee for the Protection of Serbs from The Hague Tribunal

The Committee for the Protection of Serbs from The Hague Tribunal, comprised chiefly of prominent intellectuals from Serbia, Montenegro, the Republika Srpska and the Republika Srpska Krajina, read a declaration during an open session in Belgrade on February 3, 1996. Dr. Smilja Avramov, a prominent legal scholar, organized the Committee.

With the indictments that the International War Crimes Tribunal in The Hague has brought against the President of the Republika Srpska, Dr. Radovan Karadžić, and the Commander of the Army of the Republika Srpska, Ratko Mladić, the Serbian people have borne the brunt of the game played by international circles which, from the beginning of the war, mixed causes and effects, perpetrators and victims, and attempted … to transfer the guilt for the civil war from 1991 to 1995 to the Serbian people.

Believing that we represent the good counsel and moral dignity of a great majority of Serbs in Serbia, Montenegro, the Republika Srpska, and the Republika Srpska Krajina, we wish to advise the international community of facts that The Hague's indictments have disregarded:

1. To advise them that the civil war from 1991 to 1995 was a continuation of World War II, because the previous war was not ended as wars ought be ended, with a clear determination of causes and effects, perpetrators and victims, and with the punishment of criminals. It was ended thanks to Tito's games with superficial western democracies and with an insane Russia, with a rotten compromise, which put perpetrators and victims on the same footing and subsequently permitted the neutralization of the Serbian people. He allowed the sons of [WWII] war criminals to get a

chance to continue the atrocities their fathers had begun: namely, achieving the break-up of the Yugoslav state.

2. We want to advise both the East and the West that the Serbian people were disturbed and even panic-stricken when tens of thousands of their fellow countryman left Kosovo-Metohija in a forced exodus. They took up arms only when new rulers imposed even harsher obligations on those who lived in northern Dalmatia, Kordun, Banija, Lika, Slavonija, Baranja, Western Srem, and in Bosnia-Herzegovina, when legal and constitutional measures were taken to place them in a position of second-class citizenship, when hundreds of thousands of Serbs had been perfidiously forced to flee from Federal Croatia even before the war started. Serbs offered resistance only when the new Bosnian-Herzegovian clerical representatives, in a coalition with local Croats, tried to place them under their rule. They took up arms only after arms had been taken up against them in Krajina and B-H, after the first victims had fallen.

3. The Serbian people in the aforementioned areas recognized that the symbols used by Tudjman's Croatia and Izetbegović's B-H are the same symbols used by them during World War II when they tried to exterminate the Serbs by means of genocide, when more than one and a half million Serbs, tens of thousands of Jews and patriots from other nations found martyrdom in countless death pits, concentration camps and killing fields.

If The Hague Tribunal and Justice Goldstone honor the logic of cause and effect, which distinguishes progressive world public opinion and jurisprudence founded on Roman Law, he must then realize that the Serbian position in the civil war of 1991-1995 was, as in the previous wars, characterized by self-defense....

The President of the Republika Srpska, Dr. Radovan Karadžić, and the Supreme Commander of the Army of the Republika Srpska, General Ratko Mladić, are and continue to be the representatives of an endangered people who are fighting for their survival. If the indictments that were handed down, are examined in the concrete context of national relations, they show lack of principal, and are even conspiratorial and anti-Serbian in character. The principal culprits of the current Yugoslav war drama are: Tito's anti-Serbian and anti-Yugoslav regime, which paved the way for the disintegration of Yugoslavia....

We expect The Hague Tribunal to determine the historic moral order of relations in the Yugoslav drama, and to punish the real perpetrators. We expect this Court to pierce the fog of propaganda enshrouding the innocent Serbian people, and to allow the light of truth and dignity to shine on this nation.

Western Hypocrisy Critical of Mladić

by Massimo Finia, *Il Giorno*, 11 June 1996

It is difficult to disentangle one's self of the impression that the trials being conducted in The Hague, regardless of the fact that it is an international criminal court created by super powers, are political trials of those who have been conquered by foreign powers. Three days ago the public prosecutor of this court, an American named Mark Harmon, sought a warrant for the arrest of the Serbian General Mladić and the former President Karadžić, who were indicted for "crimes against humanity" and "genocide." That being possible, however, it is then incomprehensible to leave exempt Croatian President Tudjman, since he was the author of a spectacular and colossal "ethnic cleansing" in August 1995, unprecedented in the Balkan Wars or in any other, for that matter: 200,000 Serbs fled from Croatia, 20,000 Muslims fled Srebrenica, hundreds of civilians were killed, UN peacekeepers were used as live shields, and many were killed in cold blood.

Broadening our theme, what can one say about General Schwartzkopf, who during 55 days of laying siege to Baghdad with surgical bombardments and "smart" bombs, killed 33,000 children and 33,000 women? If we wish to probe deeper into the ghastly figures of the number of children killed over the course of four years in a "purely" Slavic war versus the number of children killed in 55 days in Baghdad, the proportion is 30 to 1 ... in the Gulf. And the children of Iraq are children no less valued than

Croatian, Muslim or Serbian children; no one, however, mentions the possibility of indicting Schwartzkopf: he is a war hero!

One may suppose that the Bosnian Serbs, Karadžić and Mladić above all, are responsible for the start of the war; however, it's not as if they did not have a good reason to do so. When Slovenia and Croatia unilaterally declared their independence from Yugoslavia in 1991, the West and international organizations hurried to recognize them. It was an honest decision, based on the sacred principle of self-determination of peoples. But it must not be ignored that their independence opened the question of how to regard Bosnia. A multi-ethnic Bosnia made sense only in the federal and multi-ethnic Yugoslavia. When it ceased to exist, the Serbs from Bosnia sought to establish their own independence by forming their own state or uniting with Serbia. They considered that they had the same right of self-determination that had been accorded to the Croats and the Slovenians. However, certain western countries and international organizations went to great efforts (as they are still doing today) to establish a Bosnian state with a non-existent Muslim administration.

That was when the Serbs took up arms and began the war. Atrocities and brutal acts occurred in this war, as in every war (but also, as in every war, acts of courage, devotion, generosity and mercy). If it appears that the Serbs are more brutal than the other sides that is because they were inflicting defeat on the battlefield. But ... Croats and Muslims ... were seen to be no better. In any case, at The Hague Tribunal, Serbian soldiers, both lower and higher ranking officers, are being almost exclusively indicted, along with a token Croat or Muslim. As far as military leaders are concerned, only Mladić and Karadžić have been indicted, but not Tudjman and Izetbegović, nor Milošević, who at one moment wanted to abandon the Serbs of Bosnia to take a seat at the victor's table, since victors do not go on trial.

Therefore, the victors have put the vanquished on trial in The Hague. Another trial of this sort solemnly opened nearly half a century ago in Nuremberg. Then, as now, the hypocritical and psychoanalytic needs of the Yankee mind pushed to feel not only more powerful but also the best, but never with any regard to justice. Rather, they have merged the power of law with brute force. That concept of law coincides exactly with the notions Hitler once had.

An Indictment from the Czechs

An open letter from Dr. Rajko Dolecek, M.D., DSc. to chief prosecutor Judge Richard Goldstone was published in two parts in Novosti, *on July 12 and 13, 1996*

Honorable Prosecutor:

I am a Czech university professor who has lived for twenty years in Yugoslavia. I never belonged to any political party. Up until 1990, Western Europe, the US and NATO were respected defenders of democracy, peace and freedom. But after 1990, I realized how naïve I had been. The International Tribunal for War Crimes in The Hague, which was sponsored by the US, proved that to me. By using the principle of two weights and two measures, it became, from its very conception, an object of ridicule in the face of an honest and unbiased court. The fundamental right of *audiatur et altera pars*, i.e., let the other side be heard, has vanished entirely. The basis of the tribunal was intentionally stacked with one-sided information and disinformation, besides which Serbian information was (how can one put it?) always neglected. The Serbs were considered, *a priori*, to be war criminals, and the few Croats and Muslims who were intentionally indicted confirms it. I read Serbian accounts of Croats and Muslims who committed crimes (Vukovar, eastern and western Bosnia, Herzegovina) — in your indictment I saw practically no mention of them. Equity has been exchanged for political intentions.

Criminal Errors

No one is without blame in this civil-ethnic-religious war in Yugoslavia and it is absolutely correct to put those on trial who indeed committed war crimes, or even those who gave the orders. It is utterly dishonorable to prosecute only one side and close ones eyes to the same crimes committed by the other sides. Why not haul into court everyone who prepared the Yugoslav tragedy? The Nuremberg court tried Hitler's Foreign Minister, J. von Ribbentrop (surely he hadn't killed anyone personally), and condemned him to death for his role in the Nazi preparations for the war. Perhaps you have not been advised of the role played by German Foreign Minister Genscher and other European and American politicians and diplomats? They committed flagrant crimes against peace, and they prepared and sponsored acts of bloodshed. Why has no one indicted them?

It was a criminal (as well as planned in advance?) "mistake" when Croatia and Slovenia, but especially Bosnia-Herzegovina, were prematurely and illegally recognized, without the customary criteria for a sovereign state — and only because a powerful member of the European Union (Germany) wanted it.

Your tribunal has on its account many violators. And its legality is even dubious. What happened to a pair of Serbian officers, General Djukić and Corporal Krsmanović, would have been impossible in any civilized country. Even though they had not been indicted, they were seized by Muslims in Sarajevo, illegally and in contradiction to the Dayton Accords, and the judicial apparatus quickly turned them into war criminals, and you ordered to have them transferred as war criminals (by an American military aircraft) to a prison in The Hague, where they were illegally held for many weeks. In the end, Corporal Krsmanović was released, while the sufferings of General Djukić, who was suffering from pancreatic cancer, continued. His health ruined — he did not receive the required care in your prison — he was sent home where he died a few days later. Imagine what would have happened in a civilized country, for example in England, when a court makes such a serious violation of the law. It was routine with Stalin's show trials.

Professor of political science, Ragu G.C. Thomas (Marquette University, Milwaukee, USA) wrote of your tribunal: "The system and process would have been thrown out as a cruel farce in any Western democratic society." Dutch professor of international law, Theo van Boven,[1] warned in March 1996 of the danger that the tribunal would become an arm of American interests, and that the kidnapping of two Serbian officers (who were not on a list of 52 suspects) and their transferal to The Hague were without any legal justification, and that this was contrary to judicial statutes and contrary to human rights.

Turning a Blind Eye

After the end of the trials in Nuremberg and up until 1993, the Great Powers absolutely did not want to organize any kind of tribunal for war crimes because it was not in their interest. In the wars that have taken place in the last 50 years some 15-20 million people have died, with much more brutality and destruction than took place in Yugoslavia — but no official tribunal was ever organized. Three million people died in Bangladesh, two million in Cambodia, and one to two million in Biafra and Afghanistan. No one dragged the Vietnamese (Vietcong) or American generals into court, nor their leaders for the unbelievable savagery that took place during the Vietnam War nor French generals and Algerian nationalists during the course of the war in Algeria.

Did anyone ever indict U.S. presidents for the 150,000 deaths in Guatemala, Nicaragua, and San Salvador, of which the majority had been killed by special forces, paid for and trained by the U.S., of oppressive regimes. In that respect, no one expressed any interest in the hundreds of thousands of dead in the Sudan, Ethiopia, and Iraq, etc. The bloody massacres in Rwanda, with millions of dead and incredible violence, never had such big headlines in the newspapers as in Bosnia-Herzegovina, where the events that took place claimed far fewer lives.

According to various information, during the course of 40 months about 1% to 3% of the pre-war population, Croats, Muslims and Serbs, died. These terrible figures fall into the range of 30,000 to 150,000; the latest figures provided by Sadako Ogata (June 1996) are significantly lower, at 30,000 to 60,000. Since going into retirement in July 1995, U.S. Army General Charles G. Boyd wrote this: "Does that total after 38 months of warfare make charges of genocide a meaningful contribution to policy debate?"[2]

False Pretext

Are you at all aware, your Honor, how many innocent children, elderly, diabetics, and pregnant women have died in Yugoslavia and in the Republika Srpska, as a result of the inhuman sanctions and the loss of membership in the World Health Organization? Aren't those crimes against humanity? Is anyone going to be indicted for this?

Will U.S. President Clinton be indicted because he approved of airstrikes with Tomahawk missiles against Serbian targets that resulted in "collateral damage"? Couldn't Admiral L. Smith be indicted as a war criminal because his men killed so many

Serbian civilians and destroyed so many non-military targets in Bosnia-Herzegovina during the American (NATO) war against the Bosnian Serbs under a suspicious mandate by the UN Security Council? Admiral L. Smith could, indeed, claim that it was an order from his superiors at NATO Headquarters. But these are the same justifications given by Nazi war criminals — they were merely obeying orders.

Your Honor, you have not indicted NATO commanders for manipulating a staged massacre in Sarajevo (August 28, 1995) as a false pretext for the bombardment of Serbian targets, military and civilian. NATO commanders and brute-force diplomats like Richard Holbrooke certainly knew that the Serbs were not responsible for the massacre, which Izetbegović's men (none of whom were ever indicted for deliberately killing their own civilians for propaganda reasons) provoked NATO "to fight their war for them," as General M. Rose once said.

When asked what would result from the flood of disinformation against the Serbs that his public relations agency, Ruder Finn Global Public Affairs, introduced, its director, J. Harff, replied to French journalist Jacques Merlino (1993): "We're not paid to moralize."[3]

What do you think, should the directors of some newspapers and televisions be charged with war crimes for the media lies they told? How is it possible that many fabrications and instances of outright disinformation are given awards and that no one pays any attention to serious warnings by Yossef Bodansky about the dangers of militant Islamic fundamentalism?

No one has grasped the idea, or wanted to, that the Serbs from Bosnia-Herzegovina and from Krajina were almost annihilated during the existence of the fascist Independent State of Croatia (1941-45) by Croatian Ustashi and their Muslim allies, and that Serbs found themselves in an identical situation in 1991-1992.

The Propaganda of Murderers

In the article "U.S. Names Figures to Be Presented Over War Crimes,"[4] Lawrence Eagleburger called, without any legal justification, at the end of 1992, the Serbian leaders Radovan Karadžić and General Ratko Mladić war criminals, because their army committed acts of ethnic cleansing, and apparently mass rapes[5] (unbelievable fabrications were announced), killings, and brutal behavior. Your Honor, your obedient Tribunal immediately placed them at the head of a list of actual and alleged criminals. It is astonishing that your Honor has not drawn up indictments against Messrs. Izetbegović and Tudjman, whose armies committed the ethnic cleansing of nearly a million Serbs (a great deal of that was done with the generous aid of NATO), mass killings, rapes, and brutal behavior. The special forces of Izetbegović killed his own people in three staged explosions in Sarajevo — and the blame was put on the Serbs....

Professor C.G. Jacobsen (Political Science, Carleton University, Ottawa, Canada) commented about the Tribunal's work. He remarked that if one wanted to strengthen international law, as an abstract idea ... it was necessary for it to be understood as unbiased. In the Yugoslav situation, it meant that since Serbian leaders have been indicted, Tudjman and Izetbegović must be indicted as well, because clear and unambiguous proof exists that some of those soldiers who fought under their flags committed war crimes as well, rape and other criminal acts. It will not be enough to follow the unbiased requirements of only one side, which would ridicule the law.... Historians will later most certainly judge the Hague Tribunal as a kangaroo court.

Training for Criminals

Your Honor, your representative, C. Williamson recently stated that the Federal Republic of Yugoslavia has become a "no man's" state because it shields alleged war criminals. Can he really be such an ignoramus and so arrogant? Did anyone ever call the United States "no man's" government because there were so many real Nazis there after WWII as well as other criminals who had been welcomed as "experts on the East"? In order to better prove the absolute impartiality of your Honor's Tribunal, its president, A. Cassese, sought on June 5, 1996 in Sarajevo, to once again introduce sanctions against the Bosnian Serbs, and eventually against the Federal Republic of Yugoslavia, if they did not immediately agree to hand over their two leaders, Radovan Karadžić and General Ratko Mladić, who were treated as though they were war criminals without any legal indictment. No such requirements were announced as far as Messrs. Tudjman and

Izetbegović were concerned. The international effort to conceal the truth is astounding.

There is a private firm in Alexandria, Virginia (USA) that has the strange name of Military Professional Resources, Inc. Almost 200 elite retired American generals, admirals, and officers are employed there. They are used as mercenaries for anyone who pays. The U.S. government, which for different reasons does not want to send its own active troops to train foreign armies, sends MPRI instead.

In certain circumstances, it meant that MPRI was planning mass killings, such as those that took place in Croatia, where these elite retired officers trained the Croatian army, which had been armed during the course of the sanctions by America, Germany and others, for the well-known offensive named Operation Storm (August 1995), whose result was the expulsion of 200,000 Serbs from Krajina and the mass killing of civilians by the American-trained Croatian army. The UN did not make the slightest meaningful protest despite such a flagrant violation of the arms embargo by this influx of weapons, for which no one was indicted, pursued or arrested. Only Carl Bildt stated, and not very forcefully, something about Croatian war crimes and about Tudjman.

A Manipulated Idea

No one has had much to say about the illegal and massive supplies of weapons from Iran (America's new ally in the Balkans) to the U.S.-supported side (i.e., the Muslims and the Croats) during the embargo. The criminal destruction of UN Protected Areas by the Croatian army did not summon any significant protests. The killings of Serbs, the burglarization and destruction of their homes, were irrelevant for the U.S., the UN, your Honor's Tribunal, the EU, the Contact Group, and the Organization for Security and Cooperation in Europe. Surely, your Honor must recall how the world attacked the Serbs during the course of events surrounding the safe areas (identical to UN Protected Areas) of Srebrenica, Goražde, Tuzla, and Bihać, which were not demilitarized as had been agreed with the Serbs, and from which the Muslims attacked and destroyed surrounding Serbian areas.

Please excuse this open letter. It was written without anger. I am genuinely sad that the higher ideals of jurisprudence, [as espoused by] an unprejudiced and non-political Tribunal, which would punish war criminals, was so manipulated and debased by the interests of the Great Powers. If The Hague Tribunal continues in the same one-sided, biased manner, it will enter history as Professor Jacobson said, like a kangaroo court. I am certain that you are delighted to be completing your duties at this somewhat dubious tribunal....

The Serbs of Han Pijesak, after the incident with IFOR[6] and the issuance of international warrants for General Ratko Mladić, sent word that they would defend the commander of the Army of the Republika Srpska.

---

[1] *Theo van Boven*, professor of International Justice, University of Limburg, former UN Director for Human Rights.

[2] "Making Peace with the Guilty: The Truth about Bosnia," by General Charles G. Boyd, USAF (Ret.), *Foreign Affairs* (US), September-October 1995. General Boyd was the Deputy Commander in Chief, U.S. European Command from November 1992 to July 1995. More recent figures indicate that 100,000 people died in the Bosnian civil war. *See* p. 346.

[3] *Toutes les vérités yougoslaves ne sont pas bonnes à dire*, Jacques Merlino, Albin Michel: Paris, 1993, p. 128-129.

[4] *The New York Times*, December 12, 1992.

[5] Mass rapes, which were refuted. (*See* p. xxiv)

[6] Serbs confronted IFOR in Han Pijesak on July 6, 1996 when they came to search for General Mladić.

To the Lord Mayor and Citizens Of The Hague

by Dr. Raymond Kent

An Open Letter and Petition from Americans for International Justice Committee, Dr. Raymond Kent, secretary and Emeritus Professor of History at the University of California, Berkeley, signed on 17 July 1996, San Francisco, and published in the Haagsche Courant, *23 July 1996.*

For several centuries Holland had been regarded as one of the most civilized nations. The Hague in particular has been the seat of the World Court in the current century, a court distinguished by the application of Law to relations and disputes between nations and states. The City and the Court became intertwined, epitomizing some of the most admirable legacies of Western Civilization itself. The cases heard by the Court and its careful judicial rulings virtually defined International Law, a field now taught at most major universities. The World Court, as a global legal officer, never engaged in advocacy; it never demanded reprisals; it left the acceptance of its rulings to the parties involved; it allowed simultaneous representations to all sides in a given dispute; it did not launder or argue its finding in public before or during judicial review, while the concept of international military intervention to enforce its rulings remained alien to the World Court.

Right now, this magnificent legal bequest is being literally raped at The Hague, its respected home. Its image is being subverted by a would-be legal impostor, inserted deliberately into The Hague in search of a legal and cultural pedigree. It is presented as an international "Tribunal" on war crimes. It uses legal language. It has jurists on its panels. It has funds but, in fact, it is a fraud. It clearly has a mission that by its very nature has become a naked assault on Law itself.

Dealing with war crimes in the former Yugoslavia, it truncates the true historical context by eliminating all events before 1991, invoking the statues of limitations, which do not apply to war crimes. Disregarding rules of evidence and established legal procedure, it investigates, indicts, prosecutes and renders sentence as a single body. It demands that arbitrarily proclaimed war criminals be physically delivered to The Hague Tribunal. It issues daily accusations to the world media against two particular leaders of a single ethnicity and religion in the three-part civil war in which all sides share in brutalities. It does not allow defense attorneys to challenge the accusations, by hiding itself behind a lack of mandate for trial *in absentia*. It is even demanding that the NATO troops in Bosnia hunt and arrest the two leaders at the risk of both military and civilian bloodshed. It is deliberately sustaining a worldwide media frenzy through which the accused are pronounced guilty by association and without a trial. It is destroying and making a mockery of the judicial system and secular legal tradition by pursuing its own political objectives.

Americans for International Justice Committee believes that the decent residents of the famous city and its highest elected officials are being deceived and dishonored by the presence in their midst of a would-be court of law conceived in mischief, and motivated by political expediency and bias. It embodies the imperial arrogance of powers whose leaders mistake might for right. We, therefore, respectfully petition the Lord Mayor and the citizens of The Hague to put the Tribunal on notice that, as presently constituted and operated, it debases the true Court's historic legacy and is no longer welcome in their city. The proclamation would attest in no uncertain terms that The Hague intends to remain the permanent home and guardian of International Law, fathered by the illustrious Dutch jurist Hugo Grotius, whose immortal work *De jure belli at pacis*, 1625 (On the Law of War and Peace), has been the guiding light in the slow and painstaking evolution on international legality and morality.

UNJUST FROM THE START, Part I:
The War Crimes Tribunal
vs. General Djordje Djukić

by Dr. Kosta Čavoški [Translator Unknown]

© *1997 by Kosta Čavoški. Reprinted with permission of the author.*

Dr. Kosta Čavoški is professor at the Faculty of Law in Belgrade. Professor Čavoški obtained his master's degree after having defended a thesis wherein he provided (for the first time in Serbian) a coherent and affirmative survey of the origins and functions of the American constitutional and legal system as the most distinguished model of liberal law and politics. As an advocate of the liberal concept of "rule of law" and a very knowledgeable critic of the Bolshevik-Communist aberration of an ideological and party-controlled state, Čavoški gained a reputation as a dissident during the Communist regime. He was then ousted from the Faculty of Law in the early 70s, and only returned there in the mere capacity of a lecturer fifteen years later. He was the initiator and a founding member of the first opposition party in Serbia (The Democratic Party). He is the author of a well known book about Slobodan Milošević, as well as a number of other scholarly and journalistic works.

> Doctor Slobodan Ivković, who looked after [General] Djordje Djukić during his last days, said that "inadequate treatment and therapy during his time in [the War Crimes Tribunal] prison and hospital brought on a sudden deterioration in the General's health" and added that General Djukić received salted, greasy food which "third and fourth year medical students know that patients operated on for cancer of pancreas must not eat. *Naša Borba*, 9 February 1996. [From footnote 6 below.]

If things begin well, there is a good chance that they will end well and vice versa. The start of the first important case that was presented to the International Criminal Tribunal was a complete fiasco. The case in question was that of the Tribunal Prosecutor versus Djordje Djukić. It ended disgracefully, leaving behind a sad example of serious violation of the guarantees and institutions of criminal law which are applied and respected in all civilized countries.

Illegitimate Arrest

The arrest of a person is an exceptionally serious and dangerous act with regard to elementary human rights and should therefore be carried out with utmost caution. In civilized countries it is undertaken in accordance with procedural guarantees involving an arrest warrant when there exists reasonable doubt that a crime has been carried out, or as apprehension in the line of duty during the actual perpetration of a serious crime. General Djordje Djukić was arrested by the Muslim authorities on a road that was under the protection of the Implementation Force (IFOR). Neither the court in Muslim Sarajevo nor The Hague International Criminal Tribunal (i.e. the Prosecutor) had accused, let alone suspected him of any criminal act. Arrest implies a legal process, but he was not even arrested, he was simply kidnapped in a form of highway robbery before the eyes of the IFOR.

This took place on 30 January 1996 on a road secured by IFOR. General Lieutenant Colonel Djordje Djukić, assistant Chief of Staff of Logistics of the Republika Srpska Army in the rear, Aleksa Krsmanović, Deputy Commander of the Sarajevo-Romanija Rear Corps, and driver Radenko Todorović, were driving along this road in a car with civilian registration plates, having first informed IFOR of their route. In view of this, the arrest of General Djordje Djukić, Colonel Aleksa Krsmanović and Radenko Todorović was an arbitrary act and in violation of the well-known legal institution of *habeas corpus* — the guarantee against arbitrary arrest. At the moment of arrest none of these persons were breaking the law, neither did there exist a valid warrant for their arrest.

Following their arrest, General Djukić and Colonel Krsmanović were illegally detained for a full six days (from 30 January to 4 February 1996) in police custody, even though the current law on criminal procedure in Muslim Sarajevo states that police custody can only last 72 hours. It was only on 6 February that they were handed a ruling on custody when the Sarajevo High Court instituted proceedings (court ruling no. Ki-57/96) against General Djordje Djukić on the grounds of suspected war crimes against civilians. Until then, General Djordje Djukić was subjected to eight days of torture and mental distress as a result of interminable interrogation, sometimes lasting for 20 hours a day. All this was done in spite of Djukić's timely warning that he was seriously ill and that he needed medical care and medication.

The Prosecutor's Gullibility and Rashness

However heinous and unforgivable this illegal and arbitrary behavior on the part of the Muslim authorities, it didn't surprise anyone. In civil and religious wars, mutual hatred has provoked many worse and more dangerous crimes, particularly since the international actors in Bosnia were biased towards one side if not indifferent. What was surprising, however, was the tendency of the International Criminal Tribunal in the Hague, and especially its prosecutor Richard Goldstone, to incorrectly apply and breach the very rules that it had instituted. From November 1993 when eleven judges were appointed and the Tribunal began to work, up to 30 January 1996 (two years and two months later), the Prosecutor's office carefully collected all available data related to war crimes on the territory of former Yugoslavia, in particular in Bosnia and Herzegovina. During this time, absolutely no one marked General Djordje Djukić and Colonel Aleksa Krsmanović as suspected war criminals, even though all sides, including the Muslim authorities in Sarajevo assisted in the collection of data and the compilation of a list of suspects. This fact should have prescribed at the very least restraint and great caution on the part of Prosecutor Richard Goldstone when he heard that high rank-ing Serbian officers had been kidnapped as suspected war crimi-nals by Muslim authorities on a road supervised by IFOR. Instead of this, the ambitious Richard Goldstone decided on 7 February to instigate proceedings against General Djordje Djukić and Colonel Aleksa Krsmanović, thereby validating the lawlessness of the Muslims and their alleged suspicion of the two for being war criminals. He then sent his experts to Sarajevo to investigate this long awaited case. During talks with CSCE representatives in Vienna, Goldstone clearly stated that proof against Djukić and Krsmanović "was serious enough to call for an investigation."[1] Hence Christian Chartier, spokesman of The Hague Tribunal, announced that Goldstone "had concluded that there were ade-quate grounds to take the Bosnian charges seriously and carry out an investigation into the possible guilt of the suspects for acts under the jurisdiction of the International Tribunal."[2]

On 12 February 1996, at the request of Prosecutor Richard Goldstone, General Djordje Djukić and Colonel Aleksa Krsmanović were transferred to the International Tribunal prison in The Hague as suspects. This implied that in accordance with Rule 2 of the Tribunal "the Prosecutor possesses reliable information which tends to show that they may have committed a crime over which the Tribunal has jurisdiction." It is hardly necessary to say that the most important component of this sentence is the reliability of the information regarding alleged crimes committed by the suspects.

The Prosecutor's Violation of the Rules of Procedure and Evidence

To his great regret, Richard Goldstone very quickly realized that the information he had received from Sarajevo was not at all reliable, and that the thirty or so officials sent to The Hague by the U.S. Ministry of Justice at its own expense had not discovered anything of importance in the meantime. Only then did he realize that at the very beginning of the case he had made an unforgivable mistake and seriously violated the Tribunal's Rules of Procedure and Evidence.

According to article 8 of the Statute of the International Tribunal of 25 May 1993, the Tribunal has concurrent jurisdiction with national courts in the pursuit of people who have seriously violated international humanitarian laws on the territory of former Yugoslavia since 1 January 1991. At the same time, the primacy of the International Tribunal over national courts is stipulated. However, the practical application of such primacy occurs only if at any stage in the procedure the International Tribunal demands of the national court that it defer its competence in accordance with the Statute and its Rules of Procedure and Evidence.

Since the High Court in Sarajevo had already instituted criminal proceedings against General Djordje Djukić and Colonel Aleksa Krsmanović under its ruling no. Ki-57/96, in order to initiate his own investigation, Prosecutor Richard Goldstone should have first proposed to the Trial Chamber that it submit a formal demand for deferral of competence of the national court to that of the Tribunal. The Trial Chamber would then have had to adopt his proposal so that the International Tribunal could submit a formal demand to the state in question for its court to defer competence. Only then, the national court [having] deferred competence to the International Tribunal, could the Prosecutor initiate an investigation and seek the transferal of the suspects to The Hague. Richard Goldstone, however, did both — he initiated investigation and transferred the suspects — without having first proposed to the Trial Chamber that a formal demand for competence deferral be made, and waited for the decision of the Chamber. This would have been followed by submission of the demand and its formal acceptance. He therefore broke Rules 9 and 10, which to him should have been inviolable.

Blackmail and Extortion of Proof

If Richard Goldstone had possessed reliable and incriminating evidence against Djukić and Krsmanović, the disturbing realization that he had broken the Rules of the Tribunal would not have bothered him much. Since, however, there was no such proof or the hope that it would be found, Goldstone was forced to twist, distort and falsify the facts in an attempt to extract himself. In this he was generously assisted by the president of the First Trial Chamber, French judge Claude Jorda. The first step was to change the legal status of Djordje Djukić and Aleksa Krsmanović. To do this Richard Goldstone and the responsible judges off-handedly forgot that on 13 February 1996 The Hague Tribunal spokesman, Christian Chartier, publicly announced that investigation into two high ranking officers had begun, that as suspects they had been informed that they had the right not to answer questions, the right to choose a lawyer and that they would have at their disposal a court translator. The very next day, 14 February 1996, Goldstone himself announced that Djukić and Krsmanović had been transferred to The Hague "under suspicion that during the conflict in former Yugoslavia they had committed serious breaches of international humanitarian laws." However, instead of this qualification, on 28 February Goldstone suddenly changed the status of the prisoners to potential witnesses, to the shock of defense lawyers, Toma Fila and Milan Vujin, who immediately stated that this was "the first time" they had heard their clients were witnesses and not suspects.[3]

The real reason behind the change in the prisoners' status was due to the fact that in order to summon witnesses to The Hague it was not necessary to have either a formal demand for competence deferral by the Trial Chamber or a formal decision by the Sarajevo High Court deferring its competence to the International Tribunal. According to Rule 90 bis, which was subsequently added, the International Tribunal can demand, in the interest of a testimony, temporary access to detained persons. Thus it turns out that Djukić and Krsmanović were kidnapped and formally placed under criminal investigation in Sarajevo so that, handcuffed, they could be transferred to The Hague prison in order to supposedly testify. In this way, the Prosecutor and the judges "enriched" the international practice of criminal law by instituting the preventive arrest of witnesses — something unknown to any civilized criminal legislation. A witness can only be forcefully brought to court if he or she does not respond to a subpoena or excuse their absence.

Illegal Indictment

The act of issuing a bill of indictment against General Djordje Djukić in itself was a new and serious violation of the Rules of Procedure and Evidence. In the surprising change of Djukić's and Krsmanović's status from suspects to witnesses, Richard Goldstone tacitly admitted that the Rules had been seriously violated since there had been no previous institution of competence deferral procedures. Therefore, it could be assumed that the same mistake would not be made again. It has already been said that investigation against General Djordje Djukić and his detention in prison had been set in motion by ruling no. Ki-57/96 of the High Court bin Sarajevo of 6 February. This meant that criminal proceedings before the court of the Muslim-Croat Federation had been instigated. Under such circumstances, especially as he did not possess any proof, the Tribunal Prosecutor was not in the position to directly press charges against Djukić. To do this he first had to propose to the Trial Chamber that it submit a formal demand for deferral of competence. Only when the High Court in Sarajevo delivered its decision to defer its competence to the jurisdiction of the International Tribunal would Richard Goldstone have had the authority to issue a bill of indictment.

However, he once again broke Rules 9 and 10 of the Tribunal and did just this without the Sarajevo High Court deferring competence to the International Tribunal, or indeed the International Tribunal taking over jurisdiction of this case. To make matters worse, Goldstone was supported by Justice Adolphus Godwin Karibi-Whyte, who accepted the bill of indictment and signed the arrest warrant fully aware that formal take over of jurisdiction had not taken place. Once again, it was made clear that neither the Prosecutor nor certain of the judges afforded minimum respect to the Rules that should have been the backbone of their work.

Aside from formal default, the indictment against Djukić had inadmissible material shortcomings — Djukić's responsibility was neither specified nor backed by any reliable evidence. It was stated that General Djordje Djukić, in his capacity as assistant Chief of Staff of Logistics, was responsible for the following duties: rear area supplies to all units of the Bosnian Serb army; recommendations for all cadre appointments; issuance of orders related to the delivery of supplies for the Bosnian Serb army units, regulation of rear area transfers; decisions on the procurement and use of materials and technical equipment from the Bosnian Serb army warehouses. Furthermore, "Djordje Djukić, in agreement with others, planned, prepared or aided the actions and operations of the Bosnian Serb army and its allies," which included the bombing of civilian buildings. This bombing lasted from May 1992 until December 1995. During this time "the Bosnian Serb armed forces in Sarajevo deliberately, arbitrarily and on a widespread and systematic basis, bombed civilian targets that were of no military importance in order to kill, wound, terrorize and demoralize the civilian population of Sarajevo."

Hence, by supplying the entire Republika Srpska army, Djukić was directly responsible for the war crimes committed. This indictment, however, did not provide sufficient evidence on the basis of which a causal relationship could have been established between the deeds of the accused and their consequences that were qualified as war crimes. Instead of this, there was an attempt to "prove" that General Djordje Djukić, as assistant Chief of Staff of Logistics was directly responsible for all operations on the front surrounding Sarajevo.

Special attention should be paid to the fact that the Prosecutor did not submit the exact dates of the shelling during the given period. This would have lent support to the presumed causal relationship between Djordje Djukić's acts and their consequences — the wounding, killing, and terrorizing of the civilian population. The Prosecutor did not do this knowing that throughout the period in question, Djordje Djukić's poor state of health had resulted in his extended absence from work for treatment in the Military Medical Academy hospital in Belgrade. In fact, had the exact dates of the bombing been specified, Djukić would have had the perfect alibi — reliable proof that on the days in question he was undergoing serious medical treatment instead of planning and preparing the crimes he was allegedly responsible for.

Such incomplete and inexact charges could be used as an indictment against thousands of other Serbian soldiers simply by introducing their personal information and stressing their strict liability for action in any area of the front. This, of course, could only happen if strict liability were an accepted concept within the criminal law of the International Tribunal in The Hague. However, this is something long discarded in civilized countries.

The evidence collected by the prosecutor was the weakest aspect in the indictment against General Djordje Djukić. It was based on an overview of the organizational structure of the civil and military authority in Republika Srpska and the internal organization of certain political parties, including that of Arkan (Zeljko Raznjatović). It consisted of information related only to General Djukić, in particular the way in which he assumed his position in the Republika Srpska army and his official duties and obligations. Especially surprising is the fact that this indictment included data on Radovan Karadžić, President of the Republika Srpska, and General Ratko Mladić, Commander of the Republika Srpska army, and their alleged activities (despite the fact that Richard Goldstone had already charged the two separately). In all likelihood this was an attempt on the part of Richard Goldstone to implicate General Djordje Djukić merely because he belonged to the same military organization as Radovan Karadžić and Ratko Mladić. A tabular schedule of the alleged bombing of civilian targets and population was provided with no reference to who drew up this schedule (it could have been done by a journalist on the basis of newspaper reports), or how reliable the data were.

On the basis of such unconvincing and totally undetermined evidence, Richard Goldstone detained and indicted Djordje Djukić of alleged action that could have resulted in life imprisonment. He thereby made it clear that the Bosnian Serbs came under a special legal category subject to the rule of the Queen of Hearts from Alice in Wonderland: "Sentence first — verdict afterwards."

Professional Defeat
Portrayed As "Victory of Humanism"

The Prosecutor knew very well that the offered "facts" were no sort of proof of Djukić's individual responsibility, but he hoped that by the time the case (which was constantly postponed) came to court either something convincing would be found, or the accused, in his poor state of health, would agree to "cooperate" with the Tribunal as a witness thereby more or less validating his presence at The Hague. However, when it became clear that this last hope would come to nothing, Richard Goldstone summoned the strength to make one more desperate move: he proposed the dropping of charges. Instead of publicly admitting that he had not succeeded in collecting reliable and convincing evidence, he tried to promote his own magnanimity and humanity. Despite the fact that he knew of Djukić's incurable illness from the very beginning, Goldstone only now found it necessary to inform the Tribunal that according to the independent opinion of Danish doctors, Djukić was suffering from terminal cancer that had already metastasized to other organs, including the spine. To save face, he ended with hoping that "the withdrawal of the indictment will not be against his right to indict the accused at some time in the future for these same offenses should the medical condition of the accused change."

Had the Prosecutor been truly prepared to face up to his own professional and human conscience, he would have had to ask himself whether the kidnapping of Djordje Djukić, his long and debilitating "interrogation" and torture in the prison in Muslim Sarajevo, as well as his indictment did not exacerbate an accelerated worsening of his already fatal state of health. Would Djordje Djukić not have lived longer had he not been exposed to such maltreatment, loss of freedom and unfounded accusation?

Instead of this, Richard Goldstone coldly noted that the accused probably would not have survived his trial and even if he did, the progressive worsening of his health would make him almost incapable or meaningfully participating in his own defense. Under such conditions, his trial would be inherently unfair.

Djukić's defense lawyers, Milan Vujin and Toma Fila, immediately opposed Richard Goldstone's proposal and his attempt to wash his hands, under the guise of humanity, of his numerous mistakes and the great harm he had done Djordje Djukić. With good reason, the defense lawyers claimed that the Prosecutor had not backed his indictment with any form of evidence of the alleged guilt of Djordje Djukić. They demanded of the Tribunal that it unconditionally free Djukić due to lack of evidence. They also warned that any other resolution would leave the shadow of suspicion of Djukić's guilt as a war criminal thereby damaging his reputation and honor.

The Trial Chamber presided over by French Justice Claude Jorda immediately perceived that Richard Goldstone's proposal was not in accordance with Rule 51, which states: "The Prosecutor may withdraw an indictment without leave, at any time before its confirmation, but thereafter only with leave of the Judge who confirmed it or, if at trial only with leave of the Trial Chamber." As no conditions are specified for the withdrawal of an indictment as for example in the case of ill health of the accused, it can be assumed that this can only be done if the grounds for indictment disappear. This implies that there was no longer any suspicion, let alone evidence, that war crimes had been committed by General Djukić. Thus the withdrawal of the indictment as proposed by he Prosecutor, meant that it should never have been made. To indict again for the same offenses could not be done as a result of Djukić's improvement of health since conditional withdrawal of an indictment does not exist. He could only be indicted again on the basis of new, collected evidence.

Confronted by this state of affairs, the Trial Chamber tried to find a solution which would, at least temporarily, save the face of the Tribunal and its Prosecutor. Citing Rule 65 on provisional release, it decided to free Djukić from detention due to his poor state of health and the lack of proper medical care in the prison, leaving the indictment in force. However, this was a breach of the Rules of Procedure and Evidence that were passed by the Tribunal itself. Paragraph (B) of Rule 65 states that a detained person can be temporarily released "only in exceptional circumstances, after hearing the representatives of the host country," i.e. Holland, and possibly of the Yugoslav Federal Republic where Djukić traveled to on his release. In a feverish rush to find a way out of this worrying and humiliating position, the Trial Chamber conveniently forgot this important stipulation, and gave no hearing to either Dutch or Yugoslav Government representatives. Thereby Djukić's case ended as it began — by flagrant and shameful breach of the rules that are laid down in civilized criminal procedures. There only remained for the Appeals Chamber to rule on the Prosecutor's appeal and the complaint lodged by the defense lawyers who persistently demanded that the case be closed with a meritorious, and not procedural, verdict — meaning that Djordje Djukić be freed on lack of evidence which would preserve his reputation. Despite their professional and moral defeat, the Prosecutor and judges at The Hague at least had the satisfaction of knowing that they had shortened the life[4] of General Djordje Djukić by speeding up his death — like the riders of the Apocalypse. Djukić's death came very fast. Already on 18 May 1996, General Djordje Djukić silently passed away.

If at first glance this looked like clumsy and naive sophistry, in essence and by its consequences it was diabolical subterfuge. By changing the status of the prisoners from suspects to witnesses, the Prosecutor practically "offered" General Djukić and Colonel Krsmanović the opportunity to testify against other people in return for their own release from the charges and trial. Clearly, this was a form of blackmail and extortion. The Prosecutor must have known that such "testimony" is of doubtful credibility since it is hard to believe someone who would implicate someone else in order to be absolved. What is worse is that the blackmail was substantiated by a dangerous threat: either you "sing" here in The Hague or we'll hand you back to your torturers in Muslim Sarajevo. That this was blackmail and threat was clear to the president of the Trial Chamber, Claude Jorda, who almost incredulously asked General Djukić and his lawyer — Milan Vujin and Toma Fila — a number of times whether they were aware that if

Djukić did not "voluntarily" testify at The Hague he would be returned to Muslim Sarajevo where his only hope was the death sentence for alleged participation in genocide[5] to say nothing of abuse and torture in prison, something the Muslim police are accustomed and partial to.

In face of the firm refusal of General Djordje Djukić and Colonel Aleksa Krsmanović to "cooperate" with the Prosecutor, at the beginning of May 1996 Richard Goldstone pulled another diabolical move: he decided to separate the fates of the two Hague prisoners by indicting General Djukić and returning Colonel Krsmanović to the mercy of the Muslim police and Sarajevo judiciary. This separation was difficult because both were rear officers — Djukić was assistant Chief of Staff of Logistics of the Army of the Republika Srpska, and Krsmanović deputy commander of the Sarajevo-Romanija rear corps. If General Djukic was charged with taking part in the bombing and destruction of Sarajevo because he supplied with food and ammunition the Sarajevo-Romanija corps that had surrounded Muslim Sarajevo, why should Colonel Krsmanović, who sent the supplies he received from Djukić to the artillery batteries on the heights around Sarajevo, not answer for the same crime? However, what was impossible from the point of view of legal logic and principles, was permissible and possible from a practical point of view, and this is the only thing that seemed to govern Richard Goldstone.

And what was this practical purpose? When the Prosecutor offered Djukić and Krsmanović the opportunity to "cooperate" by implicating their seniors,[5] their refusal would have had to be so severely punished that in the future any other person forcefully brought to "testify" at The Hague would have had in mind their example and been aware there was no choice but to cooperate. This is why Krsmanović was immediately returned to Sarajevo, even though the Prosecutor and judges knew very well the danger their untried witness, against whom they could bring absolutely no charges, no matter how great their desire to do so, would be exposed to. Richard Goldstone issued a bill of indictment against General Djordje Djukić with the intention of punishing him in a likewise manner for refusing to "cooperate." Thus he offered the Tribunal its first big opportunity to bring to trial a high ranking officer of the Serbian Army. Perhaps he hoped that this indictment along with the serious state of Djukić's health would force Djukić to give in and "sing." Goldstone was not at all worried by the cruel abuse of Djukić's serious state of health since all means are allowed in carrying out of international justice.[6]

Part II: The Mistreatment of Col. Aleksa Krsmanović

No less disgraceful was the performance of The Hague Tribunal in the case of Colonel Aleksa Krsmanović. When Richard Goldstone officially sought the extradition of this high ranking Serbian officer, he explicitly stated that evidence against him "had enough substance to initiate investigation."[7] On [Colonel] Krsmanović's transfer to The Hague on 14 February 1996, Goldstone once again stated that Krsmanović was "suspected of having committed serious violations of international humanitarian law during the conflict in former Yugoslavia."

Not even two weeks had passed before Richard Goldstone changed the status of Krsmanović from suspect to witness in the hope of persuading him to "testify" against his superiors. To this end, he used blackmail, informing Krsmanović that if he refused to "cooperate" he could be returned to the Muslim prison in Sarajevo. Sure of his own innocence, Krsmanović did not give in thereby forcing Richard Goldstone and the members of the Trial Chamber to face a difficult choice: to let him go free, thus admitting their own defeat, or to disregard their own rules in order to carry out their threat of handing Krsmanović over to Muslim Sarajevo. The fact that they held no evidence of his guilt, in spite of their tireless efforts to find some, required them to free Krsmanović unconditionally, thus confirming his innocence. This is set out by the well-known legal principle *non bis in idem* which does not allow the same act to be brought to trial twice. Article 10 of the International Tribunal Statute of 26 May 1993 clearly states that "no person shall be tried before a national court for acts constituting serious violations of international humanitarian law under the present Statute, for which he or she has already been tried by the International Tribunal." Since Krsmanović was brought to The Hague as a suspect as soon as criminal proceedings were begun by the International Tribunal, withdrawal of the charges meant that the case was closed. It also meant that Krsmanović could not be tried for the same crime by any national court, including the High Court of Muslim Sarajevo. In short, following Richard Goldstone's decision to withdraw the charges, Colonel Krsmanović should have been set free.

Instead of this, The Hague Tribunal broke the inviolable principle of *non bis in idem*, and returned Colonel Aleksa Krsmanović by leased aircraft to preventive detention in Muslim Sarajevo. Encouraged by this act on the part of The Hague Tribunal, Muslim judge Izet Baždarević immediately announced that investigation against Krsmanović would be continued in order to prove "whether the Colonel was guilty of crimes."[8] In answer to the objection that the proceedings had been carried out and finalized by The Hague Tribunal, judge Bazdarević confidently added: "We have our laws, and The Hague has its own."[9] The investigation against Colonel Krsmanović were even extended on the ground that he had participated in crimes against prisoners of war in the area of his birthplace, Sokolac.

Had the Tribunal acted in accordance with its own Rules of Procedure and Evidence (Rule 13), it would have had to immediately send a reasoned order to the authorities of the Muslim-Croat Federation and High Court in Sarajevo requesting the court to permanently discontinue its proceedings against Colonel Aleksa Krsmanović. Nevertheless, it remained silent. In this manner, it tacitly validated the lawlessness in Muslim Sarajevo. As a result, the case ended in the same disgraceful way it began. On 21 April 1996 Colonel Aleksa Krsmanović was exchanged as a prisoner of war for Muslim prisoners of war captured by the Army of the Republika Srpska. Thus it would seem that Colonel Krsmanović was kidnapped after the official end of the war as a civilian in order to serve as a hostage thereby forcing the release of several Muslim soldiers that were captured during the war, all under the guise of an exchange of prisoners of war. By breaking its own Rules, whether it wanted to or not, The Hague Tribunal participated in a war crime, i.e. in covering up the taking of hostages.

Part III: The Illegal Basis of the War Crimes Tribunal

If the start of the case of the Prosecutor vs. Djordje Djukić disgraced the International Criminal Tribunal at The Hague, a more serious examination of the manner in which the Tribunal was founded and its working Rules of Procedure and Evidence would also convince us that the failure was not in the least accidental.

Moreover, it could have been expected when the Security Council Resolution 808 of 22 February 1993 was issued. In spite of the fact that the Resolution expressed the intention to found an international tribunal for the prosecution of persons responsible for committing serious violations of international humanitarian law on the territory of the former Yugoslavia since 1991, the Security Council did not feel the need to provide a legal basis for its establishment.[10] The reason for this omission is simple: the existing legal system of the UN does not provide a legal basis for it, nor can there ever be one.

Half a century has passed since the founding of the UN, and its main political and executive body, the Security Council, has never assumed the right to found a tribunal since court jurisdiction rests on international treaties as a result of the absence of a universal legislative organ. This was clearly stated by the UN Secretary General in May 1993:

> The approach which in the normal course of events would be followed in establishing an international tribunal would be the conclusion of a treaty by which the member states would establish a tribunal and approve its statute. This treaty would be drawn up and adopted by an appropriate international body (e.g. the General Assembly or a specially convened conference), following which it would be opened for signing and ratification. Such an approach would have the advantage of allowing for a detailed examination and elaboration of all issues pertaining to the establishment of the international tribunal. It would also allow the states participating in the negotiation and conclusion of the treaty to fully exercise their sovereign will in particular whether they wish to become parties to the treaty or not. (UN Secretary General's Report no. S/25704 (section 18) of 3 May 1993)

The rule whereby court jurisdiction is based on international treaties has, until now, been strictly adhered to without exception. Then in Resolution 827 of 25 May 1993, the Security Council

gave itself the right to establish *ad hoc* a tribunal whose competence was limited in time (beginning on 1 January 1991) as well
as capacity (confined to the territory of the former Socialist
Federal Republic of Yugoslavia). Since no such tribunal had ever
been established before by the Security Council,[11] it would have
been appropriate to find some sort of legal basis in order to avoid
the inference that "might is right." A legal basis was "found" in a
very loose interpretation of a clause in Chapter VII of the UN
Charter whereby the Security Council can take measures to maintain or restore international peace and security following the requisite establishment of the existence of a threat to the peace,
breach of the peace or acts of aggression. In other words, the term
"tribunal," as the requisite institution, is taken to be a "measure."
No doubt the members of the Security Council, particularly the
permanent members, assumed that "might was right," but also
that certain terms can be instilled with certain meanings that they
never had before. Thus "measures" became synonymous with
"tribunal."

The Secretary General was given the thankless task of justifying the international criminal tribunal as an enforcement measure
of the Security Council which Chapter VII of the UN Charter
grants it [the right to initiate]. As he was unable to refer to any
valid legal basis for this authority, he reverted to the principle of
expediency. "This approach," said the Secretary General, "would
have the advantage of being expeditious and immediately effective as all states would be under a binding obligation to take
whatever action is required to carry out a decision taken as an
enforcement measure under Chapter VII."[12] Thus the principle of
political expediency took precedence over that of legality and
legal validity.

The Secretary General knew of course, that the Security Council
could not simply "create" a tribunal nor did it have the legislative
authority to allow it to "create" international criminal law. He let
this slip when he said that "in assigning to the International
Tribunal the task of prosecuting persons responsible for serious
violations of international humanitarian law, the Security Council
would not be creating or purporting to 'legislate' that law. Rather,
the International Tribunal would have the task of applying existing
international humanitarian law."[13] Unfortunately this is not true.

With Resolution 827 of 25 May, the Security Council implemented its nonexistent legislative powers. It suspended the application of the Geneva Convention of 12 August 1949 with additional Protocols, as well as the Convention on the Prevention and Punishment of the Crime of Genocide of 9 December 1948, whereby prosecution is entrusted to national courts. Thus, by awarding the International Tribunal primacy over the prosecution of crimes committed on the territory of the former SFR Yugoslavia, it annulled the competence of all national courts worldwide. One has to ask in the name of what principle could the Security Council suspend and then amend international treaties of a legislative nature.

Having assumed the right to legislate, the Security Council ventured to take another step: it delegated its nonexistent legislative competency to its creature — the International Criminal Tribunal at The Hague. Under Article 15 of the Statute of the International Tribunal, it authorized its judges to adopt rules of procedure and evidence for the conduct of the pre-trial phase of proceedings, trials and appeals, the admission of evidence, the protection of victims and witnesses and other appropriate matters. In this way the Security Council not only legislated, but also authorized the Tribunal to be its own legislator with regard to criminal procedural law.

With no hesitation, the International Tribunal accepted the authority to write its own laws, i.e. to issue Rules of Procedure and Evidence that were to be applied to the prosecution of subsequent cases. The Rules were adopted by February 1994, only to be amended six more times — in May and October of 1994, January and June 1995, January and April 199. In January 1995 alone, 41 of the total 125 rules were amended, and almost half of the original rules were further changed by other amendments. To make matters worse, the Tribunal adjusted the Rules according to which it would pass judgment, having in mind the practical problems that arose in the course of the implementation of the Rules on pending cases.

Unfortunately, this was in breach of its own Rule No. 6, paragraph (C) whereby amendments shall not operate to prejudice the rights of the accused in any pending case. In this way, certain amendments took on the character of *ex post facto* law. Of special interest is the manner in which the Tribunal amended its rules. Legislative bodies usually do this at public sessions, following long and exhaustive debates over every proposed article or subsequent amendment. The International Tribunal simplified this procedure. Its Rules are adopted at plenary sessions after the decision of seven judges, and according to Rule 6, paragraph (B) this can also be done otherwise, on condition the judges accept the amendment unanimously. One asks oneself what "other way" is there for an amendment to be adopted if not by debate at a plenary session. The answer is simple: the president or some Tribunal official poses an amendment to all the judges world-wide; on the same day they fax back their approval. This is the new way of creating laws by fax that could easily revolutionize the old-fashioned procedure as exercised by the British Parliament.

This was how the Tribunal at The Hague used the legislative competence that was first usurped by the Security Council and subsequently generously delegated to it. To make for even greater paradox, the Tribunal took another step: having become its own legislator, it then passed part of its legislative power over to the Prosecutor in order to allow him to draw up the rules he would work by. Hence Rule 37, paragraph (A) stipulates that "the Prosecutor shall perform all the functions provided by the Statute in accordance with the Rules and such Regulations, consistent with the Statute and the Rules, as may be framed by him."

Antonio Cassese, President of the International Tribunal, was well aware that never in the history of a civilized country had an individual court drawn up the rules by which it would pass judgment. This would be a dangerous breach of the principle of separation of powers between the legislature and judiciary which, according to Montesquieu, is an essential guarantee of freedom. Thus it could be said that the adoption of the Rules of the Tribunal in May 1995 represented an enterprise "for which there is no precedent at the international level."[14] Had he been less self-confident and egotistic in his unexpected role of being his own legislator, he would have had to ask himself very seriously if there could possibly be a valid reason for this unprecedented breach of a practice inviolable in any civilized country.

There are, of course, countries where judge-made law is applied, e.g. common law in England. However this law is not the fruit of a premeditated and momentary enterprise by a single court but the product of all the courts as a unified system and over a considerable period of time, lasting several centuries. This is why English judges firmly believe that they are judging according to a law that was created by others. They do not have the satisfaction that was granted Antonio Cassese of creating the general rules according to which they will judge.

If the International Tribunal is only partially responsible for its role as legislator with regard to the adoption of its own Rules due to the fact that this "advantage" was delegated to it by the Security Council, it is generally responsible for its further delegation to the Prosecutor. This is also an enterprise unprecedented in recent history. Had the International Tribunal appreciated the equality of both parties, it should have gone one step further and authorized the defense counsel to prescribe its own general regulations for the defense of its client. This would also have represented a significant and unexpected innovation to modern criminal procedural law.

The Prosecutor as Organ of the Tribunal and as Privileged Party

The next feature whereby the Security Council and the International Tribunal "enriched" legal theory and practice was the exceptional position that was bestowed on the Prosecutor. In a well structured legal system, e.g. common law, the prosecutor is only one of two equal parties in a court dispute, so that with regards to the status of both sides — the prosecutor and the accused — and the possibility of their reaching a settlement, a criminal dispute assumes some of the aspects of a litigation. Under these circumstances the procedure becomes truly contradictory in that the two sides contest each other on a completely equal basis, whereas the court as a third, independent and unbiased party, resolves the litigation and passes judgment.

The Security Council and the International Tribunal discarded this concept of criminal litigation and the total equality of each party in order to award the Prosecutor a privileged position by making him a part of the court. In Article 11 of the Statute of the International Tribunal, it is explicitly stated that the Prosecutor is an organ of the Tribunal. This is followed by a series of regulations that confirm this exceptional and obviously privileged status of the Prosecutor. Rule 33 stipulates that the registrar of the Tribunal serves not only the chambers and plenum of the Tribunal but every judge and the Prosecutor, meaning that the registrar is common to them all. Under Rule 29, the Prosecutor is given the right to summon and question suspects, victims and witnesses, record their statements, collect evidence and conduct on-site investigations. Again, in a well organized judiciary system, this is done by the police up until an inquiry is instigated, whereupon it is taken over by the investigating judge. This is the only way to ensure the contradiction of procedure and the equality of both parties — the Prosecutor and accused.

However, the creators of the Statute and Rules of the International Tribunal made an unforgivable mistake. With one stroke they made the Prosecutor part of the Tribunal as well as a party before justice. Rule 2 names the prosecutor and accused as the parties, but then by virtue of a series of other regulations, their equality in the court proceedings comes under serious doubt. Thus, for instance, the Prosecutor, as a litigation party, may propose amendments to the Rules (Rule 6), while the accused and his defense counsel may not. Also, the Trial Chamber (Rule 46) may, after a warning, refuse audience to counsel if, in its opinion, his conduct is offensive, abusive or otherwise obstructive to the proper conduct of the proceedings. It occurred to none of the makers of these Rules to allow for the possible removal of the Prosecutor in the case of his behavior being offensive and abusive to the accused, his defense counsel or indeed the judges themselves. According to Rule 66 paragraph (C) the Prosecutor may, with the approval of the Trial Chamber, refuse the defense access to books, documents, photographs and tangible objects in his custody if this is considered to be contrary to public interest or affect the security interests of any state. The Trial Chamber debates this request *in camera* (in the absence of either party or the public) and the Prosecutor is obliged to give his reasons why this evidence (books, documents, photographs and tangible objects) should be confidential only to the Trial Chamber, meaning that the defense counsel does not have to be present.

The creators of this special position of the Prosecutor, who is at the same time part of the court and one of the two contesting parties, probably consider themselves to be very innovative. If they were better acquainted with the history of the Ottoman Empire they would remember that this position was held by Turkish Cadis (civil judges). That is why we [i.e., Serbs, who were ruled by the Ottoman Empire] have the saying: "the Cadi prosecutes you, the Cadi sentences you."

The Secrecy of the Indictment and the Unauthorized Collection of Evidence

This exceptional and in many ways unacceptable position of the Prosecutor is just one of the "innovations" by which the makers of the Statute and Rules of the International Tribunal "enriched" criminal procedural law. Another was the possibility of keeping secret the indictment trial and testimonies under conditions that spawn arbitrariness and considerable departures from the usual standards of modern procedural law. According to Rule 53 paragraph (B) the judges or the Trial Chamber can, after consulting the Prosecutor, prohibit the "disclosure of an indictment, or part thereof, or of all or any part of any particular document or information" if it is necessary "to protect confidential information obtained by the Prosecutor or is otherwise in the interests of justice." The Rule makers, however, did not deem it necessary to further define "confidential information" or "interests of justice," thereby leaving their interpretation open to the will or arbitrariness of the Prosecutor, judges and Trial Chamber.

Apart from facts, documents and information that can be concealed from the general public, there is information that can be denied the defense. This is information whose disclosure, for any reason "may be contrary to public interests or affect the security interests of any state" (Rule 66 paragraph (C)). This can be assumed to concern information collected by the CIA, and that is why such information should be kept secret in order to hide its source, and especially the manner in which it was collected. This involves unauthorized bugging and the recording of telephone conversations, fax messages, wireless messages, filming by satellites and pilotless aircraft unauthorized to overfly the war zones in the former Yugoslavia, as well as data and information collected by secret agents disguised as humanitarian workers or employees of the UN, Red Cross and other governmental and non-governmental organizations.

There is nothing unusual in the illegal collection of information by the US, British or Russian secret services. The trouble lies in the penchant of the Prosecutor and Hague Tribunal not only to use illegally obtained information, but also by denying the public knowledge of the indictment and trial to conceal the source of the information on which the indictment, evidence and subsequent verdict rest. With the excuse of protecting public interest and/or the security interests of a state, they are no doubt capable of going so far as to refuse the defense counsel the right to study the evidence, data, documents, photographs and tangible objects on whose existence an indictment rests. Were a prosecutor in the US to try to use unauthorized recorded telephone calls against an accused, this would be immediately rejected by the court. Unlike this civilized practice, everything was permitted to The Hague Tribunal, including the use of illegally obtained intelligence data and the concealment of its source.

Part IV: Learning from the Inquisition – Masked Witnesses

When, in the medieval age, the Inquisition wanted to protect an important witness who was ready to testify that he/she had seen a suspect communicating with the devil, the witness was allowed to appear in court with a mask, or hood, over the face. This was how the court heard the "truth," and the witness was protected from the evil eye of the witch who might take revenge after being burned at the stake.

In its fervent desire to protect the victims and witnesses of war crimes in the former Yugoslavia from the [Serbian] devil, the makers of the Rules of Procedure and Evidence similarly undertook to disguise the identity of these victims and witnesses.

Thus, according to Rule 69 "in exceptional circumstances, the Prosecutor may apply to a Trial Chamber to order the non-disclosure of the identity of a victim or witness who may be in danger or at risk until such a person is brought under the protection of the Tribunal. "This type of temporary concealment of a victim's or witnesses' identity can be understood, especially as paragraph (C) of this Rule stipulates that "the identity of the victim or witness shall be disclosed in sufficient time prior to the trial to allow adequate time for preparation of the defense."

What should not have been allowed under any circumstances was the permanent concealment of the identity of victims or witnesses, neither the allowing [*sic*] of a witness to refuse to answer a question on "grounds of confidentiality." This is foreseen in Rule 70 paragraphs (B), (C) and (D). In as much as the Prosecutor obtains information given to him on condition it remains confidential, he can not disclose its source without the agreement of the person or entity (15) who supplied it. This would not be so unusual if such information were not used as evidence at the trial. But the Prosecutor, with the consent of the person or representative of an entity, may decide to use documents and other material obtained in this way as evidence at the trial. In this case — and this is indeed something very new — "the Trial Chamber may not order either party to produce additional evidence received from the person or entity providing the initial information, nor may the Trial Chamber, for the purpose of obtaining such additional evidence itself summon that person or a representative of that entity as a witness or order their attendance." Still, the Prosecutor may call as a witness a person or entity that has offered confidential information, but the Trial Chamber may not compel the witness to answer any question the witness declines to answer on the grounds of confidentiality.

One can ask what kind of witness gives the Prosecutor confidential information and then refuses to answer further questions as to how such information was obtained when the Trial Chamber has no right to insist. As a rule, they are undercover agents who have been operating illegally in foreign countries in order to collect information that can not be obtained by regular means. They are also governmental representatives who have provided The Hague Tribunal with confidential information on condition that it conceal the source of the information as well as the manner in which it was obtained. The only remaining question is whether such "evidence" can be accepted as valid or such clandestine "witnesses" believed at all.

Another innovation that was introduced by the makers of the Rules was testimony without the obligation to appear at the trial. According to Rule 71, at the request of either party, the Trial Chamber "may, in exceptional circumstances and in the interest of justice, order a deposition be taken for use at trial and appoint for that purpose, a Presiding Officer." Naturally, it sometimes happens that an important witness, for health reasons, is unable to leave his home or hospital to attend a trial. But in such cases a hearing, under the presidency of the judge, is held in the witness' room where the witness answers the questions of the prosecution and defense. Allowing a court officer to take a deposition on his own whenever the Trial Chamber considers it to be "in the interest of justice," increases the possibility of abuse and prevents the confrontation of witnesses testifying differently about the same subject.

The greatest "innovations" introduced by the Rules was the permanent concealment of the identity of witnesses, victims or anyone related to or associated with them. Under the guise of preserving privacy and protecting a witness or victim, according to Rule 75 a judge or trial chamber can, at a session *in camera* [i.e., a closed session], take:

> measures to prevent disclosure to the public or the media of the identity or whereabouts of a victim or a witness, or of persons related to or associated with him by such means as:
>
> a) expunging names and identifying information from the Chamber's public record;
>
> b) non-disclosure to the public of any records identifying the victim;
>
> c) giving the testimony through image — or voice-altering devices or closed circuit television and
>
> d) assignment of a pseudonym.

Even this was not enough for the makers of these Rules and so they added the possibility of closed sessions and appropriate measures to facilitate the testimony of vulnerable victims and witnesses, such as one-way closed circuit television.[*]

---

[*] Consider the case of "Witness L" who testified against Dušan Tadić, the first Serb put on trial for war crimes at the ICTY. Tadic's defense attorney discovered that Witness L was Dragan Opačić (also spelled "Opachich"), a Serb soldier captured by the Muslim army. Opačić had been beaten by the Muslim secret police and forced to testify falsely against Tadić. Opachich was remanded to Bosnia. Nebojsa Malic referred to him as "The living proof of ICTY's corruption and duplicity, Opačić is Bosnia's Man in the Iron Mask. His only crime is knowing too much about his persecutors." ("Wheels of Injustice," 11/14/00, antiwar.com.) [Editor's note.]

Judicature without Sovereignty

There is no doubt whatsoever that the measures for the protection of a witness which the Holy Inquisition was capable of offering were a child's game compared to those provided by the Ruler of The Hague Tribunal. The Inquisition was only able to offer a frightened witness the possibility to enter the court by a side door under cover of night and with a hood over the head. Possibly, and very probably, the Inquisition would have taken the same measures as The Hague Tribunal Rules had it been able to use the technology at the disposal of The Hague judges today.

So as to understand more easily the "singularity" and also the exceptional possibilities of violation of the aforementioned measures for protecting a victim or witness, we will present a hypothetical example. Let us suppose that in an American city with disturbed and very strained inter-racial relations the sexual assault of a member of one race group by a member of another takes place. Terrified by the possible revenge of the relations and neighbors of the attacker, the victim asks the court to be allowed to testify under a pseudonym using image- and voice- altering devices. Would the American court allow this? Certainly not. And one of the reasons would be that such "testimony" would prevent a fair trial.

After such a convincing example, it is necessary to ask the following question. Why can American courts refuse this type of testimony and The Hague Tribunal accepts it when both are concerned with the protection of a victim or witness from possible reprisal by the accused, his relatives or friends? The answer is surprising: the American court firmly believes that the American judicature, including the police, is capable of offering such protection. And as a rule it is, except in the rare cases of organized crime. The Hague Tribunal is well aware that it is not up to this and justifiably assumes that the so-called international community, as embodied by the Security Council, has no intention whatsoever of protecting any victim or witness from the Balkan cauldron. So, if no one is ready to protect the victims or witnesses, then at least their identity can be hidden.

Had they taken one more step in forming this judgment, the Hague judges would have had to ask themselves whether, under such conditions, they should have taken on the job of judging at all if in order to protect victims and witnesses they had to use measures that were implemented by the Holy Inquisition. Had they any idea of the concept of sovereignty, they would have asked the Security Council how it thought they could take to court anyone if they were unable to provide the conditions necessary for the execution of judicature. When in his famous work "Leviathan" Thomas Hobbes demonstrated the essential traits of sovereignty, he included

> the Right of Judicature, that is to say, of hearing and deciding all Controversies which may arise concerning Law, either Civil or Natural or concerning Fact.[16]

In the execution of judicature, it is most important that sovereignty provides general and complete protection of all subjects from injustice by others. Because otherwise

> to every man remainth, from the natural and necessary appetite of his own conservation, the right of protecting himself by his private strength, which is the condition of War, and contrary to the end for which every Common-wealth is instituted.[17]

In other words, he who would judge and is able to do so, is sovereign; and as sovereign is bound to offer all subjects staunch protection from violence and the injustice of others. Who is unable of offering the second should not stand in judgment because he is not sovereign. The members of the Security Council, particularly the permanent members, wanted the first — to judge — without being capable of providing the second — reliable protection. This resulted in the concealment of the victims' and witnesses' identities and other measures as a clumsy attempt to achieve what must be provided by a well instituted and effective sovereign power.

Due to these important failings on the part of the Security Council and The Hague Tribunal, a whole series of other unusual regulations to the ridicule and shame of this Tribunal and its founders were created. Particularly characteristic is Rule 99 which allows the arrest of a suspect who has been acquitted. Truly a contradiction! However, this contradiction came about for practical reasons. When the jury of an American court of first instance brings a verdict of not guilty the accused leaves the court room a free man, able to go where he will. The prosecution can, of course, appeal against the first instance verdict but it can not demand that an acquitted person stay in detention until a second instance verdict is given. Sometimes the second instance court revokes the first instance verdict and demands a retrial. Since the suspect is free it may happen that he will not answer a summons by the first instance court. This, however, does not cause much worry as it is assumed that the police, as an organ of sovereignty, must be capable of carrying out every court order and bringing the person in question to trial.

The judges of The Hague Tribunal know very well, although they are unable to admit this publicly, that their sovereignty applies only to the court room in which they judge and the prison where witnesses, suspects and the accused are held. This forced them to make these contradictory rules. In paragraph (A) of Rule 99, they stipulate that "in case of acquittal the accused shall be released immediately." Then in paragraph (B) they recant this rule by allowing the Trial Chamber, at the mere hint of the Prosecutor submitting an appeal to "issue a warrant for the arrest of the accused to take effect immediately." Thanks to this sophistry, the accused can be freed and arrested at one stroke. Had The Hague judges the ability to think logically, they would have otherwise formulated the rule applied here: the Prosecutor shall decide on the freeing or detaining of a person acquitted by a first instance Trial Chamber. Truly in the spirit of the aforesaid Ottoman proverb: "The Cadi prosecutes, and the Cadi sentences."

To those well acquainted with constitutional and criminal law the rule that allows for a witness to testify against himself is a real surprise. Modern criminal law explicitly forbids this and a witness can refuse to answer incriminating questions. For a long time this important legal guarantee has been represented by the Fifth Amendment of the US Constitution of 1787 whereby "no person ... shall be compelled in any criminal case to be a witness against himself."

The authors of The Hague Tribunal Rules did not pay much attention to this great example and wrote Rule 90 paragraph (E) which allows for forced self-incrimination:

> A witness may object to making any statement which might tend to incriminate him. The Chamber may, however, compel the witness to answer the question. Testimony compelled in this way shall not be

used as evidence in a subsequent prosecution against the witness for any offense other than perjury.

It is worthwhile asking why the rule makers allowed for the forced self-incrimination of a witness if such evidence would not be used against him. They were probably presuming that war crimes are most often carried out by groups of people who, if they are forced to do so, will implicate each other. Supposing The Hague Tribunal had the opportunity of imprisoning two persons suspected of committing the same war crime without either knowing the fate of the other. One could be forced to testify against the other with the assurance that his testimony would not be used against him, and vice versa. In this way the Prosecutor can obtain evidence against them both without there formally having been any self-incrimination. To our great surprise, the rule makers were very perfidious in this matter, with no concern for the fact that their resourcefulness and ingeniousness was in direct contradiction to the principle of modern criminal law that self-incriminating [statements] cannot be exacted.

Finally, the above-mentioned rules contain a series of undefined concepts which allow for whimsicality and caprice. A characteristic example is given by Rule 79 which permits the exclusion of the media and public from court proceedings or part of the proceedings for the following reasons:

1) public order or morality;

2) safety, security or non-disclosure of the identity of a victim or witness, or

3) the protection of the interests of justice.

In a well founded legal system only public order and morality are considered to be valid reasons for the partial or complete exclusion of the public from court proceedings, and this only under strictly defined circumstances. The secrecy of court proceedings through concealment of the identity of a victim or witness is inadmissible, as already shown, while the "interests of justice" as a reason for the exclusion of the public, is yet another innovation whereby The Hague Tribunal "enriched" legal theory and practice. Justice is the supreme legal value and since law and judicature exist for the realization of justice, the provision of "interests of justice" as one of the reasons for the exclusion of the public was done in order to create a blanket discretionary norm which would allow the Trial Chamber to do what it wanted under the umbrella of expediency. The term was also introduced as an excuse for the taking of depositions for later use at a trial (Rule 71 paragraph A) and acceptance of evidence of a consistent pattern of conduct relevant to serious violations of international humanitarian law (Rule 93 paragraph A).

Finally, Prosecutor Richard Goldstone did not want to miss the chance of possibly using or abusing the very elastic norms containing the loose term "interests of justice." This is why he included in the regulations regarding his own power (being his own legislator), the stipulation that in certain circumstances he could grant any concessions to persons who participated in alleged offenses in order to secure their evidence in the prosecution of others (for example, by refraining from prosecuting an accomplice in return for the testimony of the accomplice against another offender), and that this "may be appropriate in the interests of justice."[18] He hereby made it known that he would be acting on his own will and not in his official capacity, and that certain executors of alleged crimes could be acquitted in return for cooperation, i.e. if they were willing to blame their accomplices. This kind of trade-off was what he called justice.

"Justice not Seen to Be Done"

Justice is taken to infer a certain type of equality, primarily an elementary equality before the law. It would appear that the members of the Security Council knew this when they introduced the following regulation into the Statute of the International Tribunal:

> All persons shall be equal before the International Tribunal. (Article 21, paragraph l)

This kind of equality is taken to mean that all detained persons at The Hague have exactly the same conditions of detention and that no exceptions will be made. However, The Hague Tribunal judges believed that justice was what they thought it to be, and so they introduced into their rules a regulation allowing for important differences in the conditions of detention. According to Rule 64

> the President of the Tribunal may, on the application of a party, request modification of the conditions of detention of an accused.

This is as if a Mafia boss in the US were to request of the judge responsible for trying his case that he be allowed to await trial in his own villa from where he had previously carried out his "business" on condition he pay from his own pocket a prison guard to prevent him from absconding.

However paradoxical this example may seem, this is what happened at The Hague. While the terminally ill Serb General Djordje Djukić was interned in a prison cell without adequate medical care, the Croat General Tihomir Blaskić, through his powerful patrons, made a deal with the Tribunal President that he await trial in a luxurious villa surrounded by guards paid by his "friends," instead of in prison. According to Antonio Cassese this was done in the interests of justice — the kind of "justice" whereby it is easy "to be a cardinal if your father is the pope."

There is an English saying: "Justice has not only to be done, but to be seen to be done." What could be seen at The Hague was not justice but caprice and injustice.

---

1   *Naša Borba*, 9 February 1996, according to FoNet report of 8 February 1996.

2   *Naša Borba*, 8 February 1996, according to a report by Mirko Klarin, correspondent in Brussels.

3   *Naša Borba*, 28 February 1996, according to a report by Mirko Klarin, correspondent in Brussels

4   *Naša Borba*, 1 March 1996 according to a report by Mirko Klarin, correspondent in Brussels.

5   In a conversation with Tribunal President Antonio Cassese, one of the attorneys asked if President Radovan Karadžić and General Ratko Mladić were those who they had in mind. Cassese answered that they needed to go much higher as if he were sure who was above Karadžić and Mladić

6   "Doctor Slobodan Ivković, who looked after Djordje Djukić during his last days, said that 'inadequate treatment and therapy during his time in prison and hospital brought on a sudden deterioration in the General's health' and added that General Djukić received salted, greasy food which 'third and fourth year medical students know that patients operated on for cancer of pancreas must not eat.' *Naša Borba*, 9 February 1996.

7   *Naša Borba*, 9 February 1996.

8   *Naša Borba*, 5 April 1996, according to a Beta/AFP report

9   *Ibid.*

10 This was noted by the UN Secretary General in his report S/25704 (section 18) of 3 May 1993.

11 The Statute of the International Court of Justice at The Hague is incorporated into the UN Charter and accepted as such by the member states

12 Report of the Secretary General S/25704 (see 23) of 3 May 1993

     Ibid, sec 29

14 Preface to a book publishing all the more important document of the International Criminal Tribunal at The Hague.

15 Being a state, one of its institutions or some organization.

16 Thomas Hobbes, "Leviathan," edited by C.B. Macpherson, Harmondsworth. Penguin Books 1982, p. 234

17 *Ibid*.

18 Regulation No. 1 of 1994, as amended 17 May 1995.

THE HAGUE TRIBUNAL: WHAT IT IS AND WHAT IT WANTS

A Review of the Basic Facts Regarding the Creation and Initial Operations of the International Criminal Tribunal for the Former Yugoslavia

Commentary by Mitar Kokolj, Professor of International Criminal Law and former President of the University of Mostar

The sanctions [imposed on Yugoslavia] and the court [The International Criminal Tribunal for the Former Yugoslavia] are two criminal tactics devised by the creators of the so-called New World Order, along with other criminal means, which include taking advantage of and abusing people who are the real victims in this war in order to subject them to experiments in social engineering and to act as executor of [all significant] actions that pertain to their existence.

The sanctions have in large part achieved this, and will continue to realize their inhuman, illegal and immoral goals, but even if these sanctions are formally suspended against the Serbian people, another criminal tactic is ready to be set in motion, the temporary (*ad hoc*) court created by the UN Security Council. The Security Council, as an executive organ of the UN authorized to protect international peace and security, whose decisions cannot be appealed, was unauthorized to assume the prerogatives of the UN General Assembly and assume the guise of an inaugural, legislative and controlling organ. The Great Powers, which issue directives to the court, have given it their blessing. According to the UN Charter and other international acts, the Security Council was not assigned the function of establishing an international temporary (*ad hoc*) court, which was established as an ancillary organ to the Security Council by reference to Article 29 of the UN Charter. The destruction of the century-old idea of the creation of a permanent international criminal court occurred in this fashion.

A chronology of the activities conducted by or in conjunction with the League of Nations up to WWII, and the UN after WWII, makes no mention of preparations to establish an *ad hoc* international criminal court in order to prosecute one government or one people.

The Nuremberg and Tokyo *ad hoc* courts were established in order to prosecute the principal war criminals of WWII for crimes without regard to geographic limitations. These precedents were created by acts of the victorious powers outside the already established Organization of the United Nations; however,[1] the actions and judgments of the Nuremberg Court were subsequently confirmed as international law.

In those courts, the victors tried the defeated, whose crimes were evident, but such legal methods have left a regrettable mark whose results can be seen today in the new *ad hoc* courts established for the former Yugoslavia and Rwanda on newly cited precedents that disregard legal criteria.

At that time, the Nuremberg and Tokyo courts polarized the victorious powers with inconsistencies with respect to the prosecution and punishment of the indicted. The case in point concerned a nation that made drastic sacrifices during WWII, but was then humiliated on legally inadmissible grounds.[2]

The basic shortcoming, with respect to international law, of the Nuremberg trials was the fact that the court did not exist at the time these crimes were committed, which meant breaking generally accepted precepts of jurisprudence.

The London Agreement of 1945 put this *ex post facto* law into effect, so that the Statutes of the International Military Court mention for the first time after WWII three categories of international crimes (crimes against peace, crimes against humanity and war crimes). According to Statute 10, subsequent punishment was foreseen for the perpetrators, so that a basic principle of jurisprudence was broken (*nullum crimen sine lege, nulla poena sine lege*, i.e., no crime without a law, no punishment without a law).

Custom and The IV Hague Convention of 1907 were cited as sources for the laws of the court in order to satisfy its legal basis. Citing custom could have meant taking into consideration Dutch law, which declined to extradite Kaiser Wilhelm II after WWI in order to put him on trial before an international court of law. With respect to The IV Hague Convention of 1907, it must be emphasized that the US opposed the prosecution and punishment of the Turks for the genocide of Armenians [1894-1896 and 1915], even though the allies had reached an agreement about it after WWI. The US argued against the prosecution of the Turks because the crimes against humanity, at the time of their occurrence, had not been foreseen by international law, even though The IV Hague Convention regarding the rights and laws of warfare was in force at the time, and on which basis the Nuremberg trials were conducted.

The founders of international law solemnly announced that this law was universal in nature, which meant that it could not be applied partially (i.e., to one part of a territory or to one people or to a part of one people). In the same manner, the law had to be applied only through an established procedure, which for the requirements of international law must be universal, i.e., one identical law for all. If that universal law were to be applied by a universal procedure, a universal court is certainly needed, which could try perpetrators of international crimes without regard to the time and place of their occurrence or by whom they were committed. In order to secure the foundations for such universality, the UN in 1968 issued a resolution stating that there is no statute of limitation for the prosecution and punishment of war criminals and the crime of genocide. That was done in answer to direct requests made by Germany to provide amnesty for crimes committed by members of its government during WWII.

If one takes into consideration the French Revolution, and documents such as the Magna Carta, the Habeas Corpus and the Declaration of the Rights of Man and of the Citizen, which emphasized equality before the law as their chief human and legal principle, then it is clear that the last decade at the UN (1990-1999), which was proclaimed as a decade of international rights, represented in fact the violation of these laws and the legalization of the use of overwhelming force in the domestic affairs of other countries.

That, however, meant the creation of a new set of laws, in direct contradiction to international acts that had already been adopted, as well as to legal acts that had been accepted over long years of work on various projects, plans and proposals put to the UN about the creation of an international judicial organ and the laws applicable to it.

Questions arose about the motives that influenced the so-called international community to abandon many of its adopted and declared principles. The creation of a permanent international court was also put into question.

The Convention against Terrorism of 1937, the Convention for Abolishing and Punishing Crimes of Apartheid of 1973 and the Convention on Preventing and Punishing Crimes of Genocide in 1948 made straightforward demands for the creation of a permanent international criminal court.

The UN General Assembly formed the International Legal Commission (ILC) and assigned it the task of preparing codices regarding crimes against peace and security (an international criminal code) and a draft of permanent statutes for a permanent international criminal court. The draft of statutes was completed in 1951, and revised in 1953, and work continued on it until 1992. That draft, which was considered to be a significant preparatory action for an international criminal court, envisioned a permanent court along with a determination of the precedents of the laws as foreseen by Article 38 of the International Court of Justice; furthermore, in addition to a determination of its precedents, including equal rights and providing *ad hoc* authority to a court, it would take into consideration the sovereignty of each individual state, even in decisions relating to extradition. This draft foresaw jurisdiction for international criminal acts perpetrated during peacetime, which was supplemented by universal principles.

The collapse of the Eastern Block and the threat this posed to the global balance of power influenced the emergence of ideas about abandoning existing international laws and creating a new set of international laws that in essence legalize the use of overwhelming force. The UN Security Council has thus become an exponent of those powers and behaves in a manner identical to the victors of WWII. The UN, namely the Security Council, has been transformed into an instrument for the execution of new international policies.

The universality of international law was transformed overnight into partial international law. It was a necessary experiment to force such a turn of events, and anticipated the foundation of an *ad hoc* Tribunal for the former Yugoslavia. That court was established by the UN Security Council, not by a resolution of the UN General Assembly, and not by any convention. A permanent international court could only have been established on a firm legal foundation and on regulations already adopted. The unsatisfactory manner in which the *ad hoc* Tribunal was created, its lack of responsibility to the UN and other concomitant inadequacies, can only lead to abuse.

The founders of the Tribunal wanted to present its creation as an act based on existing international law, which the UN General Secretary confirmed, asserting that only existing laws were applied (i.e., that no new laws were passed).[3]

Temporary committees held discussions and presented a series of comments and suggestions.

It was clear that a legal basis [for the creation of the Tribunal] did not exist, because if it had, it would have been applied and hearings would not have been necessary, nor new proposals or new resolutions. The long years of dormancy of such laws that were deemed to exist amounted to a special unintended amnesty of crimes and criminals.

The political will of the leaders of the New World Order supported the resolution of the Security Council to establish the Tribunal. It was obviously an urgent matter because they could not wait, nor did they want to go through the entire process according to existing international laws.

The UN General Secretary confirmed in a report to the Security Council that the foundation of a permanent court required much more time and that a danger of widely differing reactions from governments existed.[4]

The American creators of the draft of the *ad hoc* court for the former Yugoslavia have emphasized that a different approach to the creation of the court, which would have been based strictly on international agreements to provide it with a legal basis, was to their thinking a less effective and more lengthy procedure because it would have taken more time, prolonged the period of discussion and the signing of the agreement and its ratification.[5] Further actions and announcements indicated the great haste to establish the *ad hoc* Tribunal. Even Richard Goldstone, the Tribunal's chief prosecutor, announced that rushing the agreement was key; however, errors were made in such hastiness, and resulted in the release of a number of Serbs who had been indicted, and a cessation of legal actions against them. William Fenrick, a member of the UN Committee of Experts, Rapporteurs for On-Site Investigation in the territory of the former Yugoslavia, added that the most problematic aspect of this court was the obvious haste of some great powers to proclaim certain individuals as guilty at the expense of well-executed legal action.[6]

The draft statutes presented to the *ad hoc* Tribunal emphasized that the court and its trials had to be legal, independent and unbiased; however, it was clear from the start who the intended target of the *ad hoc* court was. The OSCE's detailed records, the first on the subject, clearly testify to this. Those records lead to one single conclusion as an absolute truth: that the Serbian side was the aggressor and invader, and that the crimes they committed were systematic, organized and planned in order to achieve the goal of a "Greater Serbia," accompanied by the maximum application of "ethnic cleansing." The activities of the other two sides were classified as sporadic, uncontrollable, incidental events or as acts committed in the heat of the moment during warfare, by which they sought to justify their actions. The Serbs were assigned the role of the criminal, and the other two sides the role of the victim. This position has not changed significantly since then.

Three OSCE investigators (Corell, Turk and Thun) visited Croatia and Bosnia-Herzegovina, but not Serbian regions. They did not visit the Federal Republic of Yugoslavia, nor did they hold any consultations with it. The investigators did not hesitate to emphasize in their report that the creation of a Tribunal was an act of political will.[7]

All the activity surrounding the creation of the international *ad hoc* court indicated the planning of the court's political character, which intended to try one side only in a three-way civil war. The war in Bosnia-Herzegovina was proclaimed to be an international affair despite the announcements of Mitterrand and Clinton that it was a civil war.

Political will turned a war in which three sides fought one another (but the Muslims fought even among themselves) into an act of aggression by one side against the other two. The united government army was transformed into an invader, and administrative boundaries into international borders.

The citizens went to sleep in one country, but woke up in another.

The act of international recognition, which legally means the confirmation of the fulfillment of conditions for such an act, was manipulated and altered for these states. Independent states were deliberately recognized in the territories of the former Yugoslavia, even though a civil war was raging there.

The message sent by the trials of war criminals in Nuremberg and Tokyo stressed that if international public opinion was seriously interested in the prosecution of perpetrators of international crimes, the prosecution had to be removed as far as possible from the sphere of political interests.[8]

Even the American Bar Association emphasized that the prosecution of war criminals in the former Yugoslavia could be successful only if the Tribunal were not used as a political instrument and if it were restricted to trying suspects for crimes against international peace.[9]

A report by the Committee for Foreign Affairs and Security of the European Parliament emphasized that the Tribunal had to be independent of political pressure, but contradicted itself by concluding that the decision to create the Tribunal was made in the short term as a result of growing political decisiveness.[10]

Those who suggested the creation of the Tribunal (namely Croatia and Bosnia-Herzegovina) also set its political goals. They pointed out that an international criminal tribunal had to be created because Belgrade was in fact creating trouble and that such a tribunal could act as a mechanism for exerting pressure on Serbia during the second phase of the Yugoslav crisis.[11]

The organization of the Tribunal's temporary operations and limited legal scope manifested its political character; for instance, crimes against peace were eliminated from the statutes of the International Criminal Tribunal, even though the International Military Tribunal in Nuremberg charged the indicted with such crimes. And the decades-long failure to establish a permanent International Criminal Court was proof of political meddling in matters of jurisprudence.

The instigators of all the events in the former Yugoslavia have carried out largely unnoticed media preparations at the expense of the Serbs for the formation of an international tribunal. Among the myriad examples of abusive public language used in the global media, one in particular stands out, which illustrates the others. When French journalist Jacques Merlino asked the director of global public relations from the public relations agency Ruder Finn, whether the firm had to bear the great responsibility for the lies and deceptions it had brought forth, the director replied that his firm was not paid to make moral judgments, but to do its job.[12]

One notices that it is "politically correct" in media campaigns to be on the side of the Bosnian Muslims and against the Serbs.[13] US journalist Peter Brock made a statistical study of 1,500 articles that appeared in various Western news agencies in 1992 and found that 40:1 took a point of view against the Serbs.[14]

It was not difficult to establish an *ad hoc* Tribunal after radical changes had taken place in global relations, and after international law had been destroyed to create a new set of international laws to suit a new world order, together with aggressive media propaganda.

The result of the vote taken in the Security Council, compared to earlier occasions, was unbelievable — 15:0 in favor of Resolution 827/1993 of May 25, 1993. An analysis of this resolution, the statutes adopted by the Tribunal, indicates the cannibalization of various paragraphs in connection with draft statutes for a permanent international criminal court that had already been adopted by the International Legal Commission; the adoption of established procedures covering authority, applicable law, legality, *non bis in idem*, the type of punishment meted out and its execution, pardons, extradition, etc., were cobbled together from various national legislatures.

Some drafts of these statutes, submitted by certain governments, upheld excessive measures that were forbidden by international law. Such suggestions could be found in the French draft of the Tribunal statutes, which proposed that the responsibility for a criminal organization be established before each trial, whereby collective responsibility, an outlawed notion, could then be applied to guilt, but they had in mind only the Srpska Demokratska Stranka (SDS, i.e. Karadžić's party) as the collective entity.[15]

Preparatory work was necessary to both establish The Hague Tribunal and commence comprehensive trials. The various so-called creators of the independent court expressed great interest in lists of alleged war criminals provided by Alija Izetbegović, Lawrence Eagleburger, Helsinki Watch, the BBC, various agencies and individuals, in which Serbian names principally appeared.

Compiling such lists and proclaiming to world public opinion the names of individual Serbs as alleged war criminals, which has no basis in reality, serves to highlight the abuses taking place. Aside from that, such behavior has decided effects on public opinion and international institutions. Taken together, it means that one single group is being prosecuted, the Serbian people: it is an attempt by Germans and Croatians to even the score from WWII and to cast collective guilt on the Serbs. Daniel Goldhagen speaks of the weight of this collective guilt for Germans and Croatians, and the mass desire of ordinary citizens to free themselves from it, in his book *Hitler's Willing Executioners*.

Resolution 780/1992 of the Security Council established a Committee of Experts, Rapporteurs for On-Site Investigation for war crimes that took place in the former Yugoslavia. The committee engaged De Paul University of Chicago for that purpose. It has been confirmed that private agencies and individuals, among them George Soros, financed the research conducted at the university.

The Serbian and Yugoslav documents delivered to the Committee of Experts from the UN have been deliberately concealed with the firm intention of misleading public opinion about the non-cooperation and the non-existence of Serbian and Yugoslav victims. The Committee of Experts delivered its unauthorized and tendentious final report to the Tribunal with the intention of prosecuting the Serbian side. The basic conclusion of the final report was that only Serbs committed and planned war crimes, which were systematic and organized, while the other two sides were exculpated because they committed crimes spontaneously.

Besides the assertion that all three sides committed various prohibited offenses, the report confirmed that only the Serbian side acted politically in order to create a greater ethnic state and that their actions were a goal, systematically planned and coordinated with local Serbian authorities and executed with the cooperation of higher authorities. The report pointed out that Muslim and Croat leaders expressed regret for such practices and that they sought to end them, emphasizing that such deeds were not part of their political agenda.

The position of the Serbian leadership on these crimes, no matter who may have committed them, was not taken into consideration. It is clear that the UN Committee of Experts received instructions to diminish the significance and pre-meditated nature of Muslim and Croatian crimes by describing them as spontaneous and sporadic in nature, while the crimes of the Serbs were described as the result of an organized plan.

Aside from the report by the OSCE, one other document was accepted by the Security Council as a reason for establishing the Tribunal. It was the EU Commission investigative report on the rape of Muslim women. The English historian Nora Beloff, a Yugoslavia expert based in London, witnessed the creation of this report and was critical of it. She wrote to the Tribunal prosecutor, Richard Goldstone, pointing out that the well-known French politician Simone Weil publicly distanced herself from the women's group, which had been sent from the EU to Zagreb solely in search of proof of the rape of Muslim women. Weil, whom Beloff knew and had interviewed on the subject, said that the procedure was so shamefully amateurish and unscientific that she had abandoned further participation in the group — but that did not prevent the EU from attaching her name to the report.

Weil said that the group had reached Zagreb without a program and without a concept, and that they opened their doors to anyone who wanted to talk. Their document in no way confirms the enormous estimation of alleged rapes, which fed the daily need for horror stories in the Western media.

When Beloff wrote a letter to Ann Warburton, the head of the group, asking why she did not look for any hard evidence that Serbian women had been raped as well, Warburton replied that it was not in the framework of her authority to do so. She had been sent to do research on Muslim victims, but a one-sided act, in Beloff's point of view, was untenable.[16]

Not only have the facts used for the formation of the Tribunal been subject to abuse and falsification, they have also grounded the Tribunal on a non-existent, untenable legal foundation. The

Tribunal was established by reference to a passage in Article 29 and Chapter VII of the UN Charter, which states that the Security Council is allowed to establish ancillary organs. Thus, the Tribunal is an ancillary organ.

In contrast to the civil International Court of Justice, which is designated in the UN Charter as its principal judicial organ, the Tribunal was designated as an ancillary organ by a resolution of the Security Council, which rendered decisions in favor of blockades, sanctions, demonization and bombardment. This court, as an ancillary organ, cannot hold a position different from that of the Security Council with respect to the trials it conducts.

The Security Council proceeded to cite Chapter VII of the UN Charter to confirm that the situation in the former Yugoslavia presented a danger to international peace and security, and that only the creation of an international court would be able to facilitate a return to peace. Representatives from a majority of the member states in the Security Council stated that they had voted for the resolution in the hope of achieving this goal.

Now the creators and representatives of this paralegal organ emphasize a specific argument: since the court has been created, it factually exists; and since its existence cannot be denied, one must cooperate with it; and, thus, the court must be acknowledged. Politically, the Tribunal is a *fait accompli*, but now the *fait accompli* is taken as the sole reason for its justification. In addition, it has been publicly pointed out that the experience acquired by this court will be the foundation for the formation of some imaginary permanent international court; the creators of this Tribunal are thereby confirming their intention of turning international law into an experiment. Besides, it is necessary to add further that the Tribunal's final goal may be to largely annihilate the Serbian people on both sides of the Drina, and to put the Tribunal's seal of approval on it. The realization of such ideas could be seen in the legal actions initiated by the Muslims of Bosnia-Herzegovina against the Serbian Republic of Yugoslavia (SRJ) before the International Court of Justice in The Hague in 1993.

The basis for the accusations [against the SFRY] was found in Article 9 of the Convention on the Prevention and Punishment of Genocide of 1948, which discussed the ability of such a court to hear claims of genocide by one state against another. Why doesn't an international court exist which can try states for criminal acts? Since the International Court of Justice chiefly hears civil cases, the problems that arose over genocide were supposed to be resolved first by the trial of individual Serbs before the Tribunal, which was established to try individuals. In this fashion, a connection between the two courts was established.

The ulterior motive of the accusations against the Socialist Federal Republic of Yugoslavia before the International Court of Justice was to hold it liable to pay reparations for all war damages that had occurred during the civil war in Bosnia-Herzegovina. To achieve this, political pressure was applied as well as threats of new sanctions for non-compliance.

As of this writing, Serbs comprise the largest number of defendants indicted by the Tribunal, which confirms all of the intentions thus far described. Permanent attention is paid to insuring that 90% of the total number of indictments is against Serbs; the basis for this is the resolution of the UN Commission on Human Rights, which itself was based on an unbelievable CIA report in which the agency confirmed that it had photographed Serbian participation in crimes in 90% of the instances.[17] Even though the CIA confirmed that it had used space satellites to photograph mass gravesites, investigators who searched for these sites on the ground were not able to find them.

The role of victim as well as that of plaintiff was reserved for the Muslims. The Muslim side actively worked with the creators of the *ad hoc* court, which can be seen from both its actions and its statements. In this fashion, the Sarajavan attorney Bekir Gavrankapetanović, president of the Government Commission for the Investigation of War Crimes in Bosnia-Herzegovina, confirmed in a report that during his meetings with the chief prosecutor of the Tribunal, Richard Goldstone, he was persuaded that none of Goldstone's political functions would be spared for the prosecution of war crimes that had taken place. Furthermore, Goldstone emphasized that, in his own estimation, the Tribunal was only going to indict Serbs and their leaders.[18]

Many stated that trials before the Tribunal would be a farce. Even the President of the Tribunal itself, Antonio Caseze, said as much. In order to rectify such appraisals, Justice Caseze began pointing out the unnoticed aggression that took place against the Serbian side.

The Tribunal farce continued after the prosecution of the innocent Serb Dušan Tadić. There was no evidence that he had committed the war crimes with which he had been charged. The
lengthy period of time that passed between his arrest and his trial
testified to the fact that the Tribunal did not succeed in providing
proof of his alleged guilt.[19]

The farce continued with the illegal arrests and deportations of
Serbian officers from Sarajevo to The Hague. Even though the
Tribunal adopted regulations that protect witnesses, individual
witnesses were nevertheless forcibly brought to The Hague. The
rules of procedure and evidence used by the Tribunal authorize
the prosecutor to change and substitute prosecution regulations at
will, which chief prosecutor Goldstone in fact does, and this
results in a situation where an indicted Croat can defend himself
while free even though all of the regulations call for preliminary
arrest of each indicted person.

Certain governments, like the US and Germany, confirmed that
they have changed their laws in order to cooperate with the
Tribunal, even going so far as to extradite suspects from their
own countries in order to goad others into cooperation with the
Tribunal. This is really a public-relations smokescreen, because
the regulations concerning extradition rule that only foreign
nationals may be delivered to the Tribunal.

To avoid any objections that might arise about the *ad hoc*
Tribunal having been created exclusively for the former
Yugoslavia, the same court with the same prosecutor was established for Rwanda in 1994, but with more charges, more statutes
and greater freedom in trial procedures and rules of evidence. A
new precedent was created which points to only one conclusion.
Crimes committed by the other side were thus amnestied. The
principle of universality and the lack of a statute of limitations for
international crimes were thwarted by the creation of courts
restricted to the former Yugoslavia and Rwanda. The Security
Council entered a situation in which it could not reply to questions about the criteria it had applied to establishing *ad hoc* international courts throughout the world.

It looks as though the New World Order ... has found the recipe
for solving the world's problems. For designated small countries,
it will create *ad hoc* courts that rely on precedents established one

after the other; then a collection of such *ad hoc* courts will unify their charges, unify their prosecution, and enjoy almost identical regulations, statutes and laws through the Security Council resolution regarding trial procedures and rules of evidence, and these courts will try to overturn the permanent International Criminal Court for smaller countries because of the wars [larger countries] provoke in them. In this fashion, an impression is being created that the formation of a permanent International Criminal Court, which, because of the way it is being established, will never be able to sue for abuses of international human rights, which larger countries perpetrate with their protégés.

Significant Events in B-H and the Confirmation of Individual Responsibility

An appraisal of the indictment against General Ratko Mladić necessitates calling to attention a few significant moments in the political life of the former republic.

From the beginning, the struggle in Bosnia-Herzegovina was characterized by manipulation, abuse, and the distortion of truth surrounding events that had taken place on the Muslim side, in conjunction with great and prejudicial aid given to it by various foreign elements. The creation of a Tribunal intended for the prosecution of Serbs, and the initiation of legal actions before the International Court of Justice in The Hague by the Muslim side against the Serbs, did not occur coincidentally.

A strong impression was created that the Muslims were victims and the Serbs were criminals as a result of the legal actions undertaken by the Muslim plaintiffs before the International Court of Justice in 1993 and 1994, as well as by the indictments against individual Serbs before the Tribunal. The plaintiffs avoided acknowledging the fact that the so-called international community recognized "Bosnia-Herzegovina as a sovereign country nearly overnight, or that those who were its "legal representatives" provided the foundation for such recognition.

This so-called legal authority [in B-H], in which Muslim and Croat representatives participated until the Serbs abandoned it, aided the civil war as it kept trying to defend all three ethnic groups on the territory of Bosnia-Herzegovina even after it had become a recognized state.

Muslim Bosnia-Herzegovina was responsible for all crimes that have taken place because, according to international law, even an armed struggle that provoked intervention from abroad could not justify a violation of the rules of warfare, the violation of human rights, and the participation in and commission of horrible crimes.

Eventually, the so-called international community admitted making a terrible mistake by recognizing a non-existent country. The act of international recognition for a state is fundamentally an acknowledgment that certain conditions have been met; it is not meant as a means to enable one warring faction or one people to found a state against the interests of other peoples living in the same territories. The fact that a Muslim state without Serbs was being planned was highlighted by the testimonies of numerous Serbian civilians who were arrested and mistreated in concentration camps and prisons, who were given a point-blank message to leave their homes, since all of Bosnia-Herzegovina was to become Muslim, ruled by Muslims. Clearly, the official Muslim government policy promised a Muslim government as well as possession of all property belonging to Serbs.

The Serbs did everything possible to avoid a conflict with the far larger Muslim-Croat coalition. The Serbian side took a significant step in that direction with an agreement, hailed as historic, signed by both the SDS and the MBO [the Muslim Bošnjak Party], calling for a peaceful resolution of problems between Serbs and Muslims.

The President of Bosnia-Herzegovina, Alija Izetbegović, rejected this agreement, and characterized it as traitorous. Adil Zulfikarpasić, the leader of the MBO, stated that he found the Serbian side to be understanding, but Izetbegović rejected the proposed agreement.

The Serbian side had many times sought to halt all military actions during the course of the civil war, and unilaterally ceased all military actions; the Serbian side even announced that the war was over as far as the Republika Srpska was concerned, and that all disputed questions should be resolved in a peaceful manner. The Serbs and the Muslims of Western Bosnia (specifically, Karadžić and Abdić) signed this agreement in Belgrade on October 20, 1993.

Alija Izetbegović essentially declared a war against the Serbs when he said that he would sacrifice peace for a sovereign, secessionist government; then, at a meeting in Tuzla, he emphasized that: "If the Croatians leave the SFRY, then we will too, but if we can't do that, then we will leave by taking actions that we can control."

Those were not empty words. Documents confirm the formation of a Muslim terrorist organization, the Patriotic League (*Patriotska Liga*, or PL) and its armed units, headquarters, shelters, hospitals, kitchens, etc., founded by the Muslim party, the SDA.

The PL was established before the civil war, and it was the result of many years of effort. Documents found in the possession of a general of the Muslim Army, a former JNA captain, revealed that the PL was designated to organize SDA [i.e., Izetbegović's party] chapters in southeastern Bosnia. Preliminary PL plans for the organization of a "defense of the sovereign republic of Bosnia-Herzegovina" were also found (document nos. 15 and 29 — Committee for the Gathering of Information about War Crimes and Genocide in SRJ, no. 590/94).

Even before the war, the PL conducted secret seminars. It organized eleven regional headquarters of which two (Priština and Novi Pazar) were in the territory of the Socialist Republic of Serbia. That was in accordance with the SDA position that Sandžak was a part of the Republic of Bosnia-Herzegovina, which Ejup Ganić, vice president of Bosnia-Herzegovina, presented.

The preparations for the foundation of a Muslim government were completed under the slogan, "a battle for sovereignty and government by its citizens." This can be clearly seen in documents concerning the planning of armed actions, regular army units, war aims, the defense of Bosnia-Herzegovina and the Muslim people, and public relations strategies for the Muslim world (document nos. 29, 35, 40 and 41).

The PL's plans encompassed missions for the seizure of territory and the removal of Muslim populations from [other] territories where they were a minority (document no. 34), which contradicts the accusation made against the Serbian side for "ethnic cleansing."

Witnesses arriving from Tuzla pointed out that anniversary celebrations commemorating the formation of the PL were held even before the war (document no. 257/94).

The fundamental characteristic of a civil war as a *bellum omnium contra omnes* was fully demonstrated in Bosnia-Herzegovina by the fact that the Muslims fought even among themselves. The fact that a civil war was being waged in Bosnia-Herzegovina was demonstrated by events taking place on the ground. First the Croats and the Muslims fought against the Serbs, then the Croats and the Muslims fought each other, and then Muslims fought Muslims. This situation absolutely fits the definition of a civil war, which is described as an armed struggle in a country between antagonistic social forces (class or ethnic group) that fight among themselves for the creation of fixed economic or political goals. A civil war is distinguished from war in general by the fact that, legally, it is waged within the borders of a state, although there is no historical example of a civil war engaging forces outside the borders of the country in which it was fought.[20]

The goal of the SDA and its armed formations was not "holding onto its own territories" but the creation of new ones. Taking notice of the dangers of Muslim and Croat secessionism in Bosnia-Herzegovina, the Serbs felt they undertook measures to which they had a right according to international laws. They voted in the referendum to remain with the SFRY on the legal basis of self-determination, and this, according to the compact of civil and political rights, belongs only to a people, and not to a state. The Muslims and the Croats held a referendum for the forced secession and formation of independent states, whose success, according to law, required two thirds (66.6%) of the vote. The organizers of the referendum announced a result of about 63% in favor of the decision, but after all, Bosnia-Herzegovina foresaw a majority vote greater than two-thirds.

The Tribunal's Indictment of General Ratko Mladić Relating to Incidents in and around Srebrenica during June 1995

Prosecutor Richard Goldstone, leveraging the powers granted to him and the laws governing trial procedure and evidence, combined 48 counts against Radovan Karadžić and Ratko Mladić into a single indictment. The charges against both these persons are in general the same, which means that the appraisal of a charge against one can be relevant to the other. Meanwhile, an analysis of the indictments exposes the thoughtlessness of the charges.

In indictment no. IT. 95-18-I of November 15, 1995, Radovan Karadžić is treated as the principal perpetrator; the Tribunal prosecutor established the charges based on the authority invested in Karadžić by the constitution of the Republika Srpska, but broadened this to include the right of self-defense and the right to govern the internal affairs of the Republika Srpska, of which Karadžić was the designated leader.

Ratko Mladić, the second person indicted, is treated as the senior head of the Army of the Republika Srpska, who discussed all-important questions of war and peace in the area of the former Bosnia-Herzegovina with representatives of the other two sides in the conflict. It is unclear at first sight why the leading senior military officer of only one side has been indicted regarding a three-sided conflict where crimes were committed by each side. In this fashion the prosecutor has selected participants in the civil war to prosecute, which amounts to manipulation. If numerous examples of hard evidence indicating that the Muslim and Croat armed forces committed terrible crimes against the Serbian population are not essential, then what criteria had the chief prosecutor of the Tribunal applied if he has considered such evidence to be without merit? In this sense, Goldstone may be granting amnesty, by default, to the two other parties in the conflict.

If the military leader of one side is indicted as a criminal with his army, but another is not, then the responsibility of the indicted person is broadened in a perfidious and unallowable manner to include all the events and all the victims during the entire civil war.

The indictment against Ratko Mladić appears to have been conceived first of all to define the events so that prosecution of the alleged crimes would fall within the jurisdiction of the Tribunal. Of the four categories of crimes addressed in the Tribunal statutes, Ratko Mladić is charged with three: violating the rules or customs of war, genocide, and crimes against humanity (Articles 3, 4, and 5). All the charges relate to alleged killings and each alleged crime is assigned to one of those categories.

The founders of the court conceived its actual authority as encompassing only those regulations of international law that are "beyond all doubt a part of established law," so that there would be no question as to whether or not individual countries would agree to the conventions. A committee on foreign affairs and security from the European Parliament took the same position. Such actions suggest that objections were considered in advance.

Regulations of the Tribunal Statutes Regarding the Alleged Responsibility of Ratko Mladić

Article 3 of the Tribunal statute authorizes the court to prosecute those who violate the laws or the customs of war as provided for by The IV Hague Convention of 1907. Article 4 of the statute adopts regulations II and III of the Convention on the Prevention and Punishment of Genocide of 1948. And Article 5 of the Tribunal statute lists the crimes that can be committed in either an armed international conflict or in a domestic one, as actions directed against the civilian population, but these were first provided for in the Constitution of the International Military Tribunal in Nuremberg and in Control Council Law No. 10, all *ex post facto* laws for offenses for which the Nuremberg Tribunal rendered judgments.

If these actions taken by the victorious powers later had to be confirmed by the UN in order to obtain legality and legitimacy, then the legitimacy of their citation of Article 5 of the statutes is brought into question.

If the founders of the Tribunal consider the statutes of the International Military Tribunal in Nuremberg to have become a precedent for international law, then how does one explain in fact that the founders of the Tribunal eliminated crimes against peace, which were one of the fundamental offenses [defined] in those statutes, but which do not appear in the statutes of The Hague Tribunal, which in turn means that no one can be held responsible for violating them. Of the 24 people who were indicted in Nuremberg, 16 were tried for war crimes and crimes against humanity, 12 for crimes against peace, and 8 were charged with conspiracy against peace.

The Hague Tribunal was created for the purpose of trying military and political leaders on the example set by the Nuremberg and Tokyo tribunals. In order to try the indicted, rules providing for individual responsibility have been adopted by the Tribunal statutes, but they have also been expanded by a rule which provides for objective and command responsibility, so, on this basis, anyone indicted by the Tribunal can be tried by it.

According to Article 7, paragraph 1 of the Tribunal statutes, which was adopted from the Nuremberg statutes, individuals who planned, incited, ordered or in some other fashion aided or participated in the planing, preparation or execution of crimes in connection with Articles 2 to 5 of the Tribunal statutes, are held responsible. It is certain that Ratko Mladić planned, prepared and executed military and humanitarian actions, but a soldier of such distinction would be unlikely to have committed the offenses with which he has been charged. In fact, he probably acted in a diametrically opposite manner. His many actions, statements and orders during the four-year war compel one to conclude that he behaved like a soldier who knew and respected the laws established by the Geneva Convention.

A rule was introduced at the suggestion of the Italian draft of the Tribunal statutes that, in fact, abandoned the principle of objective and presumed responsibility. The intent of this rule was to exclude any possibility that officials whom the Tribunal wanted to bring to trial could evade criminal responsibility, because the regulation was conceived in such a way that an indictment was at the same time a judgment.

Along with this regulation from Article 7, paragraph 3 of the statutes, the fact that some of the indictable actions, which were provided for in Articles 2 through 5 of the statutes, may have been carried out by subordinates does not free from responsibility those assumed to be guilty of crimes, if such person(s) knew or had a reason to know that a subordinate had the intention of committing such offenses or if such offenses had already been committed and the suspect did not succeed in undertaking such necessary and cognizant measures to prevent the aforesaid actions or punish the offenders thereof. Conceived in this fashion, the regulation is ideal for manipulation since it fixes responsibility on a leader for the thoughts and intentions of the incarcerated party.

It can be seen from the allegations that Ratko Mladić has not been indicted for planning and ordering crimes to be committed, but, in a sense, for being close to places where the crimes were allegedly committed. Criminal responsibility has been based on suppositions and not on the consciousness and will of the accused to commit the alleged crimes. According to this regulation, the indicted would be answerable to charges for all those acts committed by subordinates or which were imputed to them. Thus, it is impermissible to take into consideration the erroneous legal practices of such an institution, in which the criminal codes of western countries are treated for the most part as the basis for conclusive criminal responsibility, while the system of criminal justice in the former Yugoslavia is treated as being "easy going" on the punishment of criminals or as granting them immunity from prosecution.

One can hardly say that such an institution is concerned with true legal regulations, even though a similar regulation does exist in Article 86, paragraph 2 of the Amended Protocols I to the Geneva Convention of December 8, 1977, relating to international conflicts.

The legal qualifications for the indictment concerning alleged killings committed by Ratko Mladić are tied to Articles 3, 4 and 5 of the Tribunal statutes. What one notices first is that the indictment and its issuance by the officiating judge take into consideration the qualification from Article 3 regarding violations of the laws or the customs of war. In the purview of the Tribunal statutes, one can see that none of the points of Article 3 (a-d) has any bearing on killing. Thus, these points have no bearing on the situation, even as they are recounted in the allegedly factual description contained in the indictment.

Besides failures of various kinds, there appears to be crude manipulation of the statutes. In the same way, the remaining qualifications define indictable actions (Article 4/2, 5a, 56), while in the former alleged instance the qualifications were drawn from the entire Article 3, which means that in cases where such alleged acts took place, perpetrators assume the burden of all the alleged acts in that Article (Article 3 (a-d)).[21]

General Suppositions of the Indictment

The two regulations covering the criminal responsibility of individuals (i.e., Articles 7/1 and 7/3 of the statutes) are listed according to the general claims of the indictment. Along with these, even political appraisals of the situation in Bosnia-Herzegovina appear in the indictment, which contributes to an impermissibly arbitrary and judgmental picture.

The Tribunal prosecutor, as in all previous indictments handed down against Serbs, confirmed that the timeframe for the territory of Bosnia-Herzegovina and the former Yugoslavia covers the duration of the armed conflict and partial occupation.

From the following citation of violations, in accordance with Article 3 of the statutes, it appears that not one corresponds to factual confirmation.

Taking into consideration that the indictment was handed down against Serbian military and political leaders in Bosnia-Herzegovina, the judges ascribe to them crimes committed in the armed conflict and acts of limited occupation. An "occupation" would imply that there were no Serbs in Bosnia-Herzegovina, and rather that they came as aggressors and invaders to Bosnia-Herzegovina from Serbia and the Socialist Republic of Yugoslavia.

The Muslims of Bosnia-Herzegovina prepared these deceitful representations against Yugoslavia; in their charges they refer to the Serbs in Bosnia-Herzegovina as representatives, surrogates and agents. However, according to the census of 1991, the Serbs accounted for about 32% of the population in Bosnia-Herzegovina; likewise, the Serbs apparently possessed 61.4% of the land, while the Muslims possessed 27.3%.[22] David Owen emphasized in an interview that the Bosnian Serbs were the rural population even before the war and lived on 60% of the territory. The Bosnian Serbs are fighting for territory on which they have lived for centuries.[23] The French Minister of Foreign Affairs, Alain Juppé, stated "The Serbs have not come from anywhere; they are on their own land, and in significant numbers."[24]

The Tribunal prosecutor, as a general assumption, considers Ratko Mladić as though he intended to partially or completely destroy a people, ethnic and religious group, and tries to prove that the criminal act of genocide had been committed. Considering that Ratko Mladić defended the Serbian people from genocide in Croatia, and then in Bosnia-Herzegovina, how can commanding military operations against the armed forces of one side be treated as genocide, but not against the other? In that sense, genocide is fighting a war against Muslims, but not against Croats.

The commander of the Omarska camp, a Serb named Željko Meakić, was charged in one of the first indictments against Serbs for genocide, and the basis for this charge was the fact that he allegedly participated in a group that beat Muslim civilians, and that he personally kicked several of them.

Crimes against humanity are included as a general assumption in the indictment against Ratko Mladić, even though the facts speak of an armed struggle and the secession of one-third of the population, which was armed and which came from allegedly demilitarized "safe areas." By that account, the indictment does not concern a widespread, systematic and massive attack on the civilian population, but it does concern the abuse of allegedly demilitarized "safe areas."

Scene of the Alleged Crimes

The prosecutor for crimes committed in Srebrenica emphasized that the town is near the border with Serbia. Although that is true, the location could have been described differently. The location is defined in this fashion in order to establish that the armed forces from Serbia and the SRY allegedly participated in military actions around Srebrenica.

Considering that in 1992 Muslim criminals burned to the ground nearly all the Serbian villages around Bratunac, Srebrenica, Skelani and Milići, and killed large numbers of civilians, one must ask: Why didn't the regular SRY armed forces in the field take military action to defend the Serbian population? The indictment incorrectly asserts that Bosnian Serb forces occupied Bosnian Muslim villages in that region immediately after the beginning of the war and that the Muslim refugees fled to Goražde, Žepa, Tuzla and Srebrenica.

According to the 1991 census, Srebrenica had a Muslim majority, which I believe was a result of several acts of genocide committed against the Serbian population, especially in 1941. During WWI, genocide in the Srebrenica municipality cut the Serbian population in half, and acts of genocide continued during WWII with even greater ferocity.

The Muslims once again prepared to commit genocide against the Serbs throughout all of Bosnia-Herzegovina, but especially in Srebrenica. They ordered weapons and prepared terrorist cells. Patrols were organized around Serbian homes in Srebrenica and Bratunac. There is a great deal of evidence for such Muslim preparations, which includes military identification cards of paramilitary formations with dates of issue. This occurred before the war, as did the invitation to a night-time nationalist gathering of all Muslims in the neighboring town of Bratunac (a central geographic location for Muslims in the former Yugoslavia) in order to make final preparations for the creation of a Muslim state. Documents and supplementary materials indicating these motives were conscientiously gathered and included in the book *Hronika našeg groblja* (A Chronicle of Our Graveyard, Bina, Belgrade: 1994), by Milivoje Ivanišević.

Immediately after the beginning of the war, the Muslim side attacked and devastated nearly one hundred Serbian villages. People were killed, villages were put to the torch and Serbian refugees appeared. The Red Cross in Serbia registered 12,800 refugees from that area, or 45% of the total Serbian population. These attacks against Serbs had been planned much earlier and were carried out by a large number of armed units.[25]

The threat of death hung over the Serbs. They fled from Srebrenica on May 9, 1992, two days after receiving information about a massacre of Serbs on May 6, 1992 in the village of Blječeva.[26]

The allegation that Srebrenica had 7,000 inhabitants before the war and that this number grew to 60,000 is manipulated in the indictment against Ratko Mladić as well as in the charges filed against the SRY before the International Court of Justice. It seems unlikely that that so many Muslims were in Srebrenica because the county had a population of about 27,000 before the war, while the county of Bratunac had about 22,000 Muslims. Taking into consideration that the Muslims went in different directions and that the surrounding area was principally inhabited by Serbs and that Muslims from other counties did not come to Srebrenica, there is no basis for this allegation [of Srebrenica's pre-war versus wartime population], which has been manipulated on numerous occasions in order to present a greater picture of suffering. The allegation in the indictment regarding the escape of such a large number of Muslims from Srebrenica conflicts with the estimated numbers of Muslims who allegedly fled elsewhere.

International public opinion did not react to the burning, destruction, and annihilation of Serbian villages throughout 1992. Srebrenica was declared a "safe area" when Serbian forces, composed of Serbian refugees from the region, began a counter-offensive a year after the war began, and so expelled Muslim terrorist units all the way to Srebrenica.

Srebrenica was apparently the center of deadly and destructive acts against Serbs in that area. When the Army of the Republika Srpska took action in 1993 and surrounded Muslim military formations in Srebrenica, Serbs from Serbia were falsely charged with bombarding Srebrenica from their own territory, although UN observers stationed in all airports in the SRY confirmed that not one airplane took off on the alleged day. This truth was concealed until March 31, 1993, when, on the basis of earlier disinformation, the Security Council enacted Resolution 816/93 relating to the use of NATO aircraft to enforce the no-fly zone.

Aside from that, Srebrenica was not within targeting range of Serbian artillery. Rather, Muslims from Srebrenica shelled the Serbs in Bratunac, which was held by Serbs, and the Serbs in Bratunac shelled military targets in Srebrenica in reprisal. Muslim forces shelled Bratunac on February 2 and 17, and March 17, 1993, which resulted in civilian victims, as confirmed by a list of the killed and wounded issued from the *Dom Zdravlje* [health center] in Bratunac (*Komitet za prikupljanje podataka* br. 202/94). The Serbian side avenged these deaths with the shelling of Srebrenica on April 12, 1993.

Srebrenica was declared a safe area by UN Resolution 819/93, even though the warring parties and UNPROFOR anticipated a cease-fire agreement and subsequent demilitarization over a 72-hour period after the arrival of UNPROFOR. But demilitarization was not carried out, and attacks and provocations continued without interruption from the moment that Muslims came under the protection of international military forces.

The indictment omits citing the demilitarization of "safe areas," emphasizing instead that UN Security Council Resolution 819/93 requires "that all parties and others concerned treat Srebrenica and its surroundings as a safe area, which should be free from any armed attack or any other hostile act." In the same fashion, it was forbidden to call attention to the agreement that Srebrenica would not be the starting point for attacks against the Serbs. The demilitarization, which had never been carried out, led to renewed attacks from Srebrenica. NATO aircraft provisioned Srebrenica by "parachuting" weapons and munitions into it, which violated Security Council Resolution 713/91 of September 25, 1991 regarding the embargo of weapons. It must be emphasized that only Muslim areas were ever declared "safe areas." Not a single region in which Serbs were being killed was ever declared a safe area.

The killing of Serbs went unnoticed in 1992, but the protected Muslims in Srebrenica took advantage of media lies in 1993. UNPROFOR received orders to dramatize the plight of civilians in Srebrenica. With that in mind, UNPROFOR organized a convoy to transfer civilians from Srebrenica to Tuzla. They used open trucks that afforded no protection for the transported civilians at the beginning of winter. Thus, a media sensation was created — a scandal to further demonize the Serbian people. In spite of the known number of civilians who left Srebrenica, the indictment begins with the false figure of about 60,000 civilians in the town and surrounding area.

Srebrenica: Unsubstantiated Allegations

The indictment against Ratko Mladić states that the Serbian attack against Srebrenica began on June 6, 1995 and lasted until June 11, 1995. However, the attack was not directed against what was factually defined as a "safe area" as the indictment claims, but against an area that was not demilitarized and from which continuous attacks were being launched against Serbian villages as well as other targets. The attack was a reaction to and necessary defense against continuous military actions, provocations and massacres of Serbian civilians. The Serbian attack lasted six days. It was obviously an armed military conflict, but Srebrenica was not razed. Srebrenica was well armed by various foreign troops under the aegis of UNPROFOR and NATO, contrary to the stipulations of the arms embargo imposed on the former Yugoslavia. Comprehensive evidence exists of maneuvers that took place in Slovenia, the US and other countries that violated the arms embargo.

The indictment cites a figure of 60,000 Muslims in Srebrenica. This erroneous claim is made in the section dealing with the attacks on the safe area of Srebrenica (counts 4, 5 and 6). Those counts describe how 15,000 principally Muslim men, along with women and children, left Srebrenica. If we proceed from the given figure of 20,000 Muslims, one must ask where were the remaining 40,000 Muslims claimed to be in Srebrenica? The indictment states that one-third of the men from the group of 15,000 were armed, which contradicts UN statements that it had completed its assignment of demilitarizing the safe area in the allotted period of time. It is very likely that all of the men — and not one — third-were armed; therefore, they may have been essentially regarded as a military formation undertaking military actions whose goal was to cross Serbian territory.

The indictment states that two groups of Muslims, who withdrew to a UN base in Potočari, were evacuated in buses and trucks under the leadership and control of Bosnian Serb military personnel. The Serbian military command not only had a right, but an obligation to perform such an act. The obligation to evacuate protected persons from an area that was significantly exposed to the dangers of warfare originated with the Geneva Convention Relating to the Protection of Civilian Persons in Time of War from 1949 (Article 50) and with the Supplemental Protocol from the Second Geneva Convention of 1977 (Article 17). The controlled evacuation conducted by the Serbian authorities speaks for the gravity of this action and the effort expended to avoid any unwanted incidents or crimes taking place.

The indictment also claims that Ratko Mladić and members of his staff met with Dutch peacekeepers and representatives of

Muslim refugees in Bratunac. Mladić guaranteed the safety of civilians and the status of prisoner of war to Muslim soldiers who handed over their weapons. Again, this demonstrates that the safe area had not been effectively demilitarized. In fact, there were even armed soldiers among the civilians in Potočari. The indictment's claim that 50 to 60 buses arrived to evacuate civilians from Potočari implies that whatever agreements had been made during the meeting were undertaken. In the same way, the separation of the men from the group substantiates General Mladić's promise that civilians would be evacuated and that Muslim soldiers would be given prisoner-of-war status.

The indictment claims that there were several thousand Muslims around the UN base in Potočari. It was later claimed that the majority of the men were driven to Bratunac, and then to Karakaj, where they were allegedly massacred. Yet there could not have been many men in the group of civilians in Potočari. Those who had insinuated themselves into the group were separated from the civilians and treated as prisoners of war. The indictment's qualification "the majority of Muslim men," in relation to several thousand civilians who had sought shelter at the UN base, does not prove such a large figure. There is no precise information that could form the basis of an indictment or prove that there was anything more than a very small number of Muslim soldiers in Potočari at the time.

If 50 to 60 buses actually came to collect civilians as the indictment claims, then the assertion that such a large number of men was taken away and killed collapses. The chance that 60 buses can transport up to 6,000 passengers refutes the earlier claim that several thousand civilians had been there, and that several thousand were transported to Karakaj as well. If several thousand Muslims sought refuge in Potočari, and some 6,000 were evacuated, then the claim that several thousand men were separated from that group does not seem genuine.

In counts 24 through 31, the indictment goes on to cite the alleged killings of Muslim soldiers. An unsubstantiated or false claim is made that Bosnian Serb military personnel transported "thousands of Muslim prisoners" from Bratunac to Karakaj, namely those who were separated from the thousands of civilians in Potočari. Count 31 again claims that there was a "loss of thousands of lives" on June 14, 1995 after those people had been summarily judged. And furthermore, this possibly false, unconvincing, and legally incomprehensible claim does not cite a single piece of evidence. The accusation that: "At various times during 14 July 1995, Bosnian Serb military personnel killed Bosnian Muslim detainees at this school complex" appears throughout the indictment.

The indictment claims that Muslims were transported by trucks to at least two different locations in the vicinity of Karakaj. Many teams of investigators have unsuccessfully sought to discover these alleged locations. If such uncontrollable events had taken place, despite the astringent control exercised by the Serbian military leadership, only isolated individuals for whom the military command cannot be held responsible could have committed them.

Furthermore, the UN High Commission for Refugees highlighted in a resolution that the Serbs committed 90% of the war crimes, which the CIA had accurately recorded via satellite, giving the exact location of mass graves — but when teams went into the field they found nothing in those alleged "mass graves."

The indictment claims that a column of 15,000 people, composed largely of Muslim men, left Srebrenica by way of Šušnjara for Tuzla six days after the beginning of the armed conflict between Muslims and Serbs around Srebrenica. It is clear that they wanted to cross Serbian territory. If the statement that approximately 5,000 Muslims men from this column were armed is true, then it was certainly a powerful enemy formation that had not surrendered. And they were not laying down their arms. In that case, it would have been necessary to raise a defense in order to protect the Serbian villages against such a large, and evidently stronger, armed formation. It is illogical to suppose that an armed enemy formation can cross unfriendly territory during a civil war and avoid armed conflict.

That particular conflict led to the defeat and surrender of Muslim forces. The indictment tendentiously emphasized that exactly one-third, i.e. 5,000 armed Muslim soldiers, succeeded in safely reaching Tuzla, and that the remaining two-thirds were unarmed civilians who had been surrounded (count 18). The claim cannot be accurate because it would have meant that the Muslim soldiers had escaped, while leaving behind the women, children and remaining family members to be taken prisoner by the Serbs. It would make sense that Muslim soldiers rather sought to save their families and share their fates. The indictment's claim seems invented so that the alleged crimes could be treated as crimes against civilians. More likely, the group was composed of soldiers and civilians who had taken up arms. Civilians who take part in hostile actions enjoy no protection according to the Supplemental Protocols of the Second Geneva Convention of 1977.

The prosecutor made unsubstantiated charges against the Serbs for "executions" without proof of executioners, corpses and graves. The charges were made in reference to thousands of Muslims, but an analysis of counts 20.1 through 20.7 refer to a total of 715 allegedly killed. The majority are unsubstantiated claims made without a convincing argument that they had been killed.

Then there are the suspicious charges that Serbian soldiers donned stolen UN uniforms and gave guarantees of safety to Muslim prisoners. The ruse about stolen uniforms was not the first of its kind. However, couldn't those uniforms have just as well been stolen and used by the Muslims? Perhaps members of NATO forces did indeed give them guarantees of safety. In any case, the accusations against the SRY before the International Court of Justice attempt to implicate the direct participation of the JNA by claiming that Serbian forces in JNA uniforms were in the territory of Bosnia-Herzegovina. At the outbreak of the war, there were 426,000 JNA uniforms for both active and reserve units of each of the warring parties. There is a great deal of evidence that these uniforms were eventually widely used and abused.

Article I of the First Hague Convention of 1907 rules that the laws, regulations and obligations of war apply not only to the army, but also to militias and volunteer forces if those groups fulfill the conditions that relate to command personnel, identifiable insignias, the bearing of arms openly and respect for the laws and the customs of warfare. Uniforms were not foreseen as a necessary condition. The Geneva Convention upholds the same regulation, yet even the use of deceptive uniforms, considered a wartime ruse, is allowed according to Article 24 of the First Hague Convention.

Part of the indictment emphasizes that Ratko Mladić "informed some Muslim men that they would be evacuated and exchanged for Bosnian Serbs being held in Tuzla." Ratko Mladić fulfilled his promise.

The indictment also connects certain alleged events to Mladić by claiming that he met with subordinates in a nearby location and spoke to some Muslims, and that he was present at one location where executions took place. But a visit to a particular area and speaking to Muslims does not constitute proof of ordering or participating in the alleged crimes. The allegations omit proof of specific events as well as the personal responsibility of Ratko Mladić. In contrast, it has been documented that Alija Izetbegović was often seen in the company of notorious Muslim criminals, and that he visited Muslim jails on many occasions where terrible crimes were committed against Serbs *en masse*. The Tribunal does not find this to be sufficient proof to bring criminal charges against him.

In a certain sense, Ratko Mladić's conduct presents nothing that could be interpreted as a deviation from recognized international laws of warfare. US diplomats and judges, who may have groundlessly indicted Mladić for his military conduct, rendered a completely different judgment, certainly under political pressure, in similar circumstances fifty years ago[27] ....

Confirming Charges Against Ratko Mladić

Almiro Rodrigues, as presiding judge, confirmed the indictment against Ratko Mladić and Radovan Karadžić for alleged crimes in and around Srebrenica [in July 1995]. This created the basis for general court proceedings and the issue of arrest warrants.

Reading the indictment, the presiding judge repeated the facts and the alleged legal qualifications, and concluded that it appeared that a genuine horrible massacre was perpetrated against the Muslim population. Judge Rodrigues compounded the indictment's bias, because in addition to repeating the allegations, he added new ones, and even seemed to modify the allegations. The relative differences between the two versions of the indictment cast further doubt on the alleged facts.

Paragraph 20.7 of the indictment states that the executions in Karakaj lasted "approximately from noon to midnight." And "Bosnian Serb military personnel buried the executed Bosnian Muslim men in mass graves near the execution sites" (Count 28). Here, the indictment claims that all Muslims had their hands bound and were blindfolded. Besides that, it states that they were shot in small groups and that thousands were summarily executed. The indictment claims that the separation of Muslim men was carried out under the orders of Ratko Mladić (Paragraph 11). The presiding judge went further than the indictment, and claimed that Mladić personally separated them, which would seem absolutely incompatible with his status as a military commander.

Witnesses cited in the indictment have charged that on June 6, 1995 (Paragraph 10) Mladić brought military aides and a television crew with him. It makes no sense that someone who was planning to commit war crimes would bring a television crew to tape it for public relations purposes.

The [Nov. 1995] indictment concerning Srebrenica alleges a series of unbelievable executions and crimes that were not cited in the initial [July 1995] indictment. Is the Srebrenica indictment what it is supposed to be or is it a prelude to a new indictment or an annex to the original indictment? In any case, it plainly seems a violation of the rules of procedure and evidence. For example, the [Nov. 1995] Srebrenica indictment concluded that the Muslims in the safe area of Srebrenica had been disarmed; but this assertion does not exist in the initial [July 1995] indictment. Later, the [Nov. 1995] indictment claims that the group of approximately 15,000 Muslims, which headed for Tuzla, was composed mostly of unarmed men, women and children; but the indictment (Paragraph 6) stated that it was a group of Muslim men with some women and children, and that one-third of the men were armed.

The [Nov. 1995] Srebrenica indictment insists on the new fact that the army of the SRY participated directly in the actions taken in and around Srebrenica, citing their appearance, recognizable uniforms and Serbian dialect as proof. However, it was anticipated that anyone could have worn the uniforms and only the insignias constitute proof of belonging to one side or the other. In addition, various dialects existed in all the regions in question. Armed Muslim formations had been assembled with mujahideen who spoke not just another dialect but an entirely different language.

The JNA withdrew from Bosnia-Herzegovina between May 5 and May 19, 1992; from that time on it was not present in the former republic. Such was not the case with regular units of the Croatian army and units of mujahideen, whose departure was still being sought by the Security Council at the time of the indictments [in 1995].

The [Nov. 1995] Srebrenica indictment secures the initial [July 1995] indictment against Ratko Mladić for crimes against humanity and violation of the laws and customs of warfare, which "resulted in an exodus of Bosnian Muslims." Hence, an exodus becomes an act of "ethnic cleansing" and is treated as a possible form of genocide.

For actions to be qualified as genocidal, they must be a part of a pre-conceived plan. For that reason, many international documents, as well as the indictment against the SRY before the International Court of Justice, emphasize that the crimes allegedly committed by Serbs were executed in a systematic and methodical manner, while the crimes of the other two warring sides are treated as sporadic incidents that are not covered by official policies. In effect, such prejudice will conceal the crimes of the other two sides.

A criminal master plan for establishing a "Greater Serbia" was attributed to the Serbs. No one has proved that such a master plan ever existed, nor have any written orders for deploying such a plan been found. Since genocide may be committed only against a determined nationality, ethnic or religious group, the Muslim side took advantage of media lies that defined the entire population of Bosnia-Herzegovina at the very beginning of the war as the aggrieved party, thus establishing an initial, prejudicially favorable position for the Muslims as victims and the Serbs as attackers, aggressors and occupiers.

The deliberate or partial annihilation of a national, ethnic, racial or religious group is the criterion by which familiar crimes are transformed into genocide. The presiding judge considered that deliberate action could be deduced from the seriousness of the ethnic cleansing and the mass executions. This passage attempts to prove allegations, not subjective elements that unambiguously point to it. Opposed to that, statements about the observable conduct of Ratko Mladić depict an intention to prevent crimes, and specifically to respect the Geneva Convention. Even if he had violated his own straightforward and unambiguous orders to respect the Geneva Convention, it would not give them the right to try him before the Tribunal.

It is necessary to present the truth and counter these allegations of "ethnic cleansing and mass executions," as well as unsubstantiated charges about "the loss of thousands of lives." The number alone, indefinite and unsubstantiated, does not warrant qualification as a criminal act of genocide. The unambiguous and documented confirmation of genocidal intentions is necessary. They could be qualified by the presiding judge rather as a violation of humanitarian law if it could be proved that they took place *en masse*, without genocidal intention.

The so-called international community has formulated a case against Serbian leaders built on inaccuracies, while documents provided by the opposing side in the conflict unambiguously confirm similar allegations committed by them. Specifically, Franjo Tudjman, the President of the Republic of Croatia, ordered that an ultimatum be sent to Serbs to leave 27 villages in western Slavonia within 48 hours, which his armed forces carried out. The documentation of these orders, however, did not merit indictment (*see "Zločin je zločin prećutati"* (It's a Crime to Keep Quiet about Crime), Novi Sad, 1993, p. 309).

Something like ethnic cleansing was probably carried out by all three sides in the war. Indeed, the European Parliament criticized the UN Security Council for its inability to work effectively against the barbarous practice of "ethnic cleansing" in the former Yugoslavia.

The chief of the HDZ, Dario Kordić, who was indicted by the Hague Tribunal, stated the following with reference to ethnic cleansing: "In the last five to six days, around 28,000 Croats abandoned areas of the Federation, first of all from Zenica, Konjic and Kakanj. According to the information we have, and to Washington's understanding, nearly 180,000 Croatians were driven from their family homes, which they abandoned, by the Muslims" (*Oslobođenje, Muslimansko izdanje* br. 16675 od 12.11.1994).

The forced relocation of 50,000 Serbs from the Neretva Valley, as well as other forcible evictions, were not deemed worthy of indictment. Quite to the contrary, evidence of "ethnic cleansing" even included controlled evacuations of all those who voluntarily wanted to avoid war, hunger, mobilization and killing.

The forcible relocation of ethnic groups is not addressed in acts proscribed by the Convention on Genocide. The Sixth Committee of the UN, undertaken in its 56th session, rejected the Syrian amendment[28] to the convention. The voting for the Syrian amendment resulted in 5 votes in favor and 29 votes against; thus, Article 8 was upheld.[29]

The so-called international community recognized the state of Bosnia-Herzegovina and thus created obligations for it that were based on a plan that applied the Convention on Genocide. Each state signatory is obligated to prevent acts of genocide on its own territory....

The contents of these obligations are not set forth in a detailed manner in the Convention on Genocide. Article V of the convention clearly stipulated that the signatories are bound to enact regulations on behalf of the convention and especially to provide effective punishment for persons found guilty of genocide or of any act that is enumerated in Article III. Aside from that, states are obliged to undertake all other measures considered necessary and satisfactory for the prevention of genocide. If the crime of genocide is committed on the territory of a state, such state has violated its own international obligations without regard to measures that it may have undertaken

Considering the obligations of signatory states to prevent acts of genocide from being committed on their own territory, it is irrefutable that state organs are obliged not to commit acts of genocide. The Muslim leadership in Bosnia-Herzegovina, which a world forum recognized as a legal institution, thus bears responsibility for committing acts of genocide and violating its obligations to prevent it from taking place.

This analysis leads to the unambiguous conclusion that the Tribunal used unfounded allegations in the indictments to enact the initial political deceptions regarding the responsibility of the Serbian people for alleged aggression against and the occupation of Bosnia-Herzegovina by bringing its leaders to trial. Such prejudice and lack of objectivity, bias and manipulation is intolerable for any dispassionate observer.

ENDNOTES

[1] The UN was established in June 1945, several months before the London Agreement that had established the Nuremberg Court. This means that the legal basis for the creation of the Tribunal existed in the form of Article 29,

Chapter VII of the UN Charter, but was not used at that time. Now, after almost fifty years, the regulations of the UN Charter are in fact being used as such a legal basis.

2 The American Military Tribunal for the American-occupied zone brought Fieldmarshal List to trial along with a group of eleven officers on February 19, 1948 in Nuremberg (Official Transcript, 0930-1630–Justice Wenerstrum). In the decision, along with the culpability of the indicted, the court, on the one hand, took the incomprehensible position that the Nazi occupation [i.e., of Yugoslavia] was legal, and that resistance to the Nazi invaders was illegal; if, on the other hand, it is a well-known fact that Belgrade was bombed for resisting the Nazis and that the Serbian people were punished in manifold ways, while Ljubljana, Zagreb and Sarajevo had, on the other hand, prepared a festive welcome for the Nazis, then one must conclude that the Serbs had no right to resistance or to act in self-defense.

3 Report of the UN Secretary General pursuant to paragraph 2 of Security Council Resolution 808/1993 of May 3, 1993–S/25704, No. 27, p. 8.

4 Report of the UN Secretary General, No. 21, p. 7.

5 United Nations Security Council, S/25575/12.4.93.

6 William Fenrick, Reuters, London, 11/17/93.

7 Rapporteurs from the CSCE Moscow Human Dimension Mechanism to Bosnia-Herzegovina and Croatia (2/9/93), Proposal for an Integrated War Crimes Tribunal for the Former Yugoslavia, p. 12.

8 Benjamin Ferenz: Nuremberg Trial Procedure and Rights of the Accused, 39, J. Crim. I., Criminology and Police Science, 144/1948.

9 Report on the International Tribunal to Adjudicate War Crimes Committed in the Former Yugoslavia, American Bar Association (ABA), July 8, 1993, p. 8.

10 Report of the Committee for Foreign Affairs and Security of the European Parliament, 4/7/93, A3-0225/94.

11 Maroje Mihovilović, "Nuremberg in The Hague," *Novi List*, Rijeka, 10/16/94.

12 *Toutes les vérités Yougoslaves ne sont pas bonnes à dire*, by J. Merlino. Albin Michel: Paris, 1993.

13 "La Bosnie—Intoxication," M. Clos, *Le Figaro*, Paris, April 29, 1994.

14 Peter Brock, "The Partisan Press," *Foreign Policy*, Winter 1993–1994.

15 United Nations Security Council C/25266 of February 2, 1993.

16 Letter from Nora Beloff to Judge Richard Goldstone, London, August 2, 1994.

17 Robert Block, UN Indicts Belgrade for War Crimes, *The Independent*, March 10, 1995; Ian Traynor: The CIA Investigation—The Indictment of the Serbs, *The Guardian*, March 3, 1995.

18 *Vjesnik*, Zagreb, December 10, 1994.

[19] *Dušan Tadić* was acquitted of charges of murder and serious crime, and twenty of the thirty-one charges against him were found to be groundless. He was, nevertheless, sentenced to twenty years in prison for crimes against humanity, despite the fact that a key witness, Dragan Opačić, admitted that he was set up by the Bosnian government to lie to The Hague Tribunal, and that he received "training" that consisted of watching videotapes of Tadić and the Trnopolje camp before testifying (*Reuters*, October 25, 1996).

[20] *Mala politička enciklopedija*, Savremena administracija, Beograd, 1966, p. 344.

[21] The violations of law that are provided for in the conventions of war from Article 3 of the statutes are: a) the use of poison as a weapon or other weapons calculated to cause unnecessary suffering; b) careless destruction of places, cities or villages or destruction by unauthorized military means; c) the attack, destruction or intentional destruction of monuments, artistic or scholarly creations; d) the plunder of public or private property.

[22] Milena Spasovski, Dragiša Živković and Milomir Stepić: *Etnički sastav stanovništva B-H*, Stručna knjiga, Beograd, 1992.

[23] "The Future of the Balkans," by David Owen, *Foreign Affairs*, April 15, 1993.

[24] *Tanjug*, Paris, October 10, 1993.

[25] Nora Beloff: "Evidence of Crimes against Serbs in the Srebrenica-Bratunac District from April 1992 to March 1993," *Unity Herald* (UK), May 1993.

[26] Criminal acts by Muslim military formations were committed not only against the Serbian population but also against the Muslims of Srebrenica. Reports of two young Muslim girls bear witness to this. The two girls escaped from Srebrenica across a minefield into Serbian territory. Both girls were refugees from the villages of Gorovi and Pobuće, and had been relocated to Srebrenica, where they had been abused and raped on numerous occasions by Muslim soldiers who were under the command of Naser Orić. After reporting the rapes, Naser Orić's soldiers laughed at them. One of the girls was in her last month of pregnancy. Together, they fled Srebrenica, which was being held by the Muslims, to Serbian territory. The statement of one of the girls was characteristic. She said: "I was thinking of killing myself. I was so desperate that I came up with the idea of escaping from Srebrenica to Serbian territory. I got to know two Muslim girls in Srebrenica who told me that the Serbian Army had captured them, but that they never had anything bad happen to them while they were in their custody. When they were exchanged and came to Srebrenica to the Muslims, they were very quickly raped by Muslim soldiers." The witnesses were transferred to a Serbian refugee shelter in Bratunac. They stated that they were content and that they had been well treated; the Red Cross cared for the pregnant girl during the birth of her child. The girls gave information about the large number of rapes committed in Srebrenica by Muslim soldiers, especially against orphans and refugee girls. The allegations of rape were recorded and taped on video; the cassettes were deposited with the *Komitet za prikupljanje podataka* (Committee for Gathering Information) no. 158/94.

[27] *similar circumstances fifty years ago*, according to the Simon Wiesenthal Center, Adrija Artuković was the highest ranking Nazi criminal to find refuge in the United States. He served as Minister of Internal Affairs for the Nazi puppet state of Croatia. As such, he was in charge of the police and paramilitary units that imposed the Ustashi reign of terror. The Ustashi (extremist Croatian quislings) established death camps where they murdered large numbers of men, women and children. Their victims were Serbs (750,000 deaths), Jews (75,000 deaths) and Roma (50,000 deaths). As the second highest-ranking member of the Ustashi regime, Artuković was implicated in these crimes. Artuković reached the U.S. illegally through the Vatican's "rat lines" in 1948, via Dublin, on a temporary visa under the false name of Alois Anich. He used an Irish Certificate of Identity to obtain a non-immigrant visitor's visa to the U.S. as a "temporary visitor for pleasure." He stayed in the US for 38 years, and managed to fend off deportation — until 1986, when he was successfully deported, thanks to an amendment to the INA in 1978, sponsored by Congressional Representative Elizabeth Holzman, that was designed to deal with the problem of Nazi criminals in the U.S.

Before the Holzman amendment, the Yugoslav government's case for his extradition "for murder and participation in murder" was effectively dismissed because an American judge (see *United States* v. *Artuković*, 170 F. Supp 383, S.D. Calif. 1959) was not convinced by evidence presented by a Communist state. In an earlier case, Artuković's lawyers successfully argued that the Yugoslav indictment was political in nature. Like most extradition treaties, the 1902 extradition treaty between the U.S. and Serbia prohibited the extradition of fugitives for "offenses of a political character." In 1959, Artuković scored another courtroom victory when, in an opinion rarely supported and widely criticized, Commissioner Theodore Hocke concluded that Yugoslavia's evidence failed to meet the relatively lenient probable-cause standard for extradition. Hocke dismissed Yugoslavia's testimonial affidavits as not believable, noting that not only was the testimony in narrative form "drawn to incite passion and prejudice" by referring "constantly ... to children of tender years, newborn babes, aged persons, cruel and inhuman treatment," but also the use by witnesses of "the same language," such as "the so-called Independent State of Croatia"; Hocke also suggested that the Communist officials in Yugoslavia and not the witnesses had selected the language (see *Karadzole* v. *Artuković*, 170 F. Supp. 383, 390, S.D. Calif. 1959). (This information was drawn from the Simon Wiesenthal Center's Multimedia Learning Center Online [http://motlc.weisenthal.com], "The Extradition of Nazi Criminals: Ryan, Artuković and Demjanuk" by Henry Friedlander and Earlean M. McCarrick.)

[28] *Syrian amendment*, an amendment made by Syria that challenged a complicated last-minute U.S. proposal in the UN that held up agreement on an article that would have authorized the international court to order reparations for victims of war crimes, crimes against humanity and genocide. It was later defeated in a UN vote.

[29] Official Records of the third session of the UN General Assembly, Part 1. Legal questions, Sixth Committee, Summary Records of Meetings, September 21 to December 10, 1948, p. 186.

THE TEXT OF THE INDICTMENTS

THE PROSECUTOR OF THE TRIBUNAL
AGAINST
RADOVAN KARADŽIĆ
RATKO MLADIĆ
INDICTMENT

Richard J. Goldstone, Prosecutor of the International Criminal Tribunal for the Former Yugoslavia, pursuant to his authority under Article 18 of the Statute of the International Criminal Tribunal for the Former Yugoslavia ("The Statute of the Tribunal"), charges:

THE ACCUSED

1. RADOVAN KARADŽIĆ was born on 19 June 1945 in the municipality of Šavnik of the Republic of Montenegro. From on or about 13 May 1992 to the present, he has been president of the Bosnian Serb administration in Pale.

2. RATKO MLADIĆ was born on 12 March 1943 in the municipality of Kalinovik of the Republic of Bosnia and Herzegovina. He is a career military officer and holds the rank of general in the Bosnian Serb armed forces. From on or about 14 May 1992 to the present, he has been the commander of the army of the Bosnian Serb administration.

SUPERIOR AUTHORITY
RADOVAN KARADŽIĆ

3. RADOVAN KARADŽIĆ was a founding member and president of the Serbian Democratic Party (SDS) of what was then the Socialist Republic of Bosnia and Herzegovina. The SDS was the main political party among the Serbs in Bosnia and Herzegovina. As president of the SDS, he was and is the most powerful official in the party. His duties as president include representing the party, co-ordinating the work of party organs and ensuring the realisation of the programmatic tasks and goals of the party. He continues to hold this post.

4. RADOVAN KARADŽIĆ became the first president of the Bosnian Serb administration in Pale on or about 13 May 1992. At the time he assumed this position, his *de jure* powers, as described in the constitution of the Bosnian Serb administration, included, but were not limited to, commanding the army in the Bosnian Serb administration in times of war and peace and having the authority to appoint, promote and discharge officers of the army.

5. In addition to his powers described in the constitution, RADOVAN KARADŽIĆ'S powers as president of the Bosnian Serb administration are augmented by Article 6 of the Bosnian Serb Act on People's Defence which vested in him, among other powers, the authority to supervise the Territorial Defence both in peace and war and the authority to issue orders for the utilisation of the police in case of war, immediate threat and other emergencies. Article 39 of the same Act empowered him, in cases of imminent threat of war and other emergencies, to deploy Territorial Defence units for the maintenance of law and order.

6. RADOVAN KARADŽIĆ'S powers are further augmented by Article 33 of the Bosnian Serb Act on Internal Affairs, which authorised him to activate reserve police in emergency situations.

7. RADOVAN KARADŽIĆ has exercised the powers described above and has acted and been dealt with internationally as the president of the Bosnian Serb administration in Pale. In that capacity, he has, *inter alia*, participated in international negotiations and has personally made agreements on such matters as cease-fires and humanitarian relief that have been implemented.

RATKO MLADIĆ

8. RATKO MLADIĆ was, in 1991, appointed commander of the 9th Corps of the Yugoslav People's Army (JNA) in Knin in the Republic of Croatia. Subsequently, in May 1992, he assumed command of the forces of the Second Military District of the JNA which then effectively became the Bosnian Serb army. He holds the rank of general and from about 14 May 1992 to the present, has been the commander of the army of the Bosnian Serb administration.

9. RATKO MLADIĆ has demonstrated his control in military matters by negotiating, *inter alia*, cease-fire and prisoner exchange agreements; agreements relating to the opening of Sarajevo airport; agreements relating to access for humanitarian aid convoys; and anti-sniping agreements, all of which have been implemented.

GENERAL ALLEGATIONS

10. At all times relevant to this indictment, a state of armed conflict and partial occupation existed in the Republic of Bosnia and Herzegovina in the territory of the former Yugoslavia.

11. All acts or omissions herein set forth as grave breaches of the Geneva Conventions of 1949 (hereafter "grave breaches") recognised by Article 2 of the Statute of the Tribunal occurred during that armed conflict and partial occupation.

12. In each paragraph charging crimes against humanity, crimes recognised by Article 5 of the Statute of the Tribunal, the alleged acts or omissions were part of a widespread, systematic or large-scale attack directed against a civilian population.

13. The term "UN peacekeepers" used throughout this indictment includes UN military observers of the United Nations.

14. The UN peacekeepers and civilians referred to in this indictment were, at all relevant times, persons protected by the Geneva Conventions of 1949.

15. The accused in this indictment were required to abide by the laws and customs governing the conduct of war, including the Geneva Conventions of 1949.

CHARGES

16. The charges set forth in this indictment are in three parts:

Part I of the indictment, Counts 1 to 9, charges a crime of genocide, crimes against humanity and crimes that were perpetrated against the civilian population and against places of worship throughout the territory of the Republic of Bosnia and Herzegovina.

Part II of the indictment, Counts 10 to 12, charges crimes relating to the sniping campaign against civilians in Sarajevo.

Part III of the indictment, Counts 13 to 16, charges crimes relating to the taking of UN peacekeepers as hostages.

PART I

COUNTS 1-2

(GENOCIDE)

(CRIMES AGAINST HUMANITY)

17. RADOVAN KARADŽIĆ and RATKO MLADIĆ from April 1992, in the territory of the Republic of Bosnia and Herzegovina, by their acts and omissions, committed genocide.

18. Bosnian Muslim and Bosnian Croat civilians were persecuted on national, political and religious grounds throughout the Republic of Bosnia and Herzegovina. Thousands

of them were interned in detention facilities where they were subjected to widespread acts of physical and psychological abuse and to inhumane conditions. Detention facility personnel who ran and operated the Omarska, Keraterm and Luka detention facilities, among others, including, but not limited to Željko Meakić (Omarska), Duško Sikirica (Keraterm) and Goran Jelisić (Luka), intended to destroy Bosnian Muslim and Bosnian Croat people as national, ethnic, or religious groups and killed, seriously injured and deliberately inflicted upon them conditions intended to bring about their physical destruction. The conditions in the detention facilities, which are described in paragraphs 20-22 hereunder, are incorporated in full herein.

19. RADOVAN KARADŽIĆ and RATKO MLADIĆ between April 1992 and July 1995, in the territory of the Republic of Bosnia and Herzegovina, by their acts and omissions, and in concert with others, committed a crime against humanity by persecuting Bosnian Muslim and Bosnian Croat civilians on national, political and religious grounds. As set forth below, they are criminally responsible for the unlawful confinement, murder, rape, sexual assault, torture, beating, robbery and inhumane treatment of civilians; the targeting of political leaders, intellectuals and professionals; the unlawful deportation and transfer of civilians; the unlawful shelling of civilians; the unlawful appropriation and plunder of real and personal property; the destruction of homes and businesses; and the destruction of places of worship.

DETENTION FACILITIES

20. As soon as military forces from Bosnia and elsewhere in the former Yugoslavia began to attack towns and villages in the Republic of Bosnia and Herzegovina, thousands of Bosnian Muslim and Bosnian Croat civilians were systematically selected and rounded up on national, ethnic, political or religious grounds and interned in detention facilities throughout the territory occupied by the Bosnian Serbs. These facilities include, but are not limited to:

Detention facility	Dates of existence
Omarska	May – August 1992
Keraterm	May – August 1992
Trnopolje	May – December 1992
Luka	May – July 1992
Manjača	Summer 1991 – December 1992
Sušica	June 1992 – September 1992
KP Dom Foča	April – mid-1993

21. Many of these detention facilities were staffed and operated by military and police personnel and their agents, under the control of RADOVAN KARADŽIĆ and RATKO MLADIĆ. In addition, Bosnian Serb police and military interrogators had unfettered access to all of the detention facilities and operated in conjunction with the personnel in control of these detention facilities. These facilities and personnel include, but are not limited to:

Detention facility	Commander	Guards
Omarska	Željko Meakić (police)	police/military
Keraterm	Duško Sikirica (police)	police/military
Trnopolje	Slobodan Kuruzović (military)	police/military
Luka	Goran Jelisić (police)	paramilitary
Manjača	Božidar Popović (military)	military
Sušica	Dragan Nikolić (military)	military
KP Dom Foča	Milorad Krnojelac	military

22. Thousands of Bosnian Muslim and Bosnian Croat civilians, including women, children and elderly persons, were detained in these facilities for protracted periods of time.

They were not afforded judicial process and their internment was not justified by military necessity. They were detained, in large measure, because of their national, religious and political identity. The conditions in the detention facilities were inhumane and brutal. Bosnian Serb military and police personnel in charge of these facilities, including Dragan Nikolić (Sušica), Željko Meakić (Omarska), Duško Sikirica (Keraterm) and other persons over whom they had control, subjected the civilian detainees to physical and psychological abuse, intimidation and maltreatment. Detention facility personnel, intending to destroy Bosnian Muslim and Bosnian Croat people as national, ethnic or religious groups, killed, seriously injured and deliberately inflicted upon them conditions intended to bring about their physical destruction. Detainees were repeatedly subjected to and/or witnessed inhumane acts, including murder, rape, sexual assault, torture, beatings, robbery as well as other forms of mental and physical abuse. In many instances, women and girls who were detained were raped at the camps or taken from the detention centres and raped or otherwise sexually abused at other locations. Daily food rations provided to detainees were inadequate and often amounted to starvation rations. Medical care for the detainees was insufficient or non-existent and the general hygienic conditions were grossly inadequate.

TARGETING OF POLITICAL LEADERS, INTELLECTUALS AND PROFESSIONALS

23. Particularly singled out for persecution by the Bosnian Serb military, Bosnian Serb police and their agents, under the direction and control of RADOVAN KARADŽIĆ and RATKO MLADIĆ were civilian political leaders and members of the primary Bosnian Muslim political party, the Party for Democratic Action (SDA), and the principal Bosnian Croat political party, the Croatian Democratic Union (HDZ), from the cities of Prijedor, Vlasenica, Bosanski Šamac and Foča, amongst others. In many instances, lists identifying leaders of the SDA and the HDZ were provided by the SDS to personnel of the Bosnian Serb military, police and their agents. Using these lists, Bosnian Muslim and Bosnian Croat political leaders were arrested, interned, physically abused and, in many instances, murdered. Some local SDA leaders who were persecuted because of their political beliefs include, but are not limited to, Muhamed Čehajić (Prijedor), Sulejman Tihić (Bosanski Samac), and Ahmet Hadžić (Brčko).

24. In addition to persecutions of Bosnian Muslim and Bosnian Croat political leaders, the Bosnian Serb military, police and their agents systematically targeted for persecution on national or religious grounds, Bosnian Muslim and Bosnian Croat intellectuals and professionals in many towns and villages including Prijedor, Vlasenica, Bosanski Šamac and Foča, among others. Individuals who were persecuted include, but are not limited to Abdulah Puškar (academic), Žiko Crnalić (businessman) and Esad Mehmedalija (attorney) from Prijedor, and Osman Vatić (attorney) from Brčko.

DEPORTATION

25. Thousands of Bosnian Muslims and Bosnian Croats from the areas of Vlasenica, Prijedor, Bosanski Šamac, Brčko and Foča, among others, were systematically arrested and interned in detention facilities established and maintained by the Bosnian Serb military, police and their agents and thereafter unlawfully deported or transferred to locations inside and outside of the Republic of Bosnia and Herzegovina. In addition, Bosnian Muslim and Bosnian Croat civilians, including women, children and elderly persons, were taken directly from their homes and eventually used in prisoner exchanges by Bosnian Serb military and police and their agents under the control and direction of RADOVAN KARADŽIĆ and RATKO MLADIĆ. These deportations and others were not conducted as evacuations for safety, military necessity or for any other lawful purpose and have, in conjunction with other actions directed against Bosnian Muslim and Bosnian Croat civil-

ians, resulted in a significant reduction or elimination of Bosnian Muslims and Bosnian Croats in certain occupied regions.

SHELLING OF CIVILIAN GATHERINGS

26. Beginning in July 1992 and continuing through to July 1995, Bosnian Serb military forces, under the direction and control of RADOVAN KARADŽIĆ and RATKO MLADIĆ unlawfully fired on civilian gatherings that were of no military significance in order to kill, terrorise and demoralise the Bosnian Muslim and Bosnian Croat civilian population. These incidents include, but are not limited to the following:

Location/Type of civilian gathering	Municipality	Date	Casualties
Sarajevo (picnic)	Sarajevo	03/07/92	10
Sarajevo (airport)	Sarajevo	11/02/93	4
Srebrenica (playground)	Srebrenica	12/04/93	15
Dobrinja (soccer game)	Sarajevo	01/06/93	146
Dobrinja (water line)	Sarajevo	12/07/93	27
Sarajevo (residential street)	Sarajevo	28/11/93	11
Ciglane Market (fruit market)	Sarajevo	06/12/93	20
Alipašino Polje (children playing)	Sarajevo	22/01/94	10
Cetinjska St (children playing)	Sarajevo	26/10/94	7
Sarajevo (Livanjska Street)	Sarajevo	08/11/94	7
Sarajevo (flea market)	Sarajevo	22/12/94	9
Tuzla (plaza)	Tuzla	24/05/95	195

APPROPRIATION AND PLUNDER OF PROPERTY

27. Shortly after armed hostilities broke out in the Republic of Bosnia and Herzegovina, Bosnian Serb forces quickly suppressed armed resistance in most villages and cities. During and after the course of consolidating their gains, Bosnian Serb military and police personnel, and other agents of the Bosnian Serb administration, under the direction and control of RADOVAN KARADŽIĆ and RATKO MLADIĆ systematically and wantonly appropriated and looted the real and personal property of Bosnian Muslim and Bosnian Croat civilians. The appropriation of property was extensive and not justified by military necessity. It occurred from April 1992 to January 1993 in the municipalities of Prijedor, Vlasenica, and Bosanski Šamac, among others.

28. The appropriation and looting of said property was accomplished in the following manner and by the following means, among others:

A. Thousands of Bosnian Muslim and Bosnian Croat civilians were forced into detention facilities where they remained for protracted periods of time. Upon entering these internment facilities, the personnel who ran the internment facilities systematically stole the personal property of the detainees, including jewelry, watches, money and other valuables. The detainees were rarely provided receipts for the property taken from them or given their property back upon their release.

B. Civilians interned in these camps witnessed and/or were subjected to physical and psychological abuse. After witnessing or experiencing serious abuse, thousands of internees were forcibly transferred from these camps to locations inside and outside the Republic of Bosnia and Herzegovina. Before being forcibly transferred, many detainees were compelled to sign official Bosnian Serb documents wherein they "voluntarily" relinquished to the Bosnian Serb administration title to and possession of their real and personal property.

C. In many instances, Bosnian Muslim and Bosnian Croat civilian detainees were taken from internment camps to their homes and businesses and forced to turn over to their escorts money and other valuables. In other instances, they were used as labourers to load property from Bosnian Muslim and Bosnian Croat homes and businesses onto trucks for transportation to parts unknown. This occurred with the consent and approval of those in control of the detention facilities.

D. Many Bosnian Muslim and Bosnian Croat civilians who were not interned in camps were forced to stay in their communities where they were subjected to physical and psychological abuse from Bosnian Serb military and police and their agents, paramilitary forces and lawless elements of the Bosnian Serb community. Conditions for many became intolerable and they left. Before leaving, many civilians were compelled to sign official Bosnian Serb documents wherein they "voluntarily" relinquished to the Bosnian Serb administration their rights to their real and personal property. In some cases, Bosnian Muslim and Bosnian Croat civilians who left their communities were permitted to take with them limited amounts of personal property and money, but even that property was stolen from them at Bosnian Serb checkpoints or at other locations.

E. In many instances during and after the Bosnian Serb military take-over of towns and villages, Bosnian Serb military, police and their agents, entered the homes of non-Serb civilians and plundered the personal property of non-Serb civilians.

DESTRUCTION OF PROPERTY

29. Persecution throughout the occupied territory by Bosnian Serb military, police and their agents, or third parties with their acquiescence, involved the systematic destruction of Bosnian Muslim and Bosnian Croat homes and businesses. These homes and businesses were singled out and systematically destroyed in areas where hostilities had ceased or had not taken place. The purpose of this unlawful destruction was to ensure that the inhabitants could not and would not return to their homes and communities. The cities, villages and towns, or Bosnian Muslim and Bosnian Croat portions thereof, where extensive destruction of property occurred include, but are not limited to the following:

Town/Village	Municipality	Approximate dates of destruction
Grebnice	Bosanski Šamac	19-22 April 1992
Hrvatska Tišina	Bosanski Šamac	19-22 April 1992
Hasići	Bosanski Šamac	19-22 April 1992
Derventa	Derventa	4 April 1992
Vijaka	Derventa	4 April 1992
Bosanski Brod	Bosanski Brod	3 March 1992
Odžak	Odžak	July 1992
Modrica	Modrica	Late April 1992
Vidovice	Orasje	29 April and 4 May 1992
Gradačac	Gradačac	mid-1992
Piskavice	Vlasenica	22 April 1992
	Vlasenica	28 April 1992
Turalići	Vlasenica	28 April 1992
Đile	Vlasenica	1-3 May 1992
Pomol	Vlasenica 1	May 1992
Gaj	Vlasenica	1 May 1992
Besići	Vlasenica	1 May 1992
Nurići	Vlasenica 1	May 1992
Vrsinje	Vlasenica 1	May 1992
Džamdzići	Vlasenica	8 May 1992

Town/Village	Municipality	Approximate dates of destruction
Pivići	Vlasenica	11 May 1992
Hambarine	Prijedor	23 May 1992
Ljubija	Prijedor	23 May 1992
Kozarac	Prijedor	24 May 1992
Bišćani	Prijedor	20 July 1992
Čarakovo	Prijedor	20 July 1992
Rizvanovići	Prijedor	20 July 1992
Sredice	Prijedor	20 July 1992
Zikovi	Prijedor	20 July 1992

DESTRUCTION OF SACRED SITES

30. Muslim and Catholic places of worship were systematically damaged and/or destroyed by Bosnian Serb military forces and others. In many instances, where no military action had taken place or had ceased, these sacred sites were also damaged and/or destroyed. These places of worship include, but are not limited to those mentioned in paragraph 37 of this indictment. Bosnian Serb military and police forces failed to take reasonable and necessary measures to ensure that these religious sites would be protected.

31. The events described above were directed against Bosnian Muslim and Bosnian Croat civilians. Individually and collectively, these actions taken by or on behalf of the Bosnian Serb administration, have been on such a large scale and implemented in such a systematic way that they have destroyed, traumatised or dehumanised most aspects of Bosnian Muslim and Bosnian Croat life in those areas where the Bosnian Serb administration has taken control.

32. RADOVAN KARADŽIĆ and RATKO MLADIĆ knew or had reason to know that subordinates in detention facilities were about to kill or cause serious physical or mental harm to Bosnian Muslims and Bosnian Croats with the intent to destroy them, in whole or in part, as national, ethnic or religious groups or had done so and failed to take necessary and reasonable measures to prevent such acts or to punish the perpetrators thereof.

33. RADOVAN KARADŽIĆ and RATKO MLADIĆ individually and in concert with others planned, instigated, ordered or otherwise aided and abetted in the planning, preparation or execution of persecutions on political and religious grounds or knew or had reason to know that subordinates were about to do the same or had done so and failed to take necessary and reasonable measures to prevent such acts or to punish the perpetrators thereof.

By these acts and omissions, RADOVAN KARADŽIĆ and RATKO MLADIĆ committed:

Count 1: GENOCIDE as recognised by Articles 4(2)(a),(b),(c) and 7(3) of the Statute of the Tribunal.

Count 2: a CRIME AGAINST HUMANITY as recognised by Articles 5(h) and 7(1) and 7(3) of the Statute of the Tribunal.

COUNTS 3-4

(UNLAWFUL CONFINEMENT OF CIVILIANS)

34. From the outset of hostilities in the Republic of Bosnia and Herzegovina, thousands of Bosnian Muslim and Bosnian Croat civilians were unlawfully interned in detention facilities. Many of these facilities were established and operated by the Bosnian Serb military, police and their agents under the direction and control of RADOVAN KARADŽIĆ

and RATKO MLADIĆ. As described in paragraphs 18 and 20-22 of this indictment and incorporated in full herein, the conditions in these facilities were inhumane. Countless civilians were abused and many perished in these internment facilities.

35. RADOVAN KARADŽIĆ and RATKO MLADIĆ individually and in concert with others planned, ordered, instigated or otherwise aided and abetted in the planning and preparation or execution of the unlawful detention of civilians or knew or had reason to know that subordinates were unlawfully detaining civilians and failed to take necessary and reasonable measures to prevent such acts or to punish the perpetrators thereof.

By these acts and omissions, RADOVAN KARADŽIĆ and RATKO MLADIĆ committed:

Count 3: a GRAVE BREACH as recognised by Articles 2(g) (unlawful confinement of civilians), 7(1) and 7(3) of the Statute of the Tribunal.

Count 4: a VIOLATION OF THE LAWS OR CUSTOMS OF WAR (outrages upon personal dignity) as recognised by Articles 3, 7(1) and 7(3) of the Statute of the Tribunal.

COUNT 5

(SHELLING OF CIVILIAN GATHERINGS)

36. As described in paragraph 26 of this indictment, which is incorporated in full herein, Bosnian Serb military forces fired upon civilian gatherings that were of no military significance, thereby causing injury and death to hundreds of civilians. RADOVAN KARADŽIĆ and RATKO MLADIĆ individually and in concert with others planned, instigated, ordered or otherwise aided and abetted in the planning, preparation or execution of unlawful attacks against the civilian population and individual civilians with area fire weapons such as mortars, rockets and artillery or knew or had reason to know that the Bosnian Serb military forces were about to unlawfully attack the civilian population and individual civilians, or had already done so, and failed to take the necessary and reasonable steps to prevent such shelling or to punish the perpetrators thereof.

By these acts and omissions, RADOVAN KARADŽIĆ and RATKO MLADIĆ committed:

Count 5: a VIOLATION OF THE LAWS OR CUSTOMS OF WAR (deliberate attack on the civilian population and individual civilians) as recognised by Articles 3, 7(1) and 7(3) of the Statute of the Tribunal.

COUNT 6

(DESTRUCTION OF SACRED SITES)

37. Since April 1992 to the end of May 1995, in territory of the Republic of Bosnia and Herzegovina controlled by the Bosnian Serb military and police, including areas where no military conflict was ongoing, there has been widespread and systematic damage to and destruction of Muslim and Roman Catholic sacred sites. In areas such as Banja Luka, the near total obliteration of these religious sites has occurred. The sites in the Banja Luka area include the following:

MUSLIM SACRED SITES

Name of mosque	Location	Date of destruction or damage
Sefer-Beg	Banja Luka	09.04.93
Ferhadija	Banja Luka	07.05.93
Arnaudija	Banja Luka	07.05.93
Mosque in Vrbanje	Banja Luka	11.05.93
Zulfikarova	Banja Luka	15.05.93
Behram-Efendija	Banja Luka	26.05.93
Mehidibeg	Banja Luka	04.06.93
Sufi Mehmed-Paša	Banja Luka	04.06.93
Hadzi-Begzade	Banja Luka	04.06.93
Gazanferija	Banja Luka	04.06.93
Hadži-Sebenova	Banja Luka	14.06.93
Hadži-Kurt	Banja Luka	14.06.93
Hadži-Pervis	Banja Luka	06.09.93
Hadži-Osmanija	Banja Luka	08.09.93
Hadži-Omer	Banja Luka	09.09.93
Hadži-Salihija	Banja Luka	09.09.93

ROMAN CATHOLIC SACRED SITES

Name of church	City	Date of destruction or damage
Church of St. Joseph at Trno	Banja Luka	24.10.91
Parish Church	Banja Luka	00.12.91
St. Bonaventura Cathedral	Banja Luka	31.12.91
St. Vincent Monastery	Banja Luka	00.12.92
Village Church	Vujnovići	05.05.95
Parish Church	Petričevac	06.05.95
St. Anthony of Padua Church and Franciscan Monastery	Banja Luka	07.05.95
Parish Church	Sergovac	07.05.95
Village Church	Majdan	08.05.95
Parish Church	Presnace	12.05.95

38. In other areas, damage and destruction to places of worship has been widespread These sites include, but are not limited to the Aladža Mosque (Foča); the Sultan Selim Mosque (Doboj); the Church of St. Peter and St. Paul, the Obri Chapel and the Sevri-Hadži Mosque (Mostar); the parish church (Novi Šeher); and the Čaršijska Mosque (Konjić). Bosnian Serb military and police forces failed to take reasonable and necessary measures to ensure that these religious sites were protected.

39. RADOVAN KARADŽIĆ and RATKO MLADIĆ individually and in concert with others planned, instigated, ordered or otherwise aided and abetted in the planning, preparation or execution of the destruction of sacred sites or knew or had reason to know that subordinates were about to damage or destroy these sites or had done so and failed to take necessary and reasonable measures to prevent them from doing so or to punish the perpetrators thereof.

By these acts and omissions, RADOVAN KARADŽIĆ and RATKO MLADIĆ committed:

Count 6: a VIOLATION OF THE LAWS OR CUSTOMS OF WAR (destruction or willful damage to institutions dedicated to religion) as recognised by Articles 3(d), 7(1) and 7(3) of the Statute of the Tribunal.

COUNT 7

(EXTENSIVE DESTRUCTION OF PROPERTY)

40. After the take-over of Foča (8 April 1992), Bosanski Šamac (17 April 1992), Vlasenica (21 April 1992), Prijedor (30 April 1992), Brčko (30 April 1992) and other municipalities in the Republic of Bosnia and Herzegovina, Bosnian Serb military and police forces and other elements over whom they had control, under the direction and control of RADOVAN KARADŽIĆ and RATKO MLADIĆ systematically destroyed, or permitted others to destroy, for no justifiable military reasons, Bosnian Muslim and Bosnian Croat businesses and residences in occupied cities and villages. The areas where extensive destruction occurred include those areas described in paragraph 29 of this indictment, which is incorporated in full herein.

41. RADOVAN KARADŽIĆ and RATKO MLADIĆ individually and in concert with others planned, instigated, ordered or otherwise aided and abetted in the planning, preparation or execution of the extensive, wanton and unlawful destruction of Bosnian Muslim and Bosnian Croat property, not justified by military necessity or knew or had reason to know that subordinates were about to destroy or permit others to destroy the property of Bosnian Muslim or Bosnian Croat civilians or had done so and failed to take necessary and reasonable measures to prevent this destruction or to punish the perpetrators thereof.

By these acts and omissions, RADOVAN KARADŽIĆ and RATKO MLADIĆ committed:

Count 7: a GRAVE BREACH as recognised by Articles 2(d) (destruction of property), 7(1) and 7(3) of the Statute of the Tribunal.

COUNTS 8-9

(APPROPRIATION AND PLUNDER OF PROPERTY)

42. As described in paragraphs 27-28 of this indictment, which are incorporated in full herein, Bosnian Serb military and police personnel and other agents of the Bosnian Serb administration, under the direction and control of RADOVAN KARADŽIĆ and RATKO MLADIĆ systematically appropriated and looted the real and personal property of Bosnian Muslim and Bosnian Croat civilians.

43. RADOVAN KARADŽIĆ and RATKO MLADIĆ individually and in concert with others planned, instigated, ordered or otherwise aided and abetted in the planning, preparation or execution of the extensive, wanton and unlawful appropriation of real and personal property owned by Bosnian Muslim and Bosnian Croat civilians or knew or had reason to know that subordinates were about to appropriate real and personal property of Bosnian Muslim and Bosnian Croat civilians or had done so and failed to take necessary and reasonable measures to prevent this appropriation or to punish the perpetrators thereof.

By these acts and omissions, RADOVAN KARADŽIĆ and RATKO MLADIĆ committed:

Count 8: a GRAVE BREACH as recognised by Articles 2(d) (appropriation of property), 7(1) and 7(3) of the Statute of the Tribunal.

Count 9: a VIOLATION OF THE LAWS OR CUSTOMS OF WAR (plunder of public or private property) as recognised by Articles 3(e), 7(1) and 7(3) of the Statute of the Tribunal.

PART II
COUNTS 10-12
(SARAJEVO SNIPING)

44. Since 5 April 1992, the City of Sarajevo has been besieged by forces of the Bosnian Serb army. Throughout this siege, there has been a systematic campaign of deliberate targeting of civilians by snipers of the Bosnian Serb military and their agents. The sniping campaign has terrorised the civilian population of Sarajevo and has resulted in a substantial number of civilian casualties, killed and wounded, including women, children and elderly. Between 5 May 1992 and 31 May 1995, snipers have systematically, unlawfully and willfully killed and wounded civilians in the area of Sarajevo, including but not limited to the following individuals:

KILLED

Children

Elma Jakupović, age 2, at Jukićeva Street, No. 17, on 20 July 1993
Elvedina Ćolić, age 4, at Kobilja Glava on 8 August 1993
Adnan Kasapović, age 16, at Dj.A.Kuna Street on 24 October 1994
Nermina Omerović, age 11, at oure Daničića Street on 8 November 1994

Women

Almasa Konjhodžić, age 56, at the intersection of Kranjčevića and Brodska Streets on 27 June 1993
Sevda Kustura, age 50, at Špicasta Stijena on 5 August 1993
Sada Pohara, age 19, at Žarka Zgonjanina Street, No. 13, on 30 August 1993
Saliha Comaga, age 38, at Mujkića Brdo, Ugorsko, on 8 September 1993
Edina Trto, age 25, at Ivana Krndelja Street on 26 September 1993
Hatema Mukanović, age 38, at Obala 27 July 89 Street on 11 January 1994
Radmila Plainović, age 51, at Vojvode Putnika Street on 7 February 1994
Lejla Bajramović, age 24, at B. Boris Kidrić Street, No. 3, on 8 December 1994

Elderly

Hajrija Dizdarević, age 66, at Ivo Kranjčević Street 11 on 17 July 1993
Marko Stupar, age 64, at Zmaja od Bosne No. 64 Street on 12 January 1994
Fadil Zuko, age 63, at Stara Cesta Street, bb on 2 February 1994
Dragomir Ćulibrk, age 61, at Prvomajska bb on 16 June 1994

Men

Adnan Mesihović, age 34, at Hasana Brkića Street on 3 September 1993
Junuz Campara, age 59, at Milutin Đurasković Street on 6 September 1993
Augustin Vučić, age 57, at Ante Babića Street on 13 March 1994
Jasmin Podžo, age 23, at Mala Berkuša Street 10 on 4 March 1995

WOUNDED

Children

Boy, age 2, at Stara Cesta Street on 26 June 1993
Boy, age 12, at Kupališta swimming pool on 5 August 1993
Girl, age 9, at Kobilja Glava on 8 August 1993
Boy, age 14, at Džemal Bijedić Street on 3 September 1993
Girl, age 8, at Ivana Krndelja Street on 3 September 1993
Boy, age 15, at X transverzale Street bb on 4 October 1993
Boy, age 13, at Donji Hotonj II Street on 10 November 1993
Boy, age 12, at Petra Drapšina Street on 28 November 1993

Boy, age 17, at Džemala Bijedića Street on 10 January 1994
Boy, age 5, at Zmaja od Bosne Street on 19 June 1994
Girl, age 16, at Senada Mandića-Dende Street on 26 June 1994
Boy, age 13, at Miljenka Cvitkovića Street on 22 July 1994
Boy, age 7, at Zmaja od Bosne Street on 18 November 1994
Girl, age 13, at the cross-roads of Rogina and Sedrenik Streets on 22 November 1994
Boy, age 14, at Sedrenik Street on 6 March 1995

Women
Female, age 20, at Hotonj on 5 August 1993
Female, age 52, at Franca Rozmana Street on 6 August 1993
Female, age 55, at Španskih Boraca Street on 30 August 1993
Female, age 35, at Ivana Krndelja Street on 3 September 1993
Female, age 32, at Nikola Demonjač Grada Bakua Street area on 6 January 1994
Female, age 46, at Olimpijska Street, No. 15, on 18 January 1994
Female, age 42, at 21 Maj Street on 9 May 1994
Female, age 50, and female, age 62, at Nikole Demonje Street on 25 May 1994
Female, age 45, at Mojmilo-Dobrinja Road on 13 June 1994
Female, age 46, at Zaim Imamović Street, No. 15, on 20 July 1994
Female, age 54, at Baruthana Street on 8 November 1994
Female, age 28, at Zmaja od Bosne Street on 9 November 1994
Female, age 28, at Zmaja od Bosne Street on 18 November 1994
Female, age 24, at Franca Lehara Street, No. 3, on 8 December 1994
Female, age 49, at Sedrenik Street on 10 December 1994

Elderly
Female, age 71, at "Ciglane" Market on 17 September 1993
Female, age 72, at Nikole Demonje Street on 2 October 1993
Female, age 60, at Lovčenska Street on 7 December 1993
Male, age 63, at St Anto Babić on 13 March 1994
Male, age 62, at Omladinskih Radnih Brigada Street on 16 June 1994
Male, age 61, at Prvomajska bb on 16 June 1994
Male, age 67, at Senad Mandić Denda Street on 17 July 1994
Male, age 63, at Sedrenik Street on 11 December 1994
Male, age 62, at Sedrenik Street on 13 December 1994
Female, age 73, at the intersection of Zmaja od Bosne and Muzejska Streets on 18 December 1994

Men
Male, age 36, at Trg of Zavnobih on 1 February 1993
Male, age 52, at Kobilja Glava on 25 June 1993
Male, age 29, at Stara Cesta Street on 7 October 1993
Male, age 50, and male, age 56, at Brace Ribara Street on 2 November 1993
Male, age 36, at Stara Cesta Street on 14 December 1993
Male, age 27, at Zmaja od Bosne Street on 19 June 1994
Males, ages 20, 27, 34 and 34, at Zmaja od Bosne Street on 9 November 1994
Male, age 29, at Sedrenik Street on 8 December 1994
Males, ages 33 and 46, at intersection of Franje Rackog and Maršala Tita Streets on 3 March 1995
Male, age 52, at Sedrenik Street on 6 March 1995

45. RADOVAN KARADŽIĆ and RATKO MLADIĆ individually and in concert with others planned, ordered, instigated or otherwise aided and abetted in the planning, preparation or execution of the sniping of civilians or knew or had reason to know that subordinates were sniping civilians and failed to take necessary and reasonable measures to prevent such acts or to punish the perpetrators thereof.

As to the deliberate attacks by sniper fire against the civilian population and individual civilians, which resulted in death and injury to said civilians, and acts and omissions related thereto, RADOVAN KARADŽIĆ and RATKO MLADIĆ committed:

Count 10: a VIOLATION OF THE LAWS OR CUSTOMS OF WAR (deliberate attack on the civilian population and individual civilians) as recognised by Articles 3, 7(1) and 7(3) of the Statute of the Tribunal.

As to the killing by sniper fire of these civilians, among others, and acts and omissions related thereto, RADOVAN KARADŽIĆ and RATKO MLADIĆ committed:

Count 11: a CRIME AGAINST HUMANITY as recognised by Articles 5(a) (murder), 7(1) and 7(3) of the Statute of the Tribunal.

As to the wounding by sniper fire of these civilians, among others, and acts and omissions related thereto, RADOVAN KARADŽIĆ and RATKO MLADIĆ committed:

Count 12: a CRIME AGAINST HUMANITY as recognised by Articles 5(i) (inhumane acts), 7(1) and 7(3) of the Statute of the Tribunal.

PART III

COUNTS 13-16

(HOSTAGES/HUMAN SHIELDS)

46. Between 26 May 1995 and 2 June 1995, Bosnian Serb military personnel, under the direction and control of RADOVAN KARADŽIĆ and RATKO MLADIĆ seized 284 UN peacekeepers in Pale, Sarajevo, Goražde and other locations and held them hostage in order to prevent further North Atlantic Treaty Organisation (NATO) airstrikes. Bosnian Serb military personnel held the UN peacekeepers throughout their captivity by force or by the threat of force. In some instances, the UN hostages were assaulted. During and after protracted negotiations with Bosnian Serb leaders, the UN hostages were released in stages between 3 June 1995 and 19 June 1995.

47. After seizing UN peacekeepers in the Pale area, Bosnian Serb military personnel, under the direction and control of RADOVAN KARADŽIĆ and RATKO MLADIĆ immediately selected certain UN hostages to use as "human shields," including but not limited to Capt. Patrick A. Rechner (Canada), Capt. Oldrich Zidlik (Czech Republic), Capt. Teterevsky (Russia), Maj. Abdul Razak Bello (Nigeria), Capt. Ahmad Manzoor (Pakistan) and Maj. Gunnar Westlund (Sweden). From on or about 26 May 1995 through 27 May 1995, Bosnian Serb military personnel physically secured or otherwise held the UN peacekeepers against their will at potential NATO air targets, including the ammunition bunkers at Jahorinski Potok, the Jahorina radar site and a nearby communications centre in order to render these locations immune from further NATO airstrikes. High-level Bosnian Serb political and military delegations inspected and photographed the UN hostages who were handcuffed at the ammunition bunkers at Jahorinski Potok.

48. RADOVAN KARADŽIĆ and RATKO MLADIĆ individually and in concert with others planned, instigated, ordered or otherwise aided and abetted in the planning, prepa-

ration or execution of the taking of civilians, that is UN peacekeepers, as hostages and, additionally, using them as "human shields" and knew or had reason to know that subordinates were about to take and hold UN peacekeepers as hostages and about to use them as "human shields" or had done so and failed to take necessary and reasonable measures to prevent them from doing so or to punish the perpetrators thereof.

In regard to UN peacekeepers seized and held hostage between 26 May 1995 and 19 June 1995, RADOVAN KARADŽIĆ and RATKO MLADIĆ by their acts and omissions, committed:

> Count 13: a GRAVE BREACH as recognised by Articles 2(h) (taking civilians as hostage), 7(1) and 7(3) of the Statute of the Tribunal.

> Count 14: a VIOLATION OF THE LAWS OR CUSTOMS OF WAR (taking of hostages) as recognised by Articles 3, 7(1) and 7(3) of the Statute of the Tribunal.

> In regard to the UN peacekeepers used as "human shields" on 26 and 27 May 1995, RADOVAN KARADŽIĆ and RATKO MLADIĆ by their acts and omissions, committed:

> Count 15: a GRAVE BREACH as recognised by Articles 2(b) (inhuman treatment), 7(1) and 7(3) of the Statute of the Tribunal.

> Count 16: a VIOLATION OF THE LAWS OR CUSTOMS OF WAR (cruel treatment) as recognised by Articles 3, 7(1) and 7(3) of the Statute of the Tribunal.

July 1995
Richard J. Goldstone,
Prosecutor

THE PROSECUTOR OF THE TRIBUNAL
AGAINST
RADOVAN KARADŽIĆ
RATKO MLADIĆ
INDICTMENT

Richard J. Goldstone, Prosecutor of the International Criminal Tribunal for the former Yugoslavia, pursuant to his authority under Article 18 of the Statute of the International Criminal Tribunal for the former Yugoslavia ("The Statute of the Tribunal"), charges

RATKO MLADIĆ and RADOVAN KARADŽIĆ

with GENOCIDE, CRIMES AGAINST HUMANITY and VIOLATIONS OF THE LAWS OR CUSTOMS OF WAR, as set forth below:

"SAFE AREA" OF SREBRENICA

1. After war erupted in the Republic of Bosnia and Herzegovina, Bosnian Serb military forces occupied Bosnian Muslim villages in the eastern part of the country, resulting in an exodus of Bosnian Muslims to enclaves in Goražde, Žepa, Tuzla, and Srebrenica. All the events referred to in this indictment took place in the Republic of Bosnia and Herzegovina.

2. On 16 April 1993, the Security Council of the United Nations, acting pursuant to Chapter VII of its Charter, adopted resolution 819, in which it demanded that all parties to the conflict in the Republic of Bosnia and Herzegovina treat Srebrenica and its sur-

roundings as a safe area which should be free from any armed attack or any other hostile act. Resolution 819 was reaffirmed by Resolution 824 on 6 May 1993 and by Resolution 836 on 4 June 1993.

3. Before the attack by Bosnian Serb forces, as described in this indictment, the estimated Bosnian Muslim population in the safe area of Srebrenica, was approximately 60,000.

ATTACK ON THE SAFE AREA OF SREBRENICA

4. On or about 6 July 1995, the Bosnian Serb army shelled Srebrenica and attacked United Nations observation posts that were manned by Dutch soldiers and located in the safe area. The attack on the Srebrenica safe area by the Bosnian Serb army continued through 11 July 1995, when the first units of the attacking Bosnian Serb forces entered Srebrenica.

5. The Bosnian Muslim men, women and children who remained in Srebrenica after the beginning of the Bosnian Serb attack took two courses of action. Several thousand women, children and some mostly elderly men fled to the UN compound in Potočari, located within the safe area of Srebrenica, where they sought the protection of the Dutch battalion responsible for the compound. They remained at the compound from 11 July 1995 until 13 July 1995, when they were all evacuated by buses and trucks under the control of and operated by Bosnian Serb military personnel.

6. A second group of approximately 15,000 Bosnian Muslim men, with some women and children, gathered at Šušnjari during the evening hours of 11 July 1995 and fled, in a huge column, through the woods towards Tuzla. Approximately one-third of this group consisted of armed Bosnian military personnel and armed civilians. The rest were unarmed civilians.

EVENTS IN POTOČARI

7. On 11 July 1995 and 12 July 1995, RATKO MLADIĆ and members of his staff met in Bratunac with Dutch military officers and representatives of the Muslim refugees from Potočari. At these meetings, RATKO MLADIĆ informed them, among other things, that Bosnian Muslim soldiers who surrendered their weapons would be treated as prisoners of war according to the Geneva Conventions and that refugees evacuated from Potočari would not be hurt.

8. On or about 12 July 1995, Bosnian Serb military forces burned and looted Bosnian Muslim houses in and around Potočari.

9. On or about 12 July 1995, in the morning hours, Bosnian Serb military forces arrived at the UN military compound in Potočari and its environs.

10. On or about 12 July 1995, RATKO MLADIĆ arrived in Potočari, accompanied by his military aides and a television crew. He falsely and repeatedly told Bosnian Muslims in and around Potočari that they would not be harmed and that they would be safely transported out of Srebrenica.

11. On or about 12 July 1995, at the direction and in the presence of RATKO MLADIĆ approximately 50-60 buses and trucks arrived near the UN military compound in Potočari. Shortly after the arrival of these vehicles, the evacuation process of Bosnian Muslim refugees started. As Muslim women, children and men started to board the buses and trucks, Bosnian Serb military personnel separated the men from the women and children. This selection and separation of Muslim men took place in the presence of and at the direction of RATKO MLADIĆ.

12. The Bosnian Muslim men who had been separated from other refugees were taken to divers locations in and around Potočari. On or about 12 July 1995, RATKO MLADIĆ

and Bosnian Serb military personnel under his command, informed some of these Muslim men that they would be evacuated and exchanged for Bosnian Serbs being held in Tuzla.

13. Most of the Muslim men who had been separated from the other refugees in Potočari were transported to Bratunac and then to the area of Karakaj, where they were massacred by Bosnian Serb military personnel.

14. Between 12 July 1995 and 13 July 1995, Bosnian Serb military personnel summarily executed Bosnian Muslim men and women at divers locations around the UN compound where they had taken refuge. The bodies of those summarily executed were left in fields and buildings in the immediate vicinity of the compound. These arbitrary killings instilled such terror and panic amongst the Muslims remaining there that some of them committed suicide and all the others agreed to leave the enclave.

15. The evacuation of all able-bodied Muslim refugees concluded on 13 July 1995. As a result of the Bosnian Serb attack on the safe area and other actions, the Muslim population of the enclave of Srebrenica was virtually eliminated by Bosnian Serb military personnel.

SURRENDER AND EXECUTIONS

16. Between the evening of 11 July 1995 and the morning of 12 July 1995, the huge column of Muslims which had gathered in Šušnjari fled Srebrenica through the woods towards Tuzla.

17. Bosnian Serb military personnel, supported by armoured personnel carriers, tanks, anti-aircraft guns and artillery, positioned themselves along the Bratunac-Milići road in an effort to interdict the column of Bosnian Muslims fleeing towards Tuzla.

18. As soon as the column reached Bosnian Serb-held territory in the vicinity of Buljim, Bosnian Serb military forces attacked it. As a result of this and other attacks by Bosnian Serb military forces, many Muslims were killed and wounded and the column divided into several smaller parts which continued towards Tuzla. Approximately one-third of the column, mostly composed of military personnel, crossed the Bratunac-Milići road near Nova Kasaba and reached safety in Tuzla. The remaining Muslims were trapped behind the Bosnian Serb lines.

19. Thousands of Muslims were captured by or surrendered to Bosnian Serb military forces under the command and control of RATKO MLADIĆ and RADOVAN KARADŽIĆ. Many of the Muslims who surrendered did so because they were assured that they would be safe if they surrendered. In many instances, assurances of safety were provided to the Muslims by Bosnian Serb military personnel who were with other Bosnian Serb soldiers wearing stolen UN uniforms, and by Muslims who had been captured and ordered to summon their fellow Muslims from the woods.

20. Many of the Bosnian Muslims who were captured by or surrendered to Bosnian Serb military personnel were summarily executed by Bosnian Serb military personnel at the locations of their surrender or capture, or at other locations shortly thereafter. Incidents of such summary executions include, but are not limited to:

20.1. On or about 13 July 1995, near Nezuk in the Republic of Bosnia and Herzegovina, a group of 10 Bosnian Muslim men were captured. Bosnian Serb soldiers summarily executed some of these men, including Mirsad Alispahić and Hajrudin Mešanović.

20.2. On or about 13 July 1995, on the banks of the Jadar River between Konjević Polje and Drinjača, Bosnian Serb soldiers summarily executed 15 Bosnian Muslim men who had surrendered or been captured. Amongst those killed were Hamed Omerović, Azem Mujić and Ismet Ahmetović.

20.3. On or about 13 July 1995, in the vicinity of Konjević Polje, Bosnian Serb soldiers summarily executed hundreds of Muslims, including women and children.

20.4. On or about 17 July 1995 or 18 July 1995, in the vicinity of Konjević Polje, Bosnian Serb soldiers captured about 150-200 Bosnian Muslims and summarily executed about one-half of them.

20.5. On or about 18 July 1995 or 19 July 1995, in the vicinity of Nezuk, about 20 groups, each containing between 5-10 Bosnian Muslim men, surrendered to Bosnian Serb military forces. After the men surrendered, Bosnian Serb soldiers ordered them to line up and summarily executed them.

20.6. On or about 20 July 1995 or 21 July 1995, near the village of Meces, Bosnian Serb military personnel, using megaphones, urged Bosnian Muslim men who had fled Srebrenica to surrender and assured them that they would be safe. Approximately 350 Bosnian Muslim men responded to these entreaties and surrendered. Bosnian Serb soldiers then took approximately 150 of them, instructed them to dig their own graves and then summarily executed them.

20.7. On or about 21 July 1995 or 22 July 1995, near the village of Meces, an excavator dug a large pit and Bosnian Serb soldiers ordered approximately 260 Bosnian Muslim men who had been captured to stand around the hole. The Muslim men were then surrounded by armed Bosnian Serb soldiers and ordered not to move or they would be shot. Some of the men moved and were shot. The remaining men were pushed into the hole and buried alive.

21. Many of the Muslims who surrendered to Bosnian Serb military personnel were not killed at the locations of their surrender, but instead were transported to central assembly points where Bosnian Serb soldiers held them under armed guard. These assembly points included, among others, a hangar in Bratunac; soccer fields in Kasaba, Konjević Polje, Kravica, and Vlasenica; a meadow behind the bus station in Sandići and other fields and meadows along the Bratunac-Milići road.

22. Between 12 July 1995 and 14 July 1995, at various of these assembly points, including the hangar in Bratunac and the soccer stadium in Kasaba, RATKO MLADIĆ addressed the Bosnian Muslim detainees. He falsely and repeatedly assured them that they would be safe and that they would be exchanged for Bosnian Serb prisoners held by Bosnian government forces.

23. Between 12 July 1995 and 14 July 1995, Bosnian Serb military personnel arbitrarily selected Bosnian Muslim detainees and summarily executed them.

MASS EXECUTIONS NEAR KARAKAJ

24. On or about 14 July 1995, Bosnian Serb military personnel transported thousands of Muslim detainees from Bratunac, Kravica and other locations to an assembly point in a school complex near Karakaj. At this assembly point, Bosnian Serb military personnel ordered the Muslim detainees to take off their jackets, coats and other garments and place them in front of the sports hall. They were then crowded into the school building and adjacent sports hall and held under armed guard.

25. On or about 14 July 1995, at this school complex near Karakaj, RATKO MLADIĆ conferred with his military subordinates and addressed some of the Muslims detained there.

26. At various times during 14 July 1995, Bosnian Serb military personnel killed Bosnian Muslim detainees at this school complex.

27. Throughout 14 July 1995, Bosnian Serb military personnel removed all the Muslim detainees, in small groups, from the school building and sports hall and loaded them onto

trucks guarded and driven by Bosnian Serb soldiers. Before boarding the trucks, many of the detainees had their hands tied behind their backs or were blindfolded. They were then driven to at least two locations in the vicinity of Karakaj.

28. Once the trucks arrived at these locations, Bosnian Serb military personnel ordered the bound or blindfolded Muslim detainees off the trucks and summarily executed them. The summary executions took place from approximately noon to midnight on 14 July 1995.

29. Bosnian Serb military personnel buried the executed Bosnian Muslim men in mass graves near the execution sites.

30. On or about 14 July 1995, RATKO MLADIĆ was present at one of the mass execution sites when Bosnian Serb military personnel summarily executed Bosnian Muslim men.

31. The summary executions of Bosnian Muslim males, which occurred on 14 July 1995 in the vicinity of Karakaj, resulted in the loss of thousands of lives.

THE ACCUSED

32. RADOVAN KARADŽIĆ was born on 19 June 1945 in the municipality of Šavnik of the Republic of Montenegro. From on or about 13 May 1992 to the present, he has been president of the Bosnian Serb administration in Pale.

33. RATKO MLADIĆ was born on 12 March 1943 in Kalinovik municipality of the Republic of Bosnia and Herzegovina. He is a career military officer and holds the rank of general in the Bosnian Serb armed forces. From on or about 14 May 1992 to the present, he has been the commander of the army of the Bosnian Serb administration.

SUPERIOR AUTHORITY

RADOVAN KARADŽIĆ

34. RADOVAN KARADŽIĆ was a founding member and president of the Serbian Democratic Party (SDS) of what was then the Socialist Republic of Bosnia and Herzegovina. The SDS was the main political party among the Serbs in Bosnia and Herzegovina. As president of the SDS, he was and is the most powerful official in the party. His duties as president include representing the party, co-ordinating the work of party organs and ensuring the realisation of the programmatic tasks and goals of the party. He continues to hold this post.

35. RADOVAN KARADŽIĆ became the first president of the Bosnian Serb administration in Pale on or about 13 May 1992. At the time he assumed this position, his *de jure* powers, as described in the constitution of the Bosnian Serb administration, included, but were not limited to, commanding the army of the Bosnian Serb administration in times of war and peace and having the authority to appoint, promote and discharge officers of the army. As president, he was and is [in] a position of superior authority to RATKO MLADIĆ and every member of the Bosnian Serb army and all units and personnel assigned or attached to the Bosnian Serb army.

36. In addition to his powers described in the constitution, RADOVAN KARADŽIĆ's powers as president of the Bosnian Serb administration are augmented by Article 6 of the Bosnian Serb Act on People's Defence. This Act vested in him, among other powers, the authority to supervise the Territorial Defence both in peace and war and the authority to issue orders for the utilisation of the police in case of war, immediate threat and other emergencies. Article 39 of the same Act empowered him, in cases of imminent threat of war and other emergencies, to deploy Territorial Defence units for the maintenance of law and order.

37. RADOVAN KARADŽIĆ's powers are further augmented by Article 33 of the Bosnian Serb Act on Internal Affairs, which authorised him to activate reserve police in emergency situations.

38. RADOVAN KARADŽIĆ has exercised the powers described above and has acted and been dealt with internationally as the president of the Bosnian Serb administration in Pale. In that capacity, he has, *inter alia*, participated in international negotiations and has personally made agreements on such matters as cease-fires and humanitarian relief, and these agreements have been implemented.

RATKO MLADIĆ

39. RATKO MLADIĆ was, in 1991, appointed commander of the 9th Corps of the Yugoslav People's Army (JNA) in Knin in the Republic of Croatia. In May 1992, he assumed command of the forces of the Second Military District of the JNA which then effectively became the Bosnian Serb army. He holds the rank of general and from about 14 May 1992 to the present, has been the commander of the army of the Bosnian Serb administration. In that capacity, he was and is in a position of superior authority to every member of the Bosnian Serb army and all units and personnel assigned or attached to that army.

40. RATKO MLADIĆ has demonstrated his control in military matters by negotiating, *inter alia*, cease-fire and prisoner exchange agreements; agreements relating to the opening of Sarajevo airport; agreements relating to access for humanitarian aid convoys; and anti-sniping agreements, all of which have been implemented.

GENERAL ALLEGATIONS

41. At all times relevant to this indictment, a state of armed conflict and partial occupation existed in the Republic of Bosnia and Herzegovina in the territory of the former Yugoslavia.

42. In each paragraph charging genocide, a crime recognised by Article 4 of the Statute of the Tribunal, the alleged acts or omissions were committed with the intent to destroy, in whole or in part, a national, ethnical, or religious group, as such.

43. In each paragraph charging crimes against humanity, crimes recognised by Article 5 of the Statute of the Tribunal, the alleged acts or omissions were part of a widespread or systematic or large-scale attack directed against a civilian population.

44. RATKO MLADIĆ and RADOVAN KARADŽIĆ are individually responsible for the crimes alleged against them in this indictment pursuant to Article 7(1) of the Tribunal Statute. Individual criminal responsibility includes committing, planning, instigating, ordering or otherwise aiding and abetting in the planning, preparation or execution of any crimes referred to in Articles 2 to 5 of the Tribunal Statute.

45. RATKO MLADIĆ and RADOVAN KARADŽIĆ are also, or alternatively, criminally responsible as commanders for the acts of their subordinates pursuant to Article 7(3) of the Tribunal Statute. Command criminal responsibility is the responsibility of a superior officer for the acts of his subordinate if he knew or had reason to know that his subordinate was about to commit such acts or had done so and the superior failed to take the necessary and reasonable measures to prevent such acts or to punish the perpetrators thereof.

46. The general allegations contained in paragraphs 41 through 45 are realleged and incorporated into each of the charges set forth below.

CHARGES
COUNTS 1-2
(GENOCIDE)
(CRIMES AGAINST HUMANITY)

47. Between about 12 July 1995 and 13 July 1995, Bosnian Serb military personnel, under the command and control of RATKO MLADIĆ and RADOVAN KARADŽIĆ arrived in Potočari where thousands of Muslim men, women and children had sought refuge in and around the UN military compound. Bosnian Serb military personnel, under the command and control of RATKO MLADIĆ and RADOVAN KARADŽIĆ summarily executed many Bosnian Muslim refugees who remained in Potočari.

48. Between about 13 July 1995 and 22 July 1995, Bosnian Serb military personnel, under the command and control of RATKO MLADIĆ and RADOVAN KARADŽIĆ summarily executed many Bosnian Muslim men who fled to the woods and were later captured or surrendered.

49. Thousands of Bosnian Muslim men, who fled Srebrenica and who surrendered or had been captured, were transported from various assembly locations in and around Srebrenica to a main assembly point at a school complex near Karakaj.

50. On or about 14 July 1995, Bosnian Serb military personnel, under the command and control of RATKO MLADIĆ and RADOVAN KARADŽIĆ transported thousands of Muslim men from this school complex to two locations a short distance away. At these locations, Bosnian Serb soldiers, with the knowledge of RATKO MLADIĆ summarily executed these Bosnian Muslim detainees and buried them in mass graves.

51. RATKO MLADIĆ and RADOVAN KARADŽIĆ between about 6 July 1995 and 22 July 1995, individually and in concert with others, planned, instigated, ordered or otherwise aided and abetted in the planning, preparation or execution of the following crimes:

a) summary executions of Bosnian Muslim men and women in and around Potočari on 12 July 1995 and 13 July 1995,

b) summary executions, which occurred between 13 July 1995 and 22 July 1995, of Bosnian Muslims who were *hors de combat* because of injury, surrender or capture after fleeing into the woods towards Tuzla,

c) summary executions of Bosnian Muslim men, which occurred on or about 14 July 1995 at mass execution sites in and around Karakaj.

By their acts and omissions in relation to the events described in paragraphs 13, 14, 20.1 to 20.7, 23, 26 and 28, RATKO MLADIĆ and RADOVAN KARADŽIĆ committed:

Count 1: GENOCIDE as recognised by Article 4(2)(a) (killing members of the group) of the Statute of the Tribunal.

Count 2: a CRIME AGAINST HUMANITY as recognised by Article 5(b) (extermination) of the Statute of the Tribunal.

COUNTS 3-4
(CRIMES AGAINST HUMANITY)
(VIOLATION OF THE LAWS OR CUSTOMS OF WAR)

52. By their acts and omissions in relation to the summary executions of Bosnian Muslim men and women that occurred in and around Potočari between 12 July 1995 and 13 July 1995, described heretofore in paragraph 13, RATKO MLADIĆ and RADOVAN KARADŽIĆ committed:

Count 3: a CRIME AGAINST HUMANITY as recognised by Article 5(a) (murder) of the Statute of the Tribunal.

Count 4: a VIOLATION OF THE LAWS OR CUSTOMS OF WAR as recognised by Article 3 (murder) of the Statute of the Tribunal.

COUNTS 5-18
(CRIMES AGAINST HUMANITY)

(VIOLATION OF THE LAWS OR CUSTOMS OF WAR)

53. By their acts and omissions in relation the summary executions of Bosnian Muslims who fled Srebrenica into the woods between 13 July 1995 and 22 July 1995 as described heretofore in paragraphs 20.1 to 20.7, RATKO MLADIĆ and RADOVAN KARADŽIĆ committed:

Count 5: a CRIME AGAINST HUMANITY (in relation to paragraph 20.1) as recognised by Article 5(a) (murder) of the Statute of the Tribunal.

Counts 6: a VIOLATION OF THE LAWS OR CUSTOMS OF WAR (in relation to paragraph 20.1) as recognised by Article 3 (murder) of the Statute of the Tribunal.

Count 7: a CRIME AGAINST HUMANITY (in relation to paragraph 20.2) as recognised by Article 5(a) (murder) of the Statute of the Tribunal.

Counts 8: a VIOLATION OF THE LAWS OR CUSTOMS OF WAR (in relation to paragraph 20.2) as recognised by Article 3 (murder) of the Statute of the Tribunal.

Count 9: a CRIME AGAINST HUMANITY (in relation to paragraph 20.3) as recognised by Article 5(a) (murder) of the Statute of the Tribunal.

Counts 10: a VIOLATION OF THE LAWS OR CUSTOMS OF WAR (in relation to paragraph 20.3) as recognised by Article 3 (murder) of the Statute of the Tribunal.

Count 11: a CRIME AGAINST HUMANITY (in relation to paragraph 20.4) as recognised by Article 5(a) (murder) of the Statute of the Tribunal.

Counts 12: a VIOLATION OF THE LAWS OR CUSTOMS OF WAR (in relation to paragraph 20.4) as recognised by Article 3 (murder) of the Statute of the Tribunal.

Count 13: a CRIME AGAINST HUMANITY (in relation to paragraph 20.5) as recognised by Article 5(a) (murder) of the Statute of the Tribunal.

Counts 14: a VIOLATION OF THE LAWS OR CUSTOMS OF WAR (in relation to paragraph 20.5) as recognised by Article 3 (murder) of the Statute of the Tribunal.

Count 15: a CRIME AGAINST HUMANITY (in relation to paragraph 20.6) as recognised by Article 5(a) (murder) of the Statute of the Tribunal.

Counts 16: a VIOLATION OF THE LAWS OR CUSTOMS OF WAR (in relation to paragraph 20.6) as recognised by Article 3 (murder) of the Statute of the Tribunal.

Count 17: a CRIME AGAINST HUMANITY (in relation to paragraph 20.7) as recognised by Article 5(a) (murder) of the Statute of the Tribunal.

Counts 18: a VIOLATION OF THE LAWS OR CUSTOMS OF WAR (in relation to paragraph 20.7) as recognised by Article 3 (murder) of the Statute of the Tribunal.

COUNTS 19-20
(CRIMES AGAINST HUMANITY)
|(VIOLATION OF THE LAWS OR CUSTOMS OF WAR)

54. By their acts and omissions in relation to the summary executions of Bosnian Muslim men at mass execution sites in and around Karakaj, on or about 14 July 1995, as described in paragraph 28, RATKO MLADIĆ and RADOVAN KARADŽIĆ committed:

Count 19: a CRIME AGAINST HUMANITY as recognised by Article 5(a) (murder) of the Statute of the Tribunal.

Count 20: a VIOLATION OF THE LAWS OR CUSTOMS OF WAR as recognised by Article 3 (murder) of the Statute of the Tribunal.

———————————————

Richard J. Goldstone
Prosecutor
14 November 1995
The Hague, The Netherlands

Chronology of the Bosnian War

From Ratko Mladić: Hero or War Criminal,
by Ljubodrag Stojadinović

1992

February 21 — A plan is presented at the International Conference for Bosnia-Herzegovina ("B-H") in Lisbon whereby Bosnia would become a new country with three constituent nationalities, as based on census figures from 1971, 1981 and 1991.

February 29 – March 1 — A referendum for the independence and sovereignty of B-H takes place. The Bosnian Serbs boycott the referendum.

March 1 — The Serbs raise barricades around Sarajevo after several members of a Serbian wedding party are killed in cold blood in Baščaršija.

April 6 — The European Union recognizes the independence of B-H. On the same day, Sarajevo witnesses the outbreak of hostilities and the first deaths, which marks the beginning of the war in B-H.

April 7 — The Serbian Parliament in Banjaluka proclaims the independence of the Republika Srpska (the Serbian Republic) of Bosnia-Herzegovina. Biljana Plavsić and Nikola Koljević resign from the presidency of B-H, Serbian representatives walk out of Parliament and Ministries of the B-H government.

April 8 — The Presidency of B-H, now without Serbian representatives, immediately declares a state of emergency as a prelude to war in B-H.

May 3 — A convoy of Yugoslav People's Army ("YPA" or "JNA" in Serbian) units is attacked as it was withdrawing from Sarajevo with UN UNPROFOR mediation. One hundred and twenty-seven (127) JNA soldiers are killed in the ambush.

May 16 — In Tuzla, another YPA convoy is attacked and 49 YPA soldiers are killed.

May 27 — A mortar attack strikes a group of people waiting in a bread line on Vasa Miskin Street in Sarajevo. Twenty (20) are killed and another 100 injured.

May 30 — The UN Security Council adopts a resolution to impose economic sanctions against the Federal Republic of Yugoslavia.

July 17 — The leaders of the three opposing factions meet in London and sign the first in a series of cease fire agreements.

October 28 — International mediators propose a new territorial organization of B-H, which consists of a central government and ten autonomous cantons.

1993

January 14 — U.S. and UK mediators, Cyrus Vance and Lord David Owen, offer a new peace plan whereby B-H would be a decentralized country composed of three constituent nationalities with ten provinces. The Bosnian Croats sign the plan, but the Serbs and the Muslims reject it. The peace process comes to a halt, and the war continues.

April — The Muslim-Croat War begins in central and southwestern Bosnia.

May 16 — The Bosnian Serbs reject the Vance-Owen peace plan after a referendum is held in which 96% of the voters reject the plan.

June 12 — In a new round of peace negotiations, president Izetbegović is put under pressure to accept the ethnic division of B-H.

September 29 — The B-H Parliament does not accept the proposed division of B-H and demands the return of territories as well as access to the sea.

1994

January 7 — According to date supplied by the UN High Commissioner for Refugees in the former Yugoslavia, there are 3,477,000 refugees, and the largest number (2,280,000 refugees of all nationalities) are from B-H.

January 22 — Four children are killed by a mortar in Sarajevo's Alipašino Polje neighborhood.

February 4 — Seven people are killed and 17 wounded in Sarajevo's Dobrinja neighborhood.

February 5 — A mortar explosion kills 68 and wounds about 200 people at the Markale green market in Sarajevo.

February 9 — NATO demands that the Bosnian Serbs withdraw all heavy weapons from a 20 kilometer exclusion zone around Sarajevo within the next ten days.

March 18 — An agreement forming the Muslim-Croat Federation in B-H is signed in Washington in the presence of Bill Clinton.

April 10 — NATO aircraft bomb Serbian positions around Goražde.

June 3 — The U.S. officially supports a 51%-49% division of Bosnia.

June 20 — The International Contact Group for B-H in London completes maps of the new division of territories. There is a new proposal for a peace plan: one entity would be the Muslim-Croat Federation, and the other would be the Bosnian Serb entity.

August 4 — The border between Serbia and the Serbian Republic on the Drina River is closed.

August 5 — NATO airplanes bomb Serbian positions around Sarajevo.

September 30 — UNPROFOR's mandate is extended to March 31, 1995.

1995

January 1 — A four-month cease fire goes into effect in B-H, which was jointly signed by leaders of the Bosnian Muslims and the Serbs with the mediation of former U.S. President Jimmy Carter, who says that the Serbian side has not been properly heard. The cease fire is largely observed in January.

January 17 — The plenary session of the International War Crimes Tribunal for the former Yugoslavia in The Hague convenes.

February 10 — Renewed fighting in the Bihać area.

February 13 — The International War Crimes Tribunal for the former Yugoslavia indicts 21 Serbs.

March 7 — The Muslim-Croat Federation forms a joint military command.

March 29 — Clashes break out between the Bosnian Serbs and the B-H Army in Majevica and Vlasić.

March 31 — The UNPROFOR mandate is extended to November 30, 1995.

April 14 — Fighting breaks out in the Bihać "pocket."

May 1 — The four-month cease fire, which was often broken, ends.

May 25 — Mortars launched by the Bosnian Serbs kill 71 and would 150 in Tuzla.

May 26 — After NATO air strikes hit Serbian positions, the Bosnian Serbs blockade UN peacekeepers. In the matter of days, more than 370 "blue helmets" are imprisoned, and photos of UN soldiers tied to posts are broadcast around the world. The last hostages are freed on June 18.

June 14 — The B-H Army concentrates its forces north of Sarajevo. A state of general emergency is declared and curfews are imposed on the entire territory of B-H.

June 19 — The Republika Srpska proclaims a state of war alert in the Sarajevo region.

June 26 — According to a UN statement, 2,500 refugees have been drafted by the military in Serbia and pressed into service. Federal Interior Minister Vukašin Jovanović states that he doesn't know whether or not Serbia is carrying out forced mobilizations.

July 3 — The lack of food and supplies endangers the lives of 200,000 people in Bihać.

July 11 — The Bosnian Serbs take Srebrenica, a "safe area" under UN protection. Two weeks later, Žepa, another UN "safe area," is taken. More than 30,000 people, mostly women and children, are transferred to territory under the control of the Sarajevo government. Tadeusz Mazowiecki, former Polish Prime Minister and Special Rapporterur for the United Nations on Human Rights in the Former Yugoslavia, accuses the Bosnian Serbs of massive crimes in Srebrenica.

July 25 — Conflicts rage on all fronts.

July 26 — The International War Crimes Tribunal indicts Radovan Karadžić, Ratko Mladić and Milan Martić.

August 2 — The U.S. Congress decides to unilaterally end the weapons embargo on the Sarajevo government.

August 13 — The U.S. begins diplomatic action to restart the peace process in the former Yugoslavia.

August 28 — A mortar attack in Sarajevo kills 37 people and wounds 85. UN representatives accuse the Bosnian Serbs of the massacre of civilians.

August 29 — Serbian President Milošević is authorized to negotiate on behalf of the Republika Srpska delegation.

August 30 — NATO aircraft begin a series of strikes on Bosnian Serb positions, radar and communication installations. Air operations cease on September 14 when the RS leadership signs an agreement for the withdrawal of heavy weapons to a 20-kilometer exclusion zone around Sarajevo.

September 7 — The International War Crimes Tribunal indicts Ivica Rajić, one of the commanders of the HVO [Croatian Defense Forces] in Bosnia.

September 13 — HVO forces take Šipovo near Jajce, and Drvar, Ključ, and other towns in western Bosnia are under artillery attack by the B-H Army and HVO forces. More than 50,000 Serbs abandon the towns under attack and flee toward Banjaluka.

September 15 — There are about 100,000 refugees in the Banjaluka region.

September 26 — In New York, the foreign ministers of the FRY, Croatia and B-H sign a document of B-H constitutional principles, which provides for the division of B-H into two entities.

October 5 — The likelihood of peace provokes fierce fighting in Bosnia.

October 11 — The B-H Army and HVO forces enter Mrkonjić Grad and continue toward Banjaluka, Prijedor and Doboj. A curfew is imposed, and schools and restaurants are closed.

October 12 — The 35th cease fire agreement begins.

November 21 — After three weeks of negotiations at the Wright Patterson Air Force Base in Dayton, OH, representatives of Croatia, B-H, Serbia and international mediators sign a peace agreement for B-H.

November 30 — The UN Security Council extends the mandate for peacekeeping forces in Bosnia to the end of January; in Croatia to the first half of January; and in Macedonia for an additional six months.

December 5 — The foreign and defense ministers of the 16 NATO member countries approve a plan to send 60,000 soldiers to Bosnia. The largest NATO operation since its inception is to be conducted under the code name Operation "Joint Endeavour."

December 8 — The Peace Implementation Conference and discussions on the economic revival of Bosnia are held in London., which gathered the foreign ministers of more than 40 countries and representatives of numerous international organizations.

Swedish diplomat Carl Bilt is named High Representative in Bosnia; his responsibility is to coordinate the civilian aspects of the country's reconstruction.

December 14 — The Dayton Accord is signed in the palais de l'Élysée in Paris, ending 44 months of war in Bosnia.

December 16 — The UN Security Council adopts a resolution which authorizes NATO to take over peacekeeping operations in Bosnia.

December 22 — The B-H presidency decides to end the state of war.

1996

January 3 — "According to military estimates, there are between four and five million land mines in B-H. I assume that de-mining will take 30 years," sates one IFOR representative.

January 4 — The death of one person in Mostar ignites a series of incidents and raises tensions in the divided city.

January 9 — After three and one-half years, air transports of humanitarian aid to Sarajevo end. During the war, 13,000 humanitarian flights were made that shipped 160,000 tons of aid.

January 18 — The first meeting of representatives of governments of the Republika Srpska and the B-H Federation is held in Sarajevo.

January 23 — According to World Bank estimates, the cost of reconstructing B-H will be between $30 and $40 billion, while reconstructing the most basic infrastructure will cost about $4.8 billion.

January 31 — Elizabeth Rehn, the UN Special Rapporteur for Human Rights in the Former Yugoslavia, estimates that there are approximately 200-300 mass graves in Bosnia.

February 3 — 57,000 IFOR soldiers arrive in B-H, and establish headquarters for 10 brigades and 3 divisions.

February 7 — Ten IFOR soldiers are killed and fifty wounded in the first two months of operation in Bosnia. IFOR spends more than $76 million on the military occupation.

February 17 — The signatories of the Dayton Accord are once again summoned to a conference in Rome and compelled to carry out all of the provisions of the agreement. A crisis in the implementation of the peace agreement arises after the arrests of two RS Army officers (Djukić and Krsmanović), and after an attack on Hans Koschnick is carried out in Mostar.

February 26 — Hans Koschnick, EU Administrator in Mostar, resigns.

February 27 — The UN Security Council suspends the sanctions against the Republika Srpska and FR Yugoslavia that were imposed on August 4, 1994.

March 1 — The International War Crimes Tribunal in The Hague indicts General Djordje Djukić.

March 2 — The four-year-long UN mission in Bosnia ends. 38,000 soldiers, 1,500 civilians, and more than 3,000 local personnel took part in the UN peacekeeping operation.

March 5 — The European Union extends the mandate of its own administration of Mostar, which is set to expire in June, until the end of the year.

March 18 — According to a census that was conducted, one out of three inhabitants in Banjaluka is a refugee. There are 23,000 refugee and 41,500 indigenous households in the city.

March 19 — The transfer of power in Sarajevo's boroughs comes to an end with the entrance of the B-H Federation police in Grbavica. According to IFOR data, 60,000 Serbs are left in Sarajevo and according to Radovan Karadžić's statement, Sarajevo's boroughs had 80,000 remaining Serbian citizens.

March 22 — The International War Crimes Tribunal in The Hague indicts Zenjil Delalić, Zdravko Mučić, Hazim Delić and Esad Landža for crimes committed against Serbs in the Celibići camp near Konjic.

The transfer of undecided areas in B-H ends, and with it ends the D+90 phase of the Dayton Accords. The emphasis of the implementation of the peace agreement shifts from military to civilian aspects.

March 25 — Ricardo Peres Casado (Spanish), the former mayor of Valencia, is named Administrator of Mostar.

April 4 — The exhumations of mass graves in Mrkonjić Grad ends. The bodies of 181 Serbs, largely civilians, who were killed by members of the Croatian Army when it took over the town in October 1995, were exhumed.

April 13 — The conference of donor countries in Brussels ends; it is agreed to reserve $1.282 billion in 1996 for the reconstruction of Bosnia. The RS leadership refuses to attend the conference with the united B-H delegation.

May 7 — The trial of Dušan Tadić begins. It is the first trial for war crimes before an international court since the Nuremberg and Tokyo Tribunals.

May 9 — The UN Security Council demands that FR Yugoslavia extradite without delay three JNA officers indicted for war crimes to the International War Crimes Tribunal: Mile Mrksić, Miroslav Radić and Veselin Šljivčanin.

May 14 — The Republika Srpska dismisses prime minister Rajko Kasagić despite sharp protests from international mediators in Bosnia.

May 18 — Radovan Karadžić, RS President, transfers part of his presidential authority to Biljana Plavsić after being subjected to intense pressure by the international community.

June 25 — The cabinet of FRY President Zoran Lilić issues a statement demanding the leadership of the Republika Srpska to immediately name a new acting president who has full authority.

June 27 — The International War Crimes Tribunal issues 17 new indictments against Serbs and Croats. The number of persons indicted for war crimes in the former Yugoslavia reaches 74.

Evidentiary proceedings begin against Ratko Mladić, who was indicted for genocide and other war crimes in Bosnia that took place in Bosnia from May 1992 to July 1995.

June 30 — The nationalist SDA (Muslim) and HDZ (Croat) parties win in the first local post-war elections in B-H held in Mostar. Elections are carried out under the strict control of IFOR and international police. Radovan Karadžić, under intense pressure from the international community and the president of Serbia, transfers presidential authorities to RS Vice President Biljana Plavsić.

July 15 — According to a statement made by Ahmed Kapdžić, Director of the Office of Planning and Development in Sarajevo, 95% of Sarajevo's parks, 45,000 telephones, 57.5% of its apartments, approximately 90% of its cultural monuments, and between 70% to 90% of sites related to the Olympics were destroyed, in addition to countless human victims.

July 16 — A UNHCR representative stated that the results in the repatriation of refugees are very poor even seven months after the signing of the Dayton Accords. One hundred thousand refugees returned but, at the same time, 90,000 people left their homes in Bosnia.

The B-H Federation signs an agreement for military aid with the U.S.

July 17 — A team of Hague Tribunal investigators exhume the remains of a total of 86 persons from a mass grave in Cerska near Srebrenica.

July 23 — A B-H delegation led by a member of the B-H presidency and vice president of the B-H Federation, Ejup Ganić, arrives in Belgrade.

August 6 — Croats and Muslims, under pressure from international mediators, reach an agreement for the formation of a joint city government in Mostar.

August 15 — Sarajevo's airport opens after having been closed for four years. American Secretary of State Warren Christopher attends the opening ceremonies.

August 26 — A delegation from the FRY led by Vice President Nikola Sainović arrives in Sarajevo. Sainović meets President Izetbegović.

September 12 — Forty-six bodies of Serbian soldiers and civilians that were exhumed from a mass grave in the village of Kamen near Glamoč arrive in Banjaluka.

September 14 — Nationalist parties win the first postwar elections in B-H. 14,700 voters cross inter-entity borders.

October 3 — At a meeting in Paris, Presidents Slobodan Milošević of Serbia and Alija Izetbegović of B-H agree to normalize relations between their respective countries.

October 22 — The first session of the B-H presidency is held in the Sarajevo Museum, where representatives from all three nations in B-H are present. Members of the presidency reach an agreement about the the the functioning of common governmental institutions in the next six months.

November 9 — General Ratko Mladić is dismissed from the headquarters of the RS Army. The General Headquarters of the ARS (Army of the Republika Srpska) is renamed the General Staff and Pero Ćolić is named Joint Chief.

November 21 — American military aid worth $100 million for the B-H Federation Army arrives in the port of Ploče.

November 29 — The Hague Tribunal sentences Dražen Erdemović, a Croat from Bosnia, to ten years in prison after he admitted taking part in the mass murder of Muslims from Srebrenica in July of the previous year.

December 13 — The UN Security Council adopts a resolution by which the international forces that are authorized to implement peace in B-H (IFOR) are transformed into forces for the stabilization of peace (SFOR); their mandate is extended from December 20, 1996 for another 16 months.

December 31 — The EU administration mandate in Mostar ends. The primary goal of uniting the city is not achieved, despite the investment of 270 million marks in reconstruction projects. The Regional Office of the International Community High Representative in B-H assumes responsibility for the implementation of the civil aspects of the Dayton Accords.

1997

January 3 — The Constituent People's House (*Konstituisan Dom Naroda*) and the House of Representatives (*Prestavnička Dom Skupštine*) verifies the election of cabinet ministers for the central government.

January 9 — The Republika Srpska observes Constitution Day in Brčko with a celebration of the Divine Liturgy and the participation of scholars and intellectuals. The President of the RS, Biljana Plavsić, informs UN General Secretary Kofi Annan that Radovan Karadžić and Ratko Mladić would not be extradited to The Hague Tribunal.

January 13 — According to a statement issued by Ahmet Smajić, the Minister of Economics of the B-H Federation, the economic potential of B-H had been reduced to 10%-15% of pre-war levels.

Representatives of three opposition parties from the RS, three opposition parties from the B-H Federation, and one independent association of intellectuals form a shadow government ("The Alternative Cabinet Ministry").

January 14 — The B-H Federation General Rasim Delić, joint commander of the B-H Army, states that the combined military will have 35,000 professional soldiers, a common command structure, three B-H Army corps and one HVO corps.

February 3 — The International Committee for the Red Cross in B-H states that the three sides reported 18,172 persons missing, of which only 1,045 have been accounted for.

February 7 — The World Bank approves $32 million in credit for reconstruction.

February 10 — A curfew is imposed in Mostar after Croats attack Muslim believers during Ramadan when they visit cemeteries in the Croatian part of Mostar. One person is killed and 22 are wounded. SFOR representatives state that the expulsion of Muslims from their homes continues in the Croatian part of the city.

February 11 — Police in western (Croatian) Mostar state that many Croatian civilians on had been stopped and beaten on the Ploče-Sarajevo highway.

February 14 — The International Arbitration Commission rules that Brčko is to remain under international control until a final decision is reached in March 1998.

February 21 — According to data from the World Bank in Sarajevo, B-H ranks among the 63 poorest countries in the world with a per capital GDP of less than $275.

February 23 — An explosion destroys nine uninhabited Muslim houses in Mumići in the Republika Srpska.

February 25 — The trial of Novislav Djajić, who was indicted for genocide in the former Yugoslavia for the murder of 27 Muslims, begins in Munich

February 28 — The trial of Nikola Jorgić, who was indicted for genocide and the killing of Muslims in 1992, begins in Dusseldorf.

March 6 — OSCE representatives in B-H state that local elections will be held on September 13 and 14 instead of in July.

March 10 — The International War Crimes Tribunal in The Hague begins the trials of Messrs. Delalić, Mučić, Delić and Landža for crimes against Serbian civilians in central Bosnia.

The last mosque (down from a pre-war number of eight in the area) is blown up in the Celjeva suburb of Čapljina.

March 25 — The UN Security Council approves the deployment of 186 members of international police forces and 11 civilian officials who will take part in the implementation of international arbitration in Brčko.

Representatives of international police forces confirm that 87 abandoned Serbian houses were destroyed in Livno, Glamoč and Drvar between August 1996 and March 1997.

Bibliography of Suggested Reading

Books

Aarons, Mark and John Loftus. *The Unholy Trinity*. New York: St. Martin's, 1991 and 1998.

Bar, Bob. *The Meaning of Is: The Squandered Impeachment and Wasted Legacy of William Jefferson Clinton*. Stroud & Hall Publishing, 2004.

Baudson, Gerard. *Le nouvel ordre mondial et la Yougoslavie*. Paris: Gil Wern Editions, 1996.

Bokan, Branko J. *Genocide of the Serbs of Bosnia and Krayina*. Belgrade: European Letter Ltd., 1996.

Bulatovic, Ljiljana. *General Mladic*. Belgrade: Evro, 2002.

Butler, Hubert. *The Sub-Prefect Should Have Held His Tongue and Other Essays*. New York: Allen Lane, 1991.

Butler, Hubert. *Independent Spirit*. New York: Farrar, Straus & Giroux, 1996. This book of essays contains "The Artukovic File," which can also be found online at www.archipelago.org.

Butler, Smedley. *War Is a Racket*. rpt. Los Angeles: Feral House, 2003.

Eastern Orthodox Diocese for the United States of America and Canada: Chicago. *The Martyrdom of the Serbs: Persecutions of the Serbian Orthodox Church and Massacre of the Serbian People*, (1945?).

Cornwell, John. *Hitler's Pope, The Secret History of Pius XII*. New York: Viking: 1999.

Corwin, Phillip. *Duboius Mandate: A Memoir of the UN in Bosnia, Summer 1995*. Durham and London: Duke University Press, 1999.

Collon, Michel. *Liar's Poker: The Great Powers, Yugoslavia and the Wars of the Future*. Trans. Milo Yelesiyevich and Terence McGee. New York: IAC, 2002.

Dedijer, Vladimir. *The Yugoslav Auschwitz and the Vatican*: Buffalo, NY: Prometheus Books, 1992.

Dedijer, Vladimir, et al., *A History of Yugoslavia*, New York: McGraw Hill, 1974.

Draskovic, Vuk. *Knife*, Trans. Milo Yelesiyevich. New York: The Serbian Classics Press, 2000.

Falconi, Carlo. *The Silence of Pius XII*. New York: Little, Brown: 1965.

Ivanovic, Ilija. *Witness to Jasenovac's Hell*. Mt. Pleasant, TX: Dallas Publishing, 2002.

Jovanovic, Drago et al. eds. *The Eradication of Serbs (Iskorenjivanje Srba)*. Montreal: 1994.

Kostich, Dr. Lazo M. *Holocaust in the Independent State of Croatia*,

Chicago: Liberty, 1981.

Lowenthal, Dr. Zdenko, ed. *The Crimes of the Fascist Occupants and their Collaborators against Jews in Yugoslavia*. Belgrade: Federation of Jewish Communities of the FPRY, 1957.

Laurière, Hervé. *Assassins au nom de dieu*. 1951; rpt. Lausanne: L'Age d'Homme: 1993.

MacKenzie, Major General Lewis. *Peacekeeper: The Road to Sarajevo*. Vancouver/Toronto: Douglas & McIntyre, 1993.

Manhattan, Avro. *Vatican's Holocaust: The Sensational Account of the Most Horrifying Religious Massacre*. Rpt. Springfield, Missouri: Ozark Books, 1986.

Merlino, Jacques. *Les verites yougoslaves ne sont pas toutes bonnes à dire*. Paris: Albin Michel, 1993.

Mitrovic, Dr. Momcilo *Visoko. The Moslem War Prisoners Camp 1992-1993: Diary and Testimonies*. Beograd: NIU "Vojska," 1995.

Novak, Viktor. *Magnum Crimen*. 1947; rpt. Beograd: Nova Knjiga 1986.

Morse, Chuck. *The Nazi Connection to Islamic Terrorism: Adolph Hitler and Haj Amin al-Husseini*. New York: iUniverse, Inc., 2003.

Owen, David. *Balkan Odyssey*. New York: Harcourt Brace & Company, 1995.

Rivelli, Marco Aurelio. *Le Génocide Occulté*, Lausanne: L'Age d'Homme, 1998.

Sremac, Danielle S. *War of Words: Washington Tackles the Yugoslav Conflict*. Westport, CT and London: Praeger, 1999.

Trifkovic, Serge. *The Sword of the Prophet*. Boston: Regina Orthodox Press, 2002.

Vlajki, Emil. *The New Totalitarian Society and the Destruction of Yugoslavia*. New York/Ottawa, Toronto: Legas: 1999.

Wiebes, Cees. *Intelligence and the War in Bosnia, 1992-1995*. Munster, Hamburg, London: LitVerlag, 2003.

Reports

Trifunovic, Darko. *Report about Case Srebrenica (The First Part)* (also known as the "2002 Report"). Banja Luka: Documentation Centre of the Republic of Srpska Bureau of Government of RS Relation with ICTY, September 2002. (Available on the web at www.slobodan-milo-sevic.org.)

Key Articles and Papers

"Clinton-Approved Iranian Arms Transfers Help Turn Bosnia into Militant Islamic Base," United States Republican Policy Committee, Congressional Press Release, U.S. Congress, 1/16/97.

Bryce, Susan. "Will the Real Nazis Please Stand Up! The Public Relations of Modern Warfare," *New DawnMagazine* (www.newdawnmagazine.com.au), September/October, Issue 56.

Trifkovic, Srdja. "1204 and All That: Turning Allies into Foes," chroniclesmagazine.org, 12/14/04.

"Americans Used Islamists to Arm the Bosnian Muslims," by Richard J. Aldrich, The Guardian (UK), 4/22/02.

Trifkovic, Srdja. "Jihad, Then and Now" Parts I and II, chroniclesmagazine.org.

Wertz, Joachim. "On the Serbian Orthodox New Martyrs of the Secopnd World War, a Brief Historical Background" orthodoxinfo.com.

Stouffer, Bill. "The Patron Saint of Genocide," pavelicpapers.com.

Reich, Walter. "A Plan That's Bad to the Bone," *The Wall Street Journal*, 4/3/96, p. A14.

Savich, Carl. "Srebrenica and Naser Oric: An Analysis of General Philippe Morillon's Testimony at the ICTY," serbianna.com, 4/27/04.

Malic, Nebojsa. "Srebrenica Revisited: Reports, Confessions and the Elusive Truth," antiwar.com, 6/24/04.

Internet Resources

www.antiwar.com features Balkan Express, by Nebojsa Malic, who is one of the most perceptive writers on the Balkans. He has organized an series of articles on Srebrenica called "What Really Happened at Srebrenica?" which is a must read.

www.apisgroup.org is concerned with problems in the area of geopolitics, defense, strategy, politics, economics and security. It gathers the analysts from Yugoslavia as well as from the Diaspora.

www.balkanalysis.com "is one of the very few truly independent providers of news and analysis in the Balkans today. Our sometimes controversial and always informative articles cover economics, politics and current events in the Balkans and South-East Europe, and also include travel articles and book and film reviews." Kudos to Christopher Deliso, the founder.

www.chroniclesmagazine.org is a publication of The Rockford Institute, whose aim is to restore "American conservatism [which] once represented a coherent world-view, rooted in principles of individualism, liberty, moral responsibility, and social order, and expressed in the Great Tradition going back to the Scriptures and the ancient classics."

www.jasenovac.org is the official web site for the Jasenovac Research Institute, which is devoted to ongoing research about the Jasenovac Concentration Camp.

www.kosovo.com was set up with the blessing of His Grace the Bishop of Raska and Prizren, Artemije. The main focus of the Info-Service is the life of the Serbian Orthodox Church and the Serbian community in the Province of Kosovo and Metohija.

www.orthdoxinfo.com is concerned with contemporary issues facing Orthodox Christians. It also provides an excellent introduction to Orthodoxy for those who wish to know more about it.

www.pavelicpapers.com "is an independent research project exploring the history of the Ustase movement, one of the most resilient and brutal terrorist organizations in history. Our aim is to compose a narrative focusing on the entire history of the Ustase movement, from its beginnings among Croat exiles in Vienna, Austria in 1929 to the killing fields of the Independent State of Croatia and the fugitive shores of Argentina and America."

www.slobodan-milosevic.org is devoted to the defense of Slobodan Milosevic at The Hague. It is almost the only alternative source in English for news about President Milosevic's trial.

www.serbianna.com is a news and media portal about Serbia and Balkans surveying the western press and providing it to the public. It features daily news reports along with more than forty articles by Carl Savich, M. Bozinovich and Dr. Miroljub Jevtic, among others, on underreported aspects of twentieth century Serbian history.

www.serbianunity.net is the official web site of the Serbian Unity Congress. It features a wide variety of articles on cultural and historical topics, as well as an archive of news articles.

www.srebrenica-report.com. Srebrenica and the Politics of War Crimes, a report issued by the Srebrenica Research Group, led by Edward S. Hermann of Z-mag, who announced its conclusions at a UN press conference on July 11, 2005. Essential reading.

www.srpska-mreza.com is an encyclopedic compendium of news articles, book quotations, essays and studies on the Balkan Wars of Succession and twentieth century Serbian history.

www.tenc.net (The Emperor's New Clothes) is a web site devoted to investigative journalism. It broke many groundbreaking stories in the U.S. about the Balkan Wars. Most notably, it helped expose the fraudulent video Penny Marshall of ITN made about an alleged "death camp" run by the Serbs.

Index

700 ♦ *Ratko Mladić*

Michel COLLON

The Rape of Kosovo

NATO in Search
of World Conquest
via Control of Energy Corridors

Coming Soon in English!

THE RAPE OF KOSOVO

*NATO in Search of World Conquest
via Control of Energy Corridors*

(formerly titled *Monopoly: L'OTAN a la conquete du monde*)

by Michel Collon

271 pages with photographs and maps

Table of Contents

Ordering Information

Ratko Mladić: Tragic Hero can be ordered directly from Unwritten History, Inc. The price per copy is $34.95 plus $7.00 postage and handling (Priority USPS). Inquire about volume discounts.
Please make check or money order payable to:

Unwritten History, Inc.
UPS Store #1052
PMB 199, Zeckendorf Towers
111 E. 14th St.
New York, NY 10003

New York residents must add 8.25% sales tax.

Visit our website at www.unwrittenhistory.com.